TCP/IP

Protocol Suite

Behrouz A. Forouzan

with
Sophia Chung Fegan

Boston   Burr Ridge, IL   Dubuque, IA   Madison, WI   New York   San Francisco   St. Louis
Bangkok   Bogotá   Caracas   Lisbon   London   Madrid
Mexico City   Milan   New Delhi   Seoul   Singapore   Sydney   Taipei   Toronto

McGraw-Hill Higher Education ⊗

A Division of The **McGraw-Hill** *Companies*

TCP/IP PROTOCOL SUITE

This book is printed on acid-free paper.

2 3 4 5 6 7 8 9 0 DOC/DOC 9 0 9 8 7 6 5 4 3 2 1

ISBN 0-256-24166-X

Vice president/Editor-in-chief: *Kevin T. Kane*
Publisher: *Thomas Casson*
Executive editor: *Elizabeth A. Jones*
Editorial coordinator: *Emily J. Gray*
Senior marketing manager: *John T. Wannemacher*
Senior project manager: *Beth Cigler*
Senior production supervisor: *Heather D. Burbridge*
Supplement coordinator: *Matt Perry*
Compositor: *Interactive Composition Corporation*
Typeface: *10/12 Times Roman*
Printer: *R. R. Donnelley & Sons Company*

Library of Congress Cataloging-in-Publication Data

Forouzan, Behrouz A.
    TCP/IP protocols / Behrouz Forouzan.
      p. cm.
    ISBN 0-256-24166-X
    1. TCP/IP (Computer network protocol)   I. Title.
  TK5105.585.F67 2000
  004.6′2—dc21   99-26753

http://www.mhhe.com

To the memory of my father,
  the source of my inspiration

—Behrouz Forouzan

Preface

Technologies related to networks and internetworking may be the fastest growing in our culture today. One of the ramifications of that growth is a dramatic increase in the number of professions where an understanding of these technologies is essential for success—and a proportionate increase in the number and types of students taking courses to learn about them.

This is a book about TCP/IP. It provides the information necessary for students who seek a degree in data communications and networking. It is also a reference for professionals who are supporting or preparing to work with networks based on TCP/IP. In short, this book is for anyone who needs to understand the TCP/IP protocols.

The book assumes the reader has no prior knowledge of the TCP/IP protocols, although a previous course in data communications is desirable.

Organization

This book is divided into five parts. The first part, comprising Chapters 1 to 3, reviews the basic concepts and underlying technologies that, although independent from the TCP/IP protocols, are needed to support them.

The second part of the text discusses the protocols in the network and transport layer. Chapters 4 to 7 emphasize the IP protocol. Chapters 8 to 10 define protocols that give services to IP. Transport layer protocols are fully described in Chapters 11 and 12. Chapter 13 is devoted to a detailed description of routing protocols.

The text's third part discusses the application programs that use the network and transport layer protocols. Chapter 14 gives a brief review of the client-server paradigm and lays the foundation for Chapters 15 to 23, which discuss the application protocols.

The fourth part (Chapter 24) introduces network programming by giving a few examples using one of the interfaces, the socket interface. This chapter provides information to motivate those who intend to take courses in network programming.

The fifth part of the book (Chapter 25) is devoted to the next generation of TCP/IP. We describe IPv6, ICMPv6, and the transition strategies from version 4 to version 6.

Features

Several features of this text are designed to make it particularly easy for students to understand TCP/IP.

Visual Approach

The book presents highly technical subject matter without complex formulas by using a balance of text and figures. The approximately 550 figures accompanying the text provide a visual and intuitive opportunity for understanding the material. Figures are particularly important in explaining networking concepts, which are based on connections and transmission. These are both often more easily grasped visually than verbally.

Highlighted Points

We have repeated important concepts in boxes for quick reference and immediate attention.

Examples and Applications

Whenever appropriate, we have included examples that illustrate the concept introduced in the text. Also, we have added real-life applications throughout each chapter to motivate students.

Protocol Design

Although we have not tried to give the detailed code for implementing each protocol, many chapters contain a *design* section that discusses the general idea behind the implementation of each protocol. These sections provide an understanding of the ideas and issues involved in each protocol. They are optional.

Summary

Each chapter ends with a summary of the material covered by that chapter. The summary is a bulleted overview of all the key points in the chapter.

Practice Set

Each chapter includes a practice set designed to reinforce salient concepts and encourage students to apply them. It consists of three parts: multiple-choice questions, exercises, and programming exercises. Multiple-choice questions test students' grasp of basic concepts and terminology. Exercises require deeper understanding of the material. The programming exercises are for those students or readers who have taken one or two programming courses in C or a similar language. These exercises prepare students for client-server programming courses.

Appendixes

The appendixes are intended to provide quick reference material or a review of materials needed to understand the concepts discussed in the book.

Glossary and Acronyms

The book contains an extensive glossary and a list of acronyms.

How to Use the Book

This book is written for both an academic and a professional audience. The book can be used as a self-study guide for interested professionals. As a textbook, it can be used for a one-semester or one-quarter course. The chapters are organized to provide a great deal of flexibility. The following are some suggestions:

- Chapters 1 to 3 can be skipped if students have already taken a course in data communication and networking.
- Chapters 4 through 13 are essential for understanding TCP/IP.
- Chapters 14 to 23 can be covered in detail in a semester system and briefly in a quarter system.
- Chapter 24 can be skipped if there are time constraints.
- Chapter 25 can be used as a self-paced chapter.

Acknowledgments

It is obvious that the development of a book of this scope needs the support of many people. We must first thank Catherine Coombs for her many contributions. We must also thank the De Anza students and staff; their encouragement and support enabled the project to materialize and contributed to its success. In particular, we thank Richard Gilberg, Martha Kanter, Anne Oney, John Perry, George Rice, and Orva Stewart. We especially thank Scott Demouthe for his tremendous assistance in correcting and clarifying the material.

The most important contribution to the development of a book such as this comes from peer reviews. We cannot express our gratitude in words to the many reviewers who spent numerous hours reading the manuscript and providing us with helpful comments and ideas. We would especially like to acknowledge the contributions of the following reviewers:

Walter Read, California State University, Fresno
Wayne D. Smith, Mississippi State University
Ronald R. Srodawa, Oakland University
Rod Fatoohi, San Jose State University
Abdullah Abonamah, University of Akron

Special thanks go to the staff of McGraw-Hill. Betsy Jones, our senior editor, proved how a proficient editor can make the impossible, possible. Emily Gray, the assistant editor, gave us help whenever we needed it. Beth Cigler, our project manager, guided us through the production process with enormous enthusiasm. We also thank Heather Burbridge in production, Gino Cieslik in design, and Alyson Platt, the copy editor.

Trademark Notices

Throughout the text we have used several trademarks. Rather than insert a trademark symbol with each mention of the trademarked name, we acknowledge the trademarks here and state that they are used with no intention of infringing upon them. Other product names, trademarks, and registered trademarks are the property of their respective owners.

- Apple, AppleTalk, EtherTalk, LocalTalk, TokenTalk, and Macintosh are registered trademarks of Apple Computer, Inc.
- Bell and StarLan are registered trademarks of AT&T.
- DEC, DECnet, VAX, and DNA are trademarks of Digital Equipment Corp.
- IBM, SDLC, SNA, and IBM PC are registered trademarks of International Business Machines Corp.
- Novell, Netware, IPX, and SPX are registered trademarks of Novell, Inc.
- Network File System and NFS are registered trademarks of Sun Microsystems, Inc.
- PostScript is a registered trademark of Adobe Systems, Inc.
- UNIX is a registered trademark of UNIX System Laboratories, Inc., a wholly owned subsidiary of Novell, Inc.
- Xerox is a trademark, and Ethernet is a registered trademark of Xerox Corp.

CONTENTS IN BRIEF

Chapter 1   Introduction   1
Chapter 2   The OSI Model and the TCP/IP Protocol Suite   17
Chapter 3   Underlying Technologies   41
Chapter 4   IP Addressing   85
Chapter 5   Subnetting and Supernetting   109
Chapter 6   Delivery and Routing of IP Packets   131
Chapter 7   Internet Protocol (IP)   147
Chapter 8   ARP and RARP   179
Chapter 9   Internet Control Message Protocol (ICMP)   201
Chapter 10   Internet Group Management Protocol (IGMP)   227
Chapter 11   User Datagram Protocol (UDP)   247
Chapter 12   Transmission Control Protocol (TCP)   271
Chapter 13   Routing Protocols (RIP, OSPF, and BGP)   319
Chapter 14   Application Layer and Client-Server Model   369
Chapter 15   BOOTP and DHCP   387
Chapter 16   Domain Name System (DNS)   401
Chapter 17   TELNET and Rlogin   431
Chapter 18   File Transfer Protocol (FTP)   459
Chapter 19   Trivial File Transfer Protocol (TFTP)   479
Chapter 20   Simple Mail Transfer Protocol (SMTP)   495
Chapter 21   Simple Network Management Protocol (SNMP)   525
Chapter 22   Hypertext Transfer Protocol (HTTP)   551
Chapter 23   World Wide Web (WWW)   567
Chapter 24   Socket Interface   599
Chapter 25   Next Generation: IPv6 and ICMPv6   633
Appendix A   ASCII Code 677
Appendix B   Numbering Systems and Transformation 683
Appendix C   Representation of Binary Numbers 691
Appendix D   Error Detection 699
Appendix E   Encryption/Decryption 707
Appendix F   MIB Objects 713
Appendix G   High-Level Data Link Control (HDLC) 721
Appendix H   Project 802 729
Appendix I   ASN.1 733
Appendix J   Spanning Tree 737
Appendix K   Contact Addresses 743
Appendix L   RFCs 745
Appendix M   UDP and TCP Ports 747
Solutions   749
Acronyms   773
Glossary   781
References   809
Index   811

CONTENTS

Chapter 1

Introduction   1

1.1   PROTOCOLS AND STANDARDS   1
       Protocols   1
       Standards   2
1.2   STANDARDS ORGANIZATIONS   2
       Standards Creation Committees   2
       Forums   4
       Regulatory Agencies   4
1.3   INTERNET STANDARDS   4
       Maturity Levels   5
       Requirement Levels   6
1.4   INTERNET ADMINISTRATION   7
       ISOC   7
       IAB   8
       IETF   8
       IRTF   8
       IANA and ICANN   8
       NIC   9
1.5   A BRIEF HISTORY   9
       ARPANET   9
       Birth of the Internet   9
       TCP/IP   10
       MILNET   10
       CSNET   10
       NSFNET   11
       ANSNET   11
       The Internet Today   11
       Timeline   11
1.6   SUMMARY   12
1.7   PROBLEM SET   13
       Multiple Choice   13
       Exercises   15

Chapter 2

The OSI Model and the TCP/IP Protocol Suite   17

2.1   THE OSI MODEL   17
       Layered Architecture   18
       Peer-to-Peer Processes   18
2.2   LAYERS IN THE OSI MODEL   21
       Physical Layer   21
       Data Link Layer   22
       Network Layer   23
       Transport Layer   24
       Session Layer   25
       Presentation Layer   26
       Application Layer   27
2.3   TCP/IP PROTOCOL SUITE   28
       Physical and Data Link Layers   28
       Network Layer   28
       Transport Layer   30
       Application Layer   31
2.4   ADDRESSING   31
       Physical Address   31
       Internet Address   32
       Port Address   33
2.5   TCP/IP VERSIONS   34
       Version 4   34
       Version 5   35
       Version 6   35
2.6   SUMMARY   36
2.7   PRACTICE SET   36
       Multiple Choice   36
       Exercises   39

Chapter 3
Underlying Technologies   41

3.1   TRANSMISSION MEDIA   41
      Guided Media   41
      Unguided Media   45
3.2   LOCAL AREA NETWORKS (LANS)   46
      Ethernet   46
      Token Ring   51
      Fiber Distributed Data Interface (FDDI)   54
3.3   SWITCHING   56
      Circuit Switching   57
      Packet Switching   57
      Message Switching   59
3.4   WIDE AREA NETWORKS (WANS)   59
      Point-to-Point Protocol (PPP)   59
      X.25   60
      Frame Relay   62
      Asynchronous Transfer Mode (ATM)   65
3.5   CONNECTING DEVICES   68
      Repeaters   69
      Bridges   70
      Routers   72
      Gateways   73
3.6   SUMMARY   73
3.7   PRACTICE SET   76
      Multiple Choice   76
      Exercises   82
      Programming Exercises   84

Chapter 4
IP Addressing   85

4.1   DECIMAL NOTATION   86
4.2   CLASSES   87
      Class A   87
      Class B   87
      Class C   88
      Class D   88
      Class E   88
      Determining the Class of an Address   88
      Extracting Netid and Hostid   89
      Multihomed Devices   90
      Location Not Names   90
4.3   SPECIAL ADDRESSES   91
      Network Address   91
      Direct Broadcast Address   91

      Limited Broadcast Address   91
      This Host on This Network   93
      Specific Host on This Network   93
      Loopback Address   93
4.4   A SAMPLE INTERNET   95
4.5   UNICAST MULTICAST AND BROADCAST ADDRESSES   96
      Unicast Addresses   96
      Multicast Addresses   96
      Broadcast Addresses   98
4.6   APPLYING FOR IP ADDRESSES   98
      Class of Address   98
      Netids and Hostids   98
      Authorities   99
4.7   PRIVATE NETWORKS   99
4.8   SUMMARY   99
4.9   PRACTICE SET   100
      Multiple Choice   100
      Exercises   103
      Programming Exercises   107

Chapter 5
Subnetting and Supernetting   109

5.1   SUBNETTING   109
      Three Levels of Hierarchy   111
5.2   MASKING   111
      Special Addresses in Subnetting   113
      Contiguous vs. Noncontiguous Mask   113
5.3   EXAMPLES OF SUBNETTING   113
      Subnetting Class A   114
      Subnetting Class B   114
      Subnetting Class C   117
5.4   VARIABLE-LENGTH SUBNETTING   117
5.5   SUPERNETTING   119
      Supernet Mask   120
      Classless Interdomain Routing (CIDR)   121
5.6   SUMMARY   122
5.7   PRACTICE SET   123
      Multiple Choice   123
      Exercises   125

Chapter 6
Delivery and Routing of IP Packets   131

6.1   CONNECTION-ORIENTED VS. CONNECTIONLESS SERVICES   131

6.2   DIRECT VS. INDIRECT DELIVERY   132
      Direct Delivery   132
      Indirect Delivery   132
6.3   ROUTING METHODS   133
      Next-Hop Routing   133
      Network-Specific Routing   134
      Host-Specific Routing   134
      Default Routing   135
6.4   STATIC VS. DYNAMIC ROUTING   135
      Static Routing Table   136
      Dynamic Routing Table   136
6.5   ROUTING MODULE AND ROUTING
      TABLE DESIGN   137
      Routing Table   137
      Routing Module   139
      Examples   139
6.6   SUMMARY   141
6.7   PRACTICE SET   142
      Multiple Choice   142
      Exercises   144
      Programming Exercises   145

Chapter 7
Internet Protocol (IP)   147

7.1   DATAGRAM   147
7.2   FRAGMENTATION   152
      Maximum Transfer Unit (MTU)   152
      Fields Related to Fragmentation   154
7.3   OPTIONS   156
      Format   156
      Option Types   157
7.4   CHECKSUM   163
      Checksum Calculation at the Sender   163
      Checksum Calculation at the Receiver   164
      Checksum in the IP Packet   165
      Example   165
7.5   IP DESIGN   165
      Header-Adding Module   166
      Processing Module   167
      Queues   168
      Routing Table   168
      Routing Module   169
      MTU Table   169
      Fragmentation Module   169
      Reassembly Table   170
      Reassembly Module   170

7.6   SUMMARY   171
7.7   PRACTICE SET   172
      Multiple Choice   172
      Exercises   175
      Programming Exercises   176

Chapter 8
ARP and RARP   179

8.1   ARP   180
      Packet Format   182
      Encapsulation   183
      Operation   183
      Proxy ARP   184
8.2   ARP DESIGN   186
      Cache Table   186
      Queues   188
      Output Module   188
      Input Module   189
      Cache-Control Module   190
      Examples of ARP   191
8.3   RARP   193
      Packet Format   193
      Encapsulation   195
      Alternative Solutions to RARP   195
8.4   SUMMARY   195
8.5   PRACTICE SET   196
      Multiple Choice   196
      Exercises   198
      Programming Exercises   199

Chapter 9
*Internet Control Message Protocol
(ICMP)   201*

9.1   TYPES OF MESSAGES   202
9.2   MESSAGE FORMAT   203
9.3   ERROR REPORTING   203
      Destination Unreachable   204
      Source Quench   206
      Time Exceeded   208
      Parameter Problem   209
      Redirection   209
9.4   QUERY   211
      Echo Request and Reply   211
      Timestamp Request and Reply   212
      Address Mask Request and Reply   214

Router Solicitation and Advertisement   215
9.5   CHECKSUM   216
        Checksum Calculation   217
        Checksum Testing   217
        Example   217
9.6   ICMP DESIGN   217
        Input Module   218
        Output Module   219
9.7   SUMMARY   220
9.8   PRACTICE SET   220
        Multiple Choice   220
        Exercises   223
        Programming Exercises   225

Chapter 10
Internet Group Management Protocol (IGMP)   227

10.1   MULTICASTING   227
        Multicast Addresses   227
10.2   IGMP   228
        Types of Messages   228
        Message Format 228
        Operation of IGMP in a Single Network   229
        Operation of IGMP   231
        Changing IP Addresses to Physical
        Addresses   232
10.3   ENCAPSULATION   233
10.4   MULTICAST BACKBONE (MBONE)   234
10.5   IGMP DESIGN   234
        Group Table   234
        Timers   235
        Group-Joining Module   236
        Group-Leaving Module   236
        Input Module   237
        Output Module   237
        Examples of IGMP   238
10.6   SUMMARY   241
10.7   PRACTICE SET   242
        Multiple Choice   242
        Exercises   244
        Programming Exercises   246

Chapter 11
User Datagram Protocol (UDP)   247

11.1   PROCESS-TO-PROCESS

        COMMUNICATION   248
        Port Numbers   248
        Socket Addresses   252
11.2   USER DATAGRAM   253
11.3   CHECKSUM   254
        Checksum Calculation at Sender   255
        Checksum Calculation at Receiver   255
        An Example   255
        Optional Use of the Checksum   256
11.4   UDP OPERATION   256
        Connectionless Services   256
        Flow and Error Control   257
        Encapsulation and Decapsulation   257
        Queuing   258
        Multiplexing and Demultiplexing   259
11.5   USE OF UDP   260
11.6   UDP DESIGN   260
        Control-Block Table   261
        Input Queues   261
        Control-Block Module   261
        Input Module   262
        Output Module   262
        Examples   263
11.7   SUMMARY   264
11.8   PRACTICE SET   265
        Multiple Choice   265
        Exercises   268
        Programming Exercises   269

Chapter 12
Transmission Control Protocol (TCP)   271

12.1   PROCESS-TO-PROCESS
        COMMUNICATION   272
        Port Addresses   272
        Socket Addresses   274
12.2   TCP SERVICES   274
        Stream Data Service   274
        Full-Duplex Service   275
        Reliable Service   275
12.3   SEGMENT   275
12.4   OPTIONS   278
12.5   CHECKSUM   281
12.6   FLOW CONTROL   281
        Sliding Window   282
        Window Management   283
        Silly Window Syndrome   284

12.7 ERROR CONTROL 287
Error Detection and Correction 287
12.8 TCP TIMERS 290
Retransmission Timer 290
Persistence Timer 292
Keepalive Timer 292
Time-Waited Timer 293
12.9 CONNECTION 293
Connection Establishment 293
Connection Termination 295
Connection Resetting 296
12.10 STATE TRANSITION DIAGRAM 297
Client Diagram 298
Server Diagram 299
12.11 CONGESTION CONTROL 299
12.12 TCP OPERATION 301
Encapsulation and Decapsulation 301
Queuing 301
Multiplexing and Demultiplexing 301
Pushing Data 301
Urgent Data 303
12.13 TCP DESIGN 304
Transmission Control Blocks (TCBs) 304
Timers 306
Main Module 306
Input Processing Module 309
Output Processing Module 309
12.14 SUMMARY 310
12.15 PRACTICE SET 311
Multiple Choice 311
Exercises 316
Programming Exercises 318

Chapter 13
Routing Protocols (RIP, OSPF, and BGP) 319

13.1 INTERIOR AND EXTERIOR ROUTING 320
13.2 RIP 321
Distance Vector Routing 321
RIP Message Format 325
Requests and Responses 325
Timers in RIP 326
Slow Convergence 327
Instability 328

Some Remedies for Instability 329
RIP Version 2 331
Authentication 331
Encapsulation 332
13.3 OSPF 332
Areas 332
Metric 333
Link State Routing 333
Types of Packets 342
Packet Format 342
Encapsulation 350
13.4 BGP 350
Path Vector Routing 351
Types of Packets 353
Packet Format 353
Encapsulation 357
13.5 MULTICAST ROUTING 358
DVMRP 358
MOSPF 358
13.6 SUMMARY 358
13.7 PRACTICE SET 360
Multiple Choice 360
Exercises 365
Programming Exercises 368

Chapter 14
Application Layer and Client-Server Model 369

14.1 CLIENT-SERVER MODEL 370
Client 371
Server 372
14.2 CONCURRENCY 372
Concurrency in Clients 372
Concurrency in Servers 372
14.3 PROCESSES 374
Concept 375
Process Identification 376
Process Creation 377
14.4 SUMMARY 380
14.5 PRACTICE SET 381
Multiple Choice 381
Exercises 384
Programming Exercises 385

Chapter 15
BOOTP and DHCP   387

15.1   BOOTP   387
        Packet Format   387
        Operation   390
        UDP Ports   391
        Using TFTP   391
        Relay Agent   391
15.2   DYNAMIC HOST CONFIGURATION
        PROTOCOL (DHCP)   392
        Leasing   392
        DHCP Operation   392
        Packet Format   394
15.3   SUMMARY   395
15.4   PRACTICE SET   396
        Multiple Choice   396
        Exercises   398
        Programming Exercises   399

Chapter 16
Domain Name System (DNS)   401

16.1   NAME SPACE   401
        Flat Name Space   402
        Hierarchical Name Space   402
16.2   DOMAIN NAME SPACE   402
        Label   402
        Domain Name   402
        Domain   404
16.3   DISTRIBUTION OF NAME SPACE   405
        Hierarchy of Name Servers   405
        Zone   405
        Root Server   406
        Primary and Secondary Servers   407
16.4   DNS IN THE INTERNET   407
        Generic Domains   407
        Country Domains   409
        Inverse Domain   409
16.5   RESOLUTION   410
        Resolver   410
        Mapping Names to Addresses   411
        Mapping Addresses to Names   411
        Recursive Resolution   412
        Iterative Resolution   412
        Caching   412

16.6   DNS MESSAGES   413
        Header   414
16.7   TYPES OF RECORDS   416
        Question Record   416
        Resource Record   418
16.8   COMPRESSION   419
16.9   EXAMPLES   420
16.10   DDNS   423
16.11   ENCAPSULATION   424
16.12   SUMMARY   424
16.13   PRACTICE SET   425
        Multiple Choice   425
        Exercises   428

Chapter 17
TELNET and Rlogin   431

17.1   CONCEPT   431
        Timesharing Environment   431
        Login   432
17.2   NETWORK VIRTUAL TERMINAL
        (NVT)   433
17.3   NVT CHARACTER SET   434
        Data Characters   434
        Remote Control Characters   435
17.4   EMBEDDING   436
17.5   OPTIONS   436
17.6   OPTION NEGOTIATION   437
        Enabling an Option   438
        Disabling an Option   439
        Example   440
        Symmetry   441
17.7   SUBOPTION NEGOTIATION   441
17.8   CONTROLLING THE SERVER   442
17.9   OUT-OF-BAND SIGNALING   443
17.10   ESCAPE CHARACTER   444
        Default Mode   445
        Character Mode   445
        Line Mode   445
17.11   MODE OF OPERATION   445
        Default Mode   445
        Character Mode   445
        Line Mode   445
17.12   EXAMPLES   445
17.13   USER INTERFACE   447
17.14   RLOGIN (REMOTE LOGIN)   448

TCP Port   448
Connection   448
Flow Control   449
Commands   449
Mode   450
17.15 SECURITY ISSUE   452
17.16 SUMMARY   452
17.17 PRACTICE SET   453
Multiple Choice   453
Exercises   457

Chapter 18
File Transfer Protocol (FTP)   *459*

18.1 CONNECTIONS   460
Control Connection   460
Data Connection   460
18.2 COMMUNICATION   461
Communication over Control
Connection   461
Communication over Data Connection   462
18.3 COMMAND PROCESSING   464
Commands   464
Responses   467
18.4 FILE TRANSFER   469
18.5 USER INTERFACE   472
18.6 ANONYMOUS FTP   473
18.7 SUMMARY   473
18.8 PRACTICE SET   474
Multiple Choice   474
Exercises   476

Chapter 19
Trivial File Transfer Protocol (TFTP)   *479*

19.1 MESSAGES   479
RRQ   480
WRQ   480
DATA   480
ACK   481
ERROR   481
19.2 CONNECTION   482
Connection Establishment   483
Connection Termination   483
19.3 DATA TRANSFER   483
Flow Control   484
Error Control   484
Sorcerer's Apprentice Bug   485

19.4 UDP PORTS   486
19.5 TFTP EXAMPLE   487
19.6 TFTP OPTIONS   487
19.7 SECURITY   487
19.8 APPLICATIONS   489
19.9 SUMMARY   490
19.10 PRACTICE SET   490
Multiple Choice   490
Exercises   493

Chapter 20
Simple Mail Transfer Protocol (SMTP)   *495*

20.1 USER AGENT (UA)   497
Sending Mail   497
Receiving Mail   498
20.2 ADDRESSES   498
Local Part   498
Domain Name   499
20.3 DELAYED DELIVERY   499
Sender-Site Delay   499
Receiver-Site Delay   500
Intermediate Delay   501
20.4 ALIASES   501
One-to-Many Expansion   501
Many-to-One Expansion   502
20.5 MAIL TRANSFER AGENT (MTA)   502
20.6 COMMANDS AND RESPONSES   503
Commands   503
Responses   507
20.7 MAIL TRANSFER PHASES   508
Connection Establishment   508
Message Transfer   509
Connection Termination   509
20.8 MULTIPURPOSE INTERNET MAIL
EXTENSIONS (MIME)   511
MIME-Version   512
Content-Type   512
Content-Transfer-Encoding   514
Content-Id   517
Content-Description   517
20.9 POST OFFICE PROTOCOL (POP)   517
20.10 SUMMARY   518
20.11 PRACTICE SET   518
Multiple Choice   518
Exercises   522

Chapter 21
Simple Network Management Protocol (SNMP)   525

21.1   CONCEPT   525
    Managers and Agents   526
    Components   526
21.2   SMI   526
    Name   527
    Type   527
    Encoding Method   529
21.3   MIB   532
    Accessing MIB Variables   533
    Lexicographic Ordering   535
21.4   SNMP   536
    Messages   536
    Format   537
    Encoding   539
21.5   EXAMPLES   540
21.6   UDP PORTS   544
21.7   SUMMARY   545
21.8   PRACTICE SET   546
    Multiple Choice   546
    Exercises   549

Chapter 22
Hypertext Transfer Protocol (HTTP)   551

22.1   HTTP TRANSACTION   552
    Messages   552
22.2   REQUEST MESSAGES   552
    Request Line   553
    Methods   554
22.3   RESPONSE MESSAGE   555
    Status Line   556
22.4   HEADER   558
    General Header   559
    Request Header   559
    Response Header   560
    Entity Header   560
22.5   EXAMPLES   560
22.6   PRACTICE SET   563
    Multiple Choice   563
    Exercises   566

Chapter 23
World Wide Web (WWW)   567

23.1   HYPERTEXT AND HYPERMEDIA   567
23.2   BROWSER ARCHITECTURE   568
23.3   STATIC DOCUMENTS   569
23.4   HTML   569
    Structure of a Web Page   571
    Tags   571
    Examples   575
23.5   DYNAMIC DOCUMENTS   577
23.6   COMMON GATEWAY INTERFACE (CGI)   578
    CGI Program   578
    Environment Variables   579
    Input   579
    Output   580
    Examples   581
23.7   ACTIVE DOCUMENTS   583
    Creation Compilation and Execution   583
23.8   JAVA   585
    Classes and Objects   585
    Instantiation   585
    Inheritance   585
    Packages   585
    Skeleton of an Applet   586
    Creation and Compilation   587
    HTML Document   587
    Examples   587
23.9   SUMMARY   591
23.10   PRACTICE SET   592
    Multiple Choice   592
    Exercises   596
    Programming Exercises   597

Chapter 24
Socket Interface   599

24.1   SOME DEFINITIONS   599
    Data Types Defined   599
    Internet Address Structure   600
    Internet Socket Address Structure   600
24.2   SOCKETS   600
    Socket Types   602
24.3   BYTE ORDERING   602
    Big-Endian Byte Order   603
    Little-Endian Byte Order   603

Network Byte Order 604
Byte-Order Transformation 604
24.4 ADDRESS TRANSFORMATION 605
24.5 BYTE MANIPULATION FUNCTIONS 606
24.6 INFORMATION ABOUT REMOTE HOST 607
24.7 SOCKET SYSTEM CALLS 608
Socket 608
Bind 608
Connect 609
Listen 609
Accept 610
Sendto 610
Recvfrom 611
Read 611
Write 612
Close 612
24.8 CONNECTIONLESS ITERATIVE SERVER 612
Server 613
Client 614
24.9 UDP CLIENT-SERVER PROGRAMS 614
Server Program 615
Client Program 616
24.10 CONNECTION-ORIENTED CONCURRENT SERVER 618
Server 618
Client 620
24.11 TCP CLIENT-SERVER PROGRAMS 621
Server Program 622
Client Program 623
24.12 SUMMARY 625
24.13 PRACTICE SET 626
Multiple Choice 626
Exercises 631
Programming Exercises 631

Chapter 25
Next Generation: IPv6 and ICMPv6 633

25.1 IPV6 634
25.2 IPV6 ADDRESSES 634
Hexadecimal Colon Notation 634
Categories of Addresses 636
Address Space Assignment 636
25.3 IPV6 PACKET FORMAT 642

Base Header 642
Priority 644
Flow Label 645
Comparison between IPv4 and IPv6 Headers 646
Extension Headers 646
Comparison between IPv4 and IPv6 653
25.4 ICMPV6 654
Error Reporting 654
Query 658
25.5 TRANSITION FROM IPV4 TO IPV6 663
Dual Stack 664
Tunneling 664
Header Translation 665
25.6 SUMMARY 667
25.7 PRACTICE SET 668
Multiple Choice 668
Exercises 673
Programming Exercises 675

Appendix A
ASCII Code 677

Appendix B
Numbering Systems and Transformation 683

B.1 NUMBERING SYSTEMS 683
Decimal Numbers 684
Binary Numbers 684
Octal Numbers 685
Hexadecimal Numbers 686
B.2 TRANSFORMATION 687
From Other Systems to Decimal 688
From Decimal to Other Systems 688
From Binary to Octal or Hexadecimal 688
From Octal or Hexadecimal to Binary 689

Appendix C
Representation of Binary Numbers 691

C.1 UNSIGNED NUMBERS 691
C.2 SIGNED NUMBERS 692
Sign-and-Magnitude 692
One's Complement 694
Two's Complement 695
C.3 MORE ABOUT ONE'S COMPLEMENT 696

Finding the Complement 696
Adding Two Numbers 697

Appendix D
Error Detection 699

D.1 TYPES OF ERRORS 699
Single-Bit Error 700
Multiple-Bit Error 700
Burst Error 700
D.2 DETECTION 701
Redundancy 701
Vertical Redundancy Check (VRC) 702
Longitudinal Redundancy Check (LRC) 703
Cyclic Redundancy Check (CRC) 703
Checksum 706

Appendix E
Encryption/Decryption 707

E.1 CONVENTIONAL METHODS 707
DES 708
E.2 PUBLIC KEY METHODS 709
RSA Encryption 710
E.3 AUTHENTICATION 711

Appendix F
MIB Objects 713

F.1 SYSTEM GROUP 713
F.2 INTERFACE GROUP 713
F.3 IP GROUP 715
F.4 ICMP GROUP 717
F.5 TCP GROUP 718
F.6 UDP GROUP 719

Appendix G
High-Level Data Link Control (HDLC) 721

G.1 STATION TYPES 721
G.2 CONFIGURATIONS 721
G.3 MODES OF COMMUNICATION 722
NRM 723
ARM 723
ABM 723
G.4 FRAMES 724
G.5 MORE ABOUT FRAMES 726
I-frames 727
S-frames 727
U-frames 727

G.6 LINK ACCESS PROCEDURES (LAPS) 728
LAPB 728
LAPD 728
LAPM 728

Appendix H
Project 802 729

H.1 PROJECT 802.1 730
H.2 PROJECT 802.2 730
LLC 731
MAC 731

Appendix I
ASN.1 733

I.1 DATA TYPES AND VALUES 733
Simple Type 733
Structured Type 734
Tags 735
Subtyping 735
Values 735
I.2 MODULES AND MACROS 736
Modules 736
Macros 736

Appendix J
Spanning Tree 737

J.1 SPANNING TREES AND BRIDGES 738
Algorithm 739
Forming the Spanning Tree 740
Example 740
J.2 SPANNING TREES AND MULTICAST
ROUTING 742

Appendix K
Contact Addresses 743

Appendix L
RFCs 745

Appendix M
UDP and TCP Ports 747

Solutions 749

Acronyms 773

Glossary 781

References 809

Index 811

CHAPTER 1

Introduction

The Internet has revolutionized many aspects of our daily lives. It has affected the way we do business as well as the way we spend our leisure time. Count the ways you've used the Internet recently. Perhaps you've sent electronic mail (e-mail) to a business associate, paid a utility bill, read a newspaper from a distant city, or looked up a local movie schedule—all by using the Internet. Or, maybe you researched a medical topic, booked a hotel reservation, chatted with a fellow Trekkie, or comparison-shopped for a car. The Internet is a communication system that has brought a wealth of information to our fingertips and organized it for our use.

The Internet is a structured, organized system. To understand how it works and its relationship to TCP/IP, first we need to define the concepts of protocols and standards. Also, we need to be aware of the various organizations that are involved in the development of Internet standards. These standards are not developed by any specific organization, but rather through a consensus of users. We discuss the mechanism through which these standards originated and matured.

Also included in this introductory chapter are a section on Internet administrative groups and a brief section on Internet history.

1.1 PROTOCOLS AND STANDARDS

In this section, we define two widely used terms: protocols and standards. First, we define *protocols,* which are synonymous with "rules." Then we discuss *standards,* which are agreed-upon rules.

Protocols

In computer networks, communication occurs between entities in different systems. An **entity** is anything capable of sending or receiving information. However, two entities cannot simply send bit streams to each other and expect to be understood. For communication to occur, the entities must agree on a protocol. A **protocol** is a set of rules that governs data communication. A protocol defines what is communicated, how it is communicated, and when it is communicated. The key elements of a protocol are syntax, semantics, and timing.

■ **Syntax.** Syntax refers to the structure or format of the data, meaning the order in which they are presented. For example, a simple protocol might expect the first eight bits of data to be the address of the sender, the second eight bits to be the address of the receiver, and the rest of the stream to be the message itself.

■ **Semantics.** Semantics refers to the meaning of each section of bits. How is a particular pattern to be interpreted, and what action is to be taken based on that interpretation? For example, does an address identify the route to be taken or the final destination of the message?

■ **Timing.** Timing refers to two characteristics: when data should be sent and how fast it can be sent. For example, if a sender produces data at 100 Megabits per second (Mbps) but the receiver can process data at only 1 Mbps, the transmission will overload the receiver and data will be largely lost.

Standards

Standards are essential in creating and maintaining an open and competitive market for equipment manufacturers and also in guaranteeing national and international interoperability of data and telecommunications technology and processes. They provide guidelines to manufacturers, vendors, government agencies, and other service providers to ensure the kind of interconnectivity necessary in today's marketplace and in international communications.

Data communication standards fall into two categories: *de facto* (meaning "by fact" or "by convention") and *de jure* (meaning "by law" or "by regulation").

■ **De facto.** Standards that have not been approved by an organized body but have been adopted as standards through widespread use are de facto standards. De facto standards are often established originally by manufacturers that seek to define the functionality of a new product or technology.

■ **De jure.** De jure standards are those that have been legislated by an officially recognized body.

1.2   STANDARDS ORGANIZATIONS

Standards are developed through cooperation of standards creation committees, forums, and government regulatory agencies.

Standards Creation Committees

While many organizations are dedicated to the establishment of standards, data telecommunications in North America rely primarily on those published by the following:

■ **International Standards Organization (ISO).** The International Standards Organization (ISO; also referred to as the International Organization for Standardization) is a multinational body whose membership is drawn mainly from the standards creation committees of various governments throughout the world. Created in 1947, the ISO is an entirely voluntary organization dedicated to worldwide agreement on international standards. With a membership that currently includes representative bodies from 82 industrialized nations, it aims to facilitate the international exchange of goods and services by providing models for compatibility, improved quality, increased productivity, and decreased prices. The ISO is active in developing cooperation in the realms of scientific, technological, and economic activity. Of primary concern to this book are the ISO's efforts in the field of information technology, which have resulted in the creation of the Open Systems Interconnection (OSI) model for network communications. The United States is represented in the ISO by ANSI.

■ **International Telecommunications Union–Telecommunication Standards Sector (ITU-T).** By the early 1970s a number of countries were defining national standards for telecommunications, but there was still little international compatibility. The United Nations responded by forming, as part of its International Telecommunications Union (ITU), a committee, the Consultative Committee for International Telegraphy and Telephony (CCITT). This committee was devoted to the research and establishment of standards for telecommunications in general and phone and data systems in particular. On March 1, 1993, the name of this committee was changed to the International Telecommunications Union–Telecommunication Standards Sector (ITU-T).

■ **American National Standards Institute (ANSI).** Despite its name, the American National Standards Institute (ANSI) is a completely private, nonprofit corporation not affiliated with the U.S. federal government. However, all ANSI activities are undertaken with the welfare of the United States and its citizens occupying primary importance. ANSI's expressed aims include serving as the national coordinating institution for voluntary standardization in the United States, furthering the adoption of standards as a way of advancing the U.S. economy, and ensuring the participation and protection of the public interests. ANSI members include professional societies, industry associations, governmental and regulatory bodies, and consumer groups.

■ **Institute of Electrical and Electronics Engineers (IEEE).** The Institute of Electrical and Electronics Engineers (IEEE) is the largest professional engineering society in the world. International in scope, it aims to advance theory, creativity, and product quality in the fields of electrical engineering, electronics, and radio as well as in all related branches of engineering. As one of its goals, the IEEE oversees the development and adoption of international standards for computing and communication.

■ **Electronic Industries Association (EIA).** Aligned with ANSI, the Electronic Industries Association (EIA) is a nonprofit organization devoted to the promotion of electronics manufacturing concerns. Its activities include public awareness education and lobbying efforts in addition to standards development. In the field of information technology, the EIA has made significant contributions by defining physical connection interfaces and electronic signaling specifications for data communication.

Forums

Telecommunications technology development is moving faster than the ability of standards committees to ratify standards. Standards committees are procedural bodies and by nature slow moving. To accommodate the need for working models and agreements and to facilitate the standardization process, many special-interest groups have developed **forums** made up of representatives from interested corporations. The forums work with universities and users to test, evaluate, and standardize new technologies. By concentrating their efforts on a particular technology, the forums are able to speed acceptance and use of those technologies in the telecommunications community. The forums present their conclusions to the standards bodies. Some important forums for the telecommunications industry include the following:

- **Frame Relay Forum.** The Frame Relay Forum was formed by Digital Equipment Corporation, Northern Telecom, Cisco, and StrataCom to promote the acceptance and implementation of frame relay. Today, it has around 40 members representing North America, Europe, and the Pacific Rim. Issues under review include flow control, encapsulation, translation, and multicasting. The forum's results are submitted to the ISO.

- **ATM Forum.** The ATM Forum promotes the acceptance and use of Asynchronous Transfer Mode (ATM) technology. The ATM Forum is made up of Customer Premises Equipment (e.g., PBX systems) vendors and Central Office (e.g., telephone exchange) providers. It is concerned with the standardization of services to ensure interoperability. The ATM Forum is made up of vendors of hardware and software that support ATM.

Regulatory Agencies

All communications technology is subject to regulation by government agencies such as the Federal Communications Commission in the United States. The purpose of these agencies is to protect the public interest by regulating radio, television, and wire/cable communications.

- **Federal Communications Commission (FCC).** The Federal Communications Commission (FCC) has authority over interstate and international commerce as it relates to communications.

1.3   INTERNET STANDARDS

An **Internet standard** is a thoroughly tested specification that is useful to and adhered to by those who work with the Internet. It is a formalized regulation that must be followed. There is a strict procedure by which a specification attains Internet standard status. A specification begins as an Internet draft. An **Internet draft** is a working document (a work in progress) with no official status and a six-month lifetime. Upon recommendation from the Internet authorities, a draft may be published as a **Request for Comment** (RFC). Each RFC is edited, assigned a number, and made available to all interested parties.

RFCs go through maturity levels and are categorized according to their requirement level.

Maturity Levels

An RFC, during its lifetime, falls into one of six maturity levels: proposed standard, draft standard, Internet standard, historic, experimental, and informational (see Figure 1.1).

Figure 1.1   *Maturity levels of an RFC*

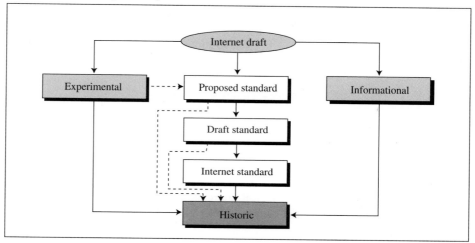

Proposed Standard

A proposed standard is a specification that is stable, well understood, and of sufficient interest to the Internet community. At this level, the specification is usually tested and implemented by several different groups.

Draft Standard

A proposed standard is elevated to draft standard status after at least two successful independent and interoperable implementations. Barring difficulties, a draft standard, with modifications if specific problems are encountered, normally becomes an Internet standard.

Internet Standard

A draft standard reaches Internet standard status after demonstrations of successful implementation.

Historic

The historic RFCs are significant from a historical perspective. They either have been superseded by later specifications or have never passed the necessary maturity levels to become an Internet standard.

Experimental

An RFC classified as experimental describes work related to an experimental situation that does not affect the operation of the Internet. Such an RFC should not be implemented in any functional Internet service.

Informational

An RFC classified as informational contains general, historical, or tutorial information related to the Internet. It is usually written by someone in a non-Internet organization, such as a vendor.

Requirement Levels

RFCs are classified into five requirement levels: required, recommended, elective, limited use, and not recommended (see Figure 1.2).

Figure 1.2 *Requirement levels of an RFC*

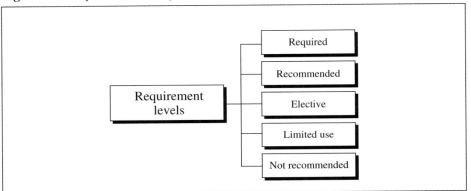

Required

An RFC is labeled *required* if it must be implemented by all Internet systems to achieve minimum conformance. For example, IP (Chapter 7) and ICMP (Chapter 9) are required protocols.

Recommended

An RFC labeled *recommended* is not required for minimum conformance; it is recommended because of its usefulness. For example, FTP (Chapter 18) and TELNET (Chapter 17) are recommended protocols.

Elective

An RFC labeled *elective* is not required and not recommended. However, a system can use it to its own benefit.

Limited Use

An RFC labeled *limited use* should be used only in limited situations. Most of the experimental RFCs fall under this category.

Not Recommended

An RFC labeled *not recommended* is inappropriate for general use. Normally a historic (obsolete) RFC may fall under this category.

1.4   INTERNET ADMINISTRATION

The Internet, with its roots primarily in the research domain, has evolved and gained a broader user base with significant commercial activity. Various groups that coordinate Internet issues have guided this growth and development. Appendix K gives the addresses, e-mail addresses, and telephone numbers for some of these groups. Figure 1.3 shows the general organization of Internet administration.

Figure 1.3   *Internet administration*

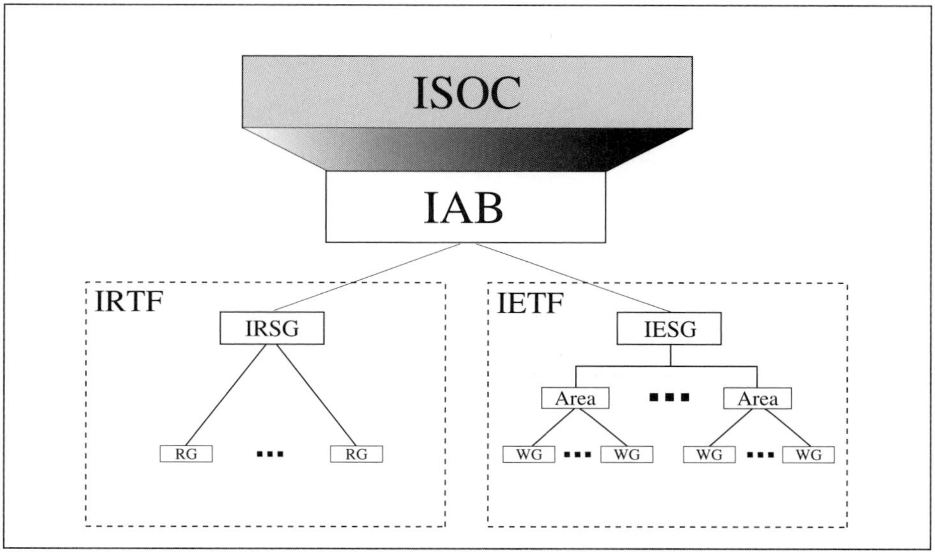

Internet Society (ISOC)

The **Internet Society** (ISOC) is an international, nonprofit organization formed in 1992 to provide support for the Internet standards process. ISOC accomplishes this through maintaining and supporting other Internet administrative bodies such as IAB, IETF, IRTF, and IANA (see the following sections). ISOC also promotes research and other scholarly activities relating to the Internet.

Internet Architecture Board (IAB)

The **Internet Architecture Board** (IAB) is the technical advisor to the ISOC. The main purposes of the IAB are to oversee the continuing development of the TCP/IP Protocol Suite and to serve in a technical advisory capacity to research members of the Internet community. IAB accomplishes this through its two primary components, the Internet Engineering Task Force (IETF) and the Internet Research Task Force (IRTF). Another responsibility of the IAB is the editorial management of the RFCs, described earlier in this chapter. IAB is also the external liaison between the Internet and other standards organizations and forums.

Internet Engineering Task Force (IETF)

The **Internet Engineering Task Force** (IETF) is a forum of working groups managed by the Internet Engineering Steering Group (IESG). IETF is responsible for identifying operational problems and proposing solutions to these problems. IETF also develops and reviews specifications intended as Internet standards. The working groups are collected into areas, and each area concentrates on a specific topic. Currently nine areas have been defined, although this is by no means a hard and fast number. The areas are:

- Applications
- Internet protocols
- Routing
- Operations
- User services
- Network management
- Transport
- Internet protocol next generation (IPng)
- Security

Internet Research Task Force (IRTF)

The **Internet Research Task Force** (IRTF) is a forum of working groups managed by the Internet Research Steering Group (IRSG). IRTF focuses on long-term research topics related to Internet protocols, applications, architecture, and technology.

Internet Assigned Numbers Authority (IANA) and Internet Corporation for Assigned Names and Numbers (ICANN)

The **Internet Assigned Numbers Authority** (IANA), supported by the U.S. government, was responsible for the management of Internet domain names and addresses until October 1998. At that time the **Internet Corporation for Assigned Names and Numbers** (ICANN), a private, nonprofit corporation managed by an international board, assumed IANA operations.

Network Information Center (NIC)

The **Network Information Center** (NIC) is responsible for collecting and distributing information about TCP/IP protocols.

1.5   A BRIEF HISTORY

A **network** is a group of connected, communicating devices such as computers and printers. An internet (note the lowercase *i*) is two or more networks that can communicate with each other. The most notable internet is called the Internet (uppercase *I*), a collaboration of more than 134,000 interconnected networks. Private individuals as well as various organizations such as government agencies, schools, research facilities, corporations, and libraries in more than 100 countries use the Internet. Millions of people are users. Yet this extraordinary communication system only came into being in 1969.

ARPANET

In the mid-1960s mainframe computers in research organizations were stand-alone devices. Computers from different manufacturers were unable to communicate with one another. The Advanced Research Projects Agency (ARPA) in the Department of Defense (DOD) was interested in finding a way to connect computers together so that the researchers they funded could share their findings, thereby reducing costs and eliminating duplication of effort.

In 1967, at an Association for Computing Machinery (ACM) meeting, ARPA presented its ideas for **ARPANET**, a small network of connected computers. The idea was that each host computer (not necessarily from the same manufacturer) would be attached to a specialized computer, called an *interface message processor* (IMP). The IMPs, in turn, would be connected to each other. Each IMP had to be able to communicate with other IMPs as well as with its own attached host.

By 1969, ARPANET was a reality. Four nodes, the University of California at Los Angeles (UCLA), the University of California at Santa Barbara (UCSB), Stanford Research Institute (SRI), and the University of Utah were connected via the IMPs to form a network. Software called the *Network Control Protocol* (NCP) provided communication between the hosts.

The ARPANET continued to grow, adding both academic and industrial sites under the aegis of ARPA.

Birth of the Internet

In 1972, Vint Cerf and Bob Kahn, both of whom were part of the core ARPANET group, collaborated on what they called the *Internetting Project*. They wanted to link different networks together so that a host on one network could communicate with a host on a second, different network. There were many problems to overcome: diverse packet sizes, diverse interfaces, and diverse transmission rates, as well as differing reliability requirements. Cerf and Kahn devised the idea of a device called a *gateway* to serve as the intermediary hardware to transfer packets from one network to another.

Transmission Control Protocol/Internetworking Protocol (TCP/IP)

Cerf and Kahn's landmark 1973 paper outlined the protocols to achieve end-to-end delivery of packets. This was a new version of NCP. This paper on transmission control protocol (TCP) included concepts such as encapsulation, the datagram, and the functions of a gateway. A radical idea was the transfer of responsibility for error correction from the IMP to the host machine. This ARPA Internet now became the major communication effort, especially since responsibility for the ARPANET had been handed over to the Defense Communication Agency (DCA).

In October 1977 an internet consisting of three different networks (ARPANET, packet radio, and packet satellite) was successfully demonstrated. Communication between networks was now possible.

Shortly thereafter, authorities made a decision to split TCP into two protocols: TCP and IP (Internetworking Protocol). IP would handle datagram routing while TCP would be responsible for higher level functions such as segmentation, reassembly, and error detection. The internetworking protocol became known as TCP/IP.

In 1981, under a DARPA contract, UC Berkeley modified the UNIX operating system to include TCP/IP. This inclusion of network software along with a popular operating system did much to further the popularity of networking. The open (non-manufacturer-specific) implementation on Berkeley UNIX gave every manufacturer a working code base on which they could build their products.

In 1983 authorities abolished the original ARPANET protocols, and TCP/IP became the official protocol for the ARPANET. Those who wanted to use the Internet to access a computer on a different network had to be running TCP/IP.

MILNET

In 1983 ARPANET split into two networks: **MILNET** for military users and ARPANET for nonmilitary users.

CSNET

Another milestone in Internet history was the creation of CSNET in 1981. **CSNET** was a network sponsored by the National Science Foundation (NSF) that was conceived by universities interested in network communication but without the defense ties to DARPA and so were thereby ineligible to join ARPANET. CSNET was a less expensive network; there were no redundant links and the transmission rate was slower. It featured connections to ARPANET and Telenet, the first commercial packet data service.

By the middle 1980s most U.S. universities with computer science departments were part of CSNET. Other institutions and companies were also forming their own networks and using TCP/IP to interconnect. The term *Internet*, originally associated with government-funded connected networks, now referred to the connected networks using TCP/IP protocols.

NSFNET

With the success of CSNET, the NSF, in 1986, sponsored **NSFNET**, a backbone that connected five supercomputer centers located throughout the United States Community networks were allowed access to this backbone, a T1 line with a 1.544 Mbps data rate, thus providing connectivity throughout the United States.

In 1990 ARPANET was officially retired and replaced by NSFNET. In 1995 NSF-NET reverted back to its original concept of a research network.

ANSNET

In 1991 the U.S. government decided that NSFNET was not capable of supporting the rapidly increasing Internet traffic. Three companies, IBM, Merit, and MCI, filled the void by forming a nonprofit organization called Advanced Network and Services (ANS) to build a new, high-speed Internet backbone called **ANSNET**.

The Internet Today

The Internet today consists of networks from around the world connected by connecting devices. More than 36 million hosts are distributed over more than 134,000 networks. Parts of the backbone operate at 155 Mbps. Figure 1.4 depicts a part of the Internet; the clouds represent networks and the square boxes represent the connecting devices.

Figure 1.4   *The Internet*

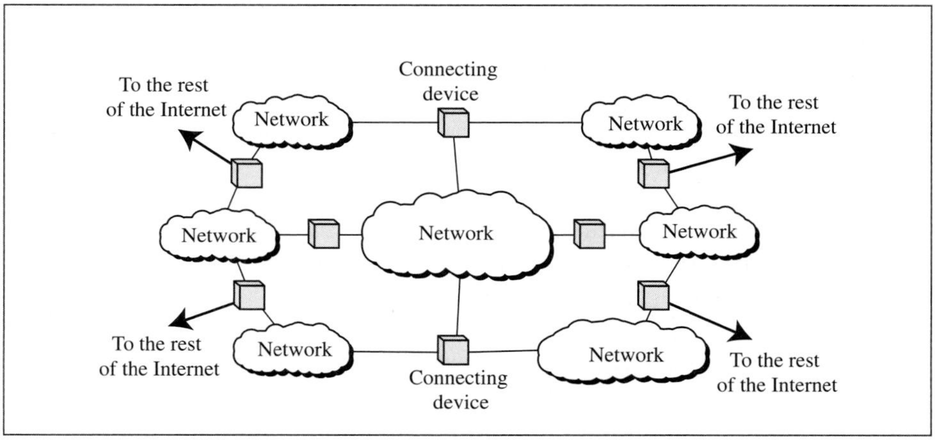

Timeline

The following is a list of important Internet events in chronological order:

- **1969.** Four-node ARPANET established.
- **1970.** ARPA hosts implement NCP.
- **1973.** Development of TCP/IP suite begins.
- **1977.** An internet tested using TCP/IP.
- **1978.** UNIX distributed to academic/research sites.
- **1981.** CSNET established.
- **1983.** TCP/IP becomes the official protocol for ARPANET.
- **1983.** MILNET was born.
- **1986.** NSFNET established.
- **1990.** ARPANET decommissioned and replaced by NSFNET.
- **1995.** NSFNET goes back to being a research network.

1.6 SUMMARY

- A protocol is a set of rules that governs data communication; the key elements of a protocol are syntax, semantics, and timing.
- Standards are necessary to ensure that products from different manufacturers can work together as expected.
- The ISO, ITU-T, ANSI, IEEE, and EIA are some of the organizations involved in standards creation.
- Forums are special-interest groups that quickly evaluate and standardize new technologies.
- Two important forums are the Frame Relay Forum and the ATM Forum.
- The FCC is a regulatory agency that regulates radio, television, and wire/cable communications.
- A Request for Comment (RFC) is an idea or concept that is a precursor to an Internet Standard.
- An RFC goes through the proposed standard level, then the draft standard level before it becomes an Internet standard.
- An RFC is categorized as required, recommended, elective, limited use, or not recommended.
- The Internet Society (ISOC) promotes research and other scholarly activities relating to the Internet.
- The Internet Architecture Board (IAB) is the technical advisor to the ISOC.
- The Internet Engineering Task Force (IETF) is a forum of working groups responsible for identifying operational problems and proposing solutions to these problems.
- The Internet Research Task Force (IRTF) is a forum of working groups focusing on long-term research topics related to Internet protocols, applications, architecture, and technology.

- The Internet Corporation for Assigned Names and Numbers (ICANN), formerly known as IANA, is responsible for the management of Internet domain names and addresses.
- The Network Information Center (NIC) is responsible for collecting and distributing information about TCP/IP protocols.
- The Internet is a collection of more than 134,000 separate networks.
- ARPANET began as a network with four nodes.
- TCP/IP is the protocol suite for the Internet.
- CSNET provided communication between networks ineligible to join ARPANET.
- NSFNET provided communication between networks throughout the United States.

1.7   PROBLEM SET

Multiple Choice

1. Which agency is the U.S. voting member to the ISO?
   a. USO
   b. IEEE
   c. NATO
   d. ANSI
2. Which organization has authority over interstate and international commerce in the communications field?
   a. ITU-T
   b. IEEE
   c. FCC
   d. ISOC
3. _____ are special-interest groups that quickly test, evaluate, and standardize new technologies.
   a. Forums
   b. Regulatory agencies
   c. Standards organizations
   d. All of the above
4. Which agency developed standards for electrical connections and the physical transfer of data between devices?
   a. EIA
   b. ITU-T
   c. ANSI
   d. ISO
5. In the original ARPANET, _____ were directly connected together.

a. IMPs

b. host computers

c. networks

d. routers

6. _____ was formed to connect universities with no defense ties.

a. ARPANET

b. CSNET

c. NFSNET

d. ANSNET

7. This was the first network.

a. CSNET

b. NFSNET

c. ANSNET

d. ARPANET

8. _____ is the protocol suite for the current Internet.

a. TCP/IP

b. NCP

c. UNIX

d. ACM

9. A version of the _____ operating system included TCP/IP.

a. DARPA

b. NCP

c. UNIX

d. ACM

10. The _____ oversees the IETF and the IRTF.

a. ISOC

b. IAB

c. IANA

d. NIC

11. The _____ maintains and supports IAB.

a. ISOC

b. IETF

c. IANA

d. ICANN

12. _____ is the precursor to ICANN.

a. ISOC

b. IETF

c. IANA

d. NIC

Exercises

13. Do some research and find some standards developed by ITU-T.

14. Do some research and find some standards developed by ANSI.

15. One of the standards developed by IEEE is project 802. Do some research and find some information about this project. What is 802.1? What is 802.2? What is 802.3? What is 802.5?

16. EIA has developed some standards for interfaces. Do some research and find some of these standards. What is EIA 232?

17. Do some research and find some regulations devised by FCC concerning AM and FM transmission.

18. Use the Internet to find the number of RFCs.

19. Use the Internet to find the subject matter of RFCs 2418 and 1603.

20. Use the Internet to find the RFC that discusses the IRTF working group guidelines and procedures.

21. Use the Internet to find two examples of an historic RFC.

22. Use the Internet to find two examples of an experimental RFC.

23. Use the Internet to find two examples of an informational RFC.

24. Use the Internet to find the RFC that discusses the FTP application.

25. Use the Internet to find the RFC for the Internet Protocol (IP).

26. Use the Internet to find the RFC for the Transmission Control Protocol (TCP).

27. Use the Internet to find the RFC that details the Internet standards process.

CHAPTER 2

The OSI Model and the TCP/IP Protocol Suite

The layered model that dominated data communication and networking literature before 1990 was the **Open Systems Interconnection** (OSI) model. Everyone believed that the OSI model would become the ultimate standard for data communication—but this did not happen. The TCP/IP protocol suite became the dominant commercial architecture because it was used and tested extensively in the Internet; the OSI model was never fully implemented.

In this chapter, we first briefly discuss the OSI as a model and then we concentrate on TCP/IP as a protocol suite.

2.1 THE OSI MODEL

Established in 1947, the **International Standards Organization** (ISO) is a multinational body dedicated to worldwide agreement on international standards. An ISO standard that covers all aspects of network communications is the OSI model. An **open system** is a set of protocols that allows any two different systems to communicate regardless of their underlying architecture. The purpose of the OSI model is to facilitate communication between different systems without requiring changes to the logic of the underlying hardware and software. The OSI model is not a protocol; it is a model for understanding and designing a network architecture that is flexible, robust, and interoperable.

ISO is the organization. OSI is the model.

The OSI model is a layered framework for the design of network systems that allows communication between all types of computer systems. It consists of seven separate but related layers, each of which defines a segment of the process of moving information across a network (see Figure 2.1). Understanding the fundamentals of the OSI model provides a solid basis for exploring data communication.

Figure 2.1   *The OSI model*

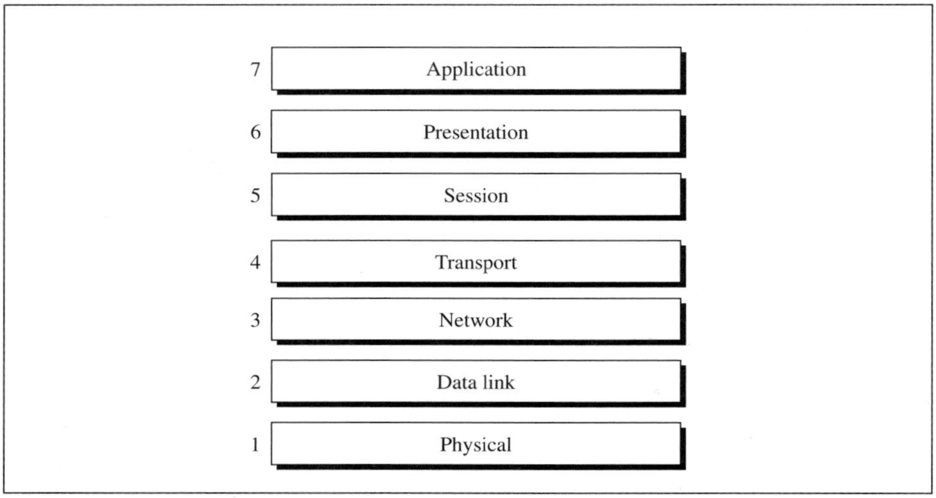

Layered Architecture

The OSI model is composed of seven ordered layers: physical (layer 1), data link (layer 2), network (layer 3), transport (layer 4), session (layer 5), presentation (layer 6), and application (layer 7). Figure 2.2 shows the layers involved when a message is sent from device A to device B. As the message travels from A to B, it may pass through many intermediate nodes. These intermediate nodes usually involve only the first three layers of the OSI model.

In developing the model, the designers distilled the process of transmitting data to its most fundamental elements. They identified which networking functions had related uses and collected those functions into discrete groups that became the layers. Each layer defines a family of functions distinct from those of the other layers. By defining and localizing functionality in this fashion, the designers created an architecture that is both comprehensive and flexible. Most important, the OSI model allows complete interoperability between otherwise incompatible systems.

Within a single machine, each layer calls upon the services of the layer just below it. Layer 3, for example, uses the services provided by layer 2 and provides services for layer 4. Between machines, layer *x* on one machine communicates with layer *x* on another machine. This communication is governed by an agreed-upon series of rules and conventions called protocols. The processes on each machine that communicate at a given layer are called **peer-to-peer processes**. Communication between machines is therefore a peer-to-peer process using the protocols appropriate to a given layer.

Peer-to-Peer Processes

At the physical layer, communication is direct: in Figure 2.2 device A sends a stream of bits to device B. At the higher layers, however, communication must move down through the layers on device A, over to device B, and then back up through the layers.

Figure 2.2   *OSI layers*

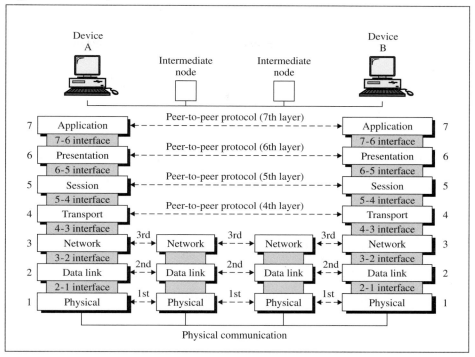

Each layer in the sending device adds its own information to the message it receives from the layer just above it and passes the whole package to the layer just below it.

> Headers are added to the data at layers 6, 5, 4, 3, and 2. Trailers are usually added only at layer 2.

At layer 1 the entire package is converted to a form that can be transferred to the receiving device. At the receiving machine, the message is unwrapped layer by layer, with each process receiving and removing the data meant for it. For example, layer 2 removes the data meant for it, then passes the rest to layer 3. Layer 3 then removes the data meant for it and passes the rest to layer 4, and so on.

Interfaces between Layers

The passing of the data and network information down through the layers of the sending device and back up through the layers of the receiving device is made possible by an *interface* between each pair of adjacent layers. Each interface defines what information and services a layer must provide for the layer above it. Well-defined interfaces and layer functions provide modularity to a network. As long as a layer provides the expected services to the layer above it, the specific implementation of its functions can be modified or replaced without requiring changes to the surrounding layers.

Organization of the Layers

The seven layers can be thought of as belonging to three subgroups. Layers 1, 2, and 3—physical, data link, and network—are the network support layers; they deal with the physical aspects of moving data from one device to another (such as electrical specifications, physical connections, physical addressing, and transport timing and reliability). Layers 5, 6, and 7—session, presentation, and application—can be thought of as the user support layers; they allow interoperability among unrelated software systems. Layer 4, the transport layer, links the two subgroups and ensures that what the lower layers have transmitted is in a form that the upper layers can use. The upper OSI layers are almost always implemented in software; lower layers are a combination of hardware and software, except for the physical layer, which is mostly hardware.

In Figure 2.3, which gives an overall view of the OSI layers, L7 data means the data unit at layer 7, L6 data means the data unit at layer 6, and so on. The process starts at layer 7 (the application layer), then moves from layer to layer in descending, sequential order. At each layer (except layers 7 and 1), a header is added to the data unit. At layer 2, a trailer is added as well. When the formatted data unit passes through the physical layer (layer 1), it is changed into an electromagnetic signal and transported along a physical link.

Figure 2.3   *An exchange using the OSI model*

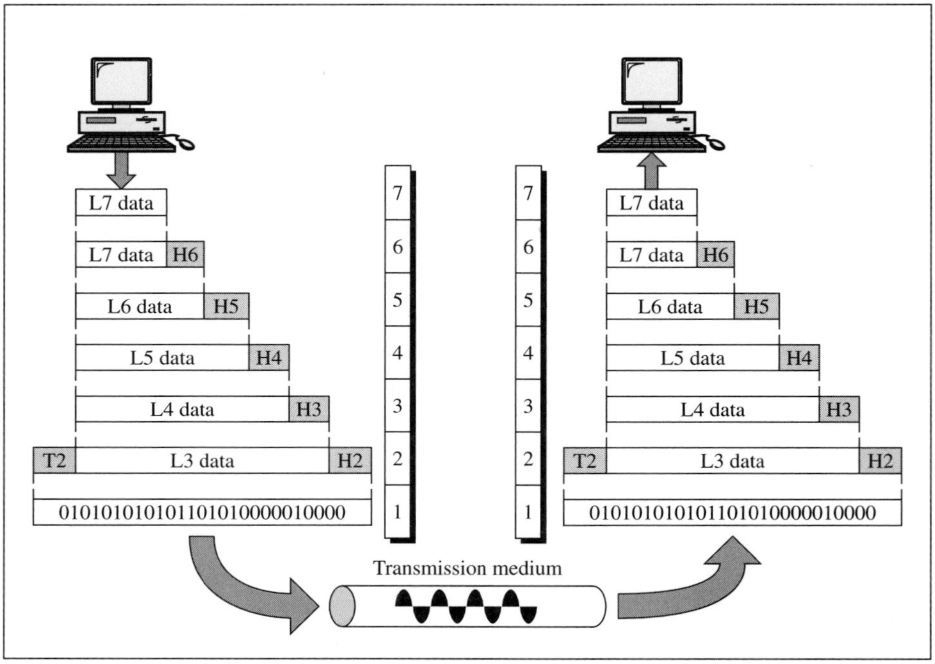

Upon reaching its destination, the signal passes into layer 1 and is transformed back into digital form. The data units then move back up through the OSI layers. As each block of data reaches the next higher layer, the headers and trailers attached to it at the corresponding sending layer are removed, and actions appropriate to that layer are taken. By the time it reaches layer 7, the message is again in a form appropriate to the application and is made available to the recipient.

2.2   LAYERS IN THE OSI MODEL

In this section we briefly describe the functions of each layer in the OSI model.

Physical Layer

The **physical layer** coordinates the functions required to transmit a bit stream over a physical medium. It deals with the mechanical and electrical specifications of the interface and transmission media. It also defines the procedures and functions that physical devices and interfaces have to perform for transmission to occur. Figure 2.4 shows the position of the physical layer with respect to the transmission media and the data link layer.

Figure 2.4   *Physical layer*

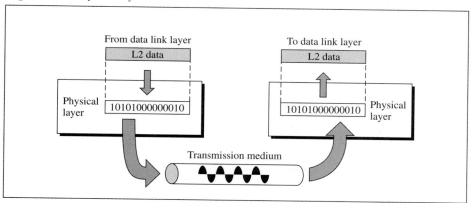

The physical layer is concerned with the following:

- **Physical characteristics of interfaces and media.** The physical layer defines the characteristics of the interface between the devices and the transmission media. It also defines the type of transmission media (see Chapter 3).

- **Representation of bits.** The physical layer data consists of a stream of **bits** (sequence of 0s or 1s) without any interpretation. To be transmitted, bits must be encoded into signals—electrical or optical. The physical layer defines the type of **encoding** (how 0s and 1s are changed to signals).

- **Data rate.** The **transmission rate**—the number of bits sent each second—is also defined by the physical layer. In other words, the physical layer defines the duration of a bit, which is how long it lasts.

- **Synchronization of bits.** The sender and receiver must not only use the same bit rate but must also be synchronized at the bit level. In other words, the sender and the receiver clocks must be synchronized.

■ **Line configuration.** The physical layer is concerned with the connection of devices to the media. In a **point-to-point configuration**, two devices are connected together through a dedicated link. In a **multipoint configuration,** a link is shared between several devices.

■ **Physical topology.** The physical topology defines how devices are connected to make a network. Devices can be connected using a **mesh topology** (every device connected to every other device), a **star topology** (devices are connected through a central device), a **ring topology** (every device is connected to the next, forming a ring), or a **bus topology** (every device on a common link).

■ **Transmission mode.** The physical layer also defines the direction of transmission between two devices: simplex, half-duplex, or full-duplex. In the **simplex mode**, only one device can send; the other can only receive. The simplex mode is a one-way communication. In the **half-duplex mode**, two devices can send and receive, but not at the same time. In a **full-duplex** (or simply duplex) **mode**, two devices can send and receive at the same time.

Data Link Layer

The **data link layer** transforms the physical layer, a raw transmission facility, to a reliable link. It makes the physical layer appear error free to the upper layer (network layer). Figure 2.5 shows the relationship of the data link layer to the network and physical layers.

Figure 2.5   *Data link layer*

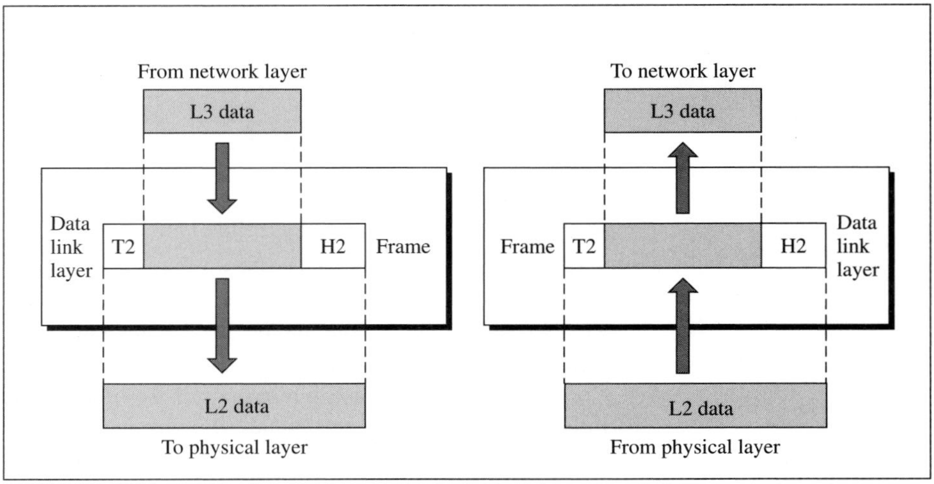

Specific responsibilities of the data link layer include the following:

■ **Framing.** The data link layer divides the stream of bits received from the network layer into manageable data units called **frames**.

■ **Physical addressing.** If frames are to be distributed to different systems on the network, the data link layer adds a header to the frame to define the sender and/or receiver of the frame. If the frame is intended for a system outside the sender's network, the receiver address is the address of the connecting device that connects the network to the next one.

- **Flow control.** If the rate in which the data is absorbed by the receiver is less than the rate produced in the sender, the data link layer imposes a flow control mechanism to prevent overwhelming the receiver.

- **Error control.** The data link layer adds reliability to the physical layer by adding mechanisms to detect and retransmit damaged or lost frames. It also uses a mechanism to prevent duplication of frames. Error control is normally achieved through a trailer added to the end of the frame.

- **Access control.** When two or more devices are connected to the same link, data link layer protocols are necessary to determine which device has control over the link at any given time.

Network Layer

The **network layer** is responsible for the source-to-destination delivery of a packet possibly across multiple networks (links). Whereas the data link layer oversees the delivery of the packet between two systems on the same network (links), the network layer ensures that each packet gets from its point of origin to its final destination.

If two systems are connected to the same link, there is usually no need for a network layer. However, if the two systems are attached to different networks (links) with connecting devices between the networks (links), there is often a need for the network layer to accomplish source-to-destination delivery. Figure 2.6 shows the relationship of the network layer to the data link transport layers.

Figure 2.6 *Network layer*

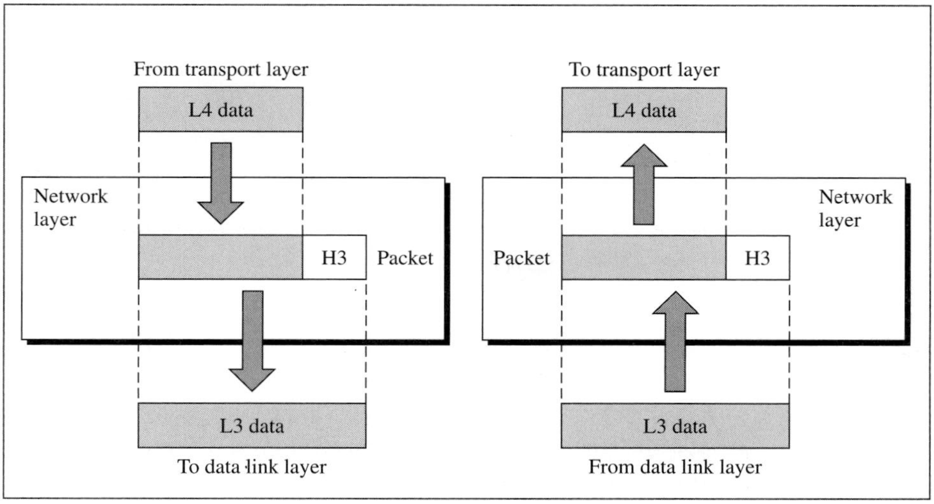

Specific responsibilities of the network layer include the following:

■ **Logical addressing.** The physical addressing implemented by the data link layer handles the addressing problem locally. If a packet passes the network boundary, we need another addressing system to help distinguish the source and destination systems. The network layer adds a header to the packet coming from the upper layer that, among other things, includes the logical addresses of the sender and receiver. We discuss logical addresses later in this chapter.

■ **Routing.** When independent networks or links are connected together to create **internetworks** (network of networks) or a large network, the connecting devices (called *routers* or *switches*) route or switch the packets to their final destination. One of the functions of the network layer is to provide this mechanism.

Transport Layer

The **transport layer** is responsible for **source-to-destination** (end-to-end) **delivery** of the entire message. Whereas the network layer oversees end-to-end delivery of individual packets, it does not recognize any relationship between those packets. It treats each one independently, as though each piece belonged to a separate message, whether or not it does. The transport layer, on the other hand, ensures that the whole message arrives intact and in order, overseeing both error control and flow control at the source-to-destination level. Figure 2.7 shows the relationship of the transport layer to the network and session layers.

Figure 2.7   *Transport layer*

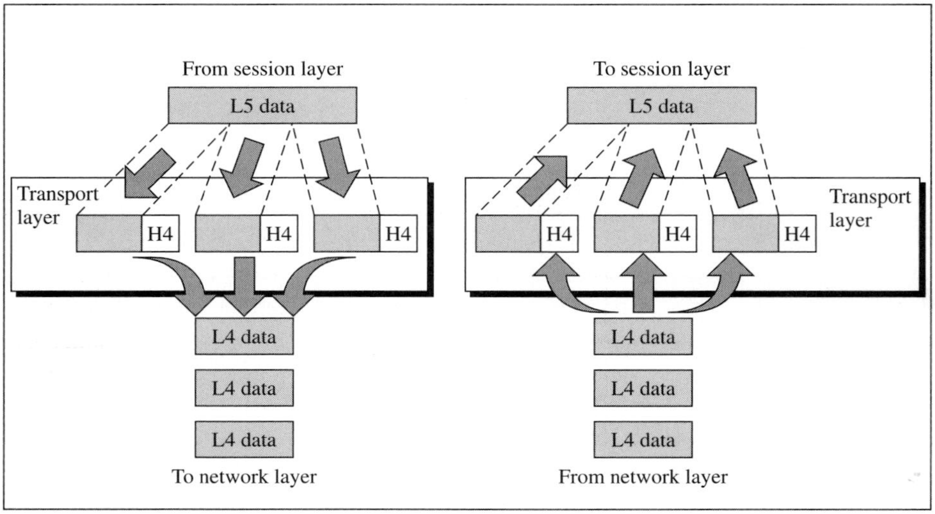

Specific responsibilities of the transport layer include the following:

■ **Service-point addressing.** Computers often run several programs at the same time. For this reason, source-to-destination delivery means delivery not only from one computer to the next but also from a specific process (running program) on one computer to a specific process (running program) on the other. The transport layer header must therefore include a type of address called a *service-point address* (or port address). The network layer gets each packet to the correct computer; the transport layer gets the entire message to the correct process on that computer.

- **Segmentation and reassembly.** A message is divided into transmittable segments, each segment containing a sequence number. These numbers enable the transport layer to reassemble the message correctly upon arriving at the destination and to identify and replace packets that were lost in the transmission.

- **Connection control.** The transport layer can be either connectionless or connection-oriented. A connectionless transport layer treats each segment as an independent packet and delivers it to the transport layer at the destination machine. A connection-oriented transport layer makes a connection with the transport layer at the destination machine first before delivering the packets. After all the data is transferred, the connection is terminated.

- **Flow control.** Like the data link layer, the transport layer is responsible for flow control. However, flow control at this layer is performed end to end rather than across a single link.

- **Error control.** Like the data link layer, the transport layer is responsible for error control. However, error control at this layer is performed end to end rather than across a single link. The sending transport layer makes sure that the entire message arrives at the receiving transport layer without **error** (damage, loss, or duplication). Error correction is usually achieved through retransmission.

Session Layer

The services provided by the first three layers (physical, data link, and network) are not sufficient for some processes. The **session layer** is the network *dialog controller*. It establishes, maintains, and synchronizes the interaction between communicating system.

Specific responsibilities of the session layer include the following:

- **Dialog control.** The session layer allows two systems to enter into a dialog. It allows the communication between two processes to take place either in half-duplex (one way at a time) or full-duplex (two ways at a time). For example, the dialog between a terminal connected to a mainframe can be half-duplex.

- **Synchronization.** The session layer allows a process to add checkpoints (synchronization points) into a stream of data. For example, if a system is sending a file of 2,000 pages, it is advisable to insert checkpoints after every 100 pages to ensure that each 100-page unit is received and acknowledged independently. In this case, if a crash happens during the transmission of page 523, the only pages that need to be resent after system recovery are pages 501 to 523. Pages 524 to 2,000 still come as well. Figure 2.8 illustrates the relationship of the session layer to the transport and presentation layers.

Figure 2.8 *Session layer*

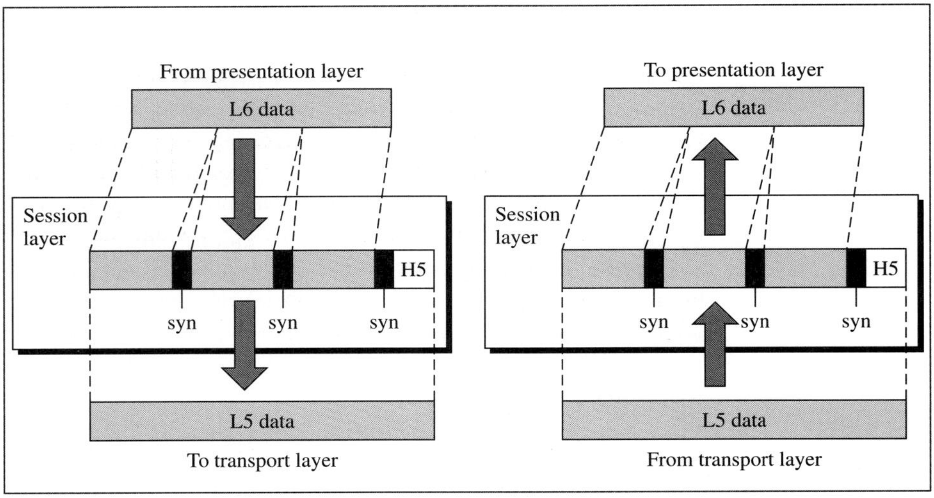

Presentation Layer

The **presentation layer** is concerned with the syntax and semantics of the information exchanged between two systems. Figure 2.9 shows the relationship between the presentation layer and the application and session layers.

Figure 2.9 *Presentation layer*

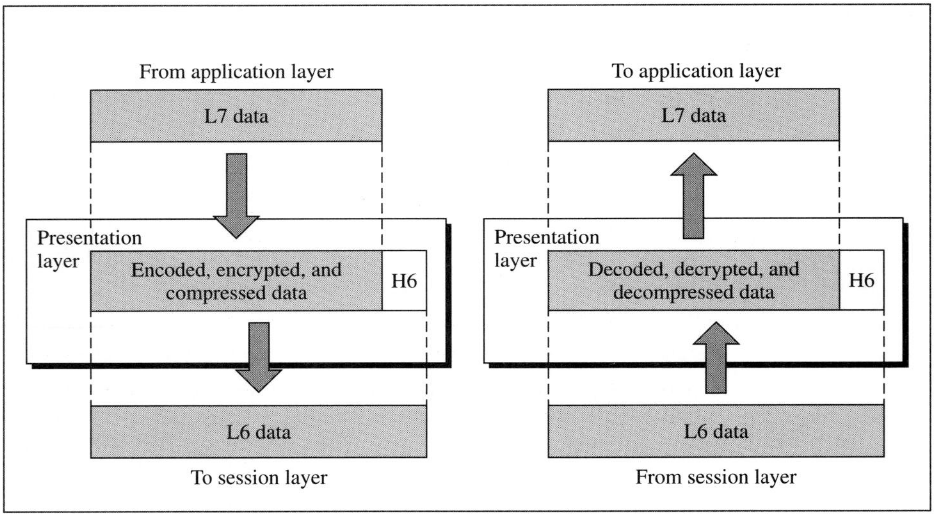

Specific responsibilities of the presentation layer include the following:

■ **Translation.** The processes (running programs) in two systems are usually exchanging information in the form of character strings, numbers, and so on. The information should be changed to bit streams before being transmitted. Because different computers use different encoding systems, the presentation layer is responsible for interoperability between these different encoding methods. The presentation layer at the sender changes the information from its sender-dependent format into a common format. The presentation layer at the receiving machine changes the common format into its receiver-dependent format.

■ **Encryption.** To carry sensitive information a system must be able to assure privacy. Encryption means that the sender transforms the original information to another form and sends the resulting message out over the network. Decryption reverses the original process to transform the message back to its original form.

■ **Compression.** Data compression reduces the number of bits contained in the information. Data compression becomes particularly important in the transmission of multimedia such as text, audio, and video.

Application Layer

The **application layer** enables the user, whether human or software, to access the network. It provides user interfaces and support for services such as electronic mail, remote file access and transfer, shared database management, and other types of distributed information services.

Figure 2.10 shows the relationship of the application layer to the user and the presentation layer. Of the many application services available, the figure shows only three: X.400 (message-handling services), X.500 (directory services), and file transfer and access management (FTAM). The user in this example uses X.400 to send an e-mail message. Note that no headers or trailers are added at this layer.

Figure 2.10   *Application layer*

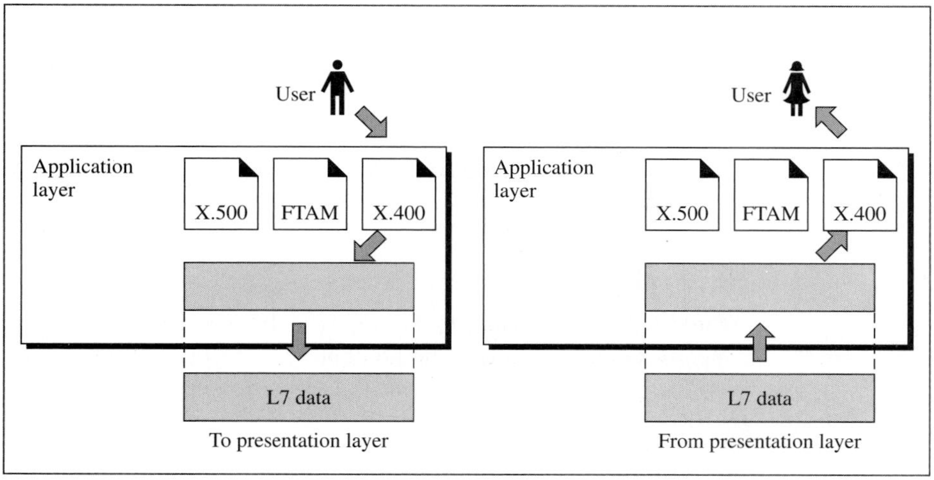

Specific services provided by the application layer include the following:

■ **Network virtual terminal.** A network virtual terminal is a software version of a physical terminal and allows a user to log on to a remote host. To do so, the application creates a software emulation of a terminal at the remote host. The user's computer talks to the software terminal, which, in turn, talks to the host, and vice versa. The remote host believes it is communicating with one of its own terminals and allows you to log on.

- **File transfer, access, and management (FTAM).** This application allows a user to access files in a remote host (to make changes or read data), to retrieve files from a remote computer for use in the local computer, and to manage or control files in a remote computer at that computer.

- **Mail services.** This application provides the basis for e-mail forwarding and storage.

- **Directory services.** This application provides distributed database sources and access for global information about various objects and services.

2.3   TCP/IP PROTOCOL SUITE

TCP was developed prior to the OSI model. Therefore, the layers in the TCP/IP protocol suite do not match exactly with those in the OSI model. The TCP/IP protocol suite is made of five layers: physical, data link, network, transport, and application. The first four layers provide physical standards, network interface, internetworking, and transport functions that correspond to the first four layers of the OSI model. The three topmost layers in the OSI model, however, are represented in TCP/IP by a single layer called the *application layer* (see Figure 2.11).

TCP/IP is a hierarchical protocol made up of interactive modules each of which provides a specific functionality, but the modules are not necessarily interdependent. Whereas the OSI model specifies which functions belong to each of its layers, the layers of the TCP/IP protocol suite contain relatively independent protocols that can be mixed and matched depending on the needs of the system. The term *hierarchical* means that each upper level protocol is supported by one or more lower level protocols.

At the transport layer, TCP/IP defines two protocols: Transmission Control Protocol (TCP) and User Datagram Protocol (UDP). At the network layer, the main protocol defined by TCP/IP is Internetworking Protocol (IP), although there are some other protocols that support data movement in this layer.

Physical and Data Link Layers

At the physical and data link layers, TCP/IP does not define any specific protocol. It supports all of the standard and proprietary protocols. A network in a TCP/IP internetwork can be a local area network (LAN), a metropolitan area network (MAN), or a wide area network (WAN).

Network Layer

At the network layer (or, more accurately, the internetwork layer), TCP/IP supports the Internetworking Protocol (IP). IP, in turn, contains four supporting protocols: ARP,

Figure 2.11   *TCP/IP and OSI model*

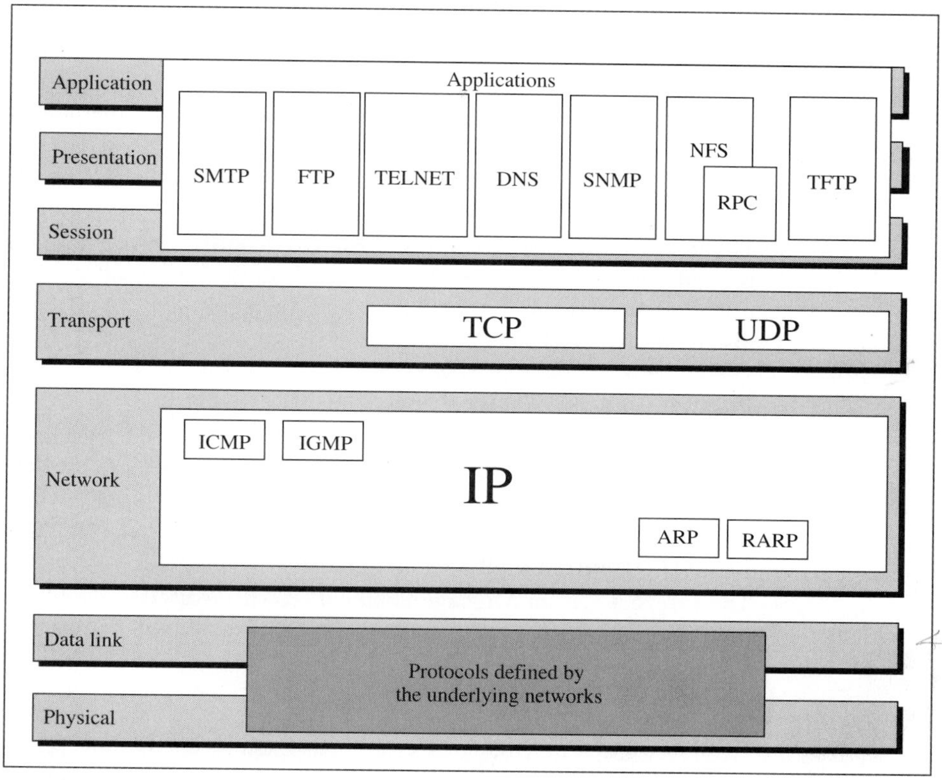

RARP, ICMP, and IGMP. Each of these protocols is described in more detail in later chapters.

Internetworking Protocol (IP)

The **Internetworking Protocol** (IP) is the transmission mechanism used by the TCP/IP protocols. It is an unreliable and connectionless datagram protocol—a best-effort delivery service. The term *best-effort* means that IP provides no error checking or tracking. IP assumes the unreliability of the underlying layers and does its best to get a transmission through to its destination, but with no guarantees.

IP transports data in packets called *datagrams*, each of which is transported separately. Datagrams can travel along different routes and can arrive out of sequence or be duplicated. IP does not keep track of the routes and has no facility for reordering datagrams once they arrive at their destination.

The limited functionality of IP should not be considered a weakness, however. IP provides bare-bones transmission functions that free the user to add only those facilities necessary for a given application and thereby allows for maximum efficiency.

Address Resolution Protocol (ARP)

The **Address Resolution Protocol** (ARP) is used to associate an IP address with the physical address. On a typical physical network, such as a LAN, each device on a link is identified by a physical or station address usually imprinted on the network interface card (NIC). ARP is used to find the physical address of the node when its Internet address is known. ARP will be discussed in Chapter 8.

Reverse Address Resolution Protocol (RARP)

The **Reverse Address Resolution Protocol** (RARP) allows a host to discover its Internet address when it knows only its physical address. It is used when a computer is connected to the network for the first time or when a diskless computer is booted. We will discuss RARP in Chapter 8.

Internet Control Message Protocol (ICMP)

The **Internet Control Message Protocol** (ICMP) is a mechanism used by hosts and gateways to send notification of datagram problems back to the sender. ICMP sends query and error reporting messages. We will thoroughly discuss ICMP in Chapter 9.

Internet Group Message Protocol (IGMP)

The **Internet Group Message Protocol** (IGMP) is used to facilitate the simultaneous transmission of a message to a group of recipients. We will thoroughly discuss IGMP in Chapter 10.

Transport Layer

The transport layer is represented in TCP/IP by two protocols: TCP and UDP. The IP is a **host-to-host protocol**, meaning that it can deliver a packet from one physical device to another. UDP and TCP are **transport level protocols** responsible for delivery of a message from a process (running program) to another process.

User Datagram Protocol (UDP)

The **User Datagram Protocol** (UDP) is the simpler of the two standard TCP/IP transport protocols. It is a process-to-process protocol that adds only port addresses, checksum error control, and length information to the data from the upper layer.

Transmission Control Protocol (TCP)

The **Transmission Control Protocol** (TCP) provides full transport layer services to applications. TCP is a reliable stream transport protocol. The term *stream,* in this context, means connection-oriented: a connection must be established between both ends of a transmission before either can transmit data.

At the sending end of each transmission, TCP divides a stream of data into smaller units called *segments*. Each segment includes a sequence number for reordering after receipt, together with an acknowledgment number for the segments received. Segments are carried across the internet inside of IP datagrams. At the receiving end, TCP collects each datagram as it comes in and reorders the transmission based on sequence numbers.

Application Layer

The **application layer** in TCP/IP is equivalent to the combined session, presentation, and application layers in the OSI model. Many protocols are defined at this layer. We cover many of the standard protocols in later chapters.

2.4   ADDRESSING

Three different levels of addresses are used in an internet using the TCP/IP protocols: physical (link) address, internetwork (IP) address, and port address (see Figure 2.12).

Figure 2.12   *Addresses in TCP/IP*

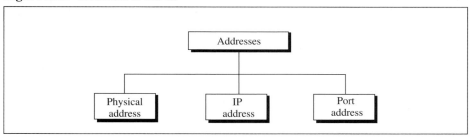

Each address belongs to a specific layer of TCP/IP architecture, as shown in Figure 2.13.

Physical Address

The **physical address**, also known as the link address, is the address of a node as defined by its LAN or WAN. It is included in the frame used by the data link layer. It is the lowest level address.

The physical addresses have authority over the network (LAN or WAN). The size and format of these addresses vary depending on the network. For example, Ethernet uses a six-byte (48-bit) physical address which is imprinted on the network interface card (NIC). LocalTalk, however, has a one-byte dynamic address which changes each time the station comes up.

Unicast, Multicast, and Broadcast Physical Addresses

Physical addresses can be either **unicast** (one single recipient), **multicast** (a group of recipients) or **broadcast** (to be received by all systems in the network). Some networks support all three addresses. For example, Ethernet (see Chapter 3) supports the unicast physical addresses (6 bytes), the multicast addresses, and the broadcast addresses. Some networks do not support the multicast or broadcast physical addresses. If a frame

Figure 2.13   *Relationship of layers and addresses in TCP/IP*

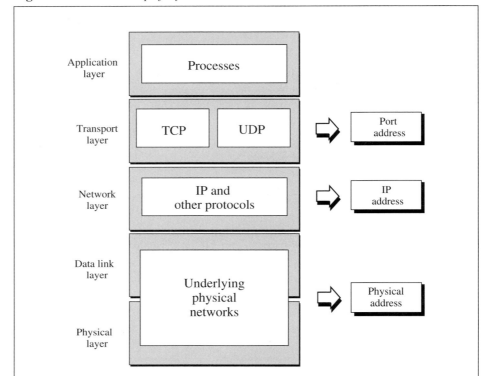

must be sent to a group of recipients or to all systems, the multicast or broadcast address must be simulated using unicast addresses. This means that multiple packets are sent out using unicast addresses.

Example 1

In Figure 2.14 a node with physical address 10 sends a frame to a node with physical address 87. The two nodes are connected by a link. At the data link level this frame contains physical (link) addresses in the header. These are the only addresses needed. The rest of the header contains other information needed at this level. The trailer usually contains extra bits needed for error detection.

Internet Address

Internet addresses are necessary for universal communication services that are independent of underlying physical networks. Physical addresses are not adequate in an inter-network environment where different networks can have different address formats. A universal addressing system in which each host can be identified uniquely, regardless of the underlying physical network, is needed.

The Internet addresses are designed for this purpose. An Internet address is currently a 32-bit address which can uniquely define a host connected to the Internet. No two hosts on the Internet can have the same IP address.

Figure 2.14 *Physical addresses*

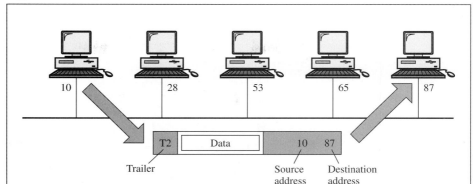

Unicast, Multicast, and Broadcast Addresses

The Internet addresses can be either unicast (one single recipient), multicast (a group of recipients), or broadcast (to be received by all systems in the network). There are limitations on broadcast addresses. We will discuss the three types of addresses in Chapter 4.

Example 2

In Figure 2.15 we want to send data from a node with network address A and physical address 10, located on one LAN, to a node with a network address P and physical address 95, located on another LAN. Because the two devices are located on different networks, we cannot use link addresses only; the link addresses have only local jurisdiction. What we need here are universal addresses that can pass through the LAN boundaries. The network (logical) addresses have this characteristic. The packet at the network layer contains the logical addresses, which remain the same from the original source to the final destination (A and P, respectively, in the figure). They will not change when we go from network to network. However, the physical addresses will change as the packet moves from one network to another. The box with the R is a router (internetwork device), which we will discuss in Chapter 3.

Port Address

The IP address and the physical address are necessary for a quantity of data to travel from a source to the destination host. However, arrival at the destination host is not the final objective of data communication on the Internet. A system that sends nothing but data from one computer to another is not complete. Today, computers are multiprocess devices that can run multiple processes at the same time. The end objective of internet communication is a process communicating with another process. For example, computer A can communicate with computer C using TELNET. At the same time, computer A communicates with computer B using File Transfer Protocol (FTP). For these processes to occur simultaneously, we need a method to label different processes. In other words, they should be given addresses. In TCP/IP architecture, the label assigned to a process is called a port address. A port address in TCP/IP is 16 bits long.

Figure 2.15 *IP addresses*

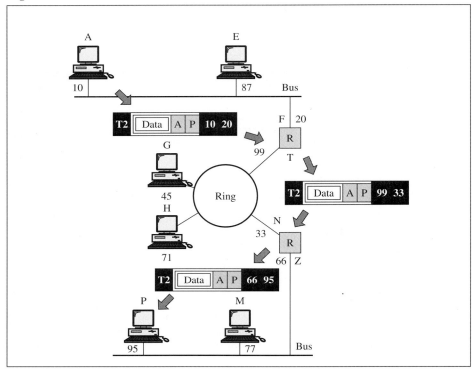

Example 3

Figure 2.16 shows an example of transport layer communication. Data coming from the upper layers have port addresses *j* and *k* (*j* is the address of the sending process, and *k* is the address of the receiving process). Since the data size is larger than the network layer can handle, the data are split into two packets, each packet retaining the service-point addresses (*j* and *k*). Then in the network layer, network addresses (A and P) are added to each packet. The packets can travel on different paths and arrive at the destination either in order or out of order. The two packets are delivered to the destination transport layer, which is responsible for removing the network layer headers and combining the two pieces of data for delivery to the upper layers.

2.5 TCP/IP VERSIONS

TCP/IP became the official protocol for the Internet (then known as ARPANET; see Chapter 1) in 1983. As the Internet has evolved, so has TCP/IP. There have been six versions since its inception. We look at the latter three versions here.

Version 4

Most of the Internet is currently using version 4. However, this version has significant shortcomings. The primary problem is that the Internet address is only 32 bits in length

Figure 2.16   *Port addresses*

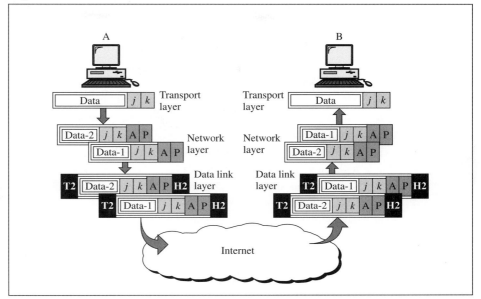

with the address space divided into different classes. With the rapid growth of the Internet, 32 bits is not sufficient to handle the projected number of users. Also, the division of the space into different classes further limits the available addresses.

Version 5

Version 5 was a proposal based on the OSI model. This version never went beyond the proposal stage due to extensive layer changes and the projected expense.

Version 6

IETF has designed a new version called version 6. In this version, the only protocols that are changed are the ones in the network layer. IPv4 (IP version 4) becomes IPv6 (IP version 6), ICMPv4 becomes ICMPv6, IGMP and ARP are merged into ICMPv6, and RARP is deleted.

IPv6, also known as IPng (IP *next generation)* uses 128-bit (16-byte) addresses, versus the 32-bit (4-byte) addresses currently used in version 4. IPv6 can thereby accommodate a larger number of users. In version 6, the packet format has been simplified, yet at the same time it is more flexible to allow for the future addition of features.

The new version supports authentication, data integrity, and confidentiality at the network layer. It is designed to handle the transmission of real-time data such as audio and video, and can carry data from other protocols. IPng can also handle congestion and route discovery better than the current version.

This book is based primarily on the fourth version, although Chapter 25 concentrates on IPng.

2.6   SUMMARY

■   The International Standards Organization (ISO) created a model called the Open Systems Interconnection (OSI), which allows diverse systems to communicate.

■   The seven-layer OSI model provides guidelines for the development of universally compatible networking protocols.

■   The physical, data link, and network layers are the network support layers.

■   The session, presentation, and application layers are the user support layers.

■   The transport layer links the network support layers and the user support layers.

■   The physical layer coordinates the functions required to transmit a bit stream over a physical medium.

■   The data link layer is responsible for delivering data units from one station to the next without errors.

■   The network layer is responsible for the source-to-destination delivery of a packet across multiple network links.

■   The transport layer is responsible for the source-to-destination delivery of the entire message.

■   The session layer establishes, maintains, and synchronizes the interactions between communicating devices.

■   The presentation layer ensures interoperability between communicating devices through transformation of data into a mutually agreed-upon format.

■   The application layer enables the users to access the network.

■   TCP/IP is a five-layer hierarchical protocol suite developed before the OSI model.

■   The TCP/IP application layer is equivalent to the combined session, presentation, and application layers of the OSI model.

■   Three types of addresses are used by systems using the TCP/IP protocol: the physical address, the internetwork address (IP address), and the port address.

■   The physical address, also known as the link address, is the address of a node as defined by its LAN or WAN.

■   The IP address uniquely defines a host on the Internet.

■   The port address identifies a process on a host.

■   Most networks use IPv4.

■   IPv6 is supposed to replace IPv4 in the near future.

2.7   PRACTICE SET

Multiple Choice

1. Why was the OSI model developed?
   a. manufacturers disliked the TCP/IP protocol suite
   b. the rate of data transfer was increasing exponentially

  c. standards were needed to allow any two systems to communicate

  d. none of the above

2. The _____ model shows how the network functions of a computer ought to be organized.

  a. CCITT

  b. OSI

  c. ISO

  d. ANSI

3. The physical layer is concerned with the transmission of _____ over the physical medium.

  a. programs

  b. dialogs

  c. protocols

  d. bits

4. The OSI model consists of _____ layers.

  a. three

  b. five

  c. seven

  d. eight

5. As a data packet moves from the lower to the upper layers, headers are _____.

  a. added

  b. subtracted

  c. rearranged

  d. modified

6. When data is transmitted from device A to device B, the header from A's layer 5 is read by B's _____ layer.

  a. physical

  b. transport

  c. session

  d. presentation

7. Which layer functions as a liaison between user support layers and network support layers?

  a. network layer

  b. physical layer

  c. transport layer

  d. session layer

8. What is the main function of the transport layer?

  a. node-to-node delivery

  b. process-to-process message delivery

  c. synchronization

     d. updating and maintenance of routing tables

9. Session layer checkpoints _____.

    a. allow just a portion of a file to be resent

    b. detect and recover errors

    c. control the addition of headers

    d. are involved in dialog control

10. Encryption and decryption are functions of the _____ layer.

    a. transport

    b. session

    c. presentation

    d. application

11. Which of the following is an application layer service?

    a. network virtual terminal

    b. file transfer, access, and management

    c. mail service

    d. all of the above

12. When a host on network A sends a message to a host on network B, which address does the router look at?

    a. port

    b. IP

    c. physical

    d. none of the above

13. To deliver a message to the correct application program running on a host, the _____ address must be consulted.

    a. port

    b. IP

    c. physical

    d. none of the above

14. IPv6 has _____ -bit addresses.

    a. 32

    b. 64

    c. 128

    d. variable

15. ICMPv6 includes _____.

    a. IGMP

    b. ARP

    c. RARP

    d. a and b

Exercises

16. How are OSI and ISO related to each other?

17. Match the following to one of the seven OSI layers:
    a. route determination
    b. flow control
    c. interface to outside world
    d. provides access to the network for the end user
    e. changes ASCII to EBCDIC
    f. packet switching

18. Match the following to one of the seven OSI layers:
    a. reliable end-to-end data transportation
    b. network selection
    c. defines frames
    d. provides user services such as e-mail and file transfer
    e. transmission of bit stream across physical medium

19. Match the following to one of the seven OSI layers:
    a. communicates directly with user's application program
    b. error correction and retransmission
    c. mechanical, electrical, and functional interface
    d. responsibility for information between adjacent nodes
    e. reassembly of data packets

20. Match the following to one of the seven OSI layers:
    a. format and code conversion services
    b. establishes, manages, and terminates sessions
    c. ensures reliable transmission of data
    d. log-in and log-out procedures
    e. provides independence from differences in data representation
    f. synchronization of users

21. Domain Name System or DNS (see Chapter 16) is an application program in the TCP/IP protocol suite. Do some research and find the equivalent of this protocol (if any) in the OSI model. Compare and contrast the two.

22. File Transfer Protocol or FTP (see Chapter 18) is an application program in the TCP/IP protocol suite. Do some research and find the equivalent of this protocol (if any) in the OSI model. Compare and contrast the two.

23. Trivial File Transfer Protocol or TFTP (see Chapter 19) is an application program in the TCP/IP protocol suite. Do some research and find the equivalent of this protocol (if any) in the OSI model. Compare and contrast the two.

24. There are several transport layer models proposed in the OSI model. Do some research and find all of them. Explain the differences between them.

25. There are several network layer models proposed in the OSI model. Do some research and find all of them. Explain the differences between them.

CHAPTER 3

Underlying Technologies

The TCP/IP protocol is designed to support a wide variety of network technologies. This chapter briefly reviews these technologies. We must mention, however, that this chapter does not attempt to describe all of these technologies in detail; it is just a review of topics that the reader should already know. A detailed discussion of all of these technologies would take an entire book. (For more information, refer to Forouzan, *Introduction to Data Communications and Networking*, 1998.)

We have chosen only five topics for review. The first section describes the transmission media. The second section discusses local area networks. The third section is devoted to the concept of switching, which is needed to understand the mechanism used in wide area networks (WANs). The fourth section discusses some common wide area networks. Finally, the fifth section discusses the functionalities of devices that connect local and wide area networks together to form an internet.

3.1 TRANSMISSION MEDIA

Computers and other telecommunication devices use signals to represent data. These signals are transmitted from one device to another using one or more types of transmission media. Transmission media can be divided into two broad categories: guided and unguided.

Guided Media

Guided media, which are those that provide a conduit from one device to another, include twisted-pair cable, coaxial cable, and fiber-optic cable (see Figure 3.1). A signal traveling along any of these media is directed and contained by the physical limits of the medium. Twisted-pair and coaxial cable use metallic (copper) conductors that accept and transport signals in the form of electrical current. Optical fiber is a glass or plastic cable that accepts and transports signals in the form of light.

Figure 3.1   *Guided media*

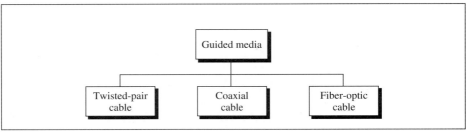

Twisted-Pair Cable

A **twisted-pair** cable is made of two insulated wires twisted together to reduce the effects of outside noise and crosstalk interference. Twisted-pair cable comes in two forms: unshielded and shielded.

Unshielded Twisted-Pair (UTP) Cable   Unshielded twisted-pair (UTP) cable is the most common type of telecommunication medium in use today. Although most familiar from its use in telephone systems, its frequency range is suitable for transmitting both data and voice (see Figure 3.2).

Figure 3.2   *Unshielded twisted-pair cable*

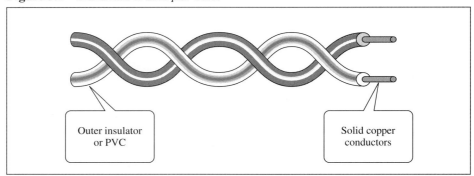

UTP is cheap, flexible, and easy to install. Higher grades of UTP are used in many LAN technologies, including Ethernet and token ring. Figure 3.3 shows a cable containing five unshielded twisted pairs.

The EIA has developed standards to grade UTP cables by quality. These categories, which follow, are determined by cable quality, with 1 as lowest and 5 as highest.

■ **Category 1.** The basic twisted-pair cabling used in telephone systems. This level of quality is fine for voice but inadequate for all but low-speed data communication.

■ **Category 2.** The next higher grade, suitable for voice and for digital data transmission that requires a bandwidth of up to 4 megahertz (MHz).

■ **Category 3.** Required to have at least three twists per foot and can be used for data transmission that requires a bandwidth of up to 16 MHz.

■ **Category 4.** Must also have at least three twists per foot as well as other conditions to bring the bandwidth to 20 MHz.

Figure 3.3 *Cable with 5 unshielded twisted pairs*

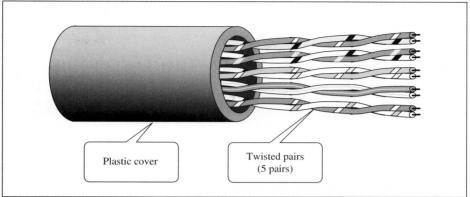

- **Category 5.** Used for data transmission that requires a bandwidth of up to 100 MHz.

Shielded Twisted-Pair (STP) Cable   Shielded twisted-pair (STP) cable has a metal foil or braided-mesh covering that encases each pair of insulated conductors (see Figure 3.4). The metal casing prevents the penetration of electromagnetic noise.

STP installation is more difficult than UTP because the shield must be connected to a ground. Materials and manufacturing requirements make STP more expensive than UTP but less susceptible to noise.

Figure 3.4 *Shielded twisted-pair cable*

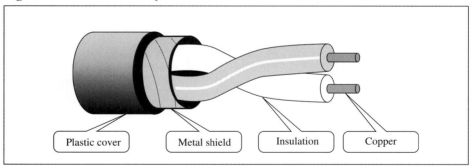

Coaxial Cable

Coaxial cable (or *coax*) carries signals of higher frequency ranges than twisted-pair cable. Instead of having two wires, coax has a central core conductor of solid or stranded wire (usually copper) enclosed in an insulating sheath, which is, in turn, encased in an outer conductor of metal foil, braid, or a combination of the two (also usually copper). The outer metallic wrapping serves both as a shield against noise and as the second conductor, which completes the circuit. This outer conductor is also enclosed in an insulating sheath, and the whole cable is protected by a plastic cover (see Figure 3.5).

Figure 3.5   *Coaxial cable*

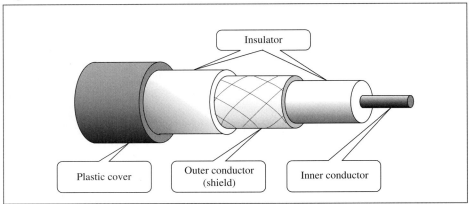

Optical Fiber

Optical fiber is made of glass or plastic and transmits signals in the form of light. If a ray of light traveling through one substance suddenly enters another substance with lower (or higher) density, the ray changes direction. This change is called **refraction** (see Figure 3.6).

Figure 3.6   *Refraction and reflection*

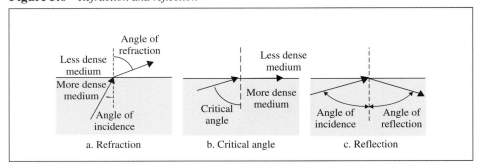

As the figure shows, if the second substance is of lower density, the angle of refraction is greater than the angle of incidence. As the angle of incidence increases, so does the angle of refraction. It, too, moves away from the vertical and closer to the horizontal. At some point in this process, a change in the incident angle results in a refracted angle of 90 degrees, with the refracted beam now lying along the horizontal. The incident angle at this point is known as the **critical angle**.

When the angle of incidence becomes greater than the critical angle, a new phenomenon occurs. Light no longer passes into the less dense medium at all. This is called **reflection**. In this case, the angle of incidence is always equal to the angle of reflection.

Optical fibers use reflection to guide light through a channel. A glass or plastic core is surrounded by a cladding of less dense glass or plastic. The difference in density of the two materials must be such that a beam of light moving through the core is reflected off the cladding instead of being refracted into it. Information is encoded onto a beam of light that represents 1 and 0 bits (see Figure 3.7).

Figure 3.7   *Fiber-optic cable*

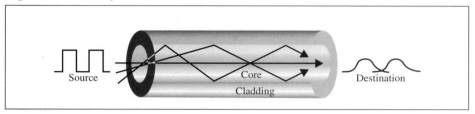

Optical fibers are defined by the ratio of the diameter of their core to the diameter of their cladding, both expressed in microns (micrometers). The common sizes are shown in Table 3.1.

Table 3.1   *Fiber types*

Fiber Type	*Core (microns)*	*Cladding (microns)*
62.5/125	62.5	125
50/125	50	125
100/140	100	140
8.3/125	8.3	125

The major advantages offered by fiber-optic cable over twisted-pair and coaxial cable are noise resistance, less signal attenuation, and higher bandwidth. The main disadvantages of fiber-optic cable are cost, installation/maintenance, and fragility.

Unguided Media

Unguided media transport electromagnetic waves without using a physical conductor. The section of the electromagnetic spectrum defined as radio communication is divided into eight ranges, called *bands*, each regulated by governmental authorities. These bands are rated from very low frequency (VLF) to extremely high frequency (EHF). Figure 3.8 shows all eight bands and their acronyms.

We can group the frequencies by use:

■ Frequencies less than 300 kilohertz (KHz) are used for long-range navigation.

■ Frequencies between 300 KHz and 3 gigahertz (GHz) are used for multidimensional radio communication.

■ Frequencies between 3 GHz and 30 GHz are called **microwave frequencies** and are used for point-to-point (line of sight) communication (terrestrial and satellite microwaves).

■ Frequencies between 30 GHz and 300 GHz are usually used for space communication.

Figure 3.8   *Radio and infrared frequencies*

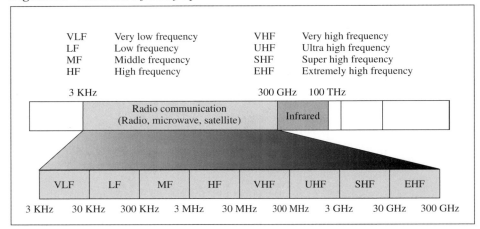

■   Frequencies between 300 GHz and 100 terahertz (THz) are infrared frequencies and are used in point-to-point or multidirectional communication in a small, confined area.

3.2   LOCAL AREA NETWORKS (LANS)

A **local area network** (LAN) is a data communication system that allows a number of independent devices to communicate directly with each other in a limited geographic area such as a single department, a single building, or a campus. LANs are dominated by three architectures: Ethernet, token ring, and fiber distributed data interface (FDDI).

Ethernet

Ethernet is a LAN standard originally developed by Xerox and later extended by a joint venture between Digital Equipment Corporation, Intel Corporation, and Xerox.

Access Method: Carrier Sense Multiple Access with Collision Detection (CSMA/CD)

The access mechanism used in an Ethernet is called **carrier sense multiple access with collision detection** (CSMA/CD). In CSMA/CD, before a station transmits data, it "listens" to the medium to check if another station is currently using the medium. If no other station is transmitting, the station can send its data.

It can happen that two or more stations send data at the same time, resulting in a collision (see Figure 3.9). For this reason, all stations must continuously "listen" to the medium to detect any collision. If a collision occurs, all stations ignore the data received. The sending stations wait for a period of time before resending data. To reduce the possibility of a second collision, the sending stations each generate a random number that determines how long the station should wait before resending.

Figure 3.9   *CSMA/CD access method*

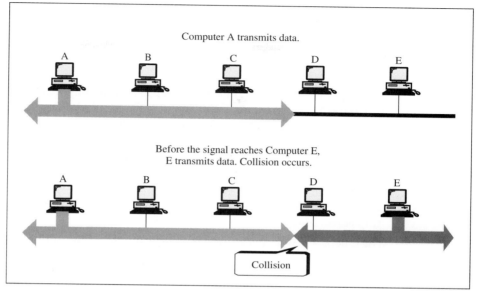

Addressing

Each station on an Ethernet network has its own NIC. The NIC usually fits inside the station and provides the station with a six-byte physical address.

Data Rate

Ethernet LANs can support data rates between 1 and 10 Mbps (Fast Ethernet supports 100 Mbps).

Frame Format

Figure 3.10 shows the format of the Ethernet frame. Ethernet does not provide any mechanism for acknowledging received frames, making it what is known as an unreliable medium. Acknowledgments must be implemented at the higher layers.

Figure 3.10   *Ethernet frame*

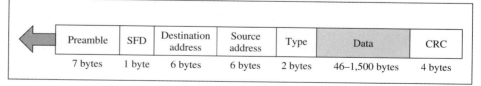

Ethernet defines a frame with seven fields:

■ **Preamble.** This field contains seven bytes (56 bits) of alternating 0s and 1s that alert the receiving system to the coming frame and enable it to synchronize its timer.

- **Start frame delimiter (SFD).** This one-byte field (10101011) is used as a flag and signals the beginning of the frame.
- **Destination address.** This six-byte field contains the physical address of the next station.
- **Source address.** This six-byte field contains the physical address of the previous station.
- **Type.** This field defines the type of the data encapsulated in the frame.
- **Data.** This field contains the data from the upper layer. The length of data should be between 46 and 1,500 bytes. If the length of data generated by the upper layer protocol is less than 46 bytes, padding should be added to make it 46 bytes. If it is more than 1,500 bytes, the upper layer should fragment the data.
- **Cyclic redundancy check (CRC).** This is a four-byte field for error detection. It uses CRC-32 (see Appendix D).

Implementation

All Ethernet LANs are configured as logical buses, although they can be physically implemented in bus or star topologies. Each frame is transmitted to every station on the link but read only by the station to which it is addressed. We discuss three implementations here.

10BASE5: Thick Ethernet   The first implementation is called 10BASE5, thick Ethernet, or Thick-net. **10BASE5** or **thick Ethernet** is a bus topology LAN that uses baseband signaling and has a maximum segment length of 500 meters.

The physical connectors and cables utilized by 10BASE5 include coaxial cable, NICs, transceivers, and attachment unit interface (AUI) cables. Figure 3.11 illustrates the interaction of these components.

10BASE2: Thin Ethernet   The second Ethernet implementation, called **10BASE2** or **thin Ethernet** (also called Thin-net, Cheapnet, and thin-wire Ethernet), provides an inexpensive alternative to 10BASE5 Ethernet, but supports the same data rate. Like 10BASE5, 10BASE2 is a bus topology LAN. The advantages of thin Ethernet are reduced cost and ease of installation (the cable is lighter weight and more flexible than that used in Thick Ethernet). The disadvantages are shorter range (185 meters as opposed to the 500 meters available with thick Ethernet) and smaller capacity (the thinner cable accommodates fewer stations).

Figure 3.12 illustrates the physical layout of 10BASE2. The connectors and cables utilized are NICs, thin coaxial cable, and BNC-T connectors. In this technology, the transceiver circuitry has moved into the NIC, and the transceiver-tap has been replaced by a connector that splices the station directly into the cable, thereby eliminating the need for AUI cables.

10BASE-T: Twisted-Pair Ethernet   The most popular implementation of an Ethernet LAN is **10BASE-T**, or **twisted-pair Ethernet**, a star topology LAN using UTP cable instead of coaxial cable. It supports a data rate of 10 Mbps and has a maximum length (measuring from hub to station) of 100 meters.

Instead of using individual transceivers, 10BASE-T Ethernet places all of its networking operations in an intelligent hub with a port for each station. Stations are linked

Figure 3.11   *Thick Ethernet*

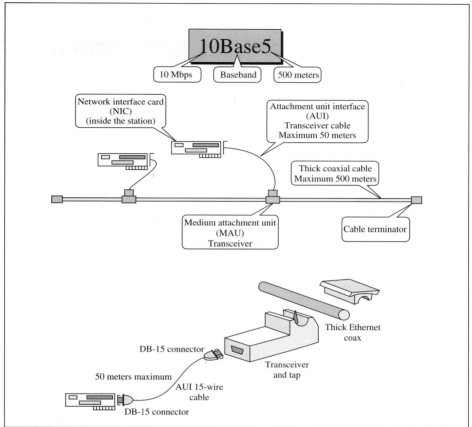

into the hub by four-pair RJ-45 cable (eight-wire UTP cable) terminating at each end in a male-type connector much like a telephone jack. The hub fans out any transmitted frame to all of its connected stations (see Figure 3.13).

Fast Ethernet

With new applications being implemented on LANs such as computer-aided design (CAD), image processing, and run-time audio and video, there is a need for a LAN with a higher data rate than 10 Mbps: **Fast Ethernet** operates at 100 Mbps.

Fortunately, the way Ethernet was designed, it is easy to increase the speed if the collision domain (the longest distance data travels between two stations) is decreased.

The collision domain of Ethernet is 2,500 meters. This collision domain is calculated to achieve the data rate of 10 Mbps using the CSMA/CD access method. For CSMA/CD to work, a station should be able to sense the collision before the whole frame is sent on the transmission media. If the whole frame is sent and collision is not detected, the station assumes that everything is fine and destroys the copy of the frame and starts sending the next one.

Figure 3.12   *Thin Ethernet*

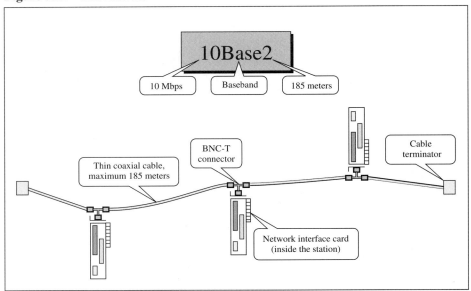

Figure 3.13   *Twisted-pair Ethernet*

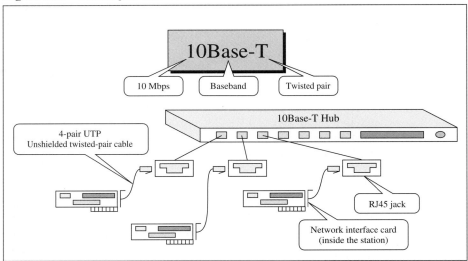

The minimum size of an Ethernet frame is 72 bytes or 576 bits. To send 576 bits at a data rate of 10 Mbps takes 57.6 microseconds (576 bits / 10 Mbps = 57.6). Before the last bit is sent, the first bit must have reached the end of the domain, and, if there is a collision, it must be sensed by the sender. This implies that during the time that the sender transmits 576 bits, the collision must be detected. In other words, the collision must be detected during 57.6 microseconds. This time is adequate to allow a signal to make a round-trip of 5,000 meters at a propagation speed in a typical transmission media such as twisted-pair cable.

To increase the data rate without changing the minimum size of a frame, we decrease the round-trip time. With the speed of 100 Mbps, the round-trip time reduces to 5.76 microseconds (576 bits / 100 Mbps). This means that the collision domain must be decreased 10 times, from 2,500 meters to 250 meters. This decrease is not a problem because LANs today connect desktop computers that are not more than 50 to 100 meters away from the central hub. This means the collision domain is between 100 to 200.

Fast Ethernet is a new version of Ethernet with a 100 Mbps data rate. There is no change in the frame format. There is no change in the access method. The only two changes are the data rate and the collision domain. The data rate is increased by a factor of 10; the collision domain is decreased by a factor of 10.

The specification developed for Fast Ethernet uses a star topology similar to 10-BASE-T. The specification defines three types of physical media: four pairs of UTP (100BASE-T4), two pairs of UTP or STP (100BASE-XT), or two optical fiber cables (100BASE-XF).

Token Ring

Token ring, a LAN standard originally developed by IBM, uses a logical ring topology. Since the access method used by Ethernet (CSMA/CD) can result in collisions, stations may attempt to send data multiple times before a transmission makes it onto the link. This redundancy can create delays of indeterminable length if the traffic is heavy. Also, there is no way to predict either the occurrence of collisions or the delays produced by multiple stations attempting to capture the link at the same time. Token ring resolves this uncertainty by requiring that stations take turns sending data: Each station can transmit only one frame during each turn.

Access Method: Token Passing

Token passing is illustrated in Figure 3.14. In token passing, the token is passed from station to station in sequence until it encounters a station with data to send. The station that has data to send waits for the token. It then captures the token and sends its data frame. This data frame proceeds around the ring, being regenerated by each station. Each intermediate station examines the destination address, finds that the frame is addressed to another station, and relays it to its neighbor. The intended recipient recognizes its own address, copies the message, checks for errors, and changes four bits in the last byte of the frame to indicate that the address has been recognized and the frame copied. The full packet then continues around the ring until it returns to the station that sent it.

The sender receives the frame and recognizes itself in the source address field. It then examines the address-recognized bits. If they are set, it knows the frame was received. The sender then discards the used data frame and releases the token back to the ring. To handle problems associated with the token, such as a lost or misused token, one of the stations in the ring is designated as the monitor station.

Figure 3.14   *Token passing access method*

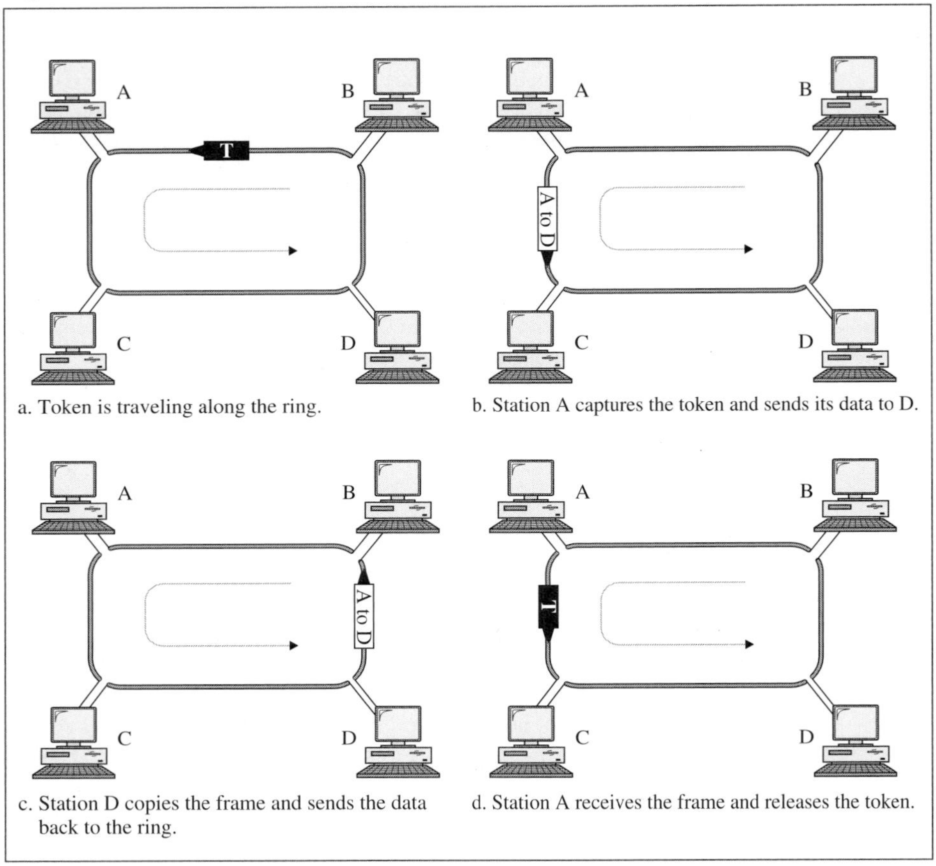

a. Token is traveling along the ring.

b. Station A captures the token and sends its data to D.

c. Station D copies the frame and sends the data back to the ring.

d. Station A receives the frame and releases the token.

Addressing

Token ring uses a six-byte address, which is imprinted on the NIC similar to Ethernet addresses.

Data Rate

Token ring supports two data rates: 4 and 16 Mbps.

Frame Formats

The token ring protocol specifies three types of frames: data, token, and abort (see Figure 3.15).

Data Frame   In token ring, the data frame is the only type of frame that can carry data. The nine fields of the data frame are as follows:

■   **Start delimiter (SD).** This one-byte field is used to alert the receiving station to the arrival of a frame.

Figure 3.15   *Token ring frames*

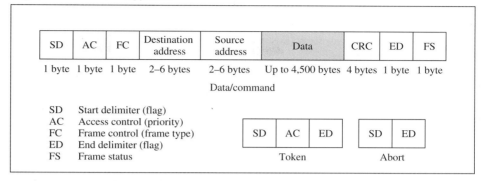

- **Access control (AC).** This one-byte field contains information about priority and reservation.
- **Frame control (FC).** This one-byte field defines the type of information contained in the data field.
- **Destination address (DA).** This variable-length (2 to 6 bytes) field contains the physical address of the next station.
- **Source address (SA).** This variable-length (2 to 6 bytes) field contains the physical address of the previous station.
- **Data.** This field contains data. Data can be up to 4,500 bytes.
- **CRC.** This field is four bytes long and contains a CRC-32 error-detection sequence (see Appendix D).
- **End delimiter (ED).** This one-byte field indicates the end of the sender's data and contains more control information.
- **Frame status (FS).** The FS field is set by the receiver to indicate that the frame has been read, or by the monitor station to indicate that the frame has already been around the ring.

Token Frame   The token frame includes only three fields: SD, AC, and ED.

Abort Frame   The abort frame includes only two fields: SD and ED. It can be used by the monitor station to abort the token passing mechanism when problems occur.

Implementation

The ring in a token ring consists of a series of 150-ohm, STP sections linking each station to its immediate neighbors. Each section connects an output port on one station to an input port on the next, creating a ring with unidirectional traffic flow. The output from the final station connects to the input of the first to complete the ring. A frame is passed to each station in sequence, where it is examined, regenerated, and then sent on to the next station

   Configuring the network as a ring introduces a potential problem: One disabled or disconnected node could stop the flow of traffic around the entire network. To solve this problem, each station is connected to an automatic switch. This switch can bypass an inactive station. While a station is disabled, the switch closes the ring to bypass it.

When the station comes on, a signal sent by the NIC moves the switch and brings the station into the ring.

For practical purposes, individual automatic switches are combined into a hub called a **multistation access unit** (MAU). This system looks like a star with the MAU in the middle, but it is, in fact, a ring (see Figure 3.16).

Figure 3.16   *Token ring implementation*

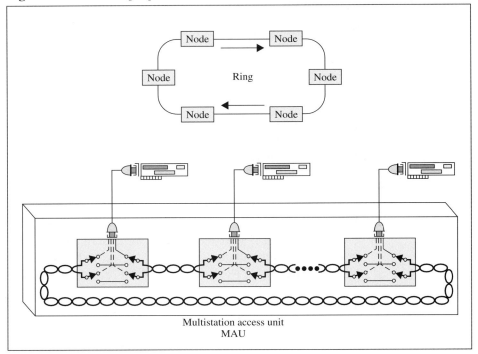

Fiber Distributed Data Interface (FDDI)

Fiber distributed data interface (FDDI) is a LAN protocol standardized by ANSI (see Chapter 1) and the ITU-T (see Chapter 1). It supports data rates of 100 Mbps and provides a high-speed alternative to Ethernet and token ring. When FDDI was designed, speeds of 100 Mbps required fiber-optic cable. Today, however, comparable speeds are available using copper cable. The copper version of FDDI is known as *CDDI*.

Access Method: Token Passing

The access method in FDDI is also called *token passing*. However, the mechanism of token passing is slightly different here. In a token ring network, a station can send only one frame each time it captures the token. In FDDI, access is limited by time. Each station keeps a timer that shows when the token should leave the station. If a station receives the token earlier than the designated time, it can keep the token and send data until the scheduled leaving time. On the other hand, if a station receives the token at or later than this time, it should let the token pass to the next station and wait for its next turn.

Addressing

FDDI uses a two- to six-byte address.

Data Rate

FDDI supports data rates of 100 Mbps.

Frame Format

FDDI uses two types of frames: data and token (see Figure 3.17). The eight fields of the frame format are as follows:

- **SD.** This one-byte field defines the starting flag.
- **FC.** This one-byte field defines the type of the frame.
- **Destination address.** This field contains the physical address of the next station.
- **Source address.** This field contains the physical address of the previous station.
- **Data.** Each data frame can carry up to 4,500 bytes of data.
- **CRC.** FDDI uses the standard IEEE four-byte cyclic redundancy check.
- **ED.** This field consists of half a byte in the data frame or a full byte in the token frame. It indicates the end of data and control information.
- **FS.** This field is similar to that of token ring. It is included only in the data frame and consists of 1.5 bytes.

Figure 3.17 *FDDI frame*

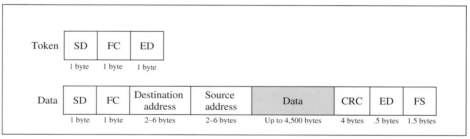

Implementation

FDDI is implemented as a dual ring. In most cases, data transmission is confined to the primary ring. The secondary ring is provided in case the primary fails. The secondary ring makes FDDI self-healing. When a problem occurs on the primary ring, the secondary can be activated to complete data circuits and maintain service (see Figure 3.18a).

Nodes connect to one or to both rings using a **media interface connector** (MIC). Every MIC has two fiber ports that allow it to connect to both ring cables. FDDI defines three types of nodes: dual attachment station (DAS), single attachment station (SAS),

Figure 3.18 *FDDI implementation*

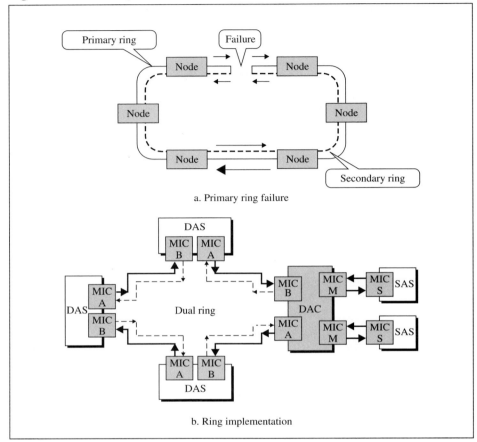

a. Primary ring failure

b. Ring implementation

and dual attachment concentrator (DAC). A DAS has two MICs (called MIC A and MIC B) and connects to both rings (see Figure 3.18b). To do so requires an expensive NIC with two inputs and two outputs. The connection to both rings gives it improved reliability and throughput. These improvements, however, are predicated on the station's remaining active (turned on). Faults are bypassed by a station's making a wrap connection from the primary ring to the secondary to switch signals from one input to another output. However, for DAS stations to make this switch, they must be active.

3.3 SWITCHING

LANs use topologies such as the bus, star, or ring, which are based on broadcasting. For example, in Ethernet, if a station sends a frame, every other station receives it. These types of topologies are not feasible in a WAN, where we want a frame to be received only by the intended recipient. The solution is to create a mesh topology, in which every computer is connected to every other computer. This involves either a huge number of links or the use of switches. WANs today use switches.

A switched network consists of a series of interlinked nodes, called *switches*. **Switches** are hardware and/or software devices capable of creating temporary connections between two or more devices linked to the switch but not to each other.

Traditionally, three methods of switching have been important: circuit switching, packet switching, and message switching. The first two are commonly used today. The third has been phased out in general communications but still has networking applications.

Circuit Switching

Circuit switching creates a direct physical connection between two devices such as telephones or computers. For example, in Figure 3.19 instead of making point-to-point connections between the three computers on the left (A, B, and C) to the four computers on the right (D, E, F, and G), requiring 12 links, we can use four switches to reduce the number and total length of the links.

Figure 3.19   *Circuit switching*

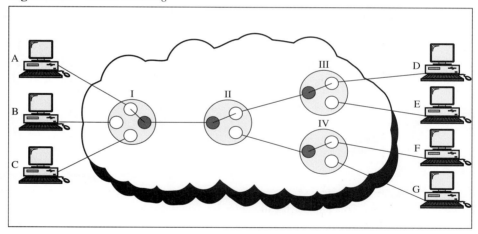

In circuit switching, after a connection is made between two systems, the path is dedicated and cannot be used by any other system. In other words, circuit switching creates a dedicated path between two end users. The end users can use the path as long as they want.

Packet Switching

A better solution for data transmission is called *packet switching*. In a **packet switched network**, data are transmitted in discrete units of potentially variable-length blocks called **packets**. The maximum length of the packet is established by the network. Longer transmissions are broken up into multiple packets. Each packet contains not only data but also a header with control information. The packets are sent over the network node-to-node. At each node, the packet is stored briefly before being routed according to the information in its header.

There are two popular approaches to packet switching: datagram and virtual circuit.

Datagram Approach

In the **datagram approach**, each packet is treated independently of all others. Even when one packet represents only a piece of a multipacket transmission, the network (and network layer functions) treats it as though it existed alone. Packets in this technology are referred to as **datagrams**.

Figure 3.20 shows how the datagram approach can be used to deliver three packets from station A to station X. In this example, all three packets (or datagrams) belong to the same message but may go by different paths to reach their destination.

Figure 3.20   *Packet switching, datagram approach*

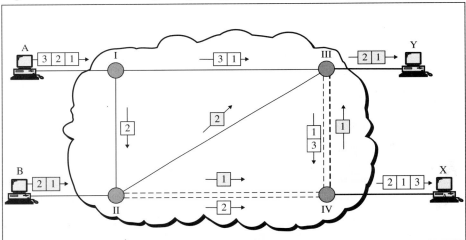

This approach can cause the datagrams of a transmission to arrive at their destination out of order. It is the responsibility of the transport layer in most protocols to reorder the datagrams before passing them on to the destination port.

The link joining each pair of nodes can contain multiple channels. Each of these channels is capable, in turn, of carrying datagrams either from several different sources simultaneously or from one source.

Virtual Circuit Approach

In the **virtual circuit** approach to packet switching, the relationship between all packets belonging to a message or session is preserved. A single route is chosen between sender and receiver at the beginning of the session. When the data are sent, all packets of the transmission travel one after another along that route (see Figure 3.21).

Although the virtual circuit approach of packet switching and circuit switching seem the same, there is a fundamental difference between them. In circuit switching,

Figure 3.21   *Packet switching, virtual circuit approach*

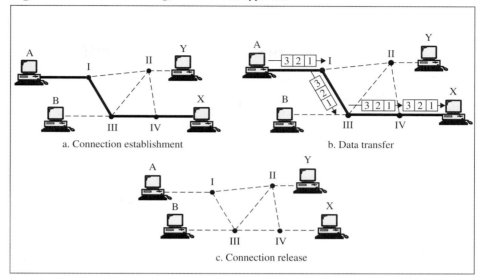

a. Connection establishment

b. Data transfer

c. Connection release

the path between the two end users is dedicated; it consists of only one channel. In the virtual circuit, on the other hand, the line is not dedicated to only two users; the line can be divided into channels. Each connection can use one of the channels in a link.

Message Switching

Message switching is best known by the descriptive term *store and forward*. In this method, a node (usually a computer) receives a message, stores it until the appropriate route is free, then sends it along. Although message switching in the network layer was common in the 1960s, it is not used today.

3.4   WIDE AREA NETWORKS (WANS)

A WAN provides long-distance transmission of data, voice, image, and video information over large geographical areas that may comprise a country, a continent, or even the whole world.

In contrast to LANs, which depend on their own hardware for transmission, WANs can utilize public, leased, or private communication devices, usually in combination.

Point-to-Point Protocol (PPP)

The **point-to-point protocol** (PPP) is designed to handle the transfer of data using asynchronous modem links or high-speed synchronous leased lines. The PPP uses a frame format very similar to what we have already seen in this chapter (see Figure 3.22). The following are the fields of the PPP frame:

Figure 3.22   *Point-to-point frame*

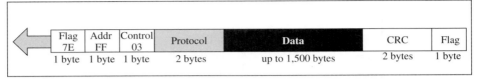

■ **Flag.** Each frame starts with a one-byte flag, which has the value of $7E_{16}$ (01111110). The flag is used for synchronization at the bit level between the sender and the receiver.

■ **Address.** The address field has the value of FF_{16}.

■ **Control.** The control field has the value of 03_{16}.

■ **Protocol.** This is a two-byte field used to define the protocol that uses the services of the line. For TCP/IP this value is 0021_{16}.

■ **CRC.** This is a two-byte cyclic redundancy check (see Appendix D).

X.25

The packet switching protocol most widely used today is called *X.25*. It was developed by the ITU-T (see Chapter 1) in 1976. According to the formal definition given in the ITU-T standard, **X.25** is an interface between data terminal equipment (DTE) and data circuit terminating equipment (DCE) for terminal operation at the packet mode on public data networks. Informally, we can say that X.25 is a packet switching protocol used in a WAN.

X.25 defines how a packet-mode terminal can be connected to a packet network for the exchange of data. It describes the procedures necessary for establishing, maintaining, and terminating connections (such as connection establishment, data exchange, acknowledgment, flow control, and data control). It also describes a set of services, called *facilities*, to provide functions such as reverse charge, call direct, and delay control.

X.25 is what is known as a *subscriber network interface* (SNI) protocol. It defines how the user's DTE, such as a computer, communicates with the network and how packets are sent over that network using DCEs, such as a router. It uses a virtual circuit approach to packet switching rather than a datagram approach.

Figure 3.23 gives a conceptual overview of X.25. Although X.25 is an end-to-end protocol, the actual movement of packets through the network is invisible to it. It sees the network as a cloud through which each packet passes on its way to the receiving DCE.

X.25 Layers

The X.25 protocol is organized into three layers: the physical layer; the link access procedure, balanced layer (LAPB); and the packet layer protocol layer (PLP). These layers define functions at the physical, data link, and network layers of the OSI model. Figure 3.24 shows the format of the packet at the PLP layer and the format of the frame at the LAPB layer.

Figure 3.23   *X.25*

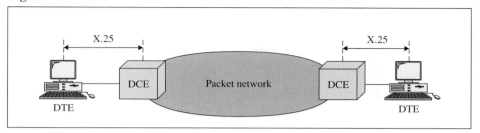

Figure 3.24   *X.25 packets and frames*

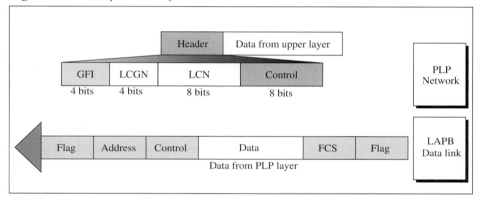

Physical Layer   At the physical layer, X.25 specifies a protocol called *X.21* (or X.21bis) which has been specifically defined for X.25 by the ITU-T. X.21, however, is close enough to other physical layer protocols, such as EIA-232, that X.25 is able to support them as well.

Data Link Layer   X.25 provides data link controls using a bit-oriented protocol (see Appendix G) called *link access procedure, balanced* (LAPB). The fields in this layer are the same as those in the frame of LANs. The control field is used for flow and error control at the data link layer. The address field is used during connection establishment. The frame check sequence (FCS) is the CRC field defined in LAN frames.

Network Layer   The network layer in X.25 is called the **packet layer protocol** (PLP). This layer is responsible for establishing the connection, transferring the data, and terminating the connection. User and system data are passed down from the upper layers. At the PLP, a header containing control information is added to transform the data into a PLP packet. PLP packets are, in turn, passed to the LAPB layer, where they are encapsulated into LAPB information frames and passed to the physical layer to be sent through the network. The following are fields of the network-layer packet:

- **General format identifier (GFI).**   This field gives general information about the header.

- **Logical channel group number (LCGN).** This is the first part of the virtual circuit number.

- **Logical channel number (LCN).** This is the second part of the virtual circuit number.
- **Control.** This field is used for flow control and error control.

Frame Relay

Frame relay is a WAN protocol designed in response to X.25 deficiencies. X.25 provides extensive error checking and flow control. Packets are checked for accuracy at each station (node) to which they are routed. Each station keeps the copy of the original frame until it receives confirmation from the next station that the frame has arrived intact. Such station-to-station checking is implemented at the data link layer of the OSI model.

But X.25 does not stop there. It also checks for errors from source to receiver at the network layer. The source keeps a copy of the original packet until it receives confirmation from the final destination. Much of the traffic on an X.25 network is devoted to error checking to ensure complete reliability of service.

Figure 3.25 shows the traffic required to transmit one packet from source to receiver. The white boxes show the data and data link acknowledgments. The shaded boxes show the network layer confirmation and acknowledgments. Only one-fourth of this traffic is message data; the rest is reliability. Such extensive traffic was necessary at the time X.25 was introduced because transmission media were more error prone then than they are today.

Improvements in traditional transmission media and a greater use of fiber-optic cable, which is far less susceptible to noise than metallic cable, have decreased the probability of transmission error to a point where this level of caution is not only unnecessary but counterproductive as well.

Frame relay does not provide error checking or require acknowledgment in the data link layer. Instead, all error checking is left to the protocols at the network and transport layers, which use the services of frame relay. (Frame relay operates at only the physical and data link layers.) Many data link layer operations are eliminated while others are combined.

Frame Format

Figure 3.26 shows the format of the frame in frame relay. The flag field is the same as the previous protocols. The FCS is the CRC (see Appendix D). The following are fields of the frame format:

- **Address fields.** The first six bits of the first byte make up part 1 of the data link connection identifier (DLCI). The second part of the DLCI uses the first four bits of the second byte. These bits are part of the 16-bit data link connection identifier defined by the standard. The function of the DLCI is discussed in the Frame Relay Operation section to follow.
- **Command/response (C/R).** The C/R bit is provided to allow upper layers to identify a frame as either a command or a response.

Figure 3.25 *Comparison between X.25 and frame relay*

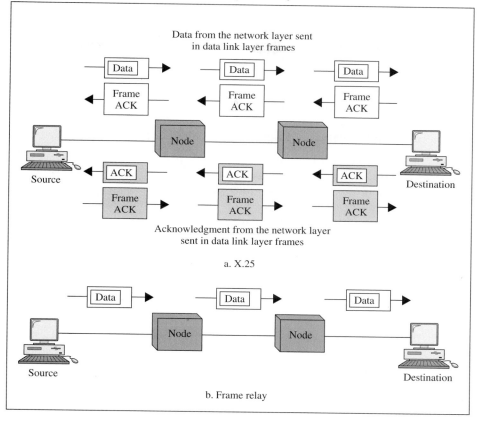

Figure 3.26 *Frame relay frame*

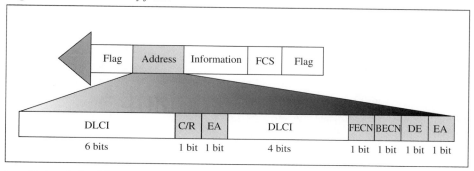

■ **Extended address (EA).** The EA bit tells whether or not the current byte is the final byte of the address. EA 0 means that another address byte is to follow. EA 1 means that the current byte is the final one.

- **Forward explicit congestion notification (FECN).** The FECN bit indicates that traffic is congested in the direction in which the frame is traveling. It informs the destination that congestion may cause the present or future frames to arrive late.

- **Backward explicit congestion notification (BECN).** The BECN bit indicates a congestion problem in the direction opposite to the one in which the frame is traveling. It informs the receiver that data sent back to the sender may be delayed by congestion.

- **Discard eligibility (DE).** The DE bit indicates the priority level of the frame.

Frame Relay Operation

Frame relay transmission is based on permanent virtual circuit (PVC) connections. Virtual circuits in other standards are implemented by the network layer. Frame relay, however, uses DLCIs, which identify a permanent virtual circuit that is set up when the system is put in place. All traffic between two given stations takes the same path.

Figure 3.27 shows a network where stations are connected directly to a frame relay network. In practice, this situation is unusual: Stations are more likely to connect to a frame relay network through another type of network or service. It is helpful to our discussion of network operation, however, to base it on this simplified model.

Figure 3.27   *Frame relay operation*

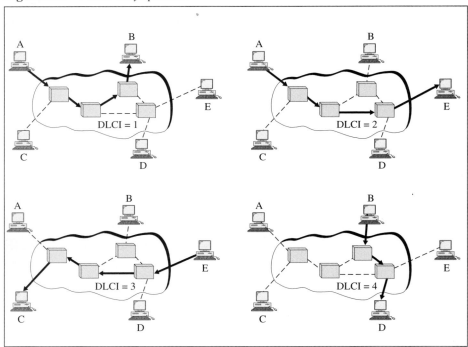

Asynchronous Transfer Mode (ATM)

Asynchronous Transfer Mode (ATM), as designed by the ATM Forum, is a revolutionary idea for restructuring the infrastructure of data communication. It is designed to support the transmission of data, voice, and video through high data-rate transmission media such as fiber-optic cable.

Cell

ATM is a protocol for transferring cells. A **cell** is a small data unit of fixed size. It is 53 bytes long, made of a five-byte header and a 48-byte payload. The header contains, among other information, a virtual path identifier (VPI) and a virtual channel identifier (VCI). These two pieces of information are used to route the cell through the network to the final destination (see Figure 3.28).

Figure 3.28   *Cell*

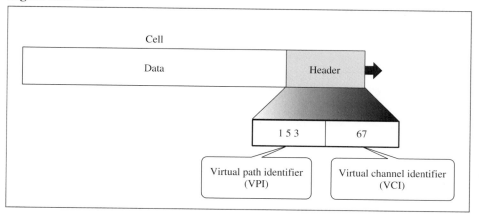

Cell Relay

An ATM network is a connection-oriented, **cell relay** (cell switching) network. This means that the unit of data is not a packet as in a packet switching network, or a frame as in frame relay, but a cell. However, ATM, like X.25 and frame relay, is a connection-oriented network, which means that before two systems can communicate, they must make a connection. To start up a connection, a system uses a 20-byte address. After the connection is established, the combination of VPI/VCI leads a cell from its source to its final destination.

The combination of VPI/VCI looks like a virtual circuit number used in packet switching networks, such as X.25. However, a virtual circuit number refers to the whole route defined during the connection establishment, whereas a VPI/VCI pair will change from switch to switch. Each switch, when receiving a cell, consults a table to find the interface through which the cell leaves the switch and the next VPI/VCI pair that must be assigned to the cell (see Figure 3.29).

Figure 3.29   *ATM switch*

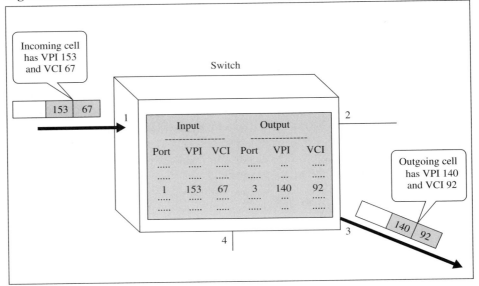

Layers

ATM uses three layers, the application adaptation layer, the ATM layer, and the physical layer (see Figure 3.30).

Figure 3.30   *Three layers in ATM*

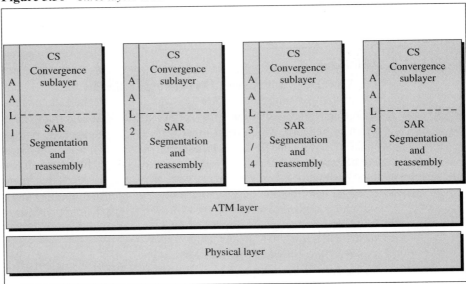

Application Adaptation Layer (AAL)   The **application adaptation layer** (AAL) allows any type of network to connect to ATM. The AAL protocol accepts data from any other protocol and encapsulates it into fixed-sized ATM cells. Each of the AAL categories is actually two sublayers: the **convergence sublayer** (CS) and the **segmentation and reassembly** (SAR) **sublayer**. The CS can add more information to the data unit; SAR breaks the data unit into small segments to be encapsulated into cells. ATM defines four different AAL categories to accommodate data from different sources with different formats. These are as follows:

- **AAL1.** AAL1 converts a stream of constant bit-rate data to cells.
- **AAL2.** AAL2 converts a stream of variable bit-rate data to cells.
- **AAL3/4.** AAL3/4 converts data from a connection-oriented packet switching network.
- **AAL5.** AAL5 converts data coming from a connectionless, packet switching network. The TCP/IP protocol suite uses this category to encapsulate the IP packets. Figure 3.31 shows how an IP packet is broken into segments of 48 bytes to be encapsulated in a cell in the lower layer.

Figure 3.31   *AAL5*

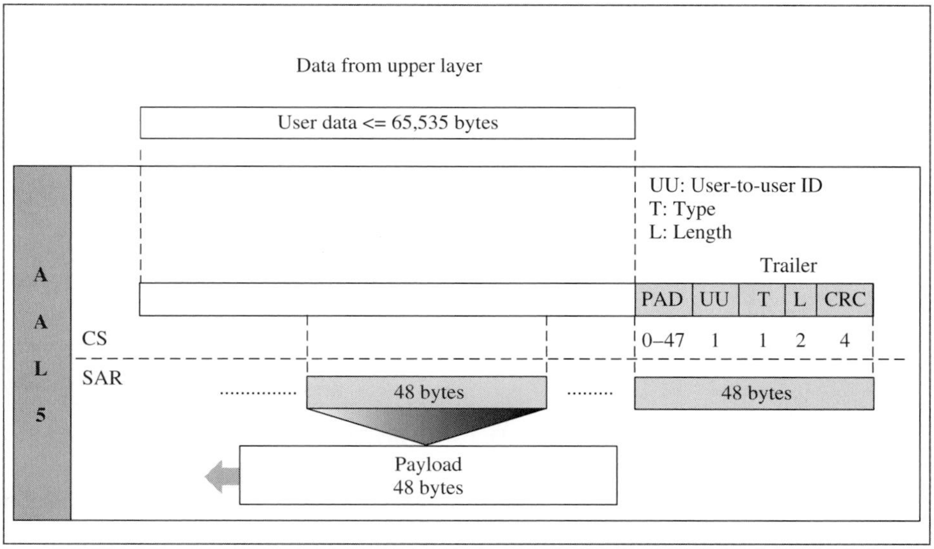

ATM Layer   The ATM layer provides routing, traffic management, switching, and multiplexing services. It processes outgoing traffic by accepting 48-byte segments from the AAL sublayers and transforming them into 53-byte cells by the addition of a five-byte header. ATM uses two formats for the header in this layer: One is for the user network interface (UNI); the other is for the network to network interface (NNI) (see Figure 3.32). The fields are as follows:

- **Generic flow control (GFC).** This field provides flow control for the UNI cell.
- **VPI.** VPI is an eight-bit field in a UNI cell and a 12-bit field in an NNI cell.
- **VCI.** VCI is a 16-bit field in both cells.
- **Payload type (PT).** This defines the type of payload.

Figure 3.32 *ATM layer*

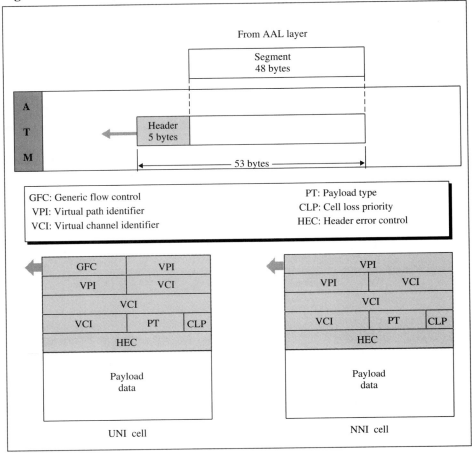

- **Cell loss priority (CLP).** This bit indicates to a switch which cell may be dropped and which must be retained.

- **Header error control (HEC).** This is an eight-bit field to detect multiple-bit errors and correct single-bit errors in the header.

Physical Layer   The physical layer defines the transmission medium, bit transmission, encoding, and electrical-to-optical transformation.

3.5   CONNECTING DEVICES

Connecting devices are used to connect the segments of a network together or to connect networks to create an internetwork or internet. We can classify these devices in four categories: repeaters, bridges, routers, and gateways (see Figure 3.33).

Each of these four device types interacts with protocols at different layers of the OSI model. Repeaters act only upon the electrical components of a signal and are there-

Figure 3.33   *Connecting devices*

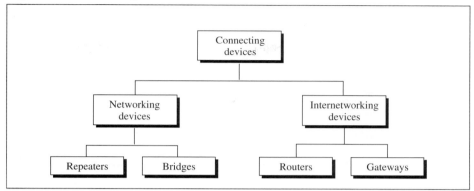

fore active only at the physical layer. Bridges utilize addressing protocols and can affect the flow control of a single LAN; they are active at the physical and data link layers. Routers provide links between two separate LANs and are active at the physical, data link, and network layers. Finally, gateways provide translation services between incompatible LANs or applications and are active in all of the layers. Each of these internetworking devices also operates in all of the layers below the one in which it is most active (see Figure 3.34).

Figure 3.34   *Connecting devices and the OSI model*

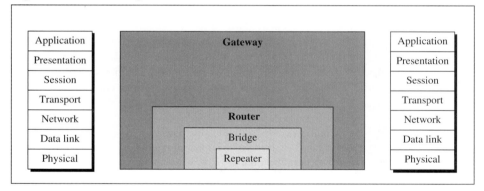

Repeaters

A **repeater** (or regenerator) is an electronic device that operates on only the physical layer of the OSI model. Signals that carry information within a network can travel a limited distance before **attenuation** (weakening of the signal) or interference from noise endangers the integrity of the data. A repeater installed on a link receives the signal before it becomes too weak or corrupted, regenerates the original bit pattern, and puts the refreshed copy back onto the link. In effect, the signal, with the corruption removed, is transmitted a second time from a location closer to the destination (see Figure 3.35).

Figure 3.35   *Repeater*

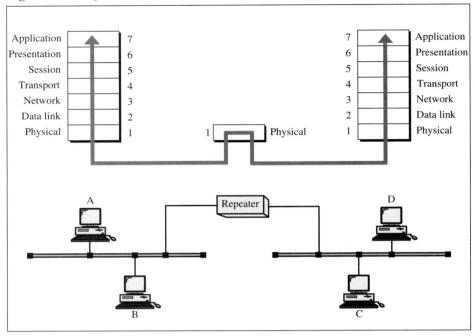

A repeater allows us to extend the physical length of a network. The two sections connected by the repeater are, in reality, one network. If station A sends a frame to station B, all stations (including C and D) will receive the frame, just as they would without the repeater. The repeater does not have the intelligence to keep the frame from passing to the right side when it is meant for a station on the left. The difference is that, with the repeater, stations C and D receive a truer copy of the frame than would otherwise have been possible.

Bridges

Bridges operate in both the physical and the data link layers of the OSI model. **Bridges** divide a large network into smaller segments. Unlike repeaters, however, bridges contain logic that allows them to keep the traffic for each segment separate. Bridges are smart enough to relay a frame only to the side of the segment containing the intended recipient. In this way they filter traffic, a fact that makes them useful for controlling congestion and isolating problem links. Bridges can also provide security through this partitioning of traffic (see Figure 3.36).

Bridges do not modify the structure or contents of a packet and can therefore be used only between segments that use the same protocol.

A bridge operates at the physical and data link layers, giving it access to the physical addresses of all stations connected to it. When a frame enters a bridge, the bridge not only regenerates the signal but checks the address of the destination and forwards the new copy only to the segment to which the address belongs. As a bridge encounters

Figure 3.36   *Bridge*

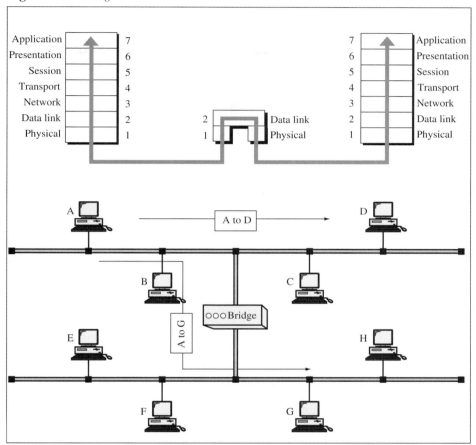

a packet, it reads the address contained in the frame and compares that address with a table of all the stations on both segments. When it finds a match, it discovers to which segment the station belongs and relays the packet only to that segment.

A multiport bridge can act as a switch to connect two or more segments of a network. It is often used to increase the real data rate of a network. For example, an Ethernet network operates at 10 Mbps. Assume exactly five devices are attached to an Ethernet network and each contends for access to the network. Since the network must be shared between these five devices, the actual data rate is 2 Mbps. To increase the data rate for each device, divide the network into five different segments using a multiport bridge (switch). This allows each segment to be independent, thereby increasing the data rate to 10 Mbps. In other words, without a bridge, all five devices share the available bandwidth; with a bridge, each device uses the whole bandwidth. The use of a bridge in an Ethernet network is often referred to as *switched Ethernet*.

Routers

Repeaters and bridges are simple hardware devices capable of executing specific tasks. Routers, however, are more sophisticated. They have access to network layer addresses and contain software that enables them to determine which of several possible paths between those addresses is the best for a particular transmission. Routers operate in the physical, data link, and network layers of the OSI model (see Figure 3.37).

Figure 3.37 *Router*

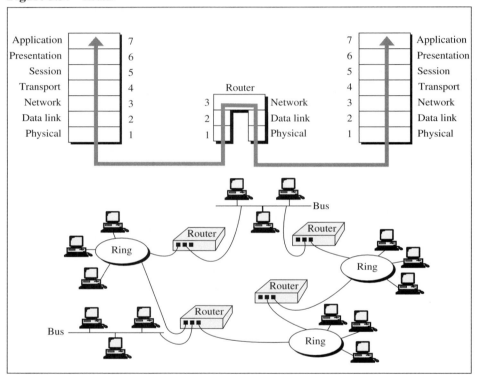

Routers relay packets among multiple interconnected networks. They route packets from one network to any of a number of potential destination networks on an internet. A packet sent from a station on one network to a station on a neighboring network goes first to the jointly held router, which switches it over to the destination network. If there is no one router connected to both the sending and receiving networks, the sending router transfers the packet across one of its connected networks to the next router in the direction of the ultimate destination. That router forwards the packet to the next router on the path, and so on, until the destination is reached.

Routers act like stations on a network. But unlike most stations, which are members of only one network, routers have addresses on, and links to, two or more networks at the same time. In their simplest function they receive packets from one connected network and pass them to a second connected network.

Gateways

Gateways potentially operate in all seven layers of the OSI model. A **gateway** is a protocol converter. A router by itself transfers, accepts, and relays packets only across networks using similar protocols. A gateway, on the other hand, can accept a packet formatted for one protocol (e.g., AppleTalk) and convert it to a packet formatted for another protocol (e.g., TCP/IP) before forwarding it.

The gateway understands the protocols used by each network linked into the router and is therefore able to translate from one to another. In some cases, the only modifications necessary are the header and trailer of the packet. In other cases, the gateway must adjust the data rate, size, and format as well (see Figure 3.38).

Figure 3.38 *Gateway*

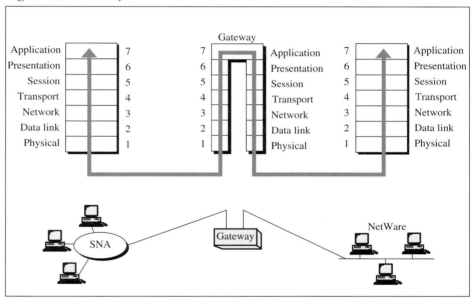

3.6 SUMMARY

- Signals travel from transmitter to receiver via a path. This path, called the medium, can be guided or unguided.

- A guided medium is contained within physical boundaries, while an unguided medium is boundless.

- The most popular types of guided media are the following:
  a. Twisted-pair cable (metallic).
  b. Coaxial cable (metallic).
  c. Optical fiber (glass or plastic).

- Unshielded twisted-pair (UTP) cable consists of two insulated copper wires twisted together.

- Shielded twisted-pair (STP) cable consists of insulated twisted pairs encased in a metal foil or braided-mesh covering.

- Coaxial cable consists of the following layers (starting from the center):

  a. A metallic rod-shaped inner conductor.

  b. An insulator covering the rod.

  c. A metallic outer conductor (shield).

  d. An insulator covering the shield.

  e. A plastic cover.

- Both twisted-pair cable and coaxial cable transmit data in the form of an electric current.

- Fiber-optic cables are composed of a glass or plastic inner core surrounded by cladding, all encased in an outside jacket.

- Fiber-optic cables carry data signals in the form of light. The signal is propagated along the inner core by reflection.

- Fiber-optic transmission is becoming increasingly popular due to its noise resistance, low attenuation, and high bandwidth capabilities.

- Radio waves can be used to transmit data. These waves use unguided media and are usually propagated through the air.

- Regulatory authorities have divided up and defined the uses for the electromagnetic spectrum dealing with radio communication.

- A local area network (LAN) is a data communication system that allows a number of independent devices to communicate directly with each other in a limited geographic area.

- Ethernet, using the CSMA/CD access method and configured in a logical bus topology, operates as follows: Any station may listen to the line to determine if the line is clear. If it is clear, transmission can commence. If a collision occurs, the data is resent after a random time-out.

- Popular methods to implement Ethernet include 10BASE5 (thick Ethernet) with thick coaxial cabling, 10BASE2 (thin Ethernet) with thin coaxial cabling, and 10BASE-T (twisted-pair Ethernet) with unshielded twisted-pair (UTP) wire.

- Fast Ethernet is a version of Ethernet with a 100 Mbps data rate.

- Token ring employs token passing as its access method. Each station has an equal opportunity to send data, and collisions are totally avoided.

- Token ring is a physical ring structure. The nodes are connected to the ring by a cable and a switch that can bypass an off node.

- Fiber distributed data interface (FDDI) is a dual-ring LAN featuring token passing, fiber-optic cable, and a data rate of 100 Mbps.

- A switch is hardware or software that temporarily links two or more devices connected to the switch but not to each other.

- There are three switching methods: circuit switching, packet switching, and message switching.

■ Circuit switching features a dedicated, physical connection between two devices.

■ Packet switching features the transmission of data in discrete units called packets.

■ In the datagram approach to packet switching each packet travels independently.

■ In the virtual circuit approach to packet switching all packets of a message take the same path.

■ In message switching, a method also known as store and forward, a node receives a message, stores it, and then sends it.

■ The point-to-point protocol (PPP) handles the transfer of data using asynchronous modem links or high-speed synchronous leased lines.

■ The most widely used packet switching protocol is X.25, an interface between data terminal equipment (DTE) and data circuit terminating equipment (DCE).

■ X.25 describes the procedures necessary for establishing, maintaining, and terminating connections between a packet-mode terminal and a packet network.

■ The X.25 protocol operates in the physical layer, the link access procedure, balanced (LAPB) layer, and the packet layer protocol (PLP) layer.

■ Frame relay eliminates the extensive error checking necessary in X.25 protocol.

■ Frame relay operates in the physical and data link layers of the OSI model.

■ Frame relay uses permanent virtual circuits (PVCs). The PVC link is identified through the data link connection identifier (DLCI).

■ Asynchronous Transfer Mode (ATM) is the cell relay protocol designed to support the transmission of data, voice, and video through high data-rate transmission media such as fiber-optic cable.

■ The ATM data packet is called a cell and is composed of 53 bytes (5 bytes of header and 48 bytes of payload).

■ A cell network is based on permanent virtual circuit routing.

■ The ATM standard defines three layers: the application adaptation layer (AAL), the ATM layer, and the physical layer.

■ The AAL is divided into two sublayers: the convergence sublayer (CS) and the segmentation and reassembly (SAR) sublayer.

■ There are four different AALs, each specific for a data type. TCP/IP uses AAL5, which converts data coming from a connectionless packet switching network.

■ Connecting devices can connect segments of a network together; they can also connect networks together to create an internet.

■ There are four types of connecting devices: repeaters, bridges, routers, and gateways.

■ Repeaters regenerate a signal in the physical layer of the OSI model.

■ Bridges have access to station addresses and can forward or filter a packet in a network. They operate in the physical and data link layers of the OSI model.

■ Routers determine the path a packet should take. They operate in the physical, data link, and network layers of the OSI model.

■ Gateways are protocol converters; they operate in all seven layers of the OSI model.

3.7   PRACTICE SET

Multiple Choice

1. Transmission media are usually categorized as _____.
   a. fixed or unfixed
   b. guided or unguided
   c. determinate or indeterminate
   d. metallic or nonmetallic

2. _____ cable consists of an inner copper core and a second conducting outer sheath.
   a. Twisted-pair
   b. Coaxial
   c. Fiber-optic
   d. Shielded twisted-pair

3. In fiber optics, the signal source is _____ waves.
   a. light
   b. radio
   c. infrared
   d. very low frequency

4. Which of the following primarily uses guided media?
   a. cellular telephone system
   b. local telephone system
   c. satellite communications
   d. radio broadcasting

5. Which of the following is not a guided medium?
   a. twisted-pair cable
   b. coaxial cable
   c. fiber-optic cable
   d. atmosphere

6. In a noisy environment, the best transmission medium would be _____.
   a. twisted-pair cable
   b. coaxial cable
   c. optical fiber
   d. the atmosphere

7. What protects the coaxial cable from noise?
   a. inner conductor
   b. diameter of cable
   c. outer conductor

    d. insulating material

8. In an optical fiber the inner core is _____ the cladding.

    a. more dense than

    b. less dense than

    c. the same density as

    d. another name for

9. The inner core of an optical fiber is _____ in composition.

    a. glass or plastic

    b. copper

    c. bimetallic

    d. liquid

10. Radio communication frequencies range from _____.

    a. 3 KHz to 300 KHz

    b. 300 KHz to 3 GHz

    c. 3 KHz to 300 GHz

    d. 3 KHz to 3,000 GHz

11. The radio communication spectrum is divided into bands based on _____.

    a. amplitude

    b. frequency

    c. cost and hardware

    d. transmission media

12. When a beam of light travels through media of two different densities, if the angle of incidence is greater than the critical angle, _____ occurs.

    a. reflection

    b. refraction

    c. incidence

    d. criticism

13. When a light beam moves to a less dense medium, the angle of refraction is _____ the angle of incidence.

    a. greater than

    b. less than

    c. equal to

    d. none of the above

14. When we talk about unguided media, usually we are referring to _____.

    a. metallic wires

    b. nonmetallic wires

    c. the atmosphere

    d. none of the above

15. 10BASE2 uses _____ cable while 10BASE5 uses _____.

    a. thick coaxial, thin coaxial

    b. twisted pair, thick coaxial

    c. thin coaxial, thick coaxial

    d. fiber optic, thin coaxial

16. 10BASE2 and 10BASE5 have different _____.

    a. signal band types

    b. fields on the frame

    c. maximum segment lengths

    d. maximum data rates

17. _____ specifies a star topology featuring a central hub and unshielded twisted-pair wire as the medium.

    a. 10BASE5

    b. 10BASE2

    c. 10BASET

    d. none of the above

18. The _____ houses the switches in token ring.

    a. NIC

    b. MAU

    c. 9-pin connector

    d. transceiver

19. What can happen at a token ring station?

    a. examination of the destination address

    b. regeneration of the frame

    c. passing of the frame to the next station

    d. all of the above

20. FDDI is more efficient than a regular token ring because _____.

    a. no timers are required

    b. the node that has the token can send more than one frame

    c. the AC field is eliminated

    d. of the added priority and reservation option

21. Which type of switching uses the entire capacity of a dedicated link?

    a. circuit switching

    b. datagram approach to packet switching

    c. virtual circuit approach to packet switching

    d. message switching

22. In which type of packet switching do all the datagrams of a message follow the same channels of a path?

    a. datagram approach to packet switching

    b. virtual circuit approach to packet switching

    c. both a and b

    d. none of the above

23. In _____, each packet of a message need not follow the same path from source to destination.
    a. circuit switching
    b. message switching
    c. the datagram approach to packet switching
    d. the virtual circuit approach to packet switching

24. X.25 protocol uses _____ for end-to-end transmission.
    a. message switching
    b. circuit switching
    c. the datagram approach to packet switching
    d. the virtual approach to packet switching

25. The physical layer protocol directly specified for the X.25 protocol is _____.
    a. RS-232
    b. X.21
    c. DB-15
    d. DB37

26. X.25 protocol requires error checking at the _____ layer.
    a. physical
    b. data link
    c. network
    d. b and c

27. Frame relay requires error checking at the _____ layer.
    a. physical
    b. data link
    c. network
    d. none of the above

28. Why is so much error checking required for the X.25 standard?
    a. X.25 requires a large bandwidth.
    b. When X.25 was first introduced, the transmission medium was unreliable.
    c. When X.25 was first introduced, the switching was unreliable.
    d. When X.25 was first introduced, no multiplexing was available.

29. Frame relay operates in the _____.
    a. physical layer
    b. data link layer
    c. physical and data link layers
    d. physical, data link, and network layers

30. In frame relay, which bit in the address field is set to one to signify the last address byte?
    a. DE (discard eligibility)
    b. EA (extended address)

   c. C/R (command/response)

   d. FECN (forward explicit congestion notification)

31. Which field contains the permanent virtual circuit address?

   a. EA

   b. FECN/BECN

   c. DE

   d. DLCI

32. The most efficient medium for ATM is _____.

   a. twisted pair

   b. coaxial cable

   c. fiber-optic cable

   d. shielded coaxial cable

33. In data communications, ATM is an acronym for _____.

   a. automatic teller machine

   b. automatic transmission model

   c. asynchronous telecommunication method

   d. Asynchronous Transfer Mode

34. Because ATM is _____, cells do not usually arrive out of order because the cells follow the same path.

   a. asynchronous

   b. multiplexed

   c. a network

   d. connection-oriented

35. Which ATM layer specifies how user data should be packaged into cells?

   a. physical

   b. ATM

   c. application adaptation

   d. data adaptation

36. Which ATM layer has a 53-byte cell as an end product?

   a. physical

   b. ATM

   c. application adaptation

   d. cell transformation

37. Which application adaptation layer type can process a data stream having a non-constant bit rate?

   a. AAL1

   b. AAL2

   c. AAL3/4

   d. AAL5

38. Which AAL type is designed to support a data stream that has a constant bit rate?

    a. AAL1

    b. AAL2

    c. AAL3/4

    d. AAL5

39. The end product of the AAL5 SAR is a data packet that is _____.

    a. variable in length

    b. 48 bytes long

    c. 44 to 48 bytes long

    d. greater than 48 bytes long

40. A _____ field on a cell header in the ATM layer determines whether a cell can be dropped.

    a. VPI (virtual path identifier)

    b. VCI (virtual channel identifier)

    c. CLP (cell loss priority)

    d. GFC (generic flow constant)

41. Which of the following is not a connecting device?

    a. bridge

    b. transceiver

    c. router

    d. repeater

42. A bridge forwards or filters a packet by comparing the information in its address table to the packet's _____.

    a. layer 2 source address

    b. source node's physical address

    c. layer 2 destination address

    d. layer 3 destination address

43. Which of the following can be handled by a gateway?

    a. protocol conversion

    b. packet re-sizing

    c. data rate adjustment

    d. all of the above

44. Gateways function in which OSI layers?

    a. lower 3

    b. upper 4

    c. all 7

    d. all but the physical layer

45. Repeaters function in the _____ layer.

    a. physical

    b. data link

    c. network

 d. a and b

46. Bridges function in the _____ layer.

 a. physical

 b. data link

 c. network

 d. a and b

47. A repeater takes a weakened or corrupted signal and _____ it.

 a. amplifies

 b. regenerates

 c. resamples

 d. reroutes

48. A bridge has access to the _____ address of a station on the same network.

 a. physical

 b. network

 c. service access point

 d. all of the above

49. Routers function in the _____ layers.

 a. physical and data link

 b. physical, data link, and network

 c. data link and network

 d. network and transport

50. A packet from an Ethernet network requires a _____ before it can be routed to an FDDI network.

 a. repeater

 b. bridge

 c. router

 d. gateway

Exercises

51. Describe the components of a fiber-optic cable. Draw a picture.

52. Why should the light ray be reflective rather than refractive in fiber optics?

53. Give three advantages and disadvantages of using fiber-optic cable over metallic cable.

54. A beam of light moves from one medium to another, less dense medium. The critical angle is 60 degrees. Draw the path of the light through both media when the angle of incidence is:

 a. 40 degrees

 b. 50 degrees

 c. 60 degrees

 d. 70 degrees

e. 80 degrees

55. Explain CSMA/CD and its use. What part of the 802 project uses CSMA/CD?

56. Discuss the placement of the transceiver in 10BASE5, 10BASE2, and 10BASET standards.

57. What is a collision?

58. What types of media are used in LANs? Give an advantage and disadvantage of each.

59. A small start-up company operating on a shoestring budget needs an Ethernet LAN to handle a maximum of 10 workstations. The company will occupy two floors of an existing building. What would be a good LAN and why?

60. How does a token ring LAN operate?

61. What types of factors must be considered when deciding which type of LAN is needed for a company?

62. Suppose there is heavy traffic on both a CSMA/CD LAN and a token ring LAN. A station on which system is more likely to wait longer to send a frame? Why?

63. What are the advantages of FDDI over a basic token ring?

64. What is more efficient, circuit switching or the virtual circuit approach to packet switching? Why?

65. How does X.25 handle error control?

66. Name some advantages of frame relay over X.25.

67. How is X.25 superior to frame relay?

68. How is flow control handled in frame relay?

69. How is a repeater different from an amplifier?

70. What are the four connecting devices? Describe their functions, rank them according to their complexity, and give the OSI layer in which they operate.

71. A token ring of three stations is connected to a second token ring of three stations by a bridge. Discuss why the network administrator used this configuration instead of just one large six-station token ring.

72. Draw three token ring LANs connected by one bridge. What happens if a fault occurs on one of the rings? What happens if the bridge fails?

73. Describe some of the factors that need to be considered in connecting networks.

74. What is the smallest size of an Ethernet frame? What is the largest size of an Ethernet frame?

75. What is the smallest size of a token ring data frame? What is the largest size of a token ring data frame?

76. What is the ratio of useful data to the entire packet for the smallest Ethernet frame? What is the ratio for the largest frame? What is the average ratio?

77. What is the ratio of useful data to the entire packet for the smallest token ring frame? What is the ratio for the largest frame? What is the average ratio?

78. What is the ratio of useful data to the entire packet for an ATM cell? Compare this to Ethernet and token ring.

79. Why do you think that an Ethernet frame should have a minimum data size?

80. Imagine the length of a 10BASE5 cable is 2,500 meters. If the speed of the propagation in a thick coaxial cable is 60 percent of the speed of light (300,000,000 meter/second), how long does it take for a bit to travel from the beginning to the end of the network? Ignore any propagation delay in the equipment.

81. Using the data in exercise 81, find the maximum time it takes to sense a collision. The worst case occurs when data is sent from one end of the cable and the collision happens at the other end. Remember that the signal needs to make a round trip.

82. The data rate of 10BASE5 is 10 Mbps. How long does it take to create the smallest frame? Show your calculation.

83. Using the data in exercises 82 and 83, find the minimum size of an Ethernet frame for collision detection to work properly.

84. Imagine the length of the ring in a token ring is 1,000 meters. If the speed of the propagation in a twisted-pair cable is 60 percent of the speed of light (300,000,000 meter/second), how long does it take for a bit to make a complete trip?

85. In a 16 Mbps token ring network, the length of the token is 3 bytes. How long does it take for a station to produce a token?

86. For a token ring to work properly, the first bit of data should not come back to the place where it was produced until the whole frame is produced. Since the token is 3 bytes long, what should be the minimum length of the ring for proper operation of the token passing method? Use the result of exercises 85 and 85.

Programming Exercises

87. Complete the following **struct** declaration for the Ethernet packet.

    struct   Ethernet
    {
    ....;
    unsigned long int   CRC ;
    } ;

88. Complete the following **struct** declaration for the token ring packet.

    struct   Token_Ring
    {
    .... ;
     unsigned long int   CRC ;
    } ;

89. Complete the following **struct** declaration for an FDDI packet.

    struct   FDDI
    {
    .... ;
     unsigned long int   CRC ;
    ....;
    } ;

CHAPTER 4

IP Addressing

At the application level, we can think of an internet as a single network connecting hosts. For a host to communicate with any other host, we need a universal identification system. In other words, we need to name each host uniquely. We will describe this naming system in Chapter 16. This system is used only in the application layer; it cannot be used in the network layer because there are other entities such as routers that also must be reached.

An internet is made of a combination of physical networks (LANs or WANs) connected by routers. When a host communicates with another host, the packets may travel from one physical network to another using these routers. This suggests that communication at this level also needs a global identification system. A host must be able to communicate with any other host without worrying about which physical network must be passed through. This means that the hosts must be identified uniquely and globally at this layer also. In addition, for efficient and optimum routing, each router must also be identified uniquely and globally at this layer.

The identifier that is used in the IP layer of the TCP/IP protocol is called the **Internet address** or **IP address**. It is a 32-bit binary address, implemented in software, that *uniquely* and *universally* defines a host or a router on the Internet.

> An IP address is a 32-bit address that uniquely defines a host or a router on the Internet.

The IP addresses are unique. They are unique in the sense that each address defines one, and only one, device (host or router) on the Internet. Two devices on the Internet can never have the same address. However, as we will see shortly, a device can have more than one IP address if it is connected to more than one physical network.

> The IP addresses are unique in the sense that two devices can never have the same address. However, a device can have more than one address.

The IP addresses are universal in the sense that the addressing system must be accepted by any host that wants to be connected to the Internet.

In addition to the physical addresses (contained on NICs) that identify individual devices, the Internet requires an additional addressing convention: an address that identifies the connection of a host to its network.

Each Internet address consists of four bytes (32 bits), defining two parts: netid and hostid. These parts are of varying lengths, depending on the class of the address. The first few bits of netid determine the class of an address as we will see shortly (see Figure 4.1).

Figure 4.1   *Internet address*

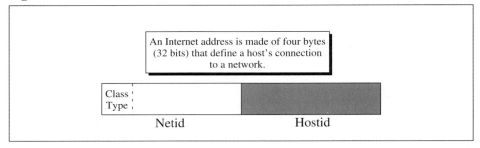

Each address is a pair (netid and hostid) where the **netid** identifies a network and the **hostid** identifies a host on that network.

Each IP address is made of two parts: netid and hostid. The netid defines a network; the hostid identifies a host on that network.

4.1   DECIMAL NOTATION

To make the 32-bit form more compact and easier to read, Internet addresses are usually written in decimal form with decimal points separating the bytes. Figure 4.2 shows an IP address in decimal point notation.

Figure 4.2   *Decimal point notation*

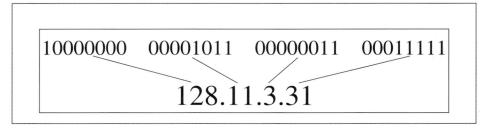

4.2   CLASSES

There are five different IP address classes: A, B, C, D, and E. These are designed to cover the needs of different types of organizations.

IP addresses are divided into five different classes: A, B, C, D, and E.

Figure 4.3 shows the structure of each class of IP address.

Figure 4.3   *Internet address classes*

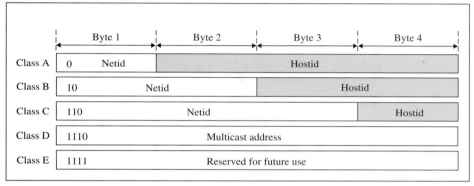

Class A

In a class A address, the first **octet** (eight bits) defines the netid. However, the leftmost bit must be zero to define the class as A. The remaining seven bits define different networks. This means that the number of networks that have class A IP addresses is very limited. We can theoretically have $2^7 = 128$ networks. However, there are actually 126 networks in class A because two of the addresses are reserved for special purposes, as we will see shortly.

In a class A network, 24 bits are used to define the hostid. This means that each network can theoretically have up to $2^{24} = 16,777,216$ hosts. However, two special addresses (hostid all 0s and hostid all 1s) are used for special address. This means that up to 16,777,214 hosts (or routers) can be connected to a class A network. We will talk about special addresses later.

Class A addresses are designed for organizations that may have a huge number of computers attached to their networks. However, it is highly improbable that an organization has so many computers, and a lot of addresses are wasted in this class.

Class B

In a class B address, two octets define the netid and two octets define the hostid. The two leftmost bits are 10 to define the class as B. The next 14 bits define different networks. This means that there are more class B networks than class A networks. We can have $2^{14} = 16,384$ class B networks.

In a class B network, 16 bits are used to define the hostid. This means each network can theoretically have up to $2^{16} = 65,536$ hosts (or routers). However, two of these addresses (hostid all 0s and hostid all 1s) are used for special addresses, as we will see shortly. This means that a class B network can have up to 65,534 hosts (or routers).

Class B addresses are designed for midsize organizations that may have a large number of computers attached to their networks. However, it is highly improbable that a midsize organization has 65,534 computers, and a lot of addresses are wasted in this class also.

Class C

In a class C address, three octets define the netid and one octet defines the hostid. The three leftmost bits are 110 to define the class as C. The next 21 bits define different networks. This means that the number of class C networks is more than class A or B. We can have $2^{21} = 2,097,152$ networks.

In a class C network, eight bits are used to define the hostid. This means each network can theoretically have up to $2^8 = 256$ hosts. However, again two addresses (hostid all 0s and hostid all 1s) are reserved for special addresses. This means that a class C network can have only up to 254 hosts (or routers).

Class C addresses are designed for small organizations that have a small number of computers attached to their networks.

Class D

The class D address is defined for multicasting. In this class, there is no netid or hostid. The whole address is used for multicasting. The first four bits define the class (1110). The remaining 28 bits define different multicast addresses. Multicasting is discussed later in this chapter.

Class E

Class E is reserved by the Internet for special use. There is no netid or hostid in this class. The first four bits define the class (1111).

Determining the Class of an Address

Given an IP address, it is very easy to determine the class of the address. If the address is in binary form, looking at the first few bits reveals the class of the address.

- If the first bit is zero, it is class A.
- If the first bit is one and the second bit is zero, it is class B.
- If the first two bits are ones and the third bit is zero, it is class C.
- If the first three bits are ones and the fourth bit is zero, it is class D.

■   If the first four bits are ones, it is class E.

If the address is defined in decimal notation, then we need look only at the first number to determine the class of the address (see Figure 4.4).

■   If the first number is between 0 and 127 (inclusive), the class is A.
■   If the first number is between 128 and 191 (inclusive), the class is B.
■   If the first number is between 192 and 223 (inclusive), the class is C.
■   If the first number is between 224 and 239 (inclusive), the class is D.
■   If the first number is between 240 and 255 (inclusive), the class is E.

Figure 4.4   *Classes using decimal notation*

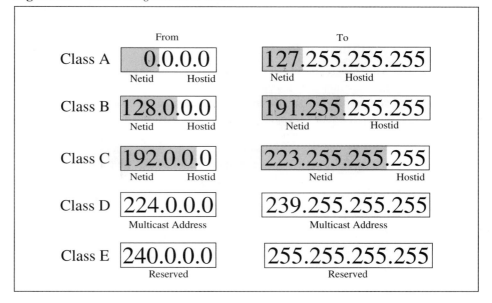

Extracting Netid and Hostid

When an IP address is given, it is very easy to extract the netid and hostid. After the class of the address is determined, note the following:

■   If it is class A, then the first octet (number) is the netid and the remaining three octets (three numbers) are the hostid.
■   If it is class B, then the left two octets (two numbers) are the netid and the remaining two octets (two numbers) are the hostid.
■   If it is class C, then the left three octets (three numbers) are the netid and the remaining one octet (one number) is the hostid.
■   If it is class D, then there is no netid or hostid. The entire address is used for multi-casting.

■ If it is class E, then there is no netid or hostid. The entire address is reserved for special use.

Table 4.1 shows the number of networks and addresses in each class.

Table 4.1   *Number of networks and hosts in each class*

Class	Number of Networks	Number of Hosts
A	$2^7 - 2 = 126$	$2^{24} - 2 = 16,777,214$
B	$2^{14} = 16,384$	$2^{16} - 2 = 65,534$
C	$2^{21} = 2,097,152$	$2^8 - 2 = 254$
D	Not applicable	Not applicable
E	Not applicable	Not applicable

Multihomed Devices

An Internet address defines the node's connection to its network. It follows, therefore, that any device connected to more than one network must have more than one Internet address. In fact, a device has a different address for each network connected to it. A computer that is connected to different networks is called a **multihomed** computer and will have more than one address, each possibly belonging to a different class. A router must be connected to more than one network, otherwise it cannot route. Therefore a router definitely has more than one IP address, one for each interface. In Figure 4.5 we have one multihomed computer and one router. The computer is connected to two networks and its two IP addresses reflect this. Likewise, the router is connected to three networks and therefore has three IP addresses.

Figure 4.5   *Multihomed devices*

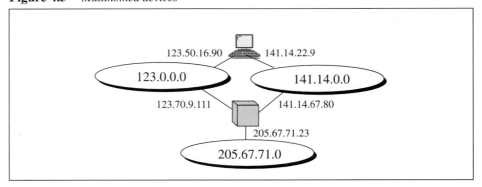

Location, Not Names

An Internet address defines the network location of a device, not its identity. In other words, because an Internet address is made of two parts (netid and hostid), it can only define the connection of a device to a specific network. One of the ramifications of this is that if we move a computer from one network to another, its IP address must be changed.

4.3   SPECIAL ADDRESSES

Some parts of the address space in class are used for special addresses (see Table 4.2).

Table 4.2   *Special addresses*

Special Address	Netid	Hostid	Source or Destination
Network address	Specific	All 0s	None
Direct broadcast address	Specific	All 1s	Destination
Limited broadcast address	All 1s	All 1s	Destination
This host on this network	All 0s	All 0s	Source
Specific host on this network	All 0s	Specific	Destination
Loopback address	127	Any	Destination

Network Address

In classes A, B, and C, an address with a hostid of all zeros is not assigned to any host; it is reserved to define the network address itself. In other words, the network itself is considered an entity with an IP address in which the hostid part is set to zero. Remember that the netid is different from the network address. The netid is only part of the IP address; the **network address** is an address with the hostid all set to 0s. Note that this address cannot be used to define a source or destination address in an IP packet. Note also that this special address reduces the number of available hostids for each netid in classes A, B, and C. Figure 4.6 shows three networks, with IP addresses for hosts and networks.

Direct Broadcast Address

In classes A, B, and C, if the hostid is all 1s, the address is called a **direct broadcast address**. It is used by a router to send a packet to all hosts in a specific network. All hosts will accept a packet having this type of destination address. Note that this address can be used only as a destination address in an IP packet. Note also that this special address also reduces the number of available hostids for each netid in classes A, B, and C. In Figure 4.7, router R sends a datagram using a destination IP address with the hostid of all 1s. All devices on this network receive and process the datagram.

Limited Broadcast Address

In classes A, B, and C, an address with all 1s for the netid and hostid (32 bits) is used to define a broadcast address in the current network. A host which wants to send a mes-

Figure 4.6   *Examples of network addresses*

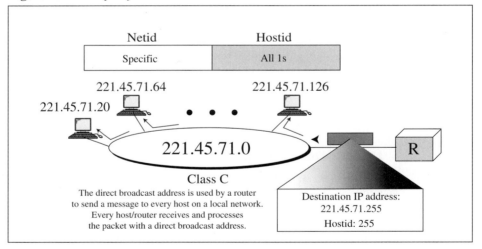

Netid	Hostid
Specific	All 0s

123.50.16.90   123.65.7.34
                123.90.123.4

123.0.0.0

(a) Class A

141.14.0.0

141.14.22.8
141.14.45.9   141.14.67.64

(b) Class B

221.45.71.64   221.45.71.126
221.45.71.20

221.45.71.0

(c) Class C

Figure 4.7   *Example of direct broadcast address*

Netid	Hostid
Specific	All 1s

221.45.71.64   221.45.71.126
221.45.71.20

221.45.71.0

R

Class C

The direct broadcast address is used by a router
to send a message to every host on a local network.
Every host/router receives and processes
the packet with a direct broadcast address.

Destination IP address:
221.45.71.255
Hostid: 255

sage to every other host can use this address as a destination address in an IP packet.
However, a router will block a packet having this type of address to confine the broadcasting to the local network. Note that this address belongs to class E. In Figure 4.8, a
host sends a datagram using a destination IP address consisting of all 1s. All devices on
this network receive and process this datagram.

Figure 4.8   *Example of limited broadcast address*

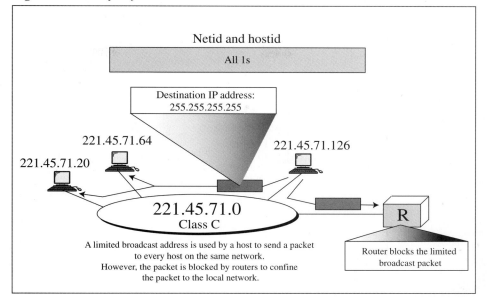

This Host on This Network

If an IP address is composed of all zeros, it means *this host on this network*. This is used by a host at bootstrap time when it does not know its IP address. The host sends an IP packet to a bootstrap server using this address as the source address and a limited broadcast address as the destination address to find its own address. Note that this address can be used only as a source address. Note also that this address is always a class A address regardless of the network. It reduces the number of networks in class A by one (see Figure 4.9).

Specific Host on This Network

An IP address with a netid of all zeros means a specific host on this network. It is used by a host to send a message to another host on the same network. Because the packet is blocked by the router, it is a way of confining the packet to the local network. Note that it can be used only for a destination address. Note also it is actually a class A address regardless of the network (see Figure 4.10).

Loopback Address

The IP address with the first byte equal to 127 is used for the **loopback address**, which is an address used to test the software on a machine. When this address is used, a packet never leaves the machine; it simply returns to the protocol software. It can be used to test the IP software. For example, an application such as "ping" can send a packet with a loopback address as the destination address to see if the IP software is capable of receiving and processing a packet. As another example, the loopback

Figure 4.9   *Examples of "this" host on "this" network address*

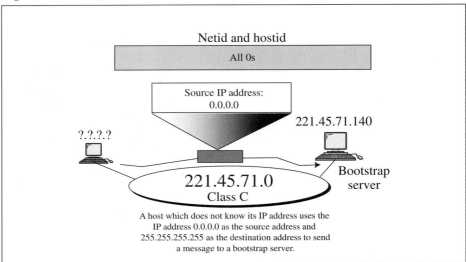

Figure 4.10   *Example of specific host on "this" network*

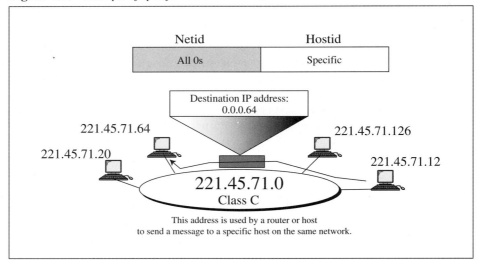

address can be used by a **client process** (a running application program) to send a message to a server process on the same machine. Note that this can be used only as a destination address in an IP packet. Note also that this is actually a class A address. It reduces the number of networks in class A by 1 (see Figure 4.11).

Figure 4.11   *Example of loopback address*

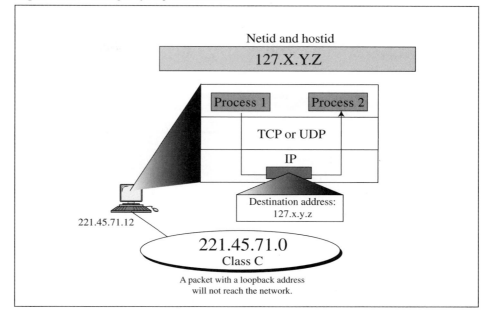

Netid and hostid

127.X.Y.Z

Process 1   Process 2

TCP or UDP

IP

Destination address:
127.x.y.z

221.45.71.12

221.45.71.0
Class C

A packet with a loopback address
will not reach the network.

4.4   A SAMPLE INTERNET

Figure 4.12 shows a part of an internet with six networks, two gateways (Gs), and two routers (Rs). One of the gateways is connected to three different networks, which is why it has three IP addresses (220.3.6.23, 129.8.14.12, and 222.13.16.40). The other gateway is connected to only two networks; it has only two addresses. One of the routers is connected to three networks; the other is connected to only two. The six networks are as follows:

■   A token ring with network address 220.3.6.0 (class C). All hosts and the gateway connected to this network have the same netid (220.3.6). However, each connection has a different hostid.

■   An Ethernet with network address 129.8.0.0 (class B). All hosts and the gateway connected to this network have the same netid (129.8). However, each connection has a different hostid.

■   A point-to-point line with network address 222.13.16.0 (class C). This network connects just two gateways together. No host is connected to this network. Although a point-to-point connection does not need a network address, we have used a network address to emphasize that a point-to-point connection is a network (a WAN).

■   Another Ethernet with network address 134.18.0.0 (class B). All hosts, the gateway, and the router connected to this network have the same netid (134.18). However, each connection has a different hostid. The router on this network connects the six networks to the rest of the internet.

Figure 4.12   *Sample internet*

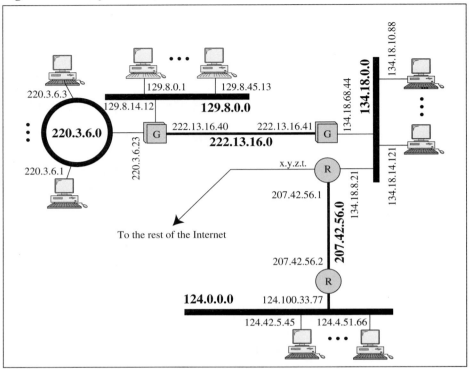

■ Another point-to-point WAN with network address 207.42.56.0 (class C). This network is used to connect two routers that are located far from each other.

■ Another Ethernet with network address 124.0.0.0 (class A).

4.5   UNICAST, MULTICAST, AND BROADCAST ADDRESSES

Communication on the Internet can be achieved using unicast, multicast, or broadcast
addresses.

Unicast Addresses

Unicast communication is *one-to-one*. When a packet is sent from an individual source
to an individual destination, a unicast communication takes place. All systems on the
Internet should have at least one unique unicast address. Unicast addresses belong to
class A, B, or C.

Multicast Addresses

Multicast communication is *one-to-many*. When a packet is sent from an individual
source to a group of destinations, a multicast communication has taken place. A multi-

cast address is a class D address. The whole address defines a groupid. A system on the Internet can have one or more class D multicast addresses (in addition to its unicast address or addresses). If a system (usually a host) has seven multicast addresses, it means it belongs to seven different groups. Note that a class D address can be used only as a destination address, not as a source address.

Multicasting on the Internet can be on the local level or global level. At the local level, hosts on a LAN can form a group and be assigned a multicast address. At the global level, hosts on different networks can form a group and be assigned a multicast address.

We will talk further about multicast delivery in Chapter 10.

Assigned Multicast Addresses

The Internet authorities have assigned some multicast addresses to some specific groups. We mention two here.

- **Category.** Some multicast addresses are assigned for some special use. These multicast addresses start with a 224.0.0 prefix. Table 4.3 shows some of these addresses.

Table 4.3   *Category addresses*

Address	Group
224.0.0.0	Reserved
224.0.0.1	All SYSTEMS on this SUBNET
224.0.0.2	All ROUTERS on this SUBNET
224.0.0.4	DVMRP ROUTERS
224.0.0.5	OSPFIGP All ROUTERS
224.0.0.6	OSPFIGP Designated ROUTERS
224.0.0.7	ST Routers
224.0.0.8	ST Hosts
224.0.0.9	RIP2 Routers
224.0.0.10	IGRP Routers
224.0.0.11	Mobile-Agents

- **Conferencing.** Some multicast addresses are assigned for conferencing and teleconferencing. These multicast addresses start with a 224.0.1 prefix. Table 4.4 shows some of these addresses.

Table 4.4   *Addresses for conferencing*

Address	Group
224.0.1.7	AUDIONEWS
224.0.1.10	IETF-1-LOW-AUDIO

Table 4.4   *Addresses for conferencing (concluded)*

Address	Group
224.0.1.11	IETF-1-AUDIO
224.0.1.12	IETF-1-VIDEO
224.0.1.13	IETF-2-LOW-AUDIO
224.0.1.14	IETF-2-AUDIO
224.0.1.15	IETF-2-VIDEO
224.0.1.16	MUSIC-SERVICE
224.0.1.17	SEANET-TELEMETRY
224.0.1.18	SEANET-IMAGE

Broadcast Addresses

Broadcast communication is *one-to-all*. The Internet allows broadcasting only at the local level. We have already seen two broadcast addresses used at the local level: limited broadcast address (all 1s) and direct broadcast address (netid: specific, hostid: all 1s).

No broadcasting is allowed at the global level. This means that a system (host or router) cannot send a message to be received by all hosts and routers in the Internet. One of the reasons for this restriction is to prevent a huge traffic jam.

4.6   APPLYING FOR IP ADDRESSES

To connect its network to the Internet, an organization needs to apply for the netid part of a class A, B, or C address.

Class of Address

An organization may apply for one of the three classes (A, B, or C). However, class A addresses are depleted, and there are few class B addresses left. To apply for a class B address, an organization needs to prove that the number of hosts in its organization cannot be accommodated by a class C address.

Netids and Hostids

When an organization is granted an address, it receives a unique netid. For example, 124 for a class A, 130.43 for a class B, and 201.45.23 for a class C. The administration of the organization is responsible for assigning hostids to the hosts and routers attached to the network.

Authorities

An application for the netid part of an IP address must be directed to one of the Network Information Centers. See Appendix K for their addresses.

4.7 PRIVATE NETWORKS

If an organization does not need access to the Internet but wants the TCP/IP protocol on its network, there are three choices for its addressing needs:

1. It can apply for a unique address and use it without being connected to the Internet. This strategy has an advantage. If in the future the organization decides to be connected to the Internet, it can do so without any hassle. However, there is also a disadvantage to doing this. It is almost impossible to obtain a class A or B address these days. Although class C addresses are available, they may not fit the needs of the organization.

2. It can use any class A, B, or C address without registering with the Internet authorities. Because the network is isolated, the address does not have to be unique. However, this strategy has a serious drawback: it could be somehow mistaken by users for a unique Internet address, resulting in confusion.

3. To overcome the problems associated with the first and second strategies, the Internet authorities have reserved three blocks of addresses, shown in Table 4.5.

Table 4.5 *Addresses for private networks*

Class	Netids	Total
A	10.0.0	1
B	172.16 to 172.31	16
C	192.168.0 to 192.168.255	256

Any organization can use an address out of this set without any permission from the Internet authorities. Everybody knows that these addresses are for private networks. They are unique inside the organization, but are not unique globally.

4.8 SUMMARY

■ At the network layer, a global identification system that uniquely identifies every host and router is necessary for delivery of a packet from network to network.

■ The Internet address (or IP address) is 32 bits that uniquely and universally defines a host or router on the Internet.

■ The portion of the IP address that identifies the network is called the netid.

■ The portion of the IP address that identifies the host or router on the network is called the hostid.

- An IP address defines a device's connection to a network.
- There are five classes of IP addresses. Classes A, B, and C differ in the number of hosts allowed per network. Class D is for multicasting and class E is for experimentation.
- The class of a network is easily determined by examination of the first byte.
- An address that has zero values for the hostid portion is a network address.
- A multihomed device is connected to multiple networks and has an IP address for each network to which it is connected.
- For classes A, B, and C, a direct broadcast address (hostid all 1s) is used by a router to send a packet to all hosts on a specific network.
- A limited broadcast address (all 1s) is used by a host to send a packet to all hosts on its network.
- A source IP address of all 0s is used by a host at bootstrap if it does not know its IP address.
- A destination IP address with a netid of all 0s is used by a host to send a packet to another host on the same network.
- A loopback address with the first byte equal to 127 is used by a host to test its internal software.
- Unicast communication is one source sending a packet to one destination.
- Multicast communication is one source sending a packet to multiple destinations.
- Hosts with the same multicast address can either be on the same network or on different networks.
- Multicast addresses are often used for information retrieval and conferencing purposes.
- Broadcast communication is one source sending a packet to all hosts on its network.
- TCP/IP can be used on a network not connected to the Internet. The network address can be:
    a. a regular network address registered with the Internet authorities.
    b. a network address not registered with the Internet authorities.
    c. a network address chosen from a block reserved by the Internet authorities.

4.9   PRACTICE SET

Multiple Choice

1. Identify the class of the following IP address: 4.5.6.7.
    a. class A
    b. class B
    c. class C
    d. class D

2. Identify the class of the following IP address: 229.1.2.3.
   a. class A
   b. class B
   c. class C
   d. class D

3. Identify the class of the following IP address: 191.1.2.3.
   a. class A
   b. class B
   c. class C
   d. class D

4. Identify the following IP address: 169.5.0.0.
   a. host IP address
   b. direct broadcast address
   c. limited broadcast address
   d. network address

5. Identify the following IP address: 169.5.1.1.
   a. host IP address
   b. direct broadcast address
   c. limited broadcast address
   d. network address

6. Identify the following IP address: 169.5.255.255.
   a. host IP address
   b. direct broadcast address
   c. limited broadcast address
   d. network address

7. Which of the following is true of the IP address 241.1.2.3?
   a. The netid is 241.
   b. The class is E.
   c. The hostid is 1.2.3.
   d. The netid is 11110.

8. A device has two IP addresses. This device could be _____.
   a. a computer
   b. a router
   c. a gateway
   d. any of the above

9. A device has two IP addresses. One address is 192.123.46.219. The other address could be _____.
   a. 192.123.46.220
   b. 192.123.46.0
   c. 192.123.47.219

      d. any of the above

10. Which of the following is true of the IP address 192.0.0.10?

      a. The netid is 192.

      b. The hostid is 0.10.

      c. The network address is 192.0.0.0.

      d. The hostid is 0.0.10.

11. Which of the following is a source IP address?

      a. this host on this network

      b. limited broadcast address

      c. loopback address

      d. specific host on this network

12. Using the direct broadcast address, a _____ sends a packet to _____ on the network.

      a. host; all other hosts

      b. router; all other hosts

      c. host; a specific host

      d. host; itself

13. Using the limited broadcast address, a _____ sends a packet to _____ on the network.

      a. host; all other hosts

      b. router; all other hosts

      c. host; a specific host

      d. host; itself

14. The loopback address is used to send a packet from the _____ to _____.

      a. host; all other hosts

      b. router; all other hosts

      c. host; a specific host

      d. host; itself

15. What destination address can be used to send a packet from a host with IP address 188.1.1.1 to all hosts on the network?

      a. 188.0.0.0

      b. 0.0.0.0

      c. 255.255.255.255

      d. b and c

16. A host can get its IP address from its server by using _____ as the source address and _____ as the destination address.

      a. 127.127.127.127; 0.0.0.0

      b. 255.255.255.255; 0.0.0.0

      c. 127.0.0.0; 255.255.255.255

      d. 0.0.0.0; 255.255.255.255

17. A host with an IP address of 142.5.0.1 needs to test internal software. What is the destination address in the packet?
    a. 127.0.0.0
    b. 127.1.1.1
    c. 127.127.127.127
    d. any of the above

18. A packet sent from a node at 198.123.46.20 to a node at 198.123.46.21 requires a _____ destination address.
    a. unicast
    b. multicast
    c. broadcast
    d. a or b

19. A packet sent from a node with IP address 198.123.46.20 to all nodes on network 198.123.46.0 requires a _____ address.
    a. unicast
    b. multicast
    c. broadcast
    d. a or b

20. A packet sent from a node with IP address 198.123.46.20 to all routers on network 198.123.46.0 requires a _____ address.
    a. unicast
    b. multicast
    c. broadcast
    d. a or b

21. A private network with 300 computers wants to use a netid reserved by the Internet authorities. What is a good netid choice?
    a. 10.0.0
    b. 172.16
    c. 192.68.0
    d. all of the above

Exercises

22. Change the following IP addresses from decimal-point notation to binary notation:
    a. 114.34.2.8
    b. 129.14.6.8
    c. 208.34.54.12
    d. 238.34.2.1
    e. 241.34.2.8

23. Change the following IP addresses from binary notation to decimal-point notation:
    a. 01111111 11110000 01100111 01111101

    b. 10101111 11000000 11111000 00011101

    c. 11011111 10110000 00011111 01011101

    d. 11101111 11110111 11000111 00011101

    e. 11110111 11110011 10000111 11011101

24. Find the class of the following IP addresses:

    a. 208.34.54.12

    b. 238.34.2.1

    c. 114.34.2.8

    d. 129.14.6.8

    e. 241.34.2.8

25. Find the class of the following IP addresses:

    a. 11110111 11110011 10000111 11011101

    b. 10101111 11000000 11110000 00011101

    c. 11011111 10110000 00011111 01011101

    d. 11101111 11110111 11000111 00011101

    e. 01111111 11110000 01100111 01111101

26. Find the netid and the hostid of the following IP addresses:

    a. 114.34.2.8

    b. 19.34.21.5

    c. 23.67.12.1

    d. 127.23.4.0

27. Find the netid and the hostid of the following IP addresses:

    a. 129.14.6.8

    b. 132.56.8.6

    c. 171.34.14.8

    d. 190.12.67.9

28. Find the netid and the hostid of the following IP addresses:

    a. 192.8.56.2

    b. 220.34.8.9

    c. 208.34.54.12

    d. 205.23.67.8

29. Find the network address of the following IP addresses:

    a. 114.34.2.8.

    b. 171.34.14.8

    c. 192.8.56.2

    d. 205.23.67.8

    e. 226.7.34.5

    f. 225.23.6.7

    g. 245.34.21.5

30. Find the network address of the following IP addresses:
    a. 23.67.12.1
    b. 127.23.4.0
    c. 190.12.67.9
    d. 220.34.8.9
    e. 237.34.8.2
    f. 240.34.2.8
    g. 247.23.4.78
31. A network has an IP address of 193.121.0.0. Find all the special addresses of this network.
32. A host with IP address 128.23.67.3 sends a message to a host with IP address 193.45.23.7. Does the message travel through any router?
33. A host with IP address 128.23.67.3 sends a message to a host with IP address 14.45.23.7. Does the message travel through any router?
34. A host with IP address 128.23.67.3 sends a message to a host with IP address 128.45.23.7. Does the message travel through any router?
35. A host with IP address 128.23.67.3 sends a message to a host with IP address 128.23.23.7. Does the message travel through any router? Assume no subnetting (subnetting is discussed in Chapter 5).
36. A host with IP address 195.23.67.3 sends a message to a host with IP address 195.23.41.7. Does the message travel through any router? Assume no subnetting (subnetting is discussed in Chapter 5).
37. A host with IP address 195.23.67.3 sends a message to a host with IP address 195.23.67.7. Does the message travel through any router? Assume no subnetting (subnetting is discussed in Chapter 5).
38. A host with IP address 9.11.67.3 sends a message to a host with IP address 11.34.2.7. Does the message travel through any router? Assume no subnetting (subnetting is discussed in Chapter 5).
39. A host with IP address 9.11.67.3 sends a message to a host with IP address 9.34.2.7. Does the message travel through any router? Assume no subnetting (subnetting is discussed in Chapter 5).
40. Draw a diagram of a network with IP address 8.0.0.0 that is connected through a router to a network with IP address 131.45.0.0. Choose IP addresses for each interface of the router. Show also some hosts on each network with their IP addresses. What is the class of each network?
41. Show three networks connected through one single router. The first network address is 14.0.0.0. The second network address is 145.25.0.0. The third network address is 202.45.78.0. Choose IP addresses for each interface of the router. Show also some hosts with their IP addresses on each network.
42. What is the class of the IP address 255.255.255.255 used in limited broadcasting?
43. What is the class of the IP address 0.0.0.0 used at bootstrap time?
44. What is the class of the IP address 0.23.56.12 used in a class A network for sending a message to a specific host located on "this" network?

45. What is the class of the IP address 0.0.52.16 used in a class B network for sending a message to a specific host located on "this" network?

46. What is the class of the IP address 0.0.0.14 used in a class C network for sending a message to a specific host located on "this" network?

47. A router is connected to network 108.0.0.0. It sends a direct broadcast packet to all hosts in this network. What are the source and destination IP addresses used in this packet?

48. A router is connected to network 140.30.0.0. It sends a direct broadcast packet to all hosts in this network. What are the source and destination IP addresses used in this packet?

49. A router is connected to network 200.74.32.0. It sends a direct broadcast packet to all hosts in this network. What are the source and destination IP addresses used in this packet?

50. A host with IP address 108.67.18.70 sends a limited broadcast packet to all hosts in the same network. What are the source and destination IP addresses used in this packet?

51. A host with IP address 180.6.8.17 sends a limited broadcast packet to all hosts in the same network. What are the source and destination IP addresses used in this packet?

52. A host with IP address 202.7.8.27 sends a limited broadcast packet to all hosts in the same network. What are the source and destination IP addresses used in this packet?

53. A host with IP address 124.67.89.34 needs loopback testing. What are the source and destination addresses?

54. A host with IP address 185.42.56.88 wants to use loopback testing. What are the source and destination addresses?

55. A host with IP address 218.34.13.89 wants to use loopback testing. What are the source and destination addresses?

56. A host with IP address 123.27.19.24 sends a message to a host with IP address 123.67.89.56 using the "Specific Host on This Network" special address. What are the source and destination addresses?

57. A host with IP address 187.12.16.38 sends a message to a host with IP address 187.12.18.99 using the "Specific Host on This Network" special address. What are the source and destination addresses?

58. A host with IP address 215.14.14.9 sends a message to a host with IP address 215.14.14.22 using the "Specific Host on This Network" special address. What are the source and destination addresses?

59. A host in class A which does not know its IP address wants to send a message to a bootstrap server to find its address. What are the source and destination addresses?

60. A host in class B which does not know its IP address wants to send a message to a bootstrap server to find its address. What are the source and destination addresses?

61. A host in class C which does not know its IP address wants to send a message to a bootstrap server to find its address. What are the source and destination addresses?

Programming Exercises

In the following exercises, write the appropriate code in C for:

62. A function to change an IP address in dotted-decimal notation to binary notation.

63. A function to change an IP address in binary notation to dotted-decimal notation.

64. A function to change an IP address in dotted-decimal notation to hexadecimal notation.

65. A function to change an IP address in binary notation to hexadecimal notation.

66. A function to change an IP address from hexadecimal notation to binary notation.

67. A function to change an IP address in hexadecimal notation to dotted-decimal notation.

CHAPTER 5

Subnetting and Supernetting

In this chapter, we discuss two important issues related to IP addressing: subnetting and supernetting. The increasing number of hosts connected to the Internet and restrictions on network size imposed by the Internet addressing system led to these concepts.

In **subnetting**, a network is divided into several smaller subnetworks with each subnetwork (or subnet) having its own subnetwork address. In **supernetting**, an organization can combine several class C addresses to create a larger range of addresses. In other words, several networks are combined to create a supernetwork.

5.1 SUBNETTING

As we learned in Chapter 4, an IP address is 32 bits long. A portion of the address indicates a network (netid), and a portion indicates the host (or router) on the network (hostid). This means that there is a sense of hierarchy in IP addressing. To reach a host on the Internet, we must first reach the network using the first portion of the address (netid). Then we must reach the host itself using the second portion (hostid). In other words, classes A, B, and C in IP addressing are designed with two levels of hierarchy.

Classes A, B, and C in IP addressing are designed with two levels of hierarchy.

However, in many cases, these two levels of hierarchy are not enough. For example, imagine an organization with a class B address. The organization has two-level hierarchical addressing, but it cannot have more than one physical network (see Figure 5.1).

With this scheme, the organization is limited to two levels of hierarchy. The hosts cannot be organized into groups, and all of the hosts are at the same level. The organization has one network with many hosts.

One solution to this problem is subnetting, the further division of a network into smaller networks called *subnetworks*. For example, Figure 5.2 shows the network in Figure 5.1 divided into three subnetworks.

Figure 5.1   *A network with two levels of hierarchy (not subnetted)*

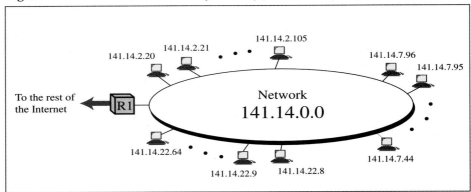

Figure 5.2   *A network with three levels of hierarchy (subnetted)*

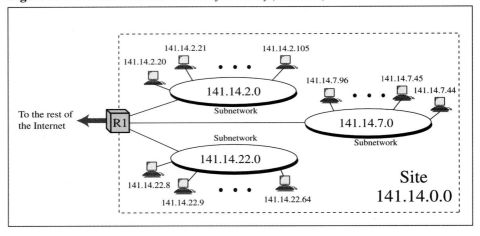

In the above example, the rest of the Internet is not aware that the network is divided into three physical subnetworks: The three subnetworks still appear as a single network to the rest of the Internet. A packet destined for host 141.14.2.21 still reaches router R1. The destination address of the IP datagram is still a class B address where 141.14 defines the netid and 2.21 defines the hostid.

However, when the datagram arrives at router R1, the interpretation of the IP address changes. Router R1 knows that the network 141.14 is physically divided into three subnetworks. It knows that the last two octets define two things: subnetid and hostid. Therefore, 2.21 must be interpreted as subnetid 2 and hostid 21. The router R1 uses the first two octets (141.14) as the netid, the third octet (2) as the subnetid, and the fourth octet (21) as the hostid.

Three Levels of Hierarchy

Adding subnetworks creates an intermediate level of hierarchy in the IP addressing system. Now we have three levels: netid, subnetid, and hostid. The netid is the first level; it defines the site. The second level is the **subnetid**; it defines the physical subnetwork. The hostid is the third level; it defines the connection of the host to the subnetwork. See Figure 5.3.

Figure 5.3 *Addresses in a network with and without subnetting*

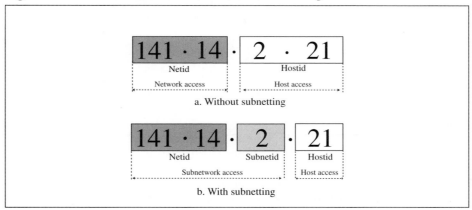

The routing of an IP datagram now involves three steps: delivery to the site, delivery to the subnetwork, and delivery to the host.

We can say that the interpretation of an IP address changes in the presence of subnetting. When a network is not subnetted, the IP address has two portions: netid and hostid. When a network is subnetted, it has three portions: netid, subnetid, and hostid.

This is analogous to the 10-digit telephone number in the United States. As Figure 5.4 shows, a telephone number is divided into three levels: area code, exchange number, and connection number.

Figure 5.4 *Hierarchy concept in a telephone number*

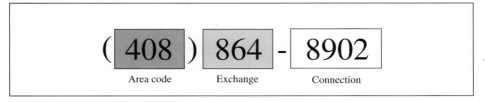

5.2 MASKING

Masking is a process that extracts the address of the physical network from an IP address. Masking can be done whether we have subnetting or not. If we have not subnetted the network, masking extracts the network address from an IP address. If we have subnetted, masking extracts the subnetwork address from an IP address (see Figure 5.5).

Figure 5.5 *Masking*

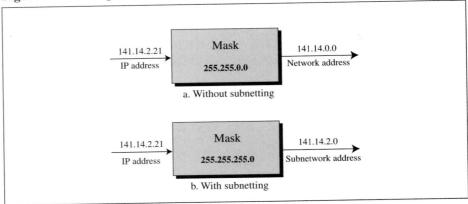

In masking, we perform a mathematical operation on a 32-bit IP address at the bit level using another 32-bit number called the *mask*. The bits in the mask are related to the corresponding bits in the IP address. The part of the mask containing 1s defines the netid (network portion) or combination of netid and subnetid (subnetwork portion). The part of the mask containing 0s defines the hostid. To get the network or subnet address, we must apply the *bit-wise-and* operation on the IP address and the mask. Figure 5.6 shows how we use masks to get the network address and the subnetwork address out of an IP address.

Figure 5.6 *Applying bit-wise-and operator to achieve masking*

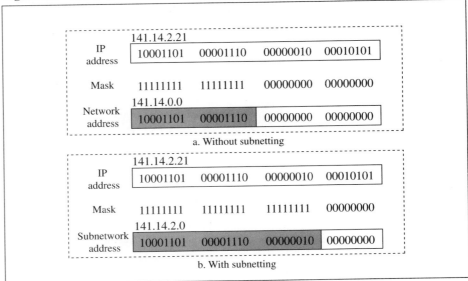

Special Addresses in Subnetting

As we learned in Chapter 4, in the absence of subnetting, some addresses are given special functionality. The netid of all 1s, the netid of all 0s, the hostid of all 1s, and the hostid of all 0s are treated as special addresses and are not assigned to any host.

In subnetting, the same idea is preserved. A subnetid of all 1s or all 0s is not assigned to any host. In addition, the address with the hostid of all 1s is reserved for broadcasting to all hosts in a specific subnet. The address with the hostid of all 0s is also reserved to define the subnetwork itself (see Figure 5.7).

Figure 5.7 *Special addresses in subnetting*

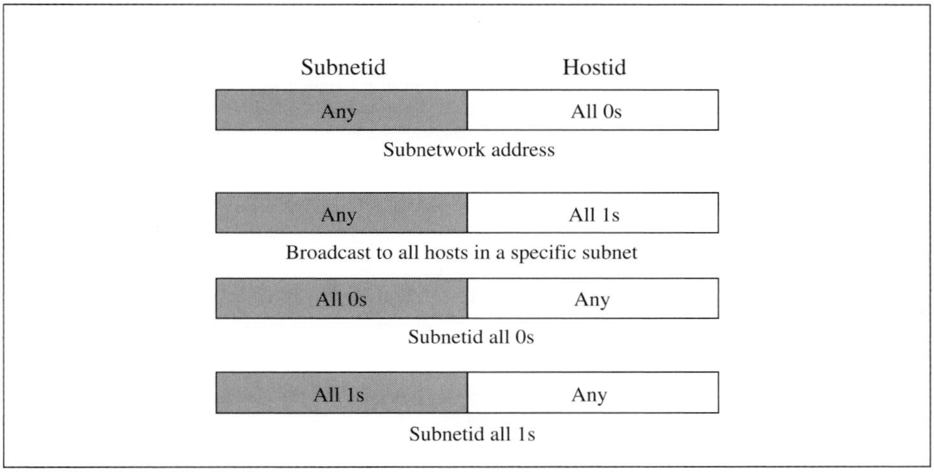

Although the above rules were originally honored by all routers, they are relaxed today. With the ideas of classless routing (defined later in this chapter) most of these rules are unnecessary and are becoming obsolete.

Contiguous versus Noncontiguous Mask

In all our examples we use a contiguous mask, which means a string of 1s precedes a string of 0s. In other words, we have all 1s to the left and all 0s to the right. Although it is possible to use a mask with intermixed 1s and 0s, it is highly discouraged because subnetting and routing become much more complex.

5.3 EXAMPLES OF SUBNETTING

In the previous section, we showed an example of subnetting using a class B address. Subnetting is allowed in all three classes: A, B, and C. In this section, we show one example of subnetting in each class.

Subnetting Class A

A class A address is made of a one-byte netid and a three-byte hostid. An organization that has been granted a class A address can have one single physical network with up to 16,777,214 ($2^{24} - 2$) hosts on that network. However, if the organization wants more physical networks, it can divide this one range into several smaller ranges. We will show one example of how this can be done.

Example 1

An organization with a class A address needs at least 1,000 subnetworks. Find the subnet mask and configuration of each subnetwork.

Solution

There is a need for at least 1,000 subnetworks. Theoretically, however, we need at least 1,002 subnetworks to allow for the all-1s and all-0s subnetids. This means that the minimum number of bits to be allocated for subnetting should be 10 ($2^9 < 1,002 < 2^{10}$). Fourteen bits are left to define the hostids. Figure 5.8 shows the subnet mask without and with subnetting.

Figure 5.8   *Masks in example 1*

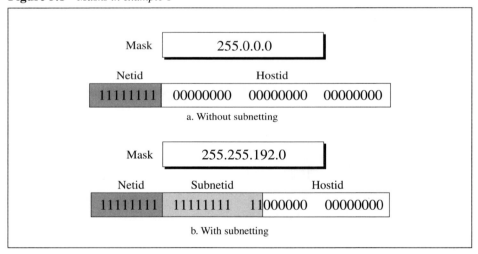

Using the above subnet mask, we have divided the original address range available for the hostids into 1,024 ranges, with two ranges to be reserved as special addresses. There are 16,384 addresses in each range. However, the first address is used to define the subnetwork (subnetwork address) and the last one is used for broadcast, which means that 16,382 computers can be attached to each subnetwork. Figure 5.9 shows the ranges; Figure 5.10 shows the configuration of each subnetwork.

Subnetting Class B

A class B address is made of a two-byte netid and a two-byte hostid. An organization that has been granted a class B address can have one single physical network and up to 65,534 ($2^{16} - 2$) hosts on that network. However, if the organization wants more physi-

Figure 5.9   *Range of addresses in example 1*

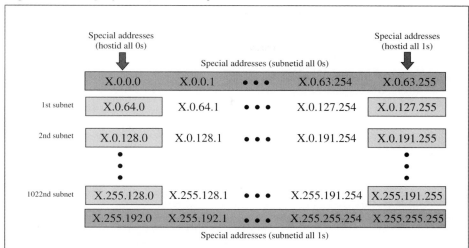

Figure 5.10   *Subnetworks in example 1*

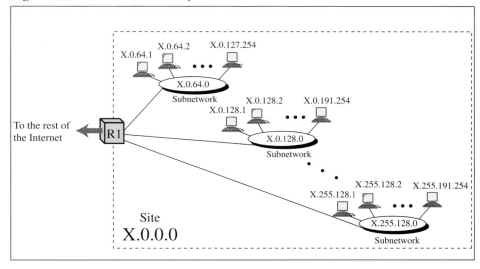

cal networks, it can divide this one big range into several smaller ranges. We have already shown one example of class B subnetting where the subnetid and hostid are at the byte boundary with 254 subnetworks and 254 hosts per each subnet. In the following example, the demarcation is not at the byte boundary.

Example 2

An organization with a class B address needs at least 12 subnetworks. Find the subnet mask and configuration of each subnetwork.

Solution

There is a need for at least 14 subnetworks, 12 as specified plus 2 reserved as special addresses. This means that the minimum number of bits should be 4 ($2^3 < 14 < 2^4$). Figure 5.11 shows the subnet mask without and with subnetting.

Figure 5.11   *Masks in example 2*

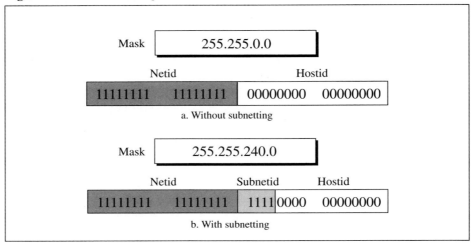

a. Without subnetting

b. With subnetting

Using the above subnet mask, we have divided the original range available for the hostids into 16 ranges, with two ranges to be reserved as special addresses. There are 4,096 addresses in each range. However, the first address is used to define the subnetwork (subnetwork address) and the last one is used for broadcast, which means that 4,094 computers can be attached to each subnetwork. Figure 5.12 shows the ranges. Figure 5.13 shows the configuration of each subnetwork.

Figure 5.12   *Range of addresses in example 2*

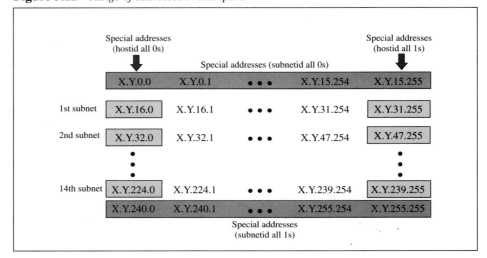

Figure 5.13   *Subnetworks in example 2*

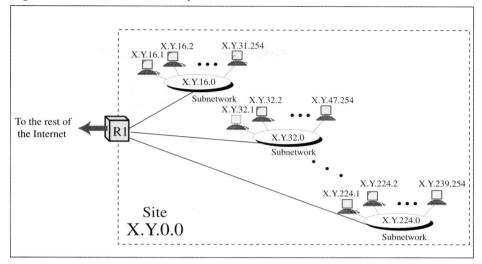

Subnetting Class C

A class C address is made of a three-byte netid and a one-byte hostid. An organization that has been granted a class C address can have one single physical network and up to 254 ($2^8 - 2$) hosts on that network. However, if the organization wants more physical networks, it can divide this one big range into several smaller ranges. We show one example of class C subnetting.

Example 3

An organization with a class C address needs at least five subnetworks. Find the subnet mask and configuration of each subnetwork.

Solution

There is a need for at least seven subnetworks, five specified and two reserved as special addresses. This means that the minimum number of bits should be 3 ($2^2 < 7 < 2^3$). Figure 5.14 shows the subnet mask without and with subnetting. Using the above subnet mask, we have divided the original range available for the hostids into eight ranges, with two ranges reserved as special addresses. There are 32 addresses in each range. However, the first address is used to define the subnetwork (subnetwork address) and the last one is used for broadcast, which means that 30 computers can be attached to each subnetwork. Figure 5.15 shows the ranges; Figure 5.16 shows the configuration of each subnetwork.

5.4   VARIABLE-LENGTH SUBNETTING

The Internet allows a site to use variable-length subnetting. For an example of when this may be desirable, consider a site that is granted a class C address and needs to have five subnets with the following number of hosts: 60, 60, 60, 30, 30. The site cannot use a subnet mask with only two bits in the subnet section because this allows only four

Figure 5.14 *Masks in example 3*

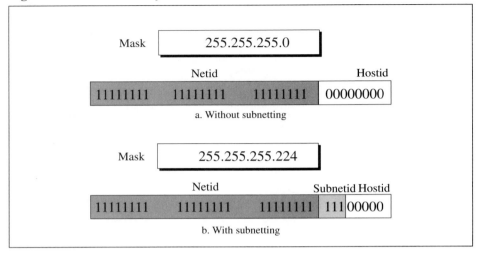

Figure 5.15 *Range of addresses in example 3*

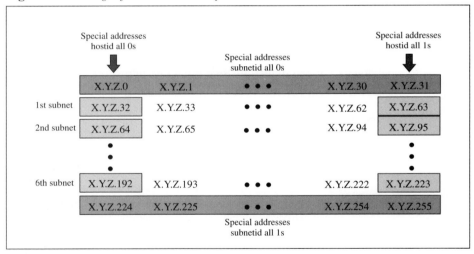

subnetworks each with 62 hosts (256/4 − 2 = 62). Nor can the site use a subnet mask with three bits in the subnet section because this allows eight subnetworks each with 30 hosts (256 / 8 − 2 = 30). Note that we are relaxing the requirement for special addresses.

One solution to this site's problem is variable-length subnetting. In this configuration, the router uses two different masks, one applied after the other. It first uses the mask with 26 1s (11111111 11111111 11111111 11000000 or 255.255.255.192) to divide the network into four subnets. Then it applies the mask with 27 1s (11111111 11111111 11111111 11100000 or 255.255.255.224) to one of the subnets to divide it into two smaller subnets (see Figure 5.17).

Figure 5.16   *Subnetworks in example 3*

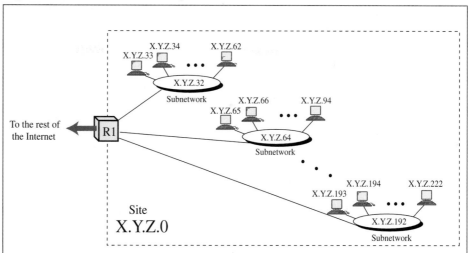

Figure 5.17   *Variable-length subnetting*

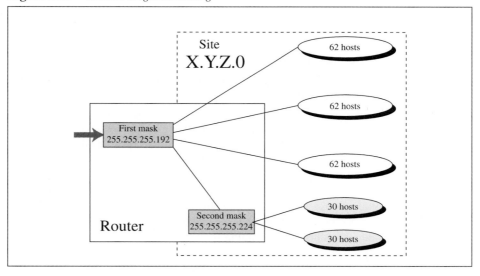

5.5   SUPERNETTING

Although class A and B addresses are almost depleted, class C addresses are still available. However, the space of a class C address, with a maximum number of 254 host addresses, may not satisfy the needs of an organization. Even a midsize organization may need more addresses.

One solution is supernetting. By doing this, an organization can apply for a block of class C addresses instead of just one. For example, an organization that needs 1,000 addresses can be granted four class C addresses. The organization can then use these addresses in one supernetwork, in four networks, or in more than four subnetworks. In Figure 5.18, four class C addresses combine to make one supernetwork.

Figure 5.18   *Supernetwork*

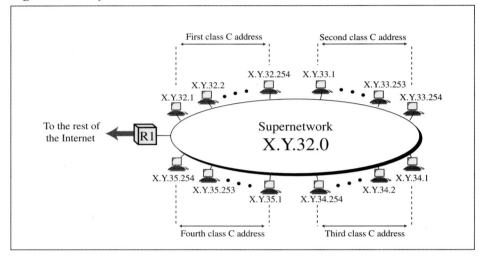

Supernet Mask

A supernet mask can be assigned to a block of class C network addresses if the number of network addresses is a power of two (2, 4, 8, 16, . . .). The default mask for a class C address is 255.255.255.0, 24 1s followed by 8 0s. If some of the 1s are changed to 0s, we can have a mask for a group of class C addresses. As Figure 5.19 shows, a supernet mask is the reverse of the subnet mask. In a subnet mask, we change some zeros in the hostid section of the default mask to 1s. In a supernet mask, we change some 1s in the netid section to 0s. Be aware that the position of 1s in the supernet mask defines the lowest address. For example, with the supernet mask shown in Figure 5.19, the beginning address can be X.Y.32.0, but it cannot be X.Y.33.0.

A combination of the lowest address and the supernet mask can uniquely define the range of addresses belonging to a supernet. Another way to define the range is to use the lowest address and the number of addresses in the range. For example, the pair shown in Figure 5.20 defines the same supernetwork.

Example

With the supernet mask of 255.255.252.0 we can have four class C addresses combined into one supernetwork. If we choose the first address to be X.Y.32.0, the other three addresses are X.Y.33.0, X.Y.34.0, and X.Y.35.0. Whenever the router receives a packet, it applies the supernet mask to the destination address and compares the result to the lowest address. If the result and the lowest address are the same, the packet belongs to the supernet.

Figure 5.19   *Supernet mask*

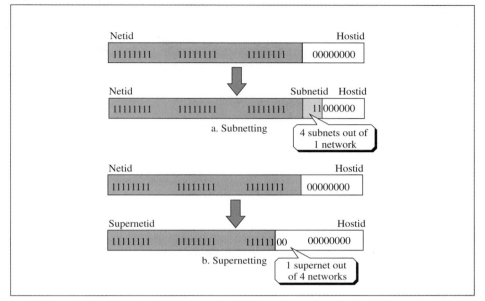

Figure 5.20   *Two ways of defining a supernet*

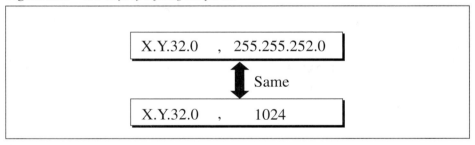

Suppose a packet arrives with the destination address X.Y.33.4. After applying the mask, the result is X.Y.32.0, which is the same as the lowest address; the packet belongs to the supernet.

Now suppose a packet arrives with the destination address X.Y.39.12. After applying the mask, the result is X.Y.36.0, which is not the same as the lowest address; the packet does not belong to the supernet (see Figure 5.21).

Classless Interdomain Routing (CIDR)

Supernetting means assigning a set of class C addresses to an organization that needs more than 254 host addresses. However, when these class C addresses are entered into the routing table (see Chapter 6), each occupies one entry in the routing table. This means that if an organization is granted 256 class C addresses (instead of one class B address), there should be 256 entries in the routing table. The **classless interdomain routing** (CIDR) technique is devised to reduce the number of routing table entries. In

Figure 5.21 *Example of supernetting*

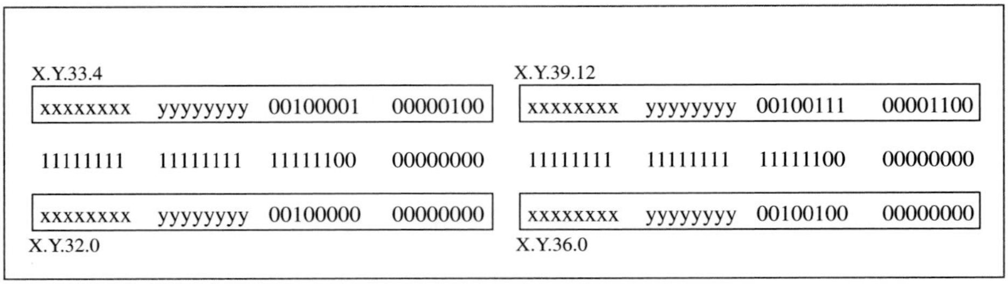

X.Y.33.4				X.Y.39.12			
xxxxxxxx	yyyyyyyy	00100001	00000100	xxxxxxxx	yyyyyyyy	00100111	00001100
11111111	11111111	11111100	00000000	11111111	11111111	11111100	00000000
xxxxxxxx	yyyyyyyy	00100000	00000000	xxxxxxxx	yyyyyyyy	00100100	00000000
X.Y.32.0				X.Y.36.0			

this technique, instead of entering each single class C address with its corresponding default mask (255.255.255.0), the router can use the supernet mask and the lowest network address in the group (see Figure 5.22).

Figure 5.22 *CIDR*

Default mask	Network address	Next hop address
255.255.255.0	X.Y.32.0	....
255.255.255.0	X.Y.33.0	....
255.255.255.0	X.Y.34.0	....
255.255.255.0	X.Y.35.0	....
⋮	⋮	⋮

a. Routing table without supernet mask

Default mask	Network address	Next hop address
255.255.252.0	X.Y.32.0	....
⋮	⋮	⋮

b. Routing table with supernet mask

5.6 SUMMARY

■ Subnetting divides one large network into several smaller ones.

■ Subnetting adds an intermediate level of hierarchy in IP addressing.

■ Class A, B, and C addresses can be subnetted.

■ The subnetid defines the physical subnetwork.

■ Masking is a process that extracts the network address from an IP address.

■ Subnet masking is a process that extracts the subnetwork address from an IP address.

■ A network or subnet address is obtained from applying the bit-wise AND operation on the IP address and the mask.

■ The concept of special addresses in IP addressing carries over to subnetting.

■ A contiguous mask (a string of 1s followed by a string of 0s) is highly recommended.

■ In variable length subnetting, more than one subnet mask is applied by the router.

■ Supernetting combines several networks into one large one.

■ Classless interdomain routing (CIDR) reduces the number of entries in a routing table by using a supernet mask and the lowest network address of a supernet to represent the member networks.

5.7   PRACTICE SET

Multiple Choice

1. In Figure 5.2, what is the mask for the network?
   a. 255.255.0.0
   b. 255.255.255.0
   c. 0.0.255.255
   d. none of the above

2. In Figure 5.2, what is the mask for the subnetwork?
   a. 255.255.0.0
   b. 255.255.255.0
   c. 0.0.255.255
   d. none of the above

3. A device has the IP address 190.1.2.3. What is its subnetid?
   a. 1
   b. 2
   c. 3
   d. insufficient information to answer the question

4. Which of the following is the default mask for the address 198.0.46.201?
   a. 255.0.0.0
   b. 255.255.0.0
   c. 255.255.255.0
   d. 255.255.255.255

5. Which of the following is the default mask for the address 98.0.46.201?
   a. 255.0.0.0
   b. 255.255.0.0
   c. 255.255.255.0
   d. 255.255.255.255

6. Which of the following is the default mask for the address 190.0.46.201?
   a. 255.0.0.0
   b. 255.255.0.0

    c. 255.255.255.0

    d. 255.255.255.255

7. Which of the following would make a good subnet mask for the address 190.0.46.201?

    a. 255.255.1.0

    b. 255.255.160.0

    c. 255.255.255.248

    d. 255.255.4.0

8. What class of IP address does the subnet mask 255.128.0.0 operate on?

    a. A

    b. B

    c. C

    d. A, B, or C

9. What class of IP address does the subnet mask 255.255.128.0 operate on?

    a. A

    b. B

    c. C

    d. A or B

10. What class of IP address does the subnet mask 255.255.255.128 operate on?

    a. A

    b. B

    c. C

    d. A, B, or C

11. A subnet mask of 255.255.255.248 allows how many hostids per subnet? (Disregard special addresses.)

    a. 3

    b. 7

    c. 8

    d. 248

12. A subnet mask of 255.255.255.224 allows how many hostids per subnet? (Disregard special addresses.)

    a. 3

    b. 7

    c. 8

    d. 32

13. The subnet mask for a class C network is 255.255.255.192. How many subnetworks are available? (Disregard special addresses.)

    a. 2

    b. 4

    c. 8

d. 192

14. The subnet mask for a class B network is 255.255.255.192. How many subnetworks are available? (Disregard special addresses.)

    a. 2

    b. 4

    c. 1,024

    d. 192

15. A supernet mask is 255.255.254.0. How many class C networks were combined to make this supernet?

    a. 1

    b. 2

    c. 3

    d. 4

16. A supernet mask is 255.255.248.0. How many class C networks were combined to make this supernet?

    a. 2

    b. 4

    c. 6

    d. 8

17. What is the supernet mask for a supernet composed of 16 class C addresses?

    a. 255.255.240.16

    b. 255.255.16.0

    c. 255.255.248.0

    d. 255.255.240.0

18. An organization is given 16 class C addresses beginning with X.Y.80.0. What is the supernet mask?

    a. 255.255.64.0

    b. 255.255.240.0

    c. 255.255.255.192

    d. 255.255.192.0

Exercises

19. The IP address of a host on a class C network is 198.123.46.237. Four subnets are allowed for this network. What is the subnet mask? Assume a contiguous subnet address space.

20. What is the subnetwork address and subnetmask for the IP address 142.45.43.44? Assume a contiguous subnet address space.

21. What is the range of hosts for the subnetwork with an address of 150.20.193.4? Assume a contiguous subnet address space.

22. Which of the following addresses are network addresses and which ones subnet addresses?

    a. 14.0.0.0

    b. 15.7.0.0

    c. 21.14.81.0

    d. 19.8.14.111

23. Which of the following addresses are network addresses and which ones subnet addresses?

    a. 128.35.0.0

    b. 131.7.23.0

    c. 180.45.23.8

    d. 190.4.0.0

24. Which of the following addresses are network addresses and which ones subnet addresses?

    a. 200.11.56.32

    b. 201.56.23.64

    c. 222.67.14.56

    d. 223.44.55.0

25. Find the class of the following subnetworks:

    a. 22.14.0.0

    b. 133.45.6.0

    c. 16.14.9.0

    d. 193.45.127.64

26. Write the following masks in binary notation:

    a. 255.255.255.0

    b. 255.255.0.0

    c. 255.0.0.0

27. Write the following masks in binary notation:

    a. 255.255.192.0

    b. 255.255.224.0

    c. 255.255.255.240

28. Write the following masks in dotted decimal notation:

    a. 11111111111111111111111111111000

    b. 11111111111111111111111111100000

    c. 11111111111111111111100000000000

29. Find the subnetwork address and the hostid for the following:
IP Address: 125.34.12.56
Mask: 255.255.0.0

30. Find the subnetwork address and the hostid for the following:
IP Address: 120.14.22.16
Mask: 255.255.128.0

31. Find the subnetwork address and the hostid for the following:
    IP Address: 140.11.36.22
    Mask: 255.255.255.0

32. Find the subnetwork address and the hostid for the following:
    IP Address: 141.181.14.16
    Mask: 255.255.224.0

33. Find the subnetwork address and the hostid for the following:
    IP Address: 200.34.22.156
    Mask: 255.255.255.240

34. Find the masks that create the following number of subnets in class A. Assume a contiguous mask.
    a. 2
    b. 6
    c. 30
    d. 62
    e. 122
    f. 250

35. Find the maximum number of hosts in each subnet in exercise 34.

36. Find the masks that create the following number of subnets in class B. Assume a contiguous mask.
    a. 2
    b. 5
    c. 30
    d. 62
    e. 120
    f. 250

37. Find the maximum number of hosts in each subnet in exercise 36.

38. Find the masks that create the following number of subnets in class C. Assume a contiguous mask.
    a. 2
    b. 6
    c. 30
    d. 62
    e. 122
    f. 250

39. Find the maximum number of hosts in each subnet in exercise 38.

40. Show the bit pattern for each of the following masks used in class A.
    a. 255.255.192.0
    b. 255.192.0.0
    c. 255.255.224.0
    d. 255.255.255.0

41. Show the bit pattern for each of the following masks used in class B.
    a. 255.255.192.0
    b. 255.255.0.0
    c. 255.255.224.0
    d. 255.255. 255.0

42. Show the bit pattern for each of the following masks used in class C.
    a. 255.255.255.192
    b. 255.255.255.224
    c. 255.255.255.240
    d. 255.255. 255.0

43. What is the maximum number of subnets in class A using the following masks?
    a. 255.255.192.0
    b. 255.192.0.0
    c. 255.255.224.0
    d. 255.255. 255.0

44. What is the maximum number of subnets in class B using the following masks?
    a. 255.255.192.0
    b. 255.255.0.0
    c. 255.255.224.0
    d. 255.255. 255.0

45. What is the maximum number of subnets in class C using the following masks?
    a. 255.255.255.192
    b. 255.255.255.224
    c. 255.255.255.240
    d. 255.255. 255.0

46. For each of the following subnet masks used in class A, find the number of 1s that define the subnet.
    a. 255.255.192.0
    b. 255.192.0.0
    c. 255.255.224.0
    d. 255.255. 255.0

47. For each of the following subnet masks used in class B, find the number of 1s that define the subnet.
    a. 255.255.192.0
    b. 255.255.0.0
    c. 255.255.224.0
    d. 255.255. 255.0

48. For each of the following subnet masks used in class C, find the number of 1s that define the subnet.
    a. 255.255.255.192

b. 255.255.255.224

c. 255.255.255.240

d. 255.255. 255.0

49. An organization is granted a class A address. The administration wants to create the maximum number of subnets with at least 50,000 hosts per subnet. Find the best mask for this situation.

50. An organization is granted a class A address. The administration wants to create at least 6,000 subnets with the maximum number of hosts per subnet. Find the best mask for this situation.

51. An organization is granted a class B address. The administration wants to create the maximum number of subnets with at least 500 hosts per subnet. Find the best mask for this situation.

52. An organization is granted a class B address. The administration wants to create at least 100 subnets with the maximum number of hosts per subnet. Find the best mask for this situation.

53. An organization is granted a class C address. The administration wants to create the maximum number of subnets with at least 30 hosts per subnet. Find the best mask for this situation.

54. An organization is granted a class C address. The administration wants to create at least 12 subnets with at least 30 hosts on each network. Find the best mask for this situation.

55. Find the appropriate subnet mask for the range of addresses from 129.42.0.0 to 129.42.255.255.

56. Find the appropriate subnet mask for the range of addresses from 62.8.0.0 to 62.8.255.255.

57. Find the appropriate subnet mask for the range of addresses from 174.88.31.1 to 174.88.63.254.

CHAPTER 6

Delivery and Routing of IP Packets

This chapter describes the delivery and routing of IP packets to their final destinations. By **delivery**, we mean the physical forwarding of the packets. Concepts such as connectionless and connection-oriented services, and direct and indirect delivery are discussed. By **routing**, we mean finding the route (next hop) for a datagram. We discuss routing methods, types of routing, the routing table, and the routing module.

6.1   CONNECTION-ORIENTED VERSUS CONNECTIONLESS SERVICES

Delivery of a packet in the network layer is accomplished using either a connection-oriented or a connectionless network service.

In a connection-oriented situation, the network layer protocol first makes a connection with the network layer protocol at the remote site before sending a packet. When the connection is established, a sequence of packets from the same source to the same destination can be sent one after another. In this case, there is a relationship between packets. They are sent on the same path where they follow each other. A packet is logically connected to the packet traveling before it and to a packet traveling after it. When all packets of a message have been delivered, the connection is terminated.

In a connection-oriented protocol, the decision about the route of a sequence of packets with the same source and destination addresses can be made only once, when the connection is established. Routers do not have to recalculate the route for each individual packet.

In a connectionless situation, the network protocol treats each packet independently, with each packet having no relationship to any other packet. The packets in a message may not travel the same path to their destination.

The IP protocol is a connectionless protocol. It is designed this way because IP, as an internetwork protocol, may have to deliver the packets through several heterogeneous networks. If IP were to be connection-oriented, all of the networks in the internet should also be connection-oriented, which is not the case.

6.2   DIRECT VERSUS INDIRECT DELIVERY

The delivery of a packet to its final destination is accomplished using two different methods of delivery: direct and indirect.

Direct Delivery

In a **direct delivery**, the final destination of the packet is a host connected to the same physical network as the deliverer. Direct delivery occurs when the source and destination of the packet are located on the same physical network or if the delivery is between the last router and the destination host (see Figure 6.1).

Figure 6.1   *Direct delivery*

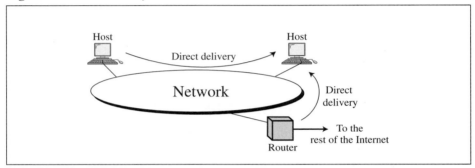

The sender can easily determine if the delivery is direct. It can extract the network address of the destination packet (setting the hostid part to all 0s) and compare this address with the addresses of the networks to which it is connected. If a match is found, the delivery is direct.

In direct delivery, the sender uses the destination IP address to find the destination physical address. The IP software then delivers the destination IP address with the destination physical address to the data link layer for actual delivery. This process is called *mapping the IP address to the physical address*. Although this mapping can be done by finding a match in a table, we will see in Chapter 8 that a protocol called address resolution protocol (ARP) dynamically maps an IP address to the corresponding physical address.

Indirect Delivery

If the destination host is not on the same network as the deliverer, the packet is delivered indirectly. In an **indirect delivery**, the packet goes from router to router until it reaches the one connected to the same physical network as its final destination (see Figure 6.2).

Note that a delivery always involves one direct delivery but zero or more indirect deliveries. Note also that the last delivery is always a direct delivery.

Figure 6.2   *Indirect delivery*

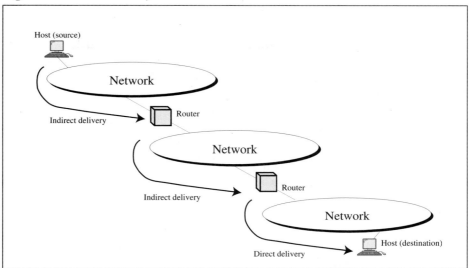

In an indirect delivery, the sender uses the destination IP address and a routing table to find the IP address of the next router to which the packet should be delivered. The sender then uses the ARP protocol to find the physical address of the next router. Note that in direct delivery, the address mapping is between the IP address of the final destination and the physical address of the final destination. In an indirect delivery, the address mapping is between the IP address of the next router and the physical address of the next router.

6.3   ROUTING METHODS

Routing requires a host or a router to have a routing table. When a host has a packet to send or when a router has received a packet to be forwarded, it looks at this table to find the route to the final destination. However, this simple solution is impossible today in an internetwork such as the Internet because the number of entries in the routing table make table lookups inefficient.

Several techniques can make the size of the routing table manageable and handle such issues as security. We will discuss these methods here.

Next-Hop Routing

One technique to make the contents of a routing table smaller is called *next-hop routing*. In this technique, the routing table holds only the address of the next hop instead of holding information about the complete route. Routing tables are thereby consistent with each other. Figure 6.3 shows how routing tables can be simplified using this technique.

Figure 6.3   *Next-hop routing*

Routing table for host A			Routing table for R1			Routing table for R2	
Destination	Route		Destination	Route		Destination	Route
Host B	R1, R2, Host B		Host B	R2, Host B		Host B	Host B

a. Routing tables based on route

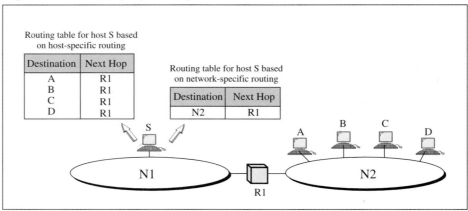

Routing table for host A			Routing table for R1			Routing table for R2	
Destination	Next Hop		Destination	Next Hop		Destination	Next Hop
Host B	R1		Host B	R2		Host B	—

b. Routing tables based on next hop

Network-Specific Routing

A second technique to make the routing table smaller and the searching process simpler is called *network-specific routing*. Here, instead of having an entry for every host connected to the same physical network, we have only one entry to define the address of the network itself. In other words, we treat all hosts connected to the same network as one single entity. For example, if 1,000 hosts are attached to the same network, only one entry exists in the routing table instead of 1,000. Figure 6.4 shows the concept.

Figure 6.4   *Network-specific routing*

Routing table for host S based on host-specific routing

Destination	Next Hop
A	R1
B	R1
C	R1
D	R1

Routing table for host S based on network-specific routing

Destination	Next Hop
N2	R1

Host-Specific Routing

In *host-specific routing*, the host address is given in the routing table. The idea of host-specific routing is the inverse of network-specific routing. Here efficiency is sacrificed for other advantages: Although it is not efficient to put the host address in the routing table, there are occasions in which the administrator wants to have more control over routing. For example, in Figure 6.5 if the administrator wants all packets arriving for host B delivered to router R3 instead of R1, one single entry in the routing table of host A can explicitly define the route.

Figure 6.5 *Host-specific routing*

Routing table for host A

Destination	Next Hop
Host B	R3
N2	R1
N3	R3
......	......

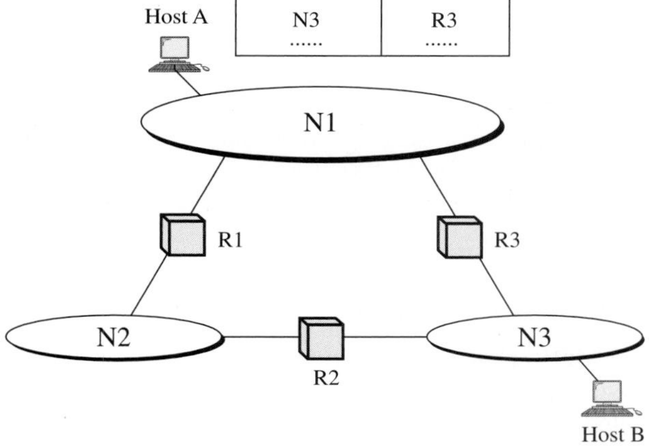

Host-specific routing is a good choice for certain purposes such as checking the route or providing security measures.

Default Routing

Another technique used to simplify routing is *default routing*. In Figure 6.6 host A is connected to a network with two routers. Router R1 is used to route the packets to hosts connected to network N2. However, for the rest of the Internet, router R2 should be used. So instead of listing all networks in the entire Internet, host A can just have one entry called the *default* (network address 0.0.0.0).

6.4 STATIC VERSUS DYNAMIC ROUTING

A host or a router keeps a routing table, with an entry for each destination, to route IP packets. The routing table can be either static or dynamic.

Figure 6.6   *Default routing*

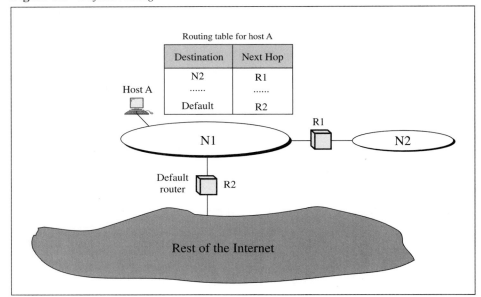

Static Routing Table

A **static routing table** contains information entered manually. The administration enters the route for each destination into the table. When a table is created, it cannot update automatically when there is a change in the Internet. The table must be manually altered by the administrator.

A static routing table can be used in a small internet that does not change very much, or in an experimental internet for troubleshooting. It is not a good strategy to use a static routing table in a big internet such as the Internet.

Dynamic Routing Table

A **dynamic routing table** is updated periodically using one of the dynamic routing protocols such as RIP, OSPF, or BGP (see Chapter 13). Whenever there is a change in the Internet, such as the shutdown of a router or breaking of a link, the dynamic routing protocols update all of the tables in the routers (and eventually in the host).

The routers in a big internet such as the Internet need to be updated dynamically for efficient delivery of the IP packets. We will discuss in detail the three dynamic routing protocols in Chapter 13.

6.5   ROUTING MODULE AND ROUTING TABLE DESIGN

In this section, we present a simplified, bare-bones routing module, which is part of the global IP module discussed in Chapter 7. This module is meant to be just a teaching tool. Details such as error checking and error handling have been omitted in an attempt to focus on the basics. Our purpose is to demystify the algorithm. In addition, we have sacrificed efficiency for the sake of simplicity. For the actual code, consult other literature such as Stevens, *TCP/IP Illustrated,* Volume 2.

When looking for the route, the router must first check for direct delivery, then host-specific delivery, then network-specific delivery, and finally default delivery. This hierarchical strategy can be implemented in the routing module or in the routing table. To make our routing module as simple as possible, we have used a routing table that is organized according to the above hierarchical scheme.

The module receives an IP packet from the IP processing module (see Chapter 7). The routing module consults the routing table to find the best route for the packet. After the route is found, the packet is sent along with the next-hop address to the fragmentation module (see Chapter 7), which makes a decision on fragmentation. See Figure 6.7.

Figure 6.7   *Routing module and routing table*

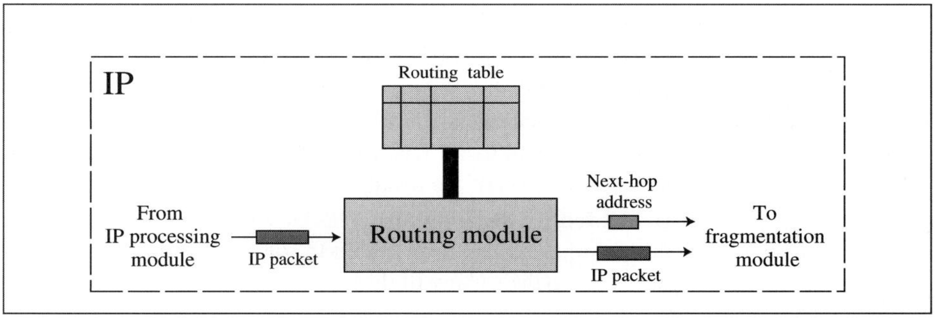

Routing Table

As mentioned previously, our routing table is organized in a hierarchical scheme with direct-delivery entries first, host-specific delivery entries next, network-specific entries next, and the default delivery entry last.

The routing table usually has these seven fields: mask, destination address, next-hop address, flags, reference-count, use, and interface (see Figure 6.8).

■   **Mask.** This field defines the mask applied to the destination IP address of the packet to find the network or subnetwork address of the destination. In host-specific and default routing the mask is 255.255.255.255. In an unsubnetted network, the mask is the default mask (255.0.0.0, 255.255.0.0, or 255.255.255.0 for class A, B, or C, respectively).

Figure 6.8   *Fields in routing table*

Mask	Destination address	Next-hop address	Flags	Reference count	Use	Interface
255.0.0.0	124.0.0.0	145.6.7.23	UG	4	20	m2
....	....	....	....	....	....	....
....	....	....	....	....	....	....

- **Destination address.** This field defines either the destination host address (host-specific address) or the destination network address (network-specific) address. A host-specific destination address gives the full destination address, netid and hostid. A network-specific address gives only the address of the network to which the destination entity is connected. The netid is specific, but the hostid is all 0s.

- **Next-hop address.** This field defines the address of the next-hop router to which the packet should be delivered.

- **Flags.** This field defines up to five flags. Flags are on/off switches that are either present or absent. The five flags are U (up), G (gateway), H (host-specific), D (added by redirection), and M (modified by redirection).

   a. **U (Up).** The U flag indicates the router is up and running. If this flag is not present, it means that the router is down. The packet cannot be forwarded and should be discarded.

   b. **G (Gateway).** The G flag means that the destination is in another network. The packet should be delivered to the next-hop router for delivery (indirect delivery). When this flag is missing, it means the destination is in this network (direct delivery).

   c. **H (Host-specific).** The H flag indicates that the entry in the destination field is a host-specific address. When it is missing, it means that the address is only the network address of the destination.

   d. **D (Added by redirection).** The D flag indicates that routing information for this destination has been added to the host routing table by a redirection message from ICMP. We will discuss redirection and the ICMP protocol in Chapter 9.

   e. **M (Modified by redirection).** The M flag indicates that the routing information for this destination has been modified by a redirection message from ICMP. We will discuss redirection and the ICMP protocol in Chapter 9.

- **Reference count.** This field gives the number of users that are using this route at any moment. For example, if five people at the same time are connecting to the same host from this router, the value of this column is 5.

- **Use.** This field shows the number of packets transmitted through this router for the corresponding destination.

- **Interface.** This field shows the name of the interface.

Routing Module

The routing module receives an IP packet from the IP processing module (see Chapter 7). In our design, the routing module goes from entry to entry trying to find a match. When it finds a match, it quits. Because the routing table is hierarchically organized, it is guaranteed that the module first looks for a direct-delivery match. If no match is found, the module looks for a host-specific delivery, and so on.

Routing Module
Receive: an IP packet
1. For each entry in the routing table
1. Apply the mask to packet destination address
2. If (the result matches the value in the destination field)
1. If (the G flag is absent)
1. Use packet destination address as next hop address
2. Send packet to fragmentation module with next hop address
3. Return
2. If no match is found, send an ICMP error message
3. Return

Examples

In this section we give some examples of routing by router R1 in Figure 6.9.

Figure 6.9   *Configuration for routing examples*

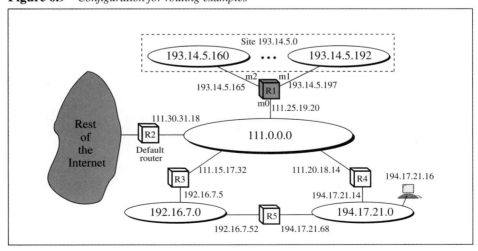

The routing table for router R1 is shown in Table 6.1.

Table 6.1   *Routing table for router R1 in Figure 6.9*

Mask	Destination	Next Hop	F.	R.C.	U.	I.
255.0.0.0	111.0.0.0	-	U	0	0	m0
255.255.255.224	193.14.5.160	-	U	0	0	m2
255.255.255.224	193.14.5.192	-	U	0	0	m1
....	....	....	....	....	...	...
....	....	....	....	....	...	...
....	....	....	....	....	...	...
255.255.255.255	194.17.21.16	111.20.18.14	UGH	0	0	m0
255.255.255.0	192.16.7.0	111.15.17.32	UG	0	0	m0
255.255.255.0	194.17.21.0	111.20.18.14	UG	0	0	m0
0.0.0.0	0.0.0.0	111.30.31.18	UG	0	0	m0

Example 1

Router R1 receives 500 packets for destination 192.16.7.14; the algorithm applies the masks row by row to the destination address until a match is found:

1. Direct delivery
    a. 192.16.7.14 & 255.0.0.0   ====> 192.0.0.0   no match
    b. 192.16.7.14 & 255.255.255.224   ====> 192.16.7.0   no match
    c. 192.16.7.14 & 255.255.255.224   ====> 192.16.7.0   no match
2. Host-specific
    a. 192.16.7.14 & 255.255.255.255   ====> 192.16.7.14   no match
3. Network-specific
    a. 192.16.7.14 & 255.255.255.0   ====> 192.16.7.0   **match**

The router sends the packet through interface m0 along with the next-hop IP address (111.15.17.32) to the fragmentation module for further processing. It increments the use field by 500 and the reference count field by 1.

Example 2

Router R1 receives 100 packets for destination 193.14.5.176; the algorithm applies the masks row by row to the destination address until a match is found:

1. Direct delivery
    a. 193.14.5.176 & 255.0.0.0   ====> 193.0.0.0   no match
    b. 193.14.5.176 & 255.255.255.224   ====> 193.14.5.160   **match**

The router sends the packet through interface m2 along with the destination IP address (193.14.5.176) to the fragmentation module for further processing. It increments the use field by 100 and the reference count field by 1.

Example 3

Router R1 receives 20 packets for destination 200.34.12.34; the algorithm applies the masks row by row to the destination address until a match is found:

1. Direct delivery
   a. 200.34.12.34 & 255.0.0.0   ====> 200.0.0.0   no match
   b. 200.34.12.34 & 255.255.255.224   ====> 200.34.12.32   no match
   c. 200.34.12.344 & 255.255.255.224   ====> 200.34.12.32   no match
2. Host-specific
   a. 200.34.12.34 & 255.255.255.255   ====> 200.34.12.34   no match
3. Network-specific
   a. 200.34.12.34 & 255.255.255.0   ====> 200.34.12.0   no match
   b. 200.34.12.34 & 255.255.255.0   ====> 200.34.12.0   no match
4. Default
   a. 200.34.12.34 & 0.0.0.0   ====> 0.0.0.0.   **match**

The router sends the packet through interface m0 along with the next hop IP address (111.30.31.18) to the fragmentation module for further processing. It increments the use field by 20 and the reference count field by 1.

6.6   SUMMARY

- The IP protocol is a connectionless protocol. Every packet is independent and has no relationship to any other packet.

- The delivery of a packet is called direct if the deliverer (host or router) and the destination are on the same network.

- The delivery of a packet is called indirect if the deliverer (host or router) and the destination are on different networks.

- Every host or router has a routing table to route IP packets.

- In next-hop routing, instead of a complete list of the stops the packet must make, only the address of the next hop is listed in the routing table.

- In network-specific routing, all hosts on a network share one entry in the routing table.

- In host-specific routing, the full IP address of a host is given in the routing table.

- In default routing, a router is assigned to receive all packets with no match in the routing table.

- A static routing table's entries are updated manually by an administrator.

- A dynamic routing table's entries are updated automatically by a routing protocol.

- The routing table can consist of seven fields: a mask, a destination address, a next-hop address, flags, a reference count, a use, and an interface.

- The routing module applies the mask, row by row, to the received destination address until a match is found.

6.7   PRACTICE SET

Multiple Choice

1. In _____ delivery, both the deliverer of the IP packet and the destination are on the same network.
   a. a connectionless
   b. a connection-oriented
   c. a direct
   d. an indirect

2. In _____ delivery, the deliverer of the IP packet and the destination are on different networks.
   a. a connectionless
   b. a connection-oriented
   c. a direct
   d. an indirect

3. In _____ delivery, packets of a message are logically connected to one another.
   a. a connectionless
   b. a connection-oriented
   c. a direct
   d. an indirect

4. In _____ delivery, a packet is not connected to any other packet.
   a. a connectionless
   b. a connection-oriented
   c. a direct
   d. an indirect

5. When a direct delivery is made, both the deliverer and receiver have the same _____.
   a. routing table
   b. IP address
   c. hostid
   d. netid

6. When an indirect delivery is made, the deliverer and receiver have _____.
   a. the same IP address
   b. different netids
   c. the same netid
   d. none of the above

7. In _____ routing, the full IP address of a destination is given in the routing table.
   a. next-hop
   b. network-specific

    c. host-specific

    d. default

8. In _____ routing, the mask and destination address are both 0.0.0.0 in the routing table.

    a. next-hop

    b. network-specific

    c. host-specific

    d. default

9. In _____ routing, the destination address is a network address in the routing table.

    a. next-hop

    b. network-specific

    c. host-specific

    d. default

10. In _____ routing, the routing table holds the address of just the next hop instead of complete route information.

    a. next-hop

    b. network-specific

    c. host-specific

    d. default

11. For a direct delivery, the _____ flag is missing.

    a. up

    b. gateway

    c. host-specific

    d. added by redirection

12. The _____ flag indicates the availability of a router.

    a. up

    b. gateway

    c. host-specific

    d. added by redirection

13. The _____ flag indicates that already existing information in the routing table has been modified by a redirection message.

    a. gateway

    b. host-specific

    c. modified by redirection

    d. added by redirection

14. The _____ flag indicates that the entry in the destination column is a host-specific address.

    a. gateway

    b. host-specific

    c. modified by redirection

d. added by redirection

15. The _____ flag indicates that a redirection message has added a new entry to the routing table.

   a. gateway

   b. host-specific

   c. modified by redirection

   d. added by redirection

16. The _____ column in the routing table indicates the number of packets transmitted through the router for the corresponding destination.

   a. destination

   b. reference count

   c. use

   d. interface

Exercises

17. A host with IP address 137.23.56.23 sends a packet to a host with IP address 137.23.67.9. Is the delivery direct or indirect? Assume no subnetting.

18. A host with IP address 137.23.56.23 sends a packet to a host with IP address 142.3.6.9. Is the delivery direct or indirect? Assume no subnetting.

19. A router with IP address 109.34.56.8 sends a packet to a host with IP address 202.34.8.9. Is the delivery direct or indirect? Assume no subnetting.

20. A host with IP address 131.23.56.23 sends a packet to a host with IP address 131.23.67.9. Is the delivery direct or indirect if there is no subnetting? Can the delivery be indirect if there is subnetting?

21. Using Table 6.1, determine the next-hop address if router R1 receives a packet destined for 111.45.32.16.

22. Using Table 6.1, determine the next-hop address if router R1 receives a packet destined for 192.16.7.31.

23. Using Table 6.1, determine the next-hop address if router R1 receives a packet destined for 194.17.21.45.

24. Using Table 6.1, determine the next-hop address if router R1 receives a packet destined for 220.7.14.7.

25. Using Table 6.1, determine the next-hop address if router R1 receives a packet destined for 193.14.5.165.

26. Using Table 6.1, determine the next-hop address if router R1 receives a packet destined for 193.14.5.196.

27. Using Table 6.1, determine the next-hop address if router R1 receives a packet destined for 115.7.3.4.

28. Using Table 6.1, determine the next-hop address if router R1 receives a packet destined for 191.61.22.7.

29. Using Table 6.1, determine the next-hop address if router R1 receives a packet destined for 189.73.43.23.

30. Show the routing table for router R2 in Figure 6.9.
31. Show the routing table for router R3 in Figure 6.9.
32. Show the routing table for router R4 in Figure 6.9.
33. Show the routing table for router R5 in Figure 6.9.

Programming Exercises

34. Create a header file to include all constants that you think are needed to implement the routing module and routing table in C. Use the **#define** directives.
35. Complete the following **struct** declaration for the routing table entry.

```
struct   Routing_Table_Entry
{
........................................   Mask;
.............................................................
.............................................................
} ;
```

36. Write a declaration for the routing table.
37. Write a function in C to simulate the routing module.

CHAPTER 7

Internet Protocol (IP)

The Internet Protocol (IP) is the transmission mechanism used by the TCP/IP protocols. It is an unreliable and connectionless datagram protocol—a best-effort delivery service. The term *best-effort* means that IP provides no error checking or tracking. IP assumes the unreliability of the underlying layers and does its best to get a transmission through to its destination, but with no guarantees.

If reliability is important, IP must be paired with a reliable protocol such as TCP. An example of a more commonly understood best-effort delivery service is the post office. The post office does its best to deliver the mail but does not always succeed. If an unregistered letter is lost, it is up to the sender or would-be recipient to discover the loss and rectify the problem. The post office itself does not keep track of every letter and cannot notify a sender of loss or damage.

IP is also a connectionless protocol designed for a packet switching network which uses the datagram approach (see Chapter 3). This means that each datagram is handled independently, and each datagram can follow a different route to the destination. This implies that if a source sends several datagrams to the same destination, they could arrive out of order. Some of them could also be lost, or some could be corrupted during transition. Again, IP relies on a higher level protocol to take care of all these problems.

7.1 DATAGRAM

Packets in the IP layer are called *datagrams*. Figure 7.1 shows the IP datagram format. A datagram is a variable-length packet consisting of two parts: header and data. The header can be from 20 to 60 bytes and contains information essential to routing and delivery. It is customary in TCP/IP to show the header in four-byte sections. A brief description of each field is in order.

■ **Version (VER).** This four-bit field defines the version of the IP protocol. Currently the version is 4. However, version 6 (or IPng) will replace version 4 in a few years. This field is an indication to the IP software running in the processing machine that the datagram has the version 4 format. All fields must be interpreted as specified in

Figure 7.1 *IP datagram*

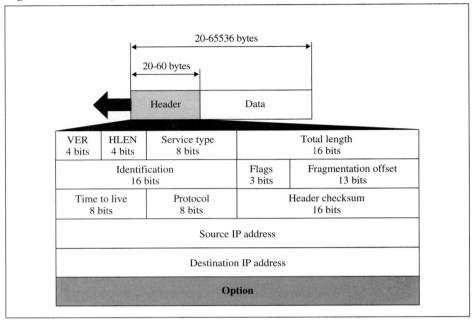

the fourth version of the protocol. If the machine is using another version of IP, the datagram is discarded rather than interpreted incorrectly.

■ **Header length (HLEN).** This four-bit field defines the total length of the datagram header in four-byte words. This field is needed because the length of the header is variable (between 20 and 60 bytes). When there are no options, the header length is 20 bytes, and the value of this field is 5 ($5 \times 4 = 20$). When the option field is at its maximum size, the value of this field is 15 ($15 \times 4 = 60$).

■ **Service type.** This eight-bit field defines how the datagram should be handled by the routers. This field is divided into two subfields: precedence (three bits) and service type (four bits). The remaining bit is unused (see Figure 7.2).

Figure 7.2 *Service type*

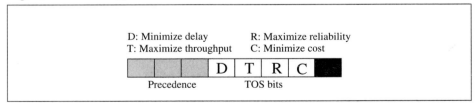

a. **Precedence** is a three-bit subfield ranging from 0 (000 in binary) to 7 (111 in binary). The precedence defines the priority of the datagram in issues such as congestion. If a router is congested and needs to discard some datagrams, those datagrams with lowest precedence are discarded first. Some datagrams in the Internet are more important than others. For example, a datagram used for network management is much more urgent and important than a datagram used for sending optional information to a group of people. At present, the precedence subfield, however, is not used. It is expected to be functional in future versions.

The precedence subfield is not used in version 4.

b. **TOS bits** is a four-bit subfield, each bit having a special meaning. Although a bit can be either 0 or 1, one and only one of the bits can have the value of 1 in each datagram. The bit patterns and their interpretations are given in Table 7.1. With only one bit set at a time, we can have five different types of services.

Table 7.1   *Types of service*

TOS Bits	Description
0000	Normal (default)
0001	Minimize cost
0010	Maximize reliability
0100	Maximize throughput
1000	Minimize delay

Application programs can request a specific type of service. However, the defaults for some applications are shown in Table 7.2.

Table 7.2   *Default types of service*

Protocol	TOS Bits	Description
ICMP	0000	Normal
BOOTP	0000	Normal
NNTP	0001	Minimize cost
IGP	0010	Maximize reliability
SNMP	0010	Maximize reliability
TELNET	1000	Minimize delay
FTP (data)	0100	Maximize throughput
FTP (control)	1000	Minimize delay
TFTP	1000	Minimize delay
SMTP (command)	1000	Minimize delay
SMTP (data)	0100	Maximize throughput
DNS (UDP query)	1000	Minimize delay
DNS (TCP query)	0000	Normal
DNS (zone)	0100	Maximize throughput

It is clear from the above table that interactive activities, activities requiring immediate attention, and activities requiring immediate response need minimum delay. Those activities that send bulk data require maximum throughput. Management activities need maximum reliability. Background activities need minimum cost.

■ **Total length.** This is a 16-bit field that defines the total length (header plus data) of the IP datagram in bytes. To find the length of the data coming from the upper layer, subtract the header length from the total length. The header length can be found by multiplying the value in the HLEN field by four.

length of data = total length – header length

Since the field length is 16 bits, the total length of the IP datagram is limited to 65,535 ($2^{16} - 1$) bytes, of which 20 to 60 bytes are the header and the rest is data from the upper layer.

> The total length field defines the total length of the datagram including the header.

A size of 65,535 bytes seems large in today's technology. However, the size of the IP datagram may increase in the near future when the underlying technology allows the use of networks with more throughput (more bandwidth).

When we discuss fragmentation in the next section, we will see that some physical networks are not able to encapsulate a datagram of 65,535 bytes in their frames. The datagram must be fragmented to be able to pass through those networks.

One may ask why we need this field anyway. When a machine (router or host) receives a frame, it drops the header and the trailer leaving the datagram. Why include an extra field that is not needed? The answer is that in many cases we really do not need the value of this field. However, there are occasions in which the datagram is not the only thing encapsulated in a frame; it may be that padding has been added. For example, the Ethernet protocol has a minimum and maximum restriction on the size of data that can be encapsulated in a frame (46 to 1,500 bytes). If the size of an IP datagram is less than 46 bytes, some padding will be added to the meet this requirement. In this case, when a machine decapsulates the datagram, it needs to check the total length field to determine how much is really data and how much is padding (see Figure 7.3).

Figure 7.3 *Encapsulation of a small datagram in an Ethernet frame*

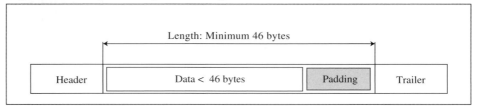

■ **Identification.** This field is used in fragmentation (discussed in the next section).

- **Flags.** This field is used in fragmentation (discussed in the next section).
- **Fragmentation offset.** This field is used in fragmentation (discussed in the next section).
- **Time to live.** A datagram should have a limited lifetime in its travel through an internet. This field was originally designed to hold a timestamp, which was decremented by each visited router. The datagram was discarded when the value became zero. However, to do so, all the machines must have synchronized clocks and must know how long it takes for a datagram to go from one machine to another. Today, this field is mostly used to control the maximum number of hops (routers) visited by the datagram. When a source host sends the datagram, it stores a number in this field. This value is approximately two times the maximum number of routes between any two hosts. Each router that processes the datagram decrements this number by one. When a router receives a datagram, it decrements the value of this field by one. If this value, after being decremented, is zero, the router discards the datagram.

  This field is needed because routers in the Internet can become corrupted. If this happens, a datagram may travel between two or more routers for a long time. Resources may become tied up without benefit. This field allows a limited life time for a datagram and prevents old datagrams from popping out of the network and perhaps confusing higher level protocols (especially TCP).

  Another use of this field is when the source wants to intentionally limit the journey of the packet. For example, if the source wants to confine the packet to the local network, it can store 1 in this field. When the packet arrives at the first router, this value is decremented to 0, and the datagram is discarded.

- **Protocol.** This eight-bit field defines the higher level protocol that uses the services of the IP layer. An IP datagram can encapsulate data from several higher level protocols such as TCP, UDP, ICMP, and IGMP. This field specifies the final destination protocol to which the IP datagram should be delivered. In other words, since the IP protocol multiplexes and demultiplexes data from different higher level protocols, the value of this field helps the process of demultiplexing when the datagram arrives at its final destination (see Figure 7.4).

Figure 7.4 *Multiplexing*

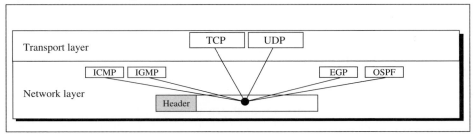

The value of this field for different higher level protocols is shown in Table 7.3.

Table 7.3   *Protocols*

Value	Protocol
1	ICMP
2	IGMP
6	TCP
8	EGP
17	UDP
41	IPv6
89	OSPF

- **Checksum.** The checksum concept and its calculation are discussed later in this chapter.
- **Source address.** This 32-bit field defines the IP address of the source. This field must remain unchanged during the time the IP datagram travels from the source host to the destination host.
- **Destination address.** This 32-bit field defines the IP address of the destination. This field must remain unchanged during the time the IP datagram travels from the source host to the destination host.

7.2   FRAGMENTATION

A datagram can travel through different networks. Each router decapsulates the IP datagram from the frame it receives, processes it, and then encapsulates it in another frame. The format and size of the received frame depend on the protocol used by the physical network through which the frame has just traveled. The format and size of the sent frame depend on the protocol used by the physical network through which the frame is going to travel. For example, if a router connects an Ethernet network to a token ring network, it receives a frame in the Ethernet format and sends a frame in the token ring format.

Maximum Transfer Unit (MTU)

Each data link layer protocol has its own frame format. One of the fields defined in the format is the maximum size of the data field. In other words, when a datagram is encapsulated in a frame, the total size of the datagram must be less than this maximum size, which is defined by the restriction imposed by the hardware and software used in the network (see Figure 7.5).

Figure 7.5   *MTU*

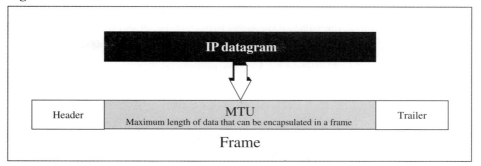

The value of the MTU differs from one physical network protocol to another. Table 7.4 shows the values for different protocols.

Table 7.4   *MTUs for different networks*

Protocol	MTU
Hyperchannel	65,535
Token ring (16 Mbps)	17,914
Token ring (4 Mbps)	4,464
FDDI	4,352
Ethernet	1,500
X.25	576
PPP	296

In order to make the IP protocol independent of the physical network, the designers decided to make the maximum length of the IP datagram equal to the largest maximum transfer unit (MTU) defined so far (65,535 bytes). This makes transmission more efficient if we use a protocol with an MTU of this size. However, for other physical networks, we must divide the datagram to make it possible to pass through these networks. This is called **fragmentation**.

When a datagram is fragmented, each fragment has its own header with most of the fields repeated, but some changed. A fragmented datagram may itself be fragmented if it encounters a network with an even smaller MTU. In other words, a datagram can be fragmented several times before it reaches the final destination.

A datagram can be fragmented by the source host or any router in the path. The reassembly of the datagram, however, is done only by the destination host because each fragment becomes an independent datagram. Whereas the fragmented datagram can travel through different routes, and we can never control or guarantee which route a fragmented datagram may take, all of the fragments belonging to the same datagram should finally arrive at the destination host. So it is logical to do the reassembly at the final destination.

When a datagram is fragmented, required parts of the header must be copied by all fragments. The option field may or may not be copied as we will see in the next section.

The host or router that fragments a datagram must change the values of three fields: flags, fragmentation offset, and total length. The rest of the fields must be copied. Of course, the value of the checksum must be recalculated regardless of fragmentation.

Fields Related to Fragmentation

The fields that are related to fragmentation and reassembly of an IP datagram are identification, flags, and fragmentation offset.

- **Identification.** This 16-bit field identifies a datagram originating from the source host. The combination of the identification and source IP address must uniquely define a datagram as it leaves the source host. To guarantee uniqueness, the IP protocol uses a counter to label the datagrams. The counter is initialized to a positive number. When the IP protocol sends a datagram, it copies the current value of the counter to the identification field and increments the counter by one. As long as the counter is kept in the main memory, uniqueness is guaranteed. When a datagram is fragmented, the value in the identification field is copied into all fragments. In other words, all fragments have the same identification number, which is also the same as the original datagram. The identification number helps the destination in reassembling the datagram. It knows that all fragments having the same identification value should be assembled into one datagram.

- **Flags.** This is a three-bit field. The first bit is reserved. The second bit is called the *do not fragment* bit. If its value is 1, the machine must not fragment the datagram. If it cannot pass the datagram through any available physical network, it discards the datagram and sends an ICMP error message to the source host (see Chapter 9). If its value is 0, the datagram can be fragmented if necessary. The third bit is called the *more fragment* bit. If its value is 1, it means the datagram is not the last fragment; there are more fragments after this one. If its value is 0, it means this is the last or only fragment (see Figure 7.6).

Figure 7.6 *Flags field*

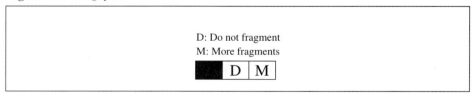

- **Fragmentation offset.** This 13-bit field shows the relative position of this fragment with respect to the whole datagram. It is the offset of the data in the original datagram measured in units of eight bytes. Figure 7.7 shows a datagram with a data size of 4,000 bytes fragmented into three fragments. The bytes in the original datagram are numbered 0 to 3,999. The first fragment carries bytes 0 to 1,399. The offset for this datagram is 0/8 = 0. The second fragment carries bytes 1,400 to 2,799; the offset value for this fragment is 1,400/8=175. Finally, the third fragment carries bytes 2,800 to 3,999. The offset value for this fragment is 2,800/8=350.

Remember that the value of the offset is measured in units of eight bytes. This is done because the length of the offset field is only 13 bits long and cannot represent a sequence of bytes greater than 8,191. This forces hosts or routers that fragment datagrams to choose the size of each fragment so that the first byte number is divisible by eight.

Figure 7.7   *Fragmentation example*

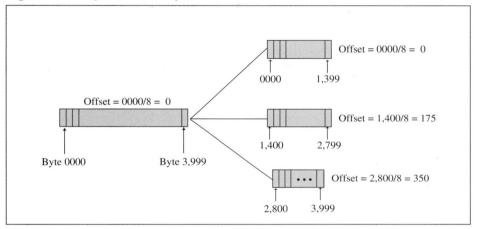

Figure 7.8 shows an expanded view of the fragments in the previous figure. Notice the value of the identification field is the same in all fragments. Notice the value of the flags field with the *more* bit set for all fragments except the last. Also, the value of the offset field for each fragment is shown.

The figure also shows what happens if a fragment itself is fragmented. In this case the value of the offset field is always relative to the original datagram. For example, in the figure, the second fragment is itself fragmented later to two fragments of 800 bytes and 600 bytes, but the offset shows the relative position of the fragments to the original data.

It is obvious that even if each fragment follows a different path and arrives out of order, the final destination host can reassemble the original datagram from the fragments received (if none of them is lost) using the following strategy:

a. The first fragment has an offset field value of zero.

b. Divide the length of the first fragment by eight. The second fragment has an offset value equal to that result.

c. Divide the total length of the first and second fragment by eight. The third fragment has an offset value equal to that result.

d. Continue the process. The last fragment has a *more* bit value of 0.

Figure 7.8 *Detailed fragmentation example*

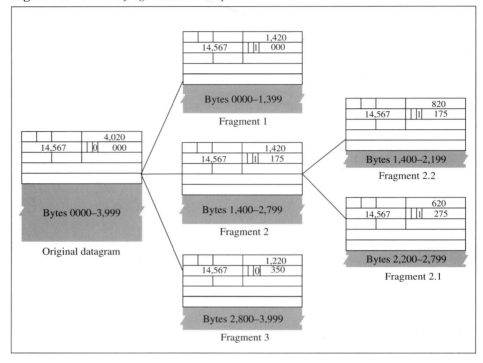

7.3 OPTIONS

The header of the IP datagram is made of two parts: the fixed part and the variable part. The fixed part is 20 bytes long and was discussed in the previous section. The variable part comprises the options which can be a maximum of 40 bytes.

Options, as the name implies, are not required for every datagram. They are used for network testing and debugging. Although options are not a required part of the IP header, option processing is a required part of the IP software. This means that all standards must be able to handle options if they are present in the header.

Format

Figure 7.9 shows the format of an option. It is composed of a one-byte code field, a one-byte length field, and a variable-sized data field.

Code

The **code field** is eight bits long and contains three subfields: copy, class, and number.

■ **Copy.** This one-bit subfield controls the presence of the option in fragmentation. When its value is 0, it means that the option must be copied only to the first fragment. If its value is 1, it means the option must be copied to all fragments.

Figure 7.9   *Option format*

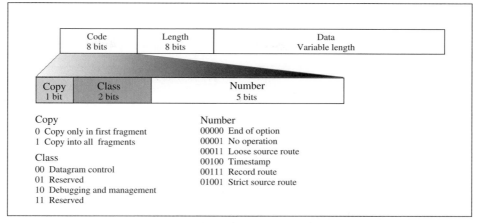

- ■   **Class.** This two-bit subfield defines the general purpose of the option. When its value is 00, it means that the option is used for datagram control. When its value is 10, it means that the option is used for debugging and management. The other two possible values (01 and 11) have not yet been defined.
- ■   **Number.** This five-bit subfield defines the type of the option. Although five bits can define up to 32 different types, currently only six types are in use. We will discuss them in a later section.

Length

The **length field** defines the total length of the option including the code field and the length field itself. This field is not present in all of the option types.

Data

The **data field** contains the data that specific options require. Like the length field, this field is also not present in all option types.

Option Types

As mentioned previously, only six options are currently being used. Two of these are one-byte options, and they do not require the length or the data fields. Four of them are multiple-byte options; they require the length and the data fields (see Figure 7.10).

No Operation

A **no operation** option is a one-byte option used as a filler between options. For example, it can be used to align the next option on a 16-bit or 32-bit boundary (see Figure 7.11).

End of Option

An **end of option** option is also a one-byte option used for padding at the end of the option field. It, however, can only be used as the last option. Only one *end of option*

Figure 7.10 *Categories of options*

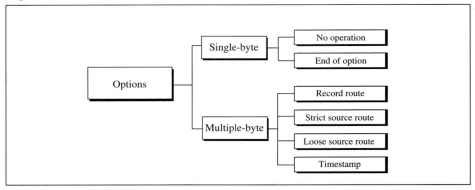

Figure 7.11 *No operation option*

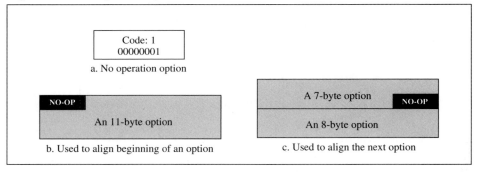

option can be used. After this option, the receiver looks for the payload data. This means that if more than one byte is needed to align the option field, some *no operation* options must be used followed by an *end of option* option (see Figure 7.12).

Figure 7.12 *End of option option*

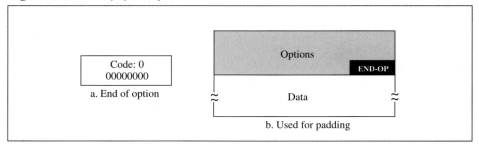

Record Route

A **record route** option is used to record the internet routers that handle the datagram. It can list up to nine router IP addresses since the maximum size of the header is 60 bytes, which must include 20 bytes for the base header. This implies that only 40 bytes are left over for the option part. The source creates placeholder fields in the option to be filled by the visited routers. Figure 7.13 shows the format of the *record route* option.

Figure 7.13   *Record route option*

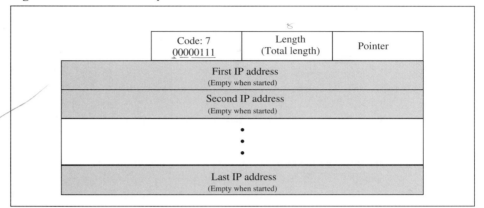

Both the code and length fields have been described above. The **pointer field** is an offset integer field containing the byte number of the first empty entry. In other words, it points to the first available entry.

The source creates empty fields for the IP address in the data field of the option. When the datagram leaves the source, all of the fields are empty. The pointer field has a value of four, pointing to the first empty field.

When the datagram is traveling, each router that processes the datagram compares the value of the pointer with the value of the length. If the value of the pointer is greater than the value of the length, the option is full and no changes are made. However, if the value of the pointer is not greater than the value of the length, the router inserts its outgoing IP address in the next empty field (remember that a router has more than one IP address). In this case, the router adds the IP address of its interface from which the datagram is leaving. The router then increments the value of the pointer by four. Figure 7.14 shows the entries as the datagram travels left to right from router to router.

Strict Source Route

A **strict source route** option is used by the source to predetermine a route for the datagram as it travels through the Internet. Dictation of a route by the source can be useful for several purposes. The sender can choose a route with a specific type of service, such as minimum delay or maximum throughput. Alternatively, it may choose a route that is safer or more reliable for the sender's purpose. For example, a sender can choose a route so that its datagram does not travel through a competitor's network.

If a datagram specifies a strict source route, all of the routers defined in the option must be visited by the datagram. A router must not be visited if its IP address is not listed in the datagram. If the datagram visits a router that is not on the list, the datagram is discarded and an error message is issued. If the datagram arrives at the destination

Figure 7.14 *Record route concept*

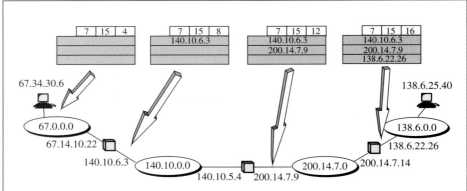

and some of the entries were not visited, it will also be discarded and an error message issued.

Nonprivileged users of the Internet, however, are not usually aware of the physical topology of the Internet. Consequently, strict source routing is not the choice of most users. Figure 7.15 shows the format of the *strict source route* option.

Figure 7.15 *Strict source route option*

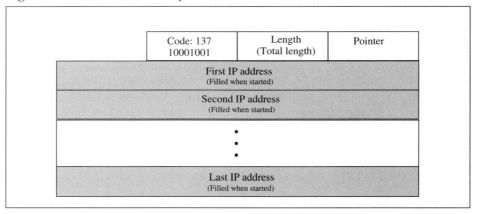

The format looks like the *record route* option with the exception that, in this case, all of the IP addresses are entered by the sender.

When the datagram is traveling, each router that processes the datagram compares the value of the pointer with the value of the length. If the value of the pointer is greater than the value of the length, the datagram has visited all of the predefined routers. The datagram cannot travel anymore; it is discarded and an error message is created. If the value of the pointer is not greater than the value of the length, the router compares the IP address pointed by the pointer with its incoming IP address: If they are equal, it processes the datagram, overwrites the current IP address with its outgoing IP address, increments the pointer value by four, and forwards the datagram. If they are not equal, it discards the datagram and issues an error message. Figure 7.16 shows the actions taken by each router as a datagram travels from source to destination.

Figure 7.16 *Strict source route concept*

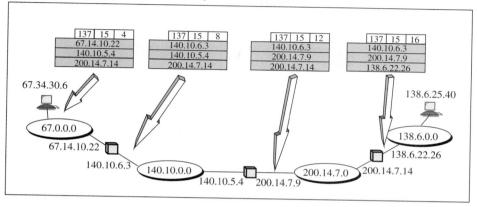

Loose Source Route

A **loose source route** option is similar to the *strict source route*, but it is more relaxed. Each router in the list must be visited, but the datagram can visit other routers as well. Figure 7.17 shows the format of the *loose source route* option.

Figure 7.17 *Loose source route option*

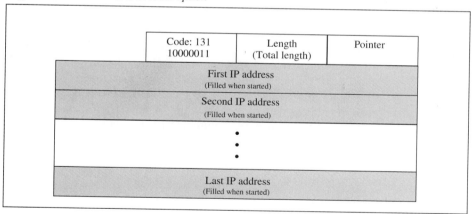

Timestamp

A **timestamp** option is used to record the time of datagram processing by a router. The time is expressed in milliseconds from midnight, Universal Time. Knowing the time a datagram is processed can help users and managers track the behavior of the routers in the Internet. We can estimate the time it takes for a datagram to go from one router to another. We say *estimate* because, although all routers may use Universal Time, their local clocks may not be synchronized.

However, nonprivileged users of the Internet are not usually aware of the physical topology of the Internet. Consequently, a timestamp option is not a choice for most users. Figure 7.18 shows the format of the *timestamp* option.

Figure 7.18   *Timestamp option*

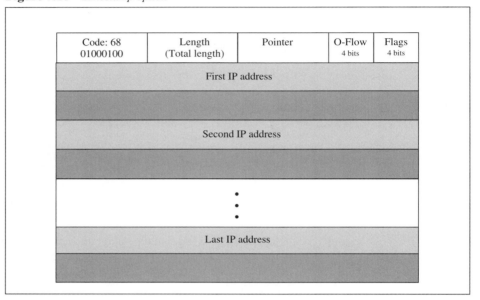

In this figure, the definition of the code and length fields are the same as before. The overflow field records the number of routers that could not add their timestamp because no more fields were available. The flags field specifies the visited router responsibilities. If the flag value is 0, each router adds only the timestamp in the provided field. If the flag value is 1, each router must add its outgoing IP address and the timestamp. If the value is 3, the IP addresses are given, and each router must check the given IP address with its own incoming IP address. If there is a match, the router overwrites the IP address with its outgoing IP address and adds the timestamp (see Figure 7.19).

Figure 7.19   *Use of flag in timestamp*

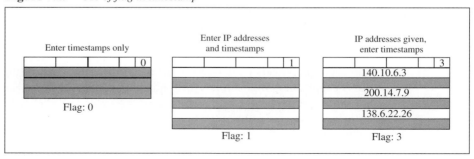

Figure 7.20 shows the actions taken by each router when a datagram travels from source to destination. The figure assumes the flag value of 1.

Figure 7.20 *Timestamp concept*

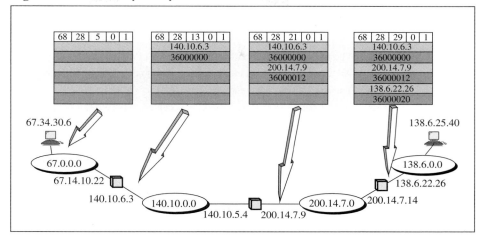

7.4 CHECKSUM

The error detection method used by most TCP/IP protocols is called the **checksum**. The checksum protects against the corruption that may occur during the transmission of a packet. It is redundant information added to the packet.

The checksum is calculated at the sender and the value obtained is sent with the packet. The receiver repeats the same calculation on the whole packet including the checksum. If the result is satisfactory (see below), the packet is accepted; otherwise, it is rejected.

Checksum Calculation at the Sender

In the sender, the packet is divided into n-bit sections (n is usually 16). These sections are added together using one's complement arithmetic (see Appendix B) in such a way that the sum is also n bits long. The sum is then complemented (changing all 0s to 1s and all 1s to 0s) to produce the checksum.

To create the checksum the sender does the following:

- The packet is divided into k sections, each of n bits.
- All sections are added together using one's complement arithmetic.
- The final result is complemented to make the checksum.

Checksum Calculation at the Receiver

The receiver divides the received packet into k sections and adds all sections. It then complements the result. If the final result is 0, the packet is accepted; otherwise, it is rejected.

> To check the validity of data, the receiver does the following:
>
> ■ The packet is divided into k sections, each of n bits.
> ■ All sections are added together using one's complement arithmetic.
> ■ The result is complemented.
> ■ If the final result is 0, the packet is accepted; otherwise, it is rejected.

Figure 7.21 shows graphically what happens at the sender and the receiver.

Figure 7.21 *Checksum concept*

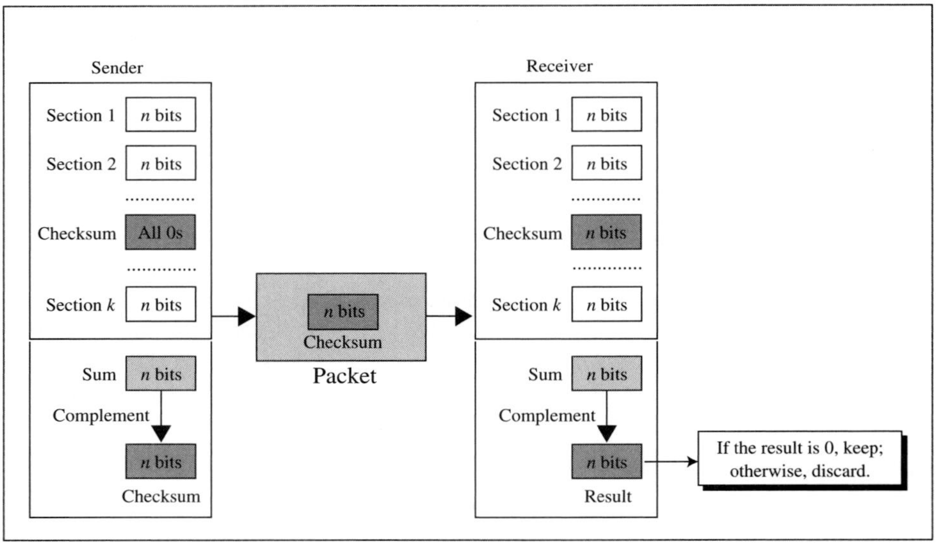

We said when the receiver adds all of the sections and complements the result, it should get zero if there is no error in the data during transmission or processing. This is true because of the rules in one's complement arithmetic.

Assume that we get a number called T when we add all the sections in the sender. When we complement the number in one's complement arithmetic, we get the negative of the number. This means that if the sum of all sections is T, the checksum is $-T$.

When the receiver receives the packet, it adds all the sections. It is adding T and $-T$ which, in one's complement, is -0 (minus zero). When the result is complemented, -0 becomes 0. Thus if the final result is 0, the packet is accepted; otherwise, it is rejected (see Figure 7.22).

Figure 7.22   *Checksum in one's complement arithmetic*

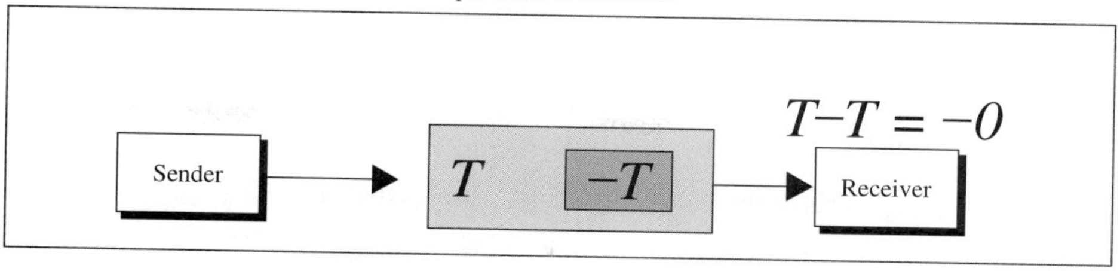

Checksum in the IP Packet

The implementation of the checksum in the IP packet follows the same principle discussed above. First, the value of the checksum field is set to 0. Then, the entire header is divided into 16-bit sections and added together. The result (sum) is complemented and inserted into the checksum field.

The checksum in the IP packet covers only the header, not the data. There are two good reasons for this. First, all higher level protocols that encapsulate data in the IP datagram have a checksum field that covers the whole packet. Therefore, the checksum for the IP datagram does not have to check the encapsulated data. Second, the header of the IP packet changes with each visited router, but the data does not. So the checksum includes only the part which has changed. If the data is included, each router must recalculate the checksum for the whole packet, which means more processing time for each router.

Example

Figure 7.23 shows an example of a checksum calculation for an IP header without options. The header is divided into 16-bit sections. All the sections are added and the sum is complemented. The result is inserted in the checksum field.

7.5   IP DESIGN

In this section, we present a simplified, bare-bones design of IP. This design is meant to be a teaching tool; details such as error checking, error handling, and packet validation have been omitted in an attempt to focus on the basics. Our purpose is to demystify the algorithms and their relationships.

Although IP supports several options, we have omitted option processing in our design to make it easier to understand at this level. In addition, we have sacrificed efficiency for the sake of simplicity. For the actual code consult other literature such as Stevens, *TCP/IP Illustrated,* Volume 2.

We can say that the IP package involves eight components: a header-adding module, a processing module, a routing module, a fragmentation module, a reassembly module, a routing table, an MTU table, and a reassembly table. In addition, the package includes input and output queues.

Figure 7.24 shows these eight components and their interactions. The package receives an IP packet, either from the data link layer or from a higher level protocol. If

Figure 7.23   *Example of checksum calculation*

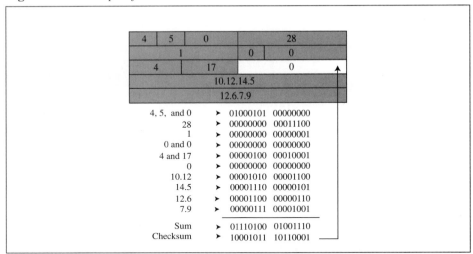

the packet comes from an upper layer protocol, it should be delivered to the data link layer for transmission except for a loopback address (127.X.Y.Z). If the packet comes from the data link layer, it should either be delivered to the data link layer for forwarding (in a router) or it should be delivered to a higher layer protocol if the destination IP address of the packet is the same as the station address.

Header-Adding Module

The **header-adding module** receives data from an upper layer protocol along with the destination IP address. It encapsulates the data in an IP datagram by adding the IP header.

Figure 7.24   *IP components*

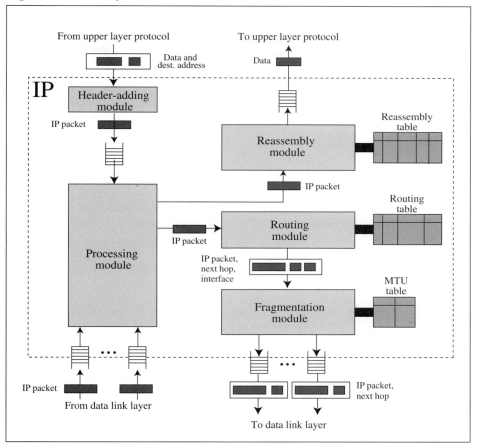

Header-Adding Module
Receive: data, destination address
1. Encapsulate the data in an IP datagram.
2. Calculate the checksum and insert it in the checksum field.
3. Send the data to the corresponding input queue.
4. Return.

Processing Module

The **processing module** is the heart of the IP package. In our design, the processing module receives a datagram from an interface or from the header-adding module. It treats both cases the same. A datagram must be processed and routed regardless of where it comes from.

The processing module first checks to see if the datagram is a loopback packet (with the destination address of 127.X.Y.Z) or a packet that has reached its final destination. In either case, the packet should be sent to the reassembly module.

If the node is a router, it decrements the time-to-live (TTL) field by one. If this value is less than or equal to zero, the datagram is discarded and an ICMP message (see Chapter 9) is sent to the original sender. If the value of TTL is greater than zero after decrement, the processing module sends the datagram to the routing module (see Chapter 6).

Processing Module
1. Remove one datagram from one of the input queues.
2. If (destination address is 127.X.Y.Z or matches one of the local addresses)
1. Send the datagram to the reassembly module.
2. Return.
3. If (machine is a router)
1. Decrement TTL.
4. If (TTL less than or equal to zero)
1. Discard the datagram.
2. Send an ICMP error message.
3. Return.
5. Send the datagram to the routing module.
6. Return.

Queues

Our design uses two types of queues: input queues and output queues. The **input queues** store the datagrams coming from the data link layer or the upper-layer protocols. The **output queues** store the datagrams going to the data link layer or the upper-layer protocols. The processing module dequeues (removes) the datagrams from the input queues. The fragmentation and reassembly modules enqueue (add) the datagrams into the output queues.

Routing Table

We discussed the routing table in Chapter 6. The routing table is used by the routing module to determine the next-hop address of the packet.

Routing Module

We discussed the routing module in Chapter 6. The **routing module** receives an IP packet from the processing module. If the packet is to be forwarded, it should be passed to this module. It finds the IP address of the next station along with the interface number from which the packet should be sent. It then sends the packet with this information to the fragmentation module.

MTU Table

The MTU table is used by the fragmentation module to find the maximum transfer unit of a particular interface. Figure 7.25 shows the format of the MTU table.

Figure 7.25 *MTU table*

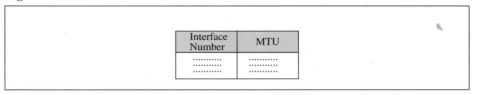

Fragmentation Module

In our design, the **fragmentation module** receives an IP datagram from the routing module. The routing module gives the IP datagram, the IP address of the next station (either the final destination in a direct delivery or the next router in an indirect delivery), and the interface number through which the datagram should be sent out.

The fragmentation module consults the MTU table to find the MTU for the specific interface number. If the length of the datagram is larger than the MTU, the fragmentation module fragments the datagram, adds the header to each fragment, and sends them to the ARP package (see Chapter 8) for address resolution and delivery.

Fragmentation Module
Receive: an IP packet from routing module
1. Extract the size of the datagram.
2. If (size > MTU of the corresponding network)
1. If (D (*do not fragment*) bit is set)
1. Discard the datagram.
2. Send an ICMP error message (see Chapter 9).
3. Return.
2. Else

Fragmentation Module (concluded)
1. Calculate the maximum size.
2. Divide the datagram into fragments.
3. Add header to each fragment.
4. Add required options to each fragment.
5. Send the datagrams.
6. Return.

3. Else

       1. Send the datagram.

4. Return.

Reassembly Table

The **reassembly table** is used by the reassembly module. In our design, the reassembly table has five fields: state, source IP address, datagram ID, time-out, and fragments. See Figure 7.26.

Figure 7.26   *Reassembly table*

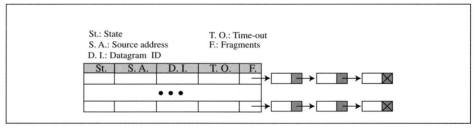

The value of the state field can be either FREE or IN-USE. The IP address field defines the source IP address of the datagram. The datagram ID is a number that uniquely defines a datagram and all of the fragments belonging to that datagram. The time-out is a predetermined amount of time in which all fragments must arrive. Finally, the fragments field is a pointer to a linked list of fragments.

Reassembly Module

The **reassembly module** receives, from the processing module, those datagram fragments that have arrived at their final destinations. In our design, the reassembly module treats an unfragmented datagram as a fragment belonging to a datagram with only one fragment.

Because the IP protocol is a connectionless protocol, there is no guarantee that the fragments arrive in order. Besides, the fragments from one datagram can be intermixed with fragments from another datagram. To keep track of these two tasks, the module uses a reassembly table with associated linked lists, as we described earlier.

The job of the reassembly module is to find the datagram to which a fragment belongs, to order the fragments belonging to the same datagram, and to reassemble all fragments of a datagram when all have arrived. If the established time-out has expired and any fragment is missing, the module discards the fragments.

Reassembly Module
Receive: an IP datagram from the processing module
1. If (offset value is zero and the M bit is 0)
1. Send the datagram to the appropriate queue.
2. Return.
2. Search the reassembly table for the corresponding entry.
3. If (not found)
1. Create a new entry.
4. Insert the fragment at the appropriate place in the link list.
1. If (all fragments have arrived)
1. Reassemble the fragments.
2. Deliver the datagram to the corresponding upper layer protocol.
3. Return.
2. Else
1. Check the time-out.
2. If (time-out expired)
1. Discard all fragments.
2. Send an ICMP error message (see Chapter 9).
5. Return.

7.6 SUMMARY

■ IP is an unreliable connectionless protocol responsible for source-to-destination delivery.

■ Packets in the IP layer are called datagrams.

■ A datagram consists of a header (20 to 60 bytes) and data.

■ The IP header contains the following information: version number, header length, type of service, datagram length, identification number, fragmentation flags, fragmentation offset, time to live, user of the protocol, checksum, source address, and destination address.

■ The maximum length of a datagram is 65,536 bytes.

■ The MTU is the maximum number of bytes that a data link protocol can encapsulate. MTUs vary from protocol to protocol.

- Fragmentation is the division of a datagram into smaller units to accommodate the MTU of a data link protocol.
- The fields in the IP header that relate to fragmentation are the identification number, the fragmentation flags, and the fragmentation offset.
- The IP datagram header consists of a fixed, 20-byte section and a variable options section with a maximum of 40 bytes.
- The options section of the IP header is used for network testing and debugging.
- The options header contains the following information: a code field that identifies the option, option length, and the specific data.
- The six IP options each have a specific function. They are as follows: filler between options for alignment purposes, padding, recording the route the datagram takes, selection of a mandatory route by the sender, selection of certain routers that must be visited, and recording of processing times at routers.
- The error detection method used by IP is the checksum.
- The checksum uses one's complement arithmetic to add equal-size sections of the IP header. The complemented result is stored in the checksum field. The receiver also uses one's complement arithmetic to check the header.
- An IP design can consist of the following: a header-adding module, a processing module, a routing module, a fragmentation module, a reassembly module, a routing table, an MTU table, and a reassembly table.

7.7   PRACTICE SET

Multiple Choice

1. What is the maximum size of the data portion of the IP datagram?
   a. 65,535 bytes
   b. 65,516 bytes
   c. 65,475 bytes
   d. 65,460 bytes
2. A best-effort delivery service such as IP does not include _____.
   a. error checking
   b. error correction
   c. datagram acknowledgment
   d. all of the above
3. An HLEN value of decimal 10 means _____.
   a. there are 10 bytes of options
   b. there are 40 bytes of options
   c. there are 10 bytes in the header
   d. there are 40 bytes in the header

4. What is the value of the total length field if the header is 28 bytes and the data field is 400 bytes?

   a. 428

   b. 407

   c. 107

   d. 427

5. What is the length of the data field given an HLEN value of 12 and total length value of 40,000?

   a. 39,988

   b. 40,012

   c. 40,048

   d. 39,952

6. A datagram is fragmented into three smaller datagrams. Which of the following is true?

   a. The *do not fragment* bit is set to 1 for all three datagrams.

   b. The *more fragment* bit is set to 0 for all three datagrams.

   c. The identification field is the same for all three datagrams.

   d. The offset field is the same for all three datagrams.

7. Which field or bit value unambiguously identifies the datagram as a fragment?

   a. Identification = 1,000

   b. *Do not fragment* bit = 0

   c. *More Fragment* bit = 0

   d. Fragment offset = 1,000

8. If the fragment offset has a value of 100, it means that _____.

   a. the datagram has not been fragmented

   b. the datagram is 100 bytes in size

   c. the first byte of the datagram is byte 100

   d. the first byte of the datagram is byte 800

9. What is needed to determine the number of the last byte of a fragment?

   a. identification number

   b. offset number

   c. total length

   d. b and c

10. The IP header size _____.

   a. is 20 to 60 bytes long

   b. is 20 bytes long

   c. is 60 bytes long

   d. depends on the MTU

11. What is the maximum number of IP addresses recorded if the value of the length field in the record route option is 27?

a. 27

b. 24

c. 12

d. 6

12. Which IP option is used if exactly four specific routers are to handle the datagram?

a. record route

b. strict source route

c. loose source route

d. timestamp

13. Which IP option always lists all routers visited?

a. record route

b. strict source route

c. loose source route

d. a and b

14. In the loose source route option, the number of routers visited may be _____ the number of routers listed.

a. greater than

b. less than

c. equal to

d. a and c

15. In the record route option, the number of routers visited may be _____ the number of routers listed.

a. greater than

b. less than

c. equal to

d. a and c

16. What is the maximum number of routers that can be recorded if the timestamp option has a flag value of 1?

a. 10

b. 9

c. 4

d. unlimited

17. The checksum in the IP packet covers _____.

a. just the header

b. just the data

c. the header and the data

d. just the source and destination addresses

18. If the value of the checksum field in an IP packet is decimal 255, what is the checksum as calculated at the receiver if the packet arrives intact (without error)?

a. 00000000 11111111

    b. 00000000 00000000

    c. 11111111 00000000

    d. 11111111 11111111

19. The _____ module takes fragments of a message and puts them back in order.

    a. processing

    b. routing

    c. fragmentation

    d. reassembly

20. The _____ module sends out an IP packet, the next-hop address, and interface information.

    a. processing

    b. routing

    c. fragmentation

    d. reassembly

21. The _____ module discards datagrams with a TTL value of zero.

    a. processing

    b. routing

    c. fragmentation

    d. reassembly

22. The output of the _____ module is an IP packet destined for an upper layer protocol.

    a. processing

    b. routing

    c. fragmentation

    d. reassembly

23. The _____ module consults the MTU table to determine the packet size necessary for transmission.

    a. processing

    b. routing

    c. fragmentation

    d. reassembly

24. Which module can send an ICMP error message?

    a. processing

    b. reassembly

    c. fragmentation

    d. all of the above

Exercises

25. Which fields of the IP header change from router to router?

26. Calculate the HLEN value if the total length is 1,200 bytes, 1,176 of which is data from the upper layer.

27. Table 7.4 lists the MTUs for many different protocols. The MTUs range from 296 to 65,535. What would be the advantages of having a large MTU? What would be the advantages of having a small MTU?

28. Given a fragmented datagram with an offset of 120, how can you determine the first and last byte number?

29. An IP datagram must go through router 128.46.10.5. There are no other restrictions on the routers to be visited. Draw the IP options with their values.

30. What is the maximum number of routers that can be recorded if the timestamp option has a flag value of 1? Why?

31. Can the value of the header length in an IP packet be less than five? When is it exactly five?

32. The value of the HLEN in an IP datagram is seven. How many option bytes are present?

33. The size of the option field of an IP datagram is 20 bytes. What is the value of HLEN? What is the value in binary?

34. The value of the total length field in an IP datagram is 36 and the value of the header length field is five. How many bytes of data is the packet carrying?

35. A datagram is carrying 1,024 bytes of data. If there is no option information, what is the value of the header length field? What is the value of the total length field?

36. A host is sending 100 datagrams to another host. If the identification number of the first datagram is 1,024, what is the identification number of the last?

37. An IP datagram arrives whose fragmentation offset is 0 and the M bit (more fragment bit) is 0. Is this a fragment?

38. An IP fragment has arrived whose offset value is 100. How many bytes of data were originally sent by the source before the data in this fragment?

39. An IP datagram has arrived with the following information in the header (in hexadecimal):

    45 00 00 54 00 03 00 00 20 06 00 00 7C 4E 03 02 B4 0E 0F 02

    a. Are there any options?
    b. Is the packet fragmented?
    c. What is the size of the data?
    d. Is a checksum used?
    e. How many more routers can the packet travel to?
    f. What is the identification number of the packet?
    g. What is the type of service?

Programming Exercises

40. Create a header file to include all constants that you think are needed to implement the IP modules in C. Use the **#define** directives.

41. Complete the following **struct** declaration for the IP header:

```
struct  IP_Header
{
.....    Ver;
....................
....................
} ;
```

42. Complete the following struct declaration for the IP datagram.

```
struct  IP_Datagram
{
        struct   IP_Header   ipHeader ;
        ..................          ipData ;
} ;
```

43. Write the declaration for an MTU table.

44. Write the declaration for a reassembly table.

45. Write a function in C to calculate the checksum for an IP header.

46. Write a function in C to simulate the header-adding module.

47. Write a function in C to simulate the processing module.

48. Write a function in C to simulate the fragmentation module.

49. Write a function in C to simulate the reassembly module.

CHAPTER 8

ARP and RARP

An internet is made of a combination of physical networks connected together by inter-networking devices such as routers and gateways. A packet starting from a source host may pass through different physical networks before finally reaching the destination host.

The hosts and routers are recognized at the network level by their logical addresses. A **logical address** is an internetwork address. Its jurisdiction is universal. A logical address is unique universally. It is called a *logical* address because it is usually implemented in software. Every protocol that deals with interconnecting networks requires logical addresses. The logical addresses in the TCP/IP protocol suite are called *IP addresses* and are 32 bits long.

However, packets pass through physical networks to reach these hosts and routers. At the physical level, the hosts and routers are recognized by their physical addresses. A physical address is a local address. Its jurisdiction is a local network. It should be unique locally, but not necessary universally. It is called a *physical* address because it is usually (not always) implemented in hardware. Examples of physical addresses are 48-bit MAC addresses in Ethernet and token ring protocols, which are imprinted on the NIC installed in the host or router.

The physical and logical addresses are two different identifiers. We need both of them because a physical network, such as an Ethernet can be used by two different protocols at the network layer such as IP and IPX (Novell) at the same time. Likewise, a packet at the network layer such as IP may pass through different physical networks such as Ethernet and LocalTalk.

This means that delivery of a packet to a host or a router requires two levels of addressing: logical and physical. We need to be able to map a logical address to its corresponding physical address and vice versa. These can be done using either static or dynamic mapping.

Static mapping means creating a table that associates a logical address with a physical address. This table is stored in each machine on the network. Each machine that knows, for example, the IP address of another machine but not its physical address, can look it up in the table. This has some limitations because physical addresses may change in the following ways:

1. A machine could change its NIC resulting in a new physical address.
2. In some LANs, such as LocalTalk, the physical address changes every time the computer is turned on.
3. A mobile computer can move from one physical network to another, resulting in a change in its physical address.

To implement these changes, a static mapping table must be updated periodically. This creates a huge overhead on the network.

In **dynamic mapping** each time a machine knows one of the two addresses (logical or physical), it can use a protocol to find the other one.

Two protocols have been designed to perform dynamic mapping: Address Resolution Protocol (ARP) and Reverse Address Resolution Protocol (RARP). The first maps a logical address to a physical address; the second maps a physical address to a logical address. Figure 8.1 shows the idea.

Figure 8.1   *ARP and RARP*

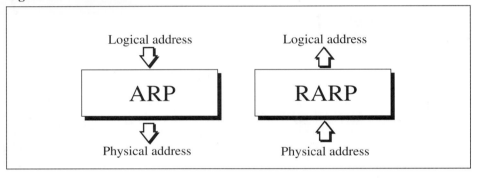

ARP and RARP use unicast and broadcast physical addresses. We discussed unicast and broadcast physical addresses in Chapter 3. We mentioned that, for example, Ethernet uses the all 1s address ($FFFFFFFFFFFF_{16}$) as the broadcast address.

8.1   ARP

Anytime a host or a router has an IP datagram to send to another host or router, it has the logical (IP) address of the receiver. But the IP datagram must be encapsulated in a frame to be able to pass through the physical network. This means that the sender needs the physical address of the receiver. A mapping corresponds a logical address to a physical address.

As we said before, this can be done either statically or dynamically. The association between logical and physical addresses can be statically stored in a table. The sender can look in the table and find the physical address corresponding to a logical address. But as we discussed before, this is not a good solution. Every time a physical address is changed, the table must be updated. Updating tables on all machines at frequent intervals is a very demanding task.

The mapping, however, can be done dynamically, which means that the sender asks the receiver to announce its physical address when needed. The ARP is designed for this purpose.

ARP associates an IP address with its physical address. On a typical physical network, such as a LAN, each device on a link is identified by a physical or station address that is usually imprinted on the NIC.

Anytime a host, or a router, needs to find the physical address of another host or router on its network, it sends an ARP query packet. The packet includes the physical and IP addresses of the sender and the IP address of the receiver. Because the sender does not know the physical address of the receiver, the query is broadcast over the network.

Every host or router on the network receives and processes the ARP query packet, but only the intended recipient recognizes its IP address and sends back an ARP response packet. The response packet contains the recipient's IP and physical addresses. The packet is unicast directly to the inquirer using the physical address received in the query packet (see Figure 8.2).

Figure 8.2 *ARP operation*

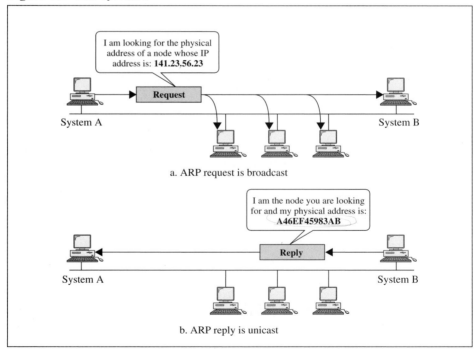

a. ARP request is broadcast

b. ARP reply is unicast

In Figure 8.2a, the system on the left (A) has a packet that should be delivered to another system (B) with IP address 141.23.56.23. System A needs to pass the packet to its data link layer for the actual delivery, but it does not know the physical address of the recipient. It uses the services of ARP by asking the ARP protocol to send a broadcast ARP request packet to ask for the physical address of a system whose IP address is 141.23.56.23.

This packet is received by every system on the physical network, but only system B will answer it, as shown in Figure 8.2b. System B sends an ARP reply packet that includes its physical address. Now system A can send all the packets it has for this destination using the physical address received.

Packet Format

Figure 8.3 shows the format of an ARP packet.

Figure 8.3 *ARP packet*

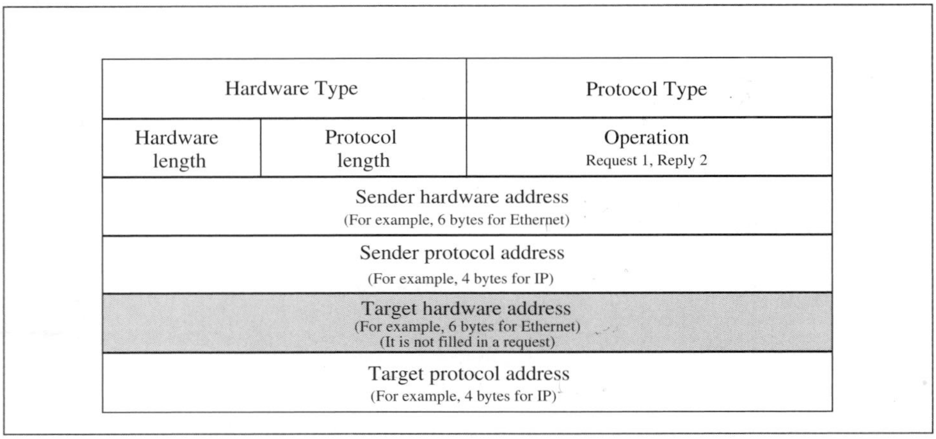

Hardware Type		Protocol Type	
Hardware length	Protocol length	Operation Request 1, Reply 2	
Sender hardware address (For example, 6 bytes for Ethernet)			
Sender protocol address (For example, 4 bytes for IP)			
Target hardware address (For example, 6 bytes for Ethernet) (It is not filled in a request)			
Target protocol address (For example, 4 bytes for IP)			

The fields are as follows:

■ **HTYPE (Hardware type).** This is a 16-bit field defining the type of the network on which ARP is running. Each LAN has been assigned an integer based on its type. For example, Ethernet is given the type 1. ARP can be used on any physical network.

■ **PTYPE (Protocol type).** This is a 16-bit field defining the protocol. For example, the value of this field for the IPv4 protocol is 0800_{16}. ARP can be used with any higher level protocol.

■ **HLEN (Hardware length).** This is an eight-bit field defining the length of the physical address in bytes. For example, for Ethernet the value is six.

■ **PLEN (Protocol length).** This is an eight-bit field defining the length of the logical address in bytes. For example, for the IPv4 protocol the value is four.

■ **OPER (Operation).** This is a 16-bit field defining the type of the packet. Two packet types are defined: ARP request (1), ARP reply (2).

■ **SHA (Sender hardware address).** This is a variable-length field defining the physical address of the sender. For example, for Ethernet this field is six bytes long.

- **SPA (Sender protocol address).** This is a variable-length field defining the logical (for example, IP) address of the sender. For the IP protocol, this field is four bytes long.

- **THA (Target hardware address).** This is a variable-length field defining the physical address of the target. For example, for Ethernet this field is six bytes long. For an ARP request message, this field is all 0s because the sender does not know the physical address of the target.

- **TPA (target protocol address).** This is a variable-length field defining the logical (for example, IP) address of the target. For the IPv4 protocol, this field is four bytes long.

Encapsulation

An ARP packet is encapsulated directly into a data link frame. For example, in Figure 8.4 an ARP packet is encapsulated in an Ethernet frame. Note that the type field indicates that the data carried by the frame is an ARP packet.

Figure 8.4 *Encapsulation of ARP packet*

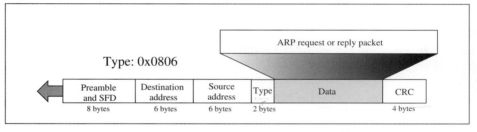

Operation

Let us see how ARP functions on a typical internet. First we describe the steps involved. Then we discuss four cases in which a host or router needs to use ARP.

Steps Involved

These are the steps involved in an ARP process:

1. The sender knows the IP address of the target. We will see how the sender obtains this shortly.

2. IP asks ARP to create a request ARP message, filling in the sender physical address, the sender IP address, and the target IP address. The target physical address field is filled with 0s.

3. The message is passed to the data link layer where it is encapsulated in a frame using the physical address of the sender as the source address and the physical broadcast address as the destination address.

4. Every host or router receives the frame. Because the frame contains a broadcast destination address, all stations remove the message and pass it to ARP. All

machines except the one targeted drop the packet. The target machine recognizes the IP address.

5. The target machine replies with an ARP message that contains its physical address. The message is unicast.

6. The sender receives the reply message. It now knows the physical address of the target machine.

7. The IP datagram, which carries data for the target machine, is now encapsulated in a frame and is unicast to the destination.

Four Different Cases

The following are four different cases in which the services of ARP can be used (see Figure 8.5).

1. The sender is a host and wants to send a packet to another host on the same network. In this case, the logical address that must be mapped to a physical address is the destination IP address in the datagram header.

2. The sender is a host and wants to send a packet to another host on another network. In this case, the host looks at its routing table and finds the IP address of the next hop (router) for this destination. If it does not have a routing table, it looks for the IP address of the default router. The IP address of the router becomes the logical address that must be mapped to a physical address.

3. The sender is a router that has received a datagram destined for a host on another network. It checks its routing table and finds the IP address of the next router. The IP address of the next router becomes the logical address that must be mapped to a physical address.

4. The sender is a router that has received a datagram destined for a host in the same network. The destination IP address of the datagram becomes the logical address that must be mapped to a physical address.

Proxy ARP

A technique called *proxy* (promiscuous) ARP can be used to create a subnetting effect. A **proxy ARP** is an ARP that acts on behalf of a set of hosts. Whenever the router running a proxy ARP receives an ARP request looking for the IP address of one of these hosts, the router sends an ARP reply announcing its own hardware (physical) address. Later when the router receives the actual IP packet, it will send the packet to the appropriate host or router.

Let us give an example. In Figure 8.6 the ARP installed on the right hand host will answer only to an ARP request with a target IP address of 141.23.56.23. We call this behavior *honest*. The other hosts or routers on the network rely on its honesty.

However, the administrator may need to create a subnet without changing the whole system to recognize subnetted addresses. One solution is to add a router running a proxy ARP. In this case, the router acts on behalf of all of the hosts installed on the subnet. When it receives an ARP request with a target IP address that matches the address of one its proteges (141.23.56.21, 141.23.56.22, and 141.23.56.23), it sends an

Figure 8.5   *Four cases using ARP*

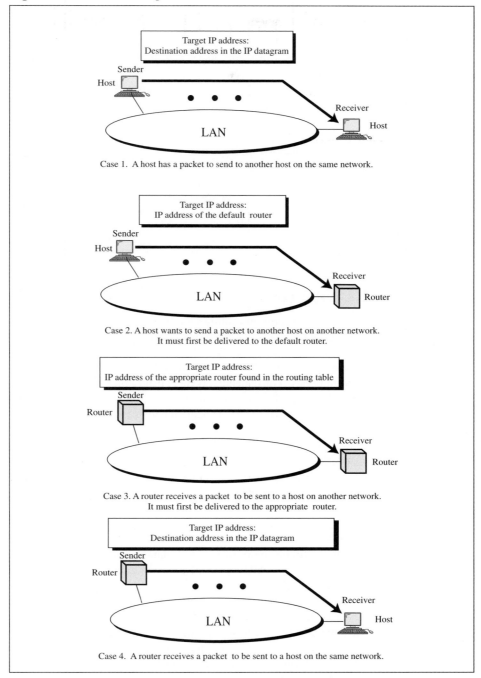

Case 1. A host has a packet to send to another host on the same network.

Case 2. A host wants to send a packet to another host on another network.
It must first be delivered to the default router.

Case 3. A router receives a packet to be sent to a host on another network.
It must first be delivered to the appropriate router.

Case 4. A router receives a packet to be sent to a host on the same network.

An ARP request is broadcast; an ARP reply is unicast.

ARP reply and announces its hardware address as the target hardware address. When the router receives the IP packet, it sends the packet to the appropriate host.

Figure 8.6   *Proxy ARP*

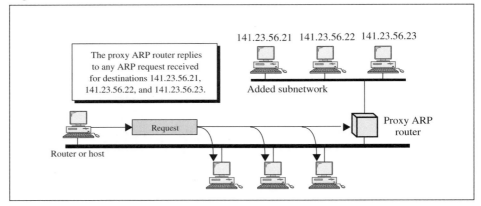

8.2   ARP DESIGN

In this section, we present a simplified, bare-bones ARP. This design is meant to be just a teaching tool. Details such as error checking, error handling, and packet validation have been omitted in an attempt to focus on the basics. Our purpose is to demystify the algorithms and their relationships. In addition, we have sacrificed efficiency for the sake of simplicity. For the actual code consult other literature such as Stevens, *TCP/IP Illustrated,* Volume 2.

We can say that the ARP package involves five components: a cache table, queues, an output module, an input module, and a cache-control module. Figure 8.7 shows these five components and their interactions. The package receives an IP datagram that needs to be encapsulated in a frame, which needs the destination physical (hardware) address. If the ARP package finds this address, it delivers the IP packet and the physical address to the data link layer for transmission.

Cache Table

A sender usually has more than one IP datagram to send to the same destination. It is inefficient to use the ARP protocol for each datagram destined for the same host or router. The solution is the cache table. When a host or router receives the corresponding physical address for an IP datagram, the address can be saved in the cache table. This address can be used for the datagrams destined for the same receiver within the next few minutes. However, as space in the cache table is very limited, mapping in the cache should not be retained for an unlimited time.

The cache table is implemented as an array of entries. In our design, each entry contains the following fields:

Figure 8.7 *ARP components*

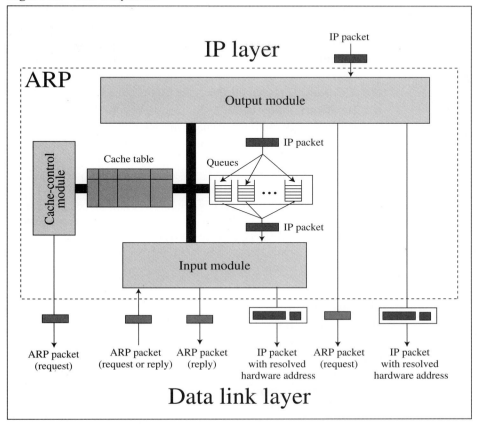

- **State.** This column shows the state of the entry. It can have one of three values: *FREE*, *PENDING*, or *RESOLVED*. The FREE state means that the time-to-live for this entry has expired. The space can be used for a new entry. The PENDING state means a request for this entry has been sent, but the reply has not yet been received. The RESOLVED state means that the entry is complete. The entry now has the physical (hardware) address of the destination. The packets waiting to be sent to this destination can use information in this entry.
- **Hardware type.** This field is the same as the corresponding field in the ARP packet.
- **Protocol type.** This field is the same as the corresponding field in the ARP packet.
- **Hardware length.** This field is the same as the corresponding field in the ARP packet.
- **Protocol length.** This field is the same as the corresponding field in the ARP packet.
- **Interface number.** A router (or a multihomed host) can be connected to different networks, each with a different interface number. Each network can have different hardware and protocol types.

- **Queue number.** ARP uses different queues to enqueue the packets waiting for address resolution. Packets for the same destination are usually enqueued in the same queue. The queue number refers to the queue whose packets are waiting for this entry to be resolved.
- **Attempts.** This column shows how many times an ARP request is sent out for this entry.
- **Time-out.** This column shows the lifetime of an entry in seconds.
- **Hardware address.** This column shows the destination hardware address. It remains empty until resolved by an ARP reply.
- **Protocol address.** This column shows the destination IP address.

Queues

In our design, the ARP package maintains a set of queues, one for each destination, to hold the IP packets while ARP tries to resolve the hardware address. The output module sends unresolved packets into the corresponding queue. The input module removes a packet from a queue and sends it, with the resolved physical address, to the data link layer for transmission.

Output Module

The **output module** waits for an IP packet from the IP software. The output module checks the cache table to find an entry corresponding to the destination IP address of this packet. The destination IP address of the IP packet must match the protocol address of the entry.

   If the entry is found and the state of the entry is RESOLVED, the packet along with the destination hardware address is passed to the data link layer for transmission.

   If the entry is found and the state of the entry is PENDING, the packet should wait until the destination hardware address is found. Because the state is PENDING, there is a queue already created for this destination. The module sends the packet to the corresponding queue.

   If no entry is found, the module creates a queue and enqueues the packet. A new entry with the state of PENDING is created for this destination and the value of the ATTEMPTS field is set to 1. An ARP request packet is then broadcast.

Output Module
1. Sleep until an IP packet is received from IP software.
2. Check the cache table to find an entry corresponding to this IP packet.
3. If (found)
1. If (the state is RESOLVED)
1. Extract the value of the hardware address from the entry.
2. Send the packet and the hardware address to data link layer.
3. Return.

Output Module (concluded)
2. If (the state is PENDING)
1. Enqueue the packet to the corresponding queue.
2. Return.
4. If (not found)
1. Create a queue.
2. Enqueue the packet.
3. Create a cache entry with state set to PENDING and ATTEMPTS set to 1.
4. Send an ARP request.
5. Return.

Input Module

The **input module** waits until an ARP packet (request or reply) arrives. The input module checks the cache table to find an entry corresponding to this ARP packet. The target protocol address should match the protocol address of the entry.

If the entry is found and the state of the entry is PENDING, the module updates the entry by copying the target hardware address in the packet to the hardware address field of the entry and changing the state to RESOLVED. The module also sets the value of the time-out for this entry. It then dequeues the packets from the corresponding queue, one by one, and delivers them along with the hardware address to the data link layer for transmission.

If the entry is found and the state is RESOLVED, the module still updates the entry. This is because the target hardware address could have been changed. The value of the TIME-OUT field is also reset.

If the entry is not found, the module creates a new entry and adds it to the table. The protocol requires that any information received should be added to the table for future use. The state is set to RESOLVED and TIME-OUT is set.

Now the module checks to see if the arrived ARP packet is a request. If it is, the module immediately creates an ARP reply message and sends it to the sender. The ARP reply packet is created by changing the value of the operation field from request to reply and filling in the target hardware address.

Input Module
1. Sleep until an ARP packet (request or reply) arrives.
2. Check the cache table to find an entry corresponding to this ARP packet.
3. If (found)
1. If (the state is PENDING)
1. Update the entry.

Input Module (concluded)
2. While the queue is not empty
1. Dequeue one packet.
2. Send the packet and the hardware address to data link.
2. If (the state is RESOLVED)
1. Update the entry.
4. If (not found)
1. Create an entry.
2. Add the entry to the table.
5. If (the packet is a request)
1. Send an ARP reply.
6. Return.

Cache-Control Module

The **cache-control module** is responsible for maintaining the cache table. It periodically (for example, every five seconds) checks the cache table, entry by entry.

If the state of the entry is FREE, it continues to the next entry. If the state is PENDING, the module increments the value of the attempts field by 1. It then checks the value of the attempts field. If this value is greater than the maximum number of attempts allowed, the state is changed to FREE and the corresponding queue is destroyed. However, if the number of attempts is less than the maximum, the module creates and sends another ARP request.

If the state of the entry is RESOLVED, the module decrements the value of the time-out field by the amount of time elapsed since the last check. If this value is less than or equal to zero, the state is changed to FREE and the queue is destroyed.

Cache-Control Module
1. Sleep until the periodic timer matures.
2. For every entry in the cache table
1. If (the state is FREE)
1. Continue.
2. If (the state is PENDING)
1. Increment the value of attempts by 1.
2. If (attempts greater than maximum)
1. Change the state to FREE.
2. Destroy the corresponding queue.
3. If (not)

Cache-Control Module (concluded)
1. Send an ARP request.
4. Continue.
3. If (the state is RESOLVED)
1. Decrement the value of time-out by the value of elapsed time.
2. If (time-out less than or equal to zero)
1. Change the state to FREE.
2. Destroy the corresponding queue.
3. Return.

Examples of ARP

Table 8.1 shows some of the fields of the beginning cache table.

Table 8.1   *Original cache table used for examples*

State	Queue	Attempt	Time-out	Protocol Addr.	Hardware Addr.
R	5		900	180.3.6.1	ACAE32457342
P	2	2		129.34.4.8	
P	14	5		201.11.56.7	
R	8		450	114.5.7.89	457342ACAE32
P	12	1		220.55.5.7	
F					
R	9		60	19.1.7.82	4573E3242ACA
P	18	3		188.11.8.71	

Example 1

The ARP output module receives an IP datagram (from the IP layer) with the destination address 114.5.7.89. It checks the cache table and finds that an entry exists for this destination with the state of RESOLVED (R in the table). It extracts the hardware address, which is 457342ACAE32, and sends the packet and the address to the data link layer for transmission. The cache table remains the same.

Example 2

Twenty seconds later, the ARP output module receives an IP datagram (from the IP layer) with the destination address 116.1.7.22. It checks the cache table and does not find this destination in the table. The module adds an entry to the table with the state PENDING and the attempts value one. It creates a new queue for this destination and enqueues the packet. It then sends an ARP request to the data link layer for this destination. The new cache table is shown in Table 8.2.

Table 8.2   *Updated cache table for example 2*

State	Queue	Attempt	Time-out	Protocol Addr.	Hardware Addr.
R	5		900	180.3.6.1	ACAE32457342
P	2	2		129.34.4.8	
P	14	5		201.11.56.7	
R	8		450	114.5.7.89	457342ACAE32
P	12	1		220.55.5.7	
P	**23**	**1**		**116.1.7.22**	
R	9		60	19.1.7.82	4573E3242ACA
P	18	3		188.11.8.71	

Example 3

Fifteen seconds later, the ARP input module receives an ARP packet with target protocol (IP) address 188.11.8.71. The module checks the table and finds this address. It changes the state of the entry to RESOLVED and sets the time-out value to 900. The module then adds the target hardware address (E34573242ACA) to the entry. Now it accesses queue 18 and sends all the packets in this queue, one by one, to the data link layer. The new cache table is shown in Table 8.3.

Table 8.3   *Updated cache table for example 3*

State	Queue	Attempt	Time-out	Protocol Addr.	Hardware Addr.
R	5		900	180.3.6.1	ACAE32457342
P	2	2		129.34.4.8	
P	14	5		201.11.56.7	
R	8		450	114.5.7.89	457342ACAE32
P	12	1		220.55.5.7	
P	23	1		116.1.7.22	
R	9		60	19.1.7.82	4573E3242ACA
R	**18**		**900**	**188.11.8.71**	**E34573242ACA**

Example 4

Twenty-five seconds later, the cache-control module updates every entry. The time-out values for the four resolved entries are decremented by 60. The state of the next-to-the last entry is changed to FREE, because the time-out is zero. For each of the three entries, the value of the attempts field is incremented by one. After incrementing, the attempts value for one entry (the one with IP protocol address 201.11.56.7) is more than the maximum; the state is changed to FREE, the queue is deleted, and an ICMP message is sent to the original destination (see Chapter 9). See Table 8.4.

Table 8.4 *Updated cache table for example 4*

State	Queue	Attempt	Time-out	Protocol Addr.	Hardware Addr.
R	5		840	180.3.6.1	ACAE32457342
P	2	3		129.34.4.8	
F					
R	8		390	114.5.7.89	457342ACAE32
P	12	2		220.55.5.7	
P	23	2		116.1.7.22	
F					
P	18		840	188.11.8.71	E34573242ACA

8.3 RARP

The RARP is designed to resolve the address mapping problem in which a machine knows its physical address but does not know its logical address.

Each host or router is assigned one or more logical (IP) addresses, which are unique and independent of the physical (hardware) address of the machine. To create an IP datagram, a host or a router needs to know its own IP address or addresses. The IP address of a machine is usually read from its configuration file stored on a disk file.

However, a diskless machine is usually booted from ROM, which has minimum booting information. The ROM is installed by the manufacturer. It cannot include the IP address because the IP addresses on a network are assigned by the administrator.

The machine can get its physical address (by reading its NIC, for example), which is unique locally. It can then use the physical address to get the logical address using the RARP protocol. A RARP request is created and broadcast on the local network. Another machine on the local network that knows all the IP addresses will respond with a RARP reply. The requesting machine must be running a RARP client program; the responding machine must be running a RARP server program (see Figure 8.8).

In Figure 8.8a, the diskless host on the left is booted. To get its IP address, it broadcasts a RARP request to all systems on the network.

This packet will be received by every host (or router) on the physical network, but only the RARP server on the right will answer it as shown in Figure 8.8b. The server sends a RARP reply packet including the IP address of the requestor.

Packet Format

The format of the RARP packet is exactly the same as the ARP packet except that the operation field is either three (RARP request) or four (RARP reply). See Figure 8.9.

Figure 8.8 *RARP operation*

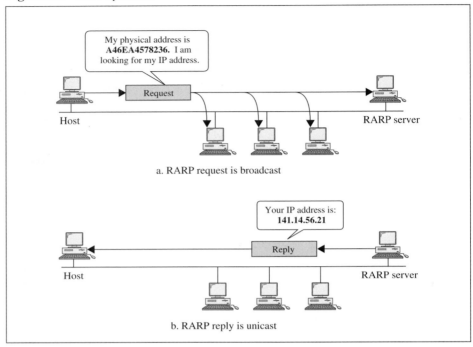

a. RARP request is broadcast

b. RARP reply is unicast

The RARP request packets are broadcast; the RARP reply packets are unicast.

Figure 8.9 *RARP packet*

Hardware type		Protocol type	
Hardware length	Protocol length	Operation Request 3, Reply 4	
Sender hardware address (For example, 6 bytes for Ethernet)			
Sender protocol address (For example, 4 bytes for IP) (It is not filled for request)			
Target hardware address (For example, 6 bytes for Ethernet) (It is not filled for request)			
Target protocol address (For example, 4 bytes for IP) (It is not filled for request)			

Encapsulation

A RARP packet is encapsulated directly into a data link frame. For example, Figure 8.10 shows a RARP packet encapsulated in an Ethernet frame. Note that the type field shows that the data carried by the frame is a RARP packet.

Figure 8.10   *Encapsulation of RARP packet*

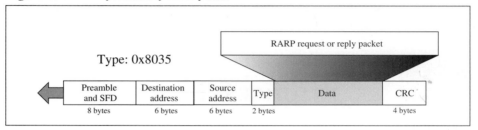

Alternative Solutions to RARP

When a diskless computer is booted, it needs more information in addition to its IP address. It needs to know its subnet mask, the IP address of a router, and the IP address of a name server. RARP cannot provide this extra information. New protocols have been developed to provide this information. In Chapter 15 we discuss two protocols, BOOTP and DHCP, that can be used instead of RARP.

8.4   SUMMARY

■ Delivery of a packet to a host or router requires two levels of addresses: logical and physical.

■ A logical address identifies a host or router at the network level. TCP/IP calls this logical address an IP address.

■ A physical address identifies a host or router at the physical level.

■ Mapping of a logical address to a physical address can be static or dynamic.

■ Static mapping involves a list of logical and physical address correspondences; maintenance of the list requires high overhead.

■ Address resolution protocol (ARP) is a dynamic mapping method that finds a physical address given a logical address.

■ An ARP request is broadcast to all devices on the network.

■ An ARP reply is unicast to the host requesting the mapping.

■ In proxy ARP (promiscuous ARP) a router represents a set of hosts. When an ARP request seeks the physical address of any host in this set, the router sends its own physical address. This creates a subnetting effect.

■ The ARP software package consists of five components: a cache table, queues, an output module, an input module, and a cache-control module.

■ The cache table has an array of entries used and updated by ARP messages.

- A queue contains packets going to the same destination.
- The output module takes a packet from the IP layer and sends it either to the data link layer or to a queue.
- The input module uses an ARP packet to update the cache table. The input module can also send an ARP reply.
- The cache control module maintains the cache table by updating entry statistics.
- Reverse address resolution protocol (RARP) is a form of dynamic mapping in which a given physical address is associated with a logical address.

8.5   PRACTICE SET

Multiple Choice

1. In _____ a protocol associates a logical address with a physical address.
   a. static mapping
   b. dynamic mapping
   c. physical mapping
   d. a and b

2. In _____ a table associating a logical address with a physical address is maintained on all devices on a network.
   a. static mapping
   b. dynamic mapping
   c. physical mapping
   d. a and b

3. The _____ is a dynamic mapping protocol in which a logical address is found for a given physical address.
   a. ARP
   b. RARP
   c. ICMP
   d. none of the above

4. The _____ is a dynamic mapping protocol in which a physical address is found for a given logical address.
   a. ARP
   b. RARP
   c. ICMP
   d. none of the above

5. A router reads the _____ address on a packet to determine the next hop.
   a. logical
   b. physical

   c. source

   d. ARP

6. The target hardware address on an Ethernet is _____ in an ARP request.

   a. 0x000000000000

   b. 0.0.0.0

   c. variable

   d. class dependent

7. An ARP reply is _____ to _____.

   a. broadcast; all hosts

   b. multicast; one host

   c. unicast; all hosts

   d. unicast; one host

8. An ARP request is _____ to _____.

   a. broadcast; all hosts

   b. multicast; one host

   c. unicast; all hosts

   d. unicast; one host

9. What does a router running proxy ARP and representing 10 hosts return in the target hardware address field in an ARP reply?

   a. any of 10 different hardware addresses

   b. any of 11 different hardware addresses

   c. just the router hardware address

   d. just the router IP address

10. The ARP component that sends an ARP reply to the data link layer is the _____.

   a. cache controller

   b. input module

   c. output module

   d. a and b

11. The ARP component that sends an IP packet to a queue is the _____.

   a. cache controller

   b. input module

   c. output module

   d. a and b

12. ARP packets are sent to the data link layer by the _____.

   a. cache-control module

   b. input module

   c. output module

   d. all of the above

13. An ARP packet from the data link layer goes to the _____.

   a. cache-control module

b. input module

c. output module

d. a and c

14. An IP packet goes directly from the _____ to the data link layer if the state of the entry is RESOLVED.

a. cache-control module

b. input module

c. output module

d. a and c

Exercises

15. Is the size of the ARP packet fixed? Explain.

16. Is the size of the RARP packet fixed? Explain.

17. What is the size of an ARP packet when the protocol is IP and the hardware is Ethernet?

18. What is the size of a RARP packet when the protocol is IP and the hardware is Ethernet?

19. What is the size of an Ethernet frame carrying an ARP packet?

20. What is the size of an Ethernet frame carrying a RARP packet?

21. What is the broadcast address for Ethernet?

22. A router with IP address 125.45.23.12 and Ethernet physical address 2345AB4F67CD has received a packet for a host destination with IP address 125.11.78.10 and Ethernet physical address AABBA24F67CD. Show the entries in the ARP request packet sent by the router. Assume no subnetting.

23. Show the entries in the ARP packet sent in response to exercise 22.

24. Encapsulate the result of exercise 22 in a data link frame. Fill in all the fields.

25. Encapsulate the result of exercise 23 in a data link frame. Fill in all the fields.

26. A router with IP address 195.5.2.12 and Ethernet physical address AA25AB1F67CD has received a packet for a destination with IP address 185.11.78.10. When the router checks its routing table, it finds out the packet should be delivered to a router with IP address 195.5.2.6 and Ethernet physical address AD345D4F67CD. Show the entries in the ARP request packet sent by the router. Assume no subnetting.

27. Show the entries in the ARP packet sent in response to exercise 26.

28. Encapsulate the result of exercise 26 in a data link frame. Fill in all the fields.

29. Encapsulate the result of exercise 27 in a data link frame. Fill in all the fields.

30. A diskless host with an Ethernet physical address 9845234F67CD has been booted. Show the entries in the RARP packet sent by this host.

31. Show the entries in the RARP packet sent in response to exercise 30 Assume that the IP address of the requesting host is 200.67.89.33. Choose appropriate physical

and logical addresses for the server. Assume the server is on the same network as the requesting host.

32. Encapsulate the result of exercise 30 in a data link frame. Fill in all the fields.

33. Encapsulate the result of exercise 31 in a data link frame. Fill in all the fields.

Programming Exercises

34. Create a header file to include all constants that you think are needed to implement the ARP module in C. Use the **#define** directives.

35. Complete the following struct declaration. It is a declaration for the ARP packet.

```
struct  ARP
{
unsigned short    HardwareType ;
...............................................
...............................................
} ;
```

36. Write the declaration for the cache table entry.

37. Write the declaration for the cache table.

38. Write a function in C to simulate the cache-control module.

39. Write a function in C to simulate the input module.

40. Write a function in C to simulate the output module.

CHAPTER 9

Internet Control Message Protocol (ICMP)

As discussed in Chapter 7, the IP provides an unreliable and connectionless datagram delivery. It was designed this way to make efficient use of network resources. The IP protocol is a best-effort delivery service that delivers a datagram from its original source to its final destination. However, it has two deficiencies: lack of error control and lack of assistance mechanisms.

The IP protocol has no error-reporting or error-correcting mechanism. What happens if something goes wrong? What happens if a router must discard a datagram because it cannot find a router to the final destination, or because the time-to-live field has a zero value? What happens if the final destination host must discard all fragments of a datagram because it has not received all fragments within a predetermined time limit? These are examples of situations where an error has occurred and the IP protocol has no built-in mechanism to notify the original host.

The IP protocol also lacks a mechanism for host and management queries. A host sometimes needs to determine if a router or another host is alive. And sometimes a network manager needs information from another host or router.

The Internet Control Message Protocol (ICMP) has been designed to compensate for the above two deficiencies. It is a companion to the IP protocol. Figure 9.1 shows the position of ICMP in relation to IP and other protocols in the network layer.

Figure 9.1 *Position of ICMP in the network layer*

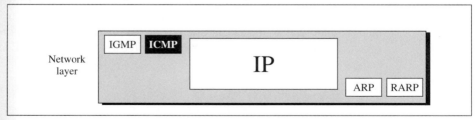

ICMP itself is a network layer protocol. However, its messages are not passed directly to the data link layer as would be expected. Instead, the messages are first encapsulated inside IP datagrams before going to the lower layer (see Figure 9.2).

Figure 9.2   *ICMP encapsulation*

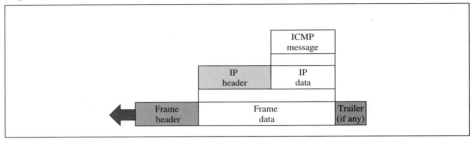

The value of the protocol field in the IP datagram is 1 to indicate that the IP data is an ICMP message.

9.1   TYPES OF MESSAGES

ICMP messages are divided into two broad categories: error-reporting messages and query messages as shown in Figure 9.3.

Figure 9.3   *ICMP messages*

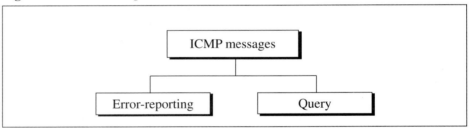

The error-reporting messages report problems that a router or a host (destination) may encounter when it processes an IP packet.

The query messages, which occur in pairs, help a host or a network manager get specific information from a router or another host. For example, nodes can discover their neighbors. Also, hosts can discover and learn about routers on their network and routers can help a node redirect its messages. Table 9.1 lists the ICMP messages in each category.

Table 9.1   *ICMP messages*

Category	Type	Message
Error-reporting messages	3	Destination unreachable
	4	Source quench
	11	Time exceeded
	12	Parameter problem
	5	Redirection

Table 9.1 *ICMP messages (concluded)*

Category	Type	Message
Query messages	8 or 0	Echo request or reply
	13 or 14	Timestamp request and reply
	17 or 18	Address mask request and reply
	10 or 9	Router solicitation and advertisement

9.2   MESSAGE FORMAT

An ICMP message has an eight-byte header and a variable-size data section. Although the general format of the header is different for each message type, the first four bytes are common to all. As Figure 9.4 shows, the first field, ICMP type, defines the type of the message. The code field specifies the reason for the particular message type. The last common field is the checksum field (to be discussed later in the chapter). The rest of the header is specific for each message type.

The data section in error messages carries information for finding the original packet which caused the error. In query messages, the data section carries extra information based on the type of the query.

Figure 9.4   *General format of ICMP messages*

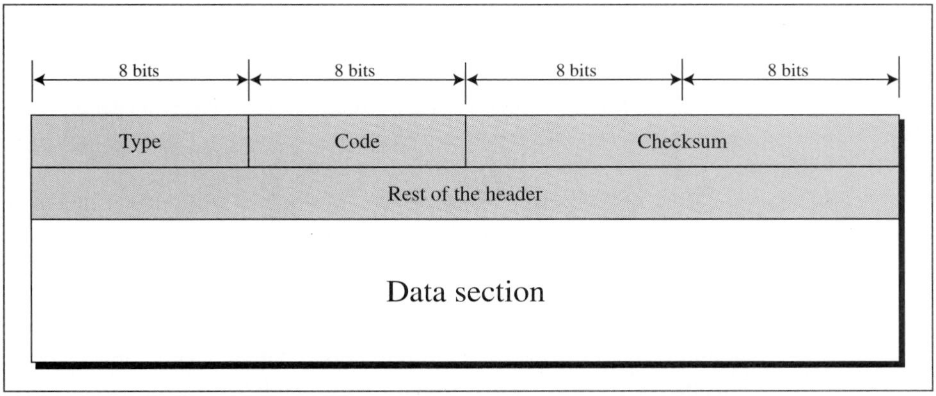

9.3   ERROR REPORTING

One of the main responsibilities of ICMP is to report errors. Although technology has produced increasingly reliable transmission media, errors still exist and must be handled. IP, as discussed in Chapter 7, is an unreliable protocol. This means that error checking and error control are not a concern of IP. ICMP was designed, in part, to compensate for this shortcoming. However, ICMP does not correct errors; it simply reports them. Error correction is left to the higher level protocols. Error messages are always sent to the original source because the only information available in the datagram about the route is the source and destination IP addresses. The ICMP uses the source IP address to send the error message to the source (originator) of the datagram.

ICMP always reports error messages to the original source.

Five types of errors are handled: destination unreachable, source quench, time exceeded, parameter problems, and redirection. See Figure 9.5.

Figure 9.5   *Error-reporting messages*

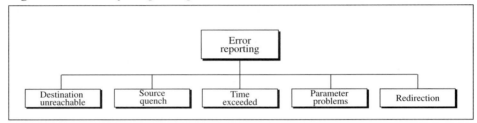

The following are important points about ICMP error messages:

■ No ICMP error message will be generated in response to a datagram carrying an ICMP error message.

■ No ICMP error message will be generated for a fragmented datagram that is not the first fragment.

■ No ICMP error message will be generated for a datagram having a multicast address.

■ No ICMP error message will be generated for a datagram having a special address such as 127.0.0.0 or 0.0.0.0.

Note that all error messages contain a data section that includes the IP header of the original datagram plus the first eight bytes of data in that datagram. The original datagram header is added to give the original source, which receives the error message, information about the datagram itself. The eight bytes of data are included because, as we will see in Chapters 11 and 12 on UDP and TCP protocols, the first eight bytes provide information about the port numbers (UDP and TCP) and sequence number (TCP). This information is needed so the source can inform the protocols (TCP or UDP) about the error situation. ICMP forms an error packet, which is then encapsulated in an IP datagram (see Figure 9.6).

Destination Unreachable

When a router cannot route a datagram or a host cannot deliver a datagram, the datagram is discarded and the router or the host sends a destination unreachable message back to the source host that initiated the datagram. Figure 9.7 shows the format of the destination unreachable message. The code field for this type specifies the reason for discarding the datagram:

Figure 9.6   *Contents of data field for the error messages*

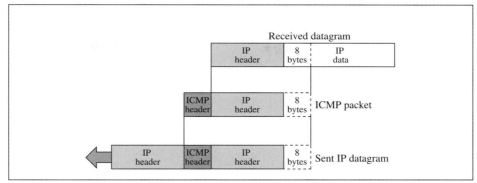

Figure 9.7   *Destination unreachable format*

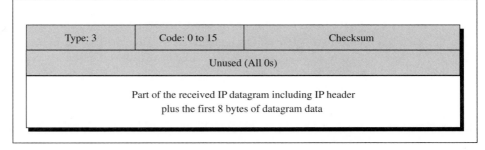

■   **Code 0.** The network is unreachable, possibly due to hardware failure. This type of message can only be generated by a router.

■   **Code 1.** The host is unreachable. This can also be due to hardware failure. This type of message can only be generated by a router.

■   **Code 2.** The protocol is unreachable. An IP datagram can carry data belonging to higher level protocols such as UDP, TCP, and OSPF. If the destination host receives a datagram that must be delivered, for example, to the TCP protocol, but the TCP protocol is not running at the moment, a code 2 message is sent. This type of message is generated only by the destination host.

■   **Code 3.** The port is unreachable. The application program (process) that the datagram is destined for is not running at the moment.

■   **Code 4.** Fragmentation is required, but the DF (do not fragment) field of the datagram has been set. In other words, the sender of the datagram has specified that the datagram should not be fragmented, but routing is impossible without fragmentation.

■   **Code 5.** Source routing cannot be accomplished. In other words, one or more routers defined in the source routing option cannot be visited.

■   **Code 6.** The destination network is unknown. This is different from code 0. In code 0, the router knows that the destination network exists, but it is unreachable at the moment. For code 6, the router has no information about the destination network.

■ **Code 7.** The destination host is unknown. This is different from code 1. In code 1, the router knows that the destination host exists, but it is unreachable at the moment. For code 7, the router is unaware of the existence of the destination host.

■ **Code 8.**   The source host is isolated.

■ **Code 9.** Communication with the destination network is administratively prohibited.

■ **Code 10.** Communication with the destination host is administratively prohibited.

■ **Code 11.** The network is unreachable for the specified type of service. This is different from code 0. Here the router can route the datagram if the source had requested an available type of service.

■ **Code 12.** The host is unreachable for the specified type of service. This is different from code 1. Here the router can route the datagram if the source had requested an available type of service.

■ **Code 13.** The host is unreachable because the administration has put a filter on it.

■ **Code 14.** The host is unreachable because the host precedence is violated. The message is sent by a router to indicate that the requested precedence is not permitted for the destination.

■ **Code 15.** The host is unreachable because its precedence was cut off. This message is generated when the network operators have imposed a minimum level of precedence for the operation of the network, but the datagram was sent with a precedence below this level.

Note that destination-unreachable messages can be created either by a router or the destination host. Code 2 or 3 messages can be created only by the destination host; the messages with the remaining codes can be created only by routers.

> Destination-unreachable messages with codes 2 or 3 can be created only by the destination host. Other destination-unreachable messages can be created only by routers.

Note that even if a router does not report a destination-unreachable message, it does not necessarily mean that the datagram has been delivered. For example, if a datagram is traveling through an Ethernet network, there is no way that a router knows that the datagram has been delivered to the destination host or the next router because Ethernet does not provide any acknowledgment mechanism.

> A router cannot detect all problems that prevent the delivery of a packet.

Source Quench

The IP protocol is a connectionless protocol. There is no communication between the source host, which produces the datagram, the routers, which forward it, and the destination host, which processes it. One of the ramifications of this lack of communication is lack of *flow control*. IP does not have a flow-control mechanism embedded in the protocol. The lack of flow control can create a major problem in the operation of IP: congestion. The source host never knows if the routers or the destination host have been overwhelmed with datagrams. The source host never knows if it is producing datagrams faster than they can be forwarded by routers or processed by the destination host.

> There is no flow-control mechanism in the IP protocol.

The lack of flow control can create congestion in routers or the destination host. A router or a host has a limited-size queue (buffer) for incoming datagrams waiting to be forwarded (in the case of a router) or to be processed (in the case of a host). If the datagrams are received much faster than they can be forwarded or processed, the queue may overflow. In this case, the router or the host has no choice but to discard some of the datagrams.

The source-quench message in ICMP has been designed to add a kind of flow control to the IP. When a router or host discards a datagram due to congestion, it sends a source-quench message to the sender of the datagram. This message has two purposes. First, it informs the source that the datagram has been discarded. Second, it warns the source that there is congestion somewhere in the path and that the source should slow down (quench) the sending process. The source-quench format is shown in Figure 9.8.

> A source-quench message informs the source that a datagram has been discarded due to congestion in a router or the destination host. The source must slow down the sending of datagrams until the congestion is relieved.

Figure 9.8   *Source-quench format*

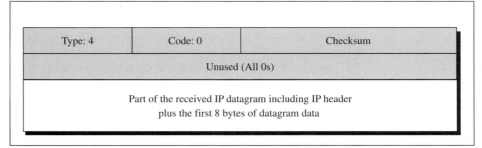

There are some points that deserve more explanation. First, the router or destination host that has experienced the congestion should send one source-quench message for each discarded datagram to the source host. Second, there is no mechanism to tell the source that the congestion has been relieved and the source can resume sending datagrams at its previous rate. The source should continue to lower the rate until no more source-quench messages are received. Third, the congestion can be created either by a one-to-one or many-to-one communication. In a one-to-one communication, a single high-speed host could create datagrams faster than a router or the destination host can handle. In this case, source-quench messages can be helpful. They tell the source to slow down. In a many-to-one communication, many sources create datagrams that must be handled by a router or the destination host. In this case, each source can be sending datagrams at different speeds, some of them at a low rate, others at a high rate. In this case, the source-quench message may not be very useful. The router or the destination host has no clue which source is responsible for the congestion. It may drop a datagram from a very slow source instead of dropping the datagram from the source that has actually created the congestion.

> One source-quench message should be sent for each datagram that is discarded due to congestion.

Time Exceeded

The time-exceeded message is generated in two cases:

■ As we saw in Chapter 6, routers use routing tables to find the next hop (next router) that must receive the packet. If there are errors in one or more routing tables, a packet can travel in a loop or a cycle, going from one router to the next or visiting a series of routers endlessly. As we saw in Chapter 7, each datagram contains a field called *time to live* that controls this situation. When a datagram visits a router, the value of this field is decremented by 1. The router that receives a datagram with a value of 0 in this field discards the datagram. However, when the datagram is discarded, a time-exceeded message must be sent by the router to the original source.

> Whenever a router receives a datagram whose time-to-live field has the value of zero, it discards the datagram and sends a time-exceeded message to the original source.

■ Second, a time-exceeded message is also generated when all fragments that make up a message do not arrive at the destination host within a certain time limit. When the first fragment arrives, the destination host starts a timer. If all the fragments have not arrived when the time expires, the destination discards all the fragments and sends a time-exceeded message to the original sender.

> When the final destination does not receive all of the fragments in a set time, it discards the received fragments and sends a time-exceeded message to the original source.

Figure 9.9 shows the format of the time-exceeded message. Code 0 is used when the datagram is discarded by the router due to a time-to-live field value of zero. Code 1 is used when arrived fragments of a datagram are discarded because some fragments have not arrived within the time limit.

> In a time-exceeded message, code 0 is used only by routers to show that the value of the time-to-live field is zero. Code 1 is used only by the destination host to show that not all of the fragments have arrived within a set time.

Figure 9.9   *Time-exceeded message format*

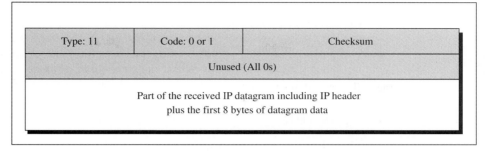

Parameter Problem

Any ambiguity in the header part of a datagram can create serious problems as the datagram travels through the Internet. If a router or the destination host discovers an ambiguous or missing value in any field of the datagram, it discards the datagram and sends a parameter-problem message back to the source.

A parameter-problem message can be created by a router or the destination host.

Figure 9.10 shows the format of the parameter-problem message. The code field in this case specifies the reason for discarding the datagram and shows exactly what has failed:

■   **Code 0.** There is error or ambiguity in one of the header fields. In this case, the value in the pointer field points to the byte with the problem. For example, if the value is zero, then the first byte is not a valid field.

■   **Code 1.** The required part of an option is missing. In this case, the pointer is not used.

Figure 9.10   *Parameter-problem message format*

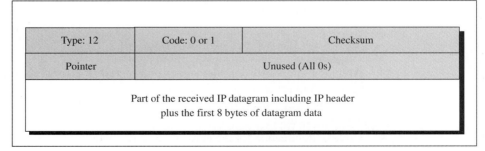

Redirection

When a router needs to send a packet destined for another network, it must know the IP address of the next appropriate router. The same is true if the sender is a host. Both routers and hosts then must have a routing table to find the address of the router or the next router. Routers take part in the routing update process as we will see in Chapter 13 and are supposed to be updated constantly. Routing is dynamic.

However, for efficiency, hosts do not take part in the routing update process because there are many more hosts in an internet than routers. Updating the routing tables of hosts dynamically produces unacceptable traffic. The hosts usually use static routing. When a host comes up, its routing table has a limited number of entries. It usually knows only the IP address of one router, the default router. For this reason, the host may send a datagram, which is destined for another network, to the wrong router. In this case, the router that receives the datagram will forward the datagram to the correct router. However, to update the routing table of the host, it sends a redirection message to the host. This concept of redirection is shown in Figure 9.11. Host A wants to send a datagram to host B. Router R2 is obviously the most efficient routing choice, but host A did not choose router R2. The datagram goes to R1 instead. R1, after consulting its table, finds that the packet should have gone to R2. It sends the packet to R2 and, at the same time, sends a redirection message to host A. Host A's routing table can now be updated.

Figure 9.11   *Redirection concept*

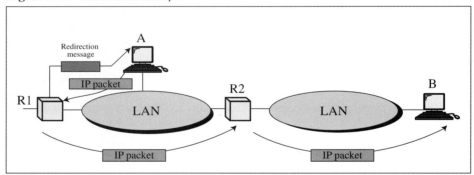

A host usually starts with a small routing table that is gradually augmented and updated. One of the tools to accomplish this is the redirection message.

The format of the redirection message is shown in Figure 9.12. Note that the IP address of the appropriate target is given in the second row.

Although the redirection message is considered an error-reporting message, it is different from other error messages. The router does not discard the datagram in this case; it is sent to the appropriate router. The code field for redirection message narrows down the redirection:

■   **Code 0.** Redirection for the network-specific route.

■   **Code 1.** Redirection for host-specific route.

■   **Code 2.** Redirection for network-specific route based on the specified type of service.

■   **Code 3.** Redirection for the host-specific route based on the specified type of service.

Figure 9.12 *Redirection message format*

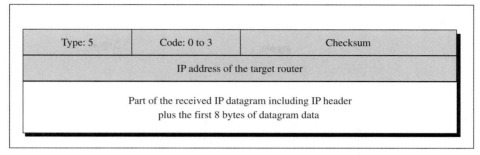

A redirection message is sent from a router to a host on the same local network.

9.4 QUERY

In addition to error reporting, ICMP can also diagnose some network problems. This is accomplished through the query messages, a group of four different pairs of messages, as shown in Figure 9.13. In this type of ICMP message, a node sends a message that is answered in a specific format by the destination node. Note that originally two other types of messages (information request and information reply) were defined, but they are now obsolete. They were designed to allow a host to get its Internet address at startup; this function is now performed by RARP (see Chapter 8) and BOOTP (see Chapter 15).

Figure 9.13 *Query messages*

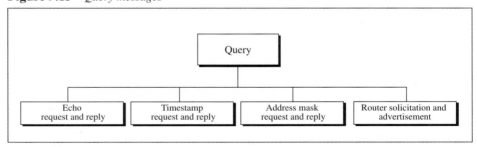

Echo Request and Reply

The echo-request and echo-reply messages are designed for diagnostic purposes. Network managers and users utilize this pair of messages to identify network problems. The combination of echo-request and echo-reply messages determines whether two systems (hosts or routers) can communicate with each other.

A host or router can send an echo-request message to another host or router. The host or router that receives an echo-request message creates an echo-reply message and returns it to the original sender.

> An echo-request message can be sent by a host or router. An echo-reply message is sent by the host or router which receives an echo-request message.

The echo-request and echo-reply messages can be used to determine if there is communication at the IP level. Because ICMP messages are encapsulated in IP datagrams, the receipt of an echo-reply message by the machine that sent the echo request is proof that the IP protocols in the sender and receiver are communicating with each other using the IP datagram. Also, it is proof that the intermediate routers are receiving, processing, and forwarding IP datagrams.

> Echo-request and echo-reply messages can be used by network managers to check the operation of the IP protocol.

The echo-request and echo-reply messages can also be used by a host to see if another host is reachable. At the user level, this is done by invoking the packet Internet groper (ping) command. Today, most systems provide a version of the ping command that can create a series of (instead of just one) echo-request or echo-reply messages, providing statistical information.

> Echo-request and echo-reply messages can test the reachability of a host. This is usually done by invoking the ping command.

Echo request, together with echo reply, can validate whether or not a node is functioning properly. The node to be tested is sent an echo-request message. The optional data field contains a message that must be repeated exactly by the responding node in its echo-reply message. Figure 9.14 shows the format of the echo-reply and echo-request message. The identifier and sequence number fields are not formally defined by the protocol and can be used arbitrarily by the sender. For example, the identifier field can define a group of problems and the sequence number can keep track of the particular echo request messages sent. The identifier is often the same as the process ID (see Chapter 24 for the definition of process ID) of the process that originated the request.

Timestamp Request and Reply

Two machines (hosts or routers) can use the timestamp-request and timestamp-reply messages to determine the round-trip time needed for an IP datagram to travel between them. It can also be used to synchronize the clocks in two machines. The format of these two messages is shown in Figure 9.15.

The three timestamp fields are each 32 bits long. Each field can hold a number representing time measured in milliseconds from midnight in Universal Time (formerly called Greenwich Mean Time). (Note that 32 bits can represent a number between 0 to

Figure 9.14 *Echo-request and echo-reply messages*

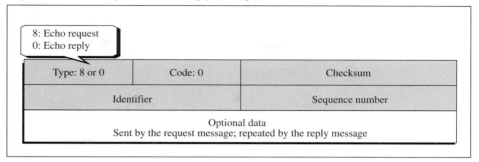

Figure 9.15 *Timestamp-request and timestamp-reply message format*

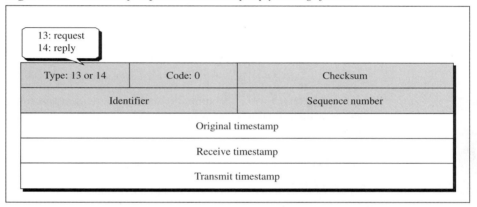

4,294,967,295, but a timestamp in this case cannot exceed 86,400,000 = 24 × 60 × 60 × 1,000.)

The source creates a timestamp-request message. The source fills the *original timestamp* field with the Universal Time shown by its clock at departure time. The other two timestamp fields are filled with zeros.

The destination creates the timestamp-reply message. The destination copies the original timestamp value from the request message into the same field in its reply message. It then fills the *receive timestamp* field with the Universal Time shown by its clock at the time the request was received. Finally, it fills the *transmit timestamp* field with the Universal Time shown by its clock at the time the reply message departs.

The timestamp-request and timestamp-reply messages can be used to compute the one-way or round-trip time required for a datagram to go from a source to a destination and then back again. The formulas are

$$
\begin{array}{lllll}
\text{Sending time} & = & \text{value of receive timestamp} & - & \text{value of original timestamp} \\
\text{Receiving time} & = & \text{time the packet returned} & - & \text{value of transmit timestamp} \\
\text{Round-trip time} & = & \text{sending time} & + & \text{receiving time}
\end{array}
$$

Note that the sending and receiving time calculations are accurate only if the two clocks in the source and destination machines are synchronized. However, the round-trip calculation is correct even if the two clocks are not synchronized because each clock contributes twice to the round-trip calculation, thus canceling any difference in synchronization.

> Timestamp-request and timestamp-reply messages can be used to measure the round-trip time between a source and a destination machine even if their clocks are not synchronized.

For example, given the following information:

Value of original timestamp: 46
Value of receive timestamp: 59
Value of transmit timestamp: 60
Time the packet arrived: 67

We can calculate the round-trip time to be 20 milliseconds:

$$
\begin{aligned}
\text{Sending time} &= 59 - 46 = 13 \quad \text{milliseconds} \\
\text{Receiving time} &= 67 - 60 = 7 \quad \text{milliseconds} \\
\text{Round-trip time} &= 13 + 7 = 20 \quad \text{milliseconds}
\end{aligned}
$$

Given the actual one-way time, the timestamp-request and timestamp-reply messages can also be used to synchronize the clocks in two machines using the following formula:

Time difference = receive timestamp − (original timestamp field + one-way time duration)

The one-way time duration can be obtained either by dividing the round-trip time duration by two (if we are sure that the duration time for sending and receiving is the same) or by other means. For example, we can tell that the two clocks in the previous example are 3 milliseconds out of synchronization because

$$\text{Time difference} = 59 - (46 + 10) = 3$$

> The timestamp-request and timestamp-reply messages can be used to synchronize two clocks in two machines if the exact one-way time duration is known.

Address Mask Request and Reply

The IP address of a host contains a network address, subnet address, and host identifier. A host may know its full IP address, but it may not know which part of the address defines the network and subnetwork address and which part corresponds to the host identifier. For example, a host may know its 32-bit IP address as

10011111. 00011111. 11100010.10101011

But it may not know that the left 20 bits are network and subnetwork addresses and the remaining 12 bits are its host identifier. In this case, the host needs the following mask:

11111111.11111111.11110000.00000000

The 1s in the mask, as we saw in Chapter 5, identify the position of the bits used for the netid and subnetid. The 0s identify the position of the bits for the hostid.

For example, applying the above mask to the above IP address, we get

Netid and subnetid ====> 10011111. 00011111. 1110

Hostid ====> 0010.10101011

To obtain its mask, a host sends an address-mask-request message to a router on the LAN. If the host knows the address of the router, it sends the request directly to the router. If it does not know, it broadcasts the message. The router receiving the address-mask-request message responds with an address-mask-reply message, providing the necessary mask for the host. This can be applied to its full IP address to get its subnet address.

The format of the address-mask request and address-mask reply is shown in Figure 9.16. The address-mask field is filled with zeros in the request message. When the router sends the address-mask reply back to the host, this field contains the actual mask (1s for the netid and subnetid and 0s for the hostid).

Figure 9.16 *Mask-request and mask-reply message format*

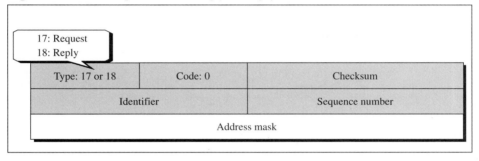

Masking is needed for diskless stations at start-up time. When a diskless station comes up for the first time, it may ask for its full IP address using the RARP protocol (see Chapter 8); after receiving its IP address, it may use the address mask request and reply to find out which part of the address defines the subnet.

Another way to get subnet mask information is through the use of the BOOTP protocol, as we will see in Chapter 15.

Router Solicitation and Advertisement

As we discussed in the redirection message section, a host that wants to send data to a host on another network needs to know the address of routers connected to its own network. Also, the host should know if the routers are alive and functioning. The router-solicitation and router-advertisement messages can help in this situation. A host can broadcast (or multicast) a router-solicitation message. The router or routers that receive the solicitation message broadcast their routing information using the router-advertisement message. A router can also periodically advertise router-advertisement messages even if no host has solicited. Note that when a router sends out an advertisement, it advertises not only its own presence but also the presence of all routers on the network of which it is aware. Figure 9.17 shows the format of the router-solicitation message.

Figure 9.17   *Router-solicitation message format*

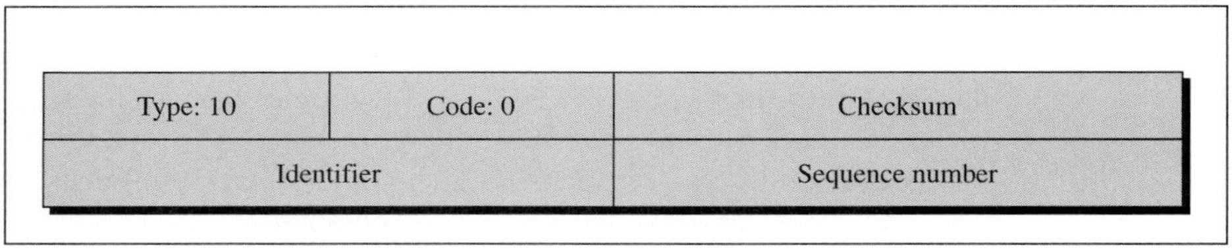

Type: 10	Code: 0	Checksum
Identifier		Sequence number

Figure 9.18 shows the format of the router-advertisement message. The lifetime field shows the number of seconds that the entries are considered to be valid. Each router entry in the advertisement contains at least two fields: the router address and the address preference level. The address preference level defines the ranking of the router. The preference level is used to select a router as the default router. If the address preference level is zero, that router is considered the default router. If the address preference level is 80000000_{16}, the router should never be selected as the default router.

Figure 9.18   *Router-advertisement message format*

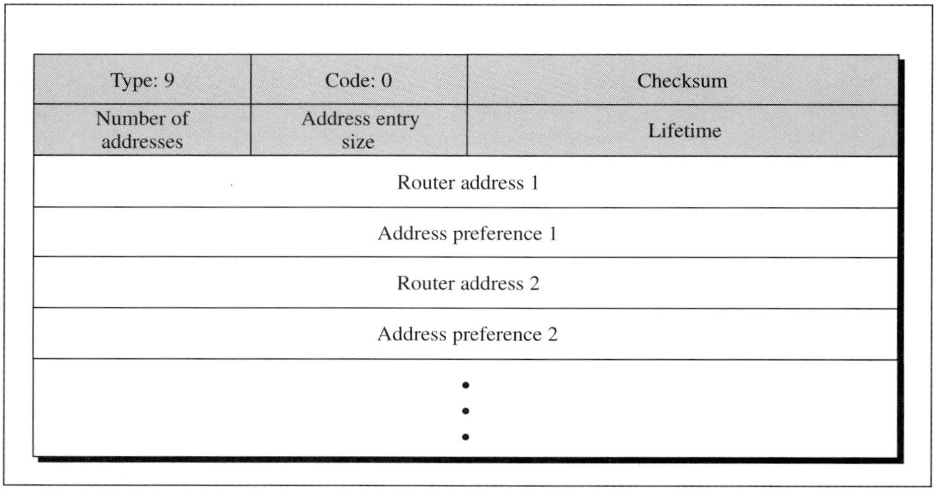

Type: 9	Code: 0	Checksum
Number of addresses	Address entry size	Lifetime
Router address 1		
Address preference 1		
Router address 2		
Address preference 2		
⋮		

9.5   CHECKSUM

In Chapter 7, we learned the concept and idea of the checksum. In ICMP the checksum is calculated over the entire message (header and data).

Checksum Calculation

The sender follows these steps using one's complement arithmetic:

1. The checksum field is set to zero.
2. The sum of all the 16-bit words (header and data) is calculated.
3. The sum is complemented to get the checksum.
4. The checksum is stored in the checksum field.

Checksum Testing

The sender follows these steps using one's complement arithmetic:

1. The sum of all words (header and data) is calculated.
2. The sum is complemented.
3. If the result obtained in step 2 is 16 0s, the message is accepted; otherwise, it is rejected.

Example

Figure 9.19 shows an example of checksum calculation for a simple echo-request message (see the section on echo request and reply). The message is divided into 16-bit (two-byte) words. The words are added together and the sum is complemented. Now the sender can put this value in the checksum field.

Figure 9.19   *Example of checksum calculation*

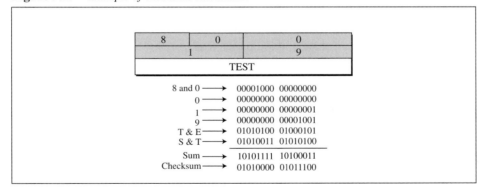

9.6   ICMP DESIGN

In this section, we present a simplified, bare-bones design of ICMP. This design is meant to be just a teaching tool. Details such as error checking, error handling, and packet validation have been omitted in an attempt to focus on the basics. Our purpose is to demystify the algorithms and their relationships. In addition, we have sacrificed efficiency for the sake of simplicity. For the actual code consult other literature such as Stevens, *TCP/IP Illustrated*, Volume 2.

In this design, the ICMP package is made of two modules: an input module and an output module. Figure 9.20 shows these two modules.

Figure 9.20 *ICMP design*

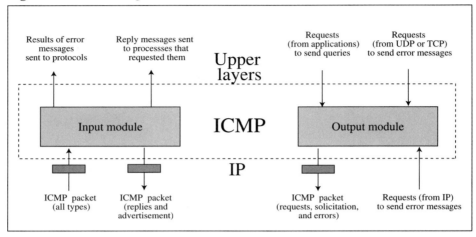

Input Module

The input module handles all received ICMP messages. It is invoked when an ICMP packet is delivered to it from the IP layer. If the received packet is a request or solicitation, the module creates a reply or an advertisement and sends it out.

If the received packet is a redirection message, the module uses the information to update the routing table. If the received packet is an error message, the module informs the protocol about the situation that caused the error. The pseudocode is shown below:

Input Module
Receive: an ICMP packet from the IP layer
1. If (the type is any of the three request types)
1. Create a reply.
2. Send the reply.
2. If (the type is a router solicitation)
1. If (station is a router)
1. Create a router advertisement.
2. Send the advertisement.
3. If (the type is one of the three reply messages or router advertisement)
1. Extract information in the data section of the packet.
2. Deliver extracted information to the process that requested it.
4. If (the type defines a redirection)

Input Module (concluded)
1. Modify the routing table.
5. If (the type defines an error message other than a redirection)
1. Inform the appropriate source protocol about the situation.
6. Return.

Output Module

The output module is responsible for creating request, solicitation, or error messages requested by a higher level or the IP protocol. The module receives a demand from IP, UDP, or TCP to send one of the ICMP error messages. If the demand is from IP, the output module must first check that the request is allowed. Remember, an ICMP message cannot be created for four situations: an IP packet carrying an ICMP error message, a fragmented IP packet, a multicast IP packet, or an IP packet having IP address 0.0.0.0 or 127.X.Y. Z.

The output module may also receive a demand from an application program to send one of the ICMP request or solicitation messages. The pseudocode is shown below:

Output Module
Receive: a demand
1. If (the demand defines an error message)
1. If (the demand is from IP)
1. If (the demand is forbidden)
1. Return.
2. If (the type defines a redirection message)
1. If (the station is not a router)
1. Return.
3. Create the error message using the type, the code, and the IP packet.
2. If (the demand defines a request or solicitation)
1.   Create a request or solicitation message.
3. Send the message.
4. Return.

9.7   SUMMARY

■ The Internet Control Message Protocol (ICMP) sends five types of error reporting messages and four pairs of query messages to support the unreliable and connectionless Internet Protocol (IP).

■ ICMP messages are encapsulated in IP datagrams.

■ The destination-unreachable error message is sent to the source host when a datagram is undeliverable.

■ The source-quench error message is sent in an effort to alleviate congestion.

■ The time-exceeded message notifies a source host that 1) the time-to-live field has reached zero, or 2) fragments of a message have not arrived in a set amount of time.

■ The parameter problem message notifies a host that there is a problem in the header field of a datagram.

■ The redirection message is sent to make the routing table of a host more efficient.

■ The echo-request and echo-reply messages test the connectivity between two systems.

■ The timestamp-request and timestamp-reply messages can determine the round-trip time between two systems or the difference in time between two systems.

■ The address-mask request and address-mask reply messages are used to obtain the subnet mask.

■ The router-solicitation and router-advertisement messages allow hosts to update their routing tables.

■ The checksum for ICMP is calculated using both the header and the data fields of the ICMP message.

■ Packet InterNet Groper (ping) is an application program that uses the services of ICMP to test the reachability of a host.

■ A simple ICMP design can consist of an input module that handles incoming ICMP packets and an output module that handles demands for ICMP services.

9.8   PRACTICE SET

Multiple Choice

1. If a host needs to synchronize its clock with another host, it sends a _____ message.

   a. timestamp-request

   b. source-quench

   c. router-advertisement

   d. time-exceeded

2. Which of the following types of ICMP messages needs to be encapsulated into an IP datagram?
    a. time exceeded
    b. multicasting
    c. echo reply
    d. all of the above

3. The purpose of echo request and echo reply is to _____.
    a. report errors
    b. check node-to-node communication
    c. check packet lifetime
    d. find IP addresses

4. In error reporting the encapsulated ICMP packet goes to _____.
    a. the sender
    b. the receiver
    c. a router
    d. any of the above

5. Which field is always present in an ICMP packet?
    a. type
    b. code
    c. checksum
    d. all of the above

6. What field uniquely identifies the kind of ICMP message (for example, echo reply versus echo request)?
    a. type
    b. code
    c. option ID
    d. a together with b

7. When the hop-count field reaches zero and the destination has not been reached, a _____ error message is sent.
    a. destination-unreachable
    b. time-exceeded
    c. parameter-problem
    d. redirection

8. When all fragments of a message have not been received within the designated amount of time, a _____ error message is sent.
    a. source-quench
    b. time-exceeded
    c. parameter-problem
    d. timestamp request

9. Errors in the header or option fields of an IP datagram require a _____ error message.
   a. parameter-problem
   b. source-quench
   c. router-solicitation
   d. redirection

10. A _____ can learn about network _____ by sending out a router-solicitation packet.
    a. router, routers
    b. router, hosts
    c. host, hosts,
    d. host, routers

11. The _____ packet contains information about a router.
    a. router-solicitation
    b. router-information
    c. router-advertisement
    d. router-reply

12. ICMP functions include:
    a. error correction
    b. detection of all unreachable datagrams
    c. reporting of some types of errors
    d. all of the above

13. Who can send ICMP error-reporting messages?
    a. routers
    b. destination hosts
    c. source hosts
    d. a and b

14. One method to alert a source host of congestion is the _____ message.
    a. redirection
    b. echo-request
    c. source-quench
    d. destination-unreachable

15. A time-exceeded message is generated if _____.
    a. the round-trip time between hosts is close to zero
    b. the time-to-live field has a zero value
    c. fragments of a message do not arrive within a set time
    d. b and c

16. To determine whether or not a node is reachable, _____ message can be sent.
    a. an echo-reply
    b. an echo-request

    c. a redirection

    d. a source-quench

17. In calculating the time difference between two clocks, a negative value indicates _____.

    a. an invalid calculation

    b. the source clock lags behind the destination clock

    c. the destination clock lags behind the source clock

    d. the one-way time has been miscalculated

18. An IP datagram (datagram A) cannot reach its destination. An ICMP error message is sent to the source. The data field of the IP datagram (datagram B) that encapsulates the ICMP packet contains _____.

    a. only the ICMP header

    b. the ICMP header plus eight bytes of datagram A

    c. only datagram A

    d. the ICMP header, datagram A's header, and eight bytes of datagram A's data field

19. ICMP packets are the output of _____.

    a. only the input module

    b. only the output module

    c. both the input and the output module

    d. neither the input nor the output module

20. ICMP packets are the input to _____.

    a. only the input module

    b. only the output module

    c. both the input and the output module

    d. neither the input nor the output module

Exercises

21. Host A sends a timestamp-request message to host B and never receives a reply. Discuss three possible causes and the corresponding course of action.

22. The IP address of a workstation is 198.123.46.219. If its subnet mask is 255.255.255.192, what is its identifier? What class does the network belong to?

23. Why is there a restriction on the generation of an ICMP message in response to a failed ICMP error message?

24. Host A sends a datagram to host B. Host B never receives the datagram and host A never receives notification of failure. Give two different explanations of what might have happened.

25. What is the purpose of including the IP header and the first eight bytes of datagram data in the error reporting ICMP messages?

26. What is the maximum value of the pointer field in a parameter-problem message?

27. Give an example of a situation in which a host would never receive a redirection message.

28. Make a table showing which ICMP messages are sent by routers, which are sent by the non-destination hosts, and which are sent by the destination hosts.

29. Can the calculated sending time, receiving time, or round-trip time have a negative value? Why or why not? Give examples.

30. Why isn't the one-way time for a packet simply the round-trip time divided by two?

31. What is the minimum size of an ICMP packet? What is the maximum size of an ICMP packet?

32. What is the minimum size of an IP packet that carries an ICMP packet? What is the maximum size?

33. What is the minimum size of an Ethernet frame that carries an IP packet which in turn carries an ICMP packet? What is the maximum size?

34. How can we determine if an IP packet is carrying an ICMP packet?

35. Calculate the checksum for the following ICMP packet:
    Type: Echo Request   Identifier: 123   Sequence Number: 25   Message: Hello

36. A router receives an IP packet with source IP address 130.45.3.3 and destination IP address 201.23.4.6. The router cannot find the destination IP address in its routing table. Fill in the fields (as much as you can) for the ICMP message sent.

37. TCP receives a segment with destination port address 234. TCP checks and cannot find an open port for this destination. Fill in the fields for the ICMP message sent.

38. An ICMP message has arrived with the header (in hexadecimal):
    03 0310 20 00 00 00 00
    What is the type of the message? What is the code? What is the purpose of the message?

39. An ICMP message has arrived with the header (in hexadecimal):
    05 00 11 12 11 0B 03 02
    What is the type of the message? What is the code? What is the purpose of the message? What is the value of the last four bytes? What do the last bytes signify?

40. A computer sends a timestamp request. If its clock shows 5:20:30 A.M. (Universal Time), show the entries for the message.

41. Repeat exercise 40 for the time of 3:40:30 P.M. (Universal Time).

42. A computer receives a timestamp request from another computer at 2:34:20 P.M. The value of the original timestamp is 52,453,000. If the sender clock is five milliseconds slow, what is the one-way time?

43. A computer sends a timestamp request to another computer. It receives the corresponding timestamp reply at 3:46:07 A.M. The values of the original timestamp, receive timestamp, and transmit timestamp are 13,560,000, 13,562,000, and 13,564,300, respectively. What is the sending trip time? What is the receiving trip time? What is the round-trip time? What is the difference between the sender clock and the receiver clock?

44. If two computers are 5,000 miles apart, what is the minimum time for a message to go from one to the other?

Programming Exercises

45. Write a program in C to calculate the time elapsed from midnight in milliseconds when the time is given as X:Y:Z A.M. or P.M. format.

46. The ICMP software package usually uses the **#define** constant to declare the different types of messages. Complete the following declarations to show all the different types covered in this chapter:

```
#define   ECHO_RP   0     /* Echo Reply              */
#define   DEST_UR   3     /* Destination Unreachable */
.........................................
```

47. The ICMP software package usually uses the **#define** constant to declare the different codes of different message types. Complete the following declarations to show all different codes covered in this chapter:

```
#define   DU_NUR   0   /* Destination Unreachable, Network Unreachable */
#define   DU_HUR   1   /* Destination Unreachable, Host Unreachable    */
................................
```

48. The ICMP software package usually uses a **struct** to declare the format of a packet header. However, the last four bytes of the header are specific for different types of messages. One solution is to use a **union** inside a **struct**. Complete the following declaration for different types of headers:

```
struct  Icmp_Header
{
          char      type :
          char      code;
          short     checksum;
          union
          {
                    ..............
                    ..............
                    ..............
          }....... ;
} ;
```

49. The ICMP software package usually uses a **struct** to declare the format of the entire ICMP packet including the data section. Using your answer in exercise 48, complete the following declaration:

```
struct  Icmp_Packet
{
          ...........          header ;
          ...........          data ;
} ;
```

50. Define a **struct** called **stateInformation** that contains all the local information that ICMP input module needs to access or modify.

51. Define a **struct** called **icmpPseudoHeader** that can hold entries for the pseudo-header needed to calculate the checksum for ICMP.

52. Using the declaration in the previous exercises, write a function called **icmpCh-Sum** to calculate the checksum field for an ICMP packet. The function takes two arguments: a pointer to an ICMP packet struct and a pointer to a pseudoheader struct.

53. Using the declarations in the previous exercises and the outline given in the text, write a C function called **icmpInput** to simulate the input module. The function accepts a pointer to an ICMP packet. It uses the stateInformation struct. It sends an ICMP reply if any, or sends the information in the data section to the higher level protocols.

54. Using the declarations in the previous exercises and the outline given in the text, write a C function called **icmpOutput** to simulate the output module. The function accepts three arguments. The first argument is a pointer to an IP packet. For error messages, this pointer points to the original IP packet with a problem. For query messages, this pointer points to NULL. The second and the third arguments are characters defining the type and the code of the message to be created. Use the stateInformation struct defined previously to access the information needed to fill in the fields.

55. Write a test program that tests all of the functions written in the previous exercises. The program can print information or the values of fields instead of sending them.

CHAPTER 10

Internet Group Management Protocol (IGMP)

In this chapter we discuss the multicasting capability of the TCP/IP protocol suite and the protocol that is involved in multicasting, the Internet Group Management Protocol (IGMP).

10.1   MULTICASTING

The IP protocol can be involved in two types of communication: unicasting and multicasting. Unicasting is the communication between one sender and one receiver. It is a one-to-one communication. However, some processes sometimes need to send the same message to a large number of receivers simultaneously. This is called *multicasting*, which is a one-to-many communication. Multicasting has many applications. For example, multiple stockbrokers can simultaneously be informed of changes in a stock price, or travel agents can be informed of a trip cancellation. Some other applications include distance learning and video-on-demand.

Multicast Addresses

As we learned in Chapter 4, IP addressing supports multicasting. All 32-bit IP addresses that start with 1110 (class D) are multicast addresses (see Figure 10.1).

Figure 10.1   *Class D address*

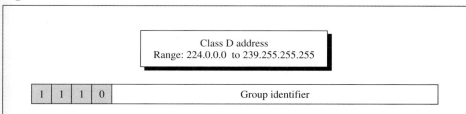

With 28 bits remaining for the group address, more than 250 million addresses are available for assignment. Some of these addresses are permanently assigned. We discussed them in Chapter 4.

It is important to remember that a multicast address can only be used as a destination address, and not as a source address.

A multicast address can only be used as a destination address.

A multicast address is also known as a *groupid*.

10.2 IGMP

The IGMP has been designed to help a multicast router identify the hosts in a LAN that are members of a multicast group. It is a companion to the IP protocol. Figure 10.2 shows the position of the IGMP protocol in relation to other protocols in the network layer.

Figure 10.2 *Position of IGMP in the network layer*

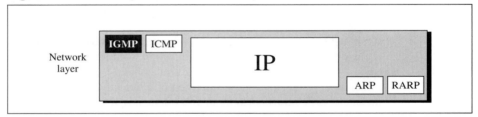

Types of Messages

IGMP has only two types of messages: report and query. The report message is sent from the host (or router) to a router. The query message is sent from a router to a host or a router. See Figure 10.3.

Figure 10.3 *IGMP messages*

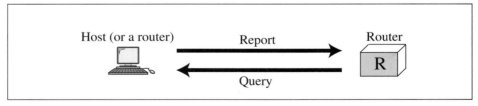

Message Format

An IGMP message has a very simple format; it consists of only eight bytes as shown in Figure 10.4.

Figure 10.4   *IGMP message format*

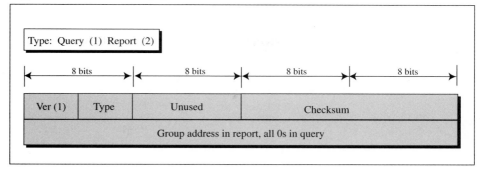

The fields of the IGMP are as follows:

- **Ver.** This four-bit field defines the version of the protocol. It is currently version 1.
- **Type.** This four-bit field defines the type of the message; 1 is for query messages and 2 is for report messages.
- **Checksum.** This is a 16-bit field carrying the checksum. The checksum is calculated on the eight-byte message.
- **Group address.** This field defines the group address in a report message. It is filled with 0s in the query message. In a report message this field is used to define either the groupid that a system wants to join or the groupid in which a system wants to continue membership. The process is discussed in a later section.

Operation of IGMP in a Single Network

Let us first find out how IGMP helps a multicast router propagate multicast packets in a single LAN. A multicast router connected to a LAN has a list of multicast addresses of the groups for which there is at least one loyal member. See Figure 10.5.

Figure 10.5   *Operation of IGMP*

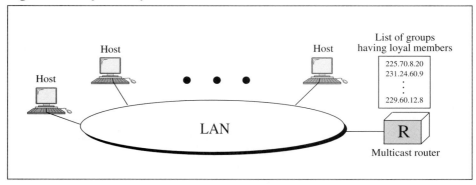

When the router receives a packet with a destination address that matches one on the list, it forwards the message, converting the IP multicast address to a physical multicast address. The mechanism of the conversion is discussed later.

There are four different situations as shown in Figure 10.6 and discussed below.

Figure 10.6 *Four situations of IGMP operation*

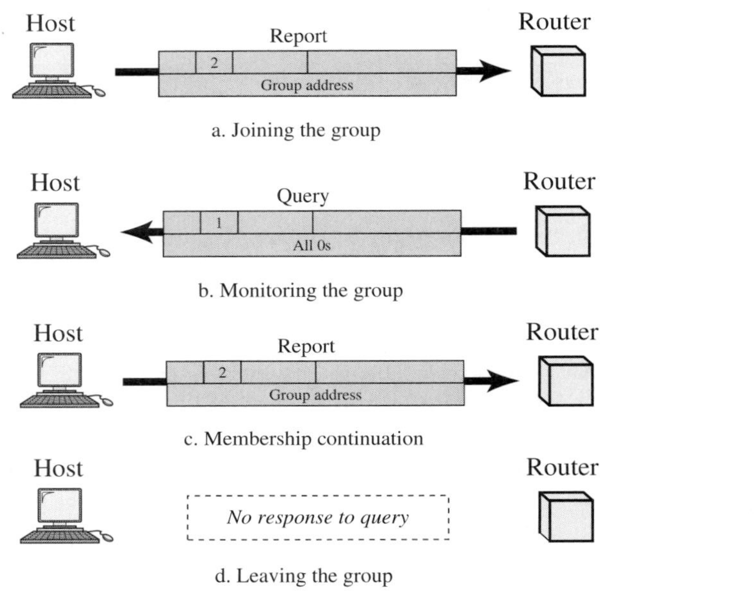

a. Joining the group

b. Monitoring the group

c. Membership continuation

d. Leaving the group

Joining a Group

Each host maintains a list of processes with membership in a group. When a process wants to join a new group, it sends its request to the host. The host will add the name of the process and the name of the requested group to its list. However, the host only sends an IGMP report to the multicast router if this is the first request for membership in that group. In other words, the host sends the report for a particular group membership only once.

Monitoring Group Membership

A multicast router is responsible for monitoring all of the hosts in a LAN to see if they want to continue their membership in a group. The router periodically sends a query message to the multicast address 224.0.0.1 (all systems on a LAN). In this message, the group address field is set to 0.0.0.0. This means the query for membership continuation is for all groups a host is involved in, not just one. The router expects an answer for each of these groups.

Continuing Membership

The host keeps a list of processes that wish to continue membership in a group. When a host receives a query, it checks this list. For each group with at least one process still interested in continuing the membership, the host must send a report. Note that a report sent in response to a query is to verify membership continuation, not for new membership. Note also that for each group, a separate report should be sent.

Leaving a Group

When a host receives a query and finds that there is not a single process interested in that group anymore, it does not respond and does not send a report about that group. If no host on the LAN sends a report for a specific group, the address of that group is purged, after a time-out, from the multicast address list of the router.

Operation of IGMP

Multicast routing in an internet is accomplished using the spanning tree algorithm (see Appendix J). Although this algorithm is not discussed here, we give a very simple example to motivate interested readers to delve deeper into the subject.

Figure 10.7 shows a subtree segment of an internet. The router R1 is at the root of the subtree, connecting the subtree to the rest of the big tree (the whole Internet).

Figure 10.7   *Operation of IGMP in a part of a spanning tree*

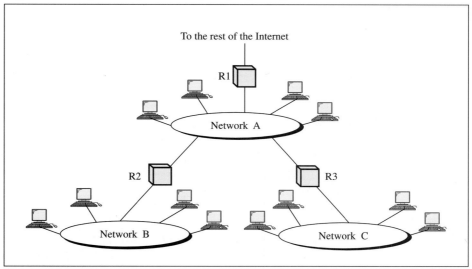

We want to see how the IGMP protocol works in this small part of an internet. Router R2, a multicast router, is responsible for monitoring network B. It keeps a list of class D addresses for which there is at least one member from network B. Router R3, also a multicast router, monitors network C in the same way. Router R1, on the other hand, is responsible for all three networks. It monitors network A in the same manner that the other two routers monitor their networks. However, R1 expects IGMP reports from routers R2 and R3. R1 expects from R2 a report for each group with a loyal member in network B. R1 expects from router R3 a report for each group having a loyal member in network C. In other words, routers R2 and R3 each have a dual duty: serving as a router to monitor the downstream networks (B and C) and serving as a host to respond to the queries of router R1.

Changing IP Addresses to Physical Addresses

When a multicast router receives a class D IP packet, it checks its list for a matching group address. If present, the router encapsulates the packet in a frame and sends it to the destination. To do that, it needs a physical address. There are two general cases: either the physical network can support multicasting or it cannot.

Case 1: Physical Multicast Support

Most LANs support physical multicast addressing. Ethernet is one of them. An Ethernet physical address (MAC address) is six octets (48 bits) long. If the first 25 bits in an Ethernet address are 0000000100000000010111100, the address defines a physical multicast address for the TCP/IP protocol. The remaining 23 bits can be used to define a group. To convert an IP multicast address into an Ethernet address, the multicast router extracts the least significant 23 bits of a class D IP address and inserts them into a multicast Ethernet physical address (see Figure 10.8).

Figure 10.8   *Mapping class D to Ethernet physical address*

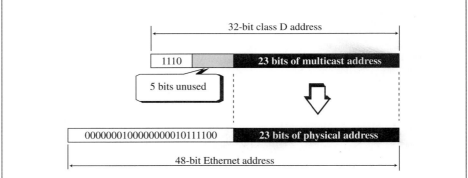

However, the group identifier of a class D IP address is 28 bits long, which implies that five bits are unused. This means that 32 (2^5) multicast addresses at the IP level are mapped to a single multicast address. In other words, the mapping is many-to-one instead of one-to-one. If the five left-most bits of the group identifier in a class D address are not all zero, a host may receive packets that do not really belong to the group in which it is involved. For this reason, the host must check the IP address and discard any packets that do not belong to it.

Other LANs support the same concept but have different methods of mapping.

Case 2: No Physical Multicast Support

Most WANs do not support physical multicast addressing. To send a multicast packet through these networks, a process called *tunneling* is used. In **tunneling**, the multicast packet is encapsulated in a unicast packet and sent through the network, where it emerges from the other side as a multicast packet (see Figure 10.9).

Figure 10.9   *Tunneling*

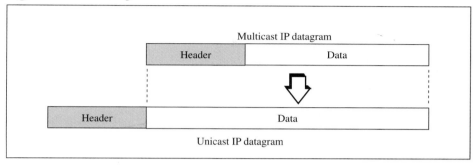

10.3   ENCAPSULATION

The IGMP message is encapsulated in an IP datagram with the protocol value of two. See Figure 10.10.

Figure 10.10   *Encapsulation of IGMP packet*

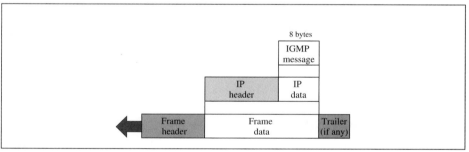

The query message is multicast using the multicast address 224.0.0.1. The report message is multicast using a destination address equal to the multicast address being reported. In this way, only one station needs to report this groupid. When it does, all other stations receive this report and know that this groupid has been reported. They should not report it again. This guarantees that only one report is generated for each group address at each network. This eliminates unnecessary reports and reduces traffic.

When the message is encapsulated in the IP datagram, the value of TTL must be one. This is required because the domain of IGMP is the LAN. No IGMP message should travel beyond the LAN. This value for TTL guarantees that the message does not leave the LAN since this value is decremented to zero by the first router and, consequently, the packet is discarded.

10.4 MULTICAST BACKBONE (MBONE)

The MBONE (multicast backbone) is a set of routers on the Internet that supports multicasting. MBONE is an experimental system supporting text, audio, and video data transmission. Although MBONE spans several continents today, its coverage is but a small part of the whole Internet.

MBONE is based on the multicasting capability of IP. At the data link layer, MBONE uses the multicasting capability of some LANs and tunneling. We can think of MBONE as made of "islands" connected by "tunnels" through which data is multicast on the Internet.

Today MBONE uses the services of UDP at the transport layer (see Chapter 11). However, it is expected that some other transport layer protocol, such as Real-Time Transport Protocol (RTP) will eventually replace UDP.

10.5 IGMP DESIGN

In this section, we present a simplified, bare-bones design of IGMP. This design is meant to be just a teaching tool. Details such as error checking, error handling, and packet validation have been omitted in an attempt to focus on the basics. Our purpose is to demystify the algorithms and their relationships. In addition, we have sacrificed efficiency for the sake of simplicity. For the actual code consult other literature such as Stevens, *TCP/IP Illustrated*, Volume 2.

Our design shows only the modules used in an IGMP host. The IGMP router will be left as an exercise. In our design an IGMP package involves a group table, a set of timers, and four software modules: a group-joining module, a group-leaving module, an input module, and an output module. Figure 10.11 shows these six components and their interactions.

Group Table

An entry in this table gives information about a multicast address that has at least one process as a member. The table has four fields: state, interface number, group address, and reference count (see Figure 10.12).

- **State.** This field defines the state of the entry. It can have one of the following values: FREE, DELAYING, and IDLE. If the state is FREE, it can be used for a new entry. If the state is DELAYING, it means that a report should be sent for this entry when the timer matures. If the state is IDLE, it means that there is no timer running for this entry.

- **Interface no.** This field defines the interface through which the multicast packet is sent and received.

- **Group address.** This is the multicast address which defines the group.

- **Reference count.** This is the number of processes still interested in this group. Every time a process joins the group, the reference count is incremented. Every

Figure 10.11   *IGMP design*

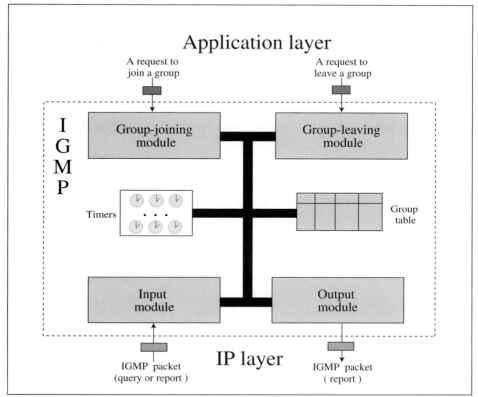

Figure 10.12   *Group table*

State	Interface No.	Group Address	Reference Count
....	....	....	....
....	....	....	....
....	....	....	....

time a process leaves the group, the reference count is decremented. When this value is zero, the entry is deleted from the table and the state is changed to FREE.

Timers

Each entry in the table in the DELAYING state has a timer to govern the sending of reports. Each timer has a randomly selected expiration time to prevent a burst of report generation. When an expiration time matures, a signal goes to the output module which then generates a report.

Group-Joining Module

A process that wants to join a group invokes this module. The module searches the group table to find an entry with the same multicast address. If found, the module increments the reference count to show that one more process has joined this group. If the multicast address is not found, the module creates a new entry and sets the reference count to one. The module then informs the data link layer to update its configuration table so that this type of multicast packet can be received. In both cases, the module changes the state of the entry to DELAYING and starts a timer so that when the timer matures, a report is generated for this entry.

Group-Joining Module
Receive: a request from a process to join a group
1. Look for the corresponding entry in the table.
2. If (found)
1. Increment the reference count.
3. If (not found)
1. Create an entry with reference count set to one.
2. Add the entry to the table.
3. Inform the data link layer to update its configuration table.
4. Set the state to DELAYING.
5. Start a timer.
6. Return.

Group-Leaving Module

A process that wants to leave a group invokes this module. The module searches the group table to find an entry with the same multicast address. If found, the module decrements the reference count. If the count is zero, the state is changed to FREE and the corresponding timer, if any, is canceled.

Group-Leaving Module
Receive: a request from a process to leave a group
1. Look for the corresponding entry in the table.
2. If (found)
1. Decrement the reference count.
2. If (reference count is zero)
1. If (any timer for this entry)
1. Cancel the timer.
2. Change the state to FREE.

Group-Leaving Module *(concluded)*
3. Return.

Input Module

The input module is invoked by an IGMP message. If the message is a query, the module starts a timer for each entry in the group table with an IDLE state and changes the state to DELAYING. To do this, the module generates a random number between zero and the maximum delay time and creates a timer with the maturation time equal to this random number. The random number generation is required so that reports will be sent by the output module at different times and thus prevent congestion.

   If the message received is a report, the module checks for a corresponding entry in its table. If it is found and the state is DELAYING, it means another host on the network has sent a report for this delaying entry and there is no need for this host to send another report. The module cancels the timer and changes the state to IDLE.

Input Module
Receive: an IGMP message
1. Check the message type.
2. If (query)
1. Start a timer for each entry in the table with the state IDLE.
2. Change each IDLE state to DELAYING state.
3. Return.
3. If (report)
1. Look for the corresponding entry in the table.
2. If (found and state is DELAYING)
1. Cancel the timer for this entry.
2. Change the state to IDLE.
4. Return.

Output Module

The output module is invoked by a matured timer. It then looks for the corresponding entry and, if the state is DELAYING, the module creates a report and sends it. It then resets the state to IDLE.

Output Module
Receive: a signal from a timer
1. Look for the corresponding entry in the table.

Output Module (concluded)
2. If (found and state is DELAYING)
1. Create a report.
2. Send the report.
3. Reset the state to IDLE.
3. Return.

Examples of IGMP

In the following examples, we assume that a host begins with the group table shown in Table 10.1.

Table 10.1   *Original group table for examples*

State	Interface No	Group Address	Reference Count
IDLE	m0	230.14.7.22	3
DELAYING	m1	229.72.14.8	1
DELAYING	m1	231.8.7.14	2
FREE			
FREE			
FREE			

Example 1

The group-joining module receives a request from a process that wants to join the group with address 229.72.14.8. The module checks the group table and finds a delaying entry in the table. The module just increments the reference count. The new group table is shown in Table 10.2.

Table 10.2   *Group table for example 1*

State	Interface No	Group Address	Reference Count
IDLE	m0	230.14.7.22	3
DELAYING	m1	229.72.14.8	**2**
DELAYING	m1	231.8.7.14	2
FREE			
FREE			
FREE			

Example 2

The group-joining module receives a request from a process that wants to join the group with address 230.14.7.22. The module checks the group table and finds an idle entry in the table. The module increments the reference count and creates a new timer for this entry. The state of the entry is changed to DELAYING. The new group table is shown in Table 10.3.

Table 10.3   *Group table for example 2*

State	Interface No	Group Address	Reference Count
DELAYING	m0	230.14.7.22	**4**
DELAYING	m1	229.72.14.8	2
DELAYING	m1	231.8.7.14	2
FREE			
FREE			
FREE			

Example 3

The timer for the second entry matures; it invokes the output module. The output module sends a report message with group address 229.72.14.8. It changes the state of this entry to IDLE. The new group table is shown in Table 10.4.

Table 10.4   *Group table for example 3*

State	Interface No	Group Address	Reference Count
DELAYING	m0	230.14.7.22	4
IDLE	m1	229.72.14.8	2
DELAYING	m1	231.8.7.14	2
FREE			
FREE			
FREE			

Example 4

The group-leaving module receives a request from a process that wants to leave the group with address 231.8.7.14. The module checks the group table and finds a delaying entry in the table. The module then decrements the reference count. The new group table is shown in Table 10.5.

Table 10.5   *Group table for example 4*

State	Interface No	Group Address	Reference Count
DELAYING	m0	230.14.7.22	4
IDLE	m1	229.72.14.8	2
DELAYING	m1	231.8.7.14	**1**
FREE			
FREE			
FREE			

Example 5

The input module receives a query. It checks the group table and finds only one entry is in the idle state. It changes the state of this entry to DELAYING and starts a timer for it. The new group table is shown in Table 10.6.

Table 10.6   *Group table for example 5*

State	Interface No	Group Address	Reference Count
DELAYING	m0	230.14.7.22	4
DELAYING	m1	229.72.14.8	2
DELAYING	m1	231.8.7.14	1
FREE			
FREE			
FREE			

Example 6

The input module receives a report about group address 230.14.7.22. The module checks the group table and finds an entry for this group. Now the input module knows that another host has sent a report for this group address and there is no need for this host to send one. The module changes the state to IDLE and cancels the timer. The new group table is shown in Table 10.7.

Table 10.7   *Group table for example 6*

State	Interface No	Group Address	Reference Count
IDLE	m0	230.14.7.22	4
DELAYING	m1	229.72.14.8	2
DELAYING	m1	231.8.7.14	1
FREE			
FREE			
FREE			

Example 7

The group-joining module receives a request from a process that wants to join the group with address 237.30.30.8. It checks the group table and does not find an entry for this group. The module adds an entry to the table for this address with the state of delaying. It also starts a timer for this entry. The new group table is shown in Table 10.8.

Table 10.8   *Group table for example 7*

State	Interface No	Group Address	Reference Count
IDLE	m0	230.14.7.22	4
DELAYING	m1	229.72.14.8	2
DELAYING	m1	231.8.7.14	1

Table 10.8   *Group table for example 7 (concluded)*

State	Interface No	Group Address	Reference Count
DELAYING	**m0**	**237.30.30.8**	**1**
FREE			
FREE			

10.6   SUMMARY

■ Multicasting is the sending of the same message to more than one receiver simultaneously.

■ IP addresses that start with 1110 are multicast addresses. Multicast addresses are class D addresses.

■ The Internet Group Management Protocol (IGMP) helps multicast routers maintain a list of multicast addresses of groups.

■ Hosts maintain a list of processes with membership in a group.

■ A host sends an IGMP report for the following cases:

a. the first request for membership in a group

b. a positive response by the host to an IGMP query concerning continued membership in a group

■ A router sends an IGMP query to determine if a host wishes to continue membership in a group.

■ A host's nonresponse to a query indicates that the host is leaving the group.

■ Using a routing algorithm based on the spanning tree concept, multicast messages travel from network to network.

■ Five bits of the class D address do not get passed to the Ethernet address on an Ethernet LAN. This can result in a misdirected multicast message that must be discarded by the host.

■ WANs that do not support physical multicast addressing can use a process called tunneling to send multicast packets.

■ The IGMP message is encapsulated in an IP datagram.

■ The multicast backbone (MBONE) is a set of routers on the Internet that supports multicasting.

■ An IGMP package can consist of a host group table, a set of timers, and four software modules: an input module, an output module, a group-joining module, and a group-leaving module.

■ The group table holds information about each multicast group of which the host is a member.

■ The timers control the sending of the reports from the host to the multicast routers.

■ The group-joining module adds and updates entries in the group table.

■ The group-leaving module deletes and updates entries in the group table.

- The input module handles incoming IGMP messages.
- The output module creates IGMP reports.

10.7   PRACTICE SET

Multiple Choice

1. The purpose of the IGMP query is to _____.
   a. solicit membership in a group
   b. monitor membership of a group
   c. continue membership in a group
   d. all of the above

2. An IGMP query is sent from a _____ to a _____.
   a. host; host
   b. host; router
   c. router; router
   d. router; host or router

3. How does a host respond when no processes in a group wish to continue membership?
   a. The host sends a report.
   b. The host sends a query.
   c. The host sends a NAK.
   d. The host does not respond.

4. The least significant 23 bits in a 48-bit Ethernet address unambiguously _____.
   a. identify a multicast router
   b. identify a host
   c. identify a multicast group
   d. none of the above

5. The _____ field of the IGMP message is all zeros in a query message.
   a. version
   b. type
   c. checksum
   d. group address

6. The _____ field of the IGMP message is one for a query message.
   a. version
   b. type
   c. checksum
   d. a and b

7. A multicast message is sent from _____ to _____.

   a. one source; one destination

   b. one source; multiple destinations

   c. multiple sources; one destination

   d. multiple sources; multiple destinations

8. In networks that do not support physical multicast addressing, multicasting can be accomplished through _____.

   a. mapping

   b. unicasting

   c. queries

   d. tunneling

9. A group table entry is in the _____ state if there is no corresponding timer running.

   a. FREE

   b. DELAYING

   c. IDLE

   d. none of the above

10. A group table entry is in the _____ state if the timer is waiting to expire.

   a. FREE

   b. DELAYING

   c. IDLE

   d. none of the above

11. The _____ module receives an IGMP report or query.

   a. input

   b. output

   c. group-joining

   d. group-leaving

12. The _____ module sends out an IGMP report.

   a. input

   b. output

   c. group-joining

   d. group-leaving

13. The _____ module can create a new entry in the group table and start a timer.

   a. input

   b. output

   c. group-joining

   d. group-leaving

14. The _____ module can decrement the reference count in the group table.

   a. input

   b. output

   c. group-joining

       d. group-leaving

Exercises

15. Why is there no need for the IGMP message to travel outside its own network?

16. A multicast router list contains four groups (W, X, Y, and Z). There are three hosts on the LAN. Host A has three loyal members belonging to group W and one loyal member belonging to group X. Host B has two loyal members belonging to group W and one loyal member belonging to group Y. Host C has no processes belonging to any group. Show the IGMP messages involved in 1) monitoring and 2) membership continuation.

17. A multicast address for a group is 231.24.60.9. What is its 48-bit Ethernet address for a LAN using TCP/IP?

18. In Figure 10.7, how does a message from a host on network B get delivered to two hosts on network C?

19. If a router has 20 entries in its group table, should it send 20 different queries periodically or just one?

20. If a host wants to continue the membership in five groups, should it send five different report message or just one?

21. A router with IP address 202.45.33.21 and physical Ethernet address 234A4512ECD2 sends an IGMP query message. Show all of the entries in the message.

22. Encapsulate the message of exercise 21 in an IP packet. Fill in all the fields.

23. Encapsulate the message of exercise 22 in an Ethernet frame. Fill in all the fields.

24. A host with IP address 124.15.13.1 and physical Ethernet address 4A224512E1E2 sends an IGMP report message about groupid 228.45.23.11. Show all of the entries in the message.

25. Encapsulate the message of exercise 24 in an IP packet. Fill in all the fields.

26. Encapsulate the message of exercise 25 in an Ethernet frame. Fill in all the fields.

27. A router on an Ethernet network has received a multicast IP packet with groupid 226.17.18.4. When the host checks its multicast group table, it finds this address. Show how the router sends this packet to the recipients by encapsulating the IP packet in an Ethernet frame. Show all of the entries of the Ethernet frame. The outgoing IP address of the router is 185.23.5.6 and its outgoing physical address is 4A224512E1E2. Does the router need the services of ARP?

28. What if the router in exercise 27 cannot find the groupid in its table?

29. Redo exercise 27 with the physical network that does not support physical multicast addressing.

30. A host with IP address 114.45.7.9 receives an IGMP query. When it checks its group table, it finds no entries. What action should the host take? Should it send any messages? If so, show the packet fields.

31. A host with IP address 222.5.7.19 receives an IGMP query. When it checks its routing table, it finds two entries in its table: 227.4.3.7 and 229.45.6.23. What

action should the host take? Should it send any messages? If so, what type and how many? Show the fields.

32. A host with IP address 186.4.77.9 receives a request from a process to join a group with groupid 230.44.101.34. When the host checks its group table, it does not find an entry for this groupid. What action should the host take? Should it send any messages? If so, show the packet field.

33. Redo exercise 32 with the host finding an entry in its table.

34. A router with IP address 184.4.7.9 receives a report from a host that wants to join a group with groupid 232.54.10.34. When the router checks its group table, it does not find an entry for this groupid. What action should the router take? Should it send any messages? If so, show the packet fields.

35. Redo exercise 34 with the router finding an entry in its table.

36. A router sends a query and receives only three reports about groupids 225.4.6.7, 225.32.56.8, and 226.34.12.9. When it checks its routing table, it finds five entries: 225.4.6.7, 225.11.6.8, 226.34.12.9, 226.23.22.67, and 229.12.4.89. What action should be taken?

37. The contents of an IGMP message in hexadecimal notation are:

    11 00 EE FF 00 00 00 00

    Answer the following questions:

    a. What is the type?

    b. What is the checksum?

    c. What is the groupid?

38. The contents of an IGMP message in hexadecimal notation are:

    12 00 F9 C0 E1 2A 13 14

    Answer the following questions:

    a. What is the type?

    b. What is the checksum?

    c. What is the groupid?

39. Is there an error in the following hexadecimal representation of an IGMP message?

    11 00 A0 11 E1 2A 13 14

40. Is there an error in the following hexadecimal representation of an IGMP message?

    12 00 A0 11 00 00 00 00

41. How many multicast addresses can be supported for IP protocol in Ethernet?

42. How many multicast addresses can be supported by IP protocol?

43. What is the size of address space lost when we transform a multicast IP address to an Ethernet multicast address?

44. Change the following IP multicast addresses to Ethernet multicast addresses. How many of them specify the same Ethernet address?

    a. 224.18.72.8

    b. 235.18.72.8

    c. 237.18.6.88

    d. 224.88.12.8

45. Modify the IGMP design in the text to be also applicable to a router.

Programming Exercises

46. Write a C function to determine if a given IP address (in the form x.y.z.t) is a multicast address.

47. Write a C function to determine if a given IP address (in the form of a long integer) is a multicast address.

48. Write a C function to determine if a given Ethernet address (in hexadecimal format) is an Ethernet multicast address.

49. Write a C function that changes a given IP multicast address (in long integer) to an Ethernet multicast address (in hexadecimal).

50. Write a C function that changes a given Ethernet multicast address (in hexadecimal) to an IP multicast address (in long integer).

CHAPTER 11

User Datagram Protocol (UDP)

The TCP/IP protocol suite specifies two protocols for the transport layer: UDP and TCP. We will first focus on UDP, the simpler of the two, before discussing TCP in Chapter 12.

Figure 11.1 shows the relationship of UDP to the other protocols and layers of the TCP/IP protocol suite: UDP lies between the application layer and the IP layer and, like TCP, serves as the intermediary between the application programs and the network operations.

Figure 11.1 *Position of UDP in the TCP/IP protocol suite*

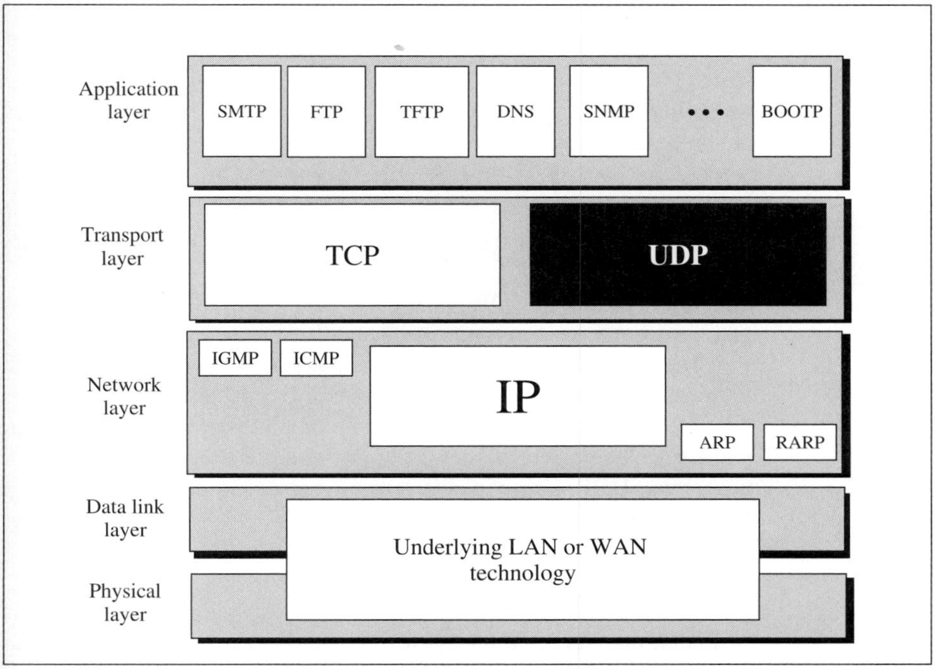

A transport layer protocol usually has several responsibilities. One is to create a process-to-process (a **process** is a running application program) communication; UDP uses port numbers to accomplish this. Another responsibility is to provide a flow-and-error control mechanism at the transport level. UDP does this task at a very minimal level. There is no flow-control mechanism and there is no acknowledgment for received packets. UDP, however, provides error control to some extent. If UDP detects an error in the received packet, it silently drops it.

The transport layer should also be responsible for providing a connection mechanism for the processes. The processes should be able to send streams of data to the transport layer. It is the responsibility of the transport layer at the sending station to make the connection with the receiver, chop the stream into transportable units, number them, and send them one by one. It is the responsibility of the transport layer at the receiving end to wait until all the different units belonging to the same process have arrived, check and pass those that are error free, and deliver them to the receiving process as a stream. After the entire stream has been sent, the transport layer should close the connection. UDP does not do any of the above. It can only receive a data unit from the processes and deliver it, unreliably, to the receiver. The data unit must be small enough to fit in a UDP packet.

UDP is called a *connectionless, unreliable* transport protocol. It does not add anything to the services of IP except for providing process-to-process communication instead of host-to-host communication. Also, it performs very limited error checking.

If UDP is so powerless, why would a process want to use it? With the disadvantages come some advantages. UDP is a very simple protocol using a minimum of overhead. If a process wants to send a small message and does not care much about reliability, it can use UDP. Sending a small message using UDP takes much less interaction between the sender and receiver than it does using TCP.

11.1   PROCESS-TO-PROCESS COMMUNICATION

Before we examine UDP, we must first understand host-to-host communication and process-to-process communication and the difference between them.

The IP is responsible for communication at the computer level (host-to-host communication). As a network layer protocol, IP can deliver the message only to the destination computer. However, this is an incomplete delivery. The message still needs to be handed to the correct process. This is where a transport layer protocol such as UDP takes over. UDP is responsible for delivery of the message to the appropriate process. Figure 11.2 shows the domain of IP and UDP.

Port Numbers

Although there are a few ways to achieve process-to-process communication, the most common one is through the **client-server** paradigm. A process on the local host, called a *client,* needs services from a process usually on the remote host, called a *server.*

Figure 11.2 *UDP versus IP*

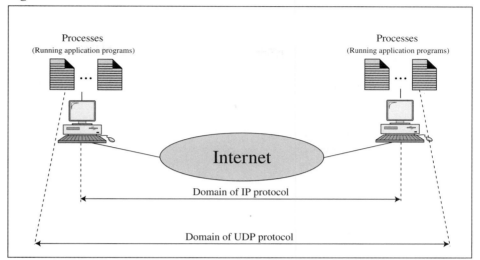

Both processes (client and server) have the same name. For example, to get the day and time from a remote machine, we need a Daytime client process running on the local host and a Daytime server process running on a remote machine.

However, operating systems today support both multiuser and multiprogramming environments. A remote computer can run several server programs at the same time, just as several local computers can run one or more client programs at the same time. For communication, we must define the

- Local host
- Local process
- Remote host
- Remote process

The local host and the remote host are defined using IP addresses. To define the processes, we need second identifiers which are called **port numbers**. In the TCP/IP protocol suite, the port numbers are integers between 0 and 65,535.

The client program defines itself with a port number, chosen randomly by the UDP software running on the client host. This is the **ephemeral port number.**

The server process must also define itself with a port number. This port number, however, cannot be chosen randomly. If the computer at the server site runs a server process and assigns a random number as the port number, the process at the client site that wants to access that server and use its services will not know the port number. Of course, one solution would be to send a special packet and request the port number of a specific server, but this requires more overhead. TCP/IP has decided to use universal port numbers for servers; these are called **well-known port numbers**. There are some exceptions to this rule; for example, there are clients that are assigned well-known port numbers. We will talk about this later when we explore the client-server paradigm in Chapter 14. Every client process knows the well-known port number of the corresponding server process. For example, while the Daytime client process, discussed above, can use an ephemeral (temporary) port number 52,000 to identify itself, the Daytime server process must use the well-known (permanent) port number 13. Figure 11.3 shows this concept.

Figure 11.3 *Port numbers*

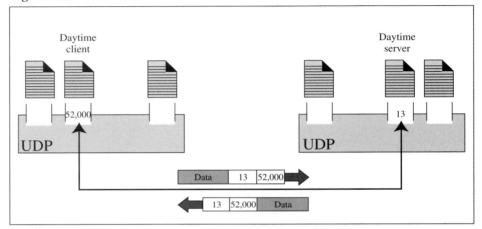

It should be clear by now that the IP addresses and port numbers play different roles in selecting the final destination of data. The destination IP address defines the host among the different hosts in the world. After the host has been selected, the port number defines one of the processes on this particular host (see Figure 11.4).

IANA Ranges

The IANA has divided the port numbers into three ranges: well-known, registered, and dynamic (or private) as shown in Figure 11.5.

■ **Well-known ports.** The ports ranging from 0 to 1,023 are assigned and controlled by IANA. These are the well-known ports.

■ **Registered ports.** The ports ranging from 1,024 to 49,151 are not assigned or controlled by IANA. They can only be registered with IANA to prevent duplication.

■ **Dynamic ports.** The ports ranging from 49,152 to 65,535 are neither controlled nor registered. They can be used by any process. These are the ephemeral ports.

Ranges Used by Other Systems

Note that other operating systems may use ranges other than IANA's for the well-known and ephemeral ports. For example, BSD Unix has three ranges: reserved, ephemeral, and nonprivileged.

Figure 11.4   *IP addresses versus port numbers*

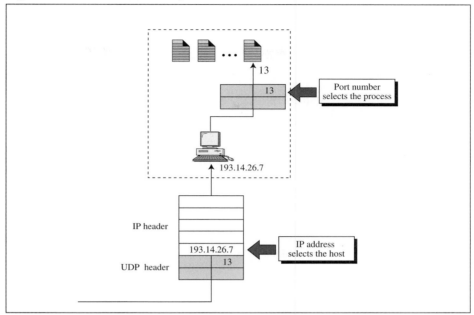

Figure 11.5   *IANA ranges*

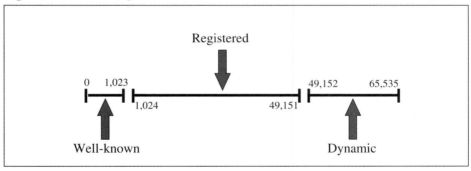

Well-Known Ports for UDP

Table 11.1 shows some well-known port numbers used by UDP. Some port numbers can be used by both UDP and TCP. We will discuss them when we talk about TCP in Chapter 12.

Table 11.1   *Well-known ports used with UDP*

Port	Protocol	Description
7	Echo	Echoes a received datagram back to the sender
9	Discard	Discards any datagram that is received
11	Users	Active users

Table 11.1   *Well-known ports used with UDP (concluded)*

Port	Protocol	Description
13	Daytime	Returns the date and the time
17	Quote	Returns a quote of the day
19	Chargen	Returns a string of characters
53	Nameserver	Domain Name Service
67	Bootps	Server port to download bootstrap information
68	Bootpc	Client port to download bootstrap information
69	TFTP	Trivial File Transfer Protocol
111	RPC	Remote Procedure Call
123	NTP	Network Time Protocol
161	SNMP	Simple Network Management Protocol
162	SNMP	Simple Network Management Protocol (trap)

Socket Addresses

As we have seen, UDP needs two identifiers, the IP address and port number, at each end to make a connection. The combination of an IP address and a port number is called a **socket address.** The client socket address defines the client process uniquely just as the server socket address defines the server process uniquely (see Figure 11.6).

Figure 11.6   *Socket address*

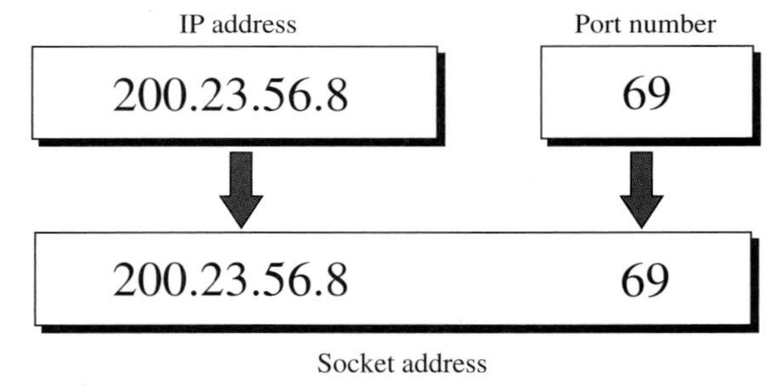

To use the services of UDP, we need a pair of socket addresses: the client socket address and the server socket address. These four pieces of information are part of the IP header and the UDP header. The IP header contains the IP addresses; the UDP header contains the port numbers.

11.2   USER DATAGRAM

UDP packets, called **user datagrams,** have a fixed-size header of eight bytes. Figure 11.7 shows the format of a user datagram.

Figure 11.7   *User datagram format*

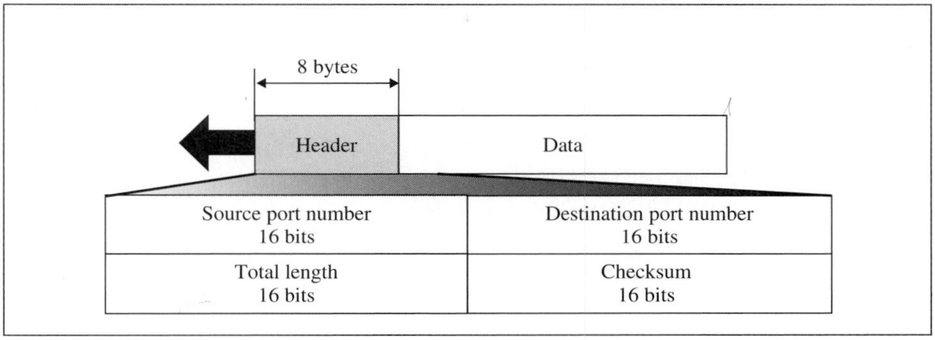

The fields are as follows:

■ **Source port number.** This is the port number used by the process running on the source host. It is 16 bits long, which means that the port number can range from 0 to 65,535. If the source host is the client (a client sending a request), the port number, in most cases, is an ephemeral port number requested by the process and chosen by the UDP software running on the source host. If the source host is the server (a server sending a response), the port number, in most cases, is a well-known port number.

■ **Destination port number.** This is the port number used by the process running on the destination host. It is also 16 bits long. If the destination host is the server (a client sending a request), the port number, in most cases, is a well-known port number. If the destination host is the client (a server sending a response), the port number, in most cases, is an ephemeral port number. In this case, the server copies the ephemeral port number it has received in the request packet.

■ **Length.** This is a 16-bit field that defines the total length of the user datagram, header plus data. The 16 bits can define a total length of 0 to 65,535 bytes. However, the minimum length is eight bytes, which indicates a user datagram with only header and no data. Therefore, the length of the data can be between 0 and 65,507 (65,535 − 20 − 8) bytes (twenty bytes for IP header and 8 bytes for UDP header).

The length field in a UDP user datagram is actually not necessary. A user datagram is encapsulated in an IP datagram. There is a field in the IP datagram that defines the total length. There is another field in the IP datagram that defines the length of the header. So if we subtract the value of the second field from the first, we can deduce the length of the UDP datagram that is encapsulated in an IP datagram.

$$\text{UDP length} = \text{IP length} - \text{IP header's length}$$

However, the designers of the UDP protocol felt that it was more efficient for the destination UDP to calculate the length of the data from the information provided in the UDP user datagram rather than asking the IP software to supply this information. We should remember that when the IP software delivers the UDP user datagram to the UDP layer, it has already dropped the IP header.

■ **Checksum.** This field is used to detect errors over the entire user datagram (header plus data). The checksum is discussed in the next section.

11.3 CHECKSUM

We have already talked about the concept of the checksum and the way it is calculated in Chapter 7. We have also shown how to calculate the checksum for the IP and ICMP packet. We now show how this is done for UDP.

UDP checksum calculation is different from the one for IP and ICMP. Here the checksum includes three sections: a pseudoheader, the UDP header, and the data coming from the application layer.

The **pseudoheader** is part of the header of the IP packet in which the user datagram is to be encapsulated for transmission with some fields filled with 0s (see Figure 11.8).

Figure 11.8 *Pseudoheader added to the UDP datagram*

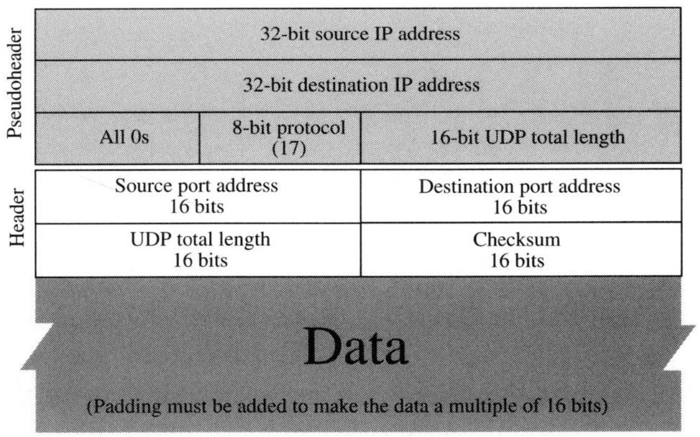

If the checksum does not include the pseudoheader, a user datagram may arrive safe and sound. However, if the IP header is corrupted, it may be delivered to a wrong host.

The protocol field is added to ensure that the packet belongs to UDP, and not to TCP. We will see later that if a process can use either UDP or TCP, the destination port number can be the same. The value of the protocol field for UDP is 17. If this value is changed during transmission, the checksum calculation at the receiver will detect it and UDP drops the packet. It is not delivered to the wrong protocol.

Note the similarities between the pseudoheader fields and the last 12 bytes of the IP header.

Checksum Calculation at Sender

The sender follows these eight steps to calculate the checksum:

1. Add the pseudoheader to the UDP user datagram.
2. Fill the checksum field with zeros.
3. Divide the total bits into 16-bit (two-byte) words.
4. If the total number of bytes is not even, add one byte of padding (all 0s). The padding is only for the purpose of calculating the checksum and will be discarded afterwards.
5. Add all 16-bit sections using one's complement arithmetic.
6. Complement the result (change all 0s to 1s and all 1s to 0s), which is a 16-bit number, and insert it in the checksum field.
7. Drop the pseudoheader and any added padding.
8. Deliver the UDP user datagram to the IP software for encapsulation.

Note that the order of the rows in the pseudoheader does not make any difference in checksum calculation. Also, adding 0s does not change the result. For this reason, the software that calculates the checksum can easily add the whole IP header (20 bytes) to the UDP datagram, set the first bytes to zero, set the TTL field to zero, replace the IP checksum with UDP length, and calculate the checksum. The result would be the same.

Checksum Calculation at Receiver

The receiver follows these six steps to calculate the checksum:

1. Add the pseudoheader to the UDP user datagram.
2. Add padding if needed.
3. Divide the total bits into 16-bit sections.
4. Add all 16-bit sections using one's complement arithmetic.
5. Complement the result.
6. If the result is all 0s, drop the pseudoheader and any added padding and accept the user datagram. If the result is anything else, discard the user datagram.

An Example

Figure 11.9 shows the checksum calculation for a very small user datagram with only seven bytes of data. Because the number of bytes of data is odd, padding is added for checksum calculation. This pseudoheader as well as the padding will be dropped when the user datagram is delivered to the IP.

Figure 11.9   *Checksum calculation of a simple UDP user datagram*

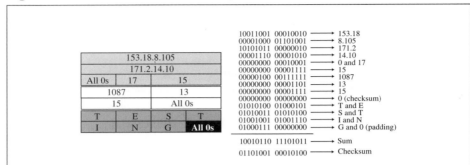

Optional Use of the Checksum

The calculation of the checksum and its inclusion in a user datagram is optional. If the checksum is not calculated, the field is filled with 0s. One might ask, when the UDP software on the destination computer receives a user datagram with a checksum value of zero, how can it determine if the checksum was not used or if it was used and the result happened to be all 0s? The answer is very simple. If the source does calculate the checksum and the result happens to be all 0s, it must be complemented. So what is sent is not all 0s, but all 1s, which is considered negative zero in one's complement arithmetic.

11.4   UDP OPERATION

UDP uses concepts common to the transport layer. These concepts will be discussed here briefly, and then expanded in the next chapter on the TCP protocol.

Connectionless Services

As mentioned previously, UDP provides a connectionless service. This means that each user datagram sent by UDP is an independent datagram. There is no relationship between the different user datagrams even if they are coming from the same source process and going to the same destination program. The user datagrams are not numbered. Also, there is no connection establishment and no connection termination as we will see in the case of the TCP protocol. This means that each user datagram can travel a different path.

One of the ramifications of being connectionless is that the process that uses UDP cannot send a stream of data to UDP and expect UDP to chop them into different related user datagrams. Instead each request must be small enough to fit into one user datagram. Only those processes sending short messages should use UDP.

Flow and Error Control

UDP is a very simple, unreliable transport protocol. There is no flow control, and hence no windowing mechanism. The receiver may overflow with incoming messages.

There is no error control mechanism in UDP except for the checksum. This means that the sender does not know if a message has been lost or duplicated. When the receiver detects an error using the checksum, the user datagram is silently discarded.

The lack of flow control and error control means that the process using UDP should provide for these mechanisms.

Encapsulation and Decapsulation

To send a message from one process to another, the UDP protocol encapsulates and decapsulates messages (see Figure 11.10).

Figure 11.10 *Encapsulation and decapsulation*

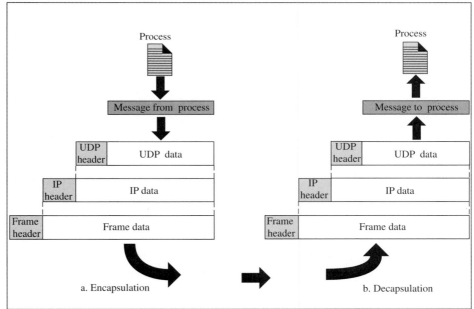

Encapsulation

When a process has a message to send through UDP, it passes the message to UDP along with a pair of socket addresses and the length of data. UDP receives the data and adds the UDP header. UDP then passes the user datagram to the IP with the socket addresses. IP adds its own header, using the value 17 in the protocol field, indicating that the data has come from the UDP protocol. The IP datagram is then passed to the data link layer. The data link layer receives the IP datagram, adds its own header (and possibly a trailer), and passes it to the physical layer. The physical layer encodes the bits into electrical or optical signals and sends it to the remote machine.

Decapsulation

When the message arrives at the destination host, the physical layer decodes the signals into bits and passes it to the data link layer. The data link layer uses the header (and the trailer) to check the data. If there is no error, the header and trailer are dropped and the datagram is passed to the IP. The IP software does its own checking. If there is no error, the header is dropped and the user datagram is passed to the UDP with the sender and receiver IP addresses. UDP uses the checksum to check the entire user datagram. If there is no error, the header is dropped and the application data along with the sender socket address is passed to the process. The sender socket address is passed to the process in case it needs to respond to the message received.

Queuing

We have talked about ports without discussing the actual implementation of them. In UDP, queues are associated with ports (see Figure 11.11).

Figure 11.11 *Queues in UDP*

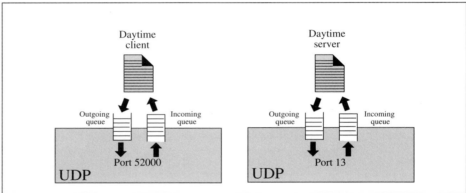

At the client site, when a process starts, it requests a port number from the operating system. Some implementations create both an incoming and an outgoing queue associated with each process. Other implementations create only an incoming queue associated with each process.

Note that even if a process wants to communicate with multiple processes, it obtains only one port number and eventually one outgoing and one incoming queue. The queues opened by the client are, in most cases, identified by ephemeral port numbers. The queues function as long as the process is running. When the process terminates, the queues are destroyed.

The client process can send messages to the outgoing queue by using the source port number specified in the request. UDP removes the messages one by one, and, after adding the UDP header delivers them to IP. An outgoing queue can overflow. If this happens, the operating system can ask the client process to wait before sending any more messages.

When a message arrives for a client, UDP checks to see if an incoming queue has been created for the port number specified in the destination port number field of the user datagram. If there is such a queue, UDP sends the received user datagram to the end of the queue. If there is no such queue, UDP discards the user datagram and asks the ICMP protocol to send a *port unreachable* message to the server. All of the incoming messages for one particular client program, whether coming from the same or a different server, are sent to the same queue. An incoming queue can overflow. If this happens, UDP drops the user datagram and asks for a *port unreachable* message to be sent to the server.

At the server site, the mechanism of creating queues is different. We will see in future chapters that there are different types of servers. However, in its simplest form, a server asks for incoming and outgoing queues using its well-known port when it starts running. The queues remain open as long as the server is running.

When a message arrives for a server, UDP checks to see if an incoming queue has been created for the port number specified in the destination port number field of the user datagram. If there is such a queue, UDP sends the received user datagram to the end of the queue. If there is no such queue, UDP discards the user datagram and asks the ICMP protocol to send a *port unreachable* message to the client. All of the incoming messages for one particular server, whether coming from the same or a different client, are sent to the same queue. An incoming queue can overflow. If this happens, UDP drops the user datagram and asks for a *port unreachable* message to be sent to the client.

When a server wants to respond to a client, it sends messages to the outgoing queue using the source port number specified in the request. UDP removes the messages one by one, and, after adding the UDP header, delivers them to IP. An outgoing queue can overflow. If this happens, the operating system asks the server to wait before sending any more messages.

Multiplexing and Demultiplexing

In a host running a TCP/IP protocol suite, there is only one UDP but possibly several processes that may want to use the services of UDP. To handle this situation, UDP multiplexes and demultiplexes (see Figure 11.12).

Multiplexing

At the sender site, there may be several processes that need to send user datagrams. However, there is only one UDP. This is a many-to-one relationship and requires multiplexing. UDP accepts messages from different processes, differentiated by their assigned port numbers. After adding the header, UDP passes the user datagram to IP.

Demultiplexing

At the receiver site, there is only one UDP. However, we may have many processes that can receive user datagrams. This is a one-to-many relationship and requires demultiplexing. UDP receives user datagrams from IP. After error checking and dropping of the header, UDP delivers each message to the appropriate process based on the port numbers.

Figure 11.12   *Multiplexing and demultiplexing*

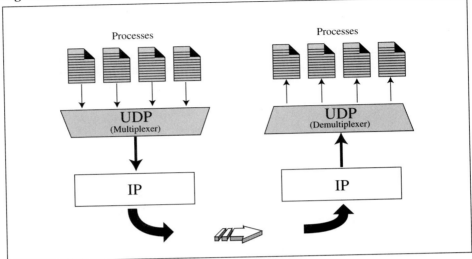

11.5   USE OF UDP

The following lists some uses of the UDP protocol:

- UDP is suitable for a process that requires simple request-response communication and with little concern for flow and error control. It is not usually used for a process that needs to send bulk data, such as FTP (see Chapter 18).

- UDP is suitable for a process with internal flow and error-control mechanisms. For example, the Trivial File Transfer Protocol (TFTP) (see Chapter 19) process includes flow and error control. It can easily use UDP.

- UDP is a suitable transport protocol for multicasting and broadcasting. Multicasting and broadcasting capabilities are embedded in the UDP software but not in the TCP software.

- UDP is used for management processes such as SNMP (see Chapter 21).

- UDP is used for some route updating protocols such as Routing Information Protocol (RIP) (see Chapter 13).

11.6   UDP DESIGN

In this section, we present a simplified, bare-bones design of UDP. This design is meant to be just a teaching tool. Details such as error checking, error handling, and packet validation have been omitted in an attempt to focus on the basics. Our purpose is to demystify the algorithms and their relationships. In addition, we have sacrificed efficiency for the sake of simplicity. For the actual code consult other literature such as Stevens, *TCP/IP Illustrated*, Volume 2.

We can say that the UDP package involves five components: a control-block table, input queues, a control-block module, an input module, and an output module. Figure 11.13 shows these five components and their interactions.

Figure 11.13   *UDP design*

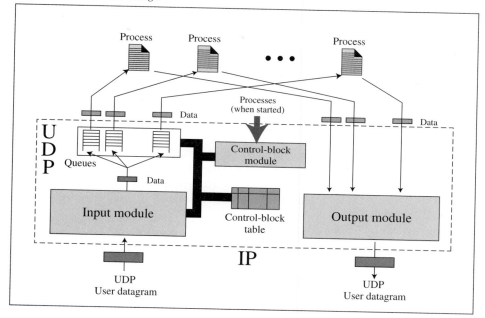

Control-Block Table

In our design, UDP has a control-block table to keep track of the open ports. Each entry in this table has a minimum of four fields: the state, which can be FREE or IN-USE, the process ID, the port number, and the corresponding queue number.

Input Queues

Our UDP design uses a set of input queues, one for each process. In this design, we do not use output queues.

Control-Block Module

The control-block module is responsible for the management of the control-block table. When a process starts, it asks for a port number from the operating system. The operating system assigns well-known port numbers to servers and ephemeral port numbers to clients. The process passes the process ID and the port number to the control-block module to create an entry in the table for the process. The module does not create the queues. The field for queue number has a value of zero. Note that we have not included a strategy to deal with a table that is full; this can be left as an exercise.

Control-Block Module
Receive: a process ID and a port number
1. Search the control block table for a FREE entry.
1. If (not found)
1. Delete an entry using a predefined strategy.
2. Create a new entry with the state IN-USE.
3. Enter the process ID and the port number.
2. Return.

Input Module

The input module receives a user datagram from IP. It searches the control-block table to find an entry having the same port number as this user datagram. If the entry is found, the module uses the information in the entry to enqueue the data. If the entry is not found, it generates an ICMP message.

Input Module
Receive: a user datagram from IP
1. Look for the corresponding entry in the control-block table.
1. If (found)
1. Check the queue field to see if a queue is allocated.
1. If (no)
1. Allocate a queue.
2. Enqueue the data in the corresponding queue.
2. If (not found)
1. Ask the ICMP module to send an "unreachable port" message.
2. Discard the user datagram.
2. Return.

Output Module

The output module is responsible for creating and sending user datagrams.

Output Module
Receive: data and information from a process
1. Create a UDP user datagram.
2. Send the user datagram.
3. Return.

Examples

In this section we will show some examples of how our design responds to input and output. The control-block table at the start of our examples is shown in Table 11.2.

Table 11.2   *The control-block table at the beginning of examples*

State	Process ID	Port Number	Queue Number
IN-USE	2,345	52,010	34
IN-USE	3,422	52,011	
FREE			
IN-USE	4,652	52,012	38
FREE			

Example 1

The first activity is the arrival of a user datagram with destination port number 52,012. The input module searches for this port number and finds it. Queue number 38 has been assigned to this port, which means that the port has been previously used. The input module sends the data to queue 38. The control-block table does not change.

Example 2

After a few seconds, a process starts. It asks the operating system for a port number and is granted port number 52,014. Now the process sends its ID (4,978) and the port number to the control-block module to create an entry in the table. The module takes the first FREE entry and inserts the information received. The module does not allocate a queue at this moment because no user datagrams have arrived for this destination (see Table 11.3).

Table 11.3   *Control-block table after example 2*

State	Process ID	Port Number	Queue Number
IN-USE	2,345	52,010	34
IN-USE	3,422	52,011	
IN-USE	**4,978**	**52,014**	
IN-USE	4,652	52,012	38
FREE			

Example 3

A user datagram now arrives for port 52,011. The input module checks the table and finds that no queue has been allocated for this destination since this is the first time a user datagram has arrived for this destination. The module creates a queue and gives it a number (43). See Table 11.4.

Table 11.4   *Control-block after example 3*

State	Process ID	Port Number	Queue Number
IN-USE	2,345	52,010	34

Table 11.4 *Control-block after example 3 (concluded)*

State	Process ID	Port Number	Queue Number
IN-USE	3,422	52,011	**43**
IN-USE	4,978	52,014	
IN-USE	4,652	52,012	38
FREE			

Example 4

After a few seconds, a user datagram arrives for port 52,222. The input module checks the table and cannot find the entry for this destination. The user datagram is dropped and a request is made to ICMP to send an "unreachable port" message to the source.

Example 5

After a few seconds, a process needs to send a user datagram. It delivers the data to the output module which adds the UDP header and sends it.

11.7 SUMMARY

■ UDP is a transport protocol that creates a process-to-process communication.

■ UDP is a (mostly) unreliable and connectionless protocol that requires little over-head and offers fast delivery.

■ In the client-server paradigm, an application program on the local host, called the client, needs services from an application program on the remote host, called a server.

■ Each application program has a unique port number that distinguishes it from other programs running at the same time on the same machine.

■ The client program is assigned a random port number called the ephemeral port number.

■ The server program is assigned a universal port number called a well-known port number.

■ The IANA has specified ranges for the different types of port numbers.

■ The combination of the IP address and the port number, called the socket address, uniquely defines a process and a host.

■ UDP requires a pair of socket addresses: the client socket address and the server socket address.

■ The UDP packet is called a user datagram.

■ UDP's only attempt at error control is the checksum.

■ Inclusion of a pseudoheader in checksum calculations allows source and destination IP address errors to be detected.

■ UDP has no flow-control mechanism.

■ A user datagram is encapsulated in the data field of an IP datagram.

■ Incoming and outgoing queues hold messages going to and from UDP.

■ UDP uses multiplexing to handle outgoing user datagrams from multiple processes on one host.

■ UDP uses demultiplexing to handle incoming user datagrams that go to different processes on the same host.

■ A UDP package can involve five components: a control-block table, a control-block module, input queues, an input module, and an output module.

■ The input queues hold incoming user datagrams.

■ The control-block module is responsible for maintenance of entries in the control-block table.

■ The input module creates input queues.

■ The output module sends out user datagrams.

11.8   PRACTICE SET

Multiple Choice

1. UDP is an acronym for _____.
   a. User Delivery Protocol
   b. User Datagram Procedure
   c. User Datagram Protocol
   d. Unreliable Datagram Protocol
2. In the sending computer, UDP receives a data unit from the _____ layer.
   a. application
   b. transport
   c. IP
   d. data link
3. In the sending computer, UDP sends a data unit to the _____ layer.
   a. application
   b. transport
   c. IP
   d. data link
4. UDP and TCP are both _____ layer protocols.
   a. physical
   b. data link
   c. network
   d. transport
5. Which of the following functions does UDP perform?
   a. process-to-process communication
   b. host-to-host communication

   c. end-to-end reliable data delivery

   d. all of the above

6. When the IP layer of a receiving host receives a datagram, _____.

   a. delivery is complete

   b. a transport layer protocol takes over

   c. a header is added

   d. b and c

7. UDP needs the _____ address to deliver the user datagram to the correct application program.

   a. port

   b. application

   c. internet

   d. physical

8. Which is a legal port address?

   a. 0

   b. 513

   c. 65,535

   d. all of the above

9. The definition of reliable delivery includes _____.

   a. error-free delivery

   b. receipt of the complete message

   c. in-order delivery

   d. all of the above

10. Which of the following does UDP guarantee?

   a. nonduplication of data

   b. in-order delivery

   c. error-free delivery

   d. a and b

11. Which of the following does UDP guarantee?

   a. sequence numbers on each user datagram

   b. acknowledgments to the sender

   c. flow control

   d. none of the above

12. Because there is no _____, UDP is considered a connectionless transport protocol.

   a. acknowledgment

   b. virtual circuit

   c. reliability

   d. data flow control

13. The source port address on the UDP user datagram header defines _____.

   a. the sending computer

   b. the receiving computer

   c. the application program of the sending computer

   d. the application program of the receiving computer

14. Which of the following is not part of the UDP user datagram header?

   a. length of header

   b. source port address

   c. checksum

   d. destination port address

15. The _____ defines the client program.

   a. ephemeral port number

   b. IP address

   c. well-known port number

   d. physical address

16. The _____ defines the server program.

   a. ephemeral port number

   b. IP address

   c. well-known port number

   d. physical address

17. If the outgoing queue of a UDP client overflows, _____.

   a. the user datagrams are discarded and a port unreachable message is sent

   b. the operating system asks the server to wait before any more messages are sent

   c. new queues are initiated

   d. the operating system asks the client process to wait before any more messages are sent

18. If the incoming queue of a UDP client overflows, _____.

   a. the user datagram is discarded and a port unreachable message is sent

   b. the operating system asks the server to wait before any more messages are sent

   c. new queues are initiated

   d. the operating system asks the client to wait before any more messages are sent

19. If the incoming queue of a UDP server overflows, _____.

   a. the user datagram is discarded and a port unreachable message is sent

   b. the operating system asks the server to wait before any more messages are sent

   c. new queues are initiated

   d. the operating system asks the client to wait before any more messages are sent

20. Which component in our UDP package allocates the queues?

   a. control-block module

   b. control-block table

   c. input module

   d. output module

21. Which component in our UDP package communicates with the ICMP software package?

    a. control-block module

    b. control-block table

    c. input module

    d. output module

22. Which component in our UDP package sends user datagrams to the IP layer?

    a. control-block module

    b. control-block table

    c. input module

    d. output module

23. Which column in the control-block table contains information from the UDP header?

    a. state

    b. process ID

    c. port number

    d. queue number

Exercises

24. In cases where reliability is not of primary importance, UDP would make a good transport protocol. Give examples of specific cases.

25. Are both UDP and IP unreliable to the same degree? Why or why not?

26. Do port addresses need to be unique? Why or why not? Why are port addresses shorter than IP addresses?

27. What is the dictionary definition of the word *ephemeral*? How does it apply to the concept of the ephemeral port number?

28. Show the entries for the header of a UDP user datagram that carries a message from a TFTP client to a TFTP server. Fill the checksum field with 0s. Choose an appropriate ephemeral port number and the correct well-known port number. The length of data is 40 bytes. Show the UDP packet using the format in Figure 11.7.

29. Show the entries for the header of a UDP user datagram that carries a message from an FTP server to an FTP client. Fill the checksum field with 0s. Choose an appropriate ephemeral port number and the correct well-known port number. The length of data is 20 bytes. Show the UDP packet using the format in Figure 11.7.

30. Calculate the checksum for the following binary numbers. Give the result in binary. Use the 16-bit format.
    11000111 11100001
    10000111 10001001
    11100101 10100011
    11111111 11100111

31. Calculate the checksum for the following decimal numbers. Give the result in decimal. Use the 16-bit format.

    23 145 78 23 114

32. Calculate the checksum for the following hexadecimal numbers. Give the result in hexadecimal. Use the16-bit format.

    3478 A233 1234 8976

33. An SNMP client residing on a host with IP address 122.45.12.7 sends a message to an SNMP server residing on a host with IP address 200.112.45.90. What is the pair of sockets used in this communication?

34. A TFTP server residing on a host with IP address 130.45.12.7 sends a message to a TFTP client residing on a host with IP address 14.90.90.33. What is the pair of sockets used in this communication?

35. What is the minimum size of a UDP datagram?

36. What is the maximum size of a UDP datagram?

37. What is the minimum size of the process data that can be encapsulated in a UDP datagram?

38. What is the maximum size of the process data that can be encapsulated in a UDP datagram?

39. A client has a packet of 68,000 bytes. Show how this packet can be transferred using only one UDP user datagram.

40. A client uses UDP to send data to a server. The data is 16 bytes. Calculate the efficiency of this transmission at the UDP level (ratio of useful bytes to total bytes).

41. Redo the previous exercise calculating the efficiency of transmission at the IP level. Assume no options for the IP header.

42. Redo the previous exercise calculating the efficiency of transmission at the data link layer. Assume no options for the IP header and use Ethernet at the data link layer.

43. The following is a dump of a UDP header in hexadecimal format.

    06 32 00 0D 00 1C E2 17

    a. What is the source port number?

    b. What is the destination port number?

    c. What is the total length of the user datagram?

    d. What is the length of the data?

    e. Is the packet directed from a client to a server or vice versa?

    f. What is the client process?

Programming Exercises

44. Create a header file to include all constants that you think are needed to implement the UDP modules in C. Use the **#define** directives.

45. Complete the following struct declaration for the UDP header.

    struct   **UDP_Header**

    {

    unsigned short   SPortAddr ;

    ....

    ....

    } ;

46. Complete the following struct declaration for the UDP user datagram.

    struct   **UDP_Packet**

    {

          struct   UDP_Header   udpHeader ;

          ....   udpData ;

    } ;

47. Write the declaration for the control-block entry.

48. Write the declaration for the control-block table.

49. Write a function that accepts a pointer to a UDP packet and a pointer to the corresponding IP header. The function should calculate and return the value of the checksum for UDP using the pseudoheader.

50. Write a function in C to simulate the control-block module.

51. Write a function in C to simulate the input module.

52. Write a function in C to simulate the output module.

CHAPTER 12

Transmission Control Protocol (TCP)

The TCP/IP protocol suite specifies two protocols for the transport layer: UDP and TCP. We studied UDP in the previous chapter; we will study TCP in this chapter.

Figure 12.1 shows the relationship of TCP to the other protocols in the TCP/IP protocol suite. TCP lies between the application layer and the network layer and serves as the intermediary between the application programs and the network operations.

Figure 12.1 *TCP/IP protocol suite*

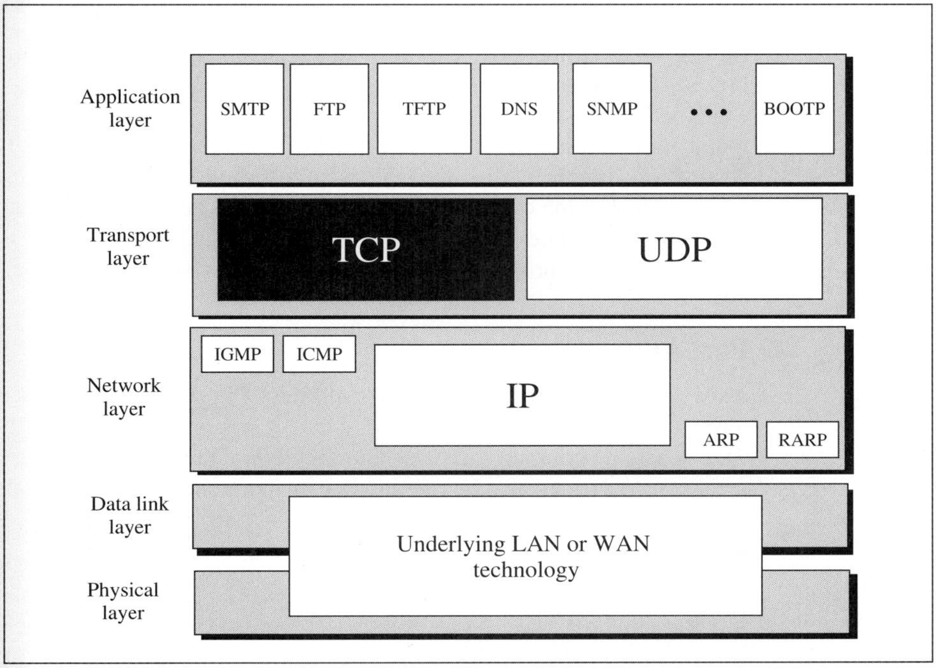

A transport layer protocol usually has several responsibilities. One is to create a process-to-process (program-to-program) communication; TCP uses port numbers to accomplish this. Another responsibility of a transport layer protocol is to create a flow-and error- control mechanism at the transport level. TCP uses a sliding window protocol to achieve flow control. It uses the acknowledgment packet, time-out, and retransmission to achieve error control.

The transport layer is also responsible for providing a connection mechanism for the application program. The application program should be able to send streams of data to the transport layer. It is the responsibility of the transport layer at the sending station to make a connection with the receiver, chop the stream into transportable units, number them, and send them one by one. It is the responsibility of the transport layer at the receiving end to wait until all the different units belonging to the same application program have arrived, check and pass those that are error free, and deliver them to the receiving application program as a stream. After the entire stream has been sent, the transport layer should close the connection. TCP performs all these tasks.

TCP is called a *connection-oriented*, *reliable* transport protocol. It adds connection-oriented and reliability features to the services of IP.

12.1 PROCESS-TO-PROCESS COMMUNICATION

Before we examine TCP, we must first understand host-to-host communication and process-to-process communication and the difference between them.

The IP is responsible for communication at the computer level (host-to-host communication). As a network layer protocol, the IP can deliver the message only to the destination computer. However, this is an incomplete delivery. The message still needs to be handed to the correct application program. This is where a transport layer protocol such as TCP takes over. TCP is responsible for delivery of the message to the appropriate application program. Figure 12.2 shows the scope of duties for IP and TCP.

Port Addresses

As we said in the previous chapter, process-to-process communication is achieved through the client/server paradigm.

A remote computer may be running several server programs at the same time. A local computer may also be running one or more client programs at the same time. For communication, we must define the

- Local host
- Local client program
- Remote host
- Remote server program

The local host and the remote host are defined using IP addresses. To define the client and server programs, we need second identifiers called *port numbers*. In the TCP/IP protocol suite, the port numbers are integers between 0 and 65,535.

Figure 12.2   *TCP versus IP*

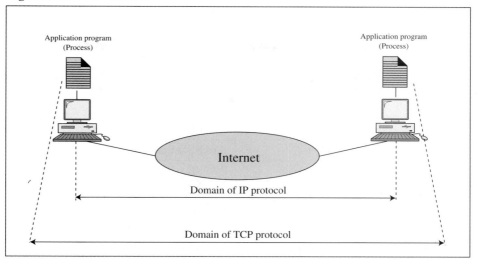

As mentioned in the UDP chapter, a client program running on the local computer defines itself with a port number, chosen randomly by the TCP software running on the local host. This is called the *ephemeral port number.*

The server program, running on the remote computer, must also define itself with a port number. As also mentioned in the UDP chapter, the server uses *well-known port numbers.* For example, in Figure 12.3 the TELNET client program uses an ephemeral (temporary) port number of 64,295 to identify itself, whereas the TELNET server program always uses the well-known (permanent) port number 23.

Figure 12.3   *Port numbers*

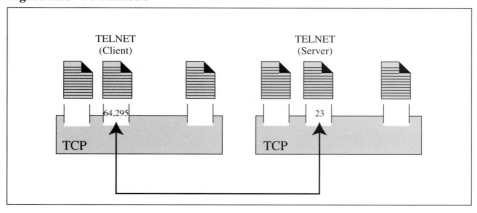

Table 12.1 lists some well-known port numbers used by TCP.

Table 12.1   *Well-known ports used by TCP*

Port	Protocol	Description
7	Echo	Echoes a received datagram back to the sender
9	Discard	Discards any datagram that is received
11	Users	Active users
13	Daytime	Returns the date and the time
17	Quote	Returns a quote of the day
19	Chargen	Returns a string of characters
20	FTP, Data	File Transfer Protocol (data connection)
21	FTP, Control	File Transfer Protocol (control connection)
23	TELNET	Terminal Network
25	SMTP	Simple Mail Transfer Protocol
53	DNS	Domain Name Server
67	BOOTP	Bootstrap Protocol
79	Finger	Finger
80	HTTP	Hypertext Transfer Protocol
111	RPC	Remote Procedure Call

Socket Addresses

Similar to UDP, TCP also needs two identifiers, the IP address and port number, for each end to make a connection. The combination of an IP address and a port number is called a **socket address.** To use the services of TCP (or UDP), we need **a pair of socket addresses**: client socket address and server socket address. The *client* socket address is what defines the client application program uniquely. The *server* socket address is what defines the server application program uniquely. These four pieces of information are part of the IP header and the TCP header. The IP header contains the IP addresses; the TCP header contains the port numbers.

12.2   TCP SERVICES

TCP offers services that are not offered by its counterpart, UDP.

Stream Data Service

TCP is considered a **stream transport layer service**, which means the sending TCP accepts a stream of characters from the sending application program, creates packets, called *segments*, of appropriate size extracted from the stream, and sends them across the network. The receiving TCP receives segments, extracts data from them, orders them if they have arrived out of order, and delivers them as a stream of characters to the receiving application program.

For stream delivery, the sending and receiving TCPs use buffers. The sending TCP uses a sending buffer to store the data coming from the sending application program. The sending application program delivers data at the rate it is created. For example, if the user is typing the data on a keyboard, the data is delivered to the sending TCP character by character. If the data is coming from a file, data may be delivered to the sending TCP line by line, or block by block. The sending application program *writes* data to the buffer of the sending TCP. However, the sending TCP does not create a segment of data for each *write* operation issued from the sending application program. TCP may choose to combine the result of several write operations into one segment to make transmission more efficient. We will see later that the application may use the *push* request to create one segment for each write operation, but TCP does not have to follow this request.

The receiving TCP receives the segments and stores them in a receiving buffer. The receiving application program uses the read operation to read the data from the receiving buffer, but it does not have to read all of the data contained in one segment in one operation. Since the rate of reading can be slower than the rate of receiving, the data is kept in the buffer until the receiving application reads it completely.

Full-Duplex Service

TCP offers **full-duplex service**, where data can flow in both directions at the same time. After two application programs are connected to each other, they can both send and receive data. One TCP connection can carry data from application A to B and, at the same time, data from B to A. When a packet is going from A to B, it can also carry an acknowledgment of the packets received from B. Likewise, when a packet is going from B to A, it can also carry an acknowledgment of the packets received from A. This is called **piggybacking** because acknowledgments can be sent with data. Of course, if one site does not have data to send, it can send just an acknowledgment, without data.

Reliable Service

TCP is a reliable transport protocol. It uses the acknowledgment mechanism to check the safe and sound arrival of data. We will discuss this feature further in section 12.7 on error control.

12.3   SEGMENT

The unit of data transfer between two devices using TCP is a **segment.** The format of a segment is shown in Figure 12.4.

The segment consists of a 20- to 60-byte header, followed by data from the application program. The header is 20 bytes if there are no options and up to 60 bytes if it contains some options. We will discuss some of the header fields in this section. The

Figure 12.4   *TCP segment format*

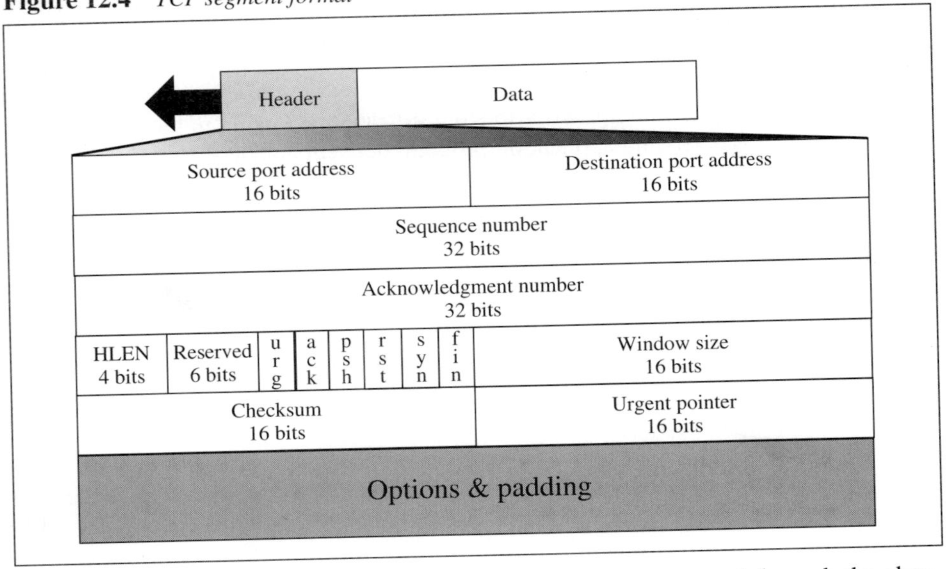

meaning and purpose of these should become clearer as we proceed through the chapter.

■   **Source port address.** This is a 16-bit field that defines the port number of the application program in the host that is sending the segment. This serves the same purpose as the source port address in the UDP header discussed in the previous chapter.

■   **Destination port address.** This is a 16-bit field that defines the port number of the application program in the host that is receiving the segment. This serves the same purpose as the destination port address in the UDP header discussed in the previous chapter.

■   **Sequence number.** This 32-bit field defines the number assigned to the first byte of data contained in this segment. As we said before, TCP is a stream transport protocol. To ensure connectivity, each byte to be transmitted is numbered. The sequence number tells the destination which byte in this sequence comprises the first byte in the segment. During connection establishment (see Section 12.9) each party uses a random number generator to create an **initial sequence number** (ISN), which is usually different in each direction. For example, if the ISN is 2,367 and the first segment is carrying 1,000 bytes, the sequence number is 2,369 (2,367 and 2,368 are used for connection establishment); the second segment, carrying 500 bytes, will have the sequence number 3,369; and so on. The destination can determine the number of the last byte by knowing the size of the data block. We will talk more about sequence number in the discussion on flow control and sliding window protocol.

■   **Acknowledgment number.** This 32-bit field defines the byte number that the source of the segment is expecting to receive from the other party. If the receiver of the segment has successfully received byte number x from the other party, it defines $x + 1$ as the acknowledgment number. As mentioned previously, acknowledgment and data can be piggybacked together.

■ **Header length.** This four-bit field indicates the number of four-byte words in the TCP header. The length of the header can be between 20 and 60 bytes. Therefore, the value of this field can be between 5 ($5 \times 4 = 20$) and 15 ($15 \times 4 = 60$).

■ **Reserved.** This is a six-bit field reserved for future use.

■ **Control.** This field defines six different control bits or flags as shown in Figure 12.5. One or more of these bits can be set at a time.

Figure 12.5 *Control field*

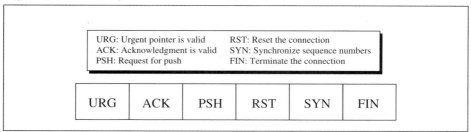

These bits enable flow control, connection establishment and termination, and the mode of data transfer in TCP. A brief description of each bit is shown in Table 12.2. We will discuss them further when we study the detailed operation of TCP later in the chapter.

Table 12.2 *Description of flags in the control field*

Flag	Description
URG	The value of the urgent pointer field is valid
ACK	The value of the acknowledgment field is valid
PSH	Push the data
RST	The connection must be reset
SYN	Synchronize sequence numbers during connection
FIN	Terminate the connection

■ **Window size.** This field defines the size of the window, in bytes, that the other party must maintain. Note that the length of this field is 16 bits, which means that the maximum size of the window is 65,535 bytes. We will talk more about this in the discussion on sliding window protocol later in the chapter.

■ **Checksum.** This 16-bit field contains the checksum. See Section 12.5 on Checksum.

■ **Urgent pointer.** This 16-bit field, which is valid only if the urgent flag is set, is used when the segment contains urgent data. It defines the number that must be added to the sequence number to obtain the number of the last urgent byte in the data section of the segment. This will be discussed later in this chapter.

■ **Options.** There can be up to 40 bytes of optional information in the TCP header. We will discuss the different options currently used in the TCP header in the next section.

12.4 OPTIONS

The TCP header can have up to 40 bytes of optional information. They are used to convey additional information to the destination or to align other options. We can define two categories of options: one-byte options and multiple-byte options. The first category contains two types of options: end of option and no operation. The second category contains three types of options: maximum segment size, window scale factor, and timestamp (see Figure 12.6).

Figure 12.6 *Options*

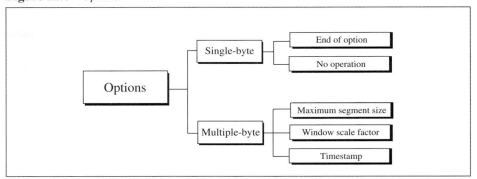

■ **End of option.** This is a one-byte option used for padding at the end of the option field. It, however, can only be used as the last option. Only one end of option can be used. After this option, the receiver looks for the payload data. This means that if more than one byte is needed to align the option field, some no-operation options must be used followed by an end of option (see Figure 12.7). End of option imparts three pieces of information to the destination:

Figure 12.7 *End of option*

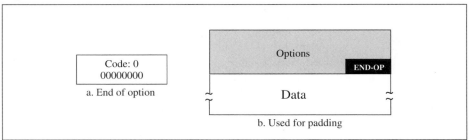

1. No more options in the header.
2. The remainder of the 32-bit word is garbage.
3. Data from the application program starts at the beginning of the next 32-bit word.

■ **No operation.** This is a one-byte option used as a filler between options. For example, it can be used to align the next option on a 16-bit or 32-bit boundary (see Figure 12.8).

Figure 12.8   *No operation option*

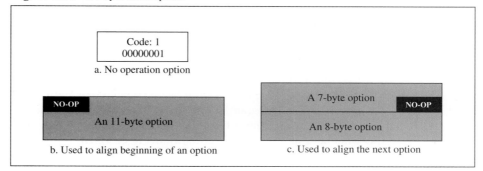

Maximum segment size (MSS). This option defines the size of the biggest chunk of data that can be received by the destination of the TCP segment. In spite of its name, it defines the maximum size of the data, not the maximum size of the segment. Since the field is 16 bits long, the value can be 0 to 65,535 bytes. The default is 536.

The maximum data size is determined during the connection establishment phase. The size is determined by the destination of the segment, not the source. So party 1 defines what should be the MSS sent by party 2. Party 2 defines what should be the MSS sent by party 1. If neither party defines the size, the default is chosen.

This option is used only in the segments that make the connections. It cannot be used in segments during data transfer. Figure 12.9 shows the format of this option.

Figure 12.9   *Maximum segment size option*

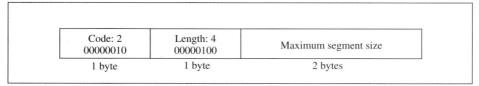

■ **Window scale factor.** The window size field in the header defines the size of the sliding window. This field is 16 bits long, which means that the window can range from 0 to 65,535 bytes. Although this seems like a very large window size, it still may not be sufficient, especially if the data is traveling on a high throughput, high-delay transmission media. Consider, for example, a fiber-optic channel (OC-24), having a throughput of 1,244.160 Mbps, connecting two computers 6,000 miles apart. When one station sends data to another, it takes at least 64 milliseconds to receive an acknowledgment. During this period, 10 Megabytes can be sent. However, the size of the window allows the station to send only 65,535 bytes.

To increase the window size, the window scale factor is used. The new window size is found by first raising 2 to the number specified in the window scale factor. Then this result is multiplied by the value of the window size in the header.

$$\text{new window size} = \text{window size defined in the header} \times 2^{\text{window scale factor}}$$

For example, if the value of the window scale factor is 3, then the actual window size is eight times the value of the window size. Although the scale factor could be as large as 255, the largest value allowed by TCP/IP is 16, which means that the maximum window size can be $2^{16} \times 2^{16} = 2^{32}$, which is the same as the maximum value for the sequence number. Note that the size of the window cannot be greater than the maximum value for the sequence number.

The window scale factor can be determined only during the connection setup phase. During data transfer, the size of the window (specified in the header) may be changed, but it must be multiplied by the same scale factor. The format of the window scale factor option is shown in Figure 12.10.

Figure 12.10   *Window scale factor option*

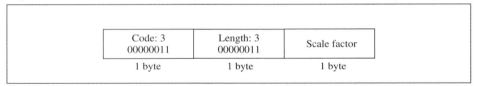

The scale factor is sometimes called the *shift count* because if you multiply a number by a power of 2, you are shifting it to the left (bitwise operation).

■   **Timestamp.** This is a 10-byte option with the format shown in Figure 12.11.

Figure 12.11   *Timestamp option*

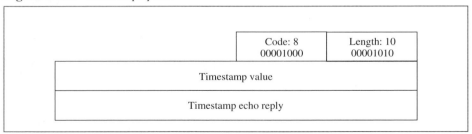

The timestamp field is filled by the source when the segment leaves. The destination receives the segment and stores the timestamp value. When the destination sends an acknowledgment for the bytes in that segment, it enters the previously stored value in the echo reply field. The source, when it receives the acknowledgment, checks the current time versus this value. The difference is the round-trip time. The round-trip time can be used by TCP to dynamically define the retransmission time-out, as we will see later.

12.5   CHECKSUM

The calculation of the checksum for TCP follows the same procedure as the one described for UDP in the previous chapter. However, the inclusion of the checksum in the UDP datagram is optional; whereas the inclusion of the checksum for TCP is mandatory.

The same pseudoheader, serving the same purpose, is added to the segment. The only field changed is the value for the protocol field: It is six in this case. See Figure 12.12.

Figure 12.12   *Pseudoheader added to the TCP datagram*

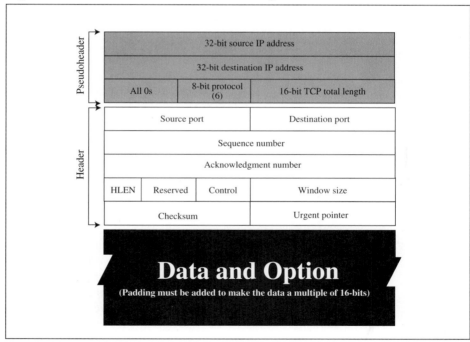

12.6   FLOW CONTROL

Flow control defines the amount of data a source can send before receiving an acknowledgment from the destination. In an extreme case, a transport layer protocol could send one byte of data and wait for an acknowledgment before sending the next byte. But this is an extremely slow process. If the data is traveling a long distance, the source is idle while it waits for an acknowledgment.

At the other extreme, a transport layer protocol can send all of the data it has without worrying about acknowledgment. This speeds up the process, but it may overwhelm the receiver. Besides, if some part of the data is lost, duplicated, received out of order, or corrupted, the source will not know until all has been checked by the destination.

TCP uses a solution that stands somewhere in between. It defines a window, which is imposed on the buffer of data delivered from the application program and is ready to be sent. TCP sends as much data as is defined by the window.

Sliding Window

To accomplish flow control, TCP uses a sliding window protocol. With this method, both hosts use a window for each connection. The window covers a portion of the buffer that a host can send before worrying about an acknowledgment from the other host. The window is called a **sliding window** because it can slide over the buffer as the receiver sends acknowledgment of the bytes received safe and sound. Figure 12.13

Figure 12.13   *Sliding window*

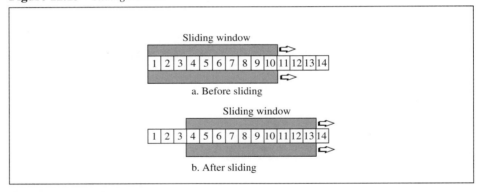

shows a sliding window of size 10. Before receiving any acknowledgment from the destination, the source can send up to 10 bytes. However, if it receives acknowledgment of the first three bytes, it can slide the window three bytes to the right. This means that now it can send 10 more bytes before worrying about an acknowledgment.

Figure 12.14 shows the previous window, but we added the pointer that the source uses to know which bytes have already been sent and which ones can be sent.

What we have shown in the previous examples is a fixed-size window. The size of the window in TCP is variable. The destination, in each acknowledgment segment, can define the size of the window. The advertised size is relative to the acknowledgment number. For example, if the receiver acknowledges the receipt of byte 3,000 and defines the size of the window to be 200, it means that the window now expands from byte 3,001 to byte 3,200.

Let us discuss the variable-size window. The size of the window can be increased or decreased depending on the advertisement by the destination.

Figure 12.14 *Sliding window with pointer*

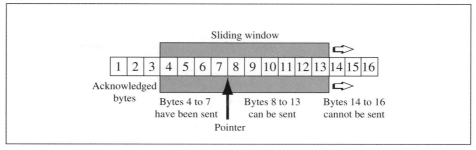

Increasing the Window Size

The destination can increase the size of the window in an acknowledgment segment. Figure 12.15 shows how the window can slide with a simultaneous increase in size.

Figure 12.15 *Increasing the window size*

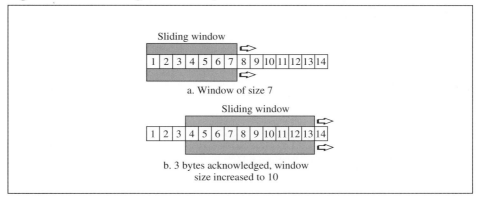

Decreasing the Window Size

The destination can decrease the size of the window in an acknowledgment segment. Figure 12.16 shows how the window can slide with a simultaneous decrease in size. However, there is a restriction: The window size cannot decrease in such a way that the leading edge of the window slides to the left.

Window Management

TCP uses two buffers and one window to control the flow of data. The sending TCP has a buffer that stores data coming from the sending application program. The application program creates data and writes it to the buffer. The sender imposes a window on this buffer and sends segments as long as the size of the window is not zero. The TCP receiver has a buffer also. It receives data, checks them, and stores them in the buffer to be consumed by the receiving application program.

We said that the size of the window in the sending TCP is determined by the receiver and is announced in the ACK segments. How does the receiver choose the size

Figure 12.16 *Decreasing the window size*

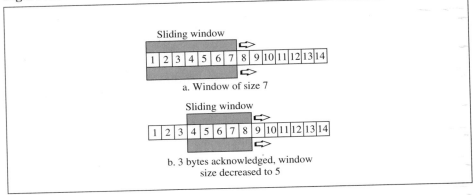

a. Window of size 7

b. 3 bytes acknowledged, window
size decreased to 5

A sliding window is used to make transmission more efficient as well as to control the flow of data so that the destination does not become overwhelmed with data. TCP's sliding windows are byte oriented.

Some Points about TCP's Sliding Windows:

■ The source does not have to send a full window's worth of data.
■ The size of the window can be increased or decreased by the destination.
■ The destination can send an acknowledgment at any time.

of the window? The size of the window, announced by the receiver, is usually the space left over in the receiving TCP buffer. Figure 12.17 shows an example. Imagine that the sending TCP has originally defined a very large buffer. The receiving TCP has defined a 4K buffer. During the connection setup, the receiving window announces the size of window to be 4K, the same size as its buffer.

The sending TCP sends 4K of data in its first segment. The buffer of the receiving window becomes full. The receiving TCP acknowledges the receipt of the segment, but announces a window size of zero. The sending TCP cannot send any more data. It must wait for acknowledgment advertising a nonzero window size.

At the receiver, the application program consumes 1K of data, resulting in 1K of available buffer space. The receiving TCP sends a new acknowledgment with a window size of 1K. The sender can now send a segment of 1K, which fills up the buffer. And so on.

Silly Window Syndrome

A serious problem can arise in the sliding window operation when either the sending application program creates data slowly or the receiving application program consumes data slowly, or both. Either of these situations results in the sending of data in very small segments, which reduces the efficiency of the operation. For example, if TCP sends segments containing only 1 byte of data, it means that we are sending a 41-byte

Figure 12.17   *Window management*

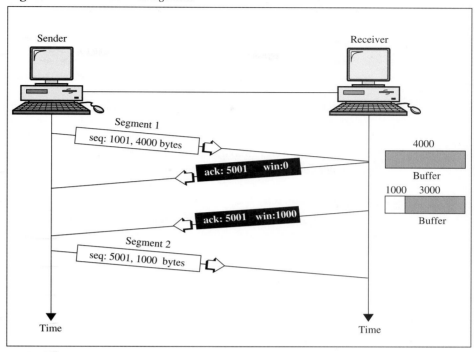

datagram (20 bytes of TCP header and 20 bytes of IP header) that transfers only 1 byte of user data. Here the overhead is 41/1, which indicates that we are using the capacity of the network very inefficiently. This problem is called the *silly window syndrome*. For each site, we first describe how the problem is created and then give the proposed solution.

Syndrome Created by the Sender

The sending TCP may create silly window syndrome if it is serving an application program that creates data slowly, for example, one byte at a time. The application program writes one byte at a time into the buffer of the sending TCP. If the sending TCP does not have any specific instructions, it may create segments containing one byte of data. The result is a lot of 41-byte segments that are traveling through an internet.

The solution is to prevent the sending TCP from sending the data byte by byte. The sending TCP must be forced to collect data and send it in a larger block. How long should the sending TCP wait? If it waits too long, it may create delay in the process. If it does not wait long enough, it may end up sending small segments. Nagle found an elegant solution.

Nagle's Algorithm   Nagle's algorithm is very simple, but it solves the problem. This algorithm is for the sending TCP:

1. The sending TCP sends the first piece of data it receives from the sending application program even if it is only one byte.

2. After sending the first segment, the sending TCP accumulates data in the output buffer and waits until either the receiving TCP sends an acknowledgment or until enough data has accumulated to fill a maximum-size segment. At this time, the sending TCP can send the segment.

3. Step 2 is repeated for the rest of the transmission. Segment 3 must be sent if an acknowledgment is received for segment 2 or enough data is accumulated to fill a maximum-size segment.

The elegance of Nagle's algorithm is in its simplicity and in the fact that it takes into account the speed of the application program that creates the data and the speed of the network that transports the data. If the application program is faster than the network, the segments are larger (maximum-size segments). If the application program is slower than the network, the segments are smaller (less than the maximum-size segment).

Syndrome Created by the Receiver

The receiving TCP may create silly window syndrome if it is serving an application program that consumes data slowly, for example, one byte at a time. Suppose that the sending application program creates data in blocks of 1K, but the receiving application program consumes data one byte at a time. Also suppose that the input buffer of the receiving TCP is 4K. The sender sends the first four kilobytes of data. The receiver stores it in its buffer. Now its buffer is full. It advertises a window size of zero, which means the sender should stop sending data. The receiving application reads the first byte of data from the input buffer of the receiving TCP. Now there is one byte of space in the incoming buffer. The receiving TCP announces a window size of one byte, which means that the sending TCP, which is eagerly waiting to send data, takes this advertisement as good news and sends a segment carrying only one byte of data. The procedure will continue. One byte of data is consumed and a segment carrying one byte of data is sent. Again we have an efficiency problem and a silly window syndrome.

Two solutions have been proposed to prevent the silly window syndrome created by an application program that consumes data slower than they arrive.

Clark's Solution   Clark's solution is to send an acknowledgment as soon as the data arrives, but to announce a window size of zero until either there is enough space to accommodate a segment of maximum size or until half of the buffer is empty.

Delayed Acknowledgment   The second solution is to delay sending the acknowledgment. This means that when a segment arrives, it is not acknowledged immediately. The receiver waits until there is a decent amount of space in its incoming buffer before acknowledging the arrived segments. The delayed acknowledgment prevents the sending TCP from sliding its window. After it has sent the data in the window, it stops. This kills the syndrome.

Delayed acknowledgment also has another advantage: It reduces traffic. The receiver does not have to acknowledge each segment. But there also is a disadvantage in that the delayed acknowledgment may force the sender to retransmit the unacknowledged segments.

The protocol balances the advantages and disadvantages. It now defines that the acknowledgment should not be delayed by more than 500 milliseconds.

12.7   ERROR CONTROL

TCP is a reliable transport layer protocol. This means that an application program that delivers a stream of data to TCP relies on TCP to deliver the entire stream to the application program on the other end in order, without error, and without any part lost or duplicated.

TCP provides reliability using error control. Error control includes mechanisms for detecting corrupted segments, lost segments, out-of-order segments, and duplicated segments. Error control also includes a mechanism for correcting errors after they are detected.

Error Detection and Correction

Error detection in TCP is achieved through the use of three simple tools: checksum, acknowledgment, and time-out. Each segment includes the checksum field, which is used to check for a corrupted segment. If the segment is corrupted, it is discarded by the destination TCP. TCP uses the acknowledgment method to confirm the receipt of those segments that have reached the destination TCP uncorrupted. No negative acknowledgment is used in TCP. If a segment is not acknowledged before the time-out, it is considered to be either corrupted or lost.

The error-correction mechanism used by TCP is also very simple. The source TCP starts one time-out counter for each segment sent. Each counter is checked periodically. When a counter matures, the corresponding segment is considered to be either corrupted or lost, and the segment will be retransmitted.

Corrupted Segment

Figure 12.18 shows a corrupted segment arriving at the destination. In this example the source sends segments 1 through 3, each 200 bytes. The sequence number begins at 1,201 on segment 1. The receiving TCP receives segments 1 and 2 and, using the checksum, finds them error free. It acknowledges the receipt of segments 1 and 2 using acknowledgment number 1,601, which means that it has received bytes 1,201 to 1,600 safe and sound, and is expecting to receive byte 1,601. However, it finds that segment 3 is corrupted and discards segment 3. Note that although it has received bytes 1,601 to 1,800 in segment 3, the destination does not consider this as a "receipt" because this segment was corrupted. After the time-out for segment 3 has matured, the source TCP will resend segment 3. After receiving segment 3, the destination sends the acknowledgment for byte 1,801, which indicates that it has received bytes 1,201 to 1,800 safe and sound.

Lost Segment

Figure 12.19 shows a lost segment. The situation is exactly the same as the corrupted segment. In other words, from the point of the source and destination, a lost segment and a corrupted segment are the same. A corrupted segment is discarded by the final destination; a lost segment is discarded by some intermediate node and never reaches the destination.

Figure 12.18 *Corrupted segment*

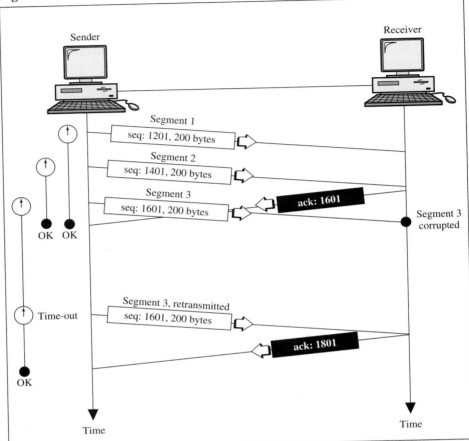

Duplicate Segment

A duplicate segment can be created, for example, by a source TCP when the acknowledgment does not arrive before the time-out. Handling the duplicated segment is a simple process for the destination TCP. The destination TCP expects a continuous stream of bytes. When a packet arrives that contains the same sequence number as another received segment, the destination TCP simply discards the packet.

Out-of-Order Segment

TCP uses the services of IP, an unreliable, connectionless network layer protocol. The TCP segment is encapsulated in an IP datagram. Each datagram is an independent entity. The routers are free to send each datagram through any route they find suitable. One datagram may follow a route with a short delay; another may follow another route with a longer delay. If datagrams arrive out of order, the TCP segments that are encapsulated in the datagrams will be out of order as well. The handling of out-of-order segments by the destination TCP is very simple: It does not acknowledge an out-of-order

Figure 12.19   *Lost segment*

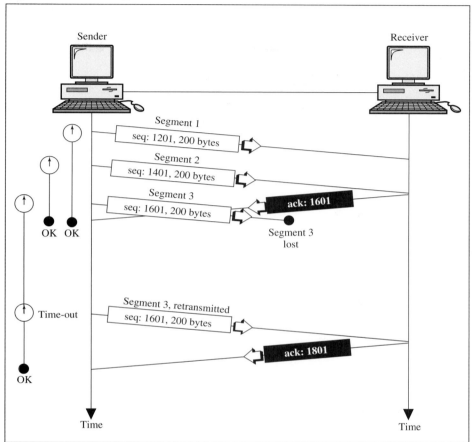

segment until it receives all of the segments that precede it. Of course, if the acknowledgment is delayed, the timer of the out-of-order segment may mature at the source TCP and the segment may be resent. The duplicates then will be discarded by the destination TCP.

Lost Acknowledgment

Figure 12.20 shows a lost acknowledgment sent by the destination. In the TCP acknowledgment mechanism, a lost acknowledgment may not even be noticed by the source TCP. TCP uses an accumulative acknowledgment system. Each acknowledgment is a confirmation that everything up to the byte specified by the acknowledgment number has been received. For example, if the destination sends an ACK segment with an acknowledgment number for byte 1,801, it is confirming that bytes 1,201 to 1,800 have been received. If the destination had previously sent an acknowledgment for byte 1,601, meaning it has received bytes 1,201 to 1,600, loss of the acknowledgment is totally irrelevant.

Figure 12.20   *Lost acknowledgment*

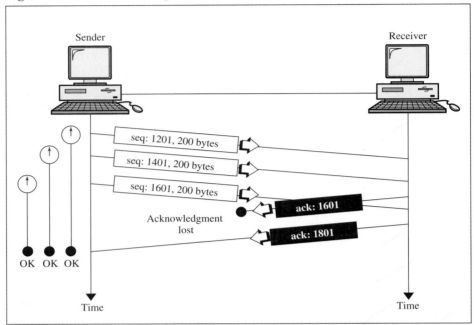

12.8   TCP TIMERS

To perform its operation smoothly, TCP uses the four timers shown in Figure 12.21.

Figure 12.21   *TCP timers*

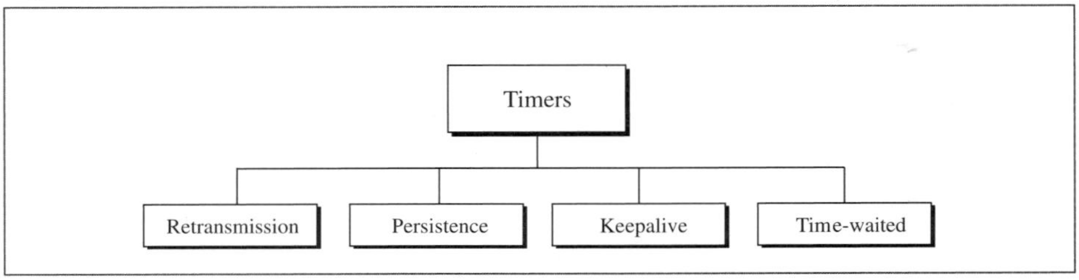

Retransmission Timer

To control a lost or discarded segment, TCP employs a retransmission timer which handles the retransmission time, the waiting time for an acknowledgment of a segment. When TCP sends a segment, it creates a retransmission timer for that particular segment. Two situations may occur:

1. If an acknowledgment is received for this particular segment before the timer goes off, the timer is destroyed.

2. If the timer goes off before the acknowledgment arrives, the segment is retransmitted and the timer is reset.

Calculation of Retransmission Time

The TCP protocol is a transport layer protocol. Each connection connects two TCPs that may be just one physical network apart or located on opposite sides of the globe. In other words, each connection creates a path with a length that may be totally different from another path created by another connection. This means that TCP cannot use the same retransmission time for all connections. Selecting a fixed retransmission time for all connections can result in serious consequences. If the retransmission time does not allow enough time for a segment to reach the destination and an acknowledgment to reach the source, it can result in retransmission of segments that are still on the way. Conversely, if the retransmission time is longer than necessary for a short path, it may result in delay for the application programs.

Even for one single connection, the retransmission time should not be fixed. A connection may be able to send segments and receive acknowledgments faster during non-traffic periods than during congestion periods. TCP uses the dynamic retransmission time-out, a transmission time-out that is different for each connection and which may be changed during the same connection.

Retransmission time-out can be made dynamic by basing it on the round-trip time (RTT). Several formulas are used for this purpose. The most common is to consider the retransmission time to be twice the RTT:

$$\text{Retransmission time} = 2 \times \text{RTT}$$

Calculation of RTT

The question now is how do we calculate the RTT itself? RTT, too, is calculated dynamically. There are two methods. In the first method, TCP uses the timestamp option as described previously. In the second method, TCP sends a segment, starts a timer, and waits for an acknowledgment. It measures the time between the sending of the segment and the receiving of the acknowledgment. Each segment has a round-trip time. The value of the RTT used in the calculation of the retransmission time of the next segment is the updated value of the RTT according to the following formula:

$$\text{RTT} = \alpha \times \text{previous RTT} + (1 - \alpha) \text{ current RTT}$$

The value of α is usually 90 percent. This means that the new RTT is 90 percent of the value of the previous RTT plus 10 percent of the value of the current RTT. For example, if the previous RTT is 250 microseconds and it takes a segment at this moment to be acknowledged in 70 microseconds, the value of the new RTT and the retransmission time would be

$$\text{RTT} = 90\% \times 250 + 10\% \times 70 = 232 \text{ microseconds}$$

$$\text{Retransmission time} = 2 \times 232 = 464 \text{ microseconds}$$

Karn's Algorithm

Suppose that a segment is not acknowledged during the retransmission period and it is therefore retransmitted. When the sending TCP receives an acknowledgment for this segment, it does not know if the acknowledgment is for the original segment or for the retransmitted one. The value of the new RTT therefore must be calculated based on the departure of the segment. But if the original segment was lost and the acknowledgment is for the retransmitted one, the value of the current RTT must be calculated from the time the segment was retransmitted. This is a dilemma that was solved by Karn. Karn's solution is very simple. Do not consider the RTT of a retransmitted segment in the calculation of the new RTT. Do not update the value of RTT until you send a segment and receive an acknowledgment without the need for retransmission.

Persistence Timer

To deal with the zero window-size advertisement, TCP needs another timer. Suppose the receiving TCP announces a window size of zero. The sending TCP then stops transmitting segments until the receiving TCP sends an acknowledgment announcing a non-zero window size. This acknowledgment can be lost. Remember that acknowledgments are not acknowledged in TCP. If this acknowledgment is lost, the receiving TCP thinks that it has done its job and waits for the sending TCP to send more segments. The sending TCP has not received an acknowledgment and waits for the other TCP to send an acknowledgment advertising the size of the window. Both TCPs can continue to wait for each other forever.

To correct this deadlock, TCP uses a persistence timer for each connection. When the sending TCP receives an acknowledgment with a window size of zero, it starts a persistence timer. When the persistence timer goes off, the sending TCP sends a special segment called a *probe.* This segment contains only one byte of data. It has a sequence number, but its sequence number is never acknowledged; it is even ignored in calculating the sequence number for the rest of the data. The probe alerts the receiving TCP that the acknowledgment was lost and should be resent.

The value of the persistence timer is set to the value of the retransmission time. However, if a response is not received from the receiver, another probe segment is sent and the value of the persistence timer is doubled and reset. The sender continues sending the probe segments and doubling and resetting the value of the persistence timer until the value reaches a threshold (usually 60 seconds). After that the sender sends one probe segment every 60 seconds until the window is reopened.

Keepalive Timer

A keepalive timer is used in some implementations to prevent a long idle connection between two TCPs. Suppose that a client opens a TCP connection to a server, transfers some data, and becomes silent. Perhaps the client has crashed. In this case, the connection remains open forever.

To remedy this situation, most implementations equip a server with a keepalive timer. Each time the server hears from a client, it resets this timer. The time-out is usually two hours. If the server does not hear from the client after two hours, it sends a probe segment. If there is no response after 10 probes, each of which is 75 seconds apart, it assumes that the client is down and terminates the connection.

Time-Waited Timer

The time-waited timer is used during connection termination. When TCP closes a connection, it does not consider the connection really closed. The connection is held in limbo for a time-waited period. This allows duplicate FIN segments, if any, to arrive at the destination to be discarded. The value for this timer is usually two times the expected lifetime of a segment.

12.9   CONNECTION

TCP is a connection-oriented protocol. A connection-oriented protocol establishes a virtual path between the source and destination. All of the segments belonging to a message are then sent over this virtual path. Using a single virtual pathway for the entire message facilitates the acknowledgment process as well as retransmission of damaged or lost frames.

In TCP, connection-oriented transmission is achieved through two procedures: connection establishment and connection termination.

Connection Establishment

TCP transmits data in full-duplex mode. When two TCPs in two machines are connected they should be able to send segments to each other simultaneously. This implies that before any data transfer, each party must initialize communication and get approval from the other party. Four actions should be taken before the two parties, called here host A and host B, can send data:

1. Host A sends a segment to announce its wish for connection and includes its initialization information about the traffic from A to B.
2. Host B sends a segment to acknowledge (confirm) the request of A.
3. Host B sends a segment that includes its initialization information about the traffic from B to A.
4. Host A sends a segment to acknowledge (confirm) the request of B.

This connection establishment implies four steps. However, since there is no time interval between steps 2 and 3, they can be combined into one step. Host B can both confirm the request of host A and send its own request.

Three-Way Handshaking

The connection establishment described above is called *three-way handshaking*. In this procedure, an application program, called the client, wants to make a connection with another application program, called the server, using TCP as the transport layer protocol.

The three-way handshaking procedure starts with the server. The server program tells its TCP that it is ready to accept a connection. This is called a request for a *passive open*. It means that although its TCP is ready to accept any connection from any machine in the world it cannot make the connection itself.

The client program makes a request for an *active open*. A client that wishes to connect to a server tells its TCP that it needs to be connected to a particular server. The TCP can now start the three-way handshaking process as shown in Figure 12.22.

Figure 12.22   *Three-way handshaking*

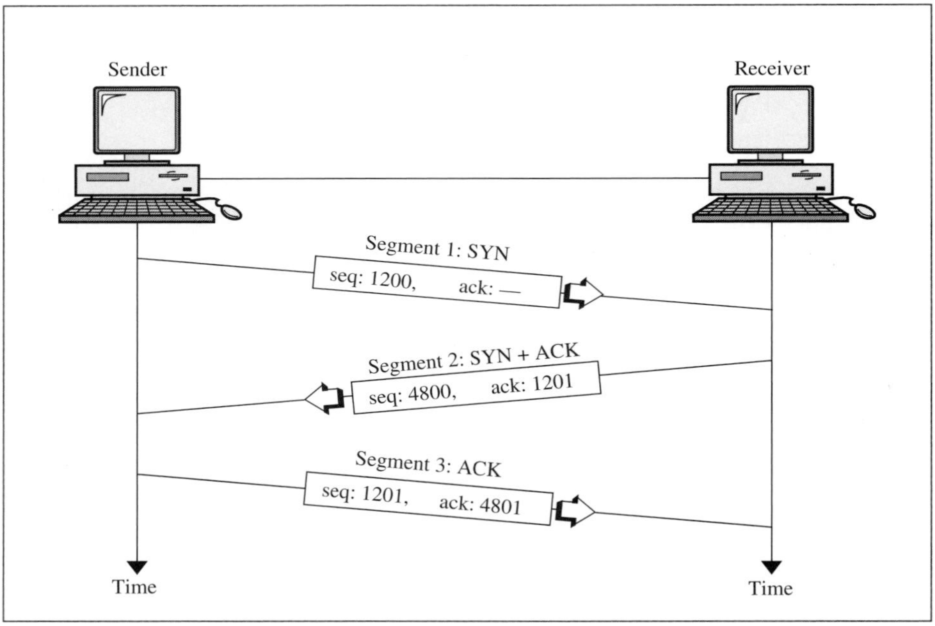

The steps of the process are as follows:

1. The client sends the first segment, a SYN segment. The segment includes the source and destination port numbers. The destination port number clearly defines the server to which the client wants to be connected. The segment also contains the client initialization sequence number (ISN) used for numbering the bytes of data sent from the client to the server. If the client wants to define the MSS that it can receive from the server, it can add the corresponding option here. Also, if the client needs a large window, it defines the window scale factor here using the appropriate option. This segment defines the wish of the client to make a connection with certain parameters. Note that this segment does not contain any acknowledgment number. It does not define the window size either; a window size definition makes sense only when a segment includes an acknowledgment.

2. The server sends the second segment, a SYN and ACK segment. This segment has a dual purpose. First, it acknowledges the receipt of the first segment using the ACK flag and acknowledgment number field. The acknowledgment number is the

client initialization sequence number plus one. The server must also define the client window size. Second, the segment is used as the initialization segment for the server. It contains the initialization sequence number used to number the bytes sent from the server to the client. It also contains the window scale factor option (if needed) to be used by the server and the MSS defined by the server. As we said before, this is two segments combined into one.

3. The client sends the third segment. This is just an ACK segment. It acknowledges the receipt of the second segment using the ACK flag and acknowledgment number field. The acknowledgment number is the server initialization sequence number plus one. The client must also define the server window size. Note that data can be sent with the third packet.

A rare situation may occur when both processes issue an active open. In this case, both TCPs transmit a SYN + ACK segment to each other and one single connection is established between them.

Connection Termination

Any of the two parties involved in exchanging data (client or server) can close the connection. When connection in one direction is terminated, the other party can continue sending data in the other direction. Therefore, four actions are needed to close the connections in both directions:

1. Host A sends a segment announcing its wish for connection termination.
2. Host B sends a segment acknowledging (confirming) the request of A. After this, the connection is closed in one direction, but not in the other. Host B can continue sending data to A.
3. When host B has finished sending its own data, it sends a segment to indicate that it wants to close the connection.
4. Host A acknowledges (confirms) the request of B.

This implies four steps. We cannot combine steps 2 and 3 here as we did in connection establishment. Steps 2 and 3 may or may not happen at the same time. The connection may be closed in one direction, but left open in the other direction.

Four-Way Handshaking

The connection termination described above is called *four-way handshaking*. In this procedure, an application program, usually the client, wants to terminate a connection.

The procedure starts with the client. The client program tells its TCP that it has finished sending data and wishes to terminate the connection. This is a request for an active close.

After receiving the request for an active close, the client TCP closes communication in the client-server direction. However, communication in the other direction is still open.

When the server program has finished sending data in the server-client direction, it can request from its TCP to close the connection in the server-client direction. This is usually a passive close. Four-way handshaking is shown in Figure 12.23.

Figure 12.23   *Four-way handshaking*

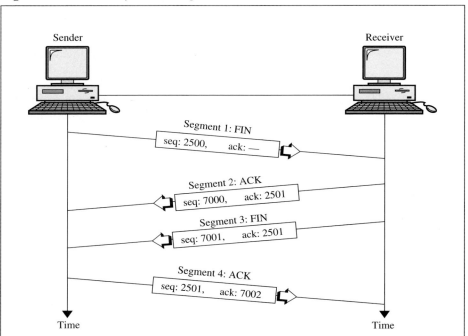

The four steps are

1. The client TCP sends the first segment, a FIN segment.

2. The server TCP sends the second segment, an ACK segment, to confirm the receipt of the FIN segment from the client. In this segment it uses the acknowledgment number, which is one plus the sequence number received in the FIN segment.

3. The server TCP can continue sending data in the server-client direction. When it does not have any more data to send, it sends the third segment. This segment is a FIN segment.

4. The client TCP sends the fourth segment, an ACK segment, to confirm the receipt of the FIN segment from the TCP server. This segment contains the acknowledgment number, which is one plus the sequence number received in the FIN segment from the server.

Connection Resetting

TCP may request the resetting of a connection. *Resetting* here means that the current connection is destroyed. This happens in one of three cases:

1. The TCP on one side has requested a connection to a nonexistent port. The TCP on the other side may send a segment with its RST bit set to annul the request.

2. One TCP may want to abort the connection due to an abnormal situation. It can send an RST segment to close the connection.

3. The TCP on one side may discover that the TCP on the other side is idle for a long time. It may send an RST segment to destroy the connection.

12.10   STATE TRANSITION DIAGRAM

To keep track of all the different events happening during connection establishment, connection termination, and data transfer, the TCP software is implemented as a finite state machine. A **finite state machine** is a machine that goes through a limited number of states. At any moment, the machine is in one of the states. It remains in that state until an event happens. The event can take the machine to a new state, or the event can also make the machine perform some actions. In other words, the event is an input applied to a state. It can change the state and can also create an output. Table 12.3 shows the states for TCP.

Table 12.3   *States for TCP*

State	Description
CLOSED	There is no connection
LISTEN	The server is waiting for calls from the client
SYN-SENT	A connection request is sent; waiting for acknowledgment
SYN-RCVD	A connection request is received
ESTABLISHED	Connection is established
FIN-WAIT-1	The application has requested the closing of the connection
FIN-WAIT-2	The other side has accepted the closing of the connection
CLOSING	Both sides have decided to close simultaneously
TIME-WAIT	Waiting for retransmitted segments to die
CLOSE-WAIT	The server is waiting for the application to close
LAST-ACK	The server is waiting for the last acknowledgment

To illustrate the concept we use a state transition diagram. The states are shown using ovals. The transition from one state to another is shown using the directed lines. Each line has two strings separated by a slash. The first string is the input, what TCP receives. The second is the output, what TCP sends. Figure 12.24 shows the state transition diagram for both client and server. The dotted lines of the figure represent the server, the solid lines represent the client, and the thin lines are for unusual situations.

Figure 12.24   *State transition diagram*

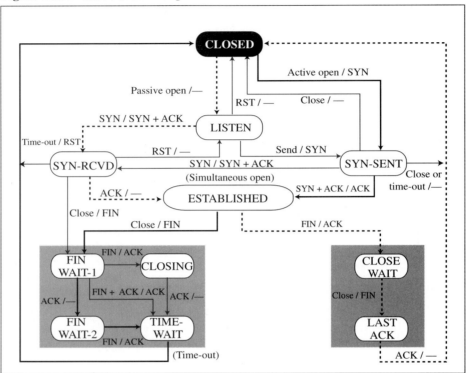

Client Diagram

The client can be in one of the following states: CLOSED, SYN-SENT, ESTAB-
LISHED, FIN-WAIT-1, FIN-WAIT-2, and TIME-WAIT.

■   The client TCP starts in the CLOSED state.

■   While in this state, the client TCP can receive an active open request from the client application program. It sends a SYN segment to the server TCP and goes to the
SYN-SENT state.

■   While in this state, the client TCP can receive an SYN + ACK segment from the
other TCP. It sends an ACK segment to the other TCP and goes to the ESTAB-
LISHED state. This is the data transfer state. The client remains in this state as
long as it is sending and receiving data.

■   While in this state, the client TCP can receive a close request from the client application program. It sends a FIN segment to the other TCP and goes to the FIN-
WAIT-1 state.

■   While in this state, the client TCP waits to receive an ACK from the server TCP.
When the ACK is received, it goes to the FIN-WAIT-2 state. It does not send anything. Now the connection is closed in one direction.

■ The client remains in this state waiting for the server to close the connection from the other end. If the client receives a FIN segment from the other end, it sends an ACK segment and goes to the TIME-WAIT state.

■ When the client is in this state, it starts a timer and waits until this timer goes off. The value of this timer is set to double the lifetime estimate of a segment of maximum size. The client remains in the state before totally closing to let all duplicate packets, if any, arrive at their destination to be discarded. After the time-out, the client goes to the CLOSED state, where it began.

Server Diagram

Although the server can be in any one of the 11 states, in normal operation it is in the following states: CLOSED, LISTEN, SYN-RCVD, ESTABLISHED, CLOSE-WAIT, and LAST-ACK.

■ The server TCP starts in the CLOSED state.

■ While in this state, the server TCP can receive a passive open request from the server application program. It goes to the LISTEN state.

■ While in this state, the server TCP can receive a SYN segment from the client TCP. It sends an SYN + ACK segment to the client TCP and then goes to the SYN-RCVD state.

■ While in this state, the server TCP can receive an ACK segment from the client TCP. It goes to the ESTABLISHED state. This is the data transfer state. The server remains in this state as long as it is receiving and sending data.

■ While in this state, the server TCP can receive a FIN segment from the client, which means that the client wishes to close the connection. It can send an ACK segment to the client and goes to the CLOSE-WAIT state.

■ While in this state, the server waits until it receives a close request from the server program. It then sends a FIN segment to the client and goes to the LAST-ACK state.

■ While in this state, the server waits for the last ACK segment. It then goes to the CLOSED state.

12.11 CONGESTION CONTROL

As we have said, an internet is a combination of networks and connecting devices (e.g., routers). A packet started at a sender may pass through several routers before reaching its final destination. A router has a buffer that stores the incoming packets, processes them, and forwards them. If a router receives packets faster than it can process them, congestion might occur, and some packets could be dropped. When a packet does not reach the destination, no acknowledgment is sent for it. The sender has no choice but to retransmit the lost packet. This may create more congestion and more dropping of packets, which means more retransmission and more congestion. A point then may be reached in which the whole system collapses and no more data can be sent. TCP therefore needs to find some way to avoid this situation.

Previously, we talked about flow control and tried to discuss solutions when the receiver is overwhelmed with data. We said that the sender window size is determined by the available buffer space in the receiver. In other words, we assumed that it is only the receiver that can dictate to the sender the size of the sender's window. We totally ignored another entity here, the network. If the network cannot deliver the data as fast as it is created by the sender, it should tell the sender to slow down. In other words, the network should be another entity that determines the size of the sender's window in addition to the receiver.

Today, TCP protocols include this feature. The sender's window size is not only determined by the receiver but also by congestion in the network.

The sender has two pieces of information: the receiver-advertised window size and the congestion window size. The actual size of the window is the minimum of these two.

Actual window size = minimum (receiver-advertised window size, congestion window size)

To determine the congestion window size, the sender TCP uses the following strategies:

- **Increasing strategy.** At the beginning of the connection, set the congestion window size to the maximum segment size. For each segment that is acknowledged, increase the size of the congestion window by one maximum segment size until you reach a threshold of half the allowable window size. This is sometimes called *slow start*, which is totally misleading because the process is not slow at all. The size of the congestion window increases exponentially. The sender sends one segment, receives one acknowledgment, increases the size to two segments, sends two segments, receives acknowledgments for two segments, increases the size to four segments, sends four segments, receives acknowledgment for four segments, increases the size to eight segments, and so on. In other words, after receiving the third acknowledgment, the size of the window has been increased to eight segments. The rate is exponential ($2^3 = 8$). To avoid congestion before it happens, one must slow down this exponential growth. After the size reaches the threshold, the size is increased one segment for each acknowledgment even if an acknowledgment is for several segments. Figure 12.25 shows the concept.

- **Decreasing strategy.** If congestion occurs, the congestion window size must be decreased. The only way the sender can guess that congestion has occurred is through a lost segment. If the sender does not receive an acknowledgment for a segment before its retransmission timer has matured, it assumes that there is congestion. Because networks today are to some extent noise free, it is more probable that a segment is lost than that it is corrupted. The strategy says if a time-out occurs, the threshold must be set to half of the last congestion window size, and the congestion window size should start from one again. In other words, the sender returns to the slow start phase.

Figure 12.25   *Window size increase strategy*

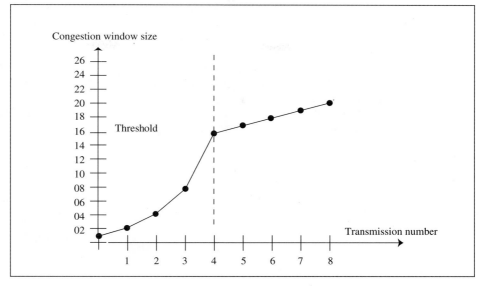

12.12   TCP OPERATION

TCP uses concepts common to the transport layer. We have seen these concepts in the UDP chapter; we will repeat them here for review.

Encapsulation and Decapsulation

To send a message from an application program to another, the TCP protocol encapsulates and decapsulates messages (see Figure 12.26).

Queuing

TCP, like UDP, uses queues (see Figure 12.27).

Multiplexing and Demultiplexing

In the TCP/IP protocol suite, there is only one TCP but there are possibly several application programs that may want to use its services. To handle this situation, TCP does multiplexing and demultiplexing (see Figure 12.28).

Pushing Data

We saw that the sending TCP uses a buffer to store the stream of data coming from the sending application program. The sending TCP has the choice to create segments of any size from the stream. The receiving TCP also buffers the data when they arrive and

Figure 12.26   *Encapsulation and decapsulation*

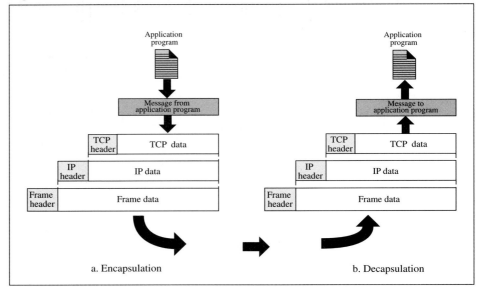

a. Encapsulation   b. Decapsulation

Figure 12.27   *Queues in TCP*

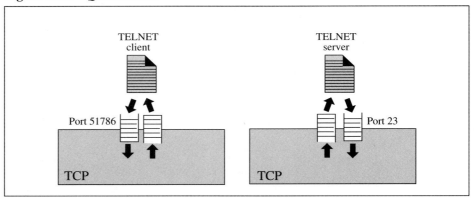

delivers them to the application program when the application program is ready or when the receiving TCP feels that it is convenient. This type of flexibility increases the efficiency of TCP.

However, there are occasions in which the application program is not comfortable with this flexibility. For example, consider an application program that communicates interactively with another application program on the other end. The application program on one site wants to send a keystroke to the application at the other site and receive an immediate response. Delayed transmission and delayed delivery of data may not be acceptable by the application program.

TCP can handle such a situation. The application program on the sending site can request a *push* operation. This means that the sending TCP should not wait for the window to be filled. It should create a segment and send it immediately. The sending TCP

Figure 12.28 *Multiplexing and demultiplexing*

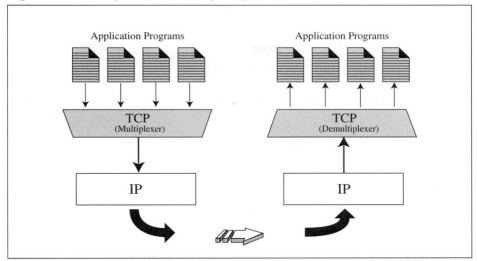

should also set the push bit (PSH) to tell the receiving TCP that the segment includes data that must be delivered to the receiving application program as soon as possible and not to wait for more data to come.

Although the push operation can be dictated by the application program, today most implementations ignore such requests. TCP has the choice to use this operation or not.

Urgent Data

TCP is a stream-oriented protocol. This means that the data is presented from the application program to the TCP as a stream of characters. Each byte of data has a position in the stream. However, there are occasions in which an application program needs to send *urgent* bytes. This means that the sending application program wants a piece of data to be read out of order by the receiving application program. Suppose that the sending application program is sending data to be processed by the receiving application program. When the result of processing comes back, the sending application program finds that everything is wrong. It wants to abort the process, but it has already sent a huge amount of data. If it issues an abort command (Control + C), these two characters will be stored at the end of the receiving TCP buffer. It will be delivered to the receiving application program after all the data has been processed.

The solution is to send a segment with the URG bit set. The sending application program tells the sending TCP that the piece of data is urgent. The sending TCP creates a segment and inserts the urgent data at the beginning of the segment. The rest of the segment can contain normal data from the buffer. The urgent pointer field in the header defines the end of the urgent data and the start of normal data.

When the receiving TCP receives a segment with the URG bit set, it extracts the urgent data from the segment, using the value of the urgent pointer, and delivers it, out of order, to the receiving application program.

12.13 TCP DESIGN

TCP is a very complex protocol. It is a stream-service, connection-oriented protocol that uses a state transition diagram. It uses flow and error control. It is so complex that actual code is tens of thousands of lines.

In this section, we present a simplified, bare-bones TCP. This design is meant to be just a teaching tool. Details such as error checking, error handling, and packet validation have been omitted in an attempt to focus on the basics. Our purpose is to show how we can simulate the heart of TCP, the state transition diagram. In addition, we have sacrificed efficiency for the sake of simplicity. For the actual code, consult other literature such as Stevens, *TCP/IP Illustrated,* Volume 2.

In our design, a TCP package involves a table called Transmission Control Blocks, a set of timers, and three software modules: a main module, an input processing module, and an output processing module. Figure 12.29 shows these five components and their interactions.

Figure 12.29 *TCP design*

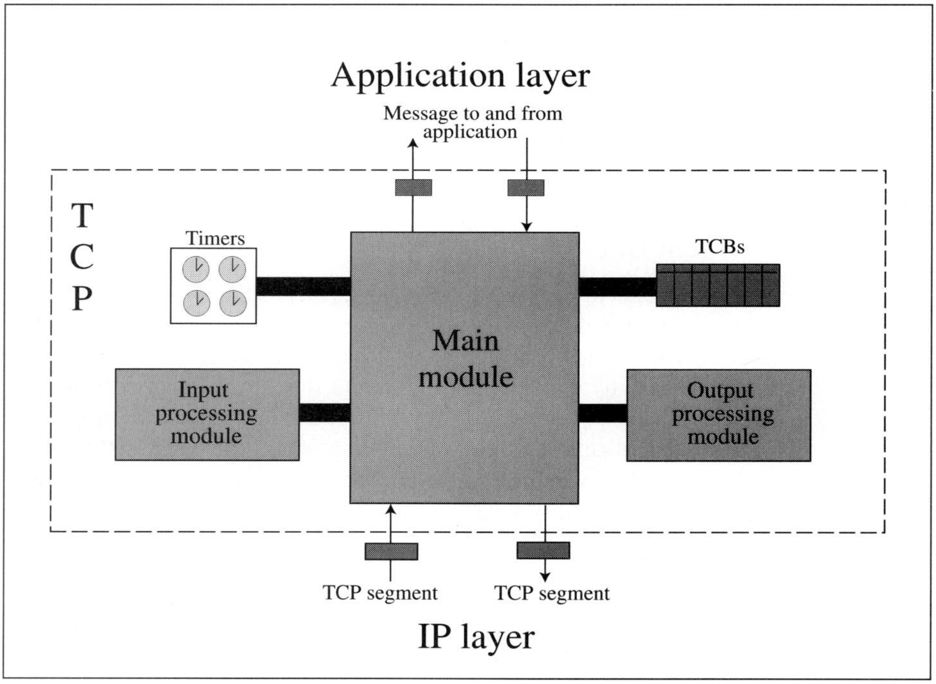

Transmission Control Blocks (TCBs)

TCP is a connection-oriented transfer protocol. A connection may be open for a long period of time. To control the connection, TCP uses a structure to hold information about each connection. This is called a *transmission control block* (TCB). Because at any time there can be several connections, TCP keeps an array of TCBs in the form of a table. The table is usually referred to as the TCB (see Figure 12.30).

Figure 12.30   *TCBs*

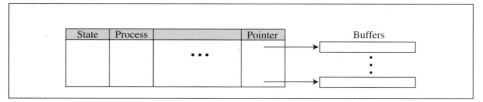

Many fields can be included in each TCB. We mention only the most common ones here.

■ **State.** This field defines the state of the connection according to the state transition diagram.

■ **Process.** This field defines the process using this connection at this machine as a client or a server.

■ **Local IP address.** This field defines the IP address of the local machine used by this connection.

■ **Local port number.** This field defines the local port number used by this connection.

■ **Remote IP address.** This field defines the IP address of the remote machine used by this connection.

■ **Remote port number.** This field defines the remote port number used by this connection.

■ **Interface.** This field defines the local interface.

■ **Local window.** This field, which can comprise several subfields, holds information about the window at the local TCP.

■ **Remote window.** This field, which can comprise several subfields, holds information about the window at the remote TCP.

■ **Sending sequence number.** This field holds the sending sequence number.

■ **Receiving sequence number.** This field holds the receiving sequence number.

■ **Sending ACK number.** This field holds the value of the ACK number sent.

■ **Round-trip time.** Several fields may be used to hold information about the RTT.

■ **Time-out values.** Several fields can be used to hold the values of the different time-out values such as the retransmission time-out, persistence time-out, keep-alive time-out, and so on.

■ **Buffer size.** This field defines the size of the buffer at the local TCP.

■ **Buffer pointer.** This field is a pointer to the buffer where the receiving data is kept until it is read by the application.

Timers

As we said before, TCP needs several timers to keep track of its operation.

Main Module

The main module is invoked by an arrived TCP segment, a time-out event, or a message from an application program. This is a very complicated module because the action to be taken depends on the current state of the TCP. Several approaches have been used to implement the state transition diagram including using a process for each state, using a table (two-dimensional array), and so on. To keep our discussion simple, we use cases to handle the state. We have 11 states; we use 11 different cases. Each state is implemented as defined in the state transition diagram. The ESTABLISHED state needs further explanation. When TCP is in this state and data or an acknowledgment segment arrives, another module, the input processing module, is called to handle the situation. Also, when TCP is in this state and a "send data" message is issued by an application program, another module, the output processing module, is called to handle the situation.

Main Module
Receive: a TCP segment, a message from an application, or a time-out event
1. Search the TCB table.
2. If (corresponding TCB is not found)
1. Create a TCB with the state CLOSED.
3. Find the state of the entry in the TCB table.
4. Case (state)
CLOSED:
1. If ("passive open" message from application received)
1. Change the state to LISTEN.
2. If ("active open" message from application received)
1. Send a SYN segment.
2. Change the state to SYN-SENT.
3. If (any segment received)
1. Send an RST segment.
4. If (any other message received)
1. Issue an error message.
5. Return.
LISTEN:
1. If ("send data" message from application received)
1. Send a SYN segment.

Main Module (continued)

2. Change the state to SYN-SENT.

  2. If (SYN segment received)

     1. Send a SYN+ACK segment.

     2. Change the state to SYN+RCVD.

  3. If (any other segment or message received)

     1. Issue an error message.

  4. Return.

SYN-SENT:

  1. If (time-out)

     1. Change the state to CLOSED.

  2. If (SYN segment received)

     1. Send a SYN+ACK segment.

     2. Change the state to SYN-RCVD.

  3. If (SYN+ACK segment received)

     1. Send an ACK segment.

     2. Change the state to ESTABLISHED.

  4. If (any other segment or message received)

     1. Issue an error message.

  5. Return.

SYN-RCVD:

  1. If (ACK segment received)

     1. Change the state to ESTABLISHED.

  2. If (time-out)

     1. Send an RST segment.

     2. Change the state to CLOSED.

  3. If ("close" message from application received)

     1. Send a FIN segment.

     2. Change the state to FIN-WAIT-1.

  4. If (RST segment received)

     1. Change the state to LISTEN.

  5. If (any other segment or message received)

     1. Issue an error message.

  6. Return.

Main Module (continued)

ESTABLISHED:

    1. If (FIN segment received)

        1. Send an ACK segment.

        2. Change the state to CLOSE-WAIT.

    2. If ("close" message from application received)

        1. Send a FIN segment.

        2. Change the state to FIN-WAIT-1.

    3. If (RST or SYN segment received)

        1. Issue an error message.

    4. If (data or ACK segment is received)

        1. Call the input module.

    5. If ("send" message from application received)

        1. Call the output module.

    6. Return.

FIN-WAIT-1:

    1. If (FIN segment received)

        1. Send an ACK segment.

        2. Change the state to CLOSING.

    2. If (FIN + ACK segment received)

        1. Send an ACK segment.

        2. Change the state to TIME-WAIT.

    3. If (ACK segment received)

        1. Change the state to FIN-WAIT-2.

    4. If (any other segment or message received)

        1. Issue an error message.

    5. Return.

FIN-WAIT-2:

    1. If (FIN segment received)

        1. Send an ACK segment.

        2. Change the state to TIME-WAIT.

    2. Return.

CLOSING:

    1. If (ACK segment received)

Main Module (concluded)
1. Change the state to TIME-WAIT.
2. If (any other segment or message received)
1. Issue an error message.
3. Return.
TIME-WAIT:
1. If (time-out)
1. Change the state to CLOSED.
2. If (any other segment or message received)
1. Issue an error message.
3. Return.
CLOSE-WAIT:
1. If ("close" message from application received)
1. Send a FIN segment.
2. Change the state to LAST-ACK.
2. If (any other segment or message received)
1. Issue an error message.
3. Return.
LAST-ACK:
1. If (ACK segment received)
1. Change the state to CLOSED.
2. If (any other segment or message received)
1. Issue an error message.
3. Return.

Input Processing Module

In our design, the input processing module handles all the details needed to process data or acknowledgment received when TCP is in the ESTABLISHED state. This module sends an ACK if needed, takes care of the window size announcement, does error checking, and so on. The details of this module are not needed for an introductory textbook.

Output Processing Module

In our design, the output processing module handles all the details needed to send out data received from application program when TCP is in the ESTABLISHED state. This module handles retransmission time-outs, persistent time-outs, and so on. One of the ways to implement this module is to use a small transition diagram to handle different output conditions. Again, the details of this module are not needed for an introductory textbook.

12.14 SUMMARY

- Transmission Control Protocol (TCP) is a connection-oriented, reliable, stream transport layer protocol in the TCP/IP protocol suite.
- TCP is responsible for process-to-process communication.
- A process can be identified by a port number.
- The socket address, a combination of an IP address and a port number, uniquely identifies a running application program.
- The unit of data transfer between two devices using TCP software is called a segment, 20 to 60 bytes of header, followed by data from the application program.
- The source and destination ports define the port numbers of the application programs that are using TCP.
- The sequence number identifies the first byte of data in the segment.
- The acknowledgment number announces the successful receipt of data.
- The header length field indicates the number of 32-bit words in the header.
- The control field bits define the use of a segment or serve as a validity check for other fields.
- The window size field defines the size of the sliding window used in flow control.
- The checksum field is used for error detection.
- The urgent pointer defines the boundary between urgent data and normal data.
- The end-of-option option is used for alignment and indicates there are no more options in the header.
- The no-operation option is used for filler and alignment purposes.
- The maximum segment size is used in connection setup to define the largest allowable data segment.
- The window scale factor is a multiplier that increases the window size.
- The timestamp option shows how much time it takes for data to travel from sender to receiver.
- TCP uses a sliding window mechanism for flow control.
- Error detection is handled by the checksum, acknowledgment, and time-out.
- Corrupted and lost segments are retransmitted and duplicate segments are discarded.
- TCP uses four timers (retransmission, persistence, keepalive, and time-waited) in its operation.
- Connection establishment requires three-way handshaking; connection termination requires four-way handshaking.
- TCP software is implemented as a finite state machine.

■ The TCP window size is determined by the sender-advertised window size or the congestion window size, whichever is smaller.

■ An increasing or decreasing strategy is used to determine the congestion window size.

■ When the push bit in the TCP header is set, a segment is sent immediately, without waiting for the window to fill with data.

■ When the urgent bit in the TCP header is set, data from the segment is delivered out of order to the receiving application program.

■ Transmission control blocks (TCBs) hold information about each TCP connection.

■ A TCP package can contain TCBs, timers, a main module, an input processing module, and an output processing module.

12.15   PRACTICE SET

Multiple Choice

1. TCP lies between the _____ and the _____ layers of the TCP/IP protocol suite.
   a. application; UDP
   b. application; transport
   c. application; network
   d. network; data link

2. IP is responsible for _____ communication while TCP is responsible for _____ communication.
   a. host-to-host; process-to-process
   b. process-to-process; host-to-host
   c. process-to-process; network-to-network
   d. network-to-network; process-to-process

3. A host can be identified by _____ while a program running on the host can be identified by _____.
   a. an IP address; a port number
   b. a port number; an IP address
   c. an IP address; a host address
   d. an IP address; a well-known port

4. The _____ address uniquely identifies a running application program.
   a. IP address
   b. host
   c. NIC
   d. socket

5. If a segment carries data along with an acknowledgment, this is called _____.

    a. backpacking

    b. piggybacking

    c. piggypacking

    d. mother's helper

6. The _____ field is used to order packets of a message.

    a. urgent pointer

    b. checksum

    c. sequence number

    d. acknowledgment number

7. The _____ field is used for error detection.

    a. urgent pointer

    b. checksum

    c. sequence number

    d. acknowledgment number

8. Multiply the header length field by _____ to find the total number of bytes in the TCP header.

    a. 2

    b. 4

    c. 6

    d. 8

9. Urgent data requires the urgent pointer field as well as the URG bit in the _____ field.

    a. control

    b. offset

    c. sequence number

    d. reserved

10. Which of the following is not a valid acknowledgment number?

    a. 0

    b. 1

    c. $2^{32} - 1$

    d. 2^{32}

11. Which field indicates the length of the TCP header?

    a. window

    b. acknowledgment

    c. header length

    d. control

12. The options field of the TCP header ranges from 0 to _____ bytes.

    a. 10

    b. 20

 c. 40

 d. 2^{32}

13. What is the maximum number of no-operation options in one 32-bit word?

 a. one

 b. two

 c. three

 d. four

14. What is the maximum number of the end-of-option options in the entire TCP header?

 a. 30

 b. 10

 c. 9

 d. 1

15. Which option defines the maximum number of bytes in a TCP segment?

 a. maximum segment size

 b. window scale factor

 c. timestamp

 d. no operation

16. In Figure 12.14 if bytes 4 and 5 are acknowledged, bytes _____ to _____ can be sent.

 a. 8; 13

 b. 6; 13

 c. 8; 15

 d. 6; 15

17. In _____, data is sent or processed at a very inefficient rate, such as one byte at a time.

 a. Nagle's syndrome

 b. silly window syndrome

 c. sliding window syndrome

 d. delayed acknowledgment

18. To prevent silly window syndrome created by a receiver that processes data at a very slow rate, _____ can be used.

 a. Clark's solution

 b. Nagle's algorithm

 c. delayed acknowledgment

 d. a or c

19. To prevent silly window syndrome created by a sender that sends data at a very slow rate, _____ can be used.

 a. Clark's solution

 b. Nagle's algorithm

    c. delayed acknowledgment

    d. a or c

20. TCP uses _____ for error detection.

    a. checksum

    b. acknowledgment

    c. time-out

    d. all of the above

21. An ACK number of 1,000 means _____.

    a. 999 bytes have been successfully received

    b. 1,000 bytes have been successfully received

    c. segment 999 has been received

    d. segment 1,000 has been received

22. The _____ timer prevents a long idle connection between two TCPs.

    a. retransmission

    b. persistence

    c. keepalive

    d. time-waited

23. The _____ timer is needed to handle the zero window-size advertisement.

    a. retransmission

    b. persistence

    c. keepalive

    d. time-waited

24. Karn's algorithm is used in calculations by the _____ timer.

    a. retransmission

    b. persistence

    c. keepalive

    d. time-waited

25. The _____ timer is used in the termination phase.

    a. retransmission

    b. persistence

    c. keepalive

    d. time-waited

26. The _____ timer keeps track of the time between the sending of a segment and the receipt of an acknowledgment.

    a. retransmission

    b. persistence

    c. keepalive

    d. time-waited

27. A server issues _____ open while a client issues _____ open.

    a. an active; a passive

b. a passive; an active

c. an ephemeral; a well-known

d. a well-known; an ephemeral

28. Connection establishment involves a _____ handshake; connection termination involves a _____ handshake.

    a. one-way; two-way

    b. two-way; three-way

    c. three-way; three-way

    d. three-way; four-way

29. In the _____ state, the server is waiting for the application to close.

    a. CLOSED

    b. ESTABLISHED

    c. CLOSE-WAIT

    d. LAST-ACK

30. In the _____ state, the server is in the data transfer state and can receive and send data.

    a. ESTABLISHED

    b. LISTEN

    c. TRANSFER

    d. OPEN

31. After the server TCP receives a passive open request from the server application program, it goes to the _____ state.

    a. CLOSED

    b. LISTEN

    c. SYN-RCVD

    d. ESTABLISHED

32. After the client TCP receives an active open request from the client application program, it goes to the _____ state.

    a. CLOSED

    b. FIN-WAIT-1

    c. SYN-SENT

    d. ESTABLISHED

33. In the _____ state, the client TCP has closed its connection to the server.

    a. CLOSED

    b. FIN-WAIT-1

    c. FIN-WAIT-2

    d. ESTABLISHED

34. In the _____ state, the client TCP waits for an ACK segment.

    a. CLOSED

    b. FIN-WAIT-1

    c. FIN-WAIT-2

    d. ESTABLISHED

35. A special segment called a probe is sent by a sending TCP when the _____ timer goes off.

    a. transmission

    b. persistence

    c. keepalive

    d. time-waited

Exercises

36. TCP sends a segment at 5:30:20. It receives the acknowledgment at 5:30:25. What is the new value for RTT if the previous RTT was four seconds?

37. TCP sends a segment at 4:30:20. It does not receive an acknowledgment. At 4:30:25, it retransmits the previous segment. It receives an acknowledgment at 4:30:27. What is the new value for RTT according to Karn's algorithm if the previous RTT was four seconds?

38. What is the maximum size of the TCP header?

39. What is the minimum size of the TCP header?

40. If the value of HLEN is 0111, how many bytes of option are included in the segment?

41. What can you say about the TCP segment in which the value of the control field is one of the following:

    a. 000000

    b. 000001

    c. 010001

    d. 000100

    e. 000010

    f. 010010

42. The control field in a TCP segment is six bits. We can have 64 different combinations of bits. How many of these combinations do you think are valid?

43. TCP opens a connection using an initial sequence number (ISN) of 14,534. The other party opens the connection with an ISN of 21,732. Show the three TCP segments during the connection establishment.

44. Following the previous exercise, show the contents of the segments during the data transmission if the initiator sends two segments containing the message "Hello Dear Customer" and the other party answers with two segments containing "Hi There Seller."

45. Following the previous two exercises, show the contents of the segments during the connection termination.

46. TCP is sending data at 1 megabyte per second (8 Mbps). If the sequence number starts with 7,000, how long does it take before the sequence number goes back to zero?

47. A TCP connection is using a window size of 10,000 bytes and the previous acknowledgment number was 22,001. It receives a segment that acknowledges bytes 24,001. Draw a diagram to show the situation of the window before and after.

48. Redo exercise 47 if the receiver has changed the window size to 11,000.

49. Redo exercise 47 if the receiver has changed the window size to 90,000.

50. In exercise 47, how low can the receiver decrease the window size?

51. A TCP connection is in the ESTABLISHED state. The following events occur one after another:

    a. A FIN segment is received.

    b. The application sends a "close" message.

    What is the state of the connection after each event? What is the action after each event?

52. A TCP connection is in the ESTABLISHED state. The following events occur one after another:

    a. The application sends a "close" message.

    b. A FIN segment is received.

    What is the state of the connection after each event? What is the action after each event?

53. A TCP connection is in the SYN-RCVD state. The following events occur one after another:

    a. The application sends a "close" message.

    b. An ACK segment is received.

    c. A FIN segment is received.

    What is the state of the connection after each event? What is the action after each event?

54. A TCP connection is in the SYN-SENT state. The following events occur one after another:

    a. A SYN+ACK segment is received.

    b. A FIN segment is received.

    What is the state of the connection after each event? What is the action after each event?

55. A TCP connection is in the FIN-WAIT-1 state. The following events occur one after another:

    a. An ACK segment is received.

    b. A FIN segment is received.

    c. Time-out occurs.

    What is the state of the connection after each event? What is the action after each event?

56. Show the entries for the header of a TCP segment that carries a message from a FTP client to a FTP server. Fill the checksum field with 0s. Choose an appropriate ephemeral port number and the correct well-known port number. The length of data is 40 bytes.

57. A client uses TCP to send data to a server. The data is 16 bytes. Calculate the efficiency of this transmission at the TCP level (ratio of useful bytes to total bytes).

58. Redo the previous exercise calculating the efficiency of transmission at the IP level. Assume no options for the IP header.

59. Redo the previous exercise calculating the efficiency of transmission at the data link layer. Assume no options for the IP header and use Ethernet at the data link layer.

60. The following is a dump of a TCP header in hexadecimal format.
05320017 00000001 00000000 500207FF 00000000
  a. What is the source port number?
  b. What is the destination port number?
  c. What the sequence number?
  d. What is the acknowledgment number?
  e. What is the length of the header?
  f. What is the type of the segment?
  g. What is the window size?

Programming Exercises

61. Create a header file to include all constants that you think are needed to implement the TCP modules in C. Use the **#define** directives.

62. Complete the following struct declaration for the TCP header.
```
struct   TCP_Header
{
unsigned short    SPortAddr ;
.................................................
.................................................
} ;
```

63. Complete the following struct declaration for the TCP segment.
```
struct   TCP_Segment
{
        struct   TCP_Header   tcpHeader ;
        .............................   tcpData ;
} ;
```
64. Write the declaration for the TCBs.

65. Write a function in C to simulate the main module.

CHAPTER 13

Routing Protocols (RIP, OSPF, and BGP)

An internet is a combination of networks connected by routers. When a datagram goes from a source to a destination, it will probably pass through many routers until it reaches the router attached to the destination network.

A router receives a packet from a network and passes it to another network. A router is usually attached to several networks. When it receives a packet, to which network should it pass the packet? The decision is based on optimization: which of the available pathways is the optimum pathway?

A **metric** is a cost assigned for passing through a network. The total metric of a particular route is equal to the sum of the metrics of networks that comprise the route. A router chooses the route with the shortest (smallest) metric.

The metric assigned to each network depends on the type of protocol. Some simple protocols, like the Routing Information Protocol (RIP), treat each network as equals. The cost of passing through each network is the same; it is one hop count. So if a packet passes through 10 networks to reach the destination, the total cost is 10 hop counts.

Other protocols, such as the Open Shortest Path First (OSPF), allow the administrator to assign a cost for passing through a network based on the type of service required. A route through a network can have different costs (metrics). For example, if maximum throughput is the desired type of service, a satellite link has a lower metric than a fiber-optic line. On the other hand, if minimum delay is the desired type of service, a fiber-optic line has a lower metric than a satellite line. OSPF allows each router to have several routing tables based on the required type of service.

Other protocols define the metric totally differently. In the Border Gateway Protocol (BGP), the criterion is the policy, which can be set by the administrator. The policy defines what paths should be chosen.

Whatever the metric, a router should have a routing table to consult when a packet is ready to be forwarded. The routing table should specify the optimum path for the packet. However, the table can be either static or dynamic. A *static table* is one that is not changed frequently. A *dynamic table*, on the other hand, is one that is updated automatically when there is a change somewhere in the internet. Today, an internet needs dynamic routing tables. The tables need to be updated as soon as there is a change in the internet. For instance, they need to be updated when a route is down, and they need to be updated whenever a better route has been created.

Routing protocols have been created in response to the demand for dynamic routing tables. A routing protocol is a combination of rules and procedures that let routers in the internet inform each other of changes. It allows routers to share whatever they know about the internet or their neighborhood. The sharing of information allows a router in San Francisco to know about the failure of a network in Texas. The routing protocols also include procedures for combining information received from other routers.

13.1   INTERIOR AND EXTERIOR ROUTING

Today, an internet can be so large that one routing protocol cannot handle the task of updating routing tables of all routers. For this reason, an internet is divided into autonomous systems. An **autonomous system** (AS) is a group of networks and routers under the authority of a single administration. Routing inside an autonomous system is referred to as *interior routing*. Routing between autonomous systems is referred to as *exterior routing*. Each autonomous system can choose an interior routing protocol to handle routing inside the autonomous system. However, only one exterior routing protocol is usually chosen to handle routing between autonomous systems.

Several interior and exterior routing protocols are in use. In this chapter, we cover only the most popular ones. We discuss two interior routing protocols, RIP and OSPF, and one exterior routing protocol, BGP (see Figure 13.1).

Figure 13.1   *Popular routing protocols*

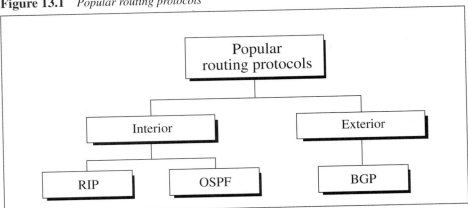

RIP and OSPF can be used to update routing tables inside an autonomous system. BGP can be used to update routing tables for routers that glue the autonomous systems together.

In Figure 13.2, routers R1, R2, R3, and R4 use an interior and an exterior routing protocol. The other routers use only interior routing protocols. The solid thin lines show the communication between routers that use interior routing protocols. The broken

Figure 13.2 *Autonomous systems*

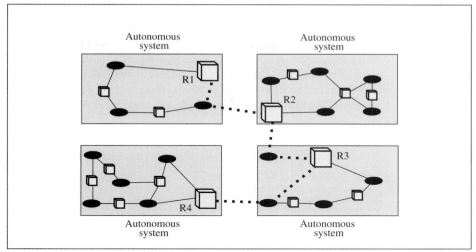

thick lines show the communication between the routers that use an exterior routing protocol.

13.2 RIP

The Routing Information Protocol is an interior routing protocol used inside an autonomous system. It is a very simple protocol based on *distance vector routing*, which uses the Bellman-Ford algorithm for calculating the routing tables. In this section, we first study the principle of distance vector routing, as it is applied to RIP, and then discuss the RIP protocol itself.

Distance Vector Routing

In **distance vector routing,** each router periodically shares its knowledge about the entire internet with its neighbors. The three keys to understanding how this algorithm works are as follows:

1. **Sharing knowledge about the entire autonomous system.** Each router shares its knowledge about the entire autonomous system with its neighbors. At the outset, a router's knowledge may be sparse. How much it knows, however, is unimportant; it sends whatever it has.

2. **Sharing only with neighbors.** Each router sends its knowledge only to neighbors. It sends whatever knowledge it has through all of its interfaces.

3. **Sharing at regular intervals.** Each router sends its knowledge to its neighbors at fixed intervals, for example, every 30 seconds.

Routing Table

Every router keeps a routing table that has one entry for each destination network of which the router is aware. The entry consists of the destination network IP address, the shortest distance to reach the destination in hop count, and the next hop (next router) to which the packet should be delivered to reach its final destination. The hop count is the number of networks a packet enters to reach its final destination.

The table may contain other information such as the time since this entry was last updated. Table 13.1 shows an example of a routing table.

Table 13.1 *A distance vector routing table*

Destination	Hop Count	Next Hop	Other Information
163.5.0.0	7	172.6.23.4	
197.5.13.0	5	176.3.6.17	
189.45.0.0	4	200.5.1.6	
115.0.0.0	6	131.4.7.19	

RIP Updating Algorithm

The routing table is updated upon receipt of a RIP response message. The following shows the updating algorithm used by RIP.

RIP Updating Algorithm
Receive: a response RIP message
1. Add one hop to the hop count for each advertised destination.
2. Repeat the following steps for each advertised destination:
1. If (destination not in the routing table)
1. Add the advertised information to the table.
2. Else
1. If (next-hop field is the same)
1. Replace entry in the table with the advertised one.
2. Else
1. If (advertised hop count smaller than one in the table)
1. Replace entry in the routing table.
2. Else
2. Do nothing.
3. Return.

In Figure 13.3 a router receives a RIP message from router C. The message lists destination networks and their corresponding hop counts. The first step according to the updating algorithm is to increase the hop count by one. Next, this updated RIP packet and the old routing table are compared. The result is a routing table with an up-to-date hop count for each destination. For Net1 there is no new information, so the Net1 entry remains the same.

For Net2, information in the table and in the message identify the same next hop (router C). Although the value of the hop count in the table (2) is less than the one in the message (5), the algorithm selects the one received in the message because the original value has come from router C. This value is now invalid because router C is advertising a new value.

Net3 is added as a new destination. For Net6, the RIP packet contains a lower hop count and this shows up on the new routing table. Both Net8 and Net9 retain their original values since the corresponding hop counts in the message are not an improvement.

Figure 13.3 *Example of updating a routing table*

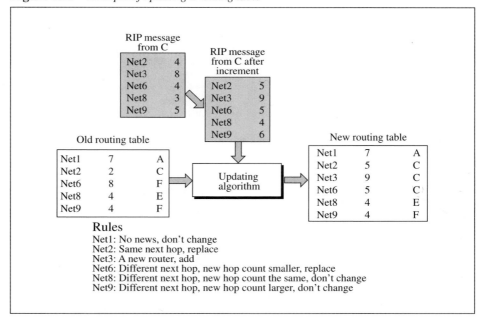

Initializing the Routing Table

When a router is added to a network, it initializes a routing table for itself using its configuration file. The table contains only the directly attached networks and the hop counts, which are initialized to 1. The next-hop field, which identifies the next router, is empty. Figure 13.4 shows the initial routing tables in a small autonomous system.

Updating the Routing Table

Each routing table is updated upon receipt of RIP messages using the RIP updating algorithm shown above. Figure 13.5 shows our previous autonomous system with final routing tables.

Figure 13.4   *Initial routing tables in a small autonomous system*

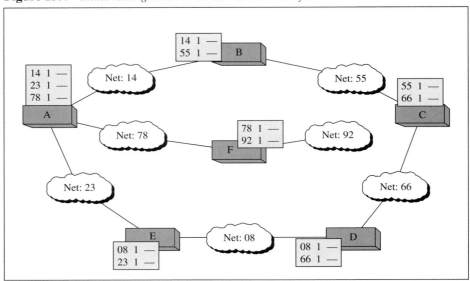

Figure 13.5   *Final routing tables for the previous figure*

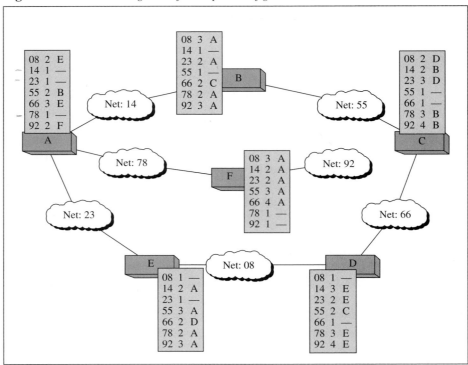

RIP Message Format

The format of the RIP message is shown in Figure 13.6.

Figure 13.6 *RIP message format*

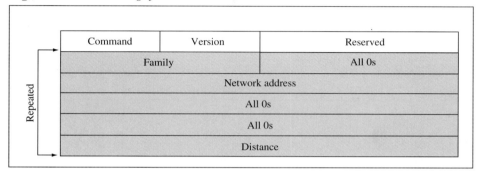

- ■ **Command.** This eight-bit field specifies the type of message: request (1) or response (2).
- ■ **Version.** This eight-bit field defines the version. In this book we use version 1, but at the end of this section, we give some new features of version 2.
- ■ **Family.** This 16-bit field defines the family of the protocol used. For TCP/IP the value is 2.
- ■ **Address.** The address field defines the address of the destination network. RIP has allocated 14 bytes for this field to be applicable to any protocol. However, IP currently uses only four bytes. The rest of the address is filled with 0s.
- ■ **Distance.** This 32-bit field defines the hop count from the advertising router to the destination network.

Note that part of the message is repeated for each destination network. We refer to this as an *entry*.

Requests and Responses

RIP uses two types of messages: request and response.

Request

A request message is sent by a router that has just come up or by a router that has some time-out entries. A request can ask about specific entries or all entries (see Figure 13.7).

Response

A response can be either solicited or unsolicited. A *solicited response* is sent only in answer to a request. It contains information about the destination specified in the corresponding request. An *unsolicited response*, on the other hand, is sent periodically, every 30 seconds, and contains information covering the whole routing table. In Figure 13.8 information about three networks is distributed by a RIP response message.

Figure 13.7 *Request messages*

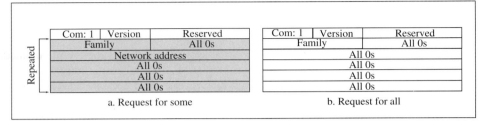

Figure 13.8 *Response message*

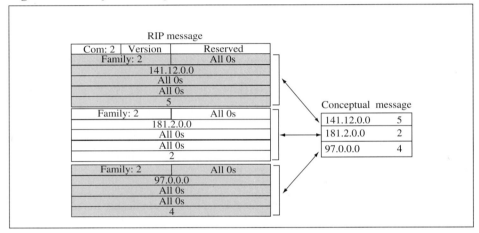

Timers in RIP

RIP uses three timers to support its operation (see Figure 13.9). The periodic timer controls the sending of messages, the expiration timer governs the validity of a route, and the garbage collection timer advertises the failure of a route.

Figure 13.9 *RIP timers*

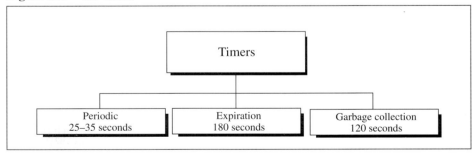

Periodic Timer

The **periodic timer** controls the advertising of regular update messages. Although the protocol specifies that this timer must be set to 30 seconds, the working model uses a random number between 25 and 35 seconds. This is to prevent any possible synchronization and therefore overload on an internet if routers update simultaneously.

Each router has one periodic timer that is set randomly to a number between 25 and 35. It counts down; when zero is reached, the update message is sent, and the timer is randomly set once again.

If RIP uses an additional timing method to send out updates (see Triggered Update, to follow), the periodic timer is not affected. The periodic update messages go out on their own schedule without regard to other update messages from other timing systems.

Expiration Timer

The **expiration timer** governs the validity of a route. When a router receives update information for a route, the expiration timer is set to 180 seconds for that particular route. Every time a new update for the route is received, the timer is reset. In normal situations this occurs every 30 seconds. However, if there is a problem on an internet and no update is received within the allotted 180 seconds, the route is considered expired and the hop count of the route is set to 16, which means the destination is unreachable. Every route has its own expiration timer.

Garbage Collection Timer

When the information about a route becomes invalid, the router does not immediately purge that route from its table. Instead, it continues to advertise the route with a metric value of 16. At the same time, a timer called the **garbage collection timer** is set to 120 seconds for that route. When the count reaches zero, the route is purged from the table. This timer allows neighbors to become aware of the invalidity of a route prior to purging.

Slow Convergence

One of the problems with RIP is slow convergence, which means that a change somewhere in the internet propagates very slowly through the rest of the internet. For example, suppose there is a change in network 1 in Figure 13.10. Router R1 updates itself immediately. However, since each router sends its periodic update every 30 seconds, this means an average of 15 seconds (range of 0 to 30 seconds) before a change reaches R2. It also takes another average 15 seconds before R3 receives the change, and so on. When the information finally reaches router Rn, $15 \times n$ seconds have passed. If n is 20, then this is 300 seconds. In this 300 seconds an ATM network can send more than one billion bits. If this change affects these bits, one billion bits are lost.

One method to deal with RIP shortcomings is limiting the hop count to 15. This prevents data packets from wandering around forever, clogging the internet. An autonomous system using RIP is limited to a diameter of 15; the number 16, therefore, is considered infinity and designates an unreachable network (see Figure 13.11).

Figure 13.10 *Slow convergence*

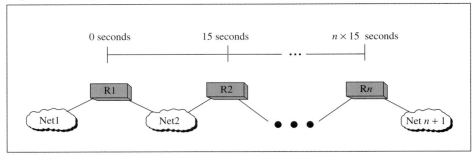

Figure 13.11 *Hop counts*

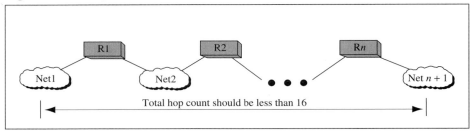

Instability

A much more important problem with RIP is instability, which means that an internet running RIP can become unstable. When this happens a packet could go from one router to another in a loop. Limiting the number of hops to 15 will improve stability but will not eliminate all of the problems.

To understand the problem, assume that the connection to Net1 in Figure 13.12 is nonfunctioning. Router A shows a cost of 1 for this network in its routing table. Router B, which can access Net1 only through router A, shows a cost of 2. When access to Net1 fails, router A immediately responds and changes the Net1 cost column to 16 (infinity). However, it may have to wait up to 30 seconds before it can send its update with this new information. In the meantime, it could happen that router B sends its own update message to A. Router A now has two entries for Net1: from its own table the cost is 16 and from router B the cost is 2. A is fooled into thinking that there is a back-door access to Net1 through B. Router A then changes the cost column for Net1 to 3 (2 + 1) and this update gets sent to B. Router B's two cost values for Net1 are now 3 (from A) and 2 (from itself). Router B knows that Net1 is accessible only through router A so it disregards its own lower cost and changes its cost to 4 (3 + 1). This back-and-forth updating continues until both routers reach a cost of 16. At this point, the routers realize there is no access to the network Net1.

Figure 13.12   *Instability*

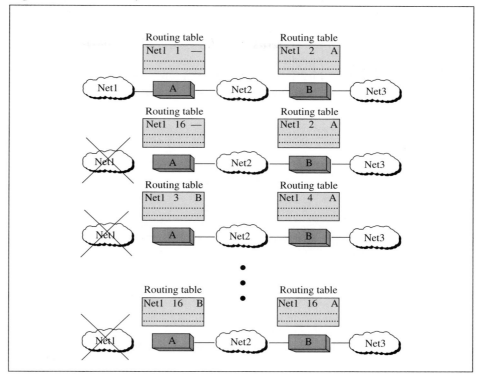

Some Remedies for Instability

Some remedies have been proposed to improve the stability. However, none of them are 100 percent effective.

Triggered Update

If there are no changes on the network, updates are sent at the usual 30-second intervals. If there is a change, however, the router springs into action immediately by sending out its new table, a process called **triggered update.**

Triggered update can improve stability. Each router that receives an update with a change sends out new information at once, in considerably less time than the 15-second average. For example, in Figure 13.12, when router A realizes that Net1 is unavailable, it changes the cost to 16 in its routing table and then immediately sends this to B. Router B then changes its table, and now both tables show a cost of 16 for Net1. The sending of update messages with incremental changes in cost has been avoided as have any looping problems.

Although triggered update can vastly improve routing, it cannot solve all routing problems. For example, router failure cannot be handled by this method.

Split Horizons

Split horizons, a second method for improving stability, utilizes selectivity in the sending of routing messages; a router must distinguish between different interfaces. If a router has received route updating information from an interface, then this same updated information must not be sent back through this interface. If an interface has passed information to help update a router, this updated information must not be sent back; it is already known and thus is not needed. Figure 13.13 illustrates this concept.

Figure 13.13   *Split horizon*

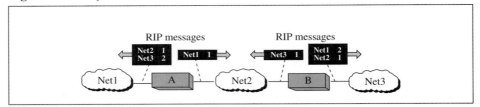

In this figure, router B has received information about Net1 and Net2 through its left interface; this information is updated and passed on through the right interface but not to the left. Similarly, information received by router B about Net3 is updated and passed on only through the left interface of B.

Split horizons can definitely improve stability. Assume that Net1 is inaccessible to router A in Figure 13.12. Router B receives its information about Net1 from A; it does not send information about Net1 to router A. Router A, therefore, has but one entry for the Net1 cost (16), and is not fooled into thinking that there is some back-door access to Net1. Router A sends its routing table to B and both will then end up with a cost of 16 for Net1.

Poison Reverse

Poison reverse is a variation of split horizons. In this method, information received by the router is used to update the routing table and then passed out to all interfaces. However, a table entry that has come through one interface is set to a metric of 16 as it goes out through the same interface.

Figure 13.14 illustrates this concept: Router B has received information about Net1 and Net2 through its left interface, so it sends information out about these networks with a metric of 16. Likewise, information about Net3 comes from the right interface, and the cost of Net3 in the update message going right is 16. Stability is

Figure 13.14   *Poison reverse*

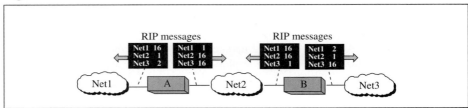

improved using poison reverse. Assume that Net1 is inaccessible to router A in Figure 13.12. Router B receives its information about Net1 from A. In each update, B sends its routing table to A with a cost of 16 for Net1. This has no effect on A if Net1 is accessible because router A will not select B's entry for Net1. However, if Net1 does go down, both cost values are 16 and instability is thereby avoided.

RIP Version 2

RIP version 2 was designed to overcome some of the shortcomings of version 1. The designers of version 2 have not augmented the length of the message for each entry. They have only replaced those fields in version 1 that were filled with 0s for the TCP/IP protocol with some new fields.

Message Format

Figure 13.15 shows the format of a RIP version 2 message. The new fields of this message are as follows:

Figure 13.15 *RIP version 2 format*

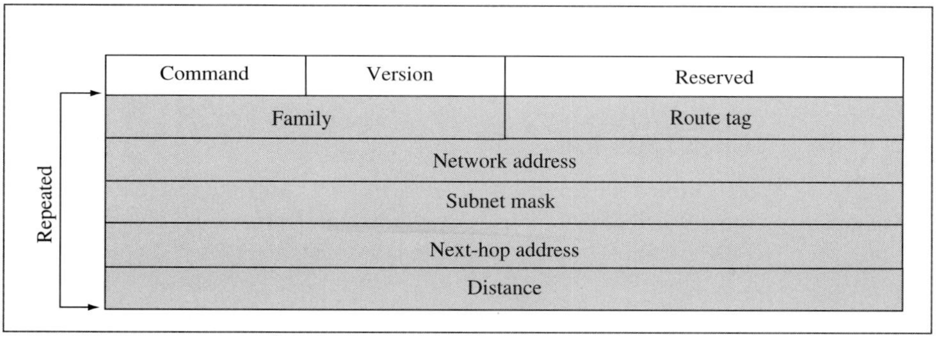

- **Route Tag.** This field carries information such as the autonomous system number. It can be used to enable RIP to receive information from an exterior routing protocol.
- **Subnet mask.** This is a four-byte field that carries the subnet mask.
- **Next-hop address.** This field shows the address of the next hop. This is particularly useful if two autonomous systems share a network (a backbone) for example. Then the message can define the router, in the same autonomous system or other autonomous systems, to which the packet should go next.

Authentication

Authentication is added to protect the message against unauthorized advertisement. No new fields are added to the packet; instead, the first entry of the message is set aside for authentication information. To indicate that the entry is authentication information and not routing information, the value of $FFFF_{16}$ is entered in the family field (see Figure

13.16). The second field, the authentication type, defines the method used for authentication, and the third field contains the actual authentication data.

Figure 13.16 *Authentication*

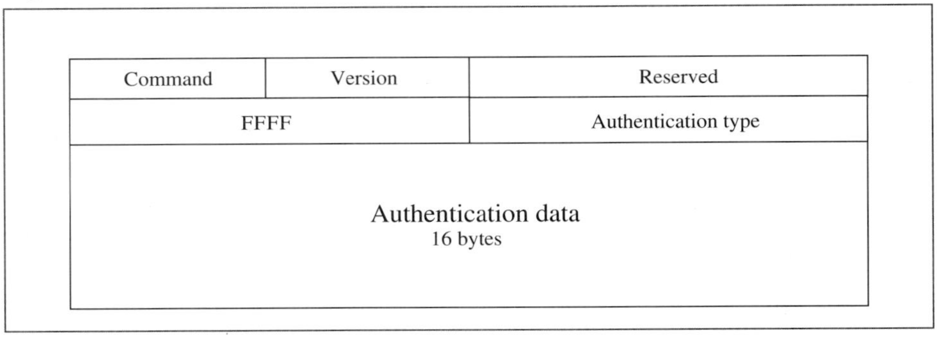

Command	Version	Reserved
FFFF		Authentication type
Authentication data 16 bytes		

Multicasting

Version 1 of RIP uses broadcasting to send RIP messages to every neighbor. In this way, not only all the routers on the network receive the packets, but all of the hosts also receive them. RIP version 2, on the other hand, uses the multicast address 224.0.0.9 to multicast RIP messages only to RIP routers in the network.

Encapsulation

RIP messages are encapsulated in UDP user datagrams. A RIP message does not include a field that indicates the length of the message. This can be determined from the UDP packet. The well-known port assigned to RIP in UDP is port 520.

> RIP uses the services of UDP on well-known port 520.

13.3 OSPF

The Open Shortest Path First (OSPF) protocol is another interior routing protocol that is becoming very popular. Its domain is also an autonomous system. Special routers called *autonomous system boundary routers* are responsible for dissipating information about other autonomous systems into the current system. To handle routing efficiently and in a timely manner, OSPF divides an autonomous system into areas.

Areas

An **area** is a collection of networks, hosts, and routers all contained within an autonomous system. An autonomous system, in turn, can be divided into many different areas. All networks inside an area must be connected.

Routers inside an area flood the area with routing information. At the border of an area, special routers called *area border routers* summarize the information about the area and send it to other areas. Among the areas inside an autonomous system is a special area called the *backbone;* all of the areas inside an autonomous system must be connected to the backbone. In other words, the backbone serves as a primary area and the other areas as the secondary areas. This does not mean that the routers within areas cannot be connected with each other, however.

The routers inside the backbone are called the *backbone routers.* Note that a backbone router can also be an area border router.

If, due to some problem, the connectivity between a backbone and an area is broken, a *virtual link* between routers must be created by the administration to allow continuity of the functions of the backbone as the primary area.

Each area has an area identification. The area identification of the backbone is zero. Figure 13.17 shows an autonomous system and its areas.

Figure 13.17   *Areas in an autonomous system*

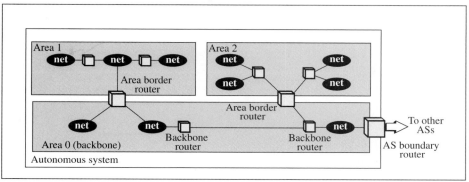

Metric

The OSPF protocol allows the administrator to assign a cost, called the *metric,* to each route. The metric can be based on a type of service (minimum delay, maximum throughput, and so on). As a matter of fact, a router can have multiple routing tables, each based on a different type of service.

Link State Routing

OSPF uses Link State Routing to update the routing tables in an area. Before discussing the details of the OSPF protocol, let us discuss **Link State Routing,** a process by which each router shares its knowledge about its neighborhood with every router in the area. The three keys to understanding how this method works are as follows:

1. **Sharing knowledge about the neighborhood.** Each router sends the *state of its neighborhood* to every other router in the area.

2. **Sharing with every other router.** Each router sends the state of its neighborhood to *every other router in the area.* It does so by **flooding,** a process whereby a router sends its information to all of its neighbors (through all of its output ports). Each neighbor sends the packet to all of its neighbors, and so on. Every router that

receives the packet sends copies to each of its neighbors. Eventually, every router (without exception) has received a copy of the same information.

3. **Sharing when there is a change.** Each router shares the state of its neighborhood only when there is a change. This rule contrasts with distance vector routing, where information is sent out at regular intervals regardless of change. This characteristic results in lower internet traffic than that required by distance vector routing.

The idea behind Link State Routing is that each router should have the exact topology of the internet at every moment. In other words, every router should have the whole "picture" of the internet. From this topology, a router can calculate the shortest path between itself and each network. The topology here means a graph consisting of nodes and edges. To represent an internet by a graph, however, we need more definitions.

Types of Links

In OSPF terminology, a network is called a *link*. Four types of links have been defined: point-to-point, transient, stub, and virtual (see Figure 13.18).

Figure 13.18   *Types of links*

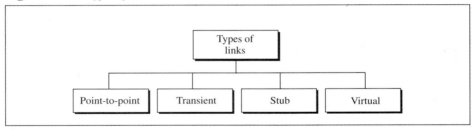

Point-to-Point Link   A point-to-point link connects two routers without any other host or router in between. In other words, the purpose of the link (network) is just to connect the two routers. An example of this type of link is two routers connected by a telephone line or a T-line. There is no need to assign a network address to this type of link. Graphically, the routers are represented by nodes, and the link is represented by a bidirectional edge connecting the nodes. The metrics, which are usually the same, are shown at the two ends, one for each direction. In other words, each router has only one neighbor at the other side of the link (see Figure 13.19).

Figure 13.19   *Point-to-point link*

Transient Link   A transient link is a network with several routers attached to it. The data can enter through any of the routers and leave through any router. All LANs and some WANs with two or more routers are of this type. In this case, each router has many neighbors. For example, consider the Ethernet in Figure 13.20a. Router A has routers B, C, D, and E as neighbors. Router B has routers A, C, D, and E as neighbors. If we want to show the neighborhood relationship in this situation, we have the graph shown in Figure 13.20b.

Figure 13.20 *Transient link*

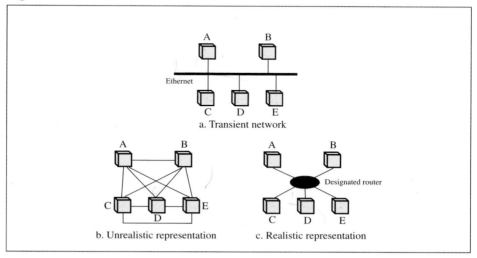

a. Transient network

b. Unrealistic representation

c. Realistic representation

This is neither efficient nor realistic. It is not efficient because each router needs to advertise the neighborhood of four other routers, for a total of 20 advertisements. It is not realistic, because there is no single network (link) between each pair of routers; there is only one network that serves as a crossroad between all five routers.

To show that each router is connected to every other router through one single network, the network itself is represented by a node. However, because a network is not a machine, it cannot function as a router. One of the routers in the network takes this responsibility. It is assigned a dual purpose; it is a true router and a designated router. We can use the topology shown in Figure 13.20c to show the connections of a transient network.

Now each router has only one neighbor, the designated router (network). On the other hand, the designated router (the network) has five neighbors. We see that the number of neighbor announcements is reduced from 20 to 10. Still, the link is represented as a bidirectional edge between the nodes. However, while there is a metric from each node to the designated router, there is no metric from the designated router to any other node. The reason is that the designated router represents the network. We can only assign a cost to a packet that is passing through the network. We cannot charge for this twice. When a packet enters a network, we assign a cost; when a packet leaves the network to go to the router, there is no charge.

Stub Link   A stub link is a network that is connected to only one router. The data packets enter the network through this single router and leave the network through this same router. This is a special case of the transient network. We can show this situation using the router as a node and using the designated router for the network. However, the link is only one-directional, from the router to the network (see Figure 13.21).

Figure 13.21   *Stub link*

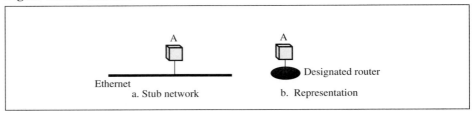

Virtual Link   When the link between two routers is broken, the administration may create a virtual link between them using a longer path that probably goes through several routers.

Graphical Representation

Let us now examine a small internet and see how we can represent it graphically with link state routing. Figure 13.22 shows a small internet with seven networks and six routers. Two of the networks are point-to-point networks. We use symbols such as N1 and N2 for transient and stub networks. There is no need to assign a number to a point-to-point network.

Figure 13.22   *Example of an internet*

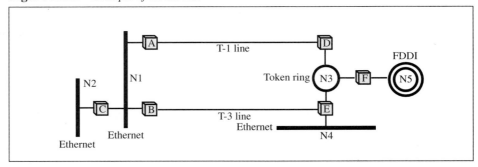

To show the above internet graphically, we use square nodes for the routers and ovals for the networks (represented by the designated router); see Figure 13.23. Note that we have three stub networks.

Link State Advertisements

To share information about their neighbors, each router distributes link state advertisements (LSAs). An LSA announces the states of router links. Depending on the type of router, we can define five different LSAs (see Figure 13.24).

Figure 13.23   *Graphical representation of an internet*

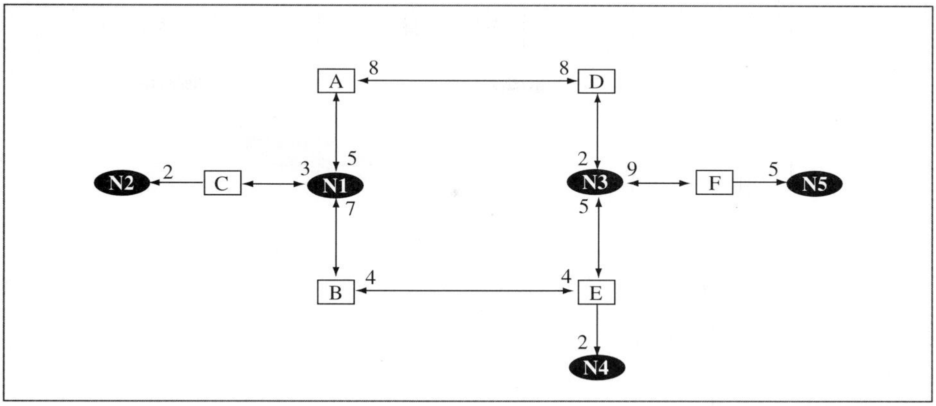

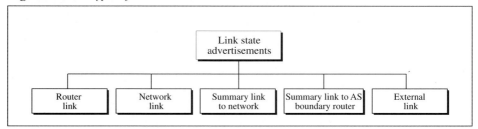

Figure 13.24   *Types of LSAs*

Link state
advertisements

| Router link | Network link | Summary link to network | Summary link to AS boundary router | External link |

Router Link   A router link defines the links of a true router. A true router uses this advertisement to announce information about all of its links and what is at the other side of the link (neighbors). See Figure 13.25 for a depiction of a router link.

Figure 13.25   *Router link*

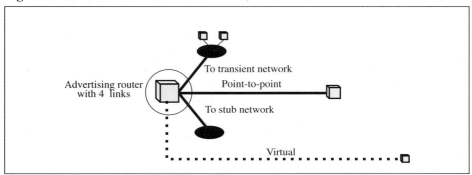

Network Link   A network link defines the links of a network. A designated router, on behalf of the transient network, distributes this type of LSA packet. The packet announces the existence of all of the routers connected to the network (see Figure 13.26).

Figure 13.26   *Network link*

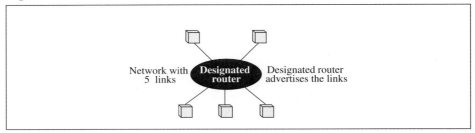

Summary Link to Network   Router link and network link advertisements flood the area with information about the router links and network links inside an area. But a router should also know about the networks outside its area, and the area border routers can provide this information. An area border router is active in more than one area. It receives router link and network link advertisements, and, as we will see, creates a routing table for each area. For example, in Figure 13.27, router R1 is an area border router. It has two routing tables, one for area 1 and one for area 0. R1 floods area 1 with information about how to reach a network located in area 0. In the same way, router R2 floods area 2 with information about how to reach the same network in area 0.

Figure 13.27   *Summary link to network*

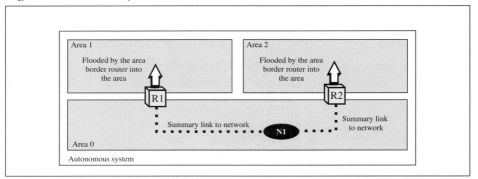

Summary Link to AS Boundary Router   The previous advertisement lets every router know the cost to reach all of the networks inside the autonomous system. But what about a network outside the autonomous system? If a router inside an area wants to send a packet outside the autonomous system, it should first know the route to an autonomous boundary router; the summary link to AS boundary router provides this information. The area border routers flood their areas with this information (see Figure 13.28).

External Link   Although the previous advertisement lets each router know the route to an AS boundary router, this information is not enough. A router inside an autonomous system wants to know which networks are available outside the autonomous system; the external link advertisement provides this information. The AS boundary router floods the autonomous system with the cost of each network outside the autonomous system using a routing table created by an exterior routing protocol. Each advertise-

Figure 13.28   *Summary link to AS boundary router*

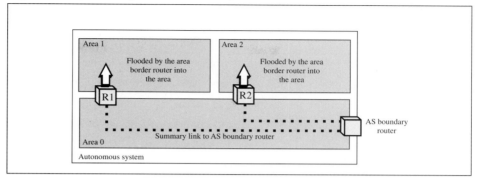

ment announces one single network. If there is more than one network, separate announcements are made. Figure 13.29 depicts an external link.

Figure 13.29   *External link*

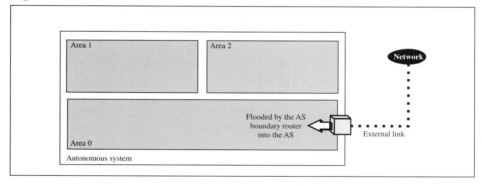

Link State Database

Every router in an area receives the router link and network link LSAs from every other router and forms a link state database. Note that every router in the same area has the same link state database.

A link state database is a tabular representation of the topology of the internet inside an area. It shows the relationship between each router and its neighbors including the metrics.

Dijkstra Algorithm

To calculate its routing table, each router applies the Dijkstra algorithm to its link state database. The **Dijkstra algorithm** calculates the shortest path between two points on a network using a graph made up of nodes and edges. The algorithm divides the nodes into two sets: tentative and permanent. It chooses nodes, makes them tentative, examines them, and if they pass the criteria, makes them permanent. We can informally define the algorithm using the following steps:

Dijkstra Algorithm
1. Start with the local node (router): the root of the tree.
2. Assign a cost of 0 to this node and make it the first permanent node.
3. Examine each neighbor node of the node that was the last permanent node.
4. Assign a cumulative cost to each node and make it tentative.
5. Among the list of tentative nodes
1. Find the node with the smallest cumulative cost and make it permanent.
2. If a node can be reached from more than one direction
1. Select the direction with the shortest cumulative cost.
6. Repeat steps 3 to 5 until every node becomes permanent.

Figure 13.30 shows the steps of the Dijkstra algorithm applied to node A of our sample internet in Figure 13.23. The number next to each node represents the cumulative cost from the root node. Note that in step h, network N3 is reached through two directions with cumulative costs of 14 and 10. The direction with the cumulative cost of 10 is kept and the other one is deleted.

Figure 13.30   *Shortest path calculation*

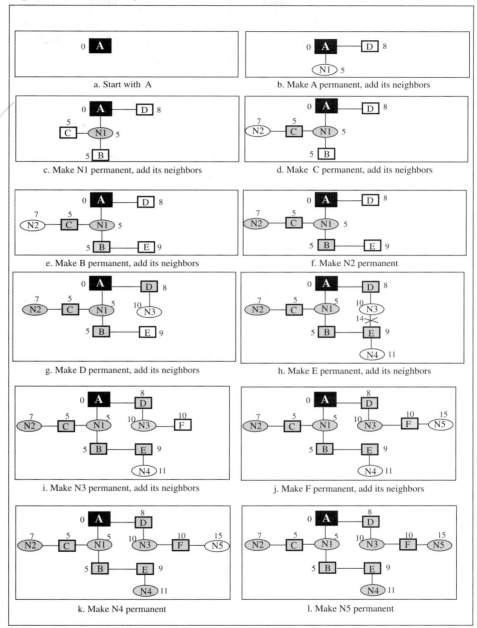

a. Start with A

b. Make A permanent, add its neighbors

c. Make N1 permanent, add its neighbors

d. Make C permanent, add its neighbors

e. Make B permanent, add its neighbors

f. Make N2 permanent

g. Make D permanent, add its neighbors

h. Make E permanent, add its neighbors

i. Make N3 permanent, add its neighbors

j. Make F permanent, add its neighbors

k. Make N4 permanent

l. Make N5 permanent

Routing Table

Each router uses the shortest path tree method to construct its routing table. The routing table shows the cost of reaching each network in the area. To find the cost of reaching networks outside of the area, the routers use the summary link to network, the summary link to boundary router, and the external link advertisements. Table 13.2 shows the routing table for router A.

Table 13.2   *Link state routing table for router A*

Network	Cost	Next Router	Other Information
N1	5		
N2	7	C	
N3	10	D	
N4	11	B	
N5	15	D	

Types of Packets

OSPF uses five different types of packets: the hello packet, database description packet, link state request packet, link state update packet, and link state acknowledgment packet (see Figure 13.31).

Figure 13.31   *Types of OSPF packets*

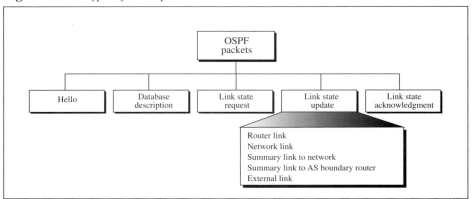

Packet Format

All OSPF packets share the same common header (see Figure 13.32). Before studying the different types of packets, let us talk about this common header.

■ **Version.** This eight-bit field defines the version of the OSPF protocol. It is currently version 2.

■ **Type.** This eight-bit field defines the type of the packet. As we said before, we have five types, with values 1 to 5 defining the types.

■ **Message length.** This 16-bit field defines the length of the total message including the header.

Figure 13.32   *OSPF packet header*

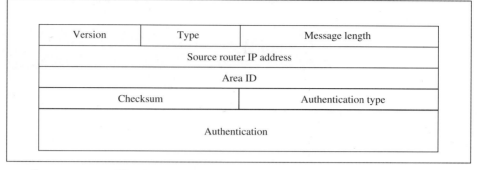

- **Source router IP address.** This 32-bit field defines the IP address of the router that sends the packet.

- **Area identification.** This 32-bit field defines the area within which the routing takes place.

- **Checksum.** This field is used for error detection on the entire packet excluding the authentication type and authentication data field.

- **Authentication type.** This 16-bit field defines the authentication method used in this area. At this time, two types of authentication are defined: 0 for none and 1 for password.

- **Authentication.** This 64-bit field is the actual value of the authentication data. In the future, when more authentication types are defined, this field will contain the result of the authentication calculation. For now, if the authentication type is 0, this field is filled with 0s. If the type is 1, this field carries an eight-character password.

Hello Message

OSPF uses the hello message to create neighborhood relationships and to test the reachability of neighbors. This is the first step in link state routing. Before a router can flood all of the other routers with information about its neighbors, it must first greet its neighbors. It must know if they are alive, and it must know if they are reachable (see Figure 13.33).

- **Network mask.** This 32-bit field defines the network mask of the network over which the hello message is sent.

- **Hello interval.** This 16-bit field defines the number of seconds between hello messages.

- **E flag.** This is a one-bit flag. When it is set, it means that the area is a stub area.

- **T flag.** This is a one-bit flag. When it is set, it means that the router supports multiple metrics.

- **Priority.** This field defines the priority of the router. The priority is used for the selection of the designated router. After all neighbors declare their priorities, the router with the highest priority is chosen as the designated router. The one with the second highest priority is chosen as the backup designated router. If the value

Figure 13.33   *Hello packet*

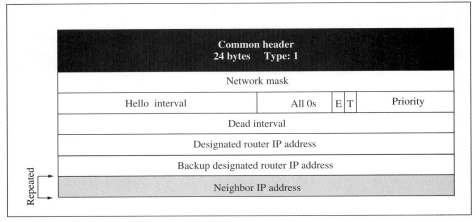

of this field is 0, it means that the router never wants to be a designated or backup designated router.

- **Dead interval.** This 32-bit field defines the number of seconds before a router assumes that a neighbor is dead.

- **Designated router IP address.** This 32-bit field is the IP address of the designated router for the network over which the message is sent.

- **Backup designated router IP address.** This 32-bit field is the IP address of the backup designated router for the network over which the message is sent.

- **Neighbor IP address.** This is a repeated 32-bit field that defines the routers that have agreed to be the neighbors of the sending router. In other words, it is a current list of all the neighbors from which the sending router has received the hello message.

Database Description Message

When a router is connected to the system for the first time or after a failure, it needs the complete link state database immediately. It cannot wait for all link state update packets to come from every other router before making its own database and calculating its routing table. Therefore, after a router is connected to the system, it sends hello packets to greet its neighbors. If this is the first time that the neighbors hear from the router, they send a database description packet. The database description packet does not contain complete database information; it only gives an outline, the title of each line in the database. The newly connected router examines the outline and finds out which lines of information it does not have. It then sends one or more link state request packets to get full information about that particular link. When two routers want to exchange database description packets, one of them takes the role of master and the other the role of slave. Because the message can be very long, the contents of the database can be divided into several messages. The format of the database description packet is shown in Figure 13.34. The fields are as follows:

- **E flag.** This one-bit flag is set to 1 if the advertising router is an autonomous boundary router (*E* stands for external).

Figure 13.34   *Database description packet*

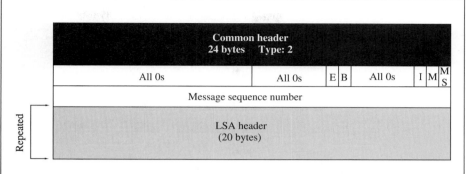

- **B flag.** This one-bit flag is set to 1 if the advertising router is an area border router.
- **I flag.** This one-bit field, the *initialization* flag, is set to 1 if the message is the first message.
- **M flag.** This one-bit field, the *more* flag, is set to 1 if this is not the last message.
- **M/S flag.** This one-bit field, the *master/slave* bit, indicates the origin of the packet: master (M/S = 1) or slave (M/S = 0).
- **Message sequence number.** This 32-bit field contains the sequence number of the message. It is used to match a request with the response.
- **LSA header.** This 20-byte field is used in each LSA. The format of this header is discussed in the link state update message section. This header gives the outline of each link, without details. It is repeated for each link in the link state database.

Link State Request Packet

The format of the link state request packet is shown in Figure 13.35. This is a packet that is sent by a router that needs information about a specific route or routes. It is answered with a link state update packet. It can be used by a newly connected router to request more information about some routes after receiving the database description packet. The three fields here are part of the LSA header which we will see shortly. Each set of the three fields is a request for one single LSA. The set is repeated if more than one advertisement is desired.

Link State Update Packet

The link state update packet is the heart of the OSPF operation. It is used by a router to advertise the states of its links. The general format of the link state update packet is shown in Figure 13.36. Each update packet may contain several different LSAs. For example, a link state update packet can contain 14 LSAs, four of which are router link advertisements, three of which are network link advertisements, two of which are summary link to network advertisements, two of which are summary link to AS boundary router advertisements, and three of which are external link advertisements. The fields are as follows:

Figure 13.35   *Link state request packet*

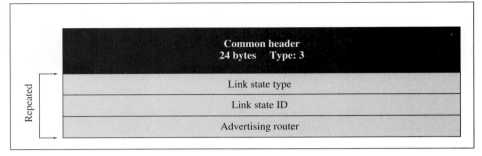

Figure 13.36   *Link state update packet*

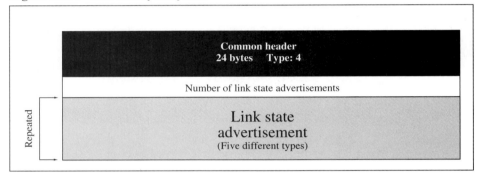

■ **Number of advertisements.** This 32-bit field defines the number of advertisements. One packet can advertise the states of several links.

■ **Link state advertisements.** There are five different LSAs, as we discussed before, all having the same header format, but different bodies. We first discuss the general header common to all of them. The format of the LSA header is shown in Figure 13.37.

Figure 13.37   *LSA header*

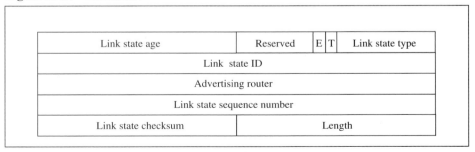

Link state age. This field indicates the number of seconds elapsed since this message was first generated. Recall that this type of message goes from router to router (flooding). When a router creates the message, the value of this field is 0. When each successive router forwards this message, it estimates the transit time and adds it to the cumulative value of this field.

E flag. If this one-bit flag is set to 1, it means that the area is a stub area. A stub area is an area that is connected to the backbone area by only one path.

T flag. If this one-bit flag is set to 1, it means that the router can handle multiple types of service.

Link state type. This field defines LSA type. As we discussed before, there are five different advertisement types: router link (1), network link (2), summary link to network (3), summary link to AS boundary router (4), and external link (5).

Link state ID. The value of this field depends on the type of link. For type 1 (router link), it is the IP address of the router. For type 2 (network link), it is the IP address of the designated router. For type 3 (summary link to network), it is the IP address of the network. For type 4 (summary link to AS boundary router), it is the IP address of the AS boundary router. For type 5 (external link), it is the IP address of the external network.

Advertising router. This is the IP address of the router advertising this message.

Link state sequence number. This is a sequence number assigned to each link state update message.

Link state checksum. This is not the usual checksum field. It uses a special checksum calculation called *Fletcher's checksum,* which is based on the whole packet except for the age field.

Length. This defines the length of the whole packet in bytes.

Router Link LSA   The router link LSA advertises all of the links of a router (true router). The format of the router link packet is shown in Figure 13.38. The fields of the router link LSA are as follows:

■   **Link ID.** The value of this field depends on the type of link. Table 13.3 shows the different link identifications based on link type.

■   **Link data.** This field gives additional information about the link. Again, the value depends on the type of the link (see Table 13.3).

■   **Link type.** Four different types of links are defined based on the type of network to which the router is connected (see Table 13.3).

Table 13.3   *Link types, link identification, and link data*

Link Type	Link Identification	Link Data
Type 1: Point-to-point connection to another router	Address of neighbor router	Interface number
Type 2: Connection to any-to-any network	Address of designated router	Router address
Type 3: Connection to stub network	Network address	Network mask
Type 4: Virtual link	Address of neighbor router	Router address

- **Number of types of service (TOS).** This field defines the number of types of services announced for each link.
- **Metric for TOS 0.** This field defines the metric for the default type of service (TOS 0).
- **TOS.** This field defines the type of service.
- **Metric.** This field defines the metric for the corresponding TOS.

Figure 13.38   *Router link LSA*

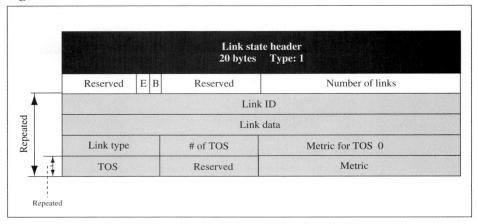

Network Link LSA   The network link advertisement announces the links connected to a network. The format of the network link advertisement is shown in Figure 13.39. The fields of the network link LSA are as follows:

- **Network mask.** This field defines the network mask.
- **Attached router.** This repeated field defines the IP addresses of all attached routers.

Figure 13.39   *Network link LSA*

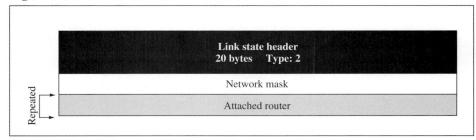

Summary Link to Network LSA   This is used by the area border router to announce the existence of other networks outside the area. The summary link to network advertisement is very simple. It consists of the network mask and the metrics for each type of service. Note that each advertisement announces only one single network. If there is more than one network, a separate advertisement must be issued for each. The reader may ask why only the mask of the network is advertised. What about the network address itself? The IP address of the advertising router is announced in the header of the link state advertisement. From this information and the mask, one can deduce the network address. The format of this advertisement is shown in Figure 13.40. The fields of the summary link to network LSA are as follows:

Figure 13.40   *Summary link to network LSA*

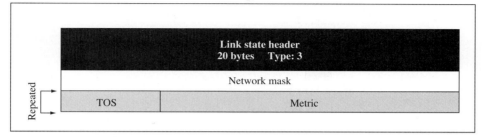

- **Network mask.** This field defines the network mask.
- **TOS.** This field defines the type of service.
- **Metric.** This field defines the metric for the type of service defined in the TOS field.

Summary Link to AS Boundary Router LSA   This packet is used to announce the route to an AS boundary router. Its format is the same as the previous summary link. The packet just defines the network to which the AS boundary router is attached. If a message can reach the network, it can be picked up by the AS boundary router. The format of the packet is shown in Figure 13.41. The fields are the same as the fields in the summary link to network advertisement message.

Figure 13.41   *Summary link to AS boundary router LSA*

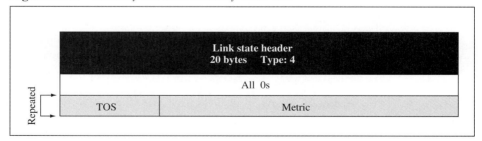

External Link LSA   This is used to announce all the networks outside the AS. The format of the LSA is similar to the summary link to AS boundary router LSA, with the addition of two fields. The AS boundary router may define a forwarding router that can provide a better route to the destination. The packet also can include an external route tag, used by other protocols, but not by OSPF. The format of the packet is shown in Figure 13.42.

Figure 13.42 *External link LSA*

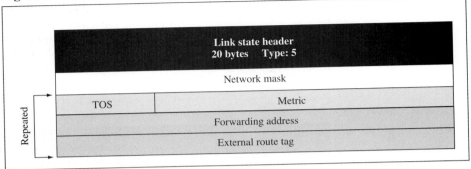

Link State Acknowledgment Packet

OSPF makes routing more reliable by forcing every router to acknowledge the receipt of every link state update packet. The format of the link state acknowledgment packet is shown in Figure 13.43. It has the common OSPF header and the generic link state update header. These two sections are sufficient to acknowledge a packet.

Figure 13.43 *Link state acknowledgment packet*

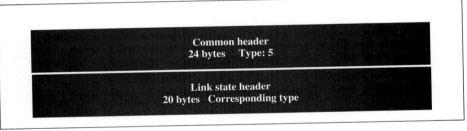

Encapsulation

OSPF packets are encapsulated in IP datagrams. They contain the acknowledgment mechanism for flow and error control. They do not need a transport layer protocol to provide these services.

OSPF packets are encapsulated in IP datagrams.

13.4 BGP

Border Gateway Protocol (BGP) is an inter-autonomous system routing protocol. It first appeared in 1989 and has gone through four versions. BGP is based on a routing method called *path vector routing*. But, before describing the principle behind path vector routing, let us see why the two previously discussed methods, namely distance vector routing and link state routing are not good candidates for inter-autonomous system routing.

Distance vector is not a good candidate because there are occasions in which the route with the smallest hop count is not the preferred route. For example, we may not want a packet to pass through an autonomous system that is not secure even though it is the shortest route. Also, distance vector routing is unstable due to the fact that the routers announce only the number of hop counts to the destination without actually defining the path that leads to that destination. A router that receives a distance vector advertisement packet may be fooled if the shortest path is actually calculated through the receiving router itself.

Link state routing is also not a good candidate for inter-autonomous system routing because an internet is too big for this routing method. To use link state routing for the whole internet would require each router to have a huge link state database. It would also take a long time for each router to calculate its routing table using the Dijkstra algorithm.

Path Vector Routing

Path vector routing is different from both distance vector routing and link state routing. Each entry in the routing table contains the destination network, the next router, and the path to reach the destination. The path is usually defined as an ordered list of autonomous systems that a packet should travel through to reach the destination. Table 13.4 shows an example of a path vector routing table.

Table 13.4 *Path vector routing table*

Network	Next Router	Path
N01	R01	AS14, AS23, AS67
N02	R05	AS22, AS67, AS05, AS89
N03	R06	AS67, AS89, AS09, AS34
N04	R12	AS62, AS02, AS09

Path Vector Messages

The autonomous boundary routers that participate in path vector routing advertise the reachability of the networks in their own autonomous systems to neighbor autonomous boundary routers. The concept of neighborhood here is the same as the one described in the RIP or OSPF protocol. Two autonomous boundary routers connected to the same network are neighbors.

We should mention here that an autonomous boundary router receives its information from an interior routing algorithm such as RIP or OSPF.

Each router that receives a path vector message verifies that the advertised path is in agreement with its policy (a set of rules imposed by the administrator controlling the routes). If it is, the router updates its routing table and modifies the message before sending it to the next neighbor. The modification consists of adding its AS number to the path and replacing the next router entry with its own identification.

For example, Figure 13.44 shows an internet with four autonomous systems. The router R1 sends a path vector message advertising the reachability of N1. Router R2 receives the message, updates its routing table, and after adding its autonomous system to the path and inserting itself as the next router, sends the message to router R3. Router R3 receives the message, updates its routing table, and sends the message, after changes, to router R4.

Figure 13.44 *Path vector packets*

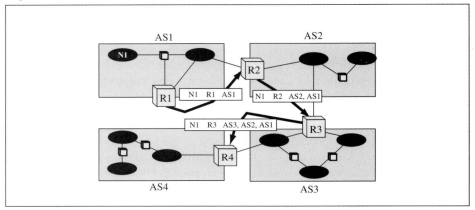

Loop Prevention

The instability of distance vector routing and the creation of loops can be avoided in path vector routing. When a router receives a message, it checks to see if its autonomous system is in the path list to the destination. If it is, looping is involved and the message is ignored.

Policy Routing

Policy routing can be easily implemented through path vector routing. When a router receives a message, it can check the path. If one of the autonomous systems listed in the path is against its policy, it can ignore that path and that destination. It does not update its routing table with this path, and it does not send this message to its neighbors. This means that the routing tables in path vector routing are not based on the smallest hop count or the minimum metric; they are based on the policy imposed on the router by the administration.

Path Attributes

In our previous example, we discussed a path for a destination network. The path was presented as a list of autonomous systems, but is, in fact, a list of attributes. Each attribute gives some information about the path. The list of attributes helps the receiving router make a better decision when applying its policy.

Attributes are divided into two broad categories: well-known and optional. A *well-known attribute* is one that every BGP router should recognize. An *optional attribute* is one that need not be recognized by every router.

Well-known attributes are themselves divided into two categories: mandatory and discretionary. A *well-known mandatory attribute* is one that must appear in the description of a route. A *well-known discretionary attribute* is one that must be recognized by each router, but is not required to be included in every update messsage. One well-known mandatory attribute is ORIGIN. This defines the source of the routing information (RIP, OSPF, and so on). Another well-known mandatory attribute is AS_PATH. This defines the list of autonomous systems through which the destination can be reached. Still another well-known mandatory attribute is NEXT-HOP, which defines the next router to which the data packet should be sent.

The optional attributes can also be subdivided into two categories: transitive and nontransitive. An *optional transitive attribute* is one that must be passed to the next router by the router that has not implemented this attribute. An *optional nontransitive attribute* is one that should be discarded if the receiving router has not implemented it.

Types of Packets

BGP uses four different types of messages: open, update, keepalive, and notification (see Figure 13.45).

Figure 13.45   *Types of BGP messages*

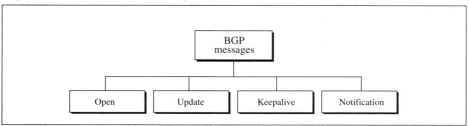

Packet Format

All BGP packets share the same common header. Before studying the different types of packets, let us talk about this common header (see Figure 13.46). The fields of this header are as follows:

Figure 13.46   *BGP packet header*

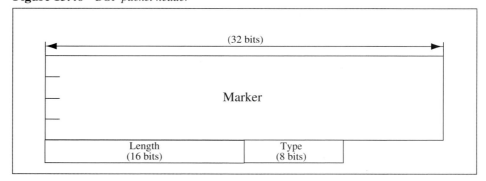

■ **Marker.** The 16-byte marker field is reserved for authentication.

■ **Length.** This two-byte field defines the length of the total message including the header.

■ **Type.** This one-byte field defines the type of the packet. As we said before, we have four types, and the values of 1 to 4 define those types.

Open Message

To create a neighborhood relationship, a router running BGP opens a TCP connection with a neighbor and sends an open message. If the neighbor accepts the neighborhood relationship, it responds with a keepalive message, which means that a relationship has been established between the two routers. See Figure 13.47 for a depiction of the open message format.

Figure 13.47   *Open message*

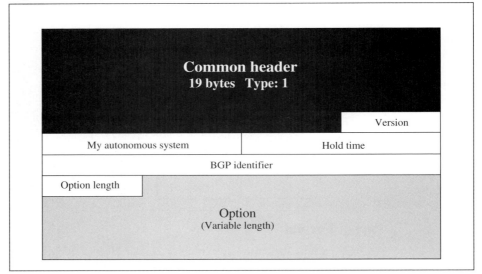

The fields of the open message are as follows:

■ **Version.** This one-byte field defines the version of BGP. The current version is 4.

■ **My autonomous system.** This two-byte field defines the autonomous system number.

■ **Hold time.** This two-byte field defines the maximum number of seconds that can elapse before one of the parties receives a keepalive or update message from the other. If a router does not receive one of these messages during the hold time period, it considers the other party dead.

■ **BGP identifier.** This is a four-byte field defining the router that sends the open message. The router usually uses one of its IP addresses (because it is unique) for this purpose.

- **Option parameter length.** The open message may also contain some option parameters. If so, this one-byte field defines the length of the total option parameters. If there are no option parameters, the value of this field is zero.

- **Option parameters.** If the value of the option parameter length is not zero, it means that there are some option parameters. Each option parameter itself has two subfields: the length of the parameter and the parameter value. The only option parameter defined so far is authentication.

Update Message

The update message is the heart of the BGP protocol. It is used by a router to withdraw destinations that have been advertised previously, announce a route to a new destination, or both. Note that BGP can withdraw several destinations that were advertised before, but it can only advertise one new destination in a single update message. The format of the update message is shown in Figure 13.48.

Figure 13.48 *Update message*

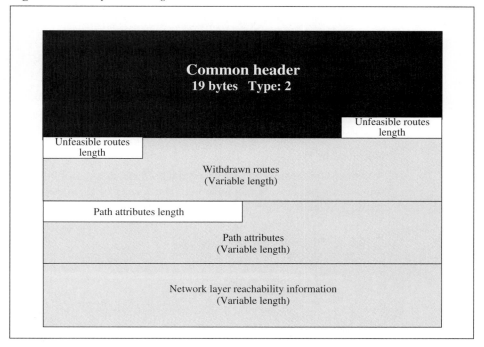

The update message fields are listed below:

- **Unfeasible routes length.** This two-byte field defines the length of the next field.

- **Withdrawn routes.**   This field lists all the routes that should be deleted from the previously advertised list.

- **Path attributes length.** This two-byte field defines the length of the next field.

■ **Path attributes.** This field defines the attributes of the path (route) to the network whose reachability is being announced in this message.

■ **Network layer reachability information (NLRI).** This field defines the network that is actually advertised by this message. It has a length field and an IP address prefix. The length defines the number of bits in the prefix. The prefix defines the netid of the network. For example, if the network is a class B address with netid 153.18, the length field value is 16 (16 bits) and the prefix is 153.18.

Keepalive Message

The routers (called *peers* in BGP parlance) running the BGP protocols, exchange keep-alive messages regularly (before their hold time expires) to tell each other that they are alive. The keepalive message consists of only the common header shown in Figure 13.49.

Figure 13.49   *Keepalive message*

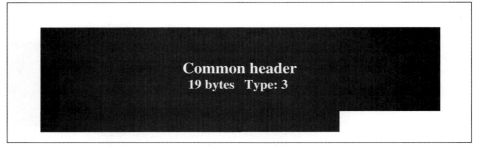

Notification Message

A notification message is sent by a router whenever an error condition is detected or a router wants to close the connection. The format of the message is shown in Figure 13.50. The fields comprising the notification message follow:

Figure 13.50   *Notification message*

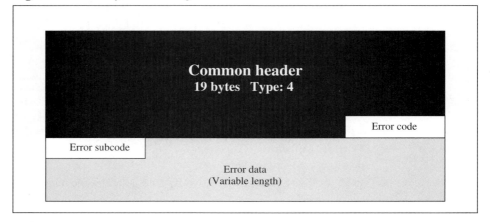

- **Error code.** This one-byte field defines the category of the error. See Table 13.5.
- **Error subcode.** This one-byte field further defines the type of error in each category.
- **Error data.** This field can be used to give more diagnostic information about the error.

Table 13.5   *Error codes*

Error Code	Error Code Description	Error Subcode Description
1	Message header error	Three different subcodes are defined for this type of error: synchronization problem (1), bad message length (2), and bad message type (3).
2	Open message error	Six different subcodes are defined for this type of error: unsupported version number (1), bad peer AS (2), bad BGP identifier (3), unsupported optional parameter (4), authentication failure (5), and unacceptable hold time (6).
3	Update message error	Eleven different subcodes are defined for this type of error: malformed attribute list (1), unrecognized well-known attribute (2), missing well-known attribute (3), attribute flag error (4), attributes length error (5), invalid origin attribute (6), AS\ routing loop (7), invalid next hop attribute (8), optional attribute error (9), invalid network field (10), malformed AS_PATH (11).
4	Hold timer expired	No subcode defined.
5	Finite state machine error	This defines the procedural error. No subcode defined.
6	Cease	No subcode defined.

Encapsulation

BGP messages are encapsulated in TCP segments using the well-known port 179. This means that there is no need for error control and flow control. When a TCP connection is opened, the exchange of update, keepalive, and notification messages is continued until a notification message of type cease is sent.

BGP uses the service of TCP on port 179.

13.5   MULTICAST ROUTING

We discussed multicast addresses and IGMP in previous chapters. In this section we briefly describe DVMRP and MOSPF, the multicasting routing protocols that are designed to handle the steadily increasing multicast traffic in the Internet.

DVMRP

Distance Vector Multicast Routing Protocol (DVMRP) is used in conjunction with IGMP to handle multicast routing. DVMRP is a simple protocol based on distance vector routing and the idea of MBONE. As described in Chapter 10, MBONE creates a set of islands connected by "tunnels." Each island uses a router that implements DVMRP.

In unicast routing, a packet has one single destination. The distance vector algorithm finds the next hop based on the optimum path. In multicast routing, using the concept of islands in MBONE, the packet has many destinations and must be delivered to every island. So each island should theoretically send the packet to other islands. However, if every island were to do so, the autonomous system would be flooded with many copies of the same packet. Optimization here means something different: which router should send out the packet through every tunnel and which one should discard it.

DVMRP uses reverse-path distance vector algorithm. The routing table is not based on destination (there are multiple destinations); it is based on source. When a packet arrives, the router calculates the reverse optimum path (from the source to itself). If the previous router is in this path, the packet is sent out; otherwise it is discarded.

MOSPF

Multicast Open Shortest Path First (MOSPF), an extension to the OSPF protocol, adds a new type of packet called the *group membership packet* to the list of link state advertisement packets.

MOSPF also uses the configuration of MBONE and islands. Each island uses one multicast router that is connected through tunnels to multicast routers in other islands. MOSPF uses the Dijkstra algorithm to create a shortest-path spanning tree (see Appendix J) between each source network and all networks with members belonging to a specific group. However, the formation of the spanning tree is dynamic; the router does not create the spanning tree until it receives a packet destined for a specific multicast address.

13.6   SUMMARY

- A metric is the cost assigned for passage of a packet through a network.
- A router consults its routing table to determine the best path for a packet.
- An autonomous system (AS) is a group of networks and routers under the authority of a single administration.

■ RIP and OSPF are popular interior routing protocols used to update routing tables in an AS.

■ RIP is based on distance vector routing, in which each router shares, at regular intervals, its knowledge about the entire AS with its neighbors.

■ A RIP routing table entry consists of a destination network address, the hop count to that destination, and the IP address of the next router.

■ RIP uses three timers: the periodic timer controls the advertising of the update message, the expiration timer governs the validity of a route, and the garbage collection timer advertises the failure of a route.

■ Two shortcomings associated with the RIP protocol are slow convergence and instability.

■ Procedures to remedy RIP instability include triggered update, split horizons, and poison reverse.

■ The RIP version 2 packet format contains fields carrying AS information and authentication information.

■ OSPF divides an AS into areas, defined as collections of networks, hosts, and routers.

■ OSPF is based on link state routing, in which each router sends the state of its neighborhood to every other router in the area. A packet is sent only if there is a change in the neighborhood.

■ OSPF defines four types of links (networks): point-to-point, transient, stub, and virtual.

■ Five types of link state advertisements (LSAs) disperse information in OSPF: router link, network link, summary link to network, summary link to AS boundary router, and external link.

■ A router compiles all the information from the LSAs it receives into a link state database. This database is common to all routers in an area.

■ OSPF routing tables are calculated using Dijkstra's algorithm.

■ There are five types of OSPF packets: hello, database description, link state request, link state update, and link state acknowledgment.

■ An LSA is a multifield entry in a link state update packet.

■ BGP is an inter-autonomous system routing protocol used to update routing tables.

■ BGP is based on a routing method called path vector routing. In this method, the ASs through which a packet must pass are explicitly listed.

■ Path vector routing does not have the instability nor looping problems of distance vector routing.

■ There are four types of BGP messages: open, update, keepalive, and notification.

■ Distance Vector Multicast Routing Protocol (DVMRP), in conjunction with MBONE, handles multicast routing using a reverse-path vector algorithm.

■ Multicast Open Shortest Path First (MOSPF) is a multicast routing protocol involving both Dijkstra's algorithm and the spanning tree algorithm.

13.7 PRACTICE SET

Multiple Choice

1. RIP is based on _____.
   a. link state routing
   b. distance vector routing
   c. Dijkstra's algorithm
   d. path vector routing

2. In distance vector routing each router receives information directly from _____.
   a. every router on the network
   b. every router less than two units away
   c. a table stored by the network hosts
   d. its neighbors only

3. In distance vector routing a router sends out information _____.
   a. at regularly scheduled intervals
   b. only when there is a change in its table
   c. only when a new host is added
   d. only when a new network is added

4. A routing table contains _____.
   a. the destination network ID
   b. the hop count to reach the network
   c. the router ID of the next hop
   d. all of the above

5. Router B receives an update from router A that indicates Net1 is two hops away. The next update from A says Net1 is five hops away. What value is entered in B's routing table for Net1? Assume the basic RIP is being used.
   a. 2
   b. 3
   c. 6
   d. 7

6. If the routing table contains four new entries, how many update messages must the router send to its one neighbor router?
   a. 1
   b. 2
   c. 3
   d. 4

7. The cost field of a router's first table from itself always has a value of _____.
   a. 0
   b. 1

   c. infinity

   d. some positive integer

8. Which field in the RIP message contains the message type?

   a. command

   b. version

   c. network address

   d. distance

9. Which field in the RIP message corresponds to the cost field of the routing table?

   a. command

   b. version

   c. network address

   d. distance

10. Which field in the RIP message corresponds to the network ID field of the routing table?

   a. command

   b. version

   c. network address

   d. distance

11. Which timer schedules the sending out of regular update messages?

   a. periodic

   b. expiration

   c. garbage collection

   d. b and c

12. Which timer can set the distance field to 16?

   a. periodic

   b. expiration

   c. garbage collection

   d. b and c

13. A periodic update message goes out at time = 37 seconds. A triggered update follows at time = 57 seconds. Assuming a period of 30 seconds, when does the next regular periodic update message go out?

   a. at time = 67 seconds

   b. at time = 87 seconds

   c. at time = 58 seconds

   d. at some random time after 57 seconds

14. Which of the following attempts to alleviate the slow convergence problem?

   a. hop count limit

   b. triggered update

   c. looping

   d. a and b

15. Which of the following features the immediate sending of an update when a change occurs?

   a. hop count limit

   b. triggered update

   c. split horizons

   d. poison reverse

16. Which of the following sets an outgoing distance field to 16 for networks which previously sent incoming information through the same interface?

   a. hop count limit

   b. triggered update

   c. split horizons

   d. poison reverse

17. Which of the following does not allow the sending of information about the same network through the same interface?

   a. hop count limit

   b. triggered update

   c. split horizons

   d. poison reverse

18. Dijkstra's algorithm is used to _____.

   a. create LSAs

   b. flood an internet with information

   c. calculate the routing tables

   d. create a link state database

19. An area is _____.

   a. part of an AS

   b. composed of at least two ASs

   c. another term for an internet

   d. a collection of stub areas

20. In an autonomous system with n areas, how many areas are connected to the backbone?

   a. 1

   b. $n - 1$

   c. n

   d. $n + 1$

21. An area border router can be connected to _____.

   a. only another router

   b. another router or another network

   c. only another network

   d. only another area border router

22. Which of the following usually has the least number of connections to other areas?

   a. an area

   b. an autonomous system

   c. a transient link

   d. a stub link

23. Which type of network using the OSPF protocol always consists of just two connected routers?

   a. point-to-point

   b. transient

   c. stub

   d. virtual

24. Which type of network using the OSPF protocol is the result of a break in a link between two routers?

   a. point-to-point

   b. transient

   c. stub

   d. virtual

25. Which type of network using the OSPF protocol can have five routers attached to it?

   a. point-to-point

   b. transient

   c. stub

   d. all of the above

26. A WAN using the OSPF protocol that connects two routers is an example of a _____ type of OSPF network.

   a. point-to-point

   b. transient

   c. stub

   d. virtual

27. An Ethernet LAN using the OSPF protocol with five attached routers can be called a _____ network.

   a. point-to-point

   b. transient

   c. stub

   d. virtual

28. Which layer produces the OSPF message?

   a. data link

   b. network

   c. transport

   d. application

29. Which OSPF packet floods the Internet with information to update the database?

    a. link state request message

    b. link state update message

    c. link state acknowledgment message

    d. database description message

30. Which type of OSPF message must be sent prior to the others?

    a. hello message

    b. link state acknowledgment message

    c. link state request message

    d. database description message

31. Which IP address is needed in the hello message?

    a. designated router

    b. backup designated router

    c. neighbor router

    d. all of the above

32. Which of the following is an exterior routing protocol?

    a. RIP

    b. OSPF

    c. BGP

    d. a and b

33. Which of the following is an interior routing protocol?

    a. RIP

    b. OSPF

    c. BGP

    d. a and b

34. RIP is based on _____.

    a. distance vector routing

    b. link state routing

    c. path vector routing

    d. a and b

35. OSPF is based on _____.

    a. distance vector routing

    b. link state routing

    c. path vector routing

    d. a and b

36. BGP is based on _____.

    a. distance vector routing

    b. link state routing

    c. path vector routing

    d. a and b

37. Which timer is reset when a new update message for a route is received?

a. garbage collection timer

b. expiration timer

c. periodic timer

d. convergence timer

38. Which timer controls the advertising of regular update messages?

a. garbage collection timer

b. expiration timer

c. periodic timer

d. convergence timer

39. Which timer is involved in purging an invalid route from a table?

a. garbage collection timer

b. expiration timer

c. periodic timer

d. convergence timer

40. Which type of BGP message creates a relationship between two routers?

a. open

b. update

c. keepalive

d. notification

41. Which type of BGP message announces a route to a new destination?

a. open

b. update

c. keepalive

d. notification

42. Which type of BGP message is sent by a system to notify another router of the sender's existence?

a. open

b. update

c. keepalive

d. notification

43. Which type of BGP message is sent by a router to close a connection?

a. open

b. update

c. keepalive

d. notification

Exercises

44. What is the purpose of RIP?

45. What are the functions of a RIP message?

46. Why is the expiration timer value six times that of the periodic timer value?

47. How does the hop count limit alleviate RIP's problems?

48. List RIP shortcomings and their corresponding fixes.

49. Compare split horizons and poison reverse. When would one be used in preference to the other?

50. What is the basis of classification for the four types of links defined by OSPF?

51. What is the purpose of the authentication type and authentication data fields?

52. Contrast and compare distance vector routing with link state routing.

53. Draw a flowchart of the steps involved when a router receives a distance vector message from a neighbor.

54. Why do OSPF messages propagate faster than RIP messages?

55. What is the size of a RIP message that advertises only one network? What is the size of a RIP message that advertises N packets? Devise a formula that shows the relationship between the number of networks advertised and the size of a RIP message.

56. A router running RIP has a routing table with 20 entries. How many periodic timers are needed to handle this table?

57. A router running RIP has a routing table with 20 entries. How many expiration timers are needed to handle this table?

58. A router running RIP has a routing table with 20 entries. How many garbage collection timers are needed to handle this table if five routes are invalid?

59. A router has the following RIP routing table:

Net1	4	B
Net2	2	C
Net3	1	F
Net4	5	G

What would be the contents of the table if the router receives the following RIP message from router C:

Net1	2
Net2	1
Net3	3
Net4	7

60. How many bytes are empty in a RIP message that advertises N networks?

61. A router has the following RIP routing table:

Net1	4	B
Net2	2	C
Net3	1	F
Net4	5	G

Show the response message sent by this router.

62. Using Figure 13.23, show the link state update/router link advertisement for router A.

63. Using Figure 13.23, show the link state update/router link advertisement for router D.

64. Using Figure 13.23, show the link state update/router link advertisement for router E.

65. Show the link state update/network link advertisement for network N2 in Figure 13.23.

66. Show the link state update/network link advertisement for network N4 in Figure 13.23.

67. Show the link state update/network link advertisement for network N5 in Figure 13.23.

68. In Figure 13.23 assume that the designated router for network N1 is router A. Show the link state update/network link advertisement for this network.

69. In Figure 13.23 assume that the designated router for network N3 is router D. Show the link state update/network link advertisement for this network.

70. Assign IP addresses to networks and routers in Figure 13.23.

71. Using the result of exercise 70, show the OSPF hello message sent by router C.

72. Using the result of exercise 70, show the OSPF database description message sent by router C.

73. Using the result of exercise 70, show the OSPF link state request message sent by router C.

74. Show the autonomous system with the following specifications:

    a. There are eight networks (N1 to N8)

    b. There are eight routers (R1 to R8)

    c. N1, N2, N3, N4, and N5 are Ethernet networks

    d. N6 is a token ring

    e. N7 and N8 are point-to-point networks

    f. R1 connects N1 and N2

    g. R2 connects N1 and N7

    h. R3 connects N2 and N8

    i. R4 connects N7 and N6

    j. R5 connects N6 and N3

    k. R6 connects N6 and N4

    l. R7 connects N6 and N5

    m. R8 connects N8 and N5

75. Draw the graphical representation of the autonomous system of exercise 74 as seen by OSPF.

76. Which of the networks in exercise 74 is a transient network? Which is a stub network?

77. Show the BGP open message for router R1 in Figure 13.44.

78. Show the BGP update message for router R1 in Figure 13.44.

79. Show the BGP keepalive message for router R1 in Figure 13.44.

80. Show the BGP notification message for router R1 in Figure 13.44.

Programming Exercises

81. Write declarations for all RIP messages in C.
82. Write declarations for all OSPF messages in C.
83. Write declarations for all BGP messages in C.
84. Write C code to implement the routing algorithm for RIP.
85. Modify the code in exercise 84 to include triggered update.
86. Modify the code in exercise 84 to include split horizon.
87. Modify the code in exercise 84 to include poison reverse.
88. Write C code to implement Dijkstra's algorithm.

CHAPTER 14

Application Layer and Client-Server Model

Because the TCP/IP protocol suite was designed before the OSI model, the layers in TCP/IP do not correspond exactly to the OSI layers. The application layer in TCP/IP is equivalent to the combined session, presentation, and application layers of the OSI model. This means that all of the functionalities associated with those three layers are handled in one single layer, the application layer (see Figure 14.1).

Figure 14.1   *Comparison between OSI and TCP/IP*

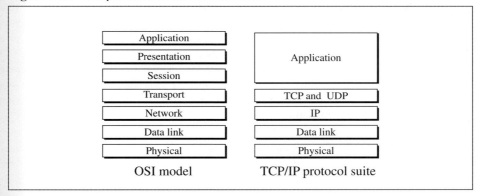

In other words, every application program must include all tasks assigned to the session, presentation, and application layers of the OSI model. This has some advantages and some disadvantages. One advantage is that each application program is independent. It requires only those functions needed for the job for which the application is designed. This saves needless calls through services that just pass parameters. One disadvantage is that the same tasks appear in different application programs, making them more complex. In addition, this kills the whole idea of modularity and layered architecture of the OSI model.

14.1   CLIENT-SERVER MODEL

The purpose of a network, or an internetwork, is to provide services to users. A user at a local site wants to receive a service from a computer at a remote site. There is only one way for a computer to do the job; it must run a program. A computer runs a program to request a service from another program and also to provide a service to another computer. This means that two computers, connected by an internet, should each run a program, one to provide a service and one to request a service.

It should be clear now that if we want to use the services available on an internet, application programs, running at two end computers and communicating with each other, are needed. In other words, in an internet, the application programs are the entities that communicate with each other, not with the computers or users.

At first glance, it looks simple to enable communication between two application programs, one running at the local site, the other running at the remote site. But many questions arise when we want to implement the approach. Some of the questions that we may ask are:

1. Should both application programs be able to request services and provide services or should the application programs just do one or the other? One solution is to have an application program, called the *client,* running on the local machine, request a service from another application program, called the *server,* running on the remote machine. In other words, the tasks of requesting a service and providing a service are separated from each other. An application program is either a requester (a client), or a provider (a server). If a machine needs to request a service and provide a service, two application programs must be installed. In other words, application programs come in pairs, client and server, both having the same name. Figure 14.2 illustrates this.

Figure 14.2   *Client-server model*

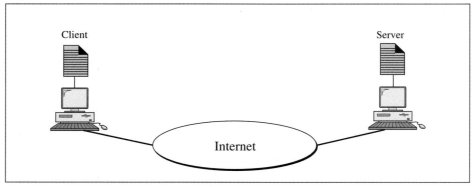

2. Should an application program provide services only to one specific application program installed somewhere in an internet or should it provide services for any application program that requests this service? The most common solution is a server providing a service for any client, not a particular client. In other words, the

client-server relationship is many-to-one. Many clients can use the services of one server (see Figure 14.3).

Figure 14.3   *Client-server relationship*

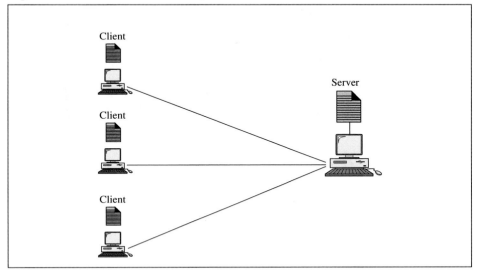

3. When should an application program be running? All of the time or just when there is a need for the service? Generally, a client program, which requests a service, should run only when it is needed. The server program, which provides a service, should run all of the time because it does not know when its service is needed.

4. Should there be only one universal application program that can provide any type of service a user wants? Or should there be one application program for each type of service? In TCP/IP, the solution is that services needed frequently and by many users have specific client-server application programs. For example, we should have client-server application programs that allow users to access files, send e-mail, and so on. For services that are more customized, we should have one generic application program that allows users to access the services available on a remote computer. For example, we should have a client-server application program that allows the user to log onto a remote computer and then use the services provided by that computer. However, we will see that there is a security problem with this type of client-server pair.

Client

A **client** is a program running on the local machine requesting service from a server. A client program is **finite,** which means it is started by the user (or another application program) and terminates when the service is complete. A client opens the communication channel using the IP address of the remote host and the well-known port address of the specific server program running on that machine. This is called an *active open.* After a channel of communication is opened, the client sends its request and receives a response. Although the request-response part may be repeated several times, the whole process is finite and eventually comes to an end. At this moment, the client closes the communication channel with an *active close*.

Server

A **server** is a program running on the remote machine providing service to the clients. When it starts, it opens the door for incoming requests from clients, but it never initiates a service until it is requested to do so. This is called a *passive open*.

A server program is an **infinite** program. When it starts it runs infinitely unless a problem arises. It waits for incoming requests from clients. When a request arrives, it responds to the request, either iteratively or concurrently as we will see shortly.

14.2 CONCURRENCY

Both clients and servers can run in concurrent mode.

Concurrency in Clients

Clients can be run on a machine either iteratively or concurrently. Running clients **iteratively** means running them one by one; one client must start, run, and terminate before the machine can start another client. Most computers today, however, allow **concurrent** clients, that is, two or more clients can run at the same time.

Concurrency in Servers

Because an iterative server can process only one request at a time, it receives a request, processes it, and sends the response to the requestor before it handles another request. A concurrent server, on the other hand, can process many requests at the same time and thus can share its time between many requests.

The servers use either UDP, a connectionless transport layer protocol, or TCP, a connection-oriented transport layer protocol. Server operation, therefore, depends on two factors: the transport layer protocol and the service method. Theoretically we can have four types of servers: connectionless iterative, connectionless concurrent, connection-oriented iterative, and connection-oriented concurrent (see Figure 14.4). However, only the first and the last are commonly used. We discuss only these two here.

Connectionless Iterative Server

The servers that use UDP are normally iterative, which, as we have said, means that the server processes one request at a time. A server gets the request received in a datagram from UDP, processes the request, and gives the response to UDP to send to the client. The server pays no attention to the other datagrams. These datagrams are stored in a queue, waiting for service. They could all be from one client or from many clients. In either case they are processed one by one in order of arrival.

Figure 14.4   *Server types*

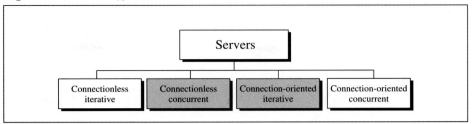

The server uses one single port for this purpose, the well-known port. All the datagrams arriving at this port wait in line to be served, as is shown in Figure 14.5.

Figure 14.5   *Connectionless iterative server*

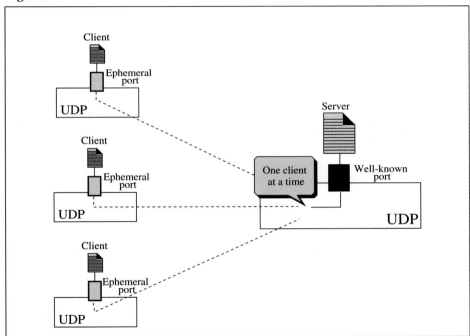

Connection-Oriented Concurrent Server

The servers that use TCP are normally concurrent. This means that the server can serve many clients at the same time. Communication is connection-oriented, which means that a request is a stream of bytes that can arrive in several segments and the response can occupy several segments. A connection is established between the server and each client, and the connection remains open until the entire stream is processed and the connection is terminated.

This type of server cannot use only one well-known port because each connection needs a port and many connections may be open at the same time. Many ports are needed, but a server can use only one well-known port. The solution is to have one well-known port and many ephemeral ports. The server makes a passive open at the well-known port. A client can make its initial approach to this port to make the connection. After the connection is made, the server assigns a temporary port to this connection to free the well-known port. Data transfer can now take place between these two temporary ports, one at the client site and the other at the server site. The well-known port is now free for another client to make the connection. The idea is to push demultiplexing to TCP instead of the server.

The server must also have one buffer for each connection. The segments come from the client, are stored in the appropriate buffer, and will be served concurrently by the server.

To provide this service, most implementations use the concept of parent and child servers. A server running infinitely and accepting connections from the clients is called a *parent server*. The parent server uses the well-known port. After it makes a connection, the parent server creates a *child server* and an ephemeral port and lets the child server handle the service. It thereby frees itself so that it can wait for another connection. See Figure 14.6 for this configuration.

Figure 14.6 *Connection-oriented concurrent server*

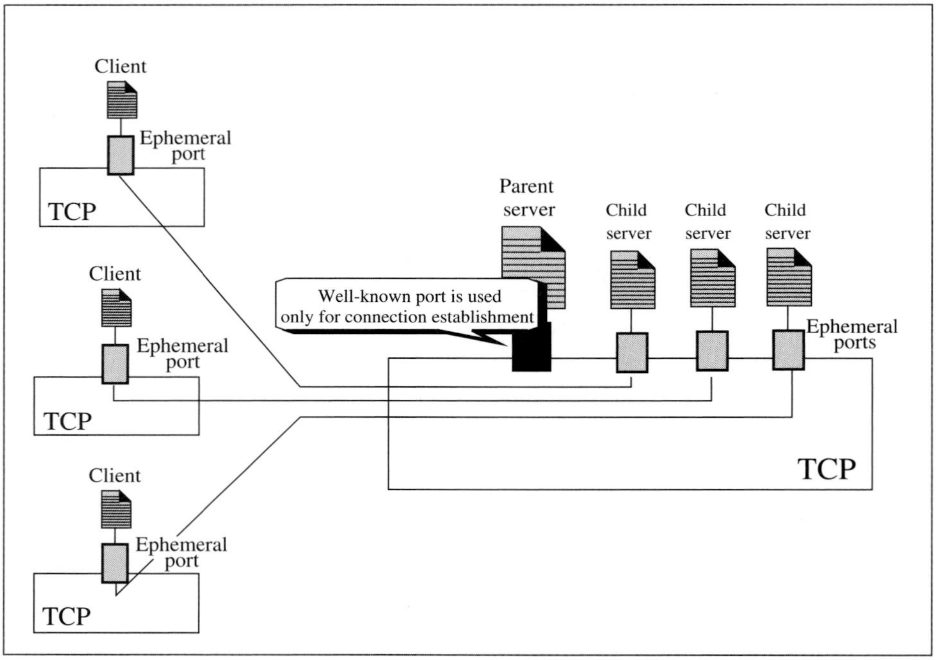

14.3 PROCESSES

Understanding the concept of a process is necessary to comprehend the client-server model. In this section, we discuss this concept and its relationship to the client-server model, particularly concurrent processing.

Concept

Most operating systems, including UNIX, distinguish a program from a process. Whereas a program and a process are related to each other, they are not the same thing. The relationship between a program and a process is similar to the relationship between a class and an object in object-oriented programming.

In object-oriented programming, a class is just a definition. One can define one single class, but many instances of that class, called *objects*, can be instantiated. The class is just the declarations and definitions of members. Memory allocation and the storing of data in the data members occur only when an instance of the class (an object) is created. Although all objects have the same types of data elements, the values stored in those data elements may be totally different for each object. Figure 14.7 shows the definition of a class and objects instantiated from that class. The class defines only two private data members: x and y. Each object has its own memory allocation and can have different values stored in it.

Figure 14.7 *Classes and object*

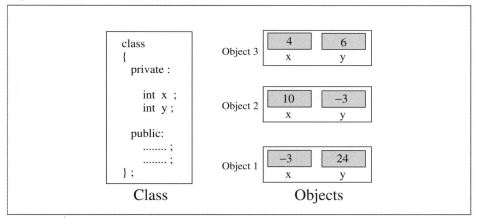

In UNIX, a program is code. The code defines all the variables and actions to be performed on those variables. A process, on the other hand, is an instance of a program. When the operating system executes a program, an instance of the program, a process, is created. The operating system can create several processes from one program, which means several instances of the same program are running at the same time (concurrently). Although all processes have the same data types, memory is allocated for each process separately. Also, the values stored in variables may be totally different from one process to another.

To handle processes, an operating system usually associates a structure with a process. The structure holds information needed to control a process. Among other things, a structure holds a pointer pointing to the line of the program being executed at this moment for this specific process, the processid, the userid, the program name, and a pointer to the memory where allocation for variables is made and data belonging to this process is stored.

Figure 14.8 shows the concept. Here the operating system is running two instances of the program, and therefore, there are two structures, one for each process.

Figure 14.8 *Program and processes*

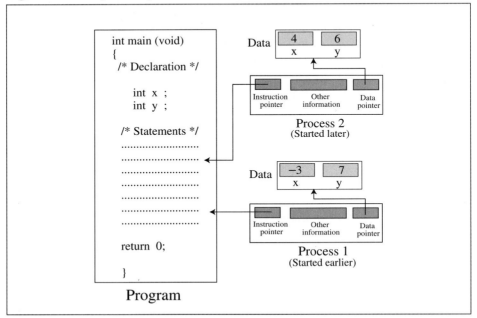

Process Identification

Each process in UNIX is uniquely defined by an integer called the *process identification* or *processid*. There is a function in UNIX that can return the process identification of a process. Figure 14.9 shows the prototype declaration. The **pid_t** is a data type that is often cast to long integer.

Figure 14.9 *Prototype for the getpid function*

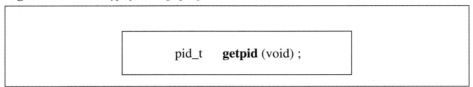

For example, the program in Figure 14.10, when run, is a process; it prints its own processid. However, the printed processid is different each time the program is run. Each time, the operating system assigns a different processid to the process.

Figure 14.10   *A program that prints its own processid*

```
#include <stdio.h>
#include <sys/types.h>
#include <unistd.h>

int main (void)
{
  printf ("My process id  is %ld", (long) getpid());

  return  0;
}
```

Process Creation

Just as creation in real life is normally done by replication, process creation in an operating system occurs the same way. In real life, a pair of parents creates a child. The child is a replica of the parents. In UNIX, a process can be created only by a parent process (except for the first process). The created process is called a *child process*. This means that for a process (the child) to be created, another process (the parent) must be running. After creation, the parent process and the child process run concurrently; they both execute the same line of codes.

We should note that not every process can create a child. For a process to create a child there must be some invocation in the program code that triggers the process. This invocation in UNIX is achieved through a function named *fork*. When the parent process encounters fork, fork creates a child process that has exactly the same image as its parent. From this time forward, the parent and child both execute all remaining lines of code. However, the lines of code prior to fork are executed only by the parent. Figure 14.11 shows the prototype of the fork function.

Figure 14.11   *Prototype for the fork function*

```
pid_t     fork (void) ;
```

Figure 14.12 shows an example of a program with the function fork. The parent process runs the program. When it encounters fork, a child process is born and, after that, both run the remaining code. The message "Hello World" is printed once and only by the parent. The message "Bye World" is printed twice; once by the parent and once by the child.

An interesting point in process creation is that a child process can also create a child (a grandchild). Figure 14.13 shows how fork is called twice in a program. The first fork is called by the parent process and creates a child; the second fork, however, is

Figure 14.12   *A program with one parent and one child*

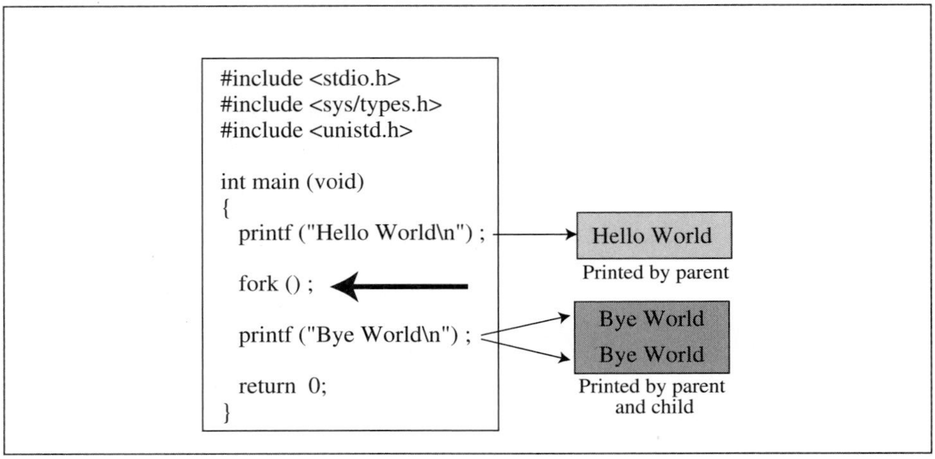

```
#include <stdio.h>
#include <sys/types.h>
#include <unistd.h>

int main (void)
{
    printf ("Hello World\n") ;          ────▶   Hello World
                                                 Printed by parent
    fork () ;   ◀────────────

    printf ("Bye World\n") ;            ────▶   Bye World
                                                 Bye World
    return  0;                                   Printed by parent
}                                                  and child
```

called by two processes: the parent and the child. When fork is called by the parent process, it creates a new child (second child). When fork is called by the first child, it creates another child (a grandchild). After the first fork, only two processes are running (the parent and the first child); after the second fork, four processes are running: the parent, the first child, the second child, and the grandchild (the child of the first child).

Figure 14.13   *A program with two fork functions*

```
#include <stdio.h>
#include <sys/types.h>
#include <unistd.h>

int main (void)
{

    printf ("Parent\n") ;
    fork () ;   ◀────────────────
    printf ("Parent and first child\n") ;
    fork () ;   ◀────────────────
    printf ("Parent, first child, second child and grandchild");

    return  0;
}
```

Figure 14.14 shows the result of the previous program. The first line is printed only once, the second line twice, and the third line four times.

A very interesting point about fork is that when it is called, it returns two values. The returned value available to the parent process is the processid of the created child. The returned value available to the child process is simply 0. These dual returned values allow the programmer to write a program to separate the parent from the child pro-

Figure 14.14   *The output of the program in Figure 14.13*

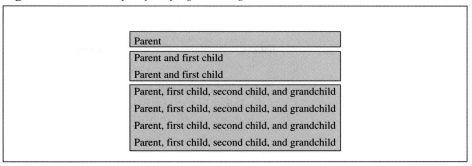

cess. The program in Figure 14.15 prints the processid of the parent and child. The program separates these two processes by testing the return value of the fork function.

Figure 14.15   *A program that prints the processids of the parent and the child*

```
#include <stdio.h>
#include <sys/types.h>
#include <unistd.h>

int main (void)
{
  pid_t  pid ;
  pid  = fork () ;
  if (pid ! = 0 )
     printf ("Parent process id  is %ld", (long) getpid());
  else
     printf ("Child process id  is %ld", (long) getpid());
  return  0;
}
```

The separation of the parent and the child is the key to the design of concurrent servers. A parent server can run infinitely and wait for a client to make a connection. As soon as a client requests the connection, the parent can create a child server to serve the client and continue to look for other clients. For every client, a new child server is created and assigned to serve that client. Figure 14.16 shows the idea. We will give more details in Chapter 24 where we discuss socket interface.

Figure 14.16   *Example of a server program with parent and child processes*

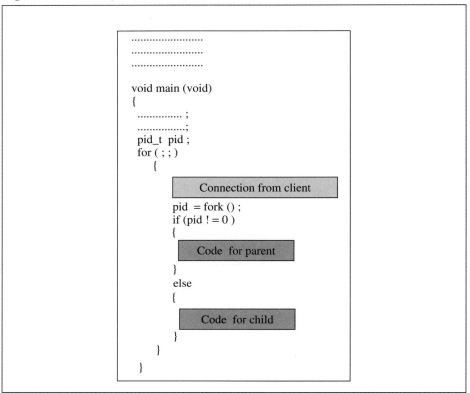

14.4   SUMMARY

■ The TCP/IP application layer corresponds to the combined session, presentation, and application layers of the OSI model.

■ In the client-server model the client runs a program to request a service and the server runs a program to provide the service. These two programs communicate with each other.

■ One server program can provide services for many client programs.

■ The server program is on at all times while the client program is run only when needed.

■ Services needed frequently and by many users have specific client-server programs.

■ A client is a finite program running on the local machine requesting service from a server.

■ A server is an infinite program running on the remote machine providing service to the clients.

■ Clients can be run either iteratively (one at a time) or concurrently (many at a time).

■ Servers can handle clients either iteratively (one at a time) or concurrently (many at a time).

■ A connectionless iterative server uses UDP as its transport layer protocol and can serve one client at a time.

■ A connection-oriented concurrent server uses TCP as its transport layer protocol and can serve many clients at the same time.

■ When the operating system executes a program, an instance of the program, called a process, is created.

■ Each program in UNIX is uniquely identified by an integer called the process identification number (processid).

■ The fork function enables the creation of a child process from a parent process.

■ The fork function returns two values that enable the separation of the parent from the child.

14.5   PRACTICE SET

Multiple Choice

1. _____ can request a service.
   a. A socket interface
   b. A port
   c. A client
   d. A server

2. _____ can provide a service.
   a. An iterative server
   b. A concurrent server
   c. A client
   d. a and b

3. The client program is _____ because it terminates after it has been served.
   a. active
   b. passive
   c. finite
   d. infinite

4. The server program is _____ because it is always available, waiting for a client request.
   a. active
   b. passive

   c. finite

   d. infinite

5. A connection-oriented concurrent server uses _____ ports.

   a. ephemeral

   b. well-known

   c. active

   d. a and b

6. A connectionless iterative server uses _____ ports.

   a. ephemeral

   b. well-known

   c. active

   d. a and b

7. The TCP/IP application layer corresponds to the OSI model's _____ layer.

   a. physical, data link, and network

   b. transport and network

   c. session and transport

   d. session, presentation, and application

8. Machine A requests service X from machine B. Machine B requests service Y from machine A. What is the total number of application programs required?

   a. 1

   b. 2

   c. 3

   d. 4

9. A client issues _____ when it needs service from a server.

   a. an active open

   b. a passive open

   c. an active request

   d. a finite open

10. A server program, once it issues _____, waits for clients to request its service.

   a. an active open

   b. a passive open

   c. an active request

   d. a finite open

11. _____ processes requests one at a time.

   a. An iterative client

   b. An iterative server

   c. A concurrent client

   d. A concurrent server

12. _____ processes many requests simultaneously.

   a. An iterative client

   b. An iterative server

   c. A concurrent client

   d. A concurrent server

13. In a connection-oriented concurrent server, the _____ is used for connection only.

   a. infinite port

   b. ephemeral port

   c. well-known port

   d. b and c

14. A _____ is an instance of a _____.

   a. process; program

   b. program; process

   c. process; service

   d. structure; process

15. Four processes from one program are created: one parent, two child, and one grandchild. How many processids are there?

   a. 1

   b. 2

   c. 3

   d. 4

16. When program A is run, its processid is 12,345. When it is run again, its processid is _____.

   a. 12,344

   b. 12,345

   c. 12,346

   d. some number assigned by the operating system

17. The _____ function creates a child process.

   a. child

   b. get_child

   c. get pid

   d. fork

18. In the program in Figure 14.13, the parent process prints _____ statements.

   a. 1

   b. 2

   c. 3

   d. 4

19. In the program in Figure 14.13, the first child process prints _____ statements.

   a. 1

   b. 2

   c. 3

    d. 4
20. In the program in Figure 14.13, the second child process prints _____ state-
    ments.
    a. 1
    b. 2
    c. 3
    d. 4
21. In the program in Figure 14.13, the grandchild process prints _____ statements.
    a. 1
    b. 2
    c. 3
    d. 4

Exercises

22. Can a child process have more than one parent process?
23. Can a parent process have more than one child process?
24. Show how a parent can print the processid of its child.
25. Show how a child can print the processid of its parent. Use the *getppid( )* function
    which is similar to *getpid*, but it prints the processid of the parent.
26. What is the output of the following program segment?

```
fork ();
printf ("Hello\n") ;
printf ("Hello\n") ;
fork ();
printf ("Bye\n") ;
return 0 ;
```

27. What is the output of the following program segment?

```
for (i =1 ; i<= 4 ; i++)
{
   pid = fork () ;
   if (pid != 0)
       printf ("%d\n", pid) ;
}
```

28. What is the output of the following program segment?

```
for (i =1 ; i<= 4 ; i++)
{
   pid = fork () ;
   if (pid == 0)
       continue ;
   else
       printf ("%d\n", pid) ;
}
```

29. What is the output of the following program segment?

```
pid  = fork ();
if (pid == 0)
        {
        printf ("Hello\n") ;
        fork ();
        printf ("Bye\n") ;
        }
else
        {
        printf ("Hi\n") ;
        fork ();
        printf ("Dear\n") ;
        fork ();
        printf ("Friend\n");
        }
```

Programming Exercises

30. Write a program that creates a child and prints the processid of the child first and the parent next.
31. Write a program that creates a child and a grandchild. The program should print the processid of the parent, the child, and the grandchild in order.
32. Write a program that creates a child and a grandchild. The program should print the processid of the grandchild, the child, and the parent in order.
33. Write a program that creates two children and four grandchildren (two for each child). The program should then print the processid of the parent, the two children, and the four grandchildren in this order.
34. Write the client program for the program in Figure 14.10.
35. Rewrite the program of Figure 14.10 as an iterative server.

CHAPTER 15

BOOTP and DHCP

Each computer that is attached to a TCP/IP internet must know the following information:

- Its IP address
- Its subnet mask
- The IP address of a router
- The IP address of a name server

This information is usually stored in a configuration file and accessed by the computer during the bootstrap process. But what about a diskless workstation or a computer with a disk that is booted for the first time?

In the case of a diskless computer, the operating system and the networking software can be stored in read-only memory (ROM). However, the above information is not known to the manufacturer and thus cannot be stored in ROM. The information is dependent on the individual configuration of the machine and defines the network to which the machine is connected.

15.1   BOOTP

BOOTP (Bootstrap Protocol) is a client/server protocol designed to provide the four previously mentioned pieces of information for a diskless computer or a computer that is booted for the first time. We have already studied one protocol, RARP, that provides the IP address for a diskless computer. Why do we need yet another protocol? The answer is that RARP provides only the IP address and not the other information. If we use BOOTP, we do not need RARP. For this reason RARP is not implemented in most systems, and it is totally removed from TCP/IP version 6.

Packet Format

Figure 15.1 shows the format of a BOOTP packet.

Figure 15.1   *BOOTP packet format*

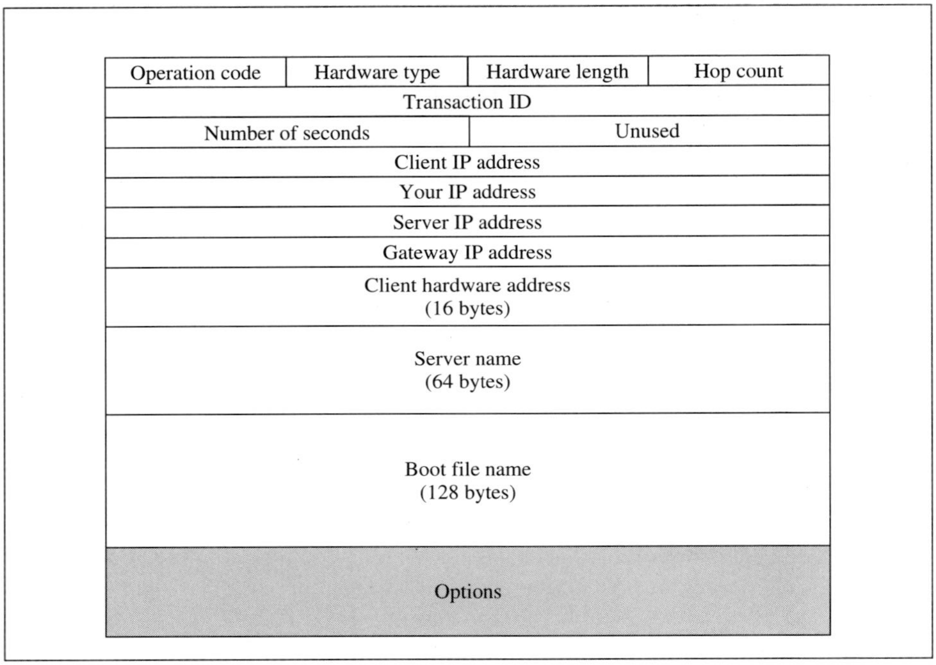

Operation code	Hardware type	Hardware length	Hop count
Transaction ID			
Number of seconds		Unused	
Client IP address			
Your IP address			
Server IP address			
Gateway IP address			
Client hardware address (16 bytes)			
Server name (64 bytes)			
Boot file name (128 bytes)			
Options			

- **Operation code.** This eight-bit field defines the type of BOOTP packet: request (1) or reply (2).

- **Hardware type.** This is an eight-bit field defining the type of physical network. Each type of local area network has been assigned an integer. For example, for Ethernet the value is 1.

- **Hardware length.** This is an eight-bit field defining the length of the physical address in bytes. For example, for Ethernet the value is 6.

- **Hop count.** This is an eight-bit field defining the maximum number of hops the packet can travel.

- **Transaction ID.** This is a four-byte field carrying an integer. The transaction identification is set by the client and is used to match a reply with the request. The server returns the same value in its reply.

- **Number of seconds.** This is a 16-bit field that indicates the number of seconds elapsed since the time the client started to boot.

- **Client IP address.** This is a four-byte field that contains the client IP address. If the client does not have this information, this field has a value of 0.

- **Your IP address.** This is a four-byte field that contains the client IP address. It is filled by the server (in the reply message) at the request of the client.

- **Server IP address.** This is a four-byte field containing the server IP address. It is filled by the server in a reply message.

- **Gateway IP address.** This is a four-byte field containing the IP address of a router. It is filled by the server in a reply message.

- **Client hardware address.** This is the physical address of the client. Although the server can retrieve this address from the frame sent by the client, it is more efficient if the address is supplied explicitly by the client in the request message.
- **Server name.** This is an optional 64-byte field filled by the server in a reply packet. It contains a null-terminated string consisting of the domain name of the server.
- **Boot filename.** This is an optional 128-byte field that can be filled by the server in a reply packet. It contains a null-terminated string consisting of the full pathname of the boot file. The client can use this path to retrieve other booting information.
- **Options.** This is a 64-byte field with a dual purpose. It can carry either additional information (such as the network mask or default router address) or some specific vendor information. The field is used only in a reply message. The server uses a number, called a *magic cookie*, in the format of an IP address with the value of 99.130.83.99. When the client finishes reading the message, it looks for this magic cookie. If present, the next 60 bytes are options. An option is composed of three fields: a one-byte tag, a one-byte length, and a variable-length value. The length field defines the length of the value field, not the whole option. See Figure 15.2.

Figure 15.2   *Option format*

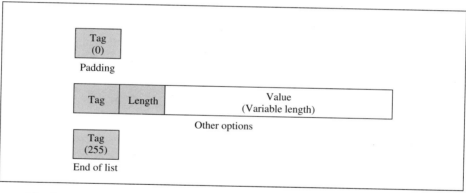

The list of options is shown in Table 15.1.

Table 15.1   *Options for BOOTP*

Description	Tag	Length	Value
Padding	0		
Subnet mask	1	4	Subnet mask
Time offset	2	4	Time of the day
Default routers	3	Variable	IP addresses
Time servers	4	Variable	IP addresses
DNS servers	6	Variable	IP addresses
Print servers	9	Variable	IP addresses

Table 15.1   *Options for BOOTP (concluded)*

Description	Tag	Length	Value
Host name	12	Variable	DNS name
Boot file size	13	2	Integer
Vendor specific	128–254	Variable	Specific information
End of list	255		

The length of the fields that contain IP addresses are multiples of four bytes. The padding option, which is only one-byte long, is used only for alignment. The end-of-list option, which is also only one-byte long, indicates the end of the option field. Vendors can use option tags 128 to 254 to supply extra information in a reply message.

Operation

Figure 15.3 shows the steps involved in using the BOOTP protocol.

Figure 15.3   *BOOTP operation*

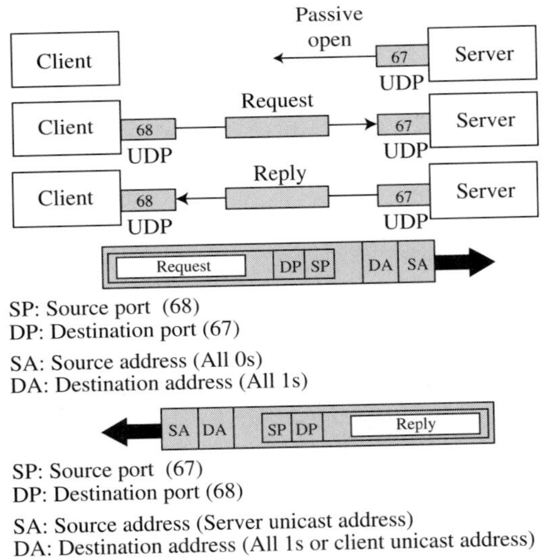

1. The BOOTP server uses UDP port number 67 and waits for a client.

2. The client sends a BOOTP request message to the server. The message is encapsulated in a UDP user datagram, using the UDP port number 68. The UDP user datagram, in turn, is encapsulated in an IP datagram. The reader may ask how the client can send an IP datagram when it knows neither its own IP address (the source address) nor the server's IP address (the destination address). The client uses all 0s

as the source address and all 1s as the destination address (see special addresses in Chapter 4).

3. The server replies to the client with either a broadcast or a unicast message using UDP destination port 68. The unicast reply message is preferred because it does not involve other hosts on the network. Note that if the server uses the unicast message to reply, it cannot use the services of ARP. The ARP protocol requires that the other party (the client) know its own IP address, which is not true in this case. This means that, instead of using ARP, the server can pass the physical address it received in the BOOTP request to its data link layer.

UDP Ports

An unusual aspect of BOOTP is the client's use of the well-known port 68 instead of an ephemeral port. This is because the reply from the server can be broadcast and therefore the response will be received by all hosts. But what if two clients, one using BOOTP, the other DAYTIME, select the same ephemeral ports? The broadcast message will be sent to both clients, and because the port numbers are the same, two clients will receive the same messages. One client is expecting a BOOTP reply, the other a DAYTIME reply. However, if the BOOTP client uses the well-known port 68, the BOOTP reply will not be received by a DAYTIME process.

The reader may ask what happens if two hosts use BOOTP at the same time. Both use the well-known port 68. If the server broadcasts the reply, both hosts receive the message. In this case, the Transaction ID field can help. It is very improbable that the two hosts used the same transaction identifier in their request. In this way, the host can recognize its reply from another host's reply.

Using TFTP

The server does not send all of the information that a client may need for booting. In the reply message, the server defines the pathname of a file in which the client can find complete booting information. The client can then use a TFTP message, which is encapsulated in a UDP user datagram, to obtain the rest of the needed information.

Relay Agent

It may happen that the administrator has decided not to include a BOOTP server for each LAN. Instead, a remote BOOTP server may serve several LANs.

In this case, if a client needs to be booted, it cannot reach the remote server using the broadcast address because an address of all 1s has only local jurisdiction. The problem is solved, however, with the use of a *relay agent*. A relay agent is a router that can help send local requests to remote servers.

The relay agent that receives the client request adds its IP address in the field provided for this purpose, and sends it to the remote server. The remote server sends the reply to the relay agent, which is then forwarded to the client.

15.2   DYNAMIC HOST CONFIGURATION PROTOCOL (DHCP)

BOOTP is not a dynamic configuration protocol. When a client requests its IP address, the BOOTP server looks up a table that matches the physical address of the client with its IP address. This implies that the binding between the physical address and the IP address of the client should already exist. The binding is predetermined.

However, what if a host moves from one physical network to another? What if a host wants a temporary IP address? BOOTP cannot handle these problems because the binding between the physical and IP addresses is static and fixed in a table until changed by the administrator. BOOTP is a static configuration protocol.

The **Dynamic Host Configuration Protocol** (DHCP) has been devised to provide dynamic configuration. DHCP is an extension to BOOTP. It enhances BOOTP and is backward compatible with BOOTP. This means a host running the BOOTP client can request a static configuration from a DHCP server.

DHCP is also needed when a host moves from network to network or is connected and disconnected from a network (like a subscriber to a service provider). DHCP provides temporary IP addresses for a limited period of time.

A DHCP server has two databases. The first database statically binds physical addresses with IP addresses. This is the same type of database a BOOTP server has. DHCP has a second database with a pool of available IP addresses. This second database makes DHCP dynamic. When a DHCP client requests a temporary IP address, the DHCP server goes to the pool of available (unused) IP addresses and assigns an IP address for a negotiable period of time.

When a DHCP client sends a request to a DHCP server, the server first checks its static database. If an entry with the requested physical address exists in the static database, the permanent IP address of the client is returned. On the other hand, if the entry does not exist in the static database, the server selects an IP address from the available pool and assigns the address to the client and adds the entry to the dynamic database.

Leasing

The addresses assigned from the pool are temporary addresses. The DHCP server issues a lease for a specific period of time. When the lease expires, the client must either stop using the IP address or renew the lease. The server has the choice to agree or disagree with renewal. If the server disagrees, the client stops using the address.

DHCP Operation

Figure 15.4 shows the operation of DHCP. To obtain an IP address, a client takes the following steps:

1. The client broadcasts a DHCPDISCOVER message using destination port 67.
2. Those servers that can give this type of service respond with a DHCPOFFER message. In these messages, the servers offer an IP address. They can also offer the duration of the lease. The default is one hour. The server that sends a DHCPOF-

Figure 15.4   *DHCP operation*

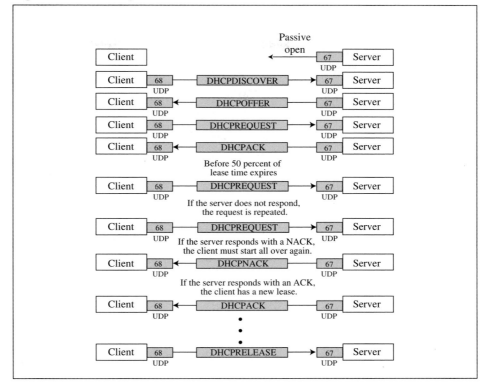

FER locks the offered IP address so that it is not available to any other clients. If the client receives no DHCPOFFER message, it will try four more times, each with a span of two seconds. If there is no reply to any of these DHCPDISCOVERs, the client sleeps for five minutes before trying again.

3. The client chooses one of the offers and sends a DHCPREQUEST message to the selected server.

4. The server responds with a DHCPACK message and creates the binding between the client physical address and its IP address. Now the client can use the IP address until the lease expires.

5. Before 50 percent of the lease period is reached, the client sends another DHCPREQUEST and asks for renewal.

6. If the server responds with a DHCPACK, the client has a new lease agreement and can reset its timer. If the server responds with a DHCPNACK, the client must immediately stop using the IP address and find another server (step 1).

7. If the server does not respond, the client sends another DHCPREQUEST when the lease time reaches 87.5 percent. If it receives a response before the end of the lease time is reached, it acts accordingly. If not, it waits until the lease time expires and starts all over again from step 1. Of course, the client can terminate the lease prematurely. In this case, it sends a DHCPRELEASE message to the server.

Packet Format

To make DHCP backward compatible with BOOTP, the designers of DHCP have decided to use almost the same packet format. They have only added a one-bit flag to the packet. However, to allow different interactions with the server, extra options have been added to the option field. Figure 15.5 shows the format of a DHCP message.

Figure 15.5   *DHCP packet*

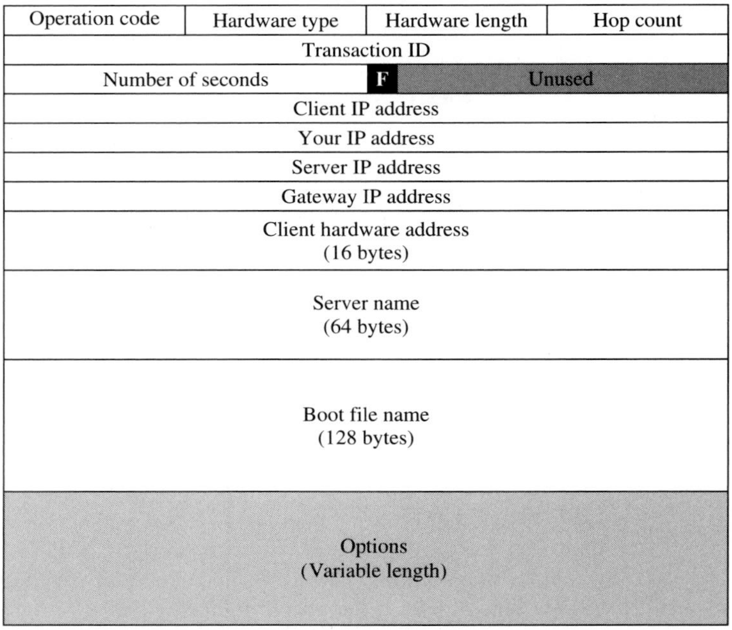

Operation code	Hardware type	Hardware length	Hop count
Transaction ID			
Number of seconds	F	Unused	
Client IP address			
Your IP address			
Server IP address			
Gateway IP address			
Client hardware address (16 bytes)			
Server name (64 bytes)			
Boot file name (128 bytes)			
Options (Variable length)			

The fields are as follows:

■ **Flag.** A one-bit flag has been added to the packet (the first bit of the unused field) to let the client specify a forced broadcast reply (instead of unicast) from the server. If the reply is unicast to the client, the destination IP address of the IP packet is the address assigned to the client. Since the client does not know its IP address, it may discard the packet. However if the IP datagram is broadcast, every host receives and processes the broadcast message.

■ **Options.** Several options have been added to the list of options. One option, with the value 53 for the tag subfield, is used to define the type of interaction between the client and the server (see Table 15.2). Other options define parameters such as lease time and so on. The options field in DHCP can be up to 312 bytes.

Table 15.2   *Options for DHCP*

Tag	Length	Value	
53	1	1	DHCPDISCOVER
		2	DHCPOFFER
		3	DHCPREQUEST
		4	DHCPDECLINE
		5	DHCPACK
		6	DHCPNACK
		7	DHCPRELEASE

15.3   SUMMARY

■ Every computer attached to a TCP/IP internet must know its IP address, the IP address of a router, the IP address of a name server, and its subnet mask (if it is part of a subnet).

■ BOOTP and Dynamic Host Configuration Protocol (DHCP) are client-server applications that deliver vital network information to either diskless computers or computers at first boot.

■ One BOOTP packet format is used for both the client request and the server reply.

■ The BOOTP server waits passively for a client request.

■ A server reply can be either broadcast or unicast.

■ A BOOTP request is encapsulated in a UDP user datagram.

■ BOOTP, a static configuration protocol, uses a table that maps IP addresses to physical addresses.

■ A relay agent is a router that helps send local BOOTP requests to remote servers.

■ DHCP is a dynamic configuration protocol with two databases: one is similar to BOOTP and the other is a pool of IP addresses available for temporary assignment.

■ The DHCP server issues a lease for an IP address to a client for a specific period of time.

■ The DHCP packet format is similar to that of BOOTP. DHCP added a flag field and extra options.

■ DHCP is backward compatible with BOOTP.

15.4 PRACTICE SET

Multiple Choice

1. The server can supply the _____ during the BOOTP process.
   a. client IP address
   b. your IP address
   c. gateway IP address
   d. all of the above

2. The _____ field in a BOOTP packet identifies a specific client request with a specific server response.
   a. operation code
   b. hardware type
   c. transaction ID
   d. hop count

3. The _____ field in a BOOTP packet identifies the type of LAN.
   a. operation code
   b. hardware type
   c. transaction ID
   d. hop count

4. The _____ field in a BOOTP packet identifies the packet as either a request or a reply.
   a. operation code
   b. hardware type
   c. transaction ID
   d. hop count

5. A relay agent is a router on LAN 1 that can help send a _____ BOOTP request to a _____ server.
   a. LAN 1; LAN 1
   b. LAN 2; LAN 2
   c. LAN 1; LAN 2
   d. LAN 2; LAN 1

6. The DHCP client may not send a _____.
   a. DHCPDISCOVER
   b. DHCPOFFER
   c. DHCPREQUEST
   d. DHCPRELEASE

7. The DHCP server may not send a _____.
   a. DHCPOFFER
   b. DHCPACK

    c. DHCPNACK

    d. DHCPRELEASE

8. The _____ message offers the client an IP address.

    a. DHCPOFFER

    b. DHCPREQUEST

    c. DHCPNACK

    d. DHCPRELEASE

9. When a client receives a _____ message, it must relinquish its IP address.

    a. DHCPOFFER

    b. DHCPDISCOVER

    c. DHCPNACK

    d. DHCPRELEASE

10. The _____ field in the reply packet is the full pathname of the boot file.

    a. server name

    b. transaction ID

    c. magic cookie

    d. boot filename

11. A computer booted for the first time has its _____ stored on ROM.

    a. IP address

    b. subnet mask

    c. IP address of a name server

    d. none of the above

12. _____ can supply a diskless computer with its IP address.

    a. RARP

    b. ARP

    c. BOOTP

    d. a and c

13. _____ can supply a diskless computer with the IP address of a router.

    a. RARP

    b. ARP

    c. BOOTP

    d. a and c

14. Which fields are most likely to contain the same information?

    a. client IP address and your IP address

    b. client IP address and server IP address

    c. client IP address and gateway IP address

    d. your IP address and server IP address

15. The BOOTP client uses _____ port number _____.

    a. ephemeral; 67

    b. ephemeral; 68

   c. well-known; 67

   d. well-known; 68

16. The server reply uses _____ as the destination address.

   a. all 0s

   b. all 1s

   c. client IP address

   d. b or c

Exercises

17. What is the minimum length of a BOOTP packet? What is the maximum length?

18. A BOOTP packet is encapsulated in a UDP packet, which is encapsulated in an IP packet, which is encapsulated in a frame. A RARP packet, on the other hand, is encapsulated only in a frame. Find the efficiency of a BOOTP packet versus a RARP packet.

19. Show an example of a BOOTP packet with a padding option.

20. Show an example of a BOOTP packet with an end-of-list option.

21. What is the maximum number of seconds that can be stored in the Number of Seconds field of a BOOTP packet?

22. Show the contents of all fields for a BOOTP request packet sent from a client with physical address 00112115EA21.

23. Show the contents of all fields for a BOOTP reply sent in response to the request in exercise 22.

24. Encapsulate the packet in exercise 22 in a UDP user datagram. Fill all the fields.

25. Encapsulate the packet in exercise 23 in a UDP user datagram. Fill all the fields.

26. Encapsulate the packet in exercise 24 in an IP datagram. Fill all the fields.

27. Encapsulate the packet in exercise 25 in an IP datagram. Fill all the fields.

28. Why does a newly added host need to know its subnetmask?

29. Why does a newly added host need to know the IP address of a router?

30. Why does a newly added host need to know the IP address of a name server?

31. Why do you think BOOTP needs to use TFTP to get additional information? Why can't all information be retrieved using BOOTP?

32. Show the format and contents of a DHCPDISCOVER message.

33. Show the format and contents of a DHCPOFFER message.

34. Show the format and contents of a DHCPREQUEST message.

35. Show the format and contents of a DHCPDECLINE message.

36. Show the format and contents of a DHCPACK message.

37. Show the format and contents of a DHCPNACK message.

38. Show the format and contents of a DHCPRELEASE message.

39. A diskless client on a Class C Ethernet network uses BOOTP. The BOOTP server is on a Class B Ethernet network. Draw a figure of the networks with appropriate

IP addresses for the client, server, and relay agent. Fill out a BOOTP request and reply packet.

40. Design an algorithm for a BOOTP client.
41. Design an algorithm for a BOOTP server.
42. Design an algorithm for a DHCP client.
43. Design an algorithm for a DHCP server.

Programming Exercises

44. Create a header file to include all constants that you think are needed to implement a BOOTP algorithm in C. Use the #define directives.
45. Create a header file to include all constants that you think are needed to implement a DHCP algorithm in C. Use the #define directives.
46. Complete the following struct declaration for the BOOTP packet.

```
struct   BOOTP
{
unsigned short    Operation_Code ;
...........................................................
...........................................................
} ;
```

47. Write a C program for the algorithm you developed in exercise 40.
48. Write a C program for the algorithm you developed in exercise 41.
49. Write a C program for the algorithm you developed in exercise 42.
50. Write a C program for the algorithm you developed in exercise 43.

CHAPTER 16

Domain Name System (DNS)

To identify an entity, TCP/IP protocols use the IP address, which uniquely identifies the connection of a host to the Internet. However, people prefer to use names instead of addresses. Therefore, we need a system that can map a name to an address or an address to a name.

When the Internet was small, mapping was done using a *host file*. The host file had only two columns comprising name and address. Every host could store the host file on its disk and update it periodically from a master host file. When a program or a user wanted to map a name to an address, the host consulted the host file and found the mapping.

Today, however, it is impossible to have one single host file to relate every address with a name or vice versa. The host file would be too large to store in every host. In addition, it would be impossible to update all the host files in the world every time there is a change.

One solution would be to store the entire host file in a single computer and allow access to this centralized information to every computer that needs mapping. But we know that this would create a huge amount of traffic on the Internet.

Another solution, the one used today, is to divide this huge amount of information into smaller parts and store each part on a different computer. In this method, the host that needs mapping can contact the closest computer holding the needed information. This method is used by the Domain Name System. In this chapter, we first discuss the concepts and ideas behind the DNS. We then describe the DNS protocol itself.

16.1   NAME SPACE

To be unambiguous, the names assigned to machines should be carefully selected from a name space with complete control over the binding between the names and IP addresses. In other words, the names should be unique because the addresses are unique. A name space that maps each address to a unique name can be organized in two ways: flat and hierarchical.

Flat Name Space

In a **flat name space,** a name is assigned to an address. A name in this space is a sequence of characters without structure. The names may or may not have a common section; if they do, it has no meaning. The main disadvantage of a flat name space is that it cannot be used in a large system such as the Internet because it must be centrally controlled to avoid ambiguity and duplication.

Hierarchical Name Space

In a **hierarchical name space,** each name is made of several parts. The first part can define the nature of the organization, the second part can define the name of an organization, the third part can define departments in the organization, and so on. In this case, the authority to assign and control the name spaces can be decentralized. A central authority can assign the part of the name that defines the nature of the organization and the name of the organization. The responsibility of the rest of the name can be given to the organization itself. The organization can add suffixes (or prefixes) to the name to define its host or resources. The management of the organization need not worry that the prefix chosen for a host is taken by another organization because, even if part of an address is the same, the whole address is different. For example, assume two colleges and a company call one of their computers *challenger*. The first college is given a name by the central authority such as *fhda.edu*, the second college is given the name *berkeley.edu*, and the company is given the name *smart.com*. When each of these organizations add the name *challenger* to the name they have already been given, the end result is three distinguishable names: *challenger.fhda.edu*, *challenger.berkeley.edu*, and *challenger.smart.com*. The names are unique without the need to be assigned by a central authority. The central authority controls only part of the name, not the whole.

16.2   DOMAIN NAME SPACE

To have a hierarchical name space, a **domain name space** was designed. In this design the names are defined in an inverted-tree structure with the root at the top. The tree can have only 128 levels: level 0 (root) to level 127. Whereas the root glues the whole tree together, each level of the tree defines a hierarchical level (see Figure 16.1).

Label

Each node in the tree has a **label,** which is a string with a maximum of 63 characters. The root label is a null string (empty string). DNS requires that children of a node (nodes which branch from the same node) have different labels, which guarantees the uniqueness of the domain names.

Domain Name

Each node in the tree has a domain name. A full **domain name** is a sequence of labels separated by dots (.). The domain names are always read from the node up to the root.

Figure 16.1   *Domain name space*

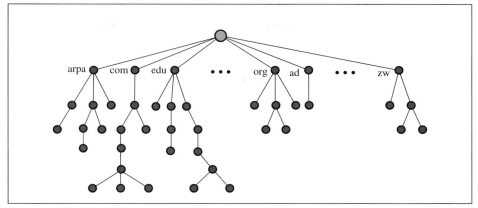

The last label is the label of the root (null). This means that a full domain name always ends in a null label, which means the last character is a dot because the null string is nothing. Figure 16.2 shows some domain names.

Figure 16.2   *Domain names and labels*

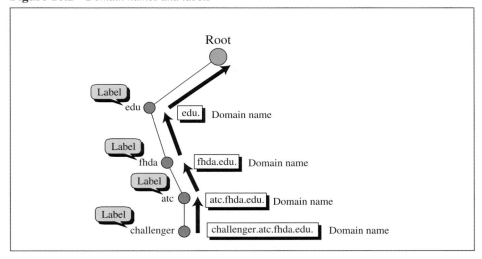

Fully Qualified Domain Name (FQDN)

If a label is terminated by a null string, it is called a fully qualified domain name (FQDN). An FQDN is a domain name that contains the full name of a host. It contains all labels, from the most specific to the most general, that uniquely defines the name of the host. For example, the domain name

challenger.atc.fhda.edu.

is the FQDN of a computer named challenger and installed at the Advanced Technology Center (ATC) at De Anza College. A DNS server can only match an FQDN to an address. Note that the name must end with a null label, but because null here means nothing, the label ends with a dot (.).

Partially Qualified Domain Name (PQDN)

If a label is not terminated by a null string, it is called a partially qualified domain name (PQDN). A PQDN starts from a node, but it does not reach the root. It is used when the name to be resolved belongs to the same site as the client. Here the resolver can supply the missing part, called the *suffix*, to create an FQDN. For example, if a user at the *fhda.edu.* site wants to get the IP address of the challenger computer, he or she can define the partial name

challenger

The DNS client adds the suffix *atc.fhda.edu.* before passing the address to the DNS server.

The DNS client normally holds a list of suffixes. The following can be the list of suffixes at De Anza College. The null suffix defines nothing. This suffix is added when the user defines an FQDN.

atc.fhda.edu
fhda.edu
null

Figure 16.3 shows some FQDNs and PQDNs.

Figure 16.3 *FQDN and PQDN*

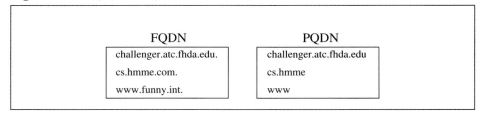

Domain

A **domain** is a subtree of the domain name space. The name of the domain is the domain name of the node at the top of the subtree. Figure 16.4 shows some domains. Note that a domain may itself be divided into domains (or *subdomains* as they are sometimes called).

Figure 16.4   *Domains*

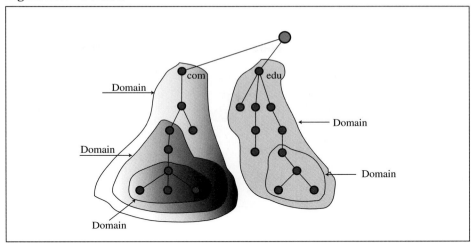

16.3   DISTRIBUTION OF NAME SPACE

The information contained in the domain name space should be stored. However, it is very inefficient and also not secure to have just one computer store such a huge amount of information. It is inefficient because the system will have a heavy load responding to requests from all over the world. It is not secure in case of failure because the whole database would be inaccessible.

Hierarchy of Name Servers

The solution to these problems is to distribute the information among many computers called *DNS servers*. One way to do this is to divide the whole space into many domains based on the first level. In other words, we let the root stand alone and create as many domains (subtrees) as there are first-level nodes. Because a domain created this way could be very large, DNS allows domains to be divided further into smaller domains (subdomains). Each server can be responsible (authoritative) for either a large or small domain. In other words, we have a hierarchy of servers in the same way that we have a hierarchy of names (see Figure 16.5).

Zone

What a server is responsible for or has authority over is called a *zone*. If a server accepts responsibility for a domain and does not divide the domain into smaller domains, the "domain" and the "zone" refer to the same thing. The server makes a database called a *zone file* and keeps all the information for every node under that domain. However, if a server divides its domain into subdomains and delegates part of its authority to other servers, "domain" and "zone" refer to different things. The informa-

Figure 16.5   *Hierarchy of name servers*

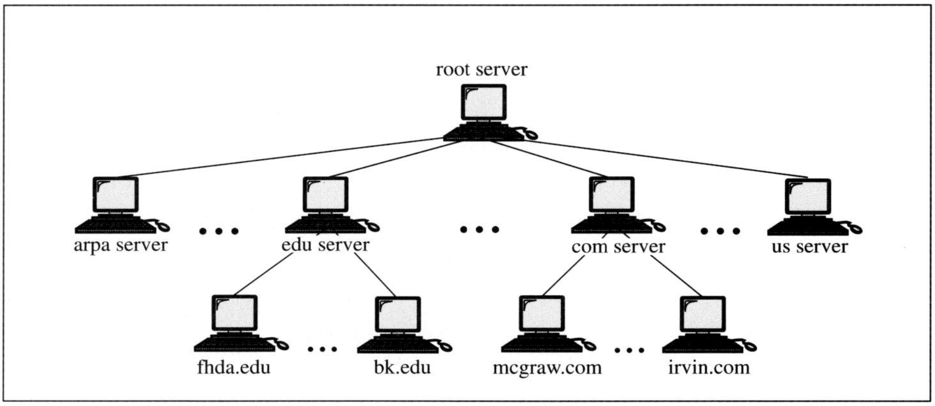

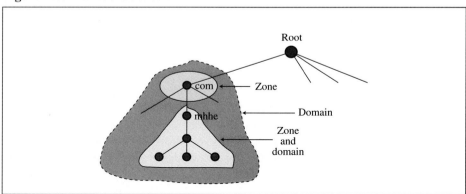

tion about the nodes in the subdomains is stored in the servers at the lower levels, with the original server keeping some sort of reference to these lower-level servers. Of course the original server does not free itself from responsibility totally: It still has a zone, but the detailed information is kept by the lower-level servers (see Figure 16.6).

Figure 16.6   *Zones and domains*

A server can also divide part of its domain and delegate responsibility but still keep part of the domain for itself. In this case, its zone is made of detailed information for the part of the domain that is not delegated and references to those parts that are delegated.

Root Server

A **root server** is a server whose zone consists of the whole tree. A root server usually does not store any information about domains but delegates its authority to other servers, keeping references to those servers. Currently there are more than 13 root servers, each covering the whole domain name space. The servers are distributed all around the world.

Primary and Secondary Servers

DNS defines two types of servers: primary and secondary. A **primary server** is a server that stores a file about the zone for which it is an authority. It it responsible for creating, maintaining, and updating the zone file. It stores the zone file on a local disk.

A **secondary server** is a server that transfers the complete information about a zone from another server (primary or secondary) and stores the file on its local disk. The secondary server neither creates nor updates the zone files. If updating is required, it must be done by the primary server, which sends the updated version to the secondary.

The primary and secondary servers are both authoritative for the zones they serve. The idea is not to put the secondary server at a lower level of authority but to create redundancy for the data so that if one server fails, the other can continue serving clients. Note also that a server can be a primary server for a specific zone and a secondary server for another zone. Therefore, when we refer to a server as a primary or secondary server, we should be careful to which zone we refer.

16.4   DNS IN THE INTERNET

DNS is a protocol that can be used in different platforms. In the Internet, the domain name space (tree) is divided into three different sections: generic domains, country domains, and inverse domain (see Figure 16.7).

Figure 16.7   *DNS used in the Internet*

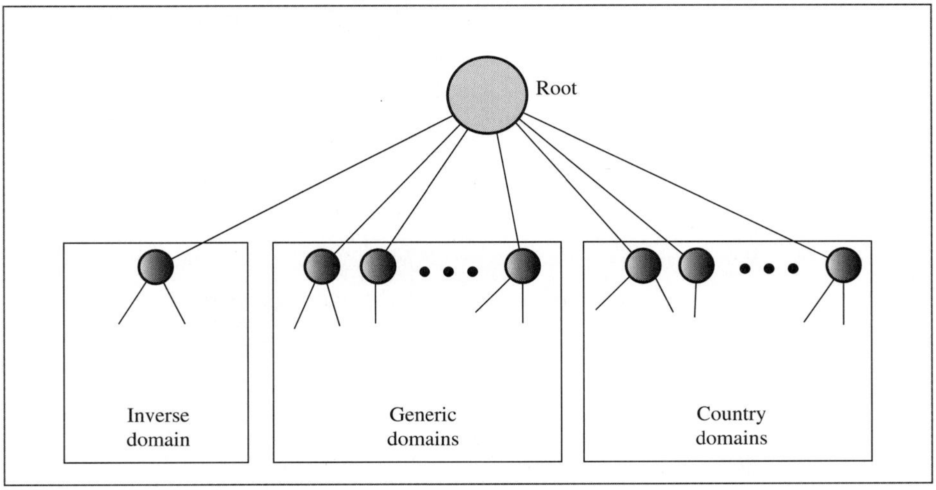

Generic Domains

The **generic domains** define registered hosts according to their generic behavior. Each node in the tree defines a domain, which is an index to the domain name space database (see Figure 16.8).

Figure 16.8 *Generic domains*

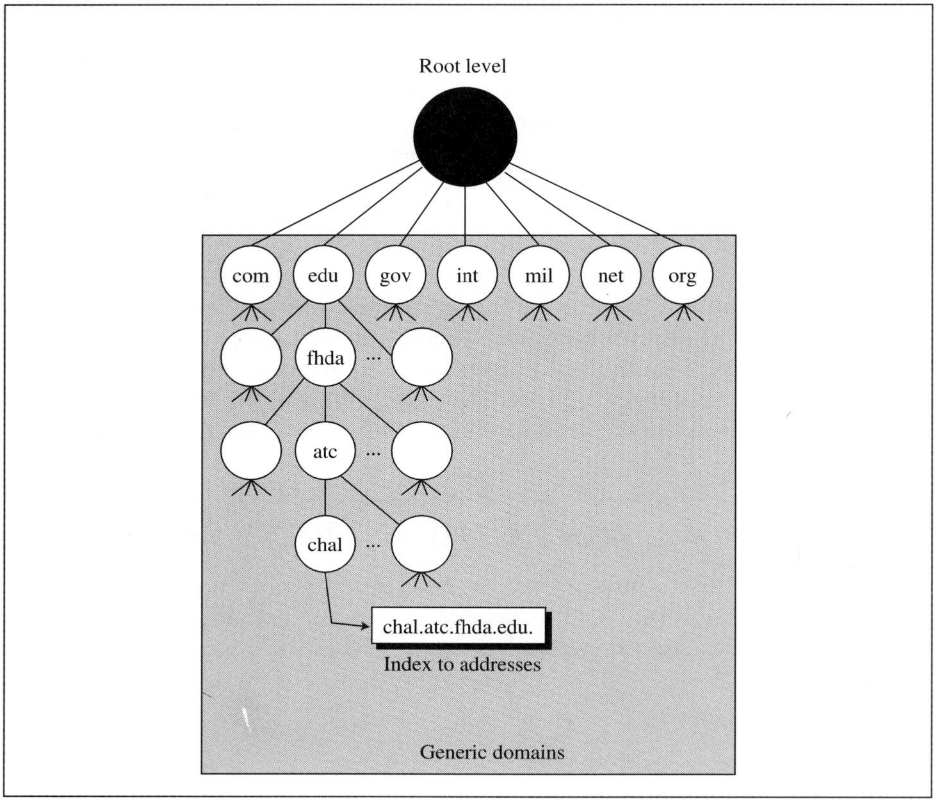

Looking at the tree, we see that the first level in the generic domains section allows seven possible three-character labels. These labels describe the organization types as listed in Table 16.1.

Table 16.1 *Generic domains labels*

Label	Description
com	Commercial organizations
edu	Educational institutions
gov	Government institutions
int	International organizations
mil	Military groups
net	Network support centers
org	Nonprofit organizations

Recently a few more first-level labels have been proposed; these are shown in Table 16.2.

Table 16.2   *Proposed generic domains labels*

Label	Description
arts	Cultural organizations
firm	Businesses or firms
info	Information service providers
nom	Personal nomenclatures
rec	Recreation/entertainment organizations
store	Businesses offering goods to purchase
web	Web-related organizations

Country Domains

The **country domains** section follows the same format as the generic domains but uses two-character country abbreviations (e.g., us for United States) in place of the three-character organizational abbreviations at the first level. Second-level labels can be organizational, or they can be more specific, national designations. The United States, for example, uses state abbreviations as a subdivision of us (e.g., ca.us.).

Figure 16.9 shows the country domains section. The address *anza.cup.ca.us* can be translated to De Anza College in Cupertino in California in the United States.

Inverse Domain

The **inverse domain** is used to map an address to a name. This may happen, for example, when a server has received a request from a client to do a task. Whereas the server has a file that contains a list of authorized clients, the server lists only the IP address of the client (extracted from the received IP packet). To determine if the client is on the authorized list, it can ask its resolver to send a query to the DNS server and ask for a mapping of address to name.

This type of query is called an inverse or pointer (PTR) query. To handle a pointer query, the inverse domain is added to the domain name space with the first-level node called *arpa* (for historical reasons). The second level is also one single node named *in-addr* (for inverse address). The rest of the domain defines IP addresses.

The servers that handle the inverse domain are also hierarchical. This means the netid part of the address should be at a higher level than the subnetid part, and the subnetid part higher than the hostid part. In this way, a server serving the whole site is at a higher level than the servers serving each subnet. This configuration makes the domain look inverted when compared to a generic or country domain. To follow the convention of reading the domain labels from the bottom to the top, an IP address such as 132.34.45.121 (a class B address with netid 132.34) is read as 121.45.34.132.in-addr.arpa. See Figure 16.10 for an illustration of the inverse domain configuration.

Figure 16.9 *Country domains*

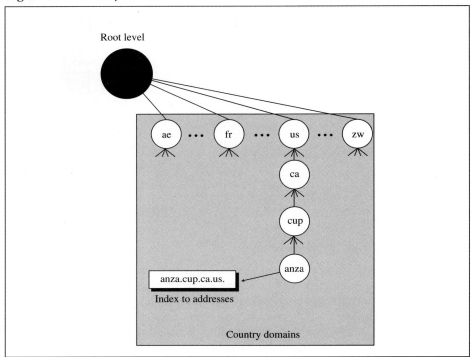

16.5 RESOLUTION

Mapping a name to an address or an address to a name is called *name-address resolution.*

Resolver

DNS is designed as a client/server application. A host that needs to map an address to a name or a name to an address calls a DNS client called a *resolver*. The resolver accesses the closest DNS server with a mapping request. If the server has the information, it satisfies the resolver; otherwise, it either refers the resolver to other servers or asks other servers to provide the information.

After the resolver receives the mapping, it interprets the response to see if it is a real resolution or an error, and finally delivers the result to the process that requested it.

Figure 16.10 *Inverse domain*

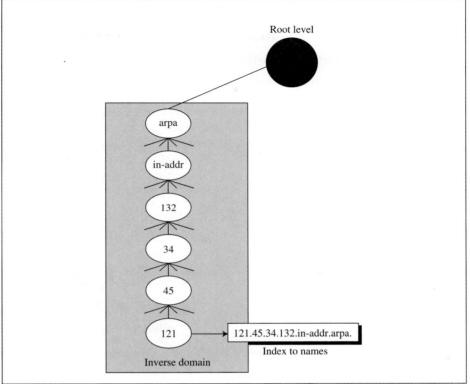

Mapping Names to Addresses

Most of the time, the resolver gives a domain name to the server and asks for the corresponding address. In this case, the server checks the generic domains or the country domains to find the mapping.

If the domain name is from the generic domains section, the resolver receives a domain name such as "*chal.atc.fhda.edu.*". The query is sent by the resolver to the local DNS server for resolution. If the local server cannot resolve the query, it either refers the resolver to other servers or asks other servers directly.

If the domain name is from the country domains section, the resolver receives a domain name such as "*ch.fhda.cu.ca.us.*". The procedure is the same.

Mapping Addresses to Names

A client can send an IP address to a server to be mapped to a domain name. As mentioned before, this is called a PTR query. To answer queries of this kind, DNS uses the inverse domain. However, in the request, the IP address should be reversed and two labels, *in-addr* and *arpa*, should be appended to create a domain acceptable by the inverse domain section. For example, if the resolver receives the IP address

132.34.45.121, the resolver first inverts the address and then adds the two labels before sending. The domain name sent is "*121.45.34.132.in-addr.arpa.*", which is received by the local DNS and resolved.

Recursive Resolution

The client (resolver) can ask for a recursive answer from a name server. This means that the resolver expects the server to supply the final answer. If the server is the authority for the domain name, it checks its database and responds. If the server is not the author-ity, it sends the request to another server (the parent usually) and waits for the response. If the parent is the authority, it responds; otherwise, it sends the query to yet another server. When the query is finally resolved, the response travels back until it finally reaches the requesting client. This is shown in Figure 16.11.

Figure 16.11 *Recursive resolution*

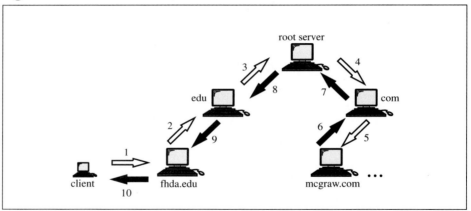

Iterative Resolution

If the client does not ask for a recursive answer, the mapping can be done iteratively. If the server is an authority for the name, it sends the answer. If it is not, it returns (to the client) the IP address of the server that it thinks can resolve the query. The client is responsible for repeating the query to this second server. If the newly addressed server can resolve the problem, it answers the query with the IP address; otherwise, it returns the IP address of a new server to the client. Now the client must repeat the query to the third server. This process is called *iterative* because the client repeats the same query to multiple servers. In Figure 16.12 the client queries four servers before it gets an answer from the mcgraw.com server.

Caching

Each time a server receives a query for a name that is not in its domain, it needs to search its database for a server IP address. Reduction of this search time would increase

Figure 16.12 *Iterative resolution*

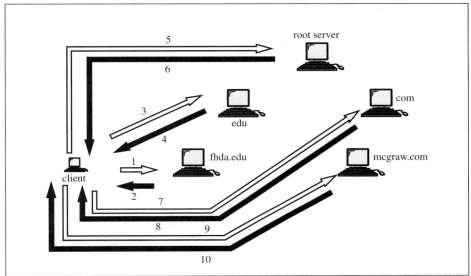

efficiency. DNS handles this with a mechanism called *caching*. When a server asks for a mapping from another server and receives the response, it stores this information in its cache memory before sending it to the client. If the same or another client asks for the same mapping, it can check its cache memory and resolve the problem. However, to inform the client that the response is coming from the cache memory and not from an authoritative source, the server marks the response as *unauthoritative*

Caching speeds up resolution, but it can also be problematic. If a server caches a mapping for a long time, it may send an outdated mapping to the client. To counter this, two techniques are used. First, the authoritative server always adds a piece of information to the mapping called *time-to-live* (TTL). It defines the time in seconds that the receiving server can cache the information. After that time, the mapping is invalid and any query must be sent again to the authoritative server. Second, DNS requires that each server keep a TTL counter for each mapping it caches. The cache memory must be searched periodically and those mappings with an expired TTL must be purged.

16.6   DNS MESSAGES

DNS has two types of messages: query and response (see Figure 16.13). Both types have the same format. The query message consists of a header and the question records; the response message consists of a header, question records, answer records, authoritative records, and additional records (see Figure 16.14).

Figure 16.13   *DNS messages*

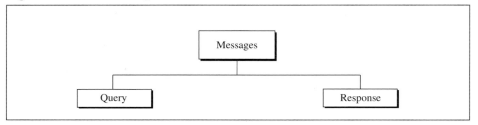

Figure 16.14   *Query and response messages*

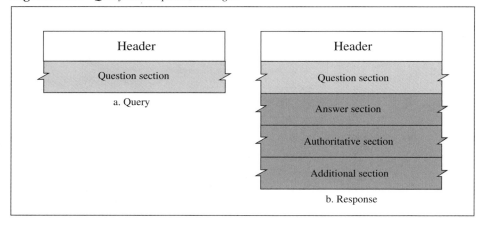

Header

Both query and response messages have the same header format with some fields set to zero for the query messages. The header is 12 bytes and its format is shown in Figure 16.15.

Figure 16.15   *Header format*

Identification	Flags
Number of question records	Number of answer records (All 0s in query message)
Number of authoritative records (All 0s in query message)	Number of additional records (All 0s in query message)

The header fields are as follows:

■ **Identification.** This is a 16-bit field used by the client to match the response with the query. The client uses a different identification number each time it sends a query. The server duplicates this number in the corresponding response.

■ **Flags.** This is a 16-bit field consisting of the subfields shown in Figure 16.16.

Figure 16.16 *Flags field*

A brief description of each flag subfield follows.

a. **QR (query/response).** This is a one-bit subfield that defines the type of message. If it is 0, the message is a query. If it is 1, the message is a response.

b. **OpCode.** This is a four-bit subfield that defines the type of query or response (0 if standard, 1 if inverse, and 2 if a server status request).

c. **AA (authoritative answer).** This is a one-bit subfield. When it is set (value of 1) it means that the name server is an authoritative server. It is used only in a response message.

d. **TC (truncated).** This is a one-bit subfield. When it is set (value of 1), it means that the response was more than 512 bytes and truncated to 512. It is used when DNS uses the services of UDP (see Section 16.11 on Encapsulation).

e. **RD (recursion desired).** This is a one-bit subfield. When it is set (value of 1) it means the client desires a recursive answer. It is set in the query message and repeated in the response message.

f. **RA (recursion available).** This is a one-bit subfield. When it is set in the response, it means that a recursive response is available. It is set only in the response message

g. **Reserved.** This is a three-bit subfield set to 000.

h. **rCode.** This is a four-bit field that shows the status of the error in the response. Of course, only an authoritative server can make such a judgment. Table 16.3 shows the possible values for this field.

Table 16.3 *Values of rCode*

Value	Meaning
0	No error
1	Format error
2	Problem at name server
3	Domain reference problem
4	Query type not supported
5	Administratively prohibited
6–15	Reserved

■ **Number of question records.** This is a 16-bit field containing the number of queries in the question section of the message.

- **Number of answer records.** This is a 16-bit field containing the number of answer records in the answer section of the response message. Its value is zero in the query message.
- **Number of authoritative records.** This is a 16-bit field containing the number of authoritative records in the authoritative section of a response message. Its value is zero in the query message.
- **Number of additional records.** This is a 16-bit field containing the number of additional records in the additional section of a response message. Its value is zero in the query message.

Question Section

This is a section consisting of one or more question records. It is present on both query and response messages. We will discuss the question records in a following section.

Answer Section

This is a section consisting of one or more resource records. It is present only on response messages. This section includes the answer from the server to the client (resolver). We will discuss resource records in a following section.

Authoritative Section

This is a section consisting of one or more resource records. It is present only on response messages.This section gives information (domain name) about one or more authoritative servers for the query.

Additional Information Section

This is a section consisting of one or more resource records. It is present only on response messages. This section provides additional information that may help the resolver. For example, a server may give the domain name of an authoritative server to the resolver in the authoritative section, and include the IP address of the same authoritative server in the additional information section.

16.7   TYPES OF RECORDS

As we saw in the previous section, two types of records are used in DNS. The question records are used in the question section of the query and response messages. The resource records are used in the answer, authoritative, and additional information sections of the response message.

Question Record

A question record is used by the client to get information from a server. This contains the domain name. Figure 16.17 shows the format of a question record. The list below describes question record fields.

Figure 16.17 *Question record format*

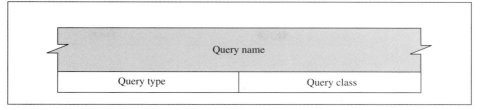

■ **Query name.** This is a variable-length field containing a domain name (see Figure 16.18).

Figure 16.18 *Query name format*

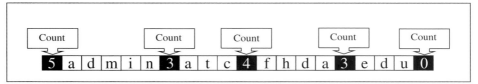

■ **Query type.** This is a 16-bit field defining the type of query. Table 16.4 shows some of the types commonly used. The last two can be used only in a query.

Table 16.4 *Types*

Type	Mnemonic	Description
1	A	Address. A 32-bit IPv4 address. It is used to convert a domain name to an IPv4 address.
2	NS	Name server. It identifies the authoritative servers for a zone.
5	CNAME	Canonical name. It defines an alias for the official name of a host.
6	SOA	Start of authority. It marks the beginning of a zone. It is usually the first record in a zone file.
11	WKS	Well-known services. It defines the network services that a host provides.
12	PTR	Pointer. It is used to convert an IP address to a domain name.
13	HINFO	Host information. It gives the description of the hardware and the operating system used by a host.
15	MX	Mail exchange. It redirects mail to a mail server.
28	AAAA	Address. An IPv6 address (see Chapter 25).
252	AXFR	A request for the transfer of the entire zone.

Table 16.4   *Types*

Type	Mnemonic	Description
255	ANY	A request for all records.

- **Query class.** This is a 16-bit field defining the specific protocol using DNS. Table 16.5 shows the current values. In this text we are interested only in class 1 (the Internet).

Table 16.5   *Classes*

Class	Mnemonic	Description
1	IN	Internet
2	CSNET	CSNET network (obsolete)
3	CS	The COAS network
4	HS	The Hesiod server developed by MIT

Resource Record

Each domain name (each node on the tree) is associated with a record called the *resource record*. The server database consists of resource records. Resource records are also what is returned by the server to the client. Figure 16.19 shows the format of a resource record.

Figure 16.19   *Resource record format*

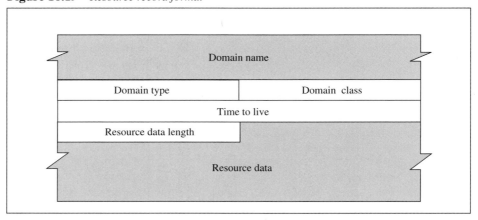

- **Domain name.** This is a variable-length field containing the domain name. It is the duplication of the domain name in the question record. Since DNS requires the use of compression everywhere a name is repeated, this field is a pointer offset to the corresponding domain name field in the question record. See Section 16.8 on Compression.

- **Domain type.** This field is the same as the query type field in the question section except the last two types are not allowed. Refer to Table 16.4 for more information.

- **Domain class.** This field is the same as the query class field in the question section (see Table 16.5).

- **Time to live.** This is a 32-bit field which defines the number of seconds the answer is valid. The receiver can cache the answer for this period of time. A zero value means that the resource record is used only in a single transaction and should not be cached.

- **Resource data length.** This is a 16-bit field defining the length of the resource data.

- **Resource data.** This is a variable-length field containing the answer to the query (in the answer section) or the domain name of the authoritative server (in the authoritative section) or additional information (in the additional information section). The format and contents of this field depend on the value of the type field. It can be one of the following:

  a. **A number.** This is written in octets. For example, an IPv4 address is a four-octet integer and an IPv6 address is a 16-octet integer.

  b. **A domain name.** Domain names are expressed as a sequence of labels. Each label is preceded by a one-byte length field that defines the number of characters in the label. Since every domain name ends with the null label, the last byte of every domain name is the length field with the value of 0. To distinguish between a length field and an offset pointer (as we will discuss later), the two high order bits of a length field should always be zero (00). This will not create a problem because the length of a label cannot be more than 63, which is a maximum of six bits (111111).

  c. **An offset pointer.** Domain names can be replaced with an offset pointer. An offset pointer is a two-byte field with the two high order bits set to 1 (11).

  d. **A character string.** A character string is represented by a one-byte length field followed by the number of characters defined in the length field. The length field is not restricted like the domain name length field. The character string can be as long as 256 characters (including the length field).

16.8 COMPRESSION

DNS requires that a domain name be replaced by an offset pointer when it is repeated. For example, in a resource record the domain name is usually a repetition of the domain name in the question record. To avoid duplication, DNS defines a two-byte offset pointer that points to a previous occurrence of the domain or part of it. The format of the field is shown in Figure 16.20.

The first two high order bits are two 1s to distinguish an offset pointer from a length field. The other 14 bits represent a number that points to the corresponding byte number in the message. The bytes in a message are counted from the beginning of the message with the first byte counted as byte 0. For example, if an offset pointer refers to byte 12 (the thirteenth byte) of the message, the value should be 1100000000001100.

Figure 16.20 *Format of an offset pointer*

11
Address of the beginning byte
2 bits
14 bits

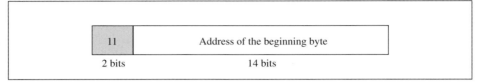

Here the two leftmost bits define the field as an offset pointer and the other bits define the decimal number 12. We will show the use of the offset pointers in the following examples.

16.9 EXAMPLES

In this section we show some examples of DNS queries and responses.

Example 1

A resolver sends a query message to a local server to find the IP address for the host "*chal.fhda.edu.*". We discuss the query and response messages separately.

Query Message Figure 16.21 shows the query message sent by the resolver. The first two bytes show the identifier (1333). It is used as a sequence number and relates a response to a query. Because a resolver may send many queries even to the same server, the identifier helps to sort responses that arrive out of order. The next bytes contain the flags with the value of 0x0100 in hexadecimal. In binary it is 0000000100000000, but it is more meaningful to divide it into the fields as shown below:

QR	OpCode	AA	TC	RD	RA	Reserved	rCode
0	0000	0	0	1	0	000	0000

Figure 16.21 *Example of a query message*

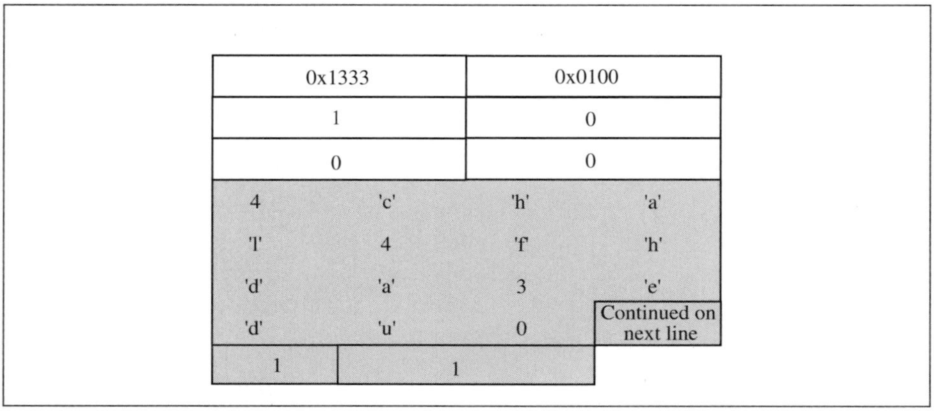

0x1333
0x0100
1
0
0
0
4 'c' 'h' 'a'
'l' 4 'f' 'h'
'd' 'a' 3 'e'
'd' 'u' 0
Continued on next line
1
1

The QR bit defines the message as a query. The OpCode is 0000, which means standard query. The recursion desired (RD) bit is set. (Refer back to Figure 16.16 for the flags field descriptions.) The message contains only one question record. The domain name is *4chal4fhda3edu0*. The next two bytes define the query type as an IP address; the last two bytes define the class as Internet.

Response Message   Figure 16.22 shows the response of the server. The response is similar to the query except that the flags are different and the number of answer records is one. The flags value is 0x8180 in hexadecimal. In binary it is 1000000110000000, but again we divide it into fields as shown below:

QR	OpCode	AA	TC	RD	RA	Reserved	rCode
1	0000	0	0	1	1	000	0000

Figure 16.22   *Example of a response message*

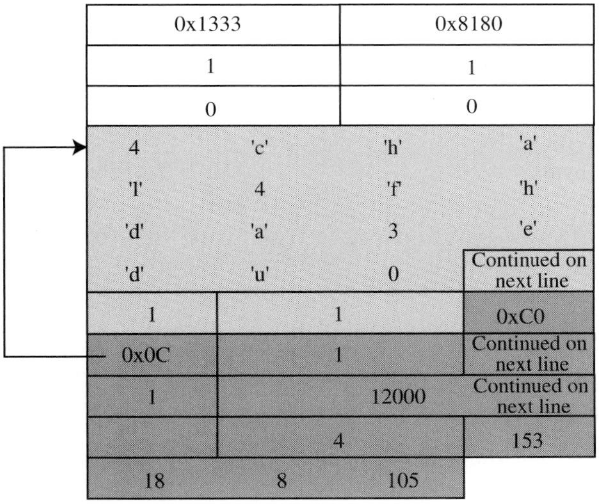

The QR bit defines the message as a response. The OpCode is 0000, which means standard query. The recursion available (RA) and RD bits are set. The message contains one question record and one answer record. The question record is repeated from the query message. The answer record has a pointer 0xC00C (split in two lines), which refers to the question record instead of repeating the domain name. The next field defines the domain type (address). The field after that defines the class (Internet). The field with the value 12,000 is the TTL (12,000 seconds). The next field is the length of the resource data, which is an IP address (153.18.8.105).

Example 2

An FTP server has received a packet from an FTP client with IP address 153.2.7.9. The FTP server wants to verify that the FTP client is an authorized client. The FTP server can consult a file containing the list of authorized clients. However, the file consists only of domain names. The FTP server has only the IP address of the requesting client, which was the source IP address in the IP datagram received. The FTP server asks the resolver (DNS client) to send an inverse query to a DNS server to ask for the name of the FTP client. We discuss the query and response messages separately.

Query Message   Figure 16.23 shows the query message sent from the resolver to the server. The first two bytes show the identifier (0x1200). The flags value is 0x0900 in hexadecimal. In binary it is 0000100100000000, and we divide it into fields as shown below:

QR	OpCode	AA	TC	RD	RA	Reserved	rCode
0	0001	0	0	1	0	000	0000

Figure 16.23   *Example of inverse query message*

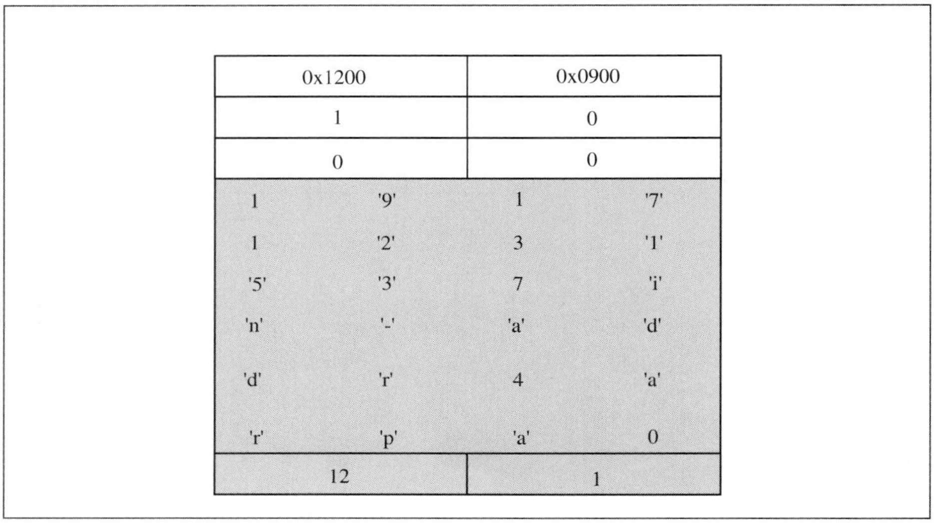

The OpCode is 0001, which means inverse query. The message contains only one question record. The domain name is *19171231537in-addr4arpa*. The next two bytes define the query type as PTR, and the last two bytes define the class as Internet.

Response Message   Figure 16.24 shows the response. The flags value is 0x8D80 in hexadecimal. In binary it is 1000110110000000, and we divide it into fields as shown below:

QR	OpCode	AA	TC	RD	RA	Reserved	rCode
1	0001	1	0	1	1	000	0000

The message contains one question record and one answer record. The question record is repeated from the query message. The answer record has a pointer 0xC00C, which refers to the question record instead of repeating the domain name. The next field defines the domain type (PTR). The field after that defines the class (Internet), and the field after that defines the TTL (24,000 seconds). The next field is the length of the resource data (10). The last field is the domain name *4mhhe3com0*, which means "mhhe.com.".

Figure 16.24   *Example of inverse response message*

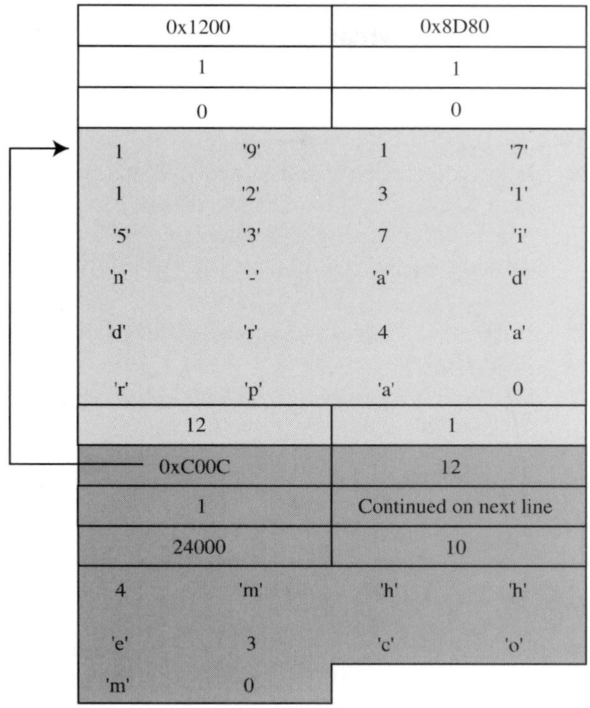

0x1200		0x8D80	
1		1	
0		0	
1	'9'	1	'7'
1	'2'	3	'1'
'5'	'3'	7	'i'
'n'	'-'	'a'	'd'
'd'	'r'	4	'a'
'r'	'p'	'a'	0
12		1	
0xC00C		12	
1		Continued on next line	
24000		10	
4	'm'	'h'	'h'
'e'	3	'c'	'o'
'm'	0		

16.10   DDNS

When the DNS was designed, no one predicted that there would be so many changes made to addresses. In DNS, when there is a change, such as adding a new host, removing a host, or changing an IP address, the change must be made to the DNS master file. These types of changes involve a lot of manual updating. The size of today's Internet does not allow this kind of manual operation.

The DNS master file must be updated dynamically. The Dynamic Domain Name System (DDNS) therefore has been devised to respond to this need. In DDNS, when a binding between a name and an address is determined, the information is sent, usually by DHCP (see Chapter 15) to a primary DNS server. The primary server updates the zone. The secondary servers are notified either actively or passively. In active notification, the primary server sends a message to the secondary servers about the change in the zone, whereas in passive notification, the secondary servers periodically check for any changes. In either case, after being notified about the change, the secondary requests information about the entire zone (zone transfer).

To provide security and prevent unauthorized changes in the DNS records, DDNS can use an authentication mechanism.

16.11   ENCAPSULATION

DNS can use either UDP or TCP. In both cases the well-known port used by the server is port 53. UDP is used when the size of the response message is less than 512 bytes because most UDP packages have a 512-byte packet size limit. If the size of the response message is more than 512 bytes, a TCP connection should be used. In that case, one of two scenarios can occur:

■   If the resolver has prior knowledge that the size of the response message is more than 512 bytes, it should use the TCP connection. For example, if a secondary name server (acting as a client) needs a zone transfer from a primary server, it should use the TCP connection because the size of the information being transferred usually exceeds 512 bytes.

■   If the resolver does not know the size of the response message, it can use the UDP port. However, if the size of the response message is more than 512 bytes, the server truncates the message and turns on the TC bit. The resolver now opens a TCP connection and repeats the request to get a full response from the server.

DNS can use the services of UDP or TCP using the well-known port 53.

16.12   SUMMARY

■   Domain Name System (DNS) is a client-server application that identifies each host on the Internet with a unique user-friendly name.

■   DNS organizes the name space in a hierarchical structure to decentralize the responsibilities involved in naming.

■   DNS can be pictured as an inverted hierarchical tree structure with one root node at the top and a maximum of 128 levels.

■   Each node in the tree has a domain name.

■   A domain is defined as any subtree of the domain name space.

■   The name space information is distributed among DNS servers. Each server has jurisdiction over its zone.

■   A root server's zone is the entire DNS tree.

■   A primary server creates, maintains, and updates information about its zone.

■   A secondary server gets its information from a primary server.

■   The domain name space is divided into three sections: generic domains, country domains, and inverse domain.

■   There are seven generic domains, each specifying an organization type.

■   Each country domain specifies a country.

■   The inverse domain finds a domain name for a given IP address. This is called address-to-name resolution.

■   Name servers, computers that run the DNS server program, are organized in a hierarchy.

■ The DNS client, called a resolver, maps a name to an address or an address to a name.

■ In recursive resolution, the client sends its request to a server that eventually returns a response.

■ In iterative resolution, the client may send its request to multiple servers before getting an answer.

■ Caching is a method whereby an answer to a query is stored in memory (for a limited time) for easy access to future requests.

■ A fully qualified domain name (FQDN) is a domain name consisting of labels beginning with the host and going back through each level to the root node.

■ A partially qualified domain name (PQDN) is a domain name that does not include all the levels between the host and the root node.

■ There are two types of DNS messages: queries and responses.

■ There are two types of DNS records: question records and resource records.

■ DNS uses an offset pointer for duplicated domain name information in its messages.

■ Dynamic DNS (DDNS) automatically updates the DNS master file.

■ DNS uses the services of UDP for messages of less than 512 bytes; otherwise, TCP is used.

16.13 PRACTICE SET

Multiple Choice

1. In the domain name chal.atc.fhda.edu _____ is the least specific label.
   a. chal
   b. atc
   c. fhda
   d. edu

2. In the domain name chal.atc.fhda.edu _____ is the most specific label.
   a. chal
   b. atc
   c. fhda
   d. edu

3. Which of the following domain names would most likely use a country domain to resolve its IP address?
   a. chal.atac.fhda.edu
   b. gsfc.nasa.gov
   c. kenz.acct.sony.jp
   d. mac.eng.sony.com

4. A DNS response is classified as _____ if the information comes from a cache memory.
   a. authoritative
   b. unauthoritative
   c. iterative
   d. recursive

5. In _____ resolution the client is in direct contact with at most one server.
   a. a recursive
   b. an iterative
   c. a cache
   d. all of the above

6. In _____ resolution the client could directly contact more than one server.
   a. a recursive
   b. an iterative
   c. a cache
   d. all of the above

7. What is the maximum length of the query name subfield?
   a. 4 bytes
   b. 63 bytes
   c. 32 bytes
   d. none of the above

8. In address-to-name resolution the _____ domain is used.
   a. inverse
   b. reverse
   c. generic
   d. country

9. How is the lifetime of a name-to-address resolution in cache memory controlled?
   a. by the time-to-live field set by the server
   b. by the time-to-live counter set by the server
   c. by the time-to-live field set by the authoritative server
   d. b and c

10. In the string 219.46.123.107.in-addr.arpa what is the network address of the host we are looking for?
    a. 219.46.123.0
    b. 107.123.0.0
    c. 107.123.46.0
    d. 107.0.0.0

11. A host with the domain name "pit.arc.nasa.gov." is on the _____ level of the DNS hierarchical tree. (The root is level one.)
    a. third

   b. fourth

   c. fifth

   d. not enough information

12. A host with the domain name "trinity.blue.vers.inc" is on the _____ level of the DNS hierarchical tree. (The root is level one.)

   a. third

   b. fourth

   c. fifth

   d. not enough information

13. A DNS _____ server gets its data from another DNS server.

   a. primary

   b. secondary

   c. root

   d. all of the above

14. A DNS _____ server creates, maintains, and updates the zone file.

   a. primary

   b. secondary

   c. root

   d. all of the above

15. A DNS _____ server's zone is the entire DNS tree.

   a. primary

   b. secondary

   c. root

   d. all of the above

16. A resolver is the _____.

   a. DNS client

   b. DNS server

   c. host machine

   d. root server

17. A pointer query involves the _____ domain.

   a. inverse

   b. reverse

   c. root

   d. recursive

18. To find the IP address of a host when the domain name is known, the _____ can be used.

   a. inverse domain

   b. generic domains

   c. country domains

   d. b or c

19. Which field has a zero value in the DNS query message?
    a. number of answer records
    b. number of authoritative records
    c. number of additional records
    d. all of the above

20. Question records are found in the _____ record section.
    a. question
    b. answer
    c. authoritative
    d. additional information

Exercises

21. Compare and contrast the DNS structure with the UNIX directory structure.

22. What is the equivalent of dots in the DNS structure in the UNIX directory structure?

23. A DNS domain name starts with a node and goes up to the root of the tree. Do the pathnames in UNIX do the same?

24. Can we say that the FQDNs in DNS are the same as absolute pathnames in UNIX and PQDNs are the same as relative pathnames in UNIX?

25. Determine which of the following is an FQDN and which is a PQDN:
    a. xxx
    b. xxx.yyy.
    c. xxx.yyy.net
    d. zzz.yyy.xxx.edu.

26. Determine which of the following is an FQDN and which one is a PQDN:
    a. mil.
    b. edu.
    c. xxx.yyy.net
    d. zzz.yyy.xxx.edu

27. Find the value of the flags field (in hexadecimal) for a query message requesting an address and demanding a recursive answer.

28. Find the value of the flags field (in hexadecimal) for an unauthoritative message carrying an inverse response. The resolver had asked for a recursive response, but the recursive answer was not available.

29. Analyze the flag 0x8F80.

30. Analyze the flag 0x0503. Is it valid?

31. Is the size of a question record fixed?

32. Is the size of a resource record fixed?

33. What is the size of a question record containing the domain name fhda.edu?

34. What is the size of a question record containing an IP address?

35. What is the size of a resource record containing the domain name fhda.edu?

36. What is the size of a resource record containing an IP address?

37. What is the size of a query message requesting the IP address for challenger.atc.fhda.edu?

38. What is the size of a query message requesting the domain name for 185.34.23.12?

39. What is the size of the response message responding to the query message in exercise 37?

40. What is the size of the response message responding to the query message in exercise 38?

41. Redo Example 1 using a response message with one answer record and one authoritative record which defines "fhda.edu." as the authoritative server.

42. Redo exercise 41, but add one additional record that defines the address of the authoritative server as 153.18.9.0.

43. A DNS client is looking for the IP address of xxx.yyy.com. Show the query message with values for each field.

44. Show the response message of a DNS server to exercise 43. Assume the IP address is 201.34.23.12.

45. A DNS client is looking for the IP addresses corresponding to xxx.yyy.com and aaa.bbb.edu. Show the query message.

46. Show the response message of a DNS server to the query in exercise 45 if the addresses are 14.23.45.12 and 131.34.67.89.

47. Show the response message of exercise 46 if the DNS server can resolve the first enquiry, but not the second.

48. A DNS client is looking for the name of the computer with IP address 132.1.17.8. Show the query message.

49. Show the response message sent by the server to the query in exercise 48.

50. Encapsulate the query message of exercise 43 in a UDP user datagram.

51. Encapsulate the response message of exercise 44 in a UDP user datagram.

CHAPTER 17

TELNET and Rlogin

The main task of the Internet and its TCP/IP protocol suite is to provide services for users. For example, users want to be able to run different application programs at a remote site and create results that can be transferred to their local site. One way to satisfy these demands is to create different client/server application programs for each desired service. Programs such as file transfer programs (FTP and TFTP), e-mail (SMTP), and so on are already available. But it would be impossible to write a specific client/server program for each demand.

The better solution is a general-purpose client/server program that lets a user access any application program on a remote computer; in other words, allow the user to log on to a remote computer. After logging on, a user can use the services available on the remote computer and transfer the results back to the local computer.

In this chapter, we discuss two client/server application programs: TELNET and Rlogin. TELNET is an abbreviation for *TErminaL NETwork*. It is the standard TCP/IP protocol for virtual terminal service as proposed by ISO. TELNET enables the establishment of a connection to a remote system in such a way that the local terminal appears to be a terminal at the remote system. Rlogin is a remote login protocol provided by BSD UNIX.

> TELNET and Rlogin are general-purpose client/server application programs.

17.1 CONCEPT

TELNET is related to several concepts that we briefly describe here.

Timesharing Environment

TELNET was designed at a time when most operating systems, such as UNIX, were operating in a timesharing environment. In a timesharing environment, a large computer supports multiple users. The interaction between a user and the computer occurs through a terminal, which is usually a combination of keyboard, monitor, and mouse. Even a microcomputer can simulate a terminal with a terminal emulator.

In a timesharing environment, all of the processing must be done by the central computer. When a user types a character on the keyboard, the character is usually sent to the computer and echoed to the monitor. Timesharing creates an environment in which each user has the illusion of a dedicated computer. The user can run a program, access the system resources, switch from one program to another, and so on.

Login

In a timesharing environment, users are part of the system with some right to access resources. Each authorized user has an identification and probably a password. The user identification defines the user as part of the system. To access the system, the user logs into the system with a user id or login name. The system also facilitates password checking to prevent an unauthorized user from accessing the resources.

Local Login

When a user logs into a local timesharing system, it is called *local login*. As a user types at a terminal or at a workstation running a terminal emulator, the keystrokes are accepted by the terminal driver. The terminal driver passes the characters to the operating system. The operating system, in turn, interprets the combination of characters and invokes the desired application program or utility (see Figure 17.1).

Figure 17.1 *Local login*

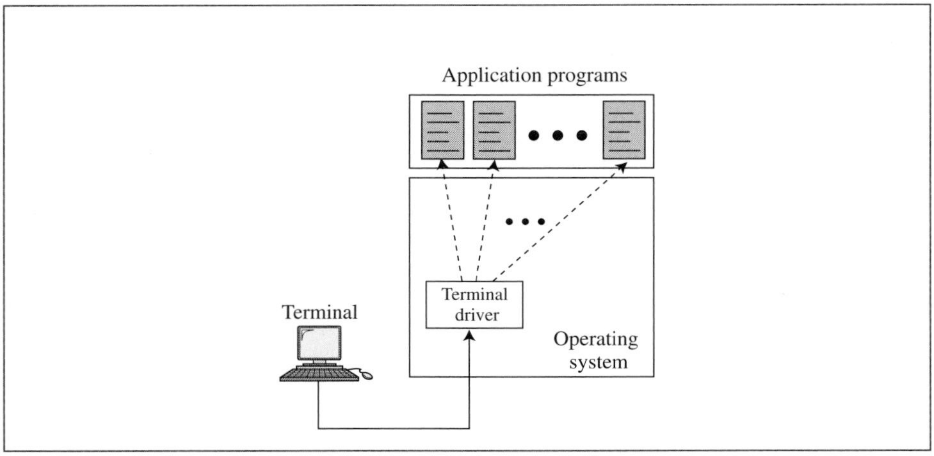

The mechanism, however, is not as simple as it seems because the operating system may assign special meanings to special characters. For example, in UNIX some combinations of characters have special meanings, such as the combination of the control character with the character "z", which means suspend; the combination of the control character with the character "c", which means abort; and so on. Whereas these special situations do not create any problem in local login because the terminal emulator and the terminal driver know the exact meaning of each character or combination of characters, they may create problems in remote login. Which process should interpret special characters? The client or the server? We will clarify this situation later in the chapter.

Remote Login

When a user wants to access an application program or utility located on a remote machine, he or she performs remote login. Here the TELNET client and server programs come into use. The user sends the keystrokes to the terminal driver where the local operating system accepts the characters but does not interpret them. The characters are sent to the TELNET client, which transforms the characters to a universal character set called *Network Virtual Terminal characters* and delivers them to the local TCP/IP stack (see Figure 17.2).

Figure 17.2   *Remote login*

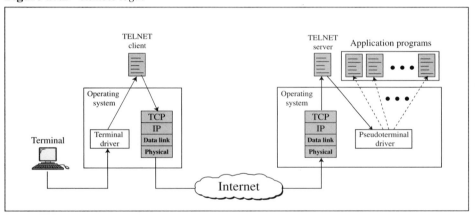

The commands or text, in NVT form, travel through the Internet and arrive at the TCP/IP stack at the remote machine. Here the characters are delivered to the operating system and passed to the TELNET server, which changes the characters to the corresponding characters understandable by the remote computer. However, the characters cannot be passed directly to the operating system because the remote operating system is not designed to receive characters from a TELNET server: It is designed to receive characters from a terminal driver. The solution is to add a piece of software called a *pseudoterminal driver* which pretends that the characters are coming from a terminal. The operating system then passes the characters to the appropriate application program.

17.2   NETWORK VIRTUAL TERMINAL (NVT)

The mechanism to access a remote computer is complex. This is because every computer and its operating system accepts a special combination of characters as tokens.

For example, the end-of-file token in a computer running the DOS operating system is Ctrl+z, while the UNIX operating system recognizes Ctrl+d.

We are dealing with heterogeneous systems. If we want to access any remote computer in the world, we must first know what type of computer we will be connected to, and we must also install the specific terminal emulator used by that computer. TELNET solves this problem by defining a universal interface called the Network Virtual Terminal (NVT) character set. Via this interface the client TELNET translates characters (data or commands) that come from the local terminal into NVT form and delivers them to the network. The server TELNET, on the other hand, translates data and commands from NVT form into the form acceptable by the remote computer. For an illustration of this concept, see Figure 17.3.

Figure 17.3   *Concept of NVT*

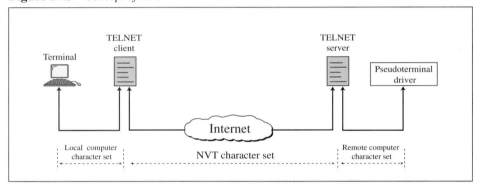

17.3   NVT CHARACTER SET

NVT uses two sets of characters, one for data and one for remote control. Both are eight-bit bytes.

Data Characters

For data, NVT normally uses what is called NVT ASCII. This is an eight-bit character set in which the seven lowest order bits are the same as US ASCII and the highest order bit is 0 (see Figure 17.4). Although it is possible to send an eight-bit ASCII (with the

Figure 17.4   *Format of data characters*

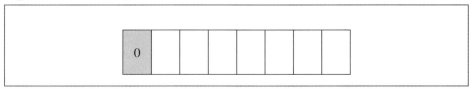

highest order bit set to be 0 or 1), this must first be agreed upon between the client and the server using option negotiation.

Remote Control Characters

To send control characters between computers (from client to server or vice versa), NVT uses an eight-bit character set in which the highest order bit is set (see Figure 17.5).

Figure 17.5   *Format of control characters*

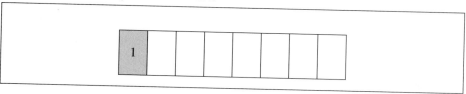

Table 17.1 lists some of the remote control characters and their meanings. We will describe these control characters later in groups based on their functionalities.

Table 17.1   *Some NVT remote control characters*

Character	Decimal	Binary	Meaning
EOF	236	11101100	End of file
EOR	239	11101111	End of record
SE	240	11110000	Suboption end
NOP	241	11110001	No operation
DM	242	11110010	Data mark
BRK	243	11110011	Break
IP	244	11110100	Interrupt process
AO	245	11110101	Abort output
AYT	246	11110110	Are you there?
EC	247	11110111	Erase character
EL	248	11111000	Erase line
GA	249	11111001	Go ahead
SB	250	11111010	Suboption begin
WILL	251	11111011	Agreement to enable option
WONT	252	11111100	Refusal to enable option
DO	253	11111101	Approval to option request
DONT	254	11111110	Denial of option request
IAC	255	11111111	Interpret (the next character) as control

17.4 EMBEDDING

TELNET uses only one TCP connection. The server uses the well-known port 23 and the client uses an ephemeral port. The same connection is used for sending both data and remote control characters. TELNET accomplishes this by embedding the control characters in a data stream. However, to distinguish data from remote control characters, each sequence of control characters is preceded by a special control character called interpret as control (IAC). For example, imagine a user wants to send a sequence of data characters to the remote server to display a file (*file1*):

cat file1

However, the name of the file has been mistyped (*filea* instead of *file1*). The user uses the backspace key to correct this situation.

cat filea<backspace>1

But in a default implementation of TELNET, the user cannot edit locally; the editing should be done at the remote server. The backspace character is translated into two remote characters (IAC EC), which is embedded in the data and sent to the remote server. What is sent to the server is shown in Figure 17.6.

Figure 17.6 *An example of embedding*

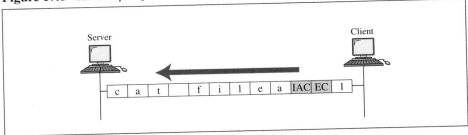

17.5 OPTIONS

TELNET lets the client and server negotiate options before or during the use of the service. Options are extra features available to a user with a more sophisticated terminal. Users with simpler terminals can use minimum features. Some of the remote control characters discussed previously are used to define options. Table 17.2 shows some common options.

Table 17.2 *Options*

Code	Option	Meaning
0	Binary	Use eight-bit binary transmission

Table 17.2 *Options (concluded)*

Code	Option	Meaning
1	Echo	Echo the data received on one side to the other
3	Suppress go ahead	Suppress go-ahead signals after data
5	Status	Request the status of TELNET
6	Timing mark	Define the timing marks
24	Terminal type	Set the terminal type
32	Terminal speed	Set the terminal speed
34	Line mode	Change to line mode

The option descriptions are as follows:

- **Binary.** This option allows the receiver to interpret every eight-bit character received, except IAC, as binary data. When IAC is received, the next character or characters are interpreted as commands. However, if two consecutive IAC characters are received, the first is discarded and the second is interpreted as data.

- **Echo.** This option allows the server to echo data received from the client. This means that every character sent by the client to the sender will be echoed back to the screen of the client terminal. In this case, the user terminal usually does not echo display characters when they are typed but waits until it receives them from the server.

- **Suppress go-ahead.** This option suppresses the go-ahead (GA) character. We will discuss the GA character in Section 17.11 on TELNET modes.

- **Status.** This option allows the user or the process running on the client machine to get the status of the options being enabled at the server site.

- **Timing mark.** This option allows one party to issue a timing mark that indicates all previously received data has been processed.

- **Terminal type.** This option allows the client to send its terminal type.

- **Terminal speed.** This option allows the client to send its terminal speed.

- **Line mode.** This option allows the client to switch to the line mode. We will discuss the line mode later.

17.6 OPTION NEGOTIATION

To use any of the options mentioned in the previous section first requires negotiation between the client and the server. Four control characters are used for this purpose; these are shown in Table 17.3.

Table 17.3   *NVT character set for option negotiation*

Character	Decimal	Binary	Meaning
WILL	251	11111011	1. Offering to enable
			2. Accepting a request to enable
WONT	252	11111100	1. Rejecting a request to enable
			2. Offering to disable
			3. Accepting a request to disable
DO	253	11111101	1. Approving an offer to enable
			2. Requesting to enable
DONT	254	11111110	1. Disapproving an offer to enable
			2. Approving an offer to disable
			3. Requesting to disable

Enabling an Option

Some options can only be enabled by the server, some only by the client, and some by both. An option is enabled either through an *offer* or a *request*.

Offer to Enable

A party can offer to enable an option if it has the right to do so. The offering can be approved or disapproved by the other party. The offering party sends the *WILL* command, which means "Will I enable the option?" The other party sends either the *DO* command, which means "Please Do," or the *DONT* command, which means "Please Don't." See Figure 17.7.

Figure 17.7   *Offer to enable an option*

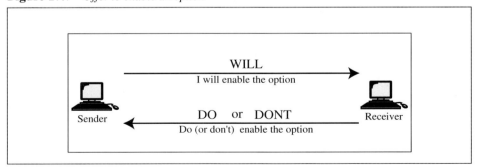

Request to Enable

A party can request from the other party the enabling of an option. The request can be accepted or refused by the other party. The requesting party sends the *DO* command, which means "Please do enable the option." The other party sends either the *WILL* command, which means "I will," or the *WONT* command, which means "I won't." See Figure 17.8.

Figure 17.8 *Request to enable an option*

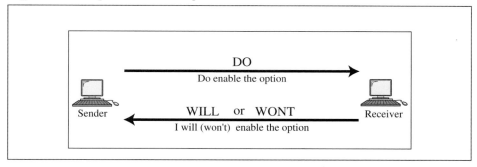

Disabling an Option

An option that has been enabled can be disabled by one of the parties. An option is disabled either through an *offer* or a *request*.

Offer to Disable

A party can offer to disable an option. The other party must approve the offering; it cannot be disapproved. The offering party sends the *WONT* command, which means "I won't use this option any more." The answer must be the *DONT* command, which means "Don't use it anymore." Figure 17.9 shows an offer to disable an option.

Figure 17.9 *Offer to disable an option*

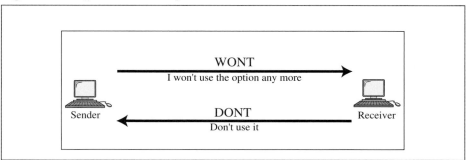

Request to Disable

A party can request from another party the disabling of an option. The other party must accept the request; it cannot be rejected. The requesting party sends the *DONT* command, which means "Please don't use this option anymore." The answer must be the *WONT* command, which means "I won't use it anymore." Figure 17.10 shows a request to disable an option.

Figure 17.10 *Request to disable an option*

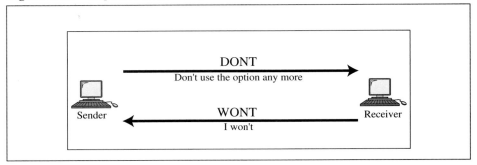

Example

Figure 17.11 shows an example of option negotiation. In this example, the client wants the server to echo each character sent to the server. In other words, when a character is typed at the user keyboard terminal, it should go to the server and be sent back to the screen of the user before being processed. The echo option should be enabled by the server because it is the server that sends the characters back to the user terminal. Therefore, the client should *request* from the server the enabling of the option using DO. The request consists of three characters: IAC, DO, and ECHO. The server accepts the request and enables the option. It informs the client by sending the three-character approval: IAC, WILL, and ECHO.

Figure 17.11 *Echo option example*

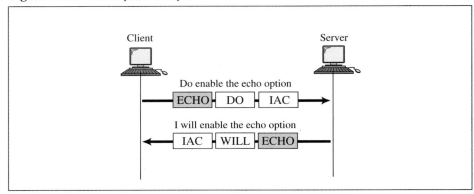

Symmetry

One interesting feature of TELNET is its symmetric option negotiation in which the client and server are given equal opportunity. This means that, at the beginning of connection, it is assumed that both sides are using a simple TELNET implementation with no options enabled. If one party wants an option enabled, it can offer or request. The other party has the right to approve the offer or reject the request if the party is not capable of using the option or does not want to use the option. This allows for the expansion of TELNET. A client or server can install a more sophisticated version of TELNET with more options. When it is connected to a party, it can offer or request these new options. If the other party also supports these options, the options can be enabled; otherwise, they are rejected.

17.7 SUBOPTION NEGOTIATION

Some options require additional information. For example, to define the type or speed of a terminal, the negotiation includes a string or a number to define the type or speed. In either case, the two suboption characters indicated in Table 17.4 are needed for suboption negotiation.

Table 17.4 *NVT character set for suboption negotiation*

Character	Decimal	Binary	Meaning
SE	240	11110000	Suboption end
SB	250	11111010	Suboption begin

For example, the type of the terminal is set by the client, as is shown in Figure 17.12 .

Figure 17.12 *Example of suboption negotiation*

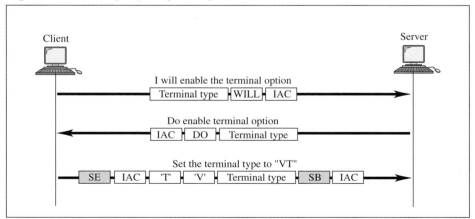

17.8   CONTROLLING THE SERVER

Some of the control characters can be used to control the remote server. When an application program is running on the local computer, special characters are used to interrupt (abort) the program (for example, Ctrl+c), or erase the last character typed (for example, delete key or backspace key), and so on. However, when a program is running on a remote computer, these control characters should be sent to the remote machine. The user still types the same sequences, but they are changed to special characters and sent to the server. Table 17.5 shows some of the characters that can be sent to the server to control the application program that is running there.

Table 17.5   *Characters used to control the application program running on remote server*

Character	Decimal	Binary	Meaning
IP	244	11110100	Interrupt process
AO	245	11110101	Abort output
AYT	246	11110110	Are you there?
EC	247	11110111	Erase the last character
EL	248	11111000	Erase line

Let's look at these characters in more detail:

- **IP (interrupt process).** When a program is being run locally, the user can interrupt (abort) the program if, for example, the program has gone into an infinite loop. The user can depress the Ctrl+c combination, the operating system calls a function, and the function aborts the program. However, if the program is running on a remote machine, the appropriate function should be called by the operating system of the remote machine. TELNET defines the IP (interrupt process) control character that is read and interpreted as the appropriate command for invoking the interrupting function in the remote machine.

- **AO (abort output).** This is the same as IP, but it allows the process to continue without creating output. This is useful if the process has another effect in addition to creating output. The user wants this effect, but not the output. For example, most commands in UNIX generate output and have an exit status. The user may want exit status for future use but is not interested in the output data.

- **AYT (are you there?).** This control character is used to determine if the remote machine is still up and running, especially after a long silence from the server. When this character is received, the server usually sends an audible or visual signal to confirm that it is running.

- **EC (erase character).** When a user sends data from the keyboard to the local machine, the delete or backspace character can erase the last character typed. To do the same in a remote machine, TELNET defines the EC control character.

- **EL (erase line).** This is used to erase the current line in the remote host.

For example, Figure 17.13 shows how to interrupt a runaway application program at the server site. The user types Ctrl+c, but the TELNET client sends the combination of IAC and IP to the server.

Figure 17.13 *Example of interrupting an application program*

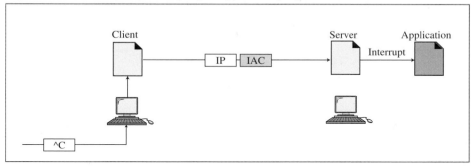

17.9 OUT-OF-BAND SIGNALING

To make control characters effective in special situations, TELNET uses out-of-band signaling. In out-of-band signaling, the control characters are preceded by IAC and are sent to the remote process out of order.

Imagine a situation in which an application program running at the server site has gone into an infinite loop and does not accept any more input data. The user wants to interrupt the application program, but the program does not read data from the buffer. The TCP at the server site has found that the buffer is full and has sent a segment specifying that the client window size should be zero. In other words, the TCP at the server site is announcing that no more regular traffic is accepted. To remedy such a situation, an urgent TCP segment should be sent from the client to the server. The urgent segment overrides the regular flow-control mechanism. Although TCP is not accepting normal segments, it must accept an urgent segment.

When a TELNET process (client or server) wants to send an out-of-band sequence of characters to the other process (client or server), it embeds the sequence in the data stream and inserts a special character called DM (data mark). However, to force the other party to handle the sequence out of order, it creates a TCP segment with the urgent bit set and the urgent pointer pointing to the DM character. When the receiving TCP receives the segment, it reads the data and discards any data preceding the control characters (IAC and IP, for example). When it reaches the DM character, the remaining data are handled normally. In other words, the DM character is used as a *synchronization* character that switches the receiving TCP from the urgent mode to the normal mode and *resynchronizes* the two ends (see Figure 17.14).

In this way, the control character (IP) is delivered out of band to the operating system, which uses the appropriate function to interrupt the running application program.

Figure 17.14 *Out-of-band signaling*

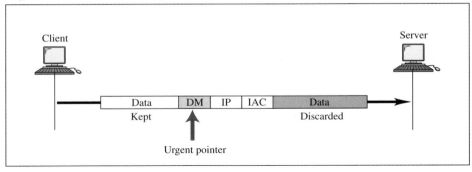

17.10 ESCAPE CHARACTER

A character typed by the user is normally sent to the server. However, sometimes the user wants characters interpreted by the client instead of the server. In this case, the user can use an *escape* character, normally Ctrl+] (shown as ^]). This is a signal to the client that the command is not for the remote server, it is for the client. Figure 17.15 compares the interruption of an application program at the remote site with the interruption of the client process at the local site using the escape character.

Figure 17.15 *Two different interruptions*

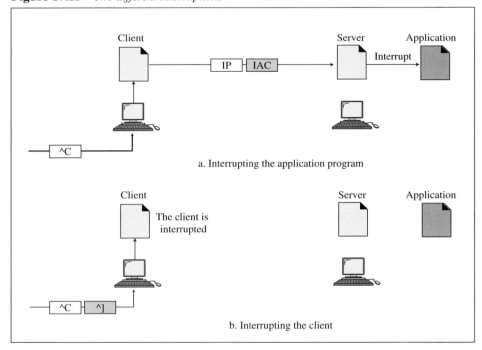

17.11   MODE OF OPERATION

Most TELNET implementations operate in one of three modes: default mode, character mode, or line mode.

Default Mode

The default mode is used if no other modes are invoked through option negotiation. In this mode, the echoing is done by the client. The user types a character and the client echoes the character on the screen (or printer), but does not send it until a whole line is completed. After sending the whole line to the server, the client waits for the GA (go ahead) command from the server before accepting a new line from the user. The operation is half-duplex. Half-duplex operation is not efficient when the TCP connection itself is full-duplex, and so this mode is becoming obsolete.

Character Mode

In the character mode, each character typed is sent by the client to the server. The server normally echoes the character back to be displayed on the client screen. In this mode the echoing of the character can be delayed if the transmission time is long (such as in a satellite connection). It also creates overhead (traffic) for the network because three TCP segments must be sent for each character of data:

1. The user enters a character which is sent to the server.
2. The server acknowledges the received character and echos the character back (in one segment).
3. The client acknowledges the receipt of the echoed character.

Line Mode

A new mode has been proposed to compensate for the deficiencies of the default mode and the character mode. In this mode, called the line mode, line editing (echoing, character erasing, line erasing, and so on) is done by the client. The client then sends the whole line to the server.

Although the line mode looks like the default mode, it is not. The default mode operates in the half-duplex mode; the line mode is full-duplex with the client sending one line after another, without the need for an intervening GA (go ahead) character from the server.

17.12   EXAMPLES

In this section, we show two examples of TELNET interaction between the client and the server.

Example 1

In this example, we use the default mode to show the concept and its deficiencies even though it is almost obsolete today. The client and the server negotiate the terminal type and terminal speed and then the server checks the login and password of the user (see Figure 17.16).

Figure 17.16 *Example 1*

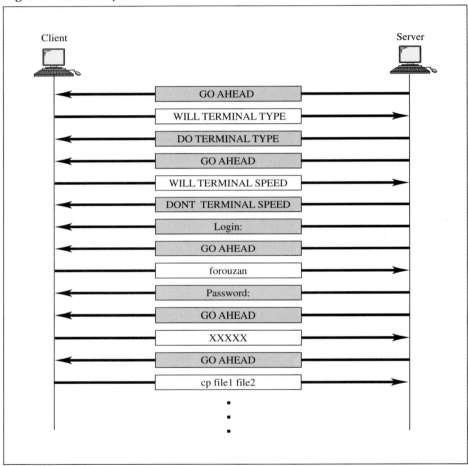

Example 2

In this example, we show how the client switches to the character mode. This requires that the client request the server to enable the SUPPRESS GO AHEAD and ECHO options (see Figure 17.17).

Figure 17.17   *Example 2*

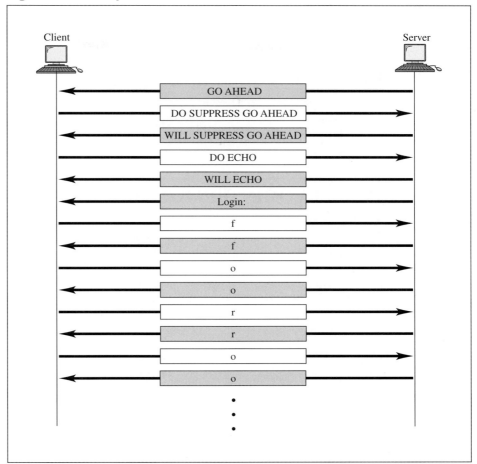

17.13   USER INTERFACE

The normal user does not use TELNET commands as defined above. Normally, the operating system (UNIX, for example) defines an interface with user-friendly commands. An example of such a set of commands can be found in Table 17.6. Note that the interface is responsible for translating the user-friendly commands to the previously defined commands in the protocol.

Table 17.6   *Example of interface commands*

Command	Meaning
open	Connect to a remote computer
close	Close the connection

Table 17.6   *Example of interface commands (concluded)*

Command	Meaning
display	Show the operating parameters
mode	Change to line mode or character mode
set	Set the operating parameters
status	Display the status information
send	Send special characters
quit	Exit TELNET

17.14   RLOGIN (REMOTE LOGIN)

Another remote login client/server application in common use is Rlogin (remote login). This is not an Internet standard but was designed by BSD UNIX to provide access to remote computers. We discuss it here briefly to compare it with TELNET.

Rlogin was originally designed to be used on the UNIX operating system as a simple remote login facility. It, therefore, does not provide option negotiation. The server accepts the terminal type of the user.

TCP Port

Rlogin uses only one TCP connection. The server uses the well-known port 513 and the client uses an ephemeral port. The one TCP connection is used both for data and commands. We will see how data and commands are distinguished by the client and the server.

The Rlogin process uses the TCP port 513.

Connection

The client starts the connection. After the usual TCP connection is established on port 513, the client sends four null-terminated strings.

1. The first string is actually empty. It is just a null character (\0).
2. The second string defines the login name of the user on the client host and terminates with a null character (\0). For example, *forouzan\0.*
3. The third string defines the login name of the user on the server host and terminates with a null character (\0). For example, *baf3652\0.*
4. The fourth string defines the name of the user's terminal followed by a slash, followed by the terminal speed, and terminated with a null character (\0). For example, *vt100/9600\0.*

The server responds with only one null character (\0). Figure 17.18 shows the interaction between the client and the server. Although everything is sent character by character and each character is echoed, we have shown only strings to conserve space.

Figure 17.18   *Connection establishment*

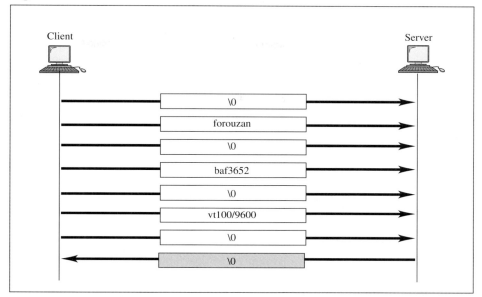

Flow Control

The output sent by the server to the client is shown on the client screen. Two special characters (Stop and Start) control the displaying of the output on the screen. The Stop and Start keys (normally Ctrl+s and Ctrl+q) can be handled either by the client or by the server.

Local Flow Control

In local flow control, the Start and Stop keys are handled by the client. The client does not send these two characters to the server. If the user types the Stop key (Ctrl+s), the client stops showing on the screen the output received from the server. It buffers them. When the user types the Start key (Ctrl+q), the buffered data is then displayed. This is the default setting. We will see that the server can change this situation.

Remote Flow Control

In remote flow control, the Start and Stop keys are handled by the server. The Stop and Start keys are passed to the server as data. When the server receives the Stop key, it stops sending data to the client. When it receives the Start key, it sends the buffered data to the client. In remote flow control, by the time the Stop key reaches the server, it may have already sent a lot of characters to the client screen.

Commands

As mentioned previously, Rlogin uses only one TCP connection. This means that data and commands are sent over the same connection. Somehow commands must be distinguished from data. In Rlogin, the commands from the server and the client are handled differently.

Commands from Server to Client

Table 17.7 shows the four commands available to the server for communication with the client. Each command is one byte and embedded in the data sent from the server to the client. The question is how the client distinguishes a command from data. When the server sends a command, it enters the urgent mode (see Chapter 12). The last byte of the urgent data is the command byte. When the client receives the TCP segment, it stores the data preceding the command byte and first handles the command before handling the data.

Table 17.7   *Rlogin commands from server to client*

Code	Description
02_{16}	The client should discard all the data received from the server. This command is sent when the client has sent an interrupt key to the server.
10_{16}	Flow control should be remote. The client should not handle the Start and Stop keys (Ctrl+s and Ctrl+q). They will be sent as data to the server. The server will handle them.
20_{16}	The client should switch to local flow control and interpret the Stop and Start keys locally.
80_{16}	The server requests the client to send its current window size.

Commands from Client to Server

The client can send commands to the server. To distinguish a command from data, the commands should started with two special characters, two FF_{16}. The next two bytes define the type of command. Note that if the client sends a stream of data starting with two FF_{16} characters, the server may be confused. However, it is very unlikely that these two characters are part of the data stream.

So far only one command has been defined. It is the *ss* (screen size) command, used to announce the screen window size. The client sends two characters of all 1s (FF_{16}) followed by ss, followed by two bytes showing the number of characters per row, followed by two bytes showing the number of characters per column, followed by two bytes showing the number of pixels (picture elements) in the X (horizontal) direction, followed by two bytes showing the number of pixels in the Y (vertical) direction (see Figure 17.19). Although everything is sent character by character and each character is echoed, we have shown strings to conserve space.

Mode

Rlogin works only in the character mode. The data is sent from the client to the server one character at a time. Each character is then echoed to the user terminal.

Figure 17.19   *Sending ss command from the client to the server*

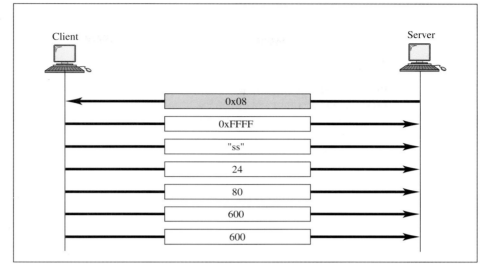

Escape Characters

During data transfer, every character typed by the user is interpreted as data and is sent to the server (unless there are two FF_{16} characters). However, sometimes the user wants the characters to be interpreted by the client instead of the server. In this case, the user can type an escape character, usually a tilde (~). Table 17.8 shows the list of characters that can be used after the escape character to accomplish a local task.

Table 17.8   *Rlogin commands used after the escape character*

Character	Description
Terminator (period or Ctrl+d)	This terminates the client process.
Job suspender (Ctrl+z)	This suspends the client. The user can run other programs and later return to Rlogin. The client program can be resumed using UNIX commands such as fg (foreground).
Input suspender (Ctrl+y)	This suspends only the client input. The user can run another program. Everything the user types is interpreted as the input for that program, not for Rlogin. However, everything sent from the server will show on the screen.

Interruption

Sometimes the user needs to interrupt (abort) the Rlogin process. It is possible to send the interrupt key (usually Ctrl+c) to the server to end the sending of data. However, when the interrupt character reaches the server, a full window of data may have already been sent to the client. The better solution would be to let the client handle the interrupt key. When the user types the interrupt key (Ctrl+c), the client discards everything in the buffer and terminates the TCP connection.

17.15 SECURITY ISSUE

Both TELNET and Rlogin suffer from security problems. Although both can use the login name and password (when exchanging text), it is often not enough. A microcomputer connected to a broadcast LAN can easily eavesdrop using some snooper software to capture a login and the corresponding password (even if it is encrypted).

TELNET, but not Rlogin, allows authentication using the AUTHENTICATION option. When this option is enabled, the client and server can communicate using one of the authentication types approved by IANA (such as Kerberos v4 or Kerberos v5).

17.16 SUMMARY

- TELNET is a client-server application that allows a user to log on to a remote machine, giving the user access to the remote system.
- When a user accesses a remote system via the TELNET process, this is comparable to a timesharing environment.
- A terminal driver correctly interprets the keystrokes on the local terminal or terminal emulator. This may not occur between a terminal and a remote terminal driver.
- TELNET uses the Network Virtual Terminal (NVT) system to encode characters on the local system. On the server machine, NVT decodes the characters to a form acceptable to the remote machine.
- NVT uses a set of characters for data and a set of characters for remote control.
- In TELNET, control characters are embedded in the data stream and preceded by the interpret as control (IAC) control character.
- Options are features that enhance the TELNET process.
- TELNET allows negotiation to set transfer conditions between the client and server before and during the use of the service.
- Some options can only be enabled by the server, some only by the client, and some by both.
- An option is enabled or disabled through an offer or a request.
- An option that needs additional information requires the use of suboption characters.
- Control characters can be used to handle the remote server.
- In out-of-band signaling, commands are sent out of order.
- A TELNET implementation operates in the default, character, or line mode.
- In the default mode, the client sends one line at a time to the server and waits for the go ahead (GA) character before a new line from the user can be accepted.
- In the character mode, the client sends one character at a time to the server.

- In the line mode, the client sends one line at a time to the server, one after the other, without the need for an intervening GA character.
- TELNET is usually not accessed directly by the user. User-friendly software acts as an interface between TELNET and the user.
- Rlogin is a BSD UNIX product that provides a simple remote login service. Options negotiation is not involved.
- Rlogin uses the TCP port 513.
- Rlogin allows either local or remote flow control.
- Rlogin allows the server to send commands to the client and vice versa.
- Rlogin supports local tasking and local program interruption.
- Security is an issue with both TELNET and Rlogin, although the former does allow an authentication option.

17.17   PRACTICE SET

Multiple Choice

1. In a timesharing environment _____.
   a. each user can access only his own computer
   b. one computer supports multiple users
   c. each user has a dedicated computer
   d. all of the above

2. In _____, the local operating system always correctly interprets the keystrokes accepted by the local terminal driver.
   a. dedicated login
   b. remote login
   c. local login
   d. b or c

3. Remote login can involve _____.
   a. NVT
   b. TELNET
   c. TCP/IP
   d. all of the above

4. When commands travel from _____ they are in NVT form.
   a. the terminal to the terminal driver
   b. the terminal driver to the TELNET client
   c. the TELNET client to the local TCP/IP stack
   d. none of the above

5. The _____ at the remote site sends received characters to the operating system.
   a. terminal driver

    b. pseudoterminal driver

    c. TELNET client

    d. TELNET server

6. The _____ translates local characters into NVT form.

    a. terminal driver

    b. pseudoterminal driver

    c. TELNET client

    d. TELNET server

7. The _____ translates NVT characters into a form acceptable by the operating system.

    a. terminal driver

    b. pseudoterminal driver

    c. TELNET client

    d. TELNET server

8. If the sender wants to disable an option, it sends a _____ command.

    a. WILL

    b. DO

    c. WONT

    d. DONT

9. If the sender wants to enable an option, it sends a _____ command.

    a. WILL

    b. DO

    c. WONT

    d. DONT

10. If the sender wants an option disabled by the receiver, it sends a _____ command.

    a. WILL

    b. DO

    c. WONT

    d. DONT

11. If the sender wants an option enabled by the receiver, it sends a _____ command.

    a. WILL

    b. DO

    c. WONT

    d. DONT

12. A TELNET control character _____.

    a. has its high-order bit set to 0

    b. has its high-order bit set to 1

    c. is the same as a command

    d. b and c

13. The _____ character precedes characters used for control.
    a. IP
    b. IAC
    c. SB
    d. GA

14. The _____ option allows the specification of terminal type.
    a. binary
    b. echo
    c. status
    d. terminal type

15. The _____ option suppresses the GA character.
    a. echo
    b. get alternate
    c. suppress go ahead
    d. terminal speed

16. The _____ option allows the server to echo data received from the client.
    a. binary
    b. echo
    c. repeat
    d. b or c

17. The _____ option conveys to the client the options enabled at the server site.
    a. echo
    b. status
    c. options
    d. terminal mode

18. What is needed to set the terminal speed?
    a. IAC
    b. terminal speed option
    c. SB
    d. all of the above

19. The _____ control character aborts a process running at the remote site.
    a. IP
    b. AO
    c. AYT
    d. EC

20. What is needed in option negotiation?
    a. an option
    b. an IAC control character
    c. an option control character (WILL, WONT, DO, or DONT)

    d. all of the above

21. The _____ control character determines whether or not the remote machine is up and running.

    a. IP

    b. AO

    c. AYT

    d. EC

22. The _____ control character allows a remote process to continue without creating output.

    a. IP

    b. AO

    c. AYT

    d. EC

23. To interrupt an application running at the remote site, type _____.

    a. Ctrl+c

    b. Ctrl+] followed by Ctrl+c

    c. Ctrl+]

    d. Ctrl+z

24. To interrupt the TELNET client, type _____.

    a. Ctrl+c

    b. Ctrl+] followed by Ctrl+c

    c. Ctrl+]

    d. Ctrl+z

25. In the TELNET _____ mode, three TCP segments are needed for each typed character.

    a. default

    b. character

    c. line

    d. b and c

26. In the TELNET _____ mode, the GA character is sent after every line of characters is received.

    a. default

    b. character

    c. line

    d. b and c

27. In the TELNET _____ mode, no GA character is sent.

    a. default

    b. character

    c. line

    d. b and c

28. In Rlogin, a command from the server to the client is accomplished through

    _____.

    a. the urgent mode

    b. the use of FF$_{16}$

    c. Ctrl+z

    d. Ctrl+c

29. In Rlogin, a command from the client to the server begins with _____.

    a. the tilde

    b. the use of FF$_{16}$

    c. Ctrl+z

    d. Ctrl+c

30. In Rlogin, a _____ can be used to let typed characters be interpreted by the client instead of the server.

    a. tilde

    b. FF$_{16}$

    c. Ctrl+z

    d. Ctrl+c

31. Which of the following is not common to both local and remote login?

    a. terminal driver

    b. local operating system

    c. application programs

    d. pseudoterminal

Exercises

32. Show the sequence of bits sent from a client TELNET for the binary transmission of 11110011 00111100 11111111.

33. If TELNET is using the character mode, how many characters are sent back and forth between the client and server to copy a file named file1 to another file named file2 in UNIX (*cp file1 file2*)?

34. What is the minimum number of bits sent at the TCP level to accomplish the task in exercise 32?

35. What is the minimum number of bits sent at the data link layer level (using Ethernet) to accomplish the task in exercise 32?

36. What is the ratio of the useful bits to the total bits in exercise 35?

37. Show the sequence of characters exchanged between the TELNET client and the server to switch from the default mode to the character mode.

38. Show the sequence of characters exchanged between the TELNET client and the server to switch from the character mode to the default mode.

39. Show the sequence of characters exchanged between the TELNET client and the server to switch from the default mode to line mode.

40. Show the sequence of characters exchanged between the TELNET client and the server to switch from the character mode to the line mode.

41. Show the sequence of characters exchanged between the TELNET client and the server to switch from the line mode to the character mode.

42. Show the sequence of characters exchanged between the TELNET client and the server to switch from the line mode to the default mode.

43. Interpret the following sequence of characters (in hexadecimal) received by a TELNET client or server:

    a. FF FB 01

    b. FF FE 01

    c. FF F4

    d. FF F9

44. Encode the interaction in Example 1 using NVT remote control characters.

45. Encode the interaction in Example 1 using hexadecimal digits.

46. Encode the interaction in Example 2 using NVT remote control characters.

47. Encode the interaction in Example 2 using hexadecimal digits.

48. Compare the modes of operations between TELNET and Rlogin.

49. Compare the escape characters in TELNET and Rlogin.

50. What is the equivalent of the IAC character in Rlogin?

51. How is the functionality of control characters in Table 14.7 accomplished in TELNET?

52. Make a table comparing the features of TELNET and Rlogin (data characters, remote control characters, escape control characters, option negotiation, etc.).

53. Do some research and find the extended options proposed for TELNET.

CHAPTER 18

File Transfer Protocol (FTP)

File transfer protocol (FTP) is the standard mechanism provided by TCP/IP for copying a file from one host to another. Transferring files from one computer to another is one of the most common tasks expected from a networking or internetworking environment.

Although transferring files from one system to another seems simple and straightforward, some problems must be dealt with first. For example, two systems may use different file name conventions. Two systems may have different ways to represent text and data. Two systems may have different directory structures. All of these problems have been solved by FTP in a very simple and elegant approach.

FTP differs from other client-server applications in that it establishes two connections between the hosts. One connection is used for data transfer, the other for control information (commands and responses). Separation of commands and data transfer makes FTP more efficient. The control connection uses very simple rules of communication. We need to transfer only a line of command or a line of response at a time. The data connection, on the other hand, needs more complex rules due to the variety of data types transferred.

FTP uses two well-known TCP ports: Port 21 is used for the control connection, and port 20 is used for the data connection.

> FTP uses the services of TCP. It needs two TCP connections. The well-known port 21 is used for the control connection and the well-known port 20 for the data connection.

Figure 18.1 shows the basic model of FTP. The client has three components: user interface, client control process, and the client data transfer process. The server has two components: the server control process and the server data transfer process. The control connection is made between the control processes. The data connection is made between the data transfer processes.

The control connection remains connected during the entire interactive FTP session. The data connection is opened and then closed for each file transferred. It opens each time commands that involve transferring files are used, and it closes when the file is transferred. In other words, when a user starts an FTP session, the control connection opens. While the control connection is open, the data connection can be opened and closed multiple times if several files are transferred.

Figure 18.1 *FTP*

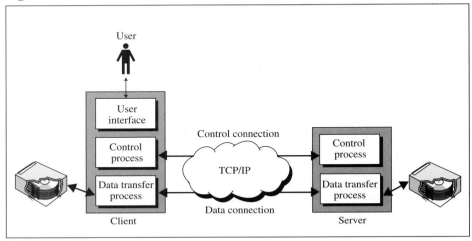

18.1 CONNECTIONS

The two FTP connections, control and data, use different strategies and different port numbers.

Control Connection

The control connection is created in the same way as other application programs described so far. There are two steps:

1. The server issues a passive open on the well-known port 21 and waits for a client.
2. The client uses an ephemeral port and issues an active open.

The connection remains open during the entire process. The service type, used by the IP protocol, is *minimize delay* because this is an interactive connection between a user (human) and a server. The user types commands and expects to receive responses without significant delay. Figure 18.2 shows the initial connection between the server and the client. Of course, after the initial connection, the server process creates a child process and assigns the duty of serving the client to the child process using an ephemeral port.

Data Connection

The data connection uses the well-known port 20 at the server site. However, the creation of a data connection is different from what we have seen so far. The following shows how FTP creates a data connection:

Figure 18.2   *Opening the control connection*

a. Passive open by server

b. Active open by client

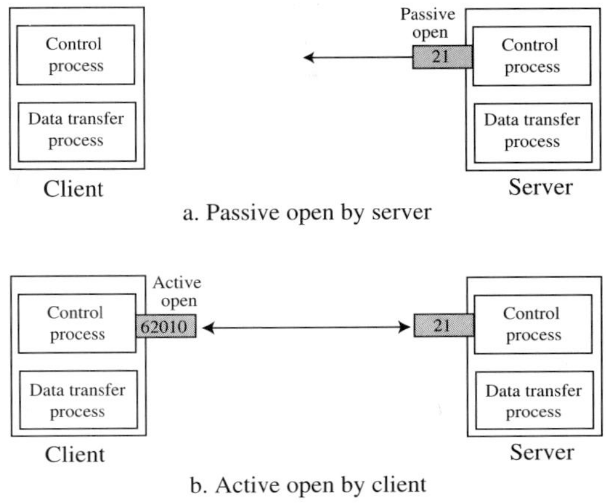

1. The client, not the server, issues a passive open using an ephemeral port. This must be done by the client because it is the client that issues the commands for transferring files.
2. The client sends this port number to the server using the PORT command (we will discuss this command shortly).
3. The server receives the port number and issues an active open using the well-known port 20 and the received ephemeral port number.

The steps for creating the initial data connection are shown in Figure 18.3. Of course, after the initial connection, the server process creates a child process and assigns the duty of serving the client to the child process using an ephemeral port.

Later we will see that these steps are changed if the PASV command is used.

18.2   COMMUNICATION

The FTP client and server, which run on different computers, must communicate with each other. These two computers may use different operating systems, different character sets, different file structures, and different file formats. FTP must make this heterogeneity compatible.

FTP has two different approaches, one for the control connection and one for the data connection. We will study each approach separately.

Communication over Control Connection

FTP uses the same approach as TELNET or SMTP to communicate across the control connection. It uses the NVT ASCII character set (see Figure 18.4). Communication is achieved through commands and responses. This simple method is adequate for the control connection because we send one command (response) at a time. Each command

Figure 18.3 *Creating the data connection*

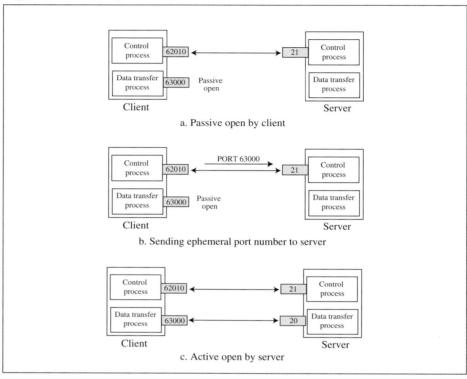

a. Passive open by client

b. Sending ephemeral port number to server

c. Active open by server

or response is only one short line so we need not worry about file format or file structure. Each line is terminated with a two-character (carriage return and line feed) end-of-line token.

Figure 18.4 *Using the control connection*

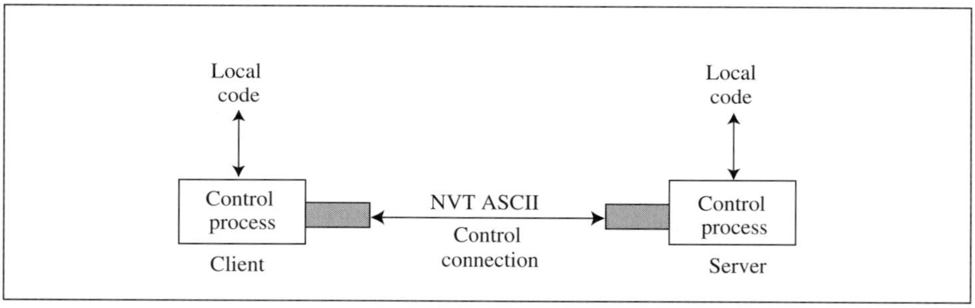

Communication over Data Connection

The purpose and implementation of the data connection are different from that of the control connection. We want to transfer files through the data connection. The client must define the type of file to be transferred, the structure of the data, and the transmission mode. Before sending the file through the data connection, we prepare for transmission through the control connection. The heterogeneity problem is resolved by defining three attributes of communication: file type, data structure, and transmission mode (see Figure 18.5).

Figure 18.5   *Using the data connection*

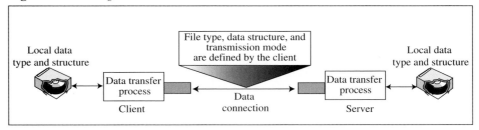

File Type

FTP can transfer one of the following file types across the data connection:

- **ASCII file.** This is the default format for transferring text files. Each character is encoded using NVT ASCII. The sender transforms the file from its own representation into NVT ASCII characters and the receiver transforms the NVT ASCII characters to its own representation.
- **EBCDIC file.** If one or both ends of the connection use EBCDIC encoding, the file can be transferred using EBCDIC encoding.
- **Image file.** This is the default format for transferring binary files. The file is sent as continuous streams of bits without any interpretation or encoding. This is mostly used to transfer binary files such as compiled programs.

If the file is encoded in ASCII or EBCDIC, another attribute must be added to define the printability of the file.

  a. **Nonprint.** This is the default format for transferring a text file. The file contains no vertical specifications for printing. This means that the file cannot be printed without further processing because there are no characters to be interpreted for vertical movement of the print head. This format is used for files that will be stored and processed later.

  b. **TELNET.** In this format the file contains NVT ASCII vertical characters such as CR (carriage return), LF (line feed), NL (new line), and VT (vertical tab). The file is printable after transfer.

Data Structure

FTP can transfer a file across the data connection using one of the following interpretations about the structure of the data:

- **File structure (default).** The file has no structure. It is a continuous stream of bytes.
- **Record structure.** The file is divided into records (or structs in C). This can be used only with text files.

■ **Page structure.** The file is divided into pages, with each page having a page number and a page header. The pages can be stored or accessed randomly or sequentially.

Transmission Mode

FTP can transfer a file across the data connection using one of the following three transmission modes:

■ **Stream mode.** This is the default mode. Data is delivered from FTP to TCP as a continuous stream of bytes. TCP is responsible for chopping data into segments of appropriate size. If the data is simply a stream of bytes (file structure), no end-of-file is needed. End-of-file in this case is the closing of the data connection by the sender. If the data is divided into records (record structure), each record will have a one-byte end-of-record (EOR) character and the end of the file will have a one-byte end-of-file (EOF) character.

■ **Block mode.** Data can be delivered from FTP to TCP in blocks. In this case, each block is preceded by a three-byte header. The first byte is called the *block descriptor*, the next two bytes define the size of the block in bytes.

■ **Compressed mode.** If the file is big, the data can be compressed. The compression method used is normally run-length encoding. In this method, consecutive appearances of a data unit are replaced by one occurrence and the number of repetitions. In a text file, this is usually spaces (blanks). In a binary file, null characters are usually compressed.

18.3 COMMAND PROCESSING

FTP uses the control connection to establish a communication between the client control process and the server control process. During this communication, the commands are sent from the client to the server and the responses are sent back from the server to the client (see Figure 18.6).

Figure 18.6 *Command processing*

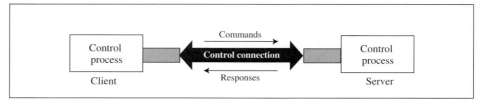

Commands

Commands, which are sent from the FTP client control process, are in the form of ASCII uppercase, which may or may not be followed by an argument. We can roughly divide the commands into six groups: access commands, file management commands, data formatting commands, port defining commands, file transferring commands, and miscellaneous commands.

- **Access commands.** These commands let the user access the remote system. Table 18.1 lists common commands in this group.

Table 18.1   *Access commands*

Command	Argument(s)	Description
USER	User id	User information
PASS	User password	Password
ACCT	Account to be charged	Account information
REIN		Reinitialize
QUIT		Log out of the system
ABOR		Abort the previous command

- **File management commands.** These commands let the user access the file system on the remote computer. They allow the user to navigate through the directory structure, create new directories, delete files, and so on. Table 18.2 gives common commands in this group.

Table 18.2   *File management commands*

Command	Argument(s)	Description
CWD	Directory name	Change to another directory
CDUP		Change to the parent directory
DELE	File name	Delete a file
LIST	Directory name	List subdirectories or files
NLIST	Directory name	List the names of subdirectories or files without other attributes
MKD	Directory name	Create a new directory
PWD		Display name of current directory
RMD	Directory name	Delete a directory
RNFR	File name (old file name)	Identify a file to be renamed
RNTO	File name (new file name)	Rename the file
SMNT	File system name	Mount a file system

- **Data formatting commands.** These commands let the user define the data structure, file type, and transmission mode. The defined format is then used by the file transfer commands. Table 18.3 shows common commands in this group.

Table 18.3   *Data formatting commands*

Command	Argument(s)	Description
TYPE	A (ASCII), E (EBCDIC), I (Image), N (Nonprint), or T (TELNET)	Define the file type and if necessary the print format
STRU	F (File), R (Record), or P (Page)	Define the organization of the data
MODE	S (Stream), B (Block), or C (Compressed)	Define the transmission mode

■ **Port defining commands.** These commands define the port number for the data connection on the client site. There are two methods to do this. In the first method, using the PORT command, the client can choose an ephemeral port number and send it to the server using a passive open. The server uses that port number and creates an active open. In the second method, using the PASV command, the client just asks the server to first choose a port number. The server does a passive open on that port and sends the port number in the response (see response numbered 227 in Table 18.7). The client issues an active open using that port number. Table 18.4 shows the port defining commands.

Table 18.4   *Port defining commands*

Command	Argument(s)	Description
PORT	6-digit identifier	Client chooses a port
PASV		Server chooses a port

■ **File transfer commands.** These commands actually let the user transfer files. Table 18.5 lists common commands in this group.

Table 18.5   *File transfer commands*

Command	Argument(s)	Description
RETR	File name(s)	Retrieve files. File(s) are transferred from server to the client.
STOR	File name(s)	Store files. File(s) are transferred from the client to the server.
APPE	File name(s)	Similar to STOR except if the file exists, data must be appended to it.
STOU	File name	Same as STOR except that the file name will be unique in the directory. However, the existing file should not be overwritten.

Table 18.5 *File transfer commands (concluded)*

Command	Argument(s)	Description
ALLO	File names	Allocate storage space for the files at the server.
REST	File name	Position the file marker at a specified data point.
STAT	File name(s)	Return the status of files.

■ **Miscellaneous commands.** These commands deliver information to the FTP user at the client site. Table 18.6 shows common commands in this group.

Table 18.6 *Miscellaneous commands*

Command	Argument(s)	Description
HELP		Ask information about the server
NOOP		Check if server is alive
SITE	Commands	Specify the site-specific commands
SYST		Ask about operating system used by the server

Responses

Every FTP command generates at least one response. A response has two parts: a three-digit number followed by text. The numeric part defines the code; the text part defines needed parameters or extra explanations. We represent the three digits as *xyz*. The meaning of each digit is described below.

First Digit

The first digit defines the status of the command. One of five digits can be used in this position:

■ **1yz (positive preliminary reply).** The action has started. The server will send another reply before accepting another command.

■ **2yz (positive completion reply).** The action has been completed. The server will accept another command.

■ **3yz (positive intermediate reply).** The command has been accepted, but further information is needed.

■ **4yz (transient negative completion reply).** The action did not take place, but the error is temporary. The same command can be sent later.

■ **5yz (permanent negative completion reply).** The command was not accepted and should not be retried again.

Second Digit

The second digit also defines the status of the command. One of six digits can be used in this position:

- x0z (syntax).
- x1z (information).
- x2z (connections).
- x3z (authentication and accounting).
- x4z (unspecified).
- x5z (file system).

Third Digit

The third digit provides additional information. Table 18.7 shows a brief list of possible responses.

Table 18.7   *Responses*

Code	Description
Positive Preliminary Reply	
120	Service will be ready shortly
125	Data connection open; data transfer will start shortly
150	File status is OK; data connection will be open shortly
Positive Completion Reply	
200	Command OK
211	System status or help reply
212	Directory status
213	File status
214	Help message
215	Naming the system type (operating system)
220	Service ready
221	Service closing
225	Data connection open
226	Closing data connection
227	Entering passive mode; server sends its IP address and port number
230	User login OK
250	Request file action OK
Positive Intermediate Reply	
331	User name OK; password is needed
332	Need account for logging
350	The file action is pending; more information needed
Transient Negative Completion Reply	
425	Cannot open data connection

Table 18.7 *Responses (concluded)*

Code	Description
426	Connection closed; transfer aborted
450	File action not taken; file not available
451	Action aborted; local error
452	Action aborted; insufficient storage
Permanent Negative Completion Reply	
500	Syntax error; unrecognized command
501	Syntax error in parameters or arguments
502	Command not implemented
503	Bad sequence of commands
504	Command parameter not implemented
530	User not logged in
532	Need account for storing file
550	Action is not done; file unavailable
552	Requested action aborted; exceeded storage allocation
553	Requested action not taken; file name not allowed

18.4   FILE TRANSFER

File transfer occurs over the data connection under the control of the commands sent over the control connection. However, we should remember that file transfer in FTP means one of three things (see Figure 18.7).

- A file is to be copied from the server to the client. This is called *retrieving a file*. It is done under the supervision of the RETR command.

- A file is to be copied from the client to the server. This is called *storing a file*. It is done under the supervision of the STOR command.

- A list of directory or file names is to be sent from the server to the client. This is done under the supervision of the LIST command. Note that FTP treats a list of directory or file names as a file. It is sent over the data connection.

Figure 18.7 *File transfer*

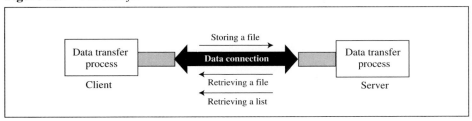

Example 1

Figure 18.8 shows an example of using FTP for retrieving a list of items in a directory.

Figure 18.8   *Example 1*

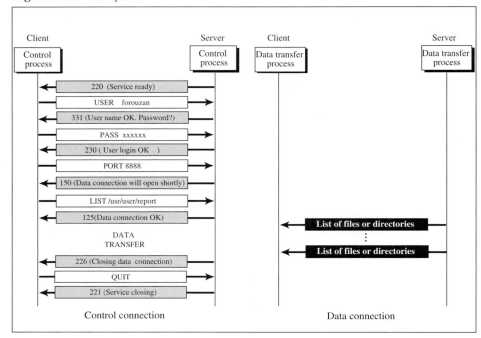

1. After the control connection to port 21 is created, the FTP server sends the 220 (service ready) response on the control connection.
2. The client sends the USER command.
3. The server responds with 331 (user name is OK, password is required).
4. The client sends the PASS command.
5. The server responds with 230 (user login is OK)
6. The client does the passive opening on an ephemeral port for data connection and sends the PORT command (over the control connection) to give this port number to the server.
7. The server does not open the connection at this time, but it prepares itself for issuing an active open on the data connection between port 20 (server side) and the ephemeral port received from the client. It sends the response 150 (data connection will be open shortly).
8. The client sends the LIST message.
9. Now the server responds with 125 and opens the data connection.
10. The server then sends the list of the files or directories (as a file) on the data connection. When the whole list (file) is sent, the server responds with 226 (closing data connection) over the control connection.
11. The client now has two choices. It can use the QUIT command to request the closing of the control or it can send another command to start another activity (and eventually open another data connection). In our example, the client sends a QUIT command.

12. After receiving the QUIT command, the server responds with 221 (service closing) and then closes the control connection.

Example 2

Figure 18.9 shows an example of how an image (binary) file is stored.

Figure 18.9 *Example 2*

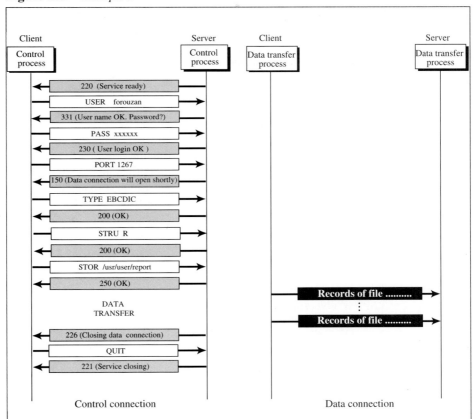

1. After the control connection to port 21 is created, the FTP server sends the 220 (service ready) response on the control connection.
2. The client sends the USER command.
3. The server responds with 331 (user name is OK, a password is required).
4. The client sends the PASS command.
5. The server responds with 230 (user login OK).
6. The client issues a passive open on an ephemeral port for data connection and sends the PORT command (over the control connection) to give this port number to the server.
7. The server does not open the connection at this time, but prepares itself for issuing an active open on the data connection between port 20 (server side) and the ephemeral port received from the client. It sends the response 150 (data connection will be open shortly).

8. The client sends the TYPE command.

9. The server responds with the response 200 (command OK).

10. The client sends the STRU command.

11. The server responds with 200 (command OK).

12. The client sends the STOR command.

13. The server opens the data connection and sends the message 250.

14. The client sends the file on the data connection. After the entire file is sent the data connection is closed. Closing the data connection means end-of-file.

15. The server sends the response 226 on the control connection.

16. The client sends the QUIT command or uses other commands to open another data connection for transferring another file. In our example, the QUIT command is sent.

17. The server responds with 221 (service closing) and it closes the control connection.

18.5 USER INTERFACE

Most operating systems provide a user-friendly interface to access the services of FTP. The interface prompts the user for the appropriate input. After the user types a line, the FTP interface reads the line and changes it to the corresponding FTP command. Table 18.8 shows the interface commands provided in UNIX FTP. Some of the commands can be abbreviated as long as there is no ambiguity.

Table 18.8 *List of FTP commands in UNIX*

Commands
!, $, account, append, ascii, bell, binary, bye, case, cd, cdup, close, cr, delete, debug, dir, discount, form, get, glob, hash, help, lcd, ls, macdef, mdelete, mdir, mget, mkdir, mls, mode, mput, nmap, ntrans, open, prompt, proxy, sendport, put, pwd, quit, quote, recv, remotehelp, rename, reset, rmdir, runique, send, status, struct, sunique, tenex, trace, type, user, verbose,?

Example 3

We show some of the user interface commands that accomplish the same task as in Example 1. The user input is shown in boldface. As shown below, some of the commands are provided automatically by the interface. For example, the user does not have to type any command corresponding to the USER, PASS, or PORT commands. The interface does this. The user receives a prompt and provides only the arguments.

> % **ftp challenger.atc.fhda.edu**
> Connected to challenger.atc.fhda.edu
> 220 Server ready
> Name: **forouzan**
> Password: **xxxxxxx**
> ftp > **ls /usr/user/report**
> 200 OK
> 150 Opening ASCII mode
> ....
> ....

```
226 transfer complete
ftp > close
221 Goodbye
ftp > quit
```

18.6   ANONYMOUS FTP

To use FTP, a user needs an account (user name) and a password on the remote server. Some sites have a set of files available for public access. To access these files, a user does not need to have an account or password. It can use the word *anonymous* as the user name and the word *guest* as the password.

User access to the system is very limited. Some sites allow anonymous users only a subset of commands. For example, most sites allow the user to copy some files, but do not allow navigation through the directories.

18.7   SUMMARY

- File transfer protocol (FTP) is a TCP/IP client-server application for copying files from one host to another.
- FTP requires two connections for data transfer: a control connection and a data connection.
- FTP employs NVT ASCII for communication between dissimilar systems.
- Prior to the actual transfer of files, the file type, data structure, and transmission mode are defined by the client through the control connection.
- There are six classes of commands sent by the client to establish communication with the server. They are:
  a. access commands
  b. file management commands
  c. data formatting commands
  d. port defining commands
  e. file transferring commands
  f. miscellaneous commands
- Responses are sent from the server to the client during connection establishment.
- There are three types of file transfer:
  a. a file is copied from the server to the client
  b. a file is copied from the client to the server
  c. a list of directories or filenames is sent from the server to the client
- Most operating systems provide a user-friendly interface between FTP and the user.
- Anonymous FTP provides a method for the general public to access files on remote sites.

18.8   PRACTICE SET

Multiple Choice

1. Which of the following is true?
    a. FTP allows systems with different directory structures to transfer files.
    b. FTP allows a system using ASCII and a system using EBCDIC to transfer files.
    c. FTP allows a PC and a SUN workstation to transfer files.
    d. all of the above

2. During an FTP session the control connection is opened _____.
    a. exactly once
    b. exactly twice
    c. as many times as necessary
    d. all of the above

3. During an FTP session the data connection is opened _____.
    a. exactly once
    b. exactly twice
    c. as many times as necessary
    d. all of the above

4. What attributes must be defined by the client prior to transmission?
    a. data type
    b. file structure
    c. transmission mode
    d. all of the above

5. A file can be organized into records, pages, or a stream of bytes. These are types of an attribute called _____.
    a. file types
    b. data structures
    c. transmission modes
    d. all of the above

6. There are three types of _____: stream, block, and compressed.
    a. file types
    b. data structures
    c. transmission modes
    d. all of the above

7. ASCII, EBCDIC, and image define an attribute called _____.
    a. file type

    b. data structure

    c. transmission mode

    d. all of the above

8. Which category of commands is used to store and retrieve files?

    a. file transfer commands

    b. access commands

    c. file management commands

    d. data formatting commands

9. Which category of commands defines the port number for the data connection on the client site?

    a. file transfer commands

    b. access commands

    c. file management commands

    d. port defining commands

10. Which category of commands sets the attributes (file type, data structure, and transmission modes) of a file to be transferred?

    a. file transfer commands

    b. access commands

    c. file management commands

    d. data formatting commands

11. Which category of commands lets a user switch directories and create or delete directories?

    a. file transfer commands

    b. access commands

    c. file management commands

    d. data formatting commands

12. When you _____ it is copied from the server to the client.

    a. retrieve a file

    b. store a file

    c. retrieve a list

    d. a and c

13. When you _____ it is copied from the client to the server.

    a. retrieve a file

    b. store a file

    c. retrieve a list

    d. a and c

14. In anonymous FTP, the user can usually _____.

    a. retrieve files

    b. navigate through directories

    c. store files

    d. all of the above

Exercises

15. What do you think would happen if the control connection is accidentally severed during an FTP transfer?

16. Explain why the client issues an active open for the control connection and a passive open for the data connection.

17. Why should there be limitations on anonymous FTP? What could an unscrupulous user do?

18. Explain why FTP does not have a message format.

19. Show a TCP segment that is carrying one of the FTP commands.

20. Show a TCP segment carrying one of the FTP responses.

21. Show a TCP segment carrying FTP data.

22. Explain what will happen if the file in Example 2 already exists.

23. Redo Example 1 using the PASV instead of the PORT command.

24. Redo Example 2 using the STOU command instead of the STOR command to store a file with a unique name. What happens if a file already exists with the same name?

25. Redo Example 2 using the RETR command instead of the STOR command to retrieve a file.

26. Give an example of the use of the HELP command. Follow the format of Example 1.

27. Give an example of the use of the NOOP command. Follow the format of Example 1.

28. Give an example of the use of the SYST command. Follow the format of Example 1.

29. A user wants to make a directory called *Jan* under the directory */usr/usrs/letters*. The host is called "*mcGraw.com.*". Show all of the commands and responses using Examples 1 and 2 as a guide.

30. A user wants to move to the parent of its current directory. The host is called "*mcGraw.com.*". Show all of the commands and responses using Examples 1 and 2 as a guide.

31. A user wants to move a file named *file1* from */usr/usrs/report* directory to */usr/usrs/letters* directory. The host is called "*mcGraw.com.*". Show all the commands and responses using Examples 1 and 2 as a guide.

32. A user wants to retrieve an EBCDIC file named *file1* from */usr/usrs/report* directory. The host is called "*mcGraw.com.*". The file is so large that the user wants to compress it before transferring. Show all the commands and responses using Examples 1 and 2 as a guide.

33. Show how the user interface commands in UNIX are translated to FTP commands (see Table 18.8).

CHAPTER 19

Trivial File Transfer Protocol (TFTP)

There are occasions when we need to simply copy a file without the need for all of the functionalities of the FTP protocol. For example, when a diskless workstation or a router is booted, we need to download the bootstrap and configuration files. Here we do not need all of the sophistication provided in FTP. We just need a protocol that quickly copies the files.

Trivial File Transfer Protocol (TFTP) is designed for these types of file transfer. It is so simple that the software package can fit into the read-only memory of a diskless workstation. It can be used at bootstrap time. TFTP can read or write a file for the client. *Reading* means copying a file from the server site to the client site. *Writing* means copying a file from the client site to the server site.

TFTP uses the services of UDP on the well-known port 69.

19.1 MESSAGES

There are five types of TFTP messages, RRQ, WRQ, DATA, ACK, and ERROR, as shown in Figure 19.1.

Figure 19.1 *Message categories*

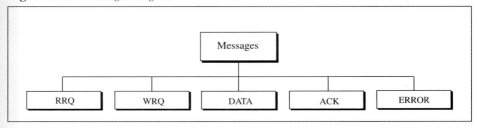

RRQ

The read request (RRQ) message is used by the client to establish a connection for reading data from the server. Its format is shown in Figure 19.2.

Figure 19.2 *RRQ format*

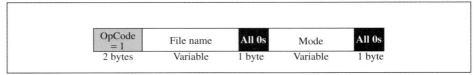

The RRQ message fields are as follows:

■ **OpCode.** The first field is a two-byte operation code. The value is 1 for the RRQ message.

■ **File name.** The next field is a variable-size string (encoded in ASCII) that defines the name of the file. Since the file name varies in length, termination is signaled by a one-byte field of 0s.

■ **Mode.** The next field is another variable-size string defining the transfer mode. The mode field is terminated by another one-byte field of 0s. The mode can be one of two strings: "netascii" (for an ASCII file) or "octet" (for a binary file). Originally there was another file mode, "mail," which is obsolete today. The file name and mode fields can be in upper- or lowercase, or a combination of both.

WRQ

The write request (WRQ) message is used by the client to establish a connection for writing data to the server. The format is the same as RRQ except that the OpCode is 2 (see Figure 19.3).

Figure 19.3 *WRQ format*

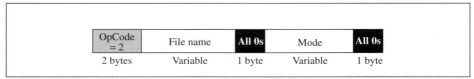

DATA

The data (DATA) message is used by the client or the server to send blocks of data. Its format is shown in Figure 19.4. The DATA message fields are as follows:

■ **OpCode.** The first field is a two-byte operation code. The value is 3 for the DATA message.

■ **Block number.** This is a two-byte field containing the block number. The sender of the data (client or server) uses this field for sequencing. All blocks are numbered

Figure 19.4 *DATA format*

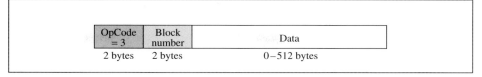

sequentially starting with 1. The block number is necessary for acknowledgment as we will see shortly.

■   **Data.** This block must be exactly 512 bytes in all DATA messages except the last block which must be between 0 and 511 bytes. A non-512 byte block is used as a signal that the sender has sent all the data. In other words, it is used as an end-of-file indicator. If the data in the file happens to be an exact multiple of 512 bytes, the sender must send one extra block of zero bytes to show the end of transmission. Data can be transferred in either NVT ASCII (netascii) or binary octet (octet).

ACK

The acknowledge (ACK) message is used by the client or server to acknowledge the receipt of a data block. The message is only four bytes long. Its format is shown in Figure 19.5.

Figure 19.5 *ACK format*

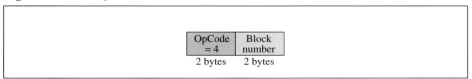

The ACK message fields are as follows:

■   **OpCode.** The first field is a two-byte operation code. The value is 4 for the ACK message.

■   **Block number.** The next field is a two-byte field containing the number of the block received.

The ACK message can also be a response to a WRQ. It is sent by the server to indicate that it is ready to receive data from the client. In this case the value of the block number field is 0. An example of an ACK message is in a later section.

ERROR

The ERROR message is used by the client or the server when a connection cannot be established or when there is a problem during data transmission. It can be sent as a negative response to RRQ or WRQ. It can also be used if the next block cannot be transferred during the actual data transfer phase. The error message is not used to declare a damaged or duplicated message. These problems are resolved by error-control mechanisms discussed later in this chapter. The format of the ERROR message is shown in Figure 19.6.

Figure 19.6   *ERROR format*

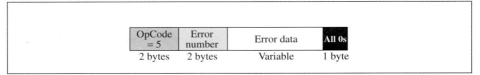

The ERROR message fields are as follows:

■ **OpCode.** The first field is a two-byte operation code. The value is 5 for the ERROR message.

■ **Error number.** This two-byte field defines the type of error. Table 19.1 shows the error numbers and their corresponding meanings.

Table 19.1   *Error numbers and their meanings*

Number	Meaning
0	Not defined
1	File not found
2	Access violation
3	Disk full or quota on disk exceeded
4	Illegal operation
5	Unknown port number
6	File already exists
7	No such user

■ **Error data.** This variable-byte field contains the textual error data and is terminated by a one-byte field of 0s.

19.2   CONNECTION

TFTP uses UDP services. Because there is no provision for connection establishment and termination in UDP, UDP transfers each block of data encapsulated in an independent user datagram. In TFTP, however, we do not want to transfer only one block of data; we do not want to transfer the file as independent blocks either. We need connections for the blocks of data being transferred as they all belong to the same file. TFTP uses RRQ, WRQ, ACK, and ERROR messages to establish connection. It uses the DATA message with a block of data of fewer than 512 bytes (0–511) to terminate connection.

Connection Establishment

Connection establishment for reading files is different from connection establishment for writing files (see Figure 19.7).

Figure 19.7 *Connection establishment*

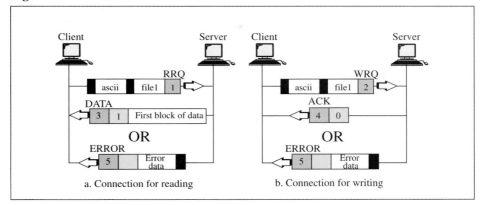

a. Connection for reading   b. Connection for writing

- **Reading.** To establish a connection for reading, the TFTP client sends the RRQ message. The name of the file and the transmission mode is defined in this message. If the server can transfer the file, it responds positively with a DATA message containing the first block of data. If there is a problem, such as difficulty in opening the file or permission restriction, the server responds negatively by sending an ERROR message.

- **Writing.** To establish a connection for writing, the TFTP client uses the WRQ message. The name of the file and the transmission mode is defined in this message. If the server can accept a copy of the file, it responds positively with an ACK message using a value of 0 for block number. If there is any problem, the server responds negatively by sending an ERROR message.

Connection Termination

After the entire file is transferred, the connection must be terminated. As mentioned previously, TFTP does not have a special message for termination. Termination is accomplished by sending the last block of data, which should be fewer than 512 bytes.

19.3   DATA TRANSFER

The data transfer phase occurs between connection establishment and termination. TFTP uses the services of UDP, which is unreliable.

The file is divided into blocks of data, in which each block except the last one is exactly 512 bytes. The last block must be between 0 and 511 bytes. TFTP can transfer data in ASCII or binary format.

UDP does not have any mechanism for flow and error control. TFTP has to create a flow- and error-control mechanism to transfer a file made of continuous blocks of data.

Flow Control

TFTP sends a block of data using the DATA message and waits for an ACK message. If the sender receives an acknowledgment before the time-out, it sends the next block. Thus, flow control is achieved by numbering the data blocks and waiting for an ACK before the next data block is sent.

Retrieve a File

When the client wants to retrieve (read) a file, it sends the RRQ message. The server responds with a DATA message sending the first block of data (if there is no problem) with a block number of 1.

Store a File

When the client wants to store (write) a file, it sends the WRQ message. The server responds with an ACK message (if there is no problem) using 0 for the block number. After receiving this acknowledgment, the client sends the first data block using the block number 1.

Error Control

The TFTP error-control mechanism is different from those of other protocols. It is *symmetric,* which means that the sender and the receiver both use time-outs. The sender uses a time-out for data messages; the receiver uses a time-out for acknowledgment messages. If a data message is lost, the sender retransmits it after time-out expiration. If an acknowledgment is lost, the receiver retransmits it after time-out expiration. This guarantees a smooth operation.

Error control is needed in four situations: damaged message, lost message, lost acknowledgment, or duplicated message.

Damaged Message

There is no negative acknowledgment. If a block of data is damaged, it will be detected by the receiver and the block is discarded. The sender waits for the acknowledgment and does not receive it within the time-out period. The block will then be sent again. Note that there is no checksum field in the DATA message of TFTP. The only way the receiver can detect data corruption is through the checksum field of the UDP user datagram.

Lost Message

If a block is lost, it never reaches the receiver and no acknowledgment is sent. The sender resends the block after the time-out.

Lost Acknowledgment

If an acknowledgment is lost, two situations can happen. If the timer of the receiver matures before the timer of the sender, the receiver retransmits the acknowledgment; otherwise, the sender retransmits the data.

Duplicate Message

Duplication of blocks can be detected by the receiver through block number. If a block is duplicated, it is simply discarded by the receiver.

Sorcerer's Apprentice Bug

Although the flow- and error-control mechanism is symmetric in TFTP, it can lead to a problem known as the *sorcerer's apprentice bug*, named for the cartoon character who inadvertently conjures up a mop that continuously replicates itself. This will happen if the ACK message for a packet is not lost, but delayed. In this situation, every succeeding block is sent twice and every succeeding acknowledgment is received twice.

Figure 19.8 shows the problem. The acknowledgment for the fifth block is delayed. After the time-out expiration, the sender retransmits the fifth block, which will be acknowledged by the receiver again. The sender receives two acknowledgments for the fifth block, which triggers it to send the sixth block twice. The receiver receives the sixth block twice and again sends two acknowledgments, which result in sending the seventh block twice. And so on.

Figure 19.8   *Sorcerer's apprentice bug*

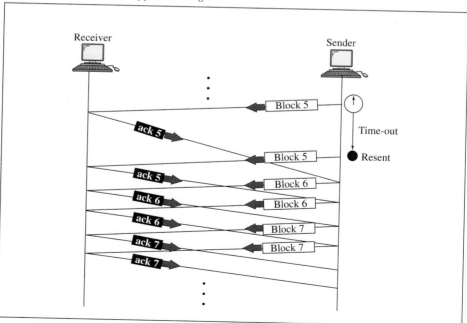

19.4   UDP PORTS

When a process uses the services of UDP, the server process issues the passive open on the well-known port and waits for the client process to issue the active open on an ephemeral port. After the connection is established, the client and server communicate using these two ports.

The situation in TFTP is different. The communication between a client TFTP and a server TFTP can last a long time (seconds or minutes). If a TFTP server uses the well-known port 69 to communicate with a single client for a long time, no other clients can use these services during that time. The solution, as shown in Figure 19.9, is to use the well-known port for the initial connection and an ephemeral port for the rest of the communication.

Figure 19.9   *UDP port numbers used by TFTP*

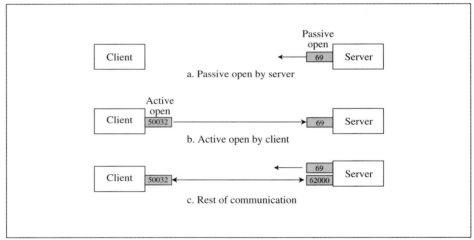

The steps are as follows:

1. The server passively opens the connection using the well-known port 69.

2. A client actively opens a connection using an ephemeral port for the source port and the well-known port 69 for the destination port. This is done using RRQ message or WRQ message.

3. The server actively opens a connection using a new ephemeral port for the source port and uses the ephemeral port received from the client as the destination port. It sends the DATA or ACK or ERROR message using these ports. The server frees the well-known port (69) to be used by other clients. When the client receives the first message from the server, it uses its own ephemeral port and the ephemeral port sent by the server for future communication.

19.5 TFTP EXAMPLE

Figure 19.10 shows a TFTP example. The client wants to retrieve the contents of a 2,000-byte file called *file1*. The client sends an RRQ message. The server sends the first block, carrying the first 512 bytes, which is received intact and acknowledged. These two messages are the connection establishment. The second block, carrying the second 512 bytes, is lost. After the time-out, the server retransmits the block, which is received. The third block, carrying the third 512 bytes, is received intact, but the acknowledgment is lost. After the time-out, the receiver retransmits the acknowledgment. The last block, carrying the remaining 464 bytes, is received damaged, so the client simply discards it. After the time-out, the server retransmits the block. This message is considered the connection termination because the block carries fewer than 512 bytes.

19.6 TFTP OPTIONS

An extension to the TFTP protocol that allows the appending of options to the RRQ and WRQ messages has been proposed. The options are mainly used to negotiate the size of the block and possibly the initial sequence number. Without the options the size of a block is 512 bytes except for the last block. The negotiation can define a size of block to be any number of bytes so long as the message can be encapsulated in a UDP user datagram.

A new type of message, option acknowledgment (OACK), to let the other party accept or reject the options, has also been proposed.

19.7 SECURITY

One important point we must remember about the TFTP is that there is no provision for security: There is no user identification or password. Today, however, precautions must be taken to prevent hackers from accessing files. One way to do this is to limit the access of TFTP to noncritical files.

Another way to add security to TFTP is to use another application program, such as TELNET. The user must first access TELNET. TELNET checks whether the user has the right to access the system and the corresponding file. It then calls the TFTP client and passes the file name to the client. The client then makes the TFTP connection to the TFTP server at the user site (see Figure 19.11).

Note that in this process the user should run the TFTP server process and the remote site should run the TFTP client process. Also note that the action performed by the user is reversed: If the user wants to read a file, the remote site now uses the write operation, and if the user wants to write a file, the remote site now uses the read operation.

Figure 19.10   *TFTP example*

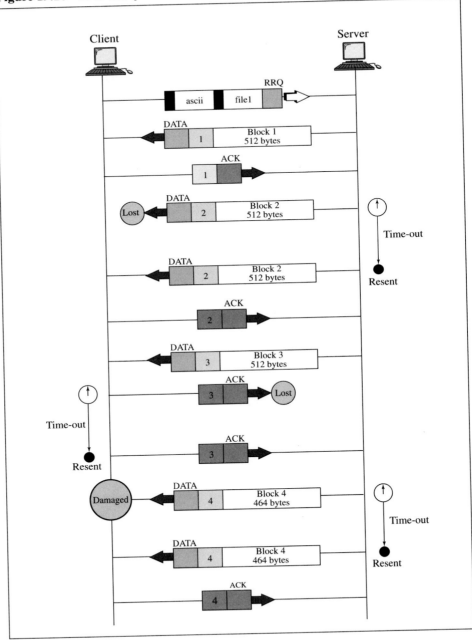

Figure 19.11   *Using TELNET in conjunction with TFTP to provide security*

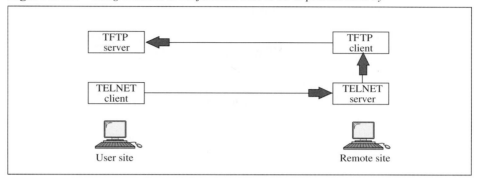

19.8   APPLICATIONS

TFTP is very useful for basic file transfer where security is not a big issue. It can be used to initialize devices such as bridges or routers. Its main application is in conjunction with the BOOTP or DHCP protocols. TFTP requires only a small amount of memory and uses only the services of UDP and IP. It can easily be configured into ROM (or PROM). When the station is powered on, TFTP will be connected to a server and can download the configuration files from there. Figure 19.12 shows the idea. The powered-on station uses the BOOTP (or DHCP) client to get the name of the configuration file from the BOOTP server. The station then passes the name of the file to the TFTP client to get the contents of the configuration file from the TFTP server.

Figure 19.12   *Use of TFTP with BOOTP*

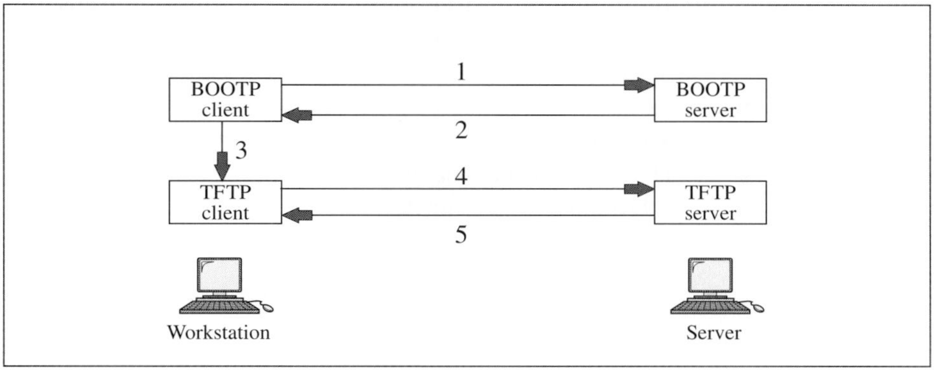

19.9   SUMMARY

■ Trivial File Transfer Protocol (TFTP) is a simple file transfer protocol without the complexities and sophistication of FTP.

■ A client uses the services of TFTP to retrieve a copy of a file or send a copy of a file to a server.

■ There are five types of TFTP messages:

   a. RRQ is a client message that establishes a connection for reading data from the server.

   b. WRQ is a client message that establishes a connection for writing data to the server.

   c. DATA is a client or server message that sends blocks of data.

   d. ACK acknowledges the receipt of a data block.

   e. ERROR is a message to convey a connection or transmission problem.

■ TFTP is an application that uses UDP for its transport mechanism.

■ TFTP uses RRQ, WRQ, ACK, and ERROR to establish connection. A DATA message with a block of data less than 512 bytes terminates connection.

■ Each DATA message, except the last, carries 512 bytes of data from the file.

■ TFTP uses a stop-and-wait protocol for flow control.

■ Error control is needed in four situations: damaged message, lost message, lost acknowledgment, or duplicated message.

■ TFTP employs symmetric transmission whereby both sender and receiver use time-outs for error handling.

■ The sorcerer's apprentice bug is the duplication of both acknowledgments and data messages caused by TFTP's flow-and error-control mechanism.

■ An extension to the TFTP protocol to allow options regarding the data block size has been proposed.

■ TFTP has no provision for security. A second application program such as TEL-NET can be used in conjunction with TFTP to provide security.

■ TFTP can be used in conjunction with BOOTP or DHCP to initialize devices by downloading configuration files.

19.10   PRACTICE SET

Multiple Choice

1. What type of message is sent in response to an RRQ that fails to establish a connection?

   a. WRQ

   b. DATA

c. ACK

d. ERROR

2. What type of message is sent to establish a connection to retrieve a file?

a. RRQ

b. WRQ

c. DATA

d. ACK

3. Which type of message is always a set number of bytes?

a. RRQ

b. WRQ

c. DATA

d. ACK

4. A DATA block is sent in response to a _____ message.

a. RRQ

b. WRQ

c. ACK

d. a or c

5. TFTP uses the _____ message for flow control.

a. RRQ

b. WRQ

c. ACK

d. ERROR

6. TFTP uses the _____ message for connection termination.

a. DATA

b. ACK

c. ERROR

d. a and b

7. An unauthorized user tries to send a file to a server using TFTP. What should be the response of the server?

a. ACK

b. ERROR

c. DATA

d. WRQ

8. The block number on a DATA message is 22. This always means _____.

a. there were 21 previous blocks

b. there were 20 previous blocks

c. this is the last block

d. none of the above

9. Which TFTP message contains a block number field?

a. ERROR

      b. DATA

      c. ACK

      d. b and c

10. The ERROR message can follow a _____ message.

      a. RRQ

      b. WRQ

      c. DATA

      d. all of the above

11. Connection termination is signaled by a DATA message with _____ bytes.

      a. any positive number of

      b. 512

      c. 0 to 511

      d. all of the above

12. The flow-control mechanism in TFTP _____.

      a. is called stop-and-wait

      b. is called sliding window

      c. is nonexistent

      d. depends on the TFTP purpose (read or write)

13. If a message is _____, it is resent.

      a. damaged

      b. lost

      c. duplicated

      d. a and b

14. If a duplicate DATA message is received, _____.

      a. the sender sends an error message

      b. the connection is terminated

      c. the sender discards the duplicate

      d. the receiver discards the duplicate

15. One symptom of the sorcerer's apprentice bug is that _____.

      a. time-outs malfunction

      b. ACKS are duplicated

      c. DATA messages are duplicated

      d. b and c

16. When TFTP services are used in conjunction with TELNET for security reasons, the user site acts as the _____ and _____.

      a. TFTP server; TELNET client

      b. TFTP client; TELNET server

      c. TFTP server; TELNET server

      d. TFTP client; TELNET client

Exercises

17. Why do we need an RRQ or WRQ message in TFTP, but not in FTP?

18. Show the encapsulation of an RRQ message in a UDP user datagram. Assume the file name is "Report" and the mode is ASCII. What is the size of the UDP datagram?

19. Show the encapsulation of a WRQ message in a UDP user datagram. Assume the file name is "Report" and the mode is ASCII. What is the size of the UDP datagram?

20. Show the encapsulation of a TFTP data message, carrying block number 7, in a UDP user datagram. What is the total size of the user datagram?

21. Host A uses TFTP to read 2,150 bytes of data from host B. Show all the TFTP commands including commands needed for connection establishment and termination. Assume no error.

22. Show all the user datagrams exchanged between the two hosts in exercise 21.

23. Redo exercise 21 but assume the second block is in error

24. Show all the user datagrams exchanged between the two hosts in exercise 23.

25. Do some research and find the format of the proposed OACK message.

26. Do some research and find the types of options proposed to be appended to the RRQ and WRQ messages.

27. Do some research and find the format of the OACK message.

CHAPTER 20

Simple Mail Transfer Protocol (SMTP)

One of the most popular network services is electronic mail (e-mail). The TCP/IP protocol that supports electronic mail on the Internet is called Simple Mail Transfer Protocol (SMTP). It is a system for sending messages to other computer users based on e-mail addresses. SMTP provides for mail exchange between users on the same or different computers. SMTP supports:

- Sending a single message to one or more recipients.
- Sending messages that include text, voice, video, or graphics.
- Sending messages to users on networks outside the Internet.

Figure 20.1 shows the basic idea. The SMTP server uses the TCP well-known port 25.

Figure 20.1 *SMTP concept*

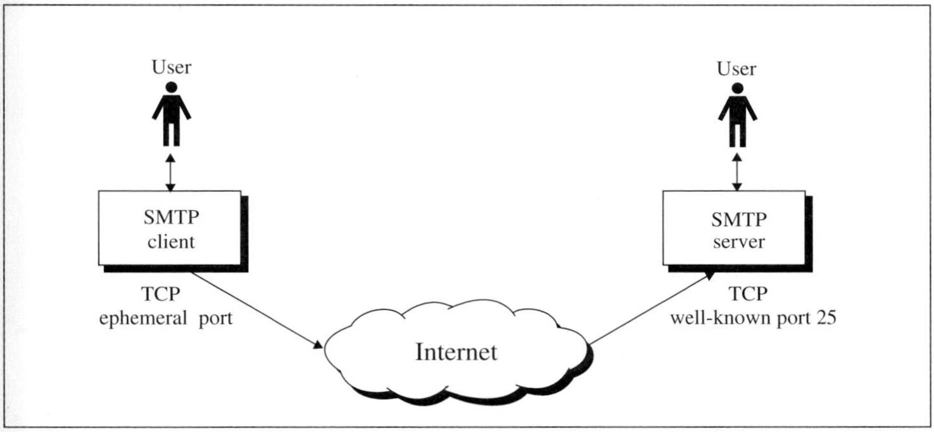

Starting with this simple figure, we will examine the components of the SMTP system, gradually adding complexity. Let us begin by breaking down both the SMTP client and server into two components: user agent (UA) and mail transfer agent (MTA).

The UA prepares the message, creates the envelope, and puts the message in the envelope. The MTA transfers the mail across the Internet. Figure 20.2 shows the previous figure with the addition of these two components.

Figure 20.2 *UAs and MTAs*

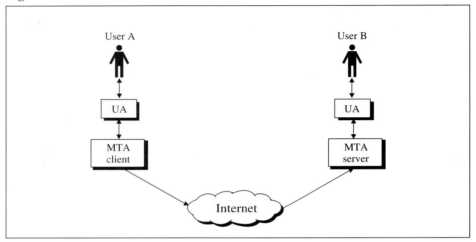

SMTP protocol allows a more complex system than the one shown. Relaying could be involved. Instead of just one MTA at the sender site and one at the receiving site, other MTAs, acting either as client or server, can relay the mail (see Figure 20.3).

Figure 20.3 *Relay MTAs*

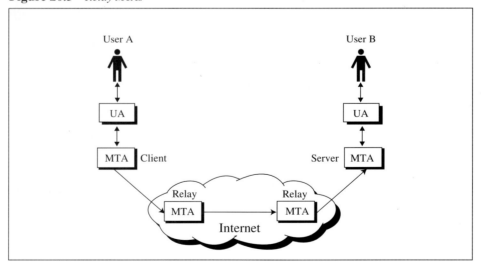

The relaying system allows sites that do not use the TCP/IP protocol suite to send e-mail to users on other sites that may or may not use the TCP/IP protocol suite. This is accomplished through the use of a **mail gateway,** which is a relay MTA that can receive mail prepared by a protocol other than SMTP and transform it to SMTP format before sending it. It can also receive mail in SMTP format and change it to another format before sending it (see Figure 20.4).

Figure 20.4   *Mail gateway*

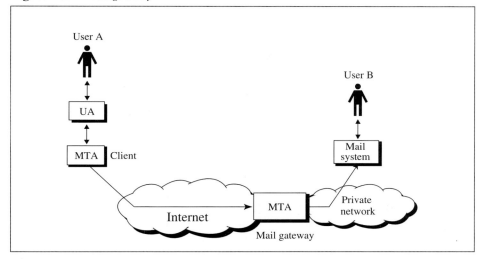

20.1   USER AGENT (UA)

A user agent is defined in SMTP, but the implementation details are not. The UA is normally a program used to send and receive mail. Popular user agent programs are MH, Berkeley Mail, Elm, Zmail, and Mush.

Some user agents have an extra user interface that allows window-type interactions with the system. Eudora is an example of this type of interface.

Sending Mail

To send mail, the user, through the UA, creates mail that looks very similar to postal mail. It has an *envelope* and a *message* (see Figure 20.5).

Envelope

The envelope usually contains the sender address, the receiver address, and other information.

Message

The message contains the *headers* and the *body.* The headers of the message define the sender, the receiver, the subject of the message, and some other information. The body of the message contains the actual information to be read by the recipient.

Figure 20.5 *Format of an e-mail*

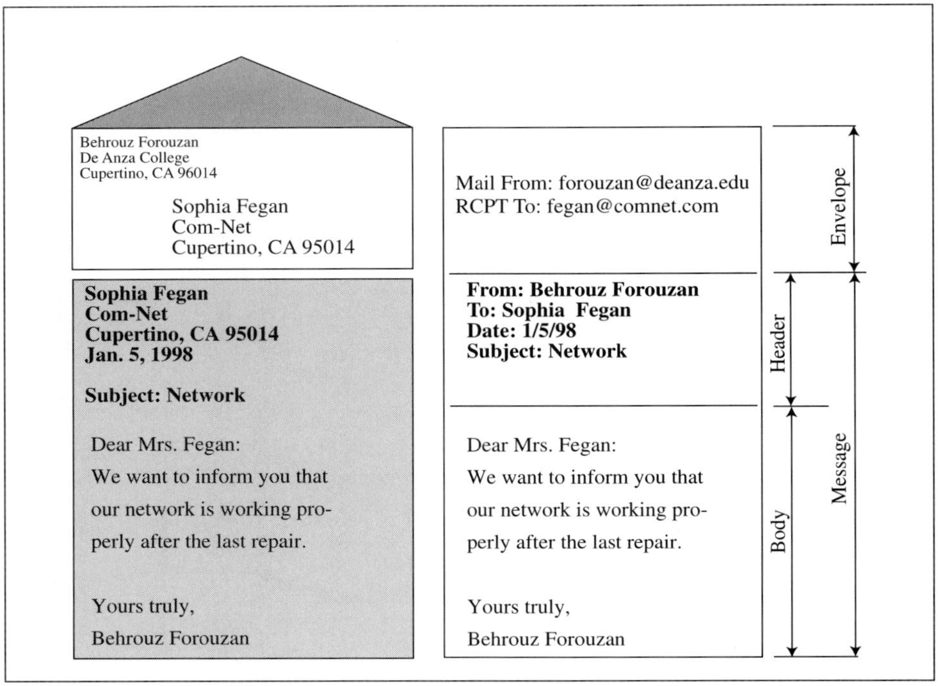

Receiving Mail

The user agent periodically checks the mailboxes. If a user has mail, the UA informs the user first by giving a notice. If the user is ready to read the mail, a list is displayed in which each line contains a summary of the information about a particular message in the mailbox. The summary usually includes the sender mail address, the subject, and the time the mail was sent or received. The user can select any of the messages and display its contents on the screen.

20.2 ADDRESSES

To deliver mail, a mail handling system must use a unique addressing system. The addressing system used by SMTP consists of two parts: a *local part* and a *domain name*, separated by an @ sign (see Figure 20.6).

Local Part

The local part defines the name of a special file, called the user mailbox, where all of the mail received for a user is stored for retrieval by the user agent.

Figure 20.6   *E-mail address*

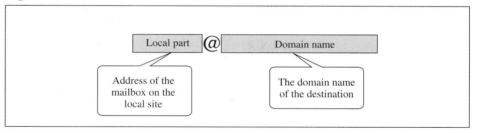

Domain Name

The second part of the address is the domain name. An organization usually selects one or more hosts to receive and send e-mail; they are sometimes called *mail exchangers*. The domain name assigned to each mail exchanger either comes from the DNS database or it is a logical name (for example, the name of the organization).

The e-mail addresses become more complex when we use mail gateways. In this case, the e-mail address must define both the address of the gateway and the address of the actual recipient. The domain name must define the name of the mail gateway in the DNS database and the local part must define the local physical network, the computer attached to that network, and the user mailbox. Because some mailing systems do not use the mailing address format defined by the SMTP, this can create problems and confusion.

20.3   DELAYED DELIVERY

SMTP is different from other application programs that we have seen so far because it allows delayed delivery. This means that the message does not necessarily have to be delivered immediately but can be delayed at the sender site, the receiver site, or the intermediate servers.

Sender-Site Delay

The sending of a message can be delayed at the sender site. SMTP stipulates that the sender site must accommodate a *spooling* system in which messages are stored before being sent. After the user agent creates a message, it is delivered to the spool, which is a storage structure. The mail transfer system periodically (every 10 to 30 minutes) checks the mail stored in the spool to see if the mail can be sent. This depends on whether the IP address of the server has been obtained through DNS, if the receiver is ready, and so on. If the message cannot be sent, it remains in the spool to be checked in the next cycle. If a message cannot be delivered in the time-out period (usually three to five days), the mail returns to the sender (see Figure 20.7).

Figure 20.7 *Sender-site delay*

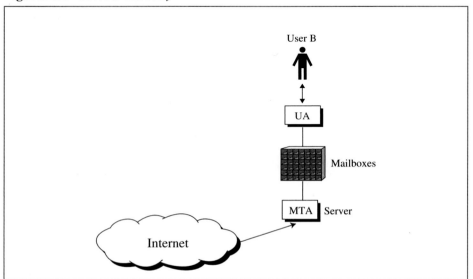

Receiver-Site Delay

After the message has been received, it does not have to be read by the recipient immediately. The mail can be stored in the mailbox of the receiver (see Figure 20.8).

Figure 20.8 *Receiver-site delay*

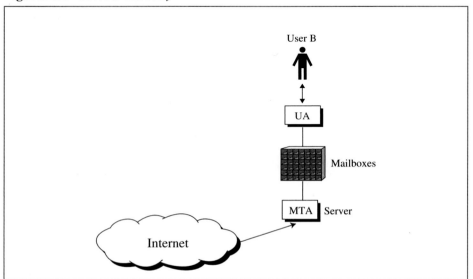

Intermediate Delay

As previously mentioned, SMTP allows intermediate MTAs to serve as clients and servers. They too can receive mail, keep mail messages in their own mailboxes and spools, and send them when appropriate.

20.4   ALIASES

SMTP allows one name, an *alias,* to represent several different e-mail addresses; this is called *one-to-many alias expansion.* Also a single user can be defined by several different e-mail addresses, called *many-to-one alias expansion.* To handle these, the system must include an alias expansion facility at both the sender and receiver site (see Figure 20.9).

Figure 20.9   *Alias expansion*

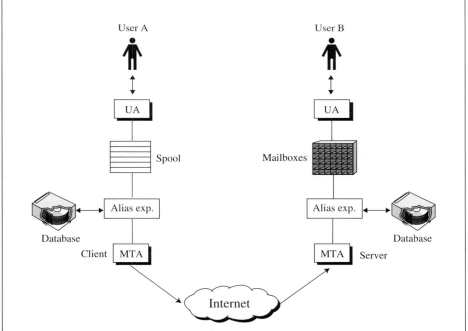

One-to-Many Expansion

In situations where the same message is to be sent to different recipients, the user can create an alias that is mapped to the list of the recipients. Every time a message is sent, the system checks the recipient's name against the alias expansion database; if there is an expansion for the defined name, separate messages, one for each entry in the expansion, must be prepared and handed to the mail delivery system. If there is no expansion for the recipient name, the name itself is the receiving address and a single message is delivered to the mail transfer entity (see Figure 20.10).

Figure 20.10   *One-to-many expansion*

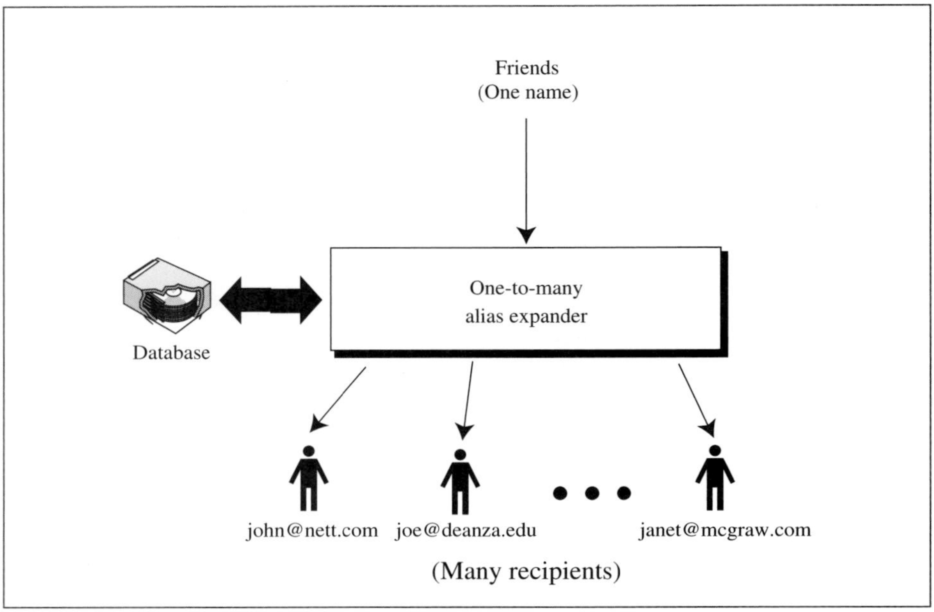

Many-to-One Expansion

A user can have several e-mail addresses, but the user agent recognizes only one mailbox name. Usually the local parts of the address will differ. When a system receives mail, it checks the many-to-one expansion database. If a mailbox name corresponding to the local part of the received address is found, the mail is sent to that mailbox; otherwise, the mail is discarded (see Figure 20.11).

20.5   MAIL TRANSFER AGENT (MTA)

The actual mail transfer is done through Mail Transfer Agents (MTAs). To send mail, a system must have the client MTA, and to receive mail, a system must have a server MTA. Although SMTP does not define a specific MTA, Sendmail is a commonly used UNIX system MTA.

SMTP simply defines how commands and responses must be sent back and forth. Each network is free to choose a software package for implementation. We will discuss the mechanism of mail transfer by the SMTP in the remainder of the chapter. However, first we present the whole picture of a bidirectional e-mail system as defined by SMTP. Figure 20.12 illustrates the process of sending and receiving e-mail as described above. For a computer to be able to send and receive mail using SMTP, it must have most of

Figure 20.11   *Many-to-one expansion*

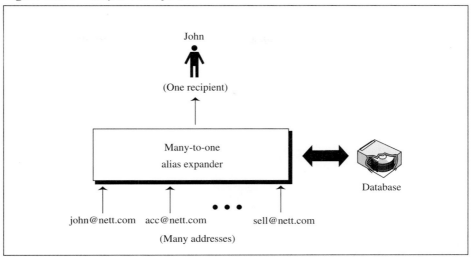

the entities (the user interface is not necessary) defined in the figure. The user interface is a component that creates a user-friendly environment. A good example of a user interface can be found in Eudora.

20.6   COMMANDS AND RESPONSES

SMTP uses commands and responses to transfer messages between an MTA client and an MTA server (see Figure 20.13).

Each command or reply is terminated by a two-character (carriage return and line feed) end-of-line token.

Commands

Commands are sent from the client to the server. The format of a command is shown in Figure 20.14. It consists of a keyword followed by zero or more arguments. SMTP defines 14 commands. The first five are mandatory; every implementation must support these five commands. The next three are often used and highly recommended. The last

Figure 20.12 *The entire e-mail system*

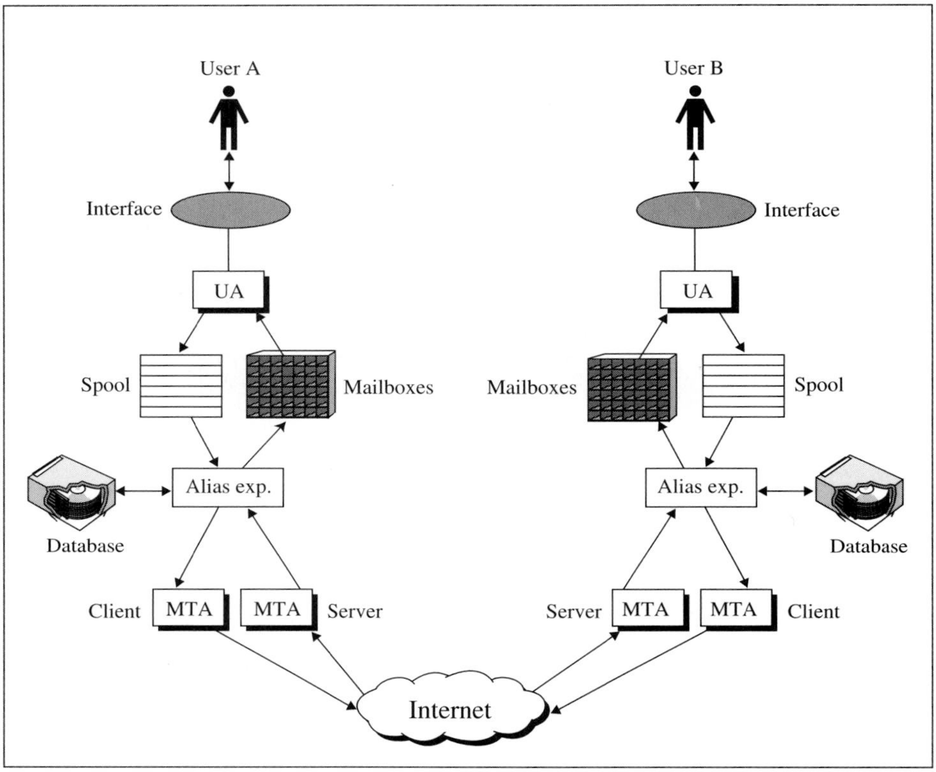

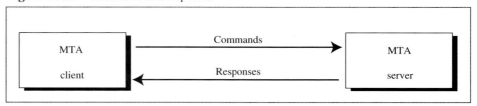

Figure 20.13 *Commands and responses*

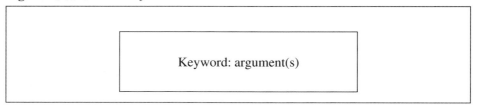

Figure 20.14 *Command format*

Keyword: argument(s)

six are seldom used. The commands are listed in Table 20.1 and described in more detail below.

Table 20.1 *Commands*

Keyword	Argument(s)
HELO	Sender's host name
MAIL	Sender of the message
RCPT	Intended recipient of the message
DATA	Body of the mail
QUIT	
RSET	
VRFY	Name of recipient to be verified
NOOP	
TURN	
EXPN	Mailing list to be expanded
HELP	Command name
SEND	Intended recipient of the message
SMOL	Intended recipient of the message
SMAL	Intended recipient of the message

- **HELO.** The HELO command is used by the client to identify itself. The argument is the domain name of the client host. The format is

    HELO: challenger.atc.fhda.edu

- **MAIL FROM.** The MAIL command is used by the client to identify the sender of the message. The argument is the e-mail address of the sender (local part plus the domain name). The format is

    MAIL FROM: forouzan@challenger.atc.fhda.edu

- **RCPT TO.** The RCPT (Recipient) command is used by the client to identify the intended recipient of the message. The argument is the e-mail address of the recipient. If there are multiple recipients, the command is repeated. The format is

    RCPT TO: betsy@mcgraw-hill.com

- **DATA.** The DATA command is used to send the actual message. All lines that follow the DATA command are treated as the mail message. The message is terminated by a line containing just a period. The format is

    DATA

    This is the message

to be sent to the McGraw-Hill

Company

.

■   **QUIT.** The QUIT command terminates the message. The format is

QUIT

■   **RSET.** The RSET (reset) command aborts the current mail transaction. The stored information about the sender and recipient is deleted. The connection will be reset.

RSET

■   **VRFY.** The VRFY (verify) command is used to verify the address of the recipient, which is sent as the argument. The sender can ask the receiver to confirm that a name identifies a valid recipient. Its format is

VRFY: betsy@mcgraw-hill.com

■   **NOOP.** The NOOP (no operation) command is used by the client to check the status of the recipient. It requires an answer from the recipient. Its format is shown below:

NOOP

■   **TURN.** The TURN command lets the sender and the recipient switch positions, whereby the sender becomes the recipient and vice versa. However, most SMTP implementations today do not support this feature. The format is

TURN

■   **EXPN.** The EXPN (expand) command asks the receiving host to expand the mailing list sent as the arguments and to return the mailbox addresses of the recipients that comprise the list. The format is

EXPN: x y z

■   **HELP.** The HELP command asks the recipient to send information about the command sent as the argument. The format is

HELP: mail

■   **SEND.** The SEND command specifies that the mail is to be delivered to the terminal of the recipient, and not the mailbox. If the recipient is not logged in, the mail is bounced back. The argument is the address of the sender. The format is

SEND FROM: forouzan@fhda.atc.edu

■   **SMOL.** The SMOL (send to the mailbox or terminal) command specifies that the mail is to be delivered to the terminal or the mailbox of the recipient. This means that if the recipient is logged in, the mail is delivered only to the terminal. If the recipient is not logged in, the mail is delivered to the mailbox. The argument is the address of the sender. The format is

SMOL FROM: forouzan@fhda.atc.edu

■ **SMAL.** The SMAL (send to the mailbox and terminal) command specifies that the mail is to be delivered to the terminal and the mailbox of the recipient. This means that if the recipient is logged in, the mail is delivered to the terminal and the mailbox. If the recipient is not logged in, the mail is delivered only to the mailbox. The argument is the address of the sender. The format is

SMAL FROM: forouzan@fhda.atc.edu

Responses

Responses are sent from the server to the client. A response is a three-digit code that may be followed by additional textual information. The meanings of the first digit are as follows:

■ **2yz (positive completion reply).** If the first digit is 2 (digit 1 is not in use today), it means that the requested command has been successfully completed and a new command can be started.

■ **3yz (positive intermediate reply).** If the first digit is 3, it means that the requested command has been accepted, but the recipient needs some more information before completion can occur.

■ **4yz (transient negative completion reply).** If the first digit is 4, it means the requested command has been rejected, but the error condition is temporary. The command can be sent again.

■ **5yz (permanent negative completion reply).** If the first digit is 5, it means the requested command has been rejected. The command cannot be sent again.

The second and the third digits provide further details about the responses. Table 20.2 lists some of the responses.

Table 20.2   *Responses*

Code	Description
Positive Completion Reply	
211	System status or help reply
214	Help message
220	Service ready
221	Service closing transmission channel
250	Request command completed
251	User not local; the message will be forwarded
Positive Intermediate Reply	
354	Start mail input
Transient Negative Completion Reply	
421	Service not available

Table 20.2   *Responses (concluded)*

Code	Description
450	Mailbox not available
451	Command aborted: local error
452	Command aborted; insufficient storage
Permanent Negative Completion Reply	
500	Syntax error; unrecognized command
501	Syntax error in parameters or arguments
502	Command not implemented
503	Bad sequence of commands
504	Command temporarily not implemented
550	Command is not executed; mailbox unavailable
551	User not local
552	Requested action aborted; exceeded storage location
553	Requested action not taken; mailbox name not allowed
554	Transaction failed

20.7   MAIL TRANSFER PHASES

The process of transferring a mail message occurs in three phases: connection establishment, mail transfer, and connection termination.

Connection Establishment

After a client has made a TCP connection to the well-known port 25, the SMTP server starts the connection phase. This phase involves the following three steps, which are illustrated in Figure 20.15.

1. The server sends code 220 (service ready) to tell the client that it is ready to receive mail. If the server is not ready, it sends code 421 (service not available).

2. The client sends the HELO message to identify itself using its domain name address. This step is necessary to inform the server of the domain name of the client. Remember that during TCP connection establishment, the sender and receiver know each other through their IP addresses.

3. The server responds with code 250 (request command completed) or some other code depending on the situation.

Figure 20.15   *Connection establishment*

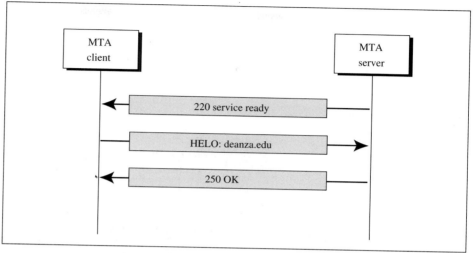

Message Transfer

After connection has been established between the SMTP client and server, a single message between a sender and one or more recipients can be exchanged. This phase involves eight steps. Steps 3 and 4 are repeated if there is more than one recipient (see Figure 20.16).

1. The client sends the MAIL message to introduce the sender of the message. It includes the mail address of the sender (mailbox and the domain name). This step is needed to give the server the return mail address for returning errors and reporting messages.
2. The server responds with code 250 or some other appropriate code.
3. The client sends the RCPT (recipient) message, which includes the mail address of the recipient.
4. The server responds with code 250 or some other appropriate code
5. The client sends the DATA message to initialize the message transfer.
6. The server responds with code 354 (start mail input) or some other appropriate message.
7. The client sends the contents of the message in consecutive lines. Each line is terminated by a two-character end-of-line token (carriage return and line feed). The message is terminated by a line containing just a period.
8. The server responds with code 250 (OK) or some other appropriate code.

Connection Termination

After the message is transferred successfully, the client terminates the connection. This phase involves two steps (see Figure 20.17).

1. The client sends the QUIT command.

Figure 20.16 *Message transfer*

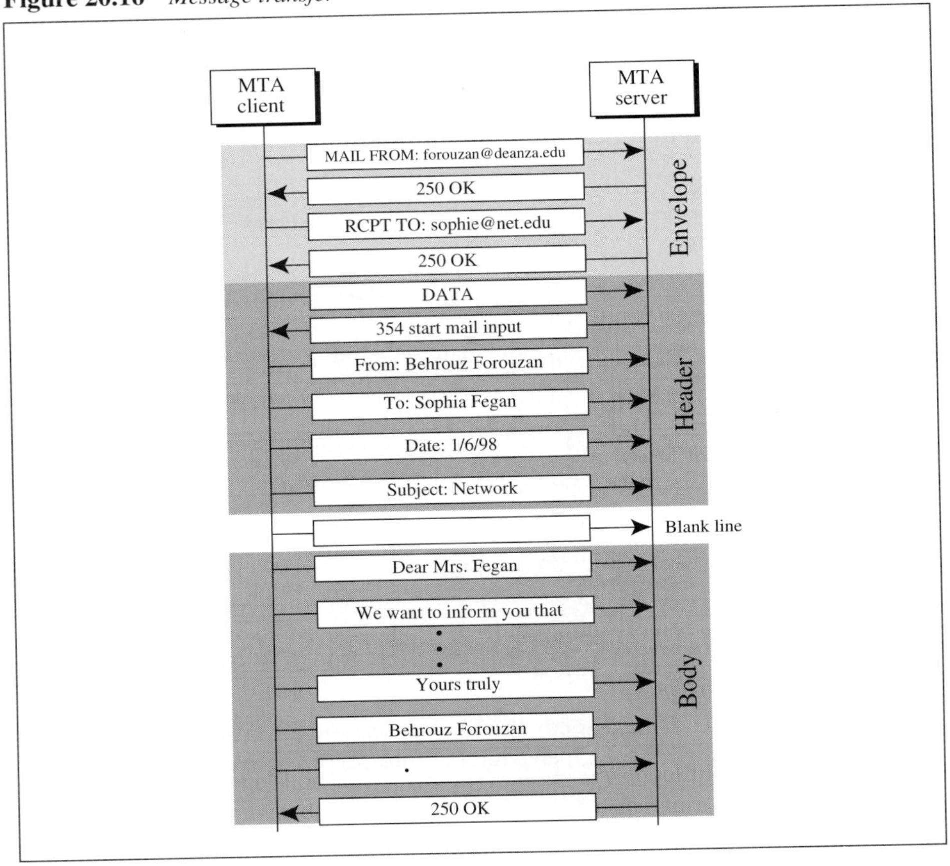

MTA
client
MTA
server
MAIL FROM: forouzan@deanza.edu
250 OK
RCPT TO: sophie@net.edu
250 OK
Envelope
DATA
354 start mail input
From: Behrouz Forouzan
To: Sophia Fegan
Date: 1/6/98
Subject: Network
Header
Blank line
Dear Mrs. Fegan
We want to inform you that
Yours truly
Behrouz Forouzan
.
250 OK
Body

Figure 20.17 *Connection termination*

MTA
client
MTA
server
QUIT
221 service closed

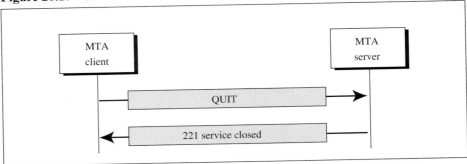

2. The server responds with code 221 or some other appropriate code.

After the connection termination phase, the TCP connection must be closed.

20.8 MULTIPURPOSE INTERNET MAIL EXTENSIONS (MIME)

SMTP is a simple mail transfer protocol. Its simplicity, however, comes with a price. SMTP can send messages only in NVT seven-bit ASCII format. In other words, it has some limitations. For example, it cannot be used for languages that are not supported by seven-bit ASCII characters (such as French, German, Hebrew, Russian, Chinese, and Japanese). Also, it cannot be used to send binary files or to send video or audio data.

Multipurpose Internet Mail Extensions (MIME) is a supplementary protocol that allows non-ASCII data to be sent through SMTP. MIME is not a mail protocol and cannot replace SMTP; it is only an extension to SMTP.

MIME transforms non-ASCII data at the sender site to NVT ASCII data and delivers it to the client SMTP to be sent through the Internet. The server SMTP at the receiving side receives the NVT ASCII data and delivers it to MIME to be transformed back to the original data.

We can think of MIME as a set of software functions that transforms non-ASCII data to ASCII data and vice versa (see Figure 20.18).

Figure 20.18 *MIME*

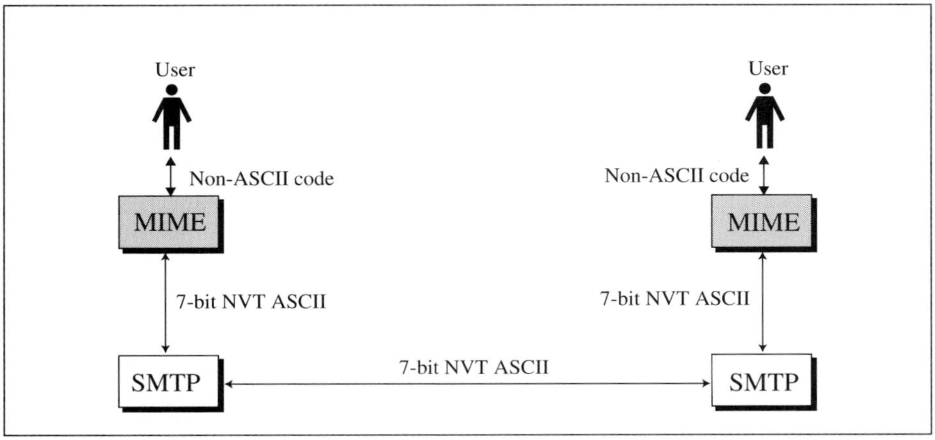

MIME defines five headers that can be added to the original SMTP header section to define the transformation parameters:

1. MIME-Version
2. Content-Type
3. Content-Transfer-Encoding
4. Content-Id
5. Content-Description

Figure 20.19 shows the original header and the extended header. We will describe each header in detail.

Figure 20.19 *MIME header*

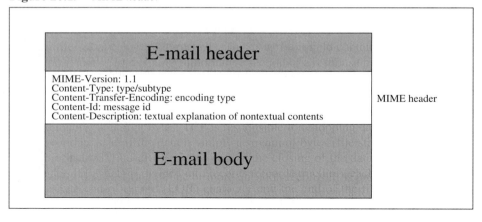

MIME-Version

This header defines the version of MIME used. The current version is 1.1.

MIME-Version: 1.1

Content-Type

This header defines the type of data used in the body of the message. The content type and the content subtype are separated by a slash. Depending on the subtype, the header may contain other parameters.

Content-Type: <type / subtype; parameters>

MIME allows seven different types of data. These are listed in Table 20.3 and described in more detail below.

Table 20.3 *Data types and subtypes in MIME*

Type	Subtype	Description
Text	Plain	Unformatted text
Multi-part	Mixed	Body contains ordered parts of different data types
	Parallel	Same as above, but no order
	Digest	Similar to Mixed, but the default is message/RFC822
	Alternative	Parts are different versions of the same message
Message	RFC822	Body is an encapsulated message
	Partial	Body is a fragment of a bigger message
	External-Body	Body is a reference to another message
Image	JPEG	Image is in JPEG format
	GIF	Image is in GIF format

Table 20.3 *Data types and subtypes in MIME*

Type	Subtype	Description
Video	MPEG	Video is in MPEG format
Audio	Basic	Single channel encoding of voice at 8 KHz
Application	PostScript	Adobe PostScript
	Octet-stream	General binary data (eight-bit bytes)

■ **Text.** The original message is in seven-bit ASCII format and no transformation by MIME is needed. There is only one subtype currently used, *plain.*

■ **Multipart.** The body contains multiple, independent parts. The multipart header needs to define the boundary between each part. The boundary is used as a parameter. It is a string token that is repeated before each part on a separate line by itself and preceded by two hyphens. The body will be terminated using the boundary token preceded and terminated by two hyphens.

Four subtypes are defined for this type: *mixed, parallel, digest,* and *alternative.* In the mixed subtype, the parts must be presented to the recipient in the exact order as in the message. Each part has a different type and is defined at the boundary. The parallel subtype is similar to the mixed subtype, except that the order of the parts is unimportant. The digest subtype is also similar to the mixed subtype except that the default type/subtype is message/rfc822 as defined below. In the alternative subtype, the same message is repeated using different formats. The following is an example of a multipart message using a mixed subtype:

```
Content-Type: multipart/mixed; boundary=xxxx

--xxxx
Content-Type: text/plain;
...........................................
...........................................
--xxxx
Content-Type: image/gif;
...........................................
...........................................
...........................................
--xxxx--
```

■ **Message.** In the message type, the body is itself a whole mail message, a part of a mail message, or a pointer to a message. Three subtypes are currently used: *rfc822, partial,* or *external-body.* The subtype rfc822 is used if the body is encapsulating another message (including header and the body). The subtype partial is used if the original message has been fragmented into different mail messages and this mail message is one of the fragments. The fragments must be reassembled at the destination by MIME. Three parameters must be added: *id, number,* and the *total.* The id identifies the message and is present in all the fragments. The number defines the sequence order of the fragment. The total defines the number of fragments that comprise the original message. The following is an example of a message with three fragments:

```
Content-Type: message/partial;
id="forouzan@challenger.atc.fhda.edu";
number=1;
total=3;
```

```
. . . . . . . . . . . . . . . . . . . . . . .
. . . . . . . . . . . . . . . . . . . . . . .
```

The subtype external-body indicates that the body does not contain the actual message, but is only a reference (pointer) to the original message. The parameters following the subtype define how to access the original message. The following is an example:

```
Content-Type: message/external-body;
name="report.txt";
site="fhda.edu";
access-type="ftp";
```

```
. . . . . . . . . . . . . . . . . . . . . . .
. . . . . . . . . . . . . . . . . . . . . . .
```

■ **Image.** The original message is a stationary image, indicating that there is no animation. The two currently used subtypes are Joint Photographic Experts Group (*JPEG*), which uses image compression, and Graphics Interchange Format (*GIF*).

■ **Video.** The original message is a time-varying image (animation). The only subtype is Motion Picture Experts Group (*MPEG*). If the animated image contains sounds, it must be sent separately using the audio content type.

■ **Audio.** The original message is a sound. The only subtype is basic, which uses 8 KHz standard audio data.

■ **Application.** The original message is a type of data not previously defined. There are only two subtypes used currently: *octet-stream* and *PostScript*. Octet-stream is used when the data must be interpreted as a sequence of eight-bit bytes (binary file). PostScript is used when the data is in Adobe PostScript format for printers that support PostScript.

Content-Transfer-Encoding

This header defines the method to encode the messages into 0s and 1s for transport:

Content-Transfer-Encoding: <type>

The five types of encoding are listed in Table 20.4.

Table 20.4 *Content-transfer-encoding*

Type	Description
7bit	NVT ASCII characters and short lines
8bit	Non-ASCII characters and short lines
binary	Non-ASCII characters with unlimited-length lines

Table 20.4   *Content-transfer-encoding (concluded)*

Type	Description
Base64	Six-bit blocks of data are encoded into eight-bit ASCII characters
Quoted-printable	Non-ASCII characters are encoded as an equal sign followed by an ASCII code

- **7bit.** This is seven-bit NVT ASCII encoding. Although no special transformation is needed, the length of the line should not exceed 1,000 characters.

- **8bit.** This is eight-bit encoding. Non-ASCII characters can be sent, but the length of the line still should not exceed 1,000 characters. MIME does not do any encoding here; the underlying SMTP protocol must be able to transfer eight-bit non-ASCII characters. It is, therefore, not recommended. Base64 and quoted-printable types are preferable.

- **Binary.** This is eight-bit encoding. Non-ASCII characters can be sent, and the length of the line can exceed 1,000 characters. MIME does not do any encoding here; the underlying SMTP protocol must be able to transfer binary data. It is, therefore, not recommended. Base64 and quoted-printable types are preferable.

- **Base64.** This is a solution for sending data made of bytes when the highest bit is not necessarily zero. Base64 transforms this type of data to printable characters, which can then be sent as ASCII characters or any type of character set supported by the underlying mail transfer mechanism.

    Base64 divides the binary data (made of streams of bits) into 24-bit blocks. Each block is then divided into four sections, each made of six bits (see Figure 20.20).

Figure 20.20   *Base64*

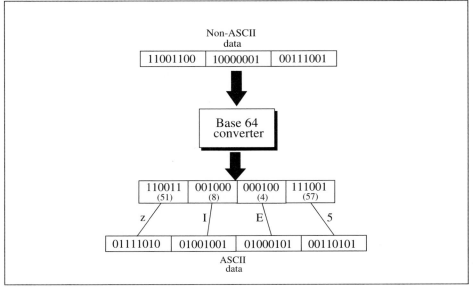

Each six-bit section is interpreted as one character according to Table 20.5.

Table 20.5   *Base64 encoding table*

Value	Code	Value	Code	Value	Code	Value	Code	Value	Code	Value	Code
0	A	11	L	22	W	33	h	44	s	55	3
1	B	12	M	23	X	34	i	45	t	56	4
2	C	13	N	24	Y	35	j	46	u	57	5
3	D	14	O	25	Z	36	k	47	v	58	6
4	E	15	P	26	a	37	l	48	w	59	7
5	F	16	Q	27	b	38	m	49	x	60	8
6	G	17	R	28	c	39	n	50	y	61	9
7	H	18	S	29	d	40	o	51	z	62	+
8	I	19	Y	30	e	41	p	52	0	63	/
9	J	20	U	31	f	42	q	53	1		
10	K	21	V	32	g	43	r	54	2		

■ **Quoted-printable.** Base64 is a redundant encoding scheme; that is, 24 bits becomes four characters, and eventually sent as 32 bits. We have an overhead of 25 percent. If the data consist of mostly ASCII characters with a small non-ASCII portion, we can use quoted-printable encoding. If a character is ASCII, it is sent as is. If a character is not ASCII, it is sent as three characters. The first character is the equal sign (=). The next two characters are the hexadecimal representation of the byte. Figure 20.21 shows an example.

Figure 20.21   *Quoted-printable*

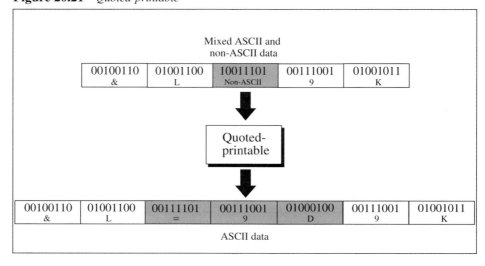

Content-Id

This header uniquely identifies the whole message in a multiple message environment.

Content-Id: id=<content-id>

Content-Description

This header defines whether the body is image, audio, or video.

Content-Description: <description>

20.9   POST OFFICE PROTOCOL (POP)

SMTP expects the destination host, the mail server receiving the mail, to be on-line all the time; otherwise, a TCP connection cannot be established. For this reason, it is not practical to establish an SMTP session with a desktop computer because desktop computers are usually powered down at the end of the day.

In many organizations, mail is received by an SMTP server that is always on-line. This SMTP server provides a mail-drop service. The server receives the mail on behalf of every host in the organization. Workstations interact with the SMTP host to retrieve messages by using a client-server protocol such as Post Office Protocol, version 3 (POP3). POP3 uses the TCP well-known port 110.

Although POP3 is used to download messages from the server, the SMTP client is still needed on the desktop to forward messages from the workstation user to its SMTP mail server (see Figure 20.22).

Figure 20.22   *POP3 and SMTP*

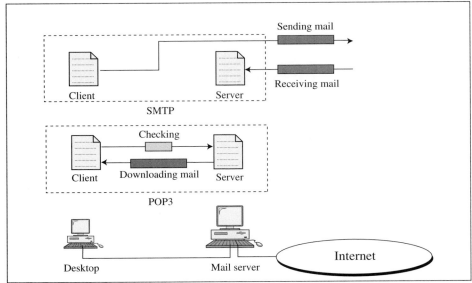

20.10   SUMMARY

- The TCP/IP protocol that supports e-mail on the Internet is called Simple Mail Transfer Protocol (SMTP).
- Both SMTP client and server require a user agent (UA) and a mail transfer agent (MTA).
- The UA prepares the message, creates the envelope, and puts the message in the envelope.
- The mail address consists of two parts: a local address (user mailbox) and a domain name. The form is localname@domainname.
- A mail gateway translates mail formats.
- Delivery of SMTP messages can be delayed at the sender site, the receiver site, or at intermediate servers.
- An alias allows one user to have multiple e-mail addresses or many users to share the same e-mail address.
- The MTA transfers the mail across the Internet.
- Sendmail is a commonly used UNIX system MTA.
- SMTP uses commands and responses to transfer messages between an MTA client and an MTA server.
- The steps in transferring a mail message are:
  a. connection establishment
  b. mail transfer
  c. connection termination
- Multipurpose Internet Mail Extension (MIME) is an extension of SMTP that allows the transfer of multimedia messages.
- Post Office Protocol (POP) is a protocol used by a mail server in conjunction with SMTP to receive and hold mail for hosts.

20.11   PRACTICE SET

Multiple Choice

1. The purpose of the UA is _____.
   a. message preparation
   b. envelope creation
   c. transferal of messages across the Internet
   d. a and b
2. The purpose of the MTA is _____.
   a. message preparation
   b. envelope creation

   c. transferal of messages across the Internet

   d. a and b

3. When a message is sent using SMTP _____ UAs are involved.

   a. only one

   b. only two

   c. only three

   d. at least two

4. E-mail cannot be sent _____.

   a. if the sending site does not use TCP/IP

   b. if the receiving site does not use TCP/IP

   c. through private networks

   d. none of the above

5. Which part of the mail created by the UA contains the sender and receiver addresses?

   a. envelope

   b. message

   c. header

   d. body

6. Which part of the mail created by the UA contains the sender and receiver names?

   a. envelope

   b. message

   c. header

   d. body

7. Hosts in a LAN that send and receive e-mail are called _____.

   a. mail spools

   b. mail gateways

   c. mail files

   d. mail exchangers

8. A _____ can transform non-SMTP mail to SMTP format and vice versa.

   a. mail spools

   b. mail gateways

   c. mail files

   d. mail exchangers

9. In the mail address mackenzie@pit.arc.nasa.gov what is the domain name?

   a. mackenzie

   b. pit.arc.nasa.gov

   c. mackenzie@pit.arc.nasa.gov

   d. a and b

10. Delayed delivery means that delivery of e-mail is delayed at _____.

   a. the sender site

b. the receiver site

c. the intermediate server

d. any of the above

11. The _____ is a storage structure that can hold outgoing mail.

a. MTA

b. alias expander

c. spool

d. mail exchanger

12. A very common MTA in use is _____.

a. Sendmail

b. Eudora

c. MIME

d. all of the above

13. This command identifies the recipient of the mail.

a. HELO

b. MAIL FROM

c. RCPT TO

d. RSET

14. This command identifies the sender of the mail.

a. HELO

b. MAIL FROM

c. RCPT TO

d. VRFY

15. This command identifies the client host.

a. HELO

b. MAIL FROM

c. RCPT TO

d. RSET

16. In the _____ command, mail is not delivered if the recipient is not logged on.

a. EXPN

b. SEND

c. SMOL

d. SMAL

17. In the _____ command, mail is delivered only to the terminal if the recipient is logged on.

a. EXPN

b. SEND

c. SMOL

d. SMAL

18. In the _____ command, mail is delivered to the terminal and mailbox if the recipient is logged on.
    a. EXPN
    b. SEND
    c. SMOL
    d. SMAL

19. A _____ reply is sent in response to a successfully completed command.
    a. positive completion
    b. positive intermediate
    c. transient negative completion
    d. permanent negative completion

20. A _____ reply is sent in response to a rejected command that cannot be resent.
    a. positive completion
    b. positive intermediate
    c. transient negative completion
    d. permanent negative completion

21. MIME allows _____ data to be sent through SMTP.
    a. audio
    b. non-ASCII data
    c. image
    d. all of the above

22. The _____ field in the MIME header is useful for mail with multiple messages.
    a. content-type
    b. content-transfer-encoding
    c. content-Id
    d. content-description

23. The _____ field in the MIME header uses text to describe the data in the body of the message.
    a. content-type
    b. content-transfer-encoding
    c. content-Id
    d. content-description

24. The _____ field in the MIME header describes the method used to encode the data.
    a. content-type
    b. content-transfer-encoding
    c. content-Id
    d. content-description

25. The _____ field in the MIME header has type and subtype subfields.
    a. content-type

    b. content-transfer-encoding

    c. content-Id

    d. content-description

26. A JPEG image is sent as e-mail. What is the content-type?

    a. multipart/mixed

    b. multipart/image

    c. image/JPEG

    d. image/basic

27. An e-mail contains a textual birthday greeting, a picture of a cake, and a song. The text must precede the image. What is the content-type?

    a. multipart/mixed

    b. multipart/parallel

    c. multipart/digest

    d. multipart/alternative

28. An e-mail contains a textual birthday greeting, a picture of a cake, and a song. The order is not important. What is the content-type?

    a. multipart/mixed

    b. multipart/parallel

    c. multipart/digest

    d. multipart/alternative

29. A message is fragmented into three mail messages. What is the content-type?

    a. multipart/mixed

    b. message/rfc822

    c. message/partial

    d. multipart/partial

30. A client machine powers off at the end of the day. It probably needs _____ to receive e-mail.

    a. only SMTP

    b. only POP

    c. both SMTP and POP

    d. none of the above

31. A client machine usually needs _____ to send e-mail.

    a. only SMTP

    b. only POP

    c. both SMTP and POP

    d. none of the above

Exercises

32. Give an example of a situation in which a one-to-many alias expander would be useful. Do the same for a many-to-one alias expander.

33. Are the HELO and MAIL FROM commands both necessary? Why or why not?

34. In Figure 20.16 what is the difference between MAIL FROM in the envelope and the FROM in the header?

35. Why is a connection establishment for mail transfer needed if TCP has already established a connection?

36. Show the connection establishment phase from aaa@xxx.com to bbb@yyy.com.

37. Show the message transfer phase from aaa@xxx.com to bbb@yyy.com. The message is "Good morning my friend."

38. Show the connection termination phase from aaa@xxx.com to bbb@yyy.com.

39. User aaa@xxx.com sends a message to user bbb@yyy.com, which is forwarded to user ccc@zzz.com. Show all SMTP commands and responses.

40. User aaa@xxx.com sends a message to user bbb@yyy.com. The latter replies. Show all SMTP commands and responses.

41. In SMTP, if we send a one-line message between two users, how many lines of commands and responses are exchanged?

42. A sender is sending unformatted text. Show the MIME header.

43. A sender is sending a JPEG message. Show the MIME header.

44. A non-ASCII message of 1,000 bytes is encoded using base64. How many bytes are in the encoded message? How many bytes are redundant? What is the ratio of redundant bytes to the total message?

45. A message of 1,000 bytes is encoded using quoted-printable. The message consists of 90 percent ASCII and 10 percent non-ASCII characters. How many bytes are in the encoded message? How many bytes are redundant? What is the ratio of redundant bytes to the total message?

46. Compare the results of exercises 44 and 45. How much is the efficiency improved if the message is a combination of ASCII and non-ASCII characters?

47. Encode the following message in base64:

    01010111 00001111 11110000 10101111 01110001 01010100

48. Encode the following message in quoted-printable:

    01010111 00001111 11110000 10101111 01110001 01010100

49. Encode the following message in base64:

    01010111 00001111 11110000 10101111 01110001

50. Encode the following message in quoted-printable:

    01010111 00001111 11110000 10101111 01110001

CHAPTER 21

Simple Network Management Protocol (SNMP)

The Simple Network Management Protocol (SNMP) is a framework for managing devices in an internet using the TCP/IP protocol suite. It provides a set of fundamental operations for monitoring and maintaining an internet.

21.1 CONCEPT

SNMP uses the concept of manager and agent. That is, a manager, usually a host, controls and monitors a set of agents, usually routers (see Figure 21.1).

Figure 21.1 *SNMP concept*

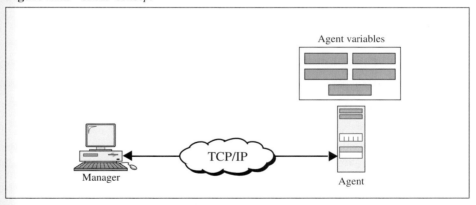

SMNP is an application-level protocol in which a few manager stations control a set of agents. The protocol is designed at the application level so that it can monitor devices made by different manufacturers and installed on different physical networks. In other words, SNMP frees management tasks from both the physical characteristics of the managed devices and the underlying networking technology. It can be used in a heterogeneous internet made of different LANs and WANs connected by routers or gateways made by different manufacturers.

Managers and Agents

A management station, called a *manager*, is a host that runs the SNMP client program. A managed station, called an *agent*, is a router (or a host) that runs the SNMP server program. Management is achieved through simple interaction between a manager and an agent.

The agent keeps performance information in a database. The manager has access to the values in the database. For example, a router can store in appropriate variables the number of packets received and forwarded. The manager can fetch and compare the values of these two variables to see if the router is congested or not.

The manager can also make the router perform certain actions. For example, a router periodically checks the value of a reboot counter to see when it should reboot itself. It reboots itself, for example, if the value of the counter is 0. The manager can use this feature to reboot the agent remotely at any time. It simply sends a packet to force a 0 value in the counter.

Agents can also contribute to the management process. The server program running on the agent can check the environment and, if it notices something unusual, it can send a warning message (called a *trap*) to the manager.

In other words, management with SNMP is based on three basic ideas:

1. A manager checks an agent by requesting information that reflects the behavior of the agent.
2. A manager forces an agent to perform a task by resetting values in the agent database.
3. An agent contributes to the management process by warning the manager of an unusual situation.

Components

Management in the Internet is achieved not only through the SNMP protocol but also by using other protocols that cooperate with SNMP. At the top level, management is accomplished with two other protocols: Structure of Management Information (SMI) and Management Information Base (MIB). SNMP uses the services provided by these two protocols to do its job. In other words, management is a team effort by SMI, MIB, and SNMP. All three use other protocols such as Abstract Syntax Notation 1 (ASN.1) and Basic Encoding Rules (BER). We discuss SMI, MIB, and SNMP in the next three sections (see Figure 21.2).

21.2   SMI

The SMI is a component used in network management. Its functions are:

1. To name objects.
2. To define the type of data that can be stored in an object.
3. To show how to encode data for transmission over the network.

SMI is a guideline for SNMP. It emphasizes three attributes to handle an object: name, data type, and encoding method (see Figure 21.3).

Figure 21.2 *Internet management components*

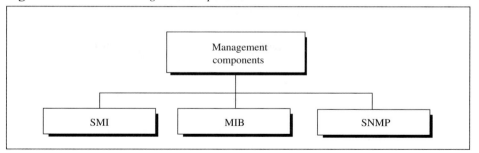

Figure 21.3 *Object attributes*

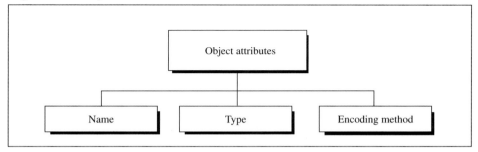

Name

SMI requires that each managed object (such as a router, a variable in a router, a value, etc.) have a unique name. To name objects globally, SMI uses an **object identifier,** which is a hierarchical identifier based on a tree structure (see Figure 21.4).

The tree structure starts with an unnamed root. Each object can be defined using a sequence of integers separated by dots. The tree structure can also define an object using a sequence of textual names separated by dots. However, the integer-dot representation is the one used in SNMP. The name-dot notation is used by humans. For example, the following shows the same object in two different notations:

iso.org.dod.internet.mgmt.mib <============> 1.3.6.1.2.1

The objects that are used in SNMP are located under the *mib* object, so their identifiers always start with 1.3.6.1.2.1.

Type

The second attribute of an object is the type of data stored in it. To define the data type, SMI uses some fundamental ASN.1 definitions but also adds some new definitions. In other words, SMI is both a subset and a superset of ASN.1.

Figure 21.4 *Object identifier*

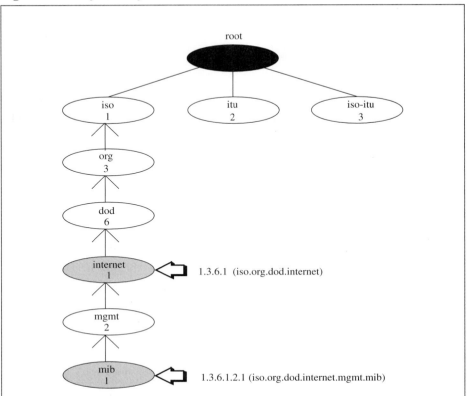

All objects managed by SNMP are given an object identifier. The object identifier always starts with 1.3.6.1.2.1.

SMI uses two broad categories of data type: *simple* and *structured*. We first define the simple types and then show how the structured types can be constructed from the simple ones (see Figure 21.5).

Figure 21.5 *Data type*

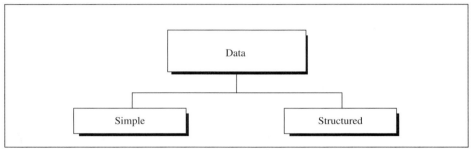

Simple Type

The simple types are atomic data types. Some of them are directly taken from ASN.1; some are added by SMI. The most important ones are given in Table 21.1. The first three are from ASN.1; the next four are defined by SMI.

Table 21.1   *Data types*

Type	Size	Description
Integer	4 bytes	A cardinal number between 0 and $2^{32}-1$
String	Variable	Zero or more ASCII characters
ObjectIdentifier	Variable	An object identifier represented in ASCII digits
IPAddress	4 bytes	An IP address made of four integers
Counter	4 bytes	An integer whose value can be incremented from zero to 4,294,967,295; when it reaches its maximum value it wraps back to zero
Gauge	4 bytes	Same as Counter, but when it reaches its maximum value, it does not wrap; it remains there until it is reset
TimeTicks	4 bytes	A counting value that records time in 1/100 seconds

Structured Type

By combining simple and structured data types, we can make new structured data types. SMI defines two structured data types: *sequence* and *sequence of*.

■ **Sequence.** A *sequence* data type is a combination of simple data types, not necessarily of the same type. It is analogous to the concept of a *struct* or a *record* used in programming languages such as C.

■ **Sequence of.** A *sequence of* data type is a combination of simple data types all of the same type or a combination of sequence data types all of the same type. It is analogous to the concept of an *array* used in programming languages such as C.

Figure 21.6 shows a conceptual view of data types.

Encoding Method

SMI uses another standard, Basic Encoding Rules (BER), to encode data to be transmitted over the network. BER specifies that each piece of data be encoded in triplet format: tag, length, and value, as illustrated in Figure 21.7.

■ **Tag.** The tag is a one-byte field that defines the type of data. It is composed of three subfields: *class* (two bits), *format* (one bit), and *number* (five bits).

The class subfield defines the scope of the data. Four classes are defined: universal (00), application-wide (01), context-specific (10), and private (11). The universal data types are those taken from ASN.1 (Integer, String, and ObjectIdentifier). The application-wide data types are those added by SMI (IPAddress, Counter, Gauge,

Figure 21.6 *Conceptual data types*

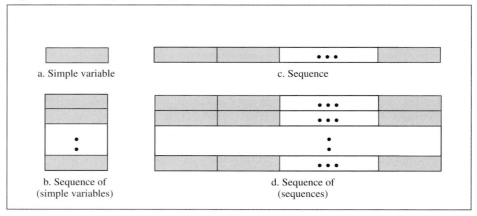

Figure 21.7 *Encoding format*

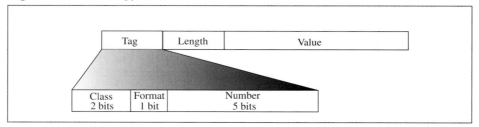

and TimeTicks). The five context-specific data types have meanings that may change from one protocol to another. The private data types are vendor-specific.

The format subfield indicates whether the data is simple (0) or structured (1). The number subfield further divides simple or structured data into subgroups. For example, in the universal class, with simple format, integer has a value of 2, string has a value of 4, and so on. Table 21.2 shows the data types we use in this chapter and their tags in binary and hexadecimal numbers.

Table 21.2 *Codes for data types*

Data Type	Class	Format	Number	Tag (Binary)	Tag (Hex)
Integer	00	0	00010	**00000010**	**02**
String	00	0	00100	**00000100**	**04**
ObjectIdentifier	00	0	00110	**00000110**	**06**
Sequence, sequence of	00	1	10000	**00110000**	**30**
IPAddress	01	0	00000	**01000000**	**40**
Counter	01	0	00001	**01000001**	**41**
Gauge	01	0	00010	**01000010**	**42**
TimeTicks	01	0	00011	**01000011**	**43**

- **Length.** The length field is one or more bytes. If it is one byte, the most significant bit must be 0. The other seven bits define the length of the data. If it is more than one byte, the most significant bit of the first byte must be 1. The other seven bits of the first byte define the number of bytes needed to define the length. See Figure 21.8 for a depiction of the length field.

Figure 21.8 *Length format*

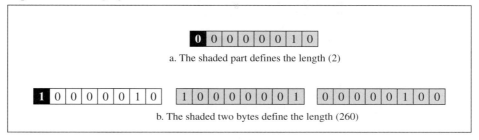

0 0 0 0 0 0 1 0
a. The shaded part defines the length (2)
1 0 0 0 0 0 1 0
1 0 0 0 0 0 0 1
0 0 0 0 0 1 0 0
b. The shaded two bytes define the length (260)

- **Value.** The value field codes the value of the data according to the rules defined in BER.

To show how these three fields—tag, length, and value— can define objects, we give some examples.

Example 1

Figure 21.9 shows how to define integer 14.

Figure 21.9 *Example 1, integer 14*

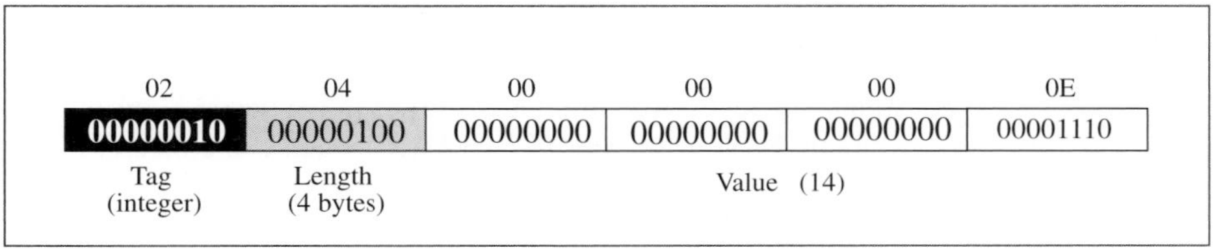

02
04
00
00
00
0E
00000010
00000100
00000000
00000000
00000000
00001110
Tag (integer)
Length (4 bytes)
Value (14)

Example 2

Figure 21.10 shows how to define the string "HI".

Figure 21.10 *Example 2, string "HI"*

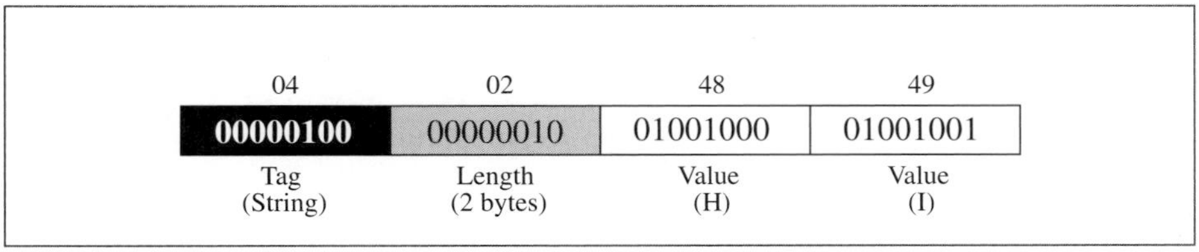

04
02
48
49
00000100
00000010
01001000
01001001
Tag (String)
Length (2 bytes)
Value (H)
Value (I)

Example 3

Figure 21.11 shows how to define object identifier 1.3.6.1 (iso.org.dod.internet).

Figure 21.11 *Example 3, ObjectIdentifier 1.3.6.1*

06
04
01
03
06
01
00000110
00000100
00000001
00000011
00000110
00000001
Tag (ObjectId)
Length (4 bytes)
Value (1)
Value (3)
Value (6)
Value (1)
1.3.6.1 (iso.org.dod.internet)

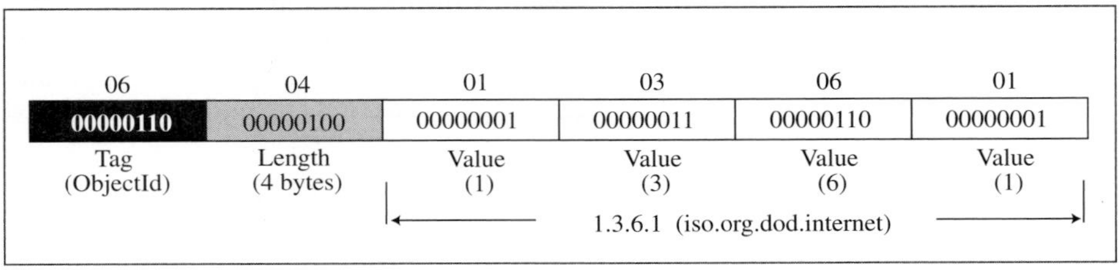

Example 4

Figure 21.12 shows how to define IP address 131.21.14.8.

Figure 21.12 *Example 4, IPAddress 131.21.14.8*

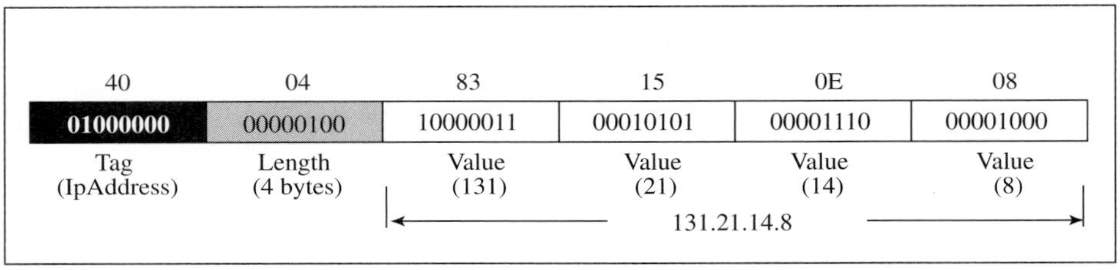

40
04
83
15
0E
08
01000000
00000100
10000011
00010101
00001110
00001000
Tag (IpAddress)
Length (4 bytes)
Value (131)
Value (21)
Value (14)
Value (8)
131.21.14.8

21.3 MIB

The Management Information Base (MIB) is the second component used in network management. Each agent has its own MIB, which is a collection of all the objects that the manager can manage. The objects in the MIB are categorized under eight different groups: system, interface, address translation, ip, icmp, tcp, udp, and egp. These groups are under the mib object in the object identifier tree (see Figure 21.13).

Figure 21.13 *MIB*

mib
1.3.6.1.2.1
sys 1
if 2
at 3
ip 4
icmp 5
tcp 6
udp 7
egp 8

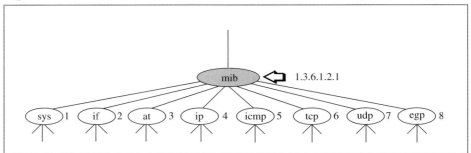

Each group has defined variables and/or tables. See Appendix F for the list of variables and tables.

Accessing MIB Variables

To show how to access different variables, we use the udp group as an example. There are four simple variables in the udp group and one sequence of (table of) records. Figure 21.14 shows the variables and the table.

Figure 21.14   *udp group*

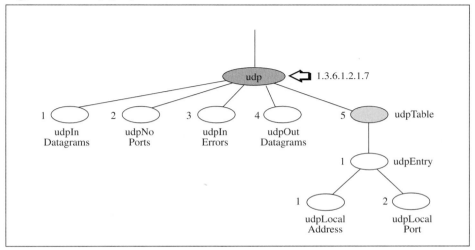

We will show how to access each entity.

Simple Variables

To access any of the simple variables, we use the id of the group (1.3.6.1.2.1.7) followed by the id of the variable. The following shows how to access each variable.

```
udpInDatagrams    ====>   1.3.6.1.2.1.7.1
udpNoPorts        ====>   1.3.6.1.2.1.7.2
udpInErrors       ====>   1.3.6.1.2.1.7.3
udpOutDatagrams   ====>   1.3.6.1.2.1.7.4
```

However, these object identifiers define the variable, not the instance (contents). To show the instance or the contents of each variable, we must add an instance suffix. The instance suffix for a simple variable is simply a zero. In other words, to show an instance of the above variables, we use the following:

```
udpInDatagrams.0    ====>   1.3.6.1.2.1.7.1.0
udpNoPorts.0        ====>   1.3.6.1.2.1.7.2.0
udpInErrors.0       ====>   1.3.6.1.2.1.7.3.0
udpOutDatagrams.0   ====>   1.3.6.1.2.1.7.4.0
```

Tables

To identify a table, we first use the table id. The udp group has only one table (with id 5) as illustrated in Figure 21.15.

Figure 21.15   *udp variables and tables*

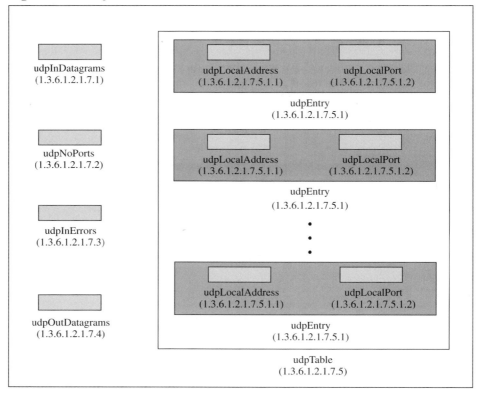

So to access the table, we should use the following:

udpTable ====> 1.3.6.1.2.1.7.5

However, the table is not at the leaf level in the tree structure. We cannot access the table; we define the entry (sequence) in the table (with id of 1), as follows:

udpEntry ====> 1.3.6.1.2.1.7.5.**1**

This entry is also not a leaf and we cannot access it. We need to define each entity (field) in the entry.

udpLocalAddress   ====> 1.3.6.1.2.1.7.5.**1.1**
udpLocalPort   ====> 1.3.6.1.2.1.7.5.**1.2**

These two variables are at the leaf of the tree. Although we can access their instances, we need to define *which* instance. At any moment, the table can have several values for each local address/local port pair. To access a specific instance (row) of the table, we should add the index to the above ids. In MIB, the indexes of arrays are not integers (like most programming languages). The indexes are based on the value of one or more fields in the entries. In our example, the udpTable is indexed based on both local address and local port number. For example, Figure 21.16 shows a table with four rows and values for each field. The index of each row is a combination of two values.

Figure 21.16   *Indexes for udpTable*

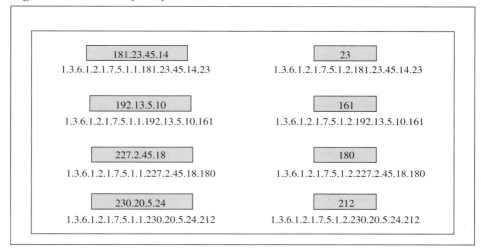

To access the instance of the local address for the first row, we use the identifier augmented with the instance index:

   udpLocalAddress.181.23.45.14.23   ====>   1.3.6.1.2.7.5.1.1.181.23.45.14.23

Note that not all tables are indexed the same way. Some tables are indexed using the value of one field, some using the value of two fields, and so on. See Appendix F for details.

Lexicographic Ordering

One interesting point about the MIB variables is that the object identifiers (including the instance identifiers) are in lexicographic order. Tables are ordered according to column-row rules, which means one should go column by column. In each column, one should go from the top to the bottom, as shown in Figure 21.17.

   The lexicographic ordering enables a manager to access a set of variables one after another by defining the first variable, as we will see in the GetNextRequest command in Section 21.4.

Figure 21.17   *Lexicographic ordering*

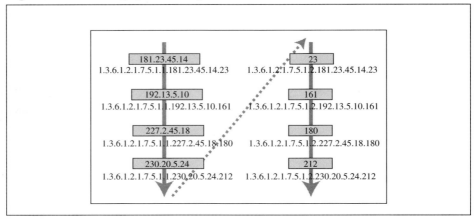

21.4   SNMP

The SNMP uses both SMI and MIB in Internet network management. It is an application program that allows:

1. A manager to retrieve the value of an object defined in an agent.
2. A manager to store a value in an object defined in an agent.
3. An agent to send an alarm message about an abnormal situation to the manager.

Messages

SNMP defines five messages: GetRequest, GetNextRequest, SetRequest, GetResponse, and Trap (see Figure 21.18).

Figure 21.18   *SNMP messages*

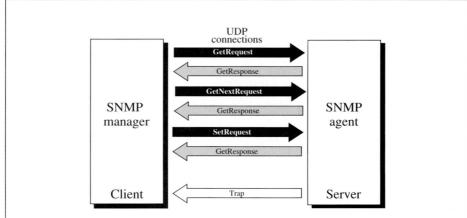

GetRequest

The GetRequest message is sent from the manager (client) to the agent (server) to retrieve the value of a variable.

GetNextRequest

The GetNextRequest message is sent from the manager to the agent to retrieve the value of a variable. The retrieved value is the value of the object following the defined ObjectId in the message. It is mostly used to retrieve the values of the entries in a table. If the manager does not know the indexes of the entries, it cannot retrieve the values. However, it can use GetNextRequest and define the ObjectId of the table. Because the first entry has the ObjectId immediately after the ObjectId of the table, the value of the first entry is returned. The manager can use this ObjectId to get the value of the next one, and so on.

GetResponse

The GetResponse message is sent from an agent to a manager in response to GetRequest and GetNextRequest. It contains the value of the variable(s) requested by the manager.

SetRequest

The SetRequest message is sent from the manager to the agent to set (store) a value in a variable.

Trap

The Trap message is sent from the agent to the manager to report an event. For example, if the agent is rebooted, it informs the manager and reports the time of rebooting.

Format

The format of the five messages is shown in Figure 21.19. Whereas the first four messages are similar in format, the Trap message is different. The fields for these messages are composed of the following:

- **Version.** This field defines the version number. Its value is actually the version number minus one. We currently use version 1 of SNMP, although version 2 has been proposed. The value of this field for our examples is 0.
- **Community.** This field defines the password. When there is no password, the value is the string "public."
- **Request ID.** This field is a sequence number used by the manager in a request message and repeated by the agent in the response. It is used to match a request to a response.

Figure 21.19 *SNMP message format*

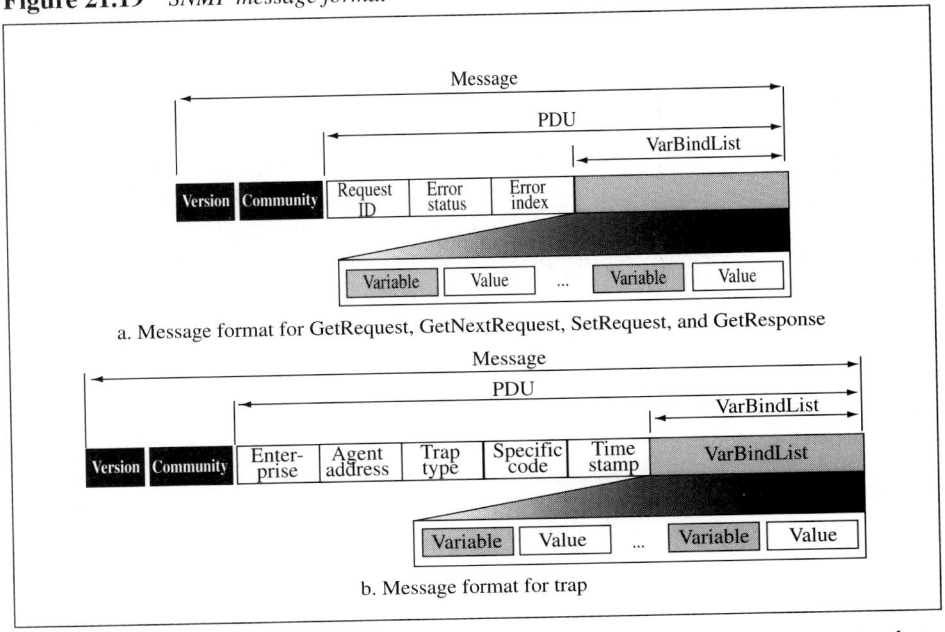

a. Message format for GetRequest, GetNextRequest, SetRequest, and GetResponse

b. Message format for trap

■ **Error status.** This is an integer that is used only in response messages to show the types of errors reported by the agent. Its value is 0 in request messages. Table Table 21.3 lists the types of errors that can occur.

Table 21.3 *Types of errors*

Status	Name	Meaning
0	noError	No error
1	tooBig	Response too big to fit in one message
2	noSuchName	Variable does not exist
3	badValue	The value to be stored is invalid
4	readOnly	The value cannot be modified
5	genErr	Other errors

■ **Error index.** The error index is an offset that tells the manager which variable caused the error.

■ **VarBindList.** This is a set of variables with the corresponding values the manager wants to retrieve or set. The values are null in GetRequest and GetNextRequest. In a Trap message, it shows the variables and values related to a specific message.

■ **Enterprise.** This field defines the ObjectId of the software package that generates the Trap.

■ **Agent address.** This defines the IP address of the agent that created the Trap.

■ **Trap type.** Seven trap types have been defined, as shown in Table 21.4.

Table 21.4 *Trap types*

Status	Name	Meaning
0	coldStart	Agent has been booted
1	warmStart	Agent has been rebooted
2	linkDown	An interface has gone down
3	linkUp	An interface has come up
4	authenticationFailure	Invalid community detected
5	egpNeighborLoss	An EGP router has gone to down state
6	enterpriseSpecific	Other messages

■ **Specific code.** If the value of Trap type is 6, this field defines the specific code used by the enterprise (vendor).

■ **Time stamp.** This shows the time elapsed since the event that caused the trap.

Encoding

To encode a message, SNMP uses the BER standard. First of all, messages are defined using tags. The class is context-sensitive (10), the format is structured (1), and the numbers are 0, 1, 2, 3, and 4 for the different types of messages (see Table 21.5).

Table 21.5 *Codes for SNMP messages*

Data	Class	Format	Number	Whole Tag (Binary)	Whole Tag (Hex)
GetRequest	10	1	00000	**10100000**	**A0**
GetNextRequest	10	1	00001	**10100001**	**A1**
GetResponse	10	1	00010	**10100010**	**A2**
SetRequest	10	1	00011	**10100011**	**A3**
Trap	10	1	00100	**10100100**	**A4**

A message is a combination of three elements: version, community, and Protocol Data Unit (PDU). The version is encoded as a triplet (tag, length, and value). The community is encoded as a triplet (tag, length, and value). The PDU contains the code for the type of PDU, the length, and the PDU data. The PDU data is made of a request id (triplet of tag, length, and value), an error status (the same), an error index (the same) and the VarBindList. The latter is a sequence of sequences (each a combination of variable and value). See Figure 21.20 for an illustration of encoding an SNMP message.

Figure 21.20 *Encoding SNMP message using BER*

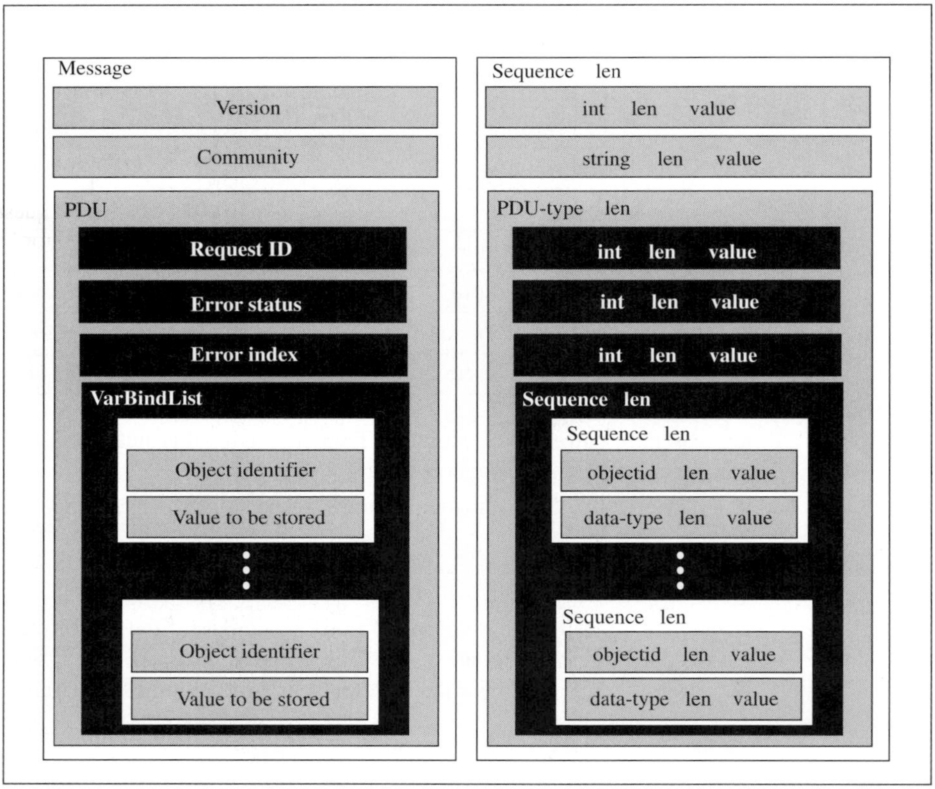

21.5 EXAMPLES

In this section, we show some examples of how SNMP works.

Example 1

In this example, a manager station (SNMP client) uses the GetRequest message to retrieve the number of UDP datagrams that a router has received. The agent (SNMP server) responds with a GetResponse message.

GetRequest Message

The GetRequest message is sent by the client (manager station). The manager wants to know how many UDP datagrams a specific router has received. The corresponding MIB variable related to this information is udpInDatagrams with the object identifier 1.3.6.1.2.1.7.1. The manager wants to retrieve a value (not to store a value), so the last section defines a null entity of value zero.

GetRequest Encoding for Example 1	
30 2A	Sequence of length $2A_{16}$
02 01 00	Integer of length 01_{16}, version=0
04 06 70 75 62 6C 69 63	String of length 06_{16}, "public"
A0 1D	GetRequest of length $1D_{16}$
02 04 00 01 06 11	Integer of length 04_{16}, Request ID=00010611_{16}
02 01 00	Integer of length 01_{16}, Error Status=00_{16}
02 01 00	Integer of length 01_{16}, Error Index=00_{16}
30 0F	Sequence of length $0F_{16}$
30 0D	Sequence of length $0D_{16}$
06 09 01 03 06 01 02 01 07 01 00	ObjectId of length 09_{16}, udpInDatagram
05 00	Null entity of length 00_{16}

Figure 21.21 shows the actual packet sent by the manager station (client) to the agent (server).

Figure 21.21   *GetRequest message*

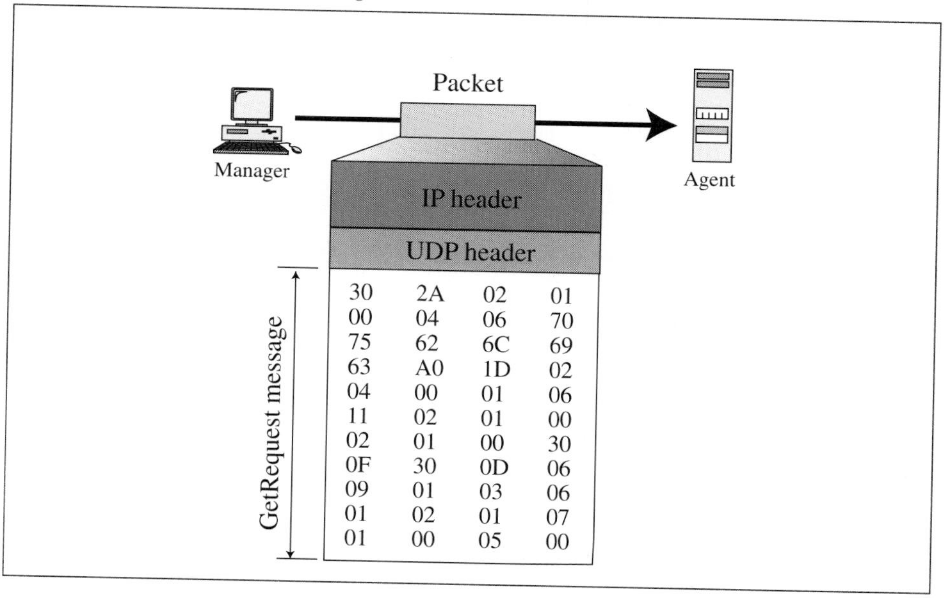

GetResponse Message

The GetResponse message is sent by the agent, which sends the number of received UDP datagrams. The corresponding MIB variable related to this piece of information is udpInDatagram with the object identifier 1.3.6.1.2.1.7.1. The VarBindList here is the object identifier followed by the value of the object.

GetResponse Encoding for Example 1	
30 2E	Sequence of length $2E_{16}$
02 01 00	Integer of length 01_{16}, version=0
04 06 70 75 62 6C 69 63	String of length 06_{16}, "public"
A2 21	GetResponse of length 21_{16}
02 04 00 01 06 11	Integer of length 04_{16}, Request ID=00010611_{16}
02 01 00	Integer of length 01_{16}, Error Status=00_{16}
02 01 00	Integer of length 01_{16}, Error Index=00_{16}
30 13	Sequence of length 13_{16}
30 11	Sequence of length 11_{16}
06 09 01 03 06 01 02 01 07 01 00	ObjectId of length 09_{16}, udpInDatagram
41 04 00 00 12 11	Counter of length 04 with the value 12 11

Example 2

In this example a manager station (SNMP client) uses the GetRequest message to retrieve the value of the subnet mask for IP address 12.44.66.71.

GetRequest Message

The GetRequest message should access the ipAddrTable, which has the id 1.3.6.1.2.1.4.21. However, the netmask (ipAdEntNetMask) is the third field in each record. So first the record must be accessed (1) and then the mask (3). The variable name thereby has the id 1.3.6.1.2.1.4.21.1.3. The table is indexed according to the IP addresses. To access the value of this variable, we add the index to the id. The resulting id is 1.3.6.1.2.1.4.21.1.3.12.44.66.71. The following shows the contents of the GetRequest message.

GetRequest Encoding for Example 2	
30 2F	Sequence of length $2F_{16}$
02 01 00	Integer of length 01_{16}, version=0
04 06 70 75 62 6C 69 63	String of length 06_{16}, "public"
A0 22	GetRequest of length 22_{16}
02 04 00 01 06 12	Integer of length 04_{16}, Request ID=00010612_{16}
02 01 00	Integer of length 01_{16}, Error Status=00_{16}
02 01 00	Integer of length 01_{16}, Error Index=00_{16}
30 14	Sequence of length 14_{16}
30 12	Sequence of length 10_{16}
06 0E 01 03 06 01 02 01 04 15 01 03 0C 2C 42 47	An objectId of length $0E_{16}$
05 00	Null entity of length 00_{16}

GetResponse Message

We leave the response as an exercise.

Example 3

In this example a manager station (SNMP client) uses the GetNextRequest message to retrieve all the interface numbers of a router (server) (see Appendix F). The client does not know the value of IP addresses corresponding to the interfaces, so it cannot access the ipAddrTable entries using indexes. Instead, it uses the GetNextRequest message and identifies the ipAddrTable to get the first value and then uses the value received to get the next value, and so on.

First GetNextRequest Message

For the first GetNextRequest message, the manager uses the object id 1.3.6.1.2.1.4.21.1.2. The id 1.3.6.1.2.1.4.21 defines the table. The id 1.3.6.1.2.1.4.21.1 defines the entry. The id 1.3.6.1.2.1.4.21.1.2 defines the ipAdEntIfInex. We leave the contents of the whole message as an exercise.

First GetResponse Message

The agent (router) responds with a GetResponse message. The agent checks the next lexicographic entity, which is 1.3.6.1.2.1.4.21.1.2.127.0.0.1 and returns the value of this variable. We leave the contents of the whole message as an exercise.

Second GetNextRequest Message

Now that the client has the id of the first object, it uses this to get the value of the next object. It uses a GetNextRequest message with object id 1.3.6.1.2.1.4.21.1.2.127.0.0.1. Again, we leave the contents of the message as an exercise.

Second GetResponse Message

The agent now sends the value of the next object with id 1.3.6.1.2.1.4.21.1.2.12.23.45.12.5.

Remainder of the GetNextRequest and Response Messages

The client uses the previous object id to get the value of the next object. This will continue until the client receives the value of an object for which it is not interested (for example, the first object in the next column).

Example 4

In this example an agent sends a Trap to a manager. A router has reinitialized itself and informs the manager with a Trap message.

Trap Message Encoding for Example 4	
30 28	Sequence of length 28_{16}
02 01 00	Integer of length 01_{16}, version=0
04 06 70 75 62 6C 69 63	String of length 06_{16}, "public"
A4 1B	Trap of length $1B_{16}$
06 07 01 03 06 01 04 12 12	ObjectId of length 07_{16}, Enterprise
06 04 12 08 23 07	ObjectId of length 04_{16}, Agent address
02 01 01	Integer of length 01_{16}, Trap type $=01_{16}$
02 01 00	Integer of length 01_{16}, Specific code=00_{16}
02 02 01 13	Integer of length 02_{16}, TimeStamp=0113_{16}
30 00	Sequence of length 00_{16}

21.6 UDP PORTS

SNMP uses the services of UDP on two well-known ports, 161 and 162. The well-known port 161 is used by the server (agent), and the well-known port 162 is used by the client (manager).

The agent (server) issues a passive open on port 161. It then waits for a connection from a manager (client). A manager (client) issues an active open using an ephemeral port. The request messages are sent from the client to the server using the ephemeral port as the source port and the well-known port 161 as the destination port. The response messages are sent from the server to the client using the well-known port 161 as the source port and the ephemeral port as the destination port.

The manager (client) issues a passive open on port 162. It then waits for a connection from an agent (server). An agent (server) issues an active open, using an ephemeral port, whenever it has a Trap message to send. This connection is only one-way, from the server to the client (see Figure 21.22).

The client-server mechanism in SNMP is different from other protocols. Here both the client and the server use well-known ports. In addition, both the client and the server should be running infinitely. The reason is that request messages are initiated by a manager (client), but Trap messages are initiated by an agent (server).

Figure 21.22   *Port numbers for SNMP*

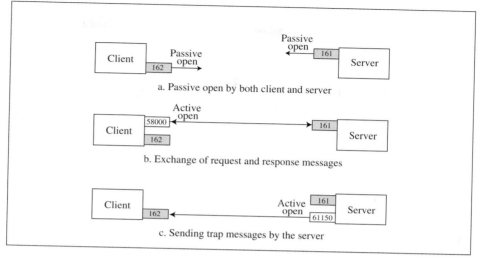

a. Passive open by both client and server

b. Exchange of request and response messages

c. Sending trap messages by the server

21.7   SUMMARY

- Simple Network Management Protocol (SNMP) is a framework for managing devices in an internet using the TCP/IP protocol suite.
- A manager, usually a host, controls and monitors a set of agents, usually routers.
- The manager is a host that runs the SNMP client program.
- The agent is a router or host that runs the SNMP server program.
- SNMP frees management tasks from both the physical characteristics of the managed devices and the underlying networking technology.
- SNMP uses the services of two other protocols: Structure of Management Information (SMI) and Management Information Base (MIB).
- SMI names objects, defines the type of data that can be stored in an object, and encodes the data.
- SMI objects are named according to a hierarchical tree structure.
- SMI data types are defined according to Abstract Syntax Notation 1 (ASN.1).
- SMI uses Basic Encoding Rules (BER) to encode data.
- MIB is a collection of groups of objects that can be managed by SNMP.
- MIB uses lexicographic ordering to manage its variables.
- SNMP functions in three ways:
  a. A manager can retrieve the value of an object defined in an agent.
  b. A manager can store a value in an object defined in an agent.
  c. An agent can send an alarm message to the manager.
- SNMP defines five messages: GetRequest, GetNextRequest, SetRequest, GetResponse, and Trap.

■   SNMP uses the services of UDP on two well-known ports, 161 and 162.

21.8   PRACTICE SET

Multiple Choice

1. Which of the following is associated with SNMP?
   a. MIB
   b. SMI
   c. BER
   d. all of the above

2. _____ runs the SNMP client program; _____ runs the SNMP server program.
   a. A manager; a manager
   b. An agent; an agent
   c. A manager; an agent
   d. An agent; a manager

3. Data types used by SNMP are defined by _____.
   a. BER
   b. SNMP
   c. ASN.1
   d. b and c

4. _____ names objects, defines the type of data that can be stored in an object, and encodes data for network transmission.
   a. MIB
   b. SMI
   c. SNMP
   d. ASN.1

5. Which of the following is a collection of objects to be managed?
   a. MIB
   b. SMI
   c. SNMP
   d. ASN.1

6. Integer, string, and object identifier are _____ definitions used by SMI.
   a. MIB
   b. SNMP
   c. ASN.1
   d. BER

7. Which of the following could be a legitimate MIB object identifier?
   a. 1.3.6.1.2.1.1

    b. 1.3.6.1.2.2.1

    c. 2.3.6.1.2.1.2

    d. 1.3.6.2.2.1.3

8. Which is a manager duty?

    a. Retrieve the value of an object defined in an agent.

    b. Store the value of an object defined in an agent.

    c. Send an alarm message to the agent.

    d. a and b

9. _____ specifies which data types are available for the MIB.

    a. BER

    b. SNMP

    c. ASN.1

    d. SMI

10. For a one-byte length field, what is the maximum value for the data length?

    a. 127

    b. 128

    c. 255

    d. 256

11. An object id defines a _____. Add a zero suffix to define the _____.

    a. variable; table

    b. table; variable

    c. variable; variable contents

    d. variable contents; variable

12. An SNMP agent can send _____ messages.

    a. GetRequest

    b. SetRequest

    c. GetNextRequest

    d. Trap

13. An SNMP manager can send _____ messages.

    a. GetRequest

    b. SetRequest

    c. GetNextRequest

    d. all of the above

14. An SNMP agent can send _____ messages.

    a. GetResponse

    b. GetRequest

    c. SetRequest

    d. GetNextRequest

15. The _____ field contains the password.

    a. community

    b. request id

    c. enterprise

    d. agent address

16. The _____ field contains a number that matches a request to a response.

    a. community

    b. request id

    c. enterprise

    d. agent address

17. The _____ field is an offset that points to the variable in error.

    a. community

    b. enterprise

    c. error status

    d. error index

18. The _____ field reports an error in a response message.

    a. community

    b. enterprise

    c. error status

    d. error index

19. The _____ field is only found in a Trap message.

    a. community

    b. enterprise

    c. error status

    d. error index

20. The _____ field is not found in a Trap message.

    a. community

    b. error status

    c. error index

    d. b and c

21. The _____ field consists of sequences of variable and value subfields.

    a. version

    b. community

    c. VarBindList

    d. agentAddress

22. A request message from the client to the server uses the _____ as the source port and the _____ as the destination port.

    a. ephemeral port; well-known port 162

    b. ephemeral port; well-known port 161

    c. well-known port 161; ephemeral port

    d. well-known port 162; ephemeral port

23. A response message from the server to the client uses the _____ as the source port and the _____ as the destination port.
    a. ephemeral port; well-known port 162
    b. ephemeral port; well-known port 161
    c. well-known port 161; ephemeral port
    d. well-known port 162; ephemeral port

24. A Trap message from the server to the client uses the _____ as the source port and the _____ as the destination port.
    a. ephemeral port; well-known port 162
    b. ephemeral port; well-known port 161
    c. well-known port 161; ephemeral port
    d. well-known port 162; ephemeral port

25. For SNMP version 1, the version field of a message consists of _____ bytes.
    a. 1
    b. 2
    c. 3
    d. 4

26. For a password of "public," the community field of a message consists of _____ bytes.
    a. 5
    b. 6
    c. 7
    d. 8

Exercises

27. Show the encoding for the integer 1456.
28. Show the encoding for the string "Hello World."
29. Show the encoding for an arbitrary string of length 1,000.
30. Show how the following record (sequence) is encoded.

Integer	String	IP Address
2345	"COMPUTER"	185.32.1.5

31. Show how the following record (sequence) is encoded.

Time Tick	Integer	Object Id
12000	14564	1.3.6.1.2.1.7

32. Show how the following array (sequence of) integers is encoded.

    2345
    1236
    122
    1236

33. Show how the following array of records (sequence of sequence) is encoded.

Integer	String	Counter
2345	"COMPUTER"	345
1123	"DISK"	1430
3456	"MONITOR"	2313

34. Decode the following:

    a. 02 04 01 02 14 32

    b. 30 06 02 01 11 02 01 14

    c. 30 09 04 03 41 43 42 02 02 14 14

    d. 30 0A 40 04 23 51 62 71 02 02 14 12

35. Show the encoding of the GetResponse message in Example 2.

36. Show the encoding of the first GetNextRequest message in Example 3.

37. Show the encoding of the first GetResponse message in Example 3.

38. A manager wants to know the value of icmpInParmProbs in a router (see Appendix F). Show the encoding of the GetRequest and GetResponse messages if the value is 167.

39. A manager wants to know the number of IP packets forwarded by a router. Show the encoding of the GetRequest and GetResponse messages if the value is 1,200.

40. A manager wants to know the subnet mask for IP address 13.67.34.2 used by a specific router. Show the encoded GetRequest and GetResponse messages if the value of the mask is 255.255.0.0.

41. A manager wants to know the subnet mask for all IP addresses used by a specific router. If there are only four entries in the table, show all encoded GetNextRequest and GetResponse messages.

42. An agent (router) wants to report that link 1,234 has gone down. Show the Trap message sent by this router. Choose an arbitrary enterprise.

CHAPTER 22

Hypertext Transfer Protocol (HTTP)

The Hypertext Transfer Protocol (HTTP) is a protocol used mainly to access data on the World Wide Web (see Chapter 23). The protocol transfers data in the form of plain text, hypertext, audio, video, and so on. However, it is called the hypertext transfer protocol because its efficiency allows its use in a hypertext environment where there are rapid jumps from one document to another.

HTTP functions like a combination of FTP and SMTP. It is similar to FTP because it transfers files and uses the services of TCP. However, it is much simpler than FTP because it uses only one TCP connection (well-known port 80). There is not a separate control connection; only data is transferred between the client and the server.

HTTP is like SMTP because the data transferred between the client and the server looks like SMTP messages. In addition, the format of the messages is controlled by MIME-like headers (see Chapter 20). However, HTTP differs from SMTP in the way the messages are sent from the client to the server and from the server to the client. Unlike SMTP, the HTTP messages are not destined to be read by humans; they are read and interpreted by the HTTP server and HTTP client (browser). SMTP messages are stored and forwarded, but the HTTP messages are delivered immediately.

The idea of HTTP is very simple. A client sends a request, which looks like mail, to the server. The server sends the response, which looks like a mail reply to the client. The request and response messages carry data in the form of a letter with MIME-like format.

The commands from the client to the server are embedded in a letterlike request message. The contents of the requested file or other information are embedded in a letterlike response message.

HTTP uses the services of TCP on well-known port 80.

551

22.1 HTTP TRANSACTION

Figure 22.1 illustrates the HTTP transaction between the client and server. Although HTTP uses the services of TCP, HTTP itself is a stateless protocol. The client initializes the transaction by sending a request message. The server replies by sending a response.

Figure 22.1 *HTTP transaction*

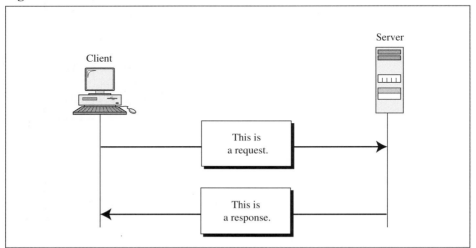

Messages

There are two general types of HTTP messages; these are shown in Figure 22.2.

Figure 22.2 *Message categories*

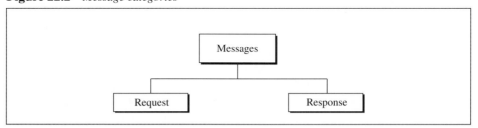

Both message types follow almost the same format.

22.2 REQUEST MESSAGES

A request message consists of a request line, a header, and sometimes a body. See Figure 22.3.

Figure 22.3 *Request message*

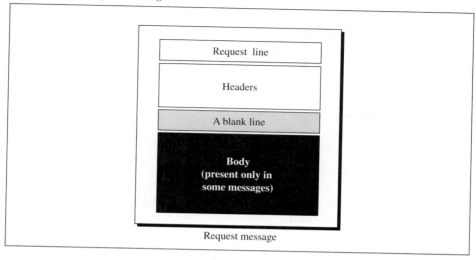

Request message

Request Line

The request line defines the request type, resource (URL), and HTTP version (see Figure 22.4). The request line consists of a request type, a space, a URL, a space, and HTTP version.

Figure 22.4 *Request line*

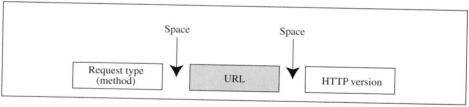

- **Request type.** In version 1.1 of HTTP, several request types are defined. The request type categorizes the request messages into several methods, which we will discuss later.

- **Uniform Resource Locator (URL).** A client that wants to access a Web page needs an address. To facilitate the access of documents distributed throughout the world, HTTP uses the concept of locators. The URL is a standard for specifying any kind of information on the Internet. The URL defines four things: method, host computer, port, and path (see Figure 22.5).

    The *method* is the protocol used to retrieve the document. Several different protocols can retrieve a document; among them are Gopher, FTP, HTTP, News, and TELNET.

Figure 22.5 *URL*

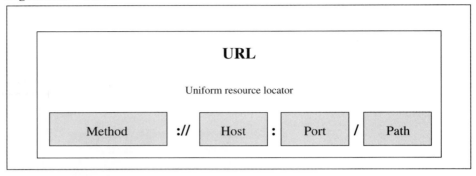

The *host* is the computer where the information is located, although the name of the computer can be an alias. Web pages are usually stored in computers, and computers are given alias names that usually begin with the characters "www". This is not mandatory, however, as the host can be any name given to the computer that hosts the Web page.

The URL optionally can contain the port number of the server. If the *port* is included, it should be inserted between the host and the path, and it should be separated from the host by a colon.

Path is the pathname of the file where the information is located. Note that the path can itself contain slashes that, in the UNIX operating system, separate the directories from the subdirectories and files.

■ **Version.** Although the most current version of HTTP is 1.1, HTTP versions 1.0 and 0.9 are still in use.

Methods

The request type field in a request message defines several kinds of messages referred to as *methods*. The request method is the actual command or request that a client issues to the server. We briefly discuss the purpose of some methods here.

GET

The GET method is used when the client wants to retrieve a document from the server. The address of the document is defined in the URL; this is the main method for retrieving a document. The server usually responds with the contents of the document in the body of the response message unless there is an error.

HEAD

The HEAD method is used when the client wants some information about a document but not the document itself. It is similar to GET, but the response from the server does not contain a body.

POST

The POST method is used when the client provides some information for the server. For example, it can be used to send input to a server.

PUT

The PUT method is used by the client to provide a new or replacement document to be stored on the server. The document is included in the body of the request and will be stored in the location defined by the URL.

PATCH

PATCH is similar to PUT except that the request contains only a list of differences that should be implemented in the existing file.

COPY

The COPY method is used to copy a file to another location. The location of the source file is given in the request line (URL); the location of the destination is given in the entity header.

MOVE

The MOVE method is used to move a file to another location. The location of the source file is given in the request line (URL); the location of the destination is given in the entity header.

DELETE

The DELETE method is used to remove a document on the server.

LINK

The LINK method is used to create a link or links from a document to another location. The location of the file is given in the request line (URL); the location of the destination is given in the entity header.

UNLINK

The UNLINK method is used to delete links created by the LINK method.

OPTION

The OPTION method is used by the client to ask the server about available options.

22.3   RESPONSE MESSAGE

A response message consists of a status line, a header, and sometimes a body. See Figure 22.6.

Figure 22.6 *Response message*

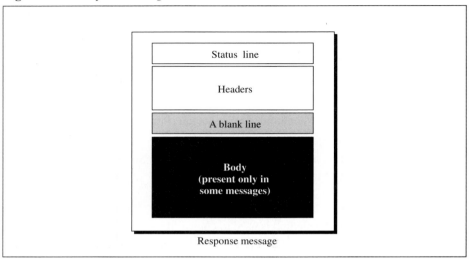

Response message

Status Line

The status line defines the status of the response message. It consists of the HTTP version, a space, a status code, a space, a status phrase. See Figure 22.7.

Figure 22.7 *Status line*

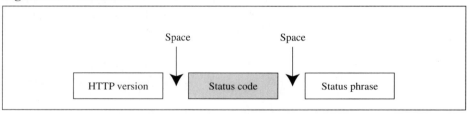

- **HTTP version.** This field is the same as the field in the request line.
- **Status code.** The status code field is similar to those in the FTP and the SMTP protocols. It consists of three digits. Whereas the codes in the 100 range are only informational, the codes in the 200 range indicate a successful request. The codes in the 300 range redirect the client to another URL, and the codes in the 400 range indicate an error at the client site. Finally, the codes in the 500 range indicate an error at the server site. We list the most common codes in Table 22.1.

Table 22.1   *Status codes*

Code	Phrase	Description
Informational		
100	Continue	The initial part of the request has been received and the client may continue with its request
101	Switching	The server is complying with a client request to switch protocols defined in the upgrade header
Success		
200	OK	The request is successful
201	Created	A new URL is created
202	Accepted	The request is accepted, but it is not immediately acted upon
204	No content	There is no content in the body
Redirection		
301	Multiple choices	The requested URL refers to more than one resource
302	Moved permanently	The requested URL is no longer used by the server
304	Moved temporarily	The requested URL has moved temporarily
Client Error		
400	Bad request	There is a syntax error in the request
401	Unauthorized	The request lacks proper authorization
403	Forbidden	Service is denied
404	Not found	The document is not found
405	Method not allowed	The method is not supported in this URL
406	Not acceptable	The format requested is not acceptable
Server Error		
500	Internal server error	There is an error, such as a crash, in the server site
501	Not implemented	The action requested cannot be performed
503	Service unavailable	The service is temporarily unavailable, but may be requested in the future

■   **Status phrase.** This field explains the status code in text form. Table 22.1 also gives the status phrase.

22.4 HEADER

The header exchanges additional information between the client and the server. For example, the client can request that the document be sent in a special format or the server can send extra information about the document.

The header can be one or more header lines. Each header line is made of a header name, a colon, a space, and a header value (see Figure 22.8). We will show some header lines in the examples at the end of this chapter.

Figure 22.8 *Header format*

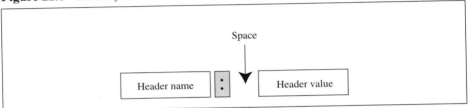

A header line belongs to one of four categories: general header, request header, response header, and entity header. A request message can contain only general, request, and entity headers. A response message, on the other hand, can contain only general, response, and entity headers. Figure 22.9 diagrams a request message and a response message.

Figure 22.9 *Headers*

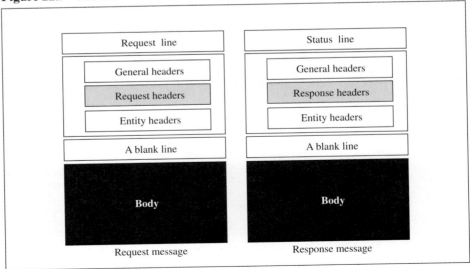

General Header

The general header gives general information about the message and can be present in both a request and a response. Table 22.2 list some general headers with their descriptions.

Table 22.2   *General headers*

Header	Description
Cache-control	Specifies information about caching
Connection	Shows whether the connection should be closed or not
Date	Shows the current date
MIME-version	Shows the MIME version used
Upgrade	Specifies the preferred communication protocol

Request Header

The request header can be present only in a request message. It specifies the client's configuration and the client's preferred document format. See Table 22.3 for a list of some request headers and their descriptions.

Table 22.3   *Request headers*

Header	Description
Accept	Shows the media format the client can accept
Accept-charset	Shows the character set the client can handle
Accept-encoding	Shows the encoding scheme the client can handle
Accept-language	Shows the language the client can accept
Authorization	Shows what permissions the client has
From	Shows the e-mail address of the user
Host	Shows the host and port number of the client
If-modified-since	Send the document if newer than specified date
If-match	Send the document only if it matches given tag
If-non-match	Send the document only if it does not match given tag
If-range	Send only the portion of the document that is missing
If-unmodified-since	Send the document if not changed since specified date
Referrer	Specifies the URL of the linked document
User-agent	Identifies the client program

Response Header

The response header can be present only in a response message. It specifies the server's configuration and special information about the request. See Table 22.4 for a list of some response headers with their descriptions.

Table 22.4   *Response headers*

Header	Description
Accept-range	Shows if server accepts the range requested by client
Age	Shows the age of the document
Public	Shows the supported list of methods
Retry-after	Specifies the date after which the server is available
Server	Shows the server name and version number

Entity Header

The entity header gives information about the body of the document. Although it is mostly present in response messages, some request messages, such as POST or PUT methods, that contain a body also use this type of header. See Table 22.5 for a list of some entity headers and their descriptions.

Table 22.5   *Entity headers*

Header	Description
Allow	List valid methods that can be used with a URL
Content-encoding	Specifies the encoding scheme
Content-language	Specifies the language
Content-length	Shows the length of the document
Content-range	Specifies the range of the document
Content-type	Specifies the media type
Etag	Gives an entity tag
Expires	Gives the date and time when contents may change
Last-modified	Gives the date and time of the last change
Location	Specifies the location of the created or moved document

22.5   EXAMPLES

In this section, we give three simple examples of request and response messages.

Example 1

This example retrieves a document. We use the GET method to retrieve an image with the path /usr/bin/image1. The request line shows the method (GET), the URL, and the HTTP version (1.1). The header has two lines that show that the client can accept images in the GIF and JPEG format. The request does not have a body. The response message contains the status line and four lines of header. The header lines define the date, server, MIME version, and length of the document. The body of the document follows the header (see Figure 22.10).

Figure 22.10   *Example 1*

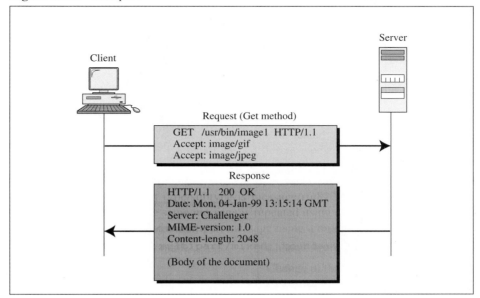

Example 2

This example retrieves information about a document. We use the HEAD method to retrieve information about an HTML document (see Chapter 23). The request line shows the method (HEAD), URL, and HTTP version (1.1). The header is one line showing that the client can accept the document in any format (wild card). The request does not have a body. The response message contains the status line and five lines of header. The header lines define the date, server, MIME version, type of document, and length of the document (see Figure 22.11). Note that the response message does not contain a body.

Example 3

In this example, the client wants to send input data to the server. We use the POST method. The request line shows the method (POST), URL, and HTTP version (1.1). There are four lines of headers. The request contains the input information in the body. The response message contains the status line and four lines of headers. The created document, which is a CGI document (see Chapter 23), is included as the body (see Figure 22.12).

Figure 22.11 *Example 2*

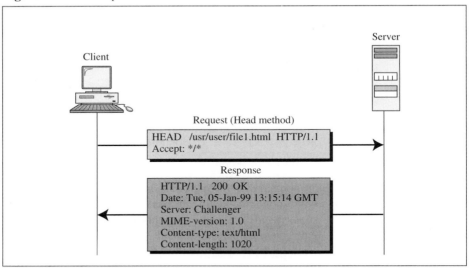

Figure 22.12 *Example 3*

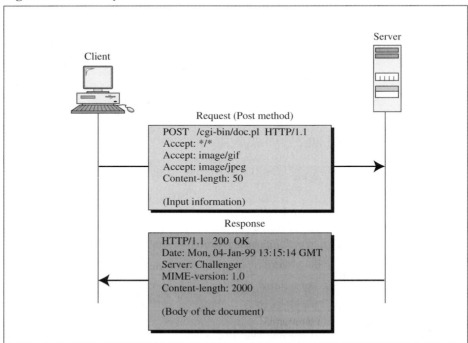

22.6   SUMMARY

■ The Hypertext Transfer Protocol (HTTP) is the main protocol used to access data on the World Wide Web (WWW).

■ HTTP uses a TCP connection to transfer files.

■ An HTTP message is similar in form to an SMTP message.

■ An HTTP message (request or response) consists of a request or status line, headers, and a body (required only for certain types of messages).

■ The request line consists of a request type, a URL, and the HTTP version number.

■ The Uniform Resource Locator (URL) consists of a method, host computer, optional port number, and pathname to locate information on the WWW.

■ The request type or method is the actual command or request issued by the client to the server.

■ The status line consists of the HTTP version number, a status code, and a status phrase.

■ The status code relays general information, information related to a successful request, redirection information, or error information.

■ The header relays additional information between the client and server.

■ A header consists of a header name and a header value.

■ A general header gives general information about the request or response message.

■ A request header specifies a client's configuration and preferred document format.

■ A response header specifies a server's configuration and special information about the request.

■ An entity header provides information about the body of a document.

22.7   PRACTICE SET

Multiple Choice

1. HTTP has similarities to both _____ and _____.
   a. FTP; SNMP
   b. FTP; SMTP
   c. FTP; MTV
   d. FTP; URL

2. A request message always contains _____.
   a. a header and a body
   b. a request line and a header
   c. a status line, a header, and a body
   d. a status line and a header

3. Which of the following is present in both a request line and a status line?

   a. HTTP version number

   b. URL

   c. status code

   d. status phrase

4. What does the URL need to access a document?

   a. pathname

   b. host computer

   c. retrieval method

   d. all of the above

5. Which of the following is a retrieval method?

   a. HTTP

   b. FTP

   c. TELNET

   d. all of the above

6. A user wants to replace a document with a newer version; the request line contains the _____ method.

   a. GET

   b. POST

   c. COPY

   d. PUT

7. A user wants to copy a file to another location; the request line contains the _____ method.

   a. PUT

   b. PATCH

   c. COPY

   d. POST

8. A user needs to retrieve a document from a remote system; the request line contains the _____ method.

   a. GET

   b. HEAD

   c. POST

   d. PUT

9. A user needs to send the server some information. The best request line method is _____.

   a. PUT

   b. PATCH

   c. MOVE

   d. POST

10. A user needs to move a file from the server to another location. The best request line method is _____.
    a. MOVE
    b. PUT
    c. GET
    d. PATCH

11. A response message always contains _____.
    a. a header and a body
    b. a request line and a header
    c. a status line, a header, and a body
    d. a status line and a header

12. Status codes that send the client to another URL are in the _____ range.
    a. 100
    b. 200
    c. 300
    d. 400

13. Status codes that indicate a successful request are in the _____ range.
    a. 100
    b. 200
    c. 300
    d. 400

14. Status codes that indicate a client error are in the _____ range.
    a. 100
    b. 200
    c. 300
    d. 400

15. The _____ header supplies information about the body of a document.
    a. general
    b. request
    c. response
    d. entity

16. The _____ header can specify the server configuration or provide information about a request.
    a. general
    b. request
    c. response
    d. entity

17. The _____ header can specify the client configuration and the client's preferred document format.
    a. general

  b. request

  c. response

  d. entity

Exercises

18. Show a request that retrieves the document /usr/users/doc/doc1. Use at least two general headers, two request headers, and one entity header.

19. Show the response to exercise 18 for a successful request.

20. Show the response to exercise 18 if the document has permanently moved to /usr/deads/doc1.

21. Show the response to exercise 18 if there is a syntax error in the request.

22. Show the response to exercise 18 if the client is unauthorized to access the document.

23. Show a request that asks for information about a document at /bin/users/file. Use at least two general headers and one request header.

24. Show the response to exercise 23 for a successful request.

25. Show the request to copy the file at location /bin/usr/bin/file1 to /bin/file1.

26. Show the response to exercise 25.

27. Show the request to delete the file at location /bin/file1.

28. Show the response to exercise 27.

29. Show a request to retrieve the file at location /bin/etc/file1. The client needs the document only if it was modified after January 23, 1999.

30. Show the response to exercise 29.

31. Show a request to retrieve the file at location /bin/etc/file1. The client should identify itself.

32. Show the response to exercise 31.

33. Show a request to store a file at location /bin/letter. The client should identify the types of documents it can accept.

34. Show the response to exercise 33. The response should show the age of the document as well as the date and time when the contents may change.

CHAPTER 23

World Wide Web (WWW)

The **World Wide Web** (WWW) is a repository of information spread all over the world and linked together. The WWW has a unique combination of flexibility, portability, and user-friendly features that distinguish it from other services provided by the Internet.

The WWW project was initiated by CERN (European Laboratory for Particle Physics) to create a system to handle distributed resources necessary for scientific research.

The WWW today is a distributed client-server service, in which a client using a browser can access a service using a server. However, the service provided is distributed over many locations called *Web sites* (see Figure 23.1).

23.1 HYPERTEXT AND HYPERMEDIA

The WWW uses the concept of hypertext and hypermedia. In a hypertext environment, information is stored in a set of documents that are linked together using the concept of pointers. An item can be associated with another document using a pointer. The reader who is browsing through the document can move to other documents by choosing (clicking) the items that are linked to other documents. Figure 23.2 shows the concept of hypertext.

Whereas hypertext documents contain only text, hypermedia documents can contain pictures, graphics, and sound.

A unit of hypertext or hypermedia available on the Web is called a *page*. The main page for an organization or an individual is known as a *homepage*.

Information about one specific subject can be undistributed or distributed. In the first case, all of the information may consist of one or more Web pages on the same server. In the second case, the information is made of multiple pages distributed on different servers.

567

Figure 23.1 *Distributed services*

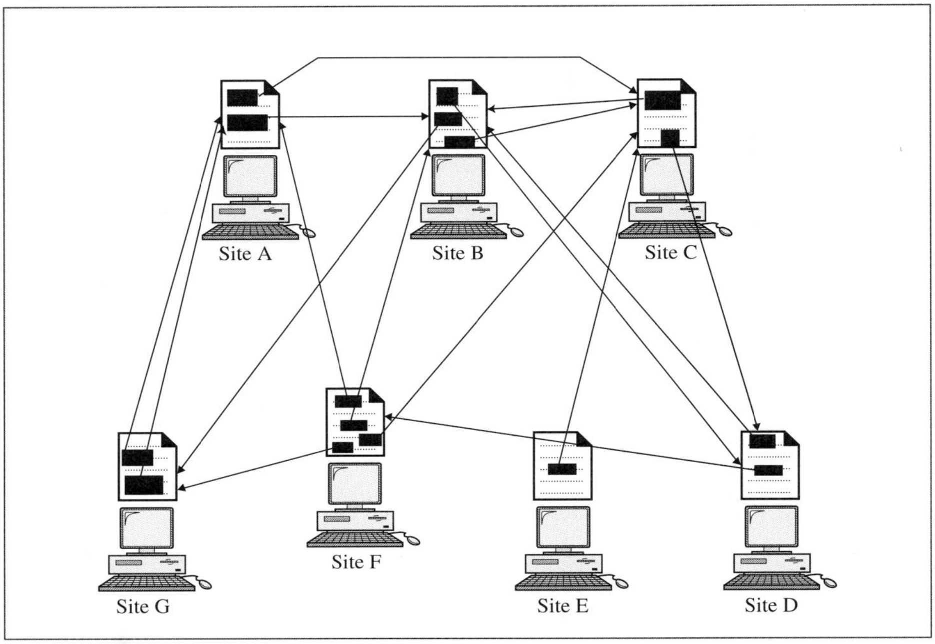

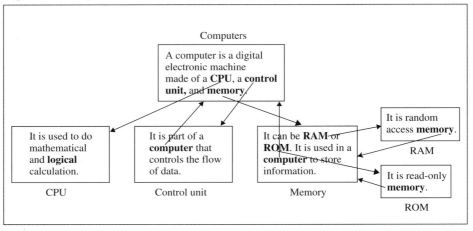

Site A
Site B
Site C
Site F
Site G
Site E
Site D

Figure 23.2 *Hypertext*

Computers

A computer is a digital electronic machine made of a **CPU**, a **control unit,** and **memory.**

It is used to do mathematical and **logical** calculation.

CPU

It is part of a **computer** that controls the flow of data.

Control unit

It can be **RAM** or **ROM**. It is used in a **computer** to store information.

Memory

It is random access **memory**.

RAM

It is read-only **memory**.

ROM

23.2   BROWSER ARCHITECTURE

A variety of vendors offer commercial browsers that interpret and display a Web document, and all of them use nearly the same architecture. Each browser usually consists of three parts: a controller, client programs, and interpreters. The controller receives input from the keyboard or the mouse and uses the client programs to access the document. After the document has been accessed, the controller uses one of the interpreters to display the document on the screen. The client programs can be one of the methods (protocols) described previously such as HTTP, FTP, Gopher, or TELNET. The interpreter can be HTML or Java, depending on the type of document (see Figure 23.3).

Figure 23.3   *Browser architecture*

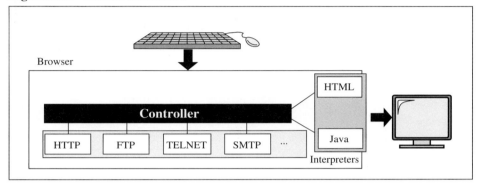

The documents in the WWW can be grouped into three broad categories: static, dynamic, and active (see Figure 23.4). The category is based on the time the contents of the document are determined.

Figure 23.4   *Categories of Web documents*

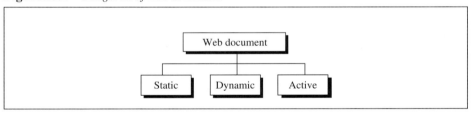

23.3   STATIC DOCUMENTS

Static documents are fixed-content documents that are created and stored in a server. The client can get only a copy of the document. In other words, the contents of the file are determined when the file is created, not when it is used. Of course, the contents in the server can be changed, but the user cannot change it. When a client accesses the document, a copy of the document is sent. The user can then use a browsing program to display the document (see Figure 23.5).

23.4   HTML

HyperText Markup Language (HTML) is a language for creating Web pages. The term *markup language* comes from the book publishing industry. Before a book is

Figure 23.5 *Static document*

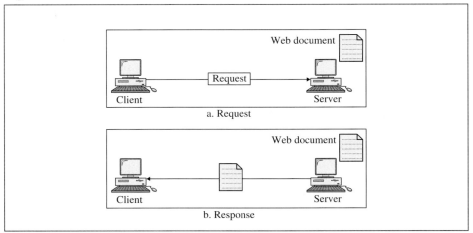

a. Request

b. Response

typeset and printed, a copy editor reads the manuscript and puts a lot of marks on it. These marks tell the designer how to format the text. For example, if the copy editor wants part of a line to be printed in boldface, he or she draws a wavy line under that part. In the same way, data for a Web page is formatted for interpretation by a browser.

Let us explain the idea with an example. To make part of a text displayed in boldface with HTML, we must include the beginning and ending boldface tags (marks) in the text as shown in Figure 23.6.

Figure 23.6 *Boldface tags*

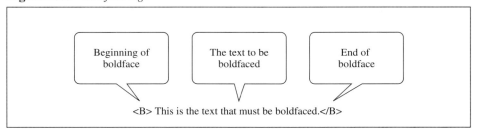

The two tags <B> and </B> are instructions for the browser. When the browser sees these two marks, it knows that the text must be boldfaced (see Figure 23.7).

A markup language such as HTML allows us to embed formatting instructions in the file itself. The instructions are stored with the text. In this way, any browser can read the instructions and format the text according to the workstation being used. One might ask why we do not use the formatting capabilities of word processors to create and save formatted text. The answer is that different word processors use different techniques or procedures for formatting text. For example, imagine that a user creates formatted text on a Macintosh computer and stores it in a Web page. Another user who is on an IBM computer is not able to receive the Web page because the two computers are using different formatting procedures.

Figure 23.7   *Effect of boldface tags*

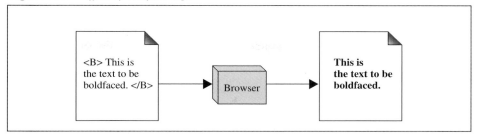

HTML lets us use only ASCII characters for both the main text and formatting instructions. In this way, every computer can receive the whole document as an ASCII document. The main text is the data, and the formatting instructions can be used by the browser to format the data.

Structure of a Web Page

A Web page is made up of two parts: the head and body.

Head

The head is the first part of a Web page. The head contains the title of the page and other parameters that the browser will use.

Body

The actual contents of a page are in the body, which includes the text and the tags. Whereas the text is the actual information contained in a page, the tags define the appearance of the document. Every HTML tag is a name followed by an optional list of attributes, all enclosed between less-than and greater-than brackets.

An attribute, if present, is followed by an equal sign and the value of the attribute. Some tags can be used alone; some must be used in pairs. Those that are used in pairs are called *starting* and *ending* tags. The starting tag can have attributes and values. The ending tag cannot have attributes or values but must have a slash before the name.

Tags

The browser makes a decision about the structure of the text based on the tags, which are marks that are embedded into the text. A tag is enclosed in two brackets (< and >) and usually comes in pairs. The beginning tag starts with the name of the tag, and the ending tag starts with a slash followed by the name of the tag.

A tag can have a list of attributes, each of which can be followed by an equal sign and a value associated with the attribute. Figure 23.8 shows the format of a tag.

Figure 23.8 *Beginning and ending tags*

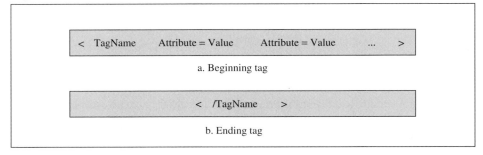

Table 23.1 shows some of the most common tags. We explain some of these tags based on their category.

Table 23.1 *Common tags*

Beginning Tag	Ending Tag	Meaning
Skeletal Tags		
<HTML>	</HTML>	Defines an HTML document
<HEAD>	</HEAD>	Defines the head of the document
<BODY>	</BODY>	Defines the body of the document
Title and Header Tags		
<TITLE>	</TITLE>	Defines the title of the document
<Hi>	</Hi>	Defines different headers (i is an integer)
Text Formatting Tags		
<B>	</B>	Boldface
<I>	</I>	Italic
<U>	</U>	Underlined
_		Subscript
[	]	Superscript
Data Flow Tags		
<CENTER>	</CENTER>	Centered
 		Line break
List Tags		
<OL>	</OL>	Ordered list
<UL>	</UL>	Unordered list
<LI>	</LI>	An item in a list
Image Tags		
<IMG>		Defines an image

Table 23.1   *Common tags (concluded)*

Beginning Tag	Ending Tag	Meaning
Hyperlink Tags		
<A>	</A>	Defines an address (hyperlink)
Executable Contents		
<APPLET>	</APPLET>	The document is an applet

Skeletal Tags

Skeletal tags show the skeleton of the document and show how it is divided into a head and body.

■ **<HTML> and </HTML>.** Every HTML document must start and finish with these two tags. They are the signals to the browser that an HTML document is embedded between these two tags.

■ **<HEAD> and </HEAD>.** The head contains information about the document itself. The head must be defined using the two head tags.

■ **<BODY> and </BODY>.** The body of the page contains the actual information. The body is encapsulated between the two body tags.

Title and Header Tags

The following tags are used to show titles or headers.

■ **<TITLE> and </TITLE>.** The title of the page is usually embedded in the head. The title is encapsulated between the two title markers. The title may or may not be displayed or printed when the page is accessed by the browser.

■ **<Hn> and </Hn>.** Headers are inserted into a page by using header tags. We can create different levels of headers, with each in a different font size. The header marker is the character H followed by a digit. For example H1 creates the biggest header, H2 is the second level header, and so on.

Text Formatting Tags

The following tags are used to recommend the format of the text.

■ **<B> and </B>.** The text between these tags should be bold.

■ **<I> and </I>.** The text between these tags should be italic.

■ **<U> and </U>.** The text between these tags should be underlined.

■ **_{and}.** The text between these tags should be subscript.

■ **^{and}.** The text between these tags should be superscript.

Data Flow Tags

The following tags are used to control the flow of data.

■ **
.** This tag inserts a line break into the text.

■ **<CENTER> and </CENTER>.** The text enclosed between these tags should be centered.

List Tags

The following tags are used to create a list of items.

■   **<UL > and </UL>.** We often need to create a list of items. HTML has a mechanism to create several types of lists. The simplest of these is the unordered list, in which items are listed one after another with a bullet in front. To create a list, use the <UL> tag at the beginning and the </UL> tag at the end of the list. Each item listed must be preceded by the <Li> tag.

■   **<OL > and </OL>.** These tags are similar to <UL> and </UL> except that the items in the list are numbered instead of bulleted.

■   **<LI> and </LI>.** These tags define an item in a list. The ending tag is usually omitted.

Image Tags

The following tag is used to insert a figure in the document.

■   **<IMG......>.** Nontextual information such as digitized photos or graphic images are not a physical part of an HTML document. But we can use an image tag to point to the file of the photo or image. The image tag defines the address of the image to be retrieved (a URL). It also specifies how the image can be inserted after retrieval. The following shows the format of the image tag. We can choose from among several attributes. The most common are SRC (source), which defines the source (address), and ALIGN, which defines the alignment of the image. The SRC attribute is required. Most browsers accept images in the GIF or JPEG formats.

<IMG   SRC= "............"   ALIGN=............. ....>

For example, the following tag can retrieve an image stored as image1.gif in the directory /bin/images:

<IMG   SRC="/bin/images/image1.gif"   ALIGN=MIDDLE >

Hyperlink Tags

The following tags are used to allow one document to be linked to another.

■   **<A......> and </A>.** A hypertext markup language needs to link documents together. Any item (word, phrase, paragraph, or image) can refer to another document. A mechanism called an *anchor* does this job. The anchor is defined by <A.....> and </A> tags, and the anchored items use the URL to refer to another document. When the document is displayed, the anchored items are underlined, blinking, or boldfaced. The user can click on the anchored item to go to another document, which may or may not be stored on the same server as the original document.

The following shows the format of the anchor tags. The reference phrase is embedded between the beginning and ending tags. The beginning tag can have several attributes, but the one required is the HREF (hyperlink reference), which defines the address (URL) of the linked document.

<A HREF="......................" >   Ref-Phrase   </A>

For example, to link to the author of a book we might see:

<A HREF= "http://www.deanza/somebody"> Author </A>

What appears in the text is the word "Author", on which the user can click to go to the author's Web page.

Executable Contents Tags

The executable contents tags show that the contents enclosed between the two tags are binary code or bytecode. They should be executed to create the output. We discuss only the tags that define a document as an applet (see the section on Java).

■   **<APPLET...> and </APPLET>.** These tags define the document as an **applet**, a small program written in Java language. Several attributes can be used with applet tags; we show only the most common ones.

> **<APPLET   CODE=.....   HEIGHT=.....   WIDTH=......>**
>
> ....
> ....
> ....
> **</APPLET>**

We will see how these tags are used when we discuss Java applets.

Examples

In this section, we give some simple examples of HTML documents to show the implementation of the tags previously described.

Example 1

This simple example shows how the skeletal tags are used to define the parts of an HTML document.

First HTML Program
<HTML>
<HEAD>
<TITLE>
First Sample Document
</TITLE>
</HEAD>
<BODY>
The body of the first sample program
....
....
</BODY>
</HTML>

Example 2

This example shows how tags are used to let the browser format the appearance of the text.

Second HTML Program

```
<HTML>
      <HEAD>
              <TITLE> Second Sample Document </TITLE>
      </HEAD>
      <BODY>
              <CENTER>
              <H1><B>  ATTENTION </B></H1>
              </CENTER>
               You can get a copy of this document by:
              <UL>
              <LI> Writing to the publisher
              <LI> Ordering on-line
              <LI> Ordering through a bookstore
              </UL>
      </BODY>
</HTML>
```

Example 3

This example shows how tags are used to import an image and insert it into the text.

Third HTML Program

```
<HTML>
      <HEAD>
              <TITLE> Third Sample Document </TITLE>
      </HEAD>
      <BODY>
          This is the picture of a book:
          <IMG SRC="Pictures/book1.gif"   ALIGN=MIDDLE>
      </BODY>
</HTML>
```

Example 4

This example shows how tags are used to make a hyperlink to another document.

Fourth HTML Program
| ```
<HTML>
      <HEAD>
            <TITLE> Fourth Sample Document </TITLE>
      </HEAD>
      <BODY>
         This is a wonderful product that can save you money and time.
         To get information about the producer, click on
         <A HREF="http://www.phony.producer">
         Producer </A>
      </BODY>
</HTML>
``` |

23.5 DYNAMIC DOCUMENTS

Dynamic documents do not exist in a predefined format. Instead, a dynamic document is created by a Web server whenever a browser requests the document. When a request arrives, the Web server runs an application program that creates the dynamic document. The server returns the output of the program as a response to the browser that requested the document. Because a fresh document is created for each request, the contents of a dynamic document can vary from one request to another. A very simple example of a dynamic document is getting the time and date from the server. Time and date are kinds of information that are dynamic in that they change from moment to moment. The client can request that the server run a program such as the *date* program in UNIX and send the result of the program to the client. Figure 23.9 illustrates the steps in sending and responding to a dynamic document.

A server that handles dynamic documents follows these steps:

1. The server examines the URL to find if it defines a dynamic document.
2. If the URL defines a dynamic document, the server executes the program.
3. It sends the output of the program to the client (browser).
```

Figure 23.9   *Dynamic document*

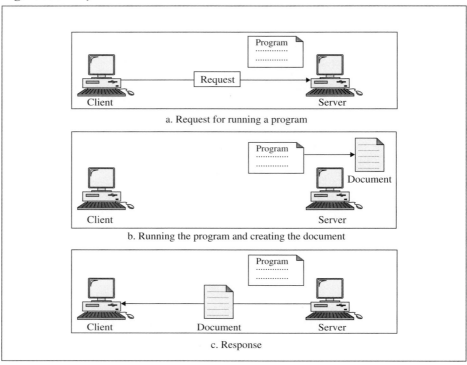

a. Request for running a program

b. Running the program and creating the document

c. Response

23.6   COMMON GATEWAY INTERFACE (CGI)

Common Gateway Interface (CGI) is a technology that creates and handles dynamic documents. CGI is a set of standards that defines how a dynamic document should be written, how input data should be supplied to the program, and how the output result should be used.

CGI is not a new language; instead, it allows programmers to use any of several languages such as C, C++, Bourne Shell, Korn Shell, C Shell, Tcl, or Perl. The only thing that CGI defines is a set of rules and terms that the programmer should follow.

The use of "common" in CGI indicates that the standard defines a set of rules that are common to any language or platform. The term "gateway" here means that a CGI program is a gateway that can be used to access other resources such as databases, graphic packages, and so on. The term "interface" here means that there are a set of predefined terms, variables, calls, and so on that can be used in any CGI program.

CGI Program

A CGI program in its simplest form is code written in one of the languages supporting the CGI. Any programmer that can encode a sequence of thoughts in a program and knows the syntax of one of the above-mentioned languages can write a simple CGI program.

Environment Variables

To answer queries from a browser and access resources, a CGI program uses a list of environment variables. These environment variables either inherit their values from the parent process or the values are supplied by the browser (input). Table 23.2 shows the list.

Table 23.2   *Environment variable in CGI*

Beginning Tag	Meaning
AUTH_TYPE	Authentication method used to validate a user
CONTENT_LENGTH	The length of data passed to CGI
CONTENT_TYPE	The MIME type of the query data
DOCUMENT_ROOT	Directory of the Web document
GATEWAY_INTERFACE	Version of CGI
HTTP_ACCEPT	A list of MIME types that client can accept
HTTP_FORM	E-mail address of the user
HTTP_REFERER	URL of the document pointed to by the client
HTTP_USER_AGENT	Name of the client program (browser)
PATH_INFO	Extra path information given by URL
PATH_TRANSLATED	Translation of the contents of PATH_INFO
QUERY_STRING	Input information supplied by the user
REMOTE_ADDR	IP address of the client
REMOTE_HOST	Name of the client
REMOTE_IDENT	Username of the user
REMOTE_USER	Authenticated name of the user
SCRIPT_NAME	Path of the script being executed
SERVER_NAME	Server name or IP address
SERVER_PORT	Port number of the server
SERVER_PROTOCOL	Name and version of protocol used to receive request
SERVER_SOFTWARE	Name and version of the protocol used to send response

Input

In traditional programming, when a program is executed, parameters can be passed to the program. Parameter passing allows the programmer to write a generic program that can be used in different situations. For example, a generic copy program can be written to copy any file to another. A user can use the program to copy a file named *x* to another file named *y* by passing *x* and *y* as parameters.

The input from a browser to a server is sent using a *form*. If the information in a form is small (such as a word), it can be appended to the URL after a question mark. For example, the following URL is carrying form information (file1, the name of a file):

http://www.deanza/cgi-bin/prog.pl?file1

When the server receives the URL, it uses the part of the URL before the question mark to access the program to be run, and it interprets the part after the question mark ("file1") as the input sent by the client. It stores this string in an environment variable called QUERY_STRING. When the CGI program is executed, it can access this value.

If input from a browser is too long to fit in the query string, the browser can request the server to send a form. The browser can then fill the form with the input data and send it to the server. The information in the form can be used as the input to the CGI program.

Output

The whole idea of CGI is to execute a CGI program at the server site and send the output to the client (browser). The output is usually plain text or a text with HTML structures; however, the output can be a variety of other things. It can be graphics or binary data, a status code, instructions to the browser to cache the result, or instructions to the server to send an existing document instead of the actual output.

To tell the client the type of document sent, a CGI program should create headers. As a matter of fact, the output of the CGI program always consists of two parts: a header and a body. The header is separated by a blank line from the body. This means any CGI program first creates the header, then a blank line, and then the body. Although the header and the blank line are not shown on the browser screen, the header is used by the browser to interpret the body.

Several different headers are defined for the output from a CGI program. They are similar to the MIME headers discussed in Chapter 20. We briefly list some common ones here.

- **CONTENT_LENGTH.** This defines the length of the output data in bytes. It is normally defined for binary data (graphics, for example). For example, a program with the header *CONTENT_LENGTH: 2000* means that the output contains 2,000 bytes of binary data.

- **CONTENT_TYPE.** This defines the type of the output data. For example, a program with the header *CONTENT_TYPE: text/plain* contains plain text while *CONTENT-TYPE: text/html* contains HTML text.

- **EXPIRES.** This shows the date and time when the document is no longer valid.

- **LOCATION.** This shows the redirection. (We will discuss redirection later.)

- **PRAGMA.** This turns document caching on and off.

- **STATUS.** This shows the status of the request.

Redirection

The output of a CGI program can be the address of a file. This is called *redirection*. The output of the program can be an address to redirect the request to a static document. The browser can now use the address (URL) to fetch that static document.

Examples

In this section, we have given some examples of CGI programming that show the concept and idea. Programs are written in different languages to show the reader that CGI is language independent.

Example 1

Example 1 is a CGI program written in Bourne shell script. The program accesses the UNIX utility (*date*) that returns the date and the time. Note that the program output is in plain text.

First Example of CGI
| ```
#!/bin/sh
# The head of the program
echo Content_type: text/plain
echo
# The body of the program
now='date'
echo  $now
exit 0
``` |

Example 2

Example 2 is similar to Example 1 except that program output is in HTML.

Second Example of CGI
| ```
#!/bin/sh
#  The head of the program
echo Content_type: text/html
echo
#  The body of the program
echo <HTML>
echo <HEAD><TITLE> Date and Time </TITLE></HEAD>
echo <BODY>
now='date'
echo <CENTER><B> $now </B></CENTER>
echo </BODY>
echo </HTML>
exit 0
``` |

Example 3
Example 3 is similar to Example 2 except that the program is written in Perl.

Third Example of CGI

```
#!/bin/perl
# The head of the program
print  "Content_type: text/html\n" ;
print "\n" ;
# The body of the program
print "<HTML>\n" ;
print "<HEAD><TITLE> Date and Time </TITLE></HEAD>\n" ;
print "<BODY>\n" ;
$now = 'date';
print "<CENTER><B>  $now </B></CENTER>\n" ;
print "</BODY>\n" ;
print "</HTML>\n"
exit 0
```

Example 4
Example 4 creates information about the server and returns it to the client.

Fourth Example of CGI

```
#!/bin/perl
# The head of the program
print  "Content/type: text/html\n" ;
print "\n" ;
# The body of the program
print "<HTML>\n" ;
print "<HEAD><TITLE> Server Information </TITLE></HEAD>\n" ;
print "<BODY>\n" ;
print " Server name:" , $ENV {'SERVER_NAME'}, "\n" ;
print " Port Number:" , $ENV {'SERVER_PORT'}, "\n" ;
print "</BODY>\n" ;
print "</HTML>\n" ;
exit 0
```

Example 5
Example 5 is a CGI program that requires user input. The program is written in C.

Fifth Example of CGI

```
#include <stdio.h>
#include <stdlib.h>
#include <string.h>
int main (void)
{
char  *query = getenv ("QUERY_STRING");
float balance;
printf ("Content_type: text/plain\n\n");
if (query == NULL)
      {
      printf ("Sorry,  you did not supply the name of the account.\n") ;
      printf ("To access the database, the account name is needed.\n") ;
      }
else
      {
      balance = Access_Balance (query) ;
      printf ("The balance is: %f\n", balance);
      }
return 0 ;
}
```

23.7   ACTIVE DOCUMENTS

For many applications, we need a program to be run at the client site. These are called
active documents. For example, imagine we want to run a program that creates animated graphics on the screen or interacts with the user. The program definitely needs to
be run at the client site where the animation or interaction takes place. When a browser
requests an active document, the server sends a copy of the document in the form of
bytecode. The document is then run at the client (browser) site (see Figure 23.10).

An active document in the server is stored in the form of binary code. However, it
does not create overhead for the server in the same way that a dynamic document does.
Although an active document is not run on the server, it is stored as a binary document
that it is retrieved by a client. When a client receives the document, it can also store it in
its own storage area. In this way, the client can run the document again without making
another request.

An active document is transported from the server to the client in binary form. This
means that it can be compressed at the server site and decompressed at the client site,
saving both bandwidth and transmission time.

Creation, Compilation, and Execution

The following steps show how an active document is created, compiled, and executed.

Figure 23.10   *Active document*

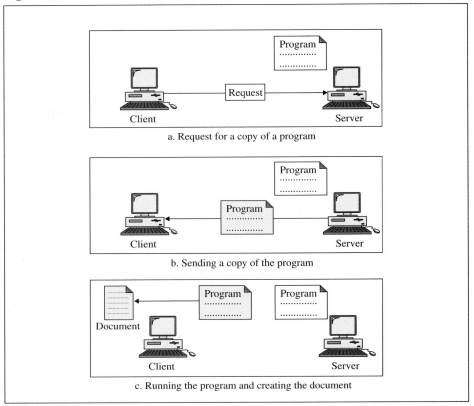

a. Request for a copy of a program

b. Sending a copy of the program

c. Running the program and creating the document

1. At the server site, a programmer writes a program, in source code, and stores it in a file.

2. At the server site, the program is compiled and binary code is created, which is stored in a file. The pathname of this file is the one used by a URL to refer to the file. In this file, each program command (statement) is in binary form and each identifier (variable, constants, function names, and so on) is referred to by a binary offset address.

3. A client (browser) requests a copy of the binary code, which is probably transported in compressed form from the server to the client (browser).

4. The client (browser) uses its own software to change the binary code into executable code. The software links all the library modules and makes it ready for execution.

5. The client (browser) runs the program and creates the result that can include animation or interaction with the user.

23.8   JAVA

Java is a combination of a high-level programming language, a run-time environment, and a class library that allows a programmer to write an active document and a browser to run it. It can also be used as a stand-alone program without using a browser. However, Java is mostly used to create an applet (a small application program).

Java is an object-oriented language which is, syntactically and semantically, very similar to C++. However, it does not have some of the complexities of C++ such as operator overloading or multiple inheritance. Java is also hardware independent and does not use pointers. In Java, like any other object-oriented language, a programmer defines a set of objects and a set of operations (methods) to operate on those objects. It is a *typed* language which means that the programmer must declare the type of any piece of data before using it. Java is also a concurrent language, which indicates the programmer can use multiple threads to create concurrency.

Classes and Objects

Java, as an object-oriented language, uses the concept of classes and objects. An object is an instance of a class that uses methods (procedures or functions) to manipulate encapsulated data.

Both data and methods can be either private or public. Public data can be accessed by any procedure or program outside the class definition. Private data, on the other hand, can be accessed only by methods defined inside the class. Public methods can be invoked by any procedure or program; private methods can be invoked only by the methods defined inside the class.

Instantiation

To use an object, a process should instantiate an object, which means it should create an instance of the object. The instance encapsulates a set of data defined in the class. The process can use any of the public methods to manipulate the data encapsulated in an object.

Inheritance

One of the main ideas in object-oriented programming is the concept of inheritance. Inheritance defines a hierarchy of objects, in which one object can inherit data and methods from other objects. In Java we can define a class as the base class that contains data and methods common to many classes. Inherited classes can inherit these data and methods and can also have their own data and methods.

Packages

Java has a rich library of classes, which allow the programmer to create and use different objects in an applet. The classes are organized in packages. Six packages are common in Java today: java.lang, java.io, java.net, java.util, java.applet, and java.awt.

- **java.lang.** This package contains methods such as threads and exception handling that are part of the language itself. Standard libraries such as mathematical and string functions are also included in this package.
- **java.io.** This package contains classes that handle input/output operations.
- **java.net.** This package contains classes that handle transmission of messages over the network. It contains methods for creating IP datagrams, accessing the socket interface, and so on.
- **java.util.** This package contains classes that handle common data structures such as stacks, vectors, time, date, and hash tables.
- **java.applet.** This package contains methods for getting and displaying Web pages. It also includes a very special class called an object class. This is an abstract class, from which all other objects are derived.
- **java.awt.** This is the Abstract Window Toolkit (AWT), which is a package designed to make the Java language portable. It contains classes and methods that make an applet capable of being run on any client environment. It contains classes and methods that enable an applet to draw on the screen. The java.awt package creates the necessary interface with the local operating system. Event handling (which includes detecting a keystroke, mouse motion, etc.) is also included in this package. This package includes two subpackages called *java.awt.image*, which manages images, and *java.awt.peer*, which is used to access the window system.

Skeleton of an Applet

An applet is a dynamic document written in Java. It is actually the definition of a publicly inherited class, which inherits from the applet class defined in the java.applet library. The programmer can define private data and public and private methods in this definition (see Figure 23.11).

Figure 23.11   *Skeleton of an applet*

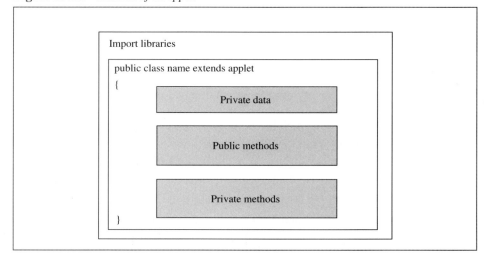

The client process (browser) creates an instance of this applet. The browser then uses the public methods defined in the applet to invoke private methods or to access data. Figure 23.12 shows this relationship.

Figure 23.12   *Instantiation of the object defined by an applet*

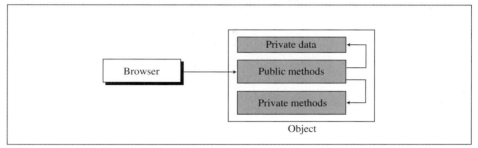

Creation and Compilation

To be used as an applet, the class definition is created using a text editor. The name of the file is the same as the name of the publicly inherited class with the "java" extension. The Java compiler creates bytecode out of this file, which has the same name with the "*class*" extension (see Figure 23.13).

HTML Document

To use the applet, an HTML document is created and the name of the applet is inserted between the <APPLET> tags. The tag also defines the size of the window used for the applet (see Figure 23.14).

Examples

In this section, we show some very simple examples of Java programs. The purpose is not to teach Java but to give some idea of how Java can be used to create active documents.

Example 1

In this example, we first import the two packages java.awt and java.applet. They contain the declarations and definitions of classes and methods that we need. Our example uses only one publicly inherited class called *First*. We define only one public method, *paint*. The browser can access the instance of First through the public method paint. The paint method, however, calls another method called *drawString*, which is defined in java.awt.*. Three parameters are passed to drawString: a string that we want to display, the x coordinate, and the y coordinate. The coordinates are measured from the top left of the browser window in pixels.

Figure 23.13 *Creation and compilation*

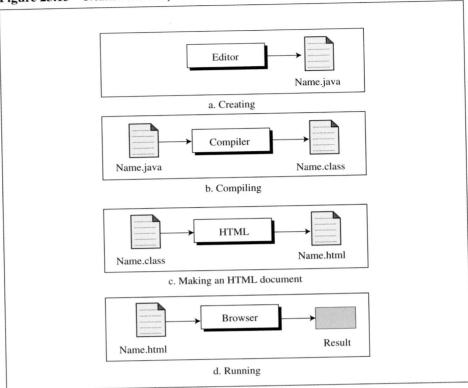

a. Creating

b. Compiling

c. Making an HTML document

d. Running

Figure 23.14 *HTML document carrying an applet*

```
<HTML>
    <APPLET   CODE = "Name.class"
    WIDTH = mmm
    HEIGHT = nnn  ....  >
    </APPLET >

</HTML>
```

First Example of Java

```
import java.applet.* ;
import java.awt.* ;

public class First extends Applet
{
    public void paint (Graphics  g)
    {
      g.drawString ("Hello World", 100, 100 ) ;
    }
}
```

Example 2

In this example, we modify the program in Example 1 to draw a line. Instead of method draw-String, we use another method called *drawLine*. This method needs four parameters, the x and y coordinates of the beginning of the line and the x and y coordinates of the end of the line. We use 0 and 0 for the beginning and 80 and 90 for the end.

Second Example of Java

```
import java.applet.* ;
import java.awt.* ;

public class Second extends Applet
{
    public void paint (Graphics  g)
    {
      g.drawLine (0, 0, 80, 90 ) ;
    }
}
```

Example 3

In this example, we modify the program in Example 2 to draw a rectangle. We use a method called *drawRect*. The drawRect method needs four parameters: The first two define the x and y coordinates of the top left corner of the rectangle, and the next two parameters define the width and the height. We also use two more methods to fill in the rectangle: The first method sets the color of filling; the second fills the rectangle we have drawn.

Third Example of Java

```
import java.applet.* ;
import java.awt.* ;

public class Third extends Applet
{
    public void paint (Graphics  g)
    {
      g.drawRect (30, 30, 80, 20 ) ;
      g.setColor (Color.black) ;
      g.fillRect (30, 30, 80, 20) ;
    }
}
```

Example 4

In this example, we draw a triangle given the coordinates of its corners. We define our own private method, called *drawTriangle*. We can use this method as many times as we want to draw different triangles in different places in the browser window.

Fourth Example of Java

```
import java.applet.* ;
import java.awt.* ;

public class Fourth extends Applet
{
        public void paint (Graphics  g)
        {
          g.drawTriangle (g, 10, 10, 10, 30, 50, 30 ) ;
          g.drawTriangle (g, 50, 30, 50, 10, 70, 10) ;
        }
        private void drawTriangle (Graphics g, int x1, int y1,
                                   int x2, int y2, int x3, int y3 )
        {
          g.drawLine (x1, y1, x2, y2 );
          g.drawLine (x2, y2, x3, y3 );
          g.drawLine (x3, y3, x1, y1 );
        }
}
```

Example 5

In all previous examples, only one public method, paint, was defined in the inherited class. This means that the browser can access the object defined by the inherited class, using only this method. Now we want to define other public methods that can be used by the browser to access the object. We use two new public methods: the *init* method that can create a new object on the screen (a scrollbar in this case) and the *handleEvent* method that is invoked by an event such as scrolling the scrollbar.

The init method creates the scrollbar. There are four numbers involved: the initial value, the increments, and the range (from and to). When the user scrolls the bar, the value associated with the bar is captured by the handleEvent method. This method uses the *repaint* method to "repaint" the value of the bar on the screen.

Fifth Example of Java

```java
import java.applet.* ;
import java.awt.* ;
public class Fifth extends Applet
{
    private Scrollbar  bar ;
    private int barValue = 0 ;

public void init ()

    {
    bar = new Scrollbar (Scrollbar.HORIZONTAL, 0, 2, 1, 100) ;
    add (bar) ;

    }


public void paint (Graphics  g)
    {
    g.drawString ("Value is " + barValue, 100, 100 ) ;
    }

public void boolean handleEvent (Event  e)

    {
    barValue = bar.getValue ( ) ;

    repaint () ;

    return true ;

    }

}
```

23.9   SUMMARY

■ The World Wide Web (WWW) is a repository of information spread all over the world and linked together.

- Hypertext and hypermedia are documents linked to one another through the concept of pointers.
- Browsers interpret and display a Web document.
- The hypertext transfer protocol (HTTP) is an advanced file-retrieving application program that can access distributed and linked documents on the WWW.
- A browser consists of a controller, client programs, and interpreters.
- A Web document can be classified as static, dynamic, or active.
- A static document is one in which the contents are fixed and stored in a server. The client can make no changes in the server document.
- HyperText Markup Language (HTML) is a language used to create static Web pages.
- Any browser can read formatting instructions (tags) embedded in an HTML document.
- A Web page has a head and a body.
- Tags provide structure to a document, define titles and headers, format text, control the data flow, insert figures, link different documents together, and define executable code.
- A dynamic Web document is created by a server only at a browser request.
- The Common Gateway Interface (CGI) is a standard for creating and handling dynamic Web documents.
- A CGI program with its embedded CGI interface tags can be written in a language such as C, C++, shell script, or Perl.
- The server receives input from a browser through a form.
- The server sends the output of the CGI program to the browser.
- The output of a CGI program can be text, graphics, binary data, status codes, instructions, or an address of a file.
- An active document is a copy of a program retrieved by the client and run at the client site.
- Java is a combination of a high-level programming language, a run-time environment, and a class library that allows a programmer to write an active document and a browser to run it.
- Java is used to create applets (small application programs).
- Java is an object-oriented typed language with a rich library of classes.

23.10 PRACTICE SET

Multiple Choice

1. Hypertext documents are linked through _____.
   a. DNS
   b. TELNET

   c. pointers

   d. homepages

2. Which of the following is not a retrieval method?

   a. gopher

   b. archie

   c. HTTP

   d. HTML

3. Which of the following is not an interpreter?

   a. HTTP

   b. HTML

   c. CGI

   d. Java

4. What are the components of a browser?

   a. retrieval method, host computer, pathname

   b. controller, client program, interpreter

   c. hypertext, hypermedia, HTML

   d. all of the above

5. Which type of Web document is run at the client site?

   a. static

   b. dynamic

   c. active

   d. all of the above

6. Which type of Web document is created at the server site only when requested by a client?

   a. static

   b. dynamic

   c. active

   d. all of the above

7. Which type of Web document is fixed-content and is created and stored at the server site?

   a. static

   b. dynamic

   c. active

   d. all of the above

8. The _____ of a Web page contains the title and parameters used by the browser.

   a. tags

   b. head

   c. body

   d. attributes

9. In   <IMG SRC="Pictures/book1.gif " ALIGN=middle> ALIGN is _____.

   a. a tag

   b. the head

   c. the body

   d. an attribute

10. An ending tag is usually of the form _____.

   a. </tagname>

   b. <\tagname>

   c. <tagname>

   d. <tagname!>

11. Which category of HTML tags inserts a figure in a document?

   a. document

   b. text formatting

   c. image

   d. list

12. Which category of HTML tags allows the listing of documents?

   a. image

   b. list

   c. hyperlink

   d. executable contents

13. The _____ tags enclose binary code or bytecode.

   a. image

   b. list

   c. hyperlink

   d. executable contents

14. A program can use _____ to write a CGI program.

   a. Bourne shell script

   b. Perl

   c. C

   d. any of the above

15. An unemployed actor has posted his resume on the Web. This is probably a(n) _____ document.

   a. active

   b. static

   c. passive

   d. dynamic

16. The server receives input from a browser through _____.

   a. an attribute

   b. a tag

   c. a form

    d. any of the above

17. Output from a CGI program is _____.

    a. text

    b. graphics

    c. binary data

    d. any of the above

18. The _____ MIME header turns document caching on and off.

    a. expires

    b. location

    c. pragma

    d. status

19. Which type of Web document is transported from the server to the client in binary form?

    a. static

    b. dynamic

    c. active

    d. all of the above

20. An applet is a small application program written in _____.

    a. C

    b. C++

    c. shell script

    d. Java

21. The _____ package contains classes that handle common data structures.

    a. java.lang

    b. java.io

    c. java.net

    d. java.util

22. The _____ package contains methods for getting and displaying Web pages.

    a. java.applet

    b. java.lang

    c. java.io

    d. java.net

23. The _____ package contains classes and methods that make an applet capable of being run on any client environment.

    a. java.applet

    b. java.lang

    c. java.io

    d. java.awt

24. _____ is used to enable the use of active documents.

    a. HTML

    b. CGI

    c. Java

    d. all of the above

25. Java is _____.

    a. a programming language

    b. a run-time environment

    c. a class library

    d. all of the above

26. An applet is _____ document application program.

    a. a static

    b. an active

    c. a passive

    d. a dynamic

27. Stock quotations are posted on the Web. This is probably a(n) _____ document.

    a. active

    b. static

    c. passive

    d. dynamic

28. Updates for a satellite's coordinates can be obtained on the WWW. This is probably a(n) _____ document.

    a. active

    b. static

    c. passive

    d. dynamic

Exercises

29. Show the effect of the tags in the following line:
    This is <BR> a line of
 HTML

30. Show the effect of the tags in the following line:
    This is

 another line of

 HTML

31. Show the effect of the tags in the following lines:
    <H1> DOCUMENT </H1>
    <H2> This is an HTML document </H2>
    <H1> It shows the effect of H-tags </H1>

32. Show the effect of the tags in the following lines:
    <UL>
    <LI> Last Name, First Name, Initial </LI>
    <LI> Street Address, City </LI>
    <LI> State, Zip Code </LI>
    </UL>

33. Where will each figure be shown on the screen?
    Look at the following picture:

    then tell me what you feel:
    <IMG SRC="Pictures/Funny1.gif " ALIGN=middle>
    <IMG SRC="Pictures/Funny2.gif " ALIGN=bottom>
    <B>What is your feeling? </B>

34. Show the effect of the following HTML segment.
    The publisher of this book is <A HREF="www.mhhe">
    McGraw-Hill Publisher </A>

Programming Exercises

35. Write an HTML document to create the following screen:
    List of items offered at *discount price:*
    1. Books
    2. Pens
    3. Pencil
    4. Notebook

36. Write an HTML document to create the following screen:
    This is the picture of a book:
    "Put the picture here. It is in a file called pic.fig"
    Look at it carefully.

37. Write an HTML document to create the following screen. Use your own URL for hyperlink connection.
    A Web document can be either **Static, Dynamic,** or **Active.**
    If you want to learn more about each type click on the boldfaced word.

38. Write the first example of CGI in Korn Shell.

39. Write the first example of CGI in C shell.

40. Write the fourth example of CGI in Bourne shell.

41. Write the fourth example of CGI in C language.

42. Write the fifth example of CGI in Perl.

43. Write a CGI program that returns the IP address of the browser.

44. Write a CGI program that returns the port number of the server.

45. Write a CGI program that echoes the query string sent by the browser.

46. Write a Java applet to draw a line from the top-left corner of the window to the bottom right of the window for a window size of 300 (horizontal) by 400 (vertical) pixels.

47. Write a Java applet to draw a line from the middle top of the window to the middle bottom of the window for a window size of 300 (horizontal) by 400 (vertical) pixels.

48. Write a Java applet to draw a line from the middle left of the window to the middle right of the window for a window size of 300 (horizontal) by 400 (vertical) pixels.

49. Write a Java applet to draw a square of size 100 pixels at the middle of the window for a window size of 300 (horizontal) by 400 (vertical) pixels.

50. Write a Java program that creates and manipulates two scrollbars, one horizontal and the other vertical. Choose the range and increments.

CHAPTER 24

Socket Interface

In a client-server model, two application programs, one running on the local system (a client for example) and the other running on the remote system (a server for example), need to communicate with one another. To standardize network programming, application programming interfaces (APIs) have been developed. An API is a set of declarations, definitions, and procedures followed by programmers to write client-server programs. Among the more common APIs are the Socket Interface, the Transport Layer Interface (TLI), the Stream Interface, the Thread Interface, and the Remote Procedure Call (RPC). The Socket Interface, which is very common today, is the implementation we will discuss in this chapter.

The Socket Interface was developed as part of UNIX BSD. It is based on UNIX and defines a set of system calls (procedures) that are an extension of system calls used in UNIX to access files.This chapter shows the fundamentals of Socket Interface programming though it by no means teaches Socket Interface programming; there are whole books devoted to this subject. Instead, we introduce the concept and idea, and, maybe, provide motivation for those readers who want to learn more.

In this chapter, we first introduce some data types and functions used in network programming. Then we define sockets and introduce socket interface calls. Finally we give two pairs of examples of client-server programs.

24.1 SOME DEFINITIONS

In this section, we introduce some data types and structures that are needed for writing client-server programs.

Data Types Defined

Figure 24.1 lists three data types used extensively in client-server programs. These are u_char, u_short, and u_long data types.

Figure 24.1 *Data types*

u_char	Unsigned 8-bit character
u_short	Unsigned 16-bit integer
u_long	Unsigned 32-bit integer

Internet Address Structure

An IPv4 address is defined as a structure (struct in C) called *in_addr*, which contains only one field called *s_addr* of type u_long. The structure holds an IP address as a 32-bit binary number. Figure 24.2 shows the structure and the corresponding declaration.

Figure 24.2 *Internet address structure*

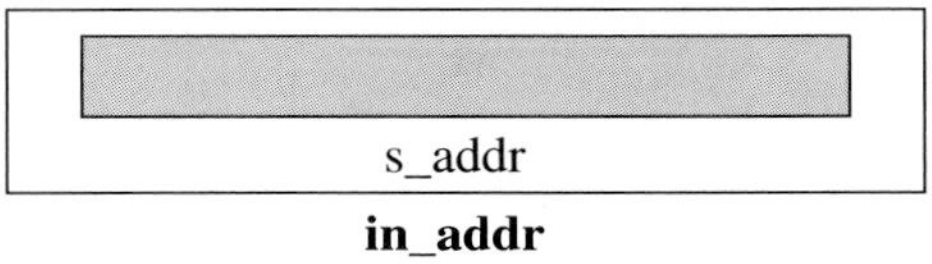

```
        s_addr
       in_addr

struct  in_addr
{
        u_long  s_addr ;
} ;
```

Internet Socket Address Structure

The application programs that use the TCP/IP protocol suite need a structure called a **socket address,** which mainly holds an IP address, a port number, and the protocol family. The structure is called *sockaddr_in* and has five fields; the first and the last field are normally not used, however. Figure 24.3 shows the structure and its declaration.

24.2 SOCKETS

The communication structure that we need in socket programming is a **socket**. A socket acts as an end point. Two processes need a socket at each end to communicate with each other.

A socket is defined in the operating system as a structure. Figure 24.4 shows a simplified version of a socket structure with five fields. These fields are listed below.

■ **Family.** This field defines the protocol group: IPv4, IPv6, UNIX domain protocols, and so on.

Figure 24.3   *Socket address structure*

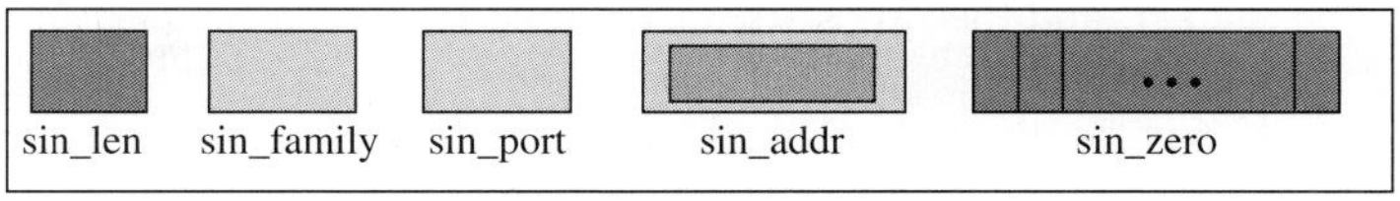

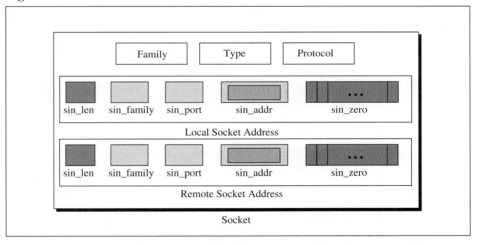

```
           sin_len  sin_family  sin_port      sin_addr           sin_zero
                              sockaddr_in

           struct    sockaddr_in
           {
                     u_char                    sin_len ;
                     u_short                   sin_family ;
                     u_short                   sin_port ;
                     struct  in_addr           sin_addr ;
                     char                      sin_zero [8] ;
           } ;
```

Figure 24.4   *Socket structure*

```
                 Family           Type           Protocol

      sin_len  sin_family  sin_port      sin_addr           sin_zero
                              Local Socket Address

      sin_len  sin_family  sin_port      sin_addr           sin_zero
                              Remote Socket Address

                                Socket
```

- **Type.** This field defines the type of socket: stream socket, datagram socket, or raw socket. These are discussed in the next section.
- **Protocol.** This field is usually set to zero for TCP and UDP.
- **Local socket address.** This field defines the local socket address, a structure of type sockaddr_in, as defined previously.
- **Remote socket address.** This field defines the remote socket address, a structure of type sockaddr_in, which was defined previously.

Socket Types

The socket interface defines three types of sockets: the stream socket, the datagram socket, and the raw socket. All three types can be used in a TCP/IP environment (see Figure 24.5).

Figure 24.5   *Socket types*

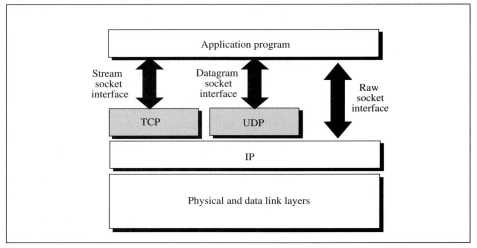

Stream Socket

A stream socket is designed to be used with a connection-oriented protocol such as TCP. TCP uses a pair of stream sockets to connect one application program to another across the Internet.

Datagram Socket

A datagram socket is designed to be used with a connectionless protocol such as UDP. UDP uses a pair of datagram sockets to send a message from one application program to another across the Internet.

Raw Socket

Some protocols such as ICMP or OSPF that directly use the services of IP use neither stream sockets nor datagram sockets. Raw sockets are designed for these types of applications.

24.3   BYTE ORDERING

Computers can be classified by the way they store data in their internal memories. Memories are addressed byte by byte. A data unit can span more than one byte, however. For example, in most computers, a short integer is two bytes (16 bits) and a long integer is four bytes (32 bits). How a two-byte short integer or a four-byte long integer is stored in bytes of memory defines the category of computer: big-endian or little-endian.

Big-Endian Byte Order

A computer that uses the **big-endian** system stores the most significant byte (the big end) of data in the starting address of the data unit. For example, an IP address such as 10.23.14.6, when expressed as a 32-bit binary number (long integer), can be stored in a big-endian computer as shown in Figure 24.6.

Figure 24.6   *Big-endian byte order*

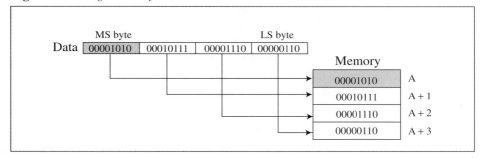

IBM mainframe computers as well as computers based on Motorola microprocessors are based on the big-endian system.

Little-Endian Byte Order

If a computer uses the **little-endian** system, it stores the least significant byte (the little end) of data in the starting address of the data unit. For example, an IP address such as 10.23.14.6, when expressed as a 32-bit binary number (long integer), can be stored in a little-endian computer as shown in Figure 24.7.

Figure 24.7   *Little-endian byte order*

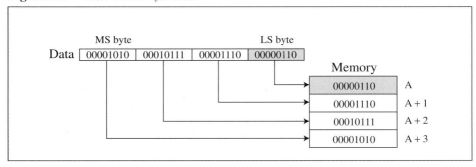

DEC VAX computers and computers using Intel microprocessors are based on the little-endian system.

Network Byte Order

Networking protocols can also choose their own byte order. The TCP/IP protocol suite has chosen the big-endian byte order.

The byte order for the TCP/IP protocol suite is big endian.

Byte-Order Transformation

To create portability in application programs, TCP/IP software provides a set of functions that transforms integers from a host byte order (big endian or little endian) to network byte order (big endian). Four functions are designed for this purpose: htons, htonl, ntohs, and ntohl (see Figure 24.8).

Figure 24.8 *Byte-order transformation functions*

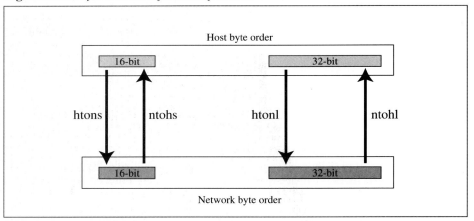

The prototypes are shown in Figure 24.9.

Figure 24.9 *Declarations for byte-order transformation*

```
u_short  htons ( u_short  host_short ) ;

u_short  ntohs ( u_short  network_short ) ;

u_long   htonl ( u_long  host_long ) ;

u_long   ntohl ( u_long  network_long ) ;
```

- **htons.** The function htons (host to network short) converts a 16-bit integer from host byte order to network byte order.
- **htonl.** The function htonl (host to network long) converts a 32-bit integer from host byte order to network byte order.
- **ntohs.** The function ntohs (network to host short) converts a 16-bit integer from network byte order to host byte order.
- **ntohl.** The function ntohl (network to host long) converts a 32-bit integer from network byte order to host byte order.

24.4 ADDRESS TRANSFORMATION

Network software provides functions to transform an IP address from ASCII dotted decimal format to 32-bit binary format and vice versa. Two of these functions are discussed here: inet_aton and inet_ntoa (see Figure 24.10).

Figure 24.10 *Address transformation*

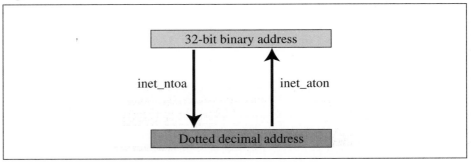

The prototypes of transformation functions are shown in Figure 24.11.

Figure 24.11 *Declarations for transformation functions*

```
int      inet_aton ( const char  *strptr , struct in_addr *addrptr ) ;

char    *inet_ntoa (struct in_addr  inaddr ) ;
```

- **inet_aton.** This function transforms an ASCII string that contains up to four segments separated by dots to a 32-bit binary address in network byte order.
- **inet_ntoa.** This function transforms a 32-bit binary address in network byte order to an ASCII string with four segments separated by dots.

24.5 BYTE MANIPULATION FUNCTIONS

In network programming, we often need to initialize a field, copy the contents of one field to another, or compare the contents of two fields. We cannot use string functions such as *strcpy* or *strcmp* because these functions assume that a field is terminated with a null character, which is not true in network programming. As a matter of fact, we may need to copy a sequence of bytes from one field to another that may contain a zero byte. The string functions interpret this zero as a terminator and stop at that point.

Several functions have been defined in the <string.h> header file for these byte manipulation purposes. We introduce the three most common: *memset*, *memcpy*, and *memcmp*. Their prototypes are shown in Figure 24.12.

Figure 24.12 *Declaration for byte-manipulation functions*

```
void *memset ( void *dest , int chr , int len ) ;

void *memcpy ( void *dest , const void *src , int len ) ;

int    memcmp ( const void *first , const void *second , int len ) ;
```

- **Memset.** This function sets a specified number of bytes to a value. The first argument is a pointer to the destination, the field to be set. The second argument is the value, and the third argument is the number of bytes. One can use the sizeof operator to fill the entire field. For example, the following stores zeros in a field called *x*:

    memset (&x , 0 , sizeof(x)) ;

- **Memcpy.** This function copies the value of one field to another. The first argument is a pointer to the destination. The second argument is a pointer to the source. The third argument is the number of bytes to be copied. For example, the following copies the value of the *y* field to the *x* field:

    memcpy (&x , &y , sizeof(x)) ;

- **Memcmp.** This function compares two fields. The first argument is a pointer to the first field. The second argument is a pointer to the second field. The third argument is the number of bytes to be compared. This function returns zero if the two fields are the same. It returns a number less than zero if the first field is smaller than the second. It returns a number greater than zero if the first field is greater than the second. For example, the following compares the first 10 bytes of fields *x* and *y*:

    memcmp (&x , &y , 10) ;

24.6 INFORMATION ABOUT REMOTE HOST

A process often needs information about a remote host. Several functions have been designed to provide this information. We discuss one such function, called *gethostbyname*. This function is actually a call to the DNS. The function accepts the domain name of the host and returns structured information called *hostent* that is actually the content of a resource record. The prototype of the function is given in Figure 24.13. The hostname is the domain name of the host in the form xxx.yyy.zzz. The function returns a pointer to the hostent structure.

Figure 24.13 *Declaration for gethostbyname*

```
struct hostent *gethostbyname ( const char *hostname ) ;
```

The struct hostent provides several pieces of information. The first field is a pointer to the name of the host. The second field is a pointer to an array of pointers with each pointer pointing to an alias by which the host can be called. The third field is the type of address (AF_INET in the Internet). The next field is the length of the address (4 bytes for IPv4). The last field is a pointer to an array of pointers with each pointer pointing to one of the host addresses (the host can be a multihomed host). See Figure 24.14.

Figure 24.14 *The hostent structure*

```
struct hostent
{
        char        *h_name ;
        char        **h_aliases ;
        int         h_addrtype ;
        int         h_length ;
        char        **h_addr_list ;
} ;
```

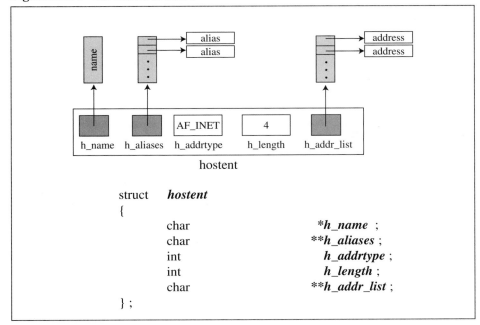

24.7   SOCKET SYSTEM CALLS

Several functions have been defined that can be called by an application program to communicate with another application program. We introduce some of these in this section for later use in our client-server programs.

Socket

The socket function is used by a process to create a socket. The prototype for this function is given in Figure 24.15. The family, type, and protocol fields were defined in Figure 24.4. For TCP/IP, the value of family is the constant AF_INET. The value of type as used in this chapter is either the constant SOCK_STREAM (used by stream sockets) or SOCK_DGRAM (used by datagram sockets).

Figure 24.15 *Declaration for socket function*

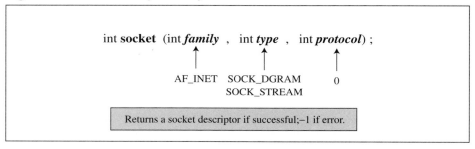

Although this function creates a socket, it sets values for only the first three fields (family, type, and protocol) of the socket structure. The other fields are set by the other functions or by the operating system, as we will discuss later.

The function returns an integer called the *socket descriptor,* which uniquely defines the created socket if the creation is successful. It returns −1 if there is an error. The socket descriptor is used by other functions to refer to the socket.

Bind

The bind function binds a socket to a local socket address by adding the local socket address to an already created socket. The prototype is given in Figure 24.16.

Figure 24.16 *Declaration for bind function*

int **bind** (int *sockfd* , const struct sockaddr_in ***localaddr** , int *localaddrlen*) ;

Returns 0 if successful; −1 if error.

Sockfd is the socket descriptor returned by the socket function; *localaddr* is a pointer to the socket address of the local machine; and *localaddrlen* is the length of the local socket address.

To use this function, the client needs first to call the socket function in order to use the returned value as the socket descriptor. The function sets values for the local socket address. Note that this function is not usually called by the client. In a client, the information about the local socket address is usually provided by the operating system. This function returns an integer, 0 for success and −1 for any error.

Connect

The connect function is used by a process (usually a client) to establish an active connection to a remote process (normally a server). The prototype is given in Figure 24.17.

Figure 24.17 *Declaration for connect function*

int **connect** (int *sockfd* , const struct sockaddr_in **serveraddr* , int *serveraddrlen*) ;

Returns 0 if successful; −1 if error.

Sockfd is the socket descriptor returned by the socket function; *serveraddr* is a pointer to the remote socket address; and *serveraddrlen* is the length of that address.

To use this function, the client needs first to call the socket function in order to use the returned value as the socket descriptor. This function sets values for the remote socket address. The local socket address is either provided by the bind function or set by the operating system. The function returns an integer, 0 for success and −1 for any error.

Listen

The listen function is called only by the TCP server. It creates a passive socket from an unconnected socket. Before calling the listen function, the socket must already be created and the local socket address fields set. This function informs the operating system that the server is ready to accept connection through this socket. Figure 24.18 shows the prototype.

Figure 24.18 *Declaration for listen function*

int **listen** (int *sockfd* , int *backlog*) ;

Returns 0 if successful; −1 if error.

Sockfd is the socket descriptor returned by the socket function; *backlog* is the number of requests that can be queued for this connection.   This function returns an integer, 0 for success and −1 for any error.

Accept

The accept function is called by a TCP server to remove the first connection request from the corresponding queue. If there are no requests (the queue is empty), the accept function is put to sleep. The prototype is given in Figure 24.19.

Figure 24.19   *Declaration for accept function*

int **accept** (int *sockfd* , const struct sockaddr_in ***clientaddr** , int ***clientaddrlen***) ;

Returns a socket descriptor if successful; −1 if error.

Sockfd is the socket descriptor; *clientaddr* is the pointer to the address of the client that has requested the connection; and *clientaddrlen* is a pointer to the client address length. Note that the socket address is not passed to the function but is returned from it. The length, however, is passed to the function as a value; it is also returned as a result.

This function actually creates a new socket (child socket) that can be used by a child server to connect to the client. All of the information needed for a new socket is provided by the operating system. The return value is the new socket descriptor.

Sendto

The sendto function is used by a process using UDP to send a message to another process usually running on a remote machine. The prototype is given in Figure 24.20.

Figure 24.20   *Declaration for sendto function*

int **sendto** (int *sockfd* , const void ***buf** , int buflen , int *flags* ,
const struct sockaddr_in ***toaddr** , int **toaddrlen***) ;

Returns number of bytes sent if successful; −1 if error.

Sockfd is the socket descriptor; *buf* is a pointer to the buffer holding the message to be sent; *buflen* defines the length of the buffer; and the *flags* field specifies out-of-band data or lookahead messages. Normally it is set to zero. *Toaddr* is a pointer to the socket address of the receiver and *toaddrlen* is the length of the socket address. The function returns the number of characters sent if there is no error and −1 otherwise.

Recvfrom

The recvfrom function extracts the next message that arrives at a socket. It also extracts the sender's socket address. In this way, the process that uses this function can record the socket address and use it to send a reply back to the sender. It is used mostly by a UDP process. The prototype is given in Figure 24.21.

Figure 24.21 *Declaration for recvfrom function*

int **recvfrom** (int *sockfd* , const void ***buf*** , int ***buflen*** , int ***flags***
const struct sockaddr_in ***fromaddr*** , int ***fromaddrlen***) ;

Returns number of bytes received if successful; −1 if error.

Sockfd is the socket descriptor; *buf* is a pointer to the buffer where the message will be stored; *buflen* defines the length of the buffer; and the *flags* field specifies out-of-band data or lookahead messages. Normally it is set to zero. *Fromaddr* is a pointer to the socket address of the sender, and *fromaddrlen* is a pointer to the length of the socket address. The function returns the number of characters received if there is no error and −1 otherwise. Note that the socket address is not passed to the function, it is returned from it. It can be used by the process to respond to the remote process. The length, however, is passed as a value and is also returned as a result.

Read

The read function is used by a process to receive data from another process running on a remote machine. This function assumes that there is already an open connection between two machines; therefore, it can only be used by TCP processes. The prototype is given in Figure 24.22.

Figure 24.22 *Declaration for read function*

int **read** (int *sockfd* , const void ***buf*** , int ***buflen***) ;

Returns number of bytes read if successful; 0 for end of file; −1 if error.

Sockfd is the socket descriptor; *buf* is a pointer to the buffer where data will be stored; and *buflen* is the length of the buffer. This function returns the number of bytes received (read) if successful, 0 if an end-of-file condition is detected, and −1 if there is an error.

Write

The write function is used by a process to send data to another process running on a remote machine. This function assumes that there is already an open connection between two machines. Therefore, it can only be used by TCP processes. The prototype is given in Figure 24.23.

Figure 24.23   *Declaration for write function*

int **write** (int *sockfd* , const void **buf* , int *buflen*) ;

Returns number of bytes written if successful;−1 if error.

Sockfd is the socket descriptor; *buf* is a pointer to the buffer where data to be sent is stored; and *buflen* is the length the buffer. This function returns the number of bytes sent (written) if successful and −1 if there is an error.

Close

The close function is used by a process to close a socket and terminate a TCP connection. The prototype is given in Figure 24.24.

Figure 24.24   *Declaration for close function*

int **close** (int *sockfd*) ;

Returns 0 if successful;−1 if error.

The socket descriptor is not valid after calling this function. The socket returns an integer, 0 for success and −1 for error.

24.8   CONNECTIONLESS ITERATIVE SERVER

In this section, we discuss connectionless, iterative client-server communication using UDP and datagram sockets. As we discussed in Chapter 14, a server that uses UDP is usually connectionless iterative. This means that the server serves one request at a time. A server gets the request received in a datagram from UDP, processes the request, and gives the response to UDP to send to the client. The server pays no attention to the other datagrams. These datagrams, which could all be from one client or from many clients, are stored in a queue, waiting for service. They are processed one by one in order of arrival.

The server uses one single port for this purpose, the well-known port. All the datagrams arriving at this port wait in line to be served. Figure 24.25 shows the flowchart of events in connectionless iterative communication.

Figure 24.25   *Socket interface for connectionless iterative server*

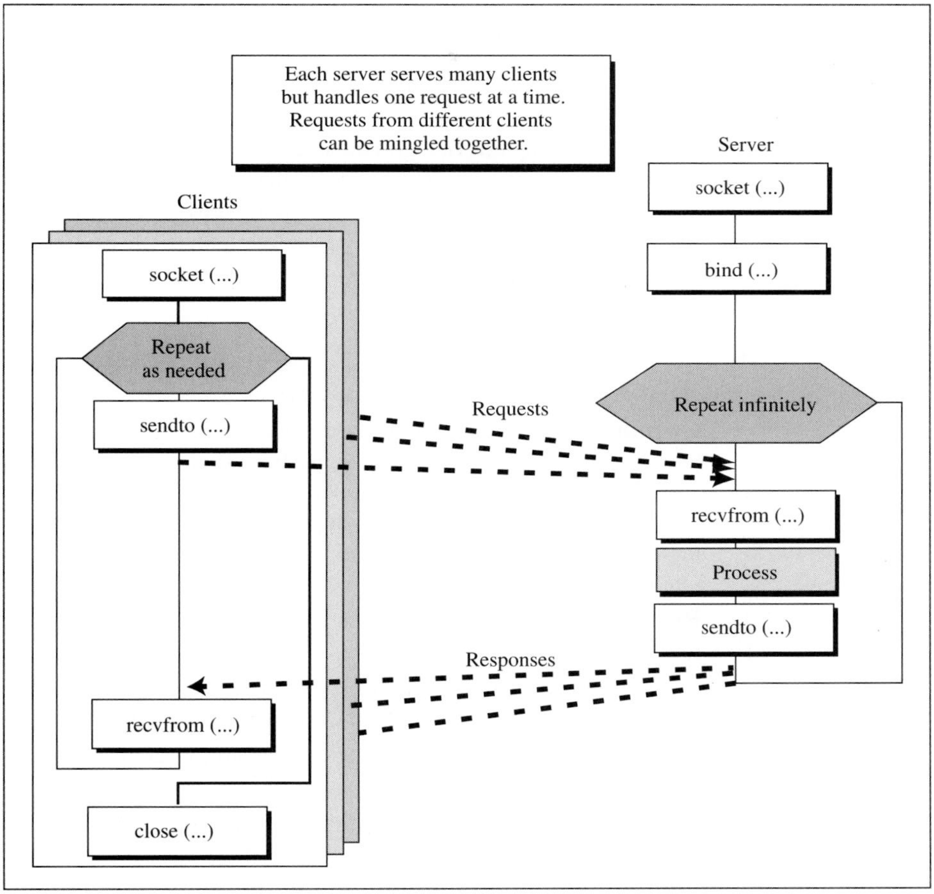

Server

The server performs the following functions:

1. **Opening a socket.** The server issues the socket call to ask the operating system to create a socket. The socket call in the socket interface is like the open call in the file interface. The socket call creates a new socket structure, and the open call creates a new file structure. The application program makes this call and passes three pieces of information: family, type, and protocol. The operating system creates a socket and enters the received information. However, the information for the socket is not complete. The operating system returns an integer to define the socket

uniquely. This integer is called the *socket descriptor* and is used to refer to the socket in the following calls.

2. **Binding.** The server issues the bind call to ask the operating system to enter information in the socket structure created in the previous step. This information consists of the local socket address.

3. **Repeating the steps.** The server repeats the following steps infinitely:

   a. **Receiving.** The server issues the recvfrom call to read, from the incoming queue, a datagram sent by a client.

   b. **Sending.** After processing the datagram, the server issues the sendto call to send the datagram that contains the result to the outgoing queue. Because the communication is connectionless, the sendto call provides the remote socket address (client IP address and the client ephemeral port address) for each datagram to be sent to the client. These two pieces of information are obtained by the recvfrom system call.

Client

The client performs the following functions:

1. **Opening a socket.** The client issues the socket call to ask the operating system to create a socket. The client does not have to do binding because the local socket address can be provided by the operating system. The operating system enters the local IP address and the ephemeral port number in the local socket address field of the created socket. In some implementations, the client also issues the bind call so that stray data from another program do not enter that port.

2. **Repeating the steps.** The client repeats the following steps as long as it has requests to make:

   a. **Sending.** After receiving the socket descriptor from the operating system, the client issues the sendto calls to send its request to the server.

   b. **Receiving.** The client issues the recvfrom to obtain the response of its request from the operating system.

3. **Closing.** When the client has no more requests, it issues a close call to destroy the socket.

24.9   UDP CLIENT-SERVER PROGRAMS

This section contains one simple server program and one simple client program. The server is a generic server. We have included one PROCESS call that is used to define the server function. For the sake of simplicity, we have not included any error-checking or error-handling statements.

Server Program

The server program is shown below:

UDP Iterative Server Program
1   #include <sys/types.h>
2   #include <sys/socket.h>
3   #include <netdb.h>
4   #include <netinet/in.h>
5   #include <stdio.h>
6   #include <string.h>
7
8   #define MAXBUF   256
9
10   void main (void)
11   {
12   char buf [MAXBUF] ;
13   int passiveSocket ;
14   int clientAddrLen ;
15   struct sockaddr_in   serverAddr ;
16   struct sockaddr_in   clientAddr ;
17   passiveSocket = socket (AF_INET, SOCK_DGRAM, 0) ;
18   memset (&serverAddr , 0 , sizeof (serverAddr)) ;
19   serverAddr.sin_family = AF_INET ;
20   serverAddr.sin_port = htons (a-well-known-port) ;
21   serverAddr.sin_addr.s_addr = htonl (INADDR_ANY) ;
22   bind (passiveSocket, &serverAddr, sizeof(serverAddr));
23   clientAddLen = sizeof (serverAddr) ;
24   memset (buf , 0, MAXBUF) ;
25   for (; ;)
26   {
27   while (recvfrom (passiveSocket, buf, MAXBUF, 0,
28   &clientAddr, &clientAddrLen) > 0)
29   {
30   PROCESS (............) ;
31   memset (buf, 0, MAXBUF);
32   sendto (passiveSocket, buf , MAXBUF , 0 ,
33   &clientAddr , clientAddrLen) ;

UDP Iterative Server Program (concluded)	
34	memset (buf , 0 , MAXBUF) ;
35	}
36	}
37	}

- Lines 1–6 are the header files.
- Line 8 defines the buffer size.
- Line 17 creates a socket.
- Line 18 initializes a server socket address.
- Lines 19–21 sets the values for the server socket address. Note that we use htons and htonl to create network byte order integers.
- Line 22 binds the created socket to the local socket address (server socket address).
- Line 24 initializes the buffer.
- Line 25 starts an infinite loop.
- Line 27 receives the client messages.
- Line 30 uses a procedure to process the data.
- Line 32 sends the results back to the client.
- Line 34 reinitializes the buffer for the next iteration.

Client Program

The client program is shown below:

UDP Iterative Client Program	
1	#include <sys/types.h>
2	#include <sys/socket.h>
3	#include <netdb.h>
4	#include <netinet/in.h>
5	#include <stdio.h>
6	#include <string.h>
7	
8	#define MAXBUF 256
9	
10	void main (void)
11	{
12	char buf [MAXBUF] ;
13	int activeSocket ;
14	int remoteAddrLen ;
15	struct sockaddr_in remoteAddr ;

UDP Iterative Client Program (concluded)
16	struct sockaddr_in localAddr ;
17	struct hostent *hptr ;
18	ctiveSocket = socket (AF_INET, SOCK_DGRAM, 0) ;
19	memset (&remoteAddr , 0 , sizeof (remoteAddr)) ;
20	remoteAddr.sin_family = AF_INET ;
21	remoteAddr.sin_port = htons (a-well-known-port) ;
22	hptr = gethostbyname (" a-domain-name") ;
23	memcpy ((char*) &remoteAddr.sin_addr.s_addr,
24	hptr ->h_addr_list[0], hptr ->h_lengh) ;
25	connect (activeSocket, &remoteAddr, sizeof (remoteAddr)) ;
26	memset (buf , 0, MAXBUF) ;
27	remoteAddLen = sizeof (remoteAddr) ;
28	while (gets (buf))
29	{
30	sendto (activeSocket, buf , sizeof (buf) , 0 ,
31	&remoteAddr , sizeof(remoteAddr)) ;
32	memset (buf, 0, sizeof(buf);
33	recvfrom (activeSocket, buf , MAXBUF, 0 ,
34	&remoteAddr , &remoteAddrLen) ;
35	printf ("%s\n", buf) ;
36	memset (buf , 0 , sizeof (buf)) ;
37	}
38	close (activeSocket) ;
39	}

- Lines 1–6 are the header files.
- Line 8 defines the buffer size.
- Line 18 creates a socket.
- Line 19 initializes a remote socket address.
- Lines 20–24 set the values for the remote socket address.
- Line 25 connects the created socket to the server.
- Line 26 initializes the buffer.
- Line 30 sends the buffer contents to the server.
- Line 33 receives the responses from the server.
- Line 35 prints the received message.
- Line 36 reinitializes the buffer for the next iteration.
- Line 38 closes the connection.

24.10   CONNECTION-ORIENTED CONCURRENT SERVER

In this section, we discuss connection-oriented, concurrent client-server communication using TCP and stream sockets. As mentioned in Chapter 14, the servers that use TCP are normally concurrent. This means that the server serves many clients at the same time. Communication is connection-oriented, which means that a request is a stream of bytes that could arrive in several segments, and the response could occupy several segments. A connection is established between the server and each client; the connection remains open until the entire stream is processed, and the connection is terminated.

For this type of server, many connections may be open at the same time. Many ports are needed, but the server can use only one well-known port. The solution is to use one well-known port and many ephemeral ports. The server issues a passive open at the well-known port. A client makes its initial approach to this port to make the connection. After the connection is made, the server assigns an ephemeral port to this connection to free the well-known port. Data transfer can now take place between these two ephemeral ports, one at the client site and the other at the server site. The well-known port is now free for another client connection.

The server must have one buffer for each connection. The segments from the clients are stored in the appropriate buffers and handled concurrently by the server.

To provide this service, most implementations use the concept of parent and child servers. A server running infinitely and accepting connections from clients is called a *parent server*. The parent server uses the well-known port. After the connection is made, the parent server creates a *child server* and an ephemeral port and lets the child server handle the client. It frees itself so that it can wait for another connection. In this section, we show how a server can serve several clients concurrently using the services of TCP. Figure 24.26 shows the flowchart of events for a server and a client.

Server

The server performs the following functions:

1. **Opening a socket.** The server issues the socket call to ask the operating system to create a socket.
2. **Binding.** The server issues the bind call to ask the operating system to enter information in the socket structure created in the previous step. This information consists of the local socket address.
3. **Listening.** The server issues the listen call to convert a socket into a passive socket, usually called the listening socket. A listening socket does not connect itself to a socket at the other end; it just waits for a connection from the other end. The server passes the socket descriptor and the maximum number of requests for connection.

Figure 24.26   *Socket interface for connection-oriented concurrent server*

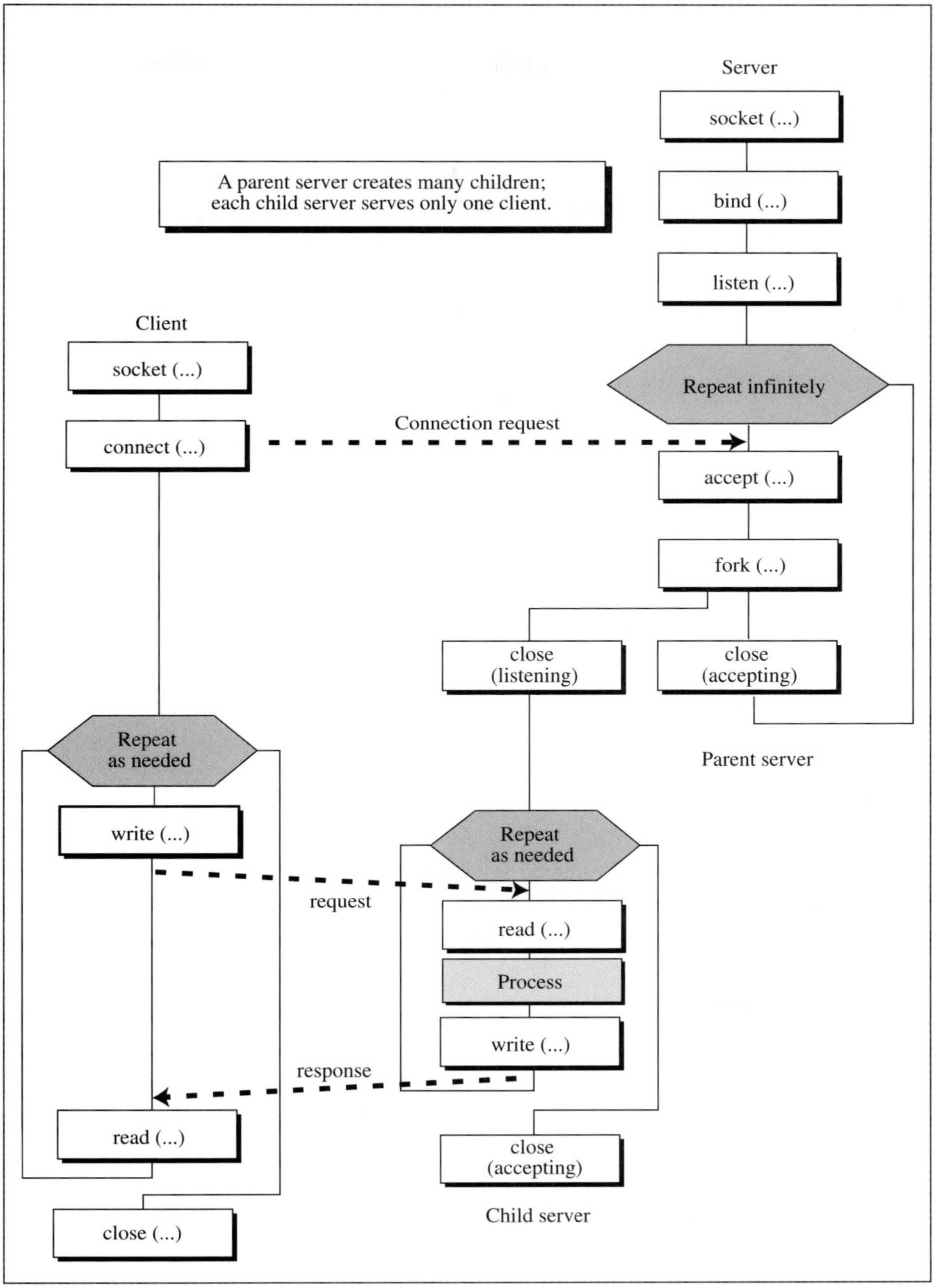

4. **Repeating the steps.** The server repeats the following steps infinitely:

    a. **Accepting.** The accept call creates a new socket, called the *accepting socket*, for actual communication and connects the next client in line. After this call, the client is connected to the new socket and the previous socket is freed.

    b. **Forking.** The server now uses the fork call (see Chapter 14) to create a process just like itself. This is called the *child process*; and the creator is called the *parent process*. After this operation, the client is connected to both the parent and the child. Both parent and child have a listening and accepting socket.

    c. **Closing the accepting socket.** The parent issues the close call to close its accepting socket, but its listening socket remains open for the next client.

    d. **Closing the listening socket.** The child issues the close call to close its listening socket, but its accepting socket remains open.

    e. **Repeating.** The child repeats the following steps as long as it has requests from the client:

        Reading. The child issues the read call to read as much data as it can process in one shot from the incoming buffer assigned to the client.
        Processing. The child processes the data read from the buffer.
        Writing. The child issues the write call to write the result of processing to the outgoing buffer assigned to the client.

    f. **Closing the communicating socket.** After the client has been served, the child issues the close call to close the communicating socket.

Client

The client performs the following functions:

1. **Opening a socket.** The client issues the socket call to ask the operating system to create a socket.

2. **Connecting.** The client issues the connect call to ask the operating system to enter the socket address of the server into the created socket structure. This call also requests a connection with the TCP on the other side.

3. **Repeating the steps.** The client repeats the following steps as long as it has requests to make.

    a. **Writing.** The client issues the write call to write data into the outgoing TCP buffer.

    b. **Reading.** The client issues the read call to get data from the incoming buffer.

4. **Closing.** After the client has finished, it issues a close call to request TCP to close the connection. It also sends an application-defined "quit" packet to notify the server.

Figure 24.27 shows the relationships between the client, the parent server, and the child server.

Figure 24.27 *Relationship between the client and the server.*

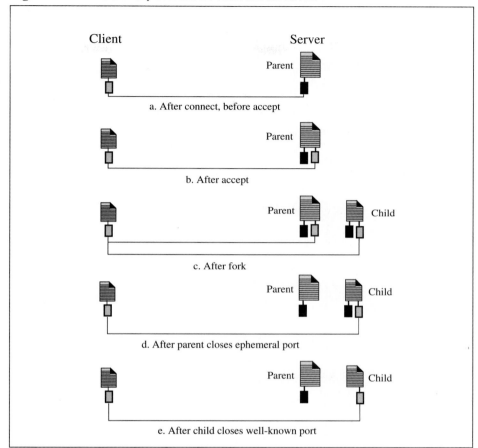

24.11 TCP CLIENT-SERVER PROGRAMS

This section contains one simple server program and one simple client program. The server is a generic server. We have included one PROCESS call that is used to define the server function. For the sake of simplicity, we have not included any error-checking or error-handling statements.

Server Program

The following shows the server program:

	TCP Concurrent Server Program
1	#include <sys/types.h>
2	#include <sys/socket.h>
3	#include <netdb.h>
4	#include <netinet/in.h>
5	#include <stdio.h>
6	#include <string.h>
7	
8	#define MAXBUF 256
9	
10	void main (void)
11	{
12	char buf [MAXBUF] ;
13	int listenSocket ;
14	int acceptSocket ;
15	int clientAddrLen ;
16	struct sockaddr_in serverAddr ;
17	struct sockaddr_in clientAddr ;
18	listSocket = socket (AF_INET, SOCK_STREAM, 0) ;
19	memset (&serverAddr , 0 , sizeof (serverAddr)) ;
20	serverAddr.sin_family = AF_INET ;
21	serverAddr.sin_port = htons (a-well-known-port) ;
22	serverAddr.sin_addr.s_addr = htonl(INADDR_ANY) ;
23	bind (listenSocket, &serverAddr, sizeof(serverAddr)) ;
24	listen (listenSocket , 1) ;
25	clientAddrLen = sizeof (clientAddr) ;
26	for (; ;)
27	{
28	acceptSocket = accept (listSocket &clientAddr,
29	&clientAddrLen) ;
30	pid = fork () ;
31	if (pid != 0) /* parent */
32	{
33	close (acceptSocket) ;

	TCP Concurrent Server Program (concluded)
34	continue ;
35	}
36	else /* child */
37	{
38	close (listenSocket) ;
39	memset (buf , 0, MAXBUF) ;
40	while (read (acceptSocket , buf, MAXBUF)> 0)
41	{
42	PROCESS (............) ;
43	memset (buf, 0, MAXBUF);
44	write (acceptSocket, buf , MAXBUF) ;
45	memset (buf , 0 , MAXBUF) ;
46	} /* while */
47	close (acceptSocket) ;
48	} /* else */
49	} /* for */
50	}

- Lines 1–6 are the header files.
- Line 8 defines the buffer size.
- Line 18 creates a passive socket.
- Line 23 binds the passive socket to the server socket address.
- Line 24 creates a listening socket from the passive socket.
- Line 28 creates an accepting socket.
- Line 30 creates the child process using fork.
- Line 33 closes the parent accepting socket.
- Line 38 closes the child listening socket.
- Line 40 makes the child read from the accepting socket in a loop.
- Line 42 processes the data read.
- Line 44 makes the child write the result to the accepting socket.
- Line 47 closes the accepting socket.

Client Program

The client program is shown below:

	TCP Concurrent Client Program
1	#include <sys/types.h>
2	#include <sys/socket.h>

TCP Concurrent Client Program (concluded)	
3	#include <netdb.h>
4	#include <netinet/in.h>
5	#include <stdio.h>
6	#include <string.h>
7	
8	#define MAXBUF 256
9	
10	void main (void)
11	{
12	char buf [MAXBUF] ;
13	int activeSocket ;
14	struct sockaddr_in remoteAddr ;
15	struct sockaddr_in localAddr ;
16	struct hostent *hptr ;
17	activeSocket = socket (AF_INET, SOCK_STREAM, 0) ;
18	memset (&remoteAddr , 0 , sizeof (remoteAddr)) ;
19	remoteAddr.sin_family = AF_INET ;
20	remoteAddr.sin_port = htons (a-well-known-port) ;
21	hptr = gethostbyname (" a-domain-name") ;
22	memcpy ((char*) &remoteAddr.sin_addr.s_addr ,
23	hptr ->h_addr_list[0], hptr ->h_length) ;
24	memset (buf , 0, MAXBUF) ;
25	while (gets (buf))
26	{
27	write (activeSocket, buf , MAXBUF) ;
28	memset (buf, 0, MAXBUF);
29	read (sockds , buf , MAXBUF) ;
30	printf ("%s\n", buf) ;
31	memset (buf , 0 , MAXBUF) ;
32	}
33	close (activeSocket) ;
34	}

- Lines 1–6 are the header files.
- Line 8 defines the buffer size.
- Line 17 creates an active socket.

- Line 21 gets information about the remote host (server) and stores it in a variable pointing to a hostent structure.
- Lines 22–23 copy the socket address in hostent to the remote socket address structure.
- Line 25 uses a loop to get data from the user and stores it in a buffer.
- Line 27 writes the buffer contents to the active socket.
- Line 29 reads from the active socket what is received from the server.
- Line 30 prints the contents of the received buffer.
- Line 33 closes the active socket.

24.12   SUMMARY

- If two application programs, one running on a local system and the other running on the remote system, need to communicate with each other, network programming is required.
- The socket interface is a set of declarations, definitions, and procedures for writing client-server programs.
- The communication structure needed for socket programming is called a socket.
- A stream socket is used with a connection-oriented protocol such as TCP.
- A datagram socket is used with a connectionless protocol such as UDP.
- A raw socket is used by protocols such as ICMP or OSPF that directly use the services of IP.
- In big-endian byte order, the most significant byte is stored in the starting address of the data unit.
- In little-endian byte order, the least significant byte is stored in the starting address of the data unit.
- TCP/IP uses the big-endian byte order.
- Three functions to manipulate bytes in network programming are memset, memcpy, and memcmp.
- A function to provide information about the remote host is gethostbyname.
- The socket system call creates a socket.
- The bind system call adds the local socket address to an already created socket.
- The connect system call establishes an active connection to a remote process.
- The listen system call converts a socket into a passive socket.
- The accept system call creates a new socket for actual communication and connects the next client in line.
- A connectionless process issues the sendto system call to send data to a remote process.
- A connectionless process issues the recvfrom system call to receive, from the incoming queue, the datagrams sent by a remote process.

■ A connection-oriented process issues the read system call to receive datagrams from a remote process.

■ A connection-oriented process issues the write system call to send datagrams to a remote process.

■ The close system call closes a socket and terminates a TCP connection.

■ A connectionless, iterative server uses the services of UDP and can serve only one client at a time.

■ A connection-oriented, concurrent server uses the services of TCP and can serve many clients simultaneously.

■ A server running infinitely and accepting connections from clients is called a parent server.

■ A parent server creates a child server that actually handles the client.

24.13   PRACTICE SET

Multiple Choice

1. An API is a set of _____.
   a. declarations
   b. definitions
   c. procedures
   d. all of the above

2. The structure to define an IPv4 address is called a _____ and contains a field called _____.
   a. u_long; s_addr
   b. s_addr; in_addr
   c. in_addr; s_addr
   d. in_addr; u_long

3. The _____ field in the socket structure is usually set to 0 for a process using the services of TCP or UDP.
   a. family
   b. type
   c. protocol
   d. local socket address

4. The _____ field in the socket structure defines the protocol group.
   a. family
   b. type
   c. protocol
   d. local socket address

5. The _____ field in the socket structure is a structure of type sockaddr_in.
   a. family
   b. local socket address
   c. remote socket address
   d. b and c

6. The _____ socket is used with a connection-oriented protocol.
   a. stream
   b. datagram
   c. raw
   d. remote

7. The _____ socket is used with a connectionless protocol.
   a. stream
   b. datagram
   c. raw
   d. remote

8. The _____ socket is used with a protocol that directly uses the services of IP.
   a. stream
   b. datagram
   c. raw
   d. remote

9. On an IBM mainframe computer, the starting address in memory for the IP address 7.8.9.10 contains _____.
   a. 00000111
   b. 00001000
   c. 00001001
   d. 00001010

10. On a PC with an Intel processor, the starting address in memory for the IP address 7.8.9.10 contains _____.
    a. 00000111
    b. 00001000
    c. 00001001
    d. 00001010

11. To convert a dotted decimal address to a 32-bit binary address, use the _____ function.
    a. htons
    b. htonl
    c. inet_ntoa
    d. inet_aton

12. To convert a 16-bit word to network byte order, use the _____ function.
    a. htons

    b. ntohs

    c. htonl

    d. ntohl

13. To convert a 32-bit integer from network byte order to host byte order, use the _____ function.

    a. htons

    b. ntohs

    c. htonl

    d. ntohl

14. In network programming, the _____ function copies the value of one field to another.

    a. memset

    b. memcpy

    c. memcmp

    d. memstr

15. In network programming, the _____ function inserts a specified byte in a field.

    a. memset

    b. memcpy

    c. memcmp

    d. memstr

16. If the memcmp function returns a value of 1, it means _____.

    a. the first field is the same as the second field

    b. the first field is greater than the second field

    c. the first field is less than the second field

    d. the first field has a value of 1

17. The _____ function provides information about the remote host.

    a. hostent

    b. hostname

    c. gethostbyname

    d. getnameofhost

18. A connectionless process issues the _____ system call to receive, from the incoming queue, the datagrams sent by a remote process.

    a. listen

    b. receive

    c. bind

    d. recvfrom

19. A connection-oriented process issues the _____ system call to send datagrams to a remote process.

    a. sendto

    b. bind

   c. accept

   d. write

20. A connectionless process issues the _____ system call to send data to a remote process.

   a. sendto

   b. bind

   c. listen

   d. remote

21. The _____ system call adds the local socket address to an already created socket.

   a. address

   b. create

   c. bind

   d. socket

22. The _____ system call creates a socket.

   a. create

   b. socket

   c. open

   d. bind

23. The _____ system call closes a socket and terminates a TCP connection.

   a. recvfrom

   b. close

   c. shut

   d. bind

24. The _____ system call creates a new socket for actual communication and connects the next client in line.

   a. accept

   b. connect

   c. bind

   d. create

25. The _____ system call converts a socket into a passive socket.

   a. convert

   b. listen

   c. socket

   d. bind

26. The _____ system call establishes an active connection to a remote process.

   a. accept

   b. bind

   c. socket

   d. connect

27. A connection-oriented process issues the _____ system call to receive data-grams from a remote process.

   a. read

   b. recvfrom

   c. listen

   d. sendto

28. The client program is _____ because it terminates after it has been served.

   a. active

   b. passive

   c. finite

   d. infinite

29. The server program is _____ because it is always available, waiting for a client request.

   a. active

   b. passive

   c. finite

   d. infinite

30. A connection-oriented concurrent server uses _____ ports.

   a. ephemeral

   b. well-known

   c. active

   d. a and b

31. A connectionless iterative concurrent server uses _____ ports.

   a. ephemeral

   b. well-known

   c. active

   d. a and b

32. A _____ server serves multiple clients, handling one request at a time.

   a. connection-oriented iterative

   b. connection-oriented concurrent

   c. connectionless iterative

   d. connectionless concurrent

33. A _____ server serves multiple clients simultaneously.

   a. connection-oriented iterative

   b. connection-oriented concurrent

   c. connectionless iterative

   d. connectionless concurrent

34. A _____ server uses the sendto and recvfrom system.

   a. connection-oriented iterative

   b. connection-oriented concurrent

    c. connectionless iterative

    d. connectionless concurrent

35. A _____ server uses the read and write system calls.

    a. connection-oriented iterative

    b. connection-oriented concurrent

    c. connectionless iterative

    d. connectionless concurrent

Exercises

36. Explain the difference between the bind function and the connect function.
37. Explain the difference between the bind function and the listen function.
38. Explain the difference between the socket function and the accept function.
39. Write the necessary lines of code to connect a socket to the remote TELNET server at site xxx.yyy.edu.
40. Write the necessary lines of code to connect a socket to the remote FTP server at site yy.zz.edu.
41. Write the necessary lines of code to bind a socket to the local server.
42. Write the necessary lines of code to create a listening socket with a queue size of 100.
43. Write the necessary lines of code to create a child socket.
44. Describe the differences between the sendto and the write functions.
45. Describe the differences between the recvfrom and the read functions.
46. Describe the relationship between the connect function and the TCP state transition diagram. (See Chapter 12.) What is the state of TCP after the connect function?
47. Describe the relationship between the bind function and the TCP state transition diagram. (See Chapter 12.) What is the state of TCP after the bind function?
48. Describe the relationship between the listen function and the TCP state transition diagram. (See Chapter 12.) What is the state of TCP after the listen function?
49. Describe the relationship between the accept function and the TCP state transition diagram. (See Chapter 12.) What is the state of TCP after the accept function?

Programming Exercises

50. Write a UDP client program that sends a string of characters to a server. The client does not use a loop.
51. Write a UDP server program that receives a string of characters from a client. The server receives the string from the client program in exercise 50.
52. Write a TCP client program that does the same job as the client program in exercise 50.
53. Write a TCP server program that does the same job as the server program in exercise 51.

54. Write a UDP client program that asks for the time from a UDP server.
55. Write a UDP server program that responds to the client in exercise 54.
56. Write a TCP client program that asks for the time from a TCP server.
57. Write a TCP server program that responds to the client in exercise 56.
58. Write a UDP client program that behaves like a simple TFTP client.
59. Write a UDP server program that behaves like a simple TFTP server.
60. Write a TCP client program that behaves like a simple FTP client.
61. Write a TCP server program that behaves like a simple FTP server.
62. Write a TCP client program that behaves like a simple TELNET client.
63. Write a TCP server program that behaves like a simple TELNET server.

CHAPTER 25

Next Generation:
IPv6 and ICMPv6

The network layer protocol in the TCP/IP protocol suite is currently IPv4 (Internetworking Protocol, version 4). IPv4 provides the host-to-host communication between systems in the Internet. Although IPv4 is well designed, data communication has evolved since the inception of IPv4 in the 1970s. IPv4 has some deficiencies that make it unsuitable for the fast-growing Internet, including the following:

■ IPv4 has a two-level address structure (netid and hostid) categorized into five classes (A, B, C, D, and E). The use of address space is inefficient. For instance, when an organization is granted a class A address, 16 million addresses from the address space are assigned for the organization's exclusive use. If an organization is granted a class C address, on the other hand, only 256 addresses are assigned to this organization, which may not be a sufficient number. Also, millions of addresses are wasted in classes D and E. This method of addressing has depleted the address space of IPv4, and soon there will not be any addresses left to assign to any new system that wants to be connected to the Internet. Although the subnetting and supernetting strategies have alleviated some of the addressing problems, subnetting and supernetting make routing more complicated as we have seen in the previous chapters.

■ The Internet must accommodate real-time audio and video transmission. This type of transmission requires minimum delay strategies and reservation of resources not provided in the IPv4 design.

■ The Internet must accommodate encryption and authentication of data for some applications. No encryption or authentication is provided by IPv4.

To overcome these deficiencies, IPv6 (Internet Protocol, version 6), also known as IPng (Internetworking Protocol, next generation) was proposed and is now a standard. In IPv6, the Internet protocol was extensively modified to accommodate the unforeseen growth of the Internet. The format and the length of the IP addresses were changed along with the packet format. Related protocols, such as ICMP, were also modified. Other protocols in the network layer, such as ARP, RARP, and IGMP, were either deleted or included in the ICMP protocol. Routing protocols, such as RIP and OSPF, were also slightly modified to accommodate these changes. Communication experts predict that IPv6 and its related protocols will soon replace the current IP version. In this chapter we talk first about IPv6. Then we discuss ICMPv6. Finally we explore the strategies used for the transition from version 4 to version 6.

25.1   IPV6

The next-generation IP, or IPv6, has some advantages over IPv4 that can be summarized as follows:

- **Larger address space.** An IPv6 address is 128 bits long. Compared with the 32-bit address of IPv4, this is a four-time increase in the address space.
- **Better header format.** IPv6 uses a new header format in which options are separated from the base header and inserted, when needed, between the base header and the upper-layer data. This simplifies and speeds up the routing process because most of the options do not need to be checked by routers.
- **New options.** IPv6 has new options to allow for additional functionalities.
- **Allowance for extension.** IPv6 is designed to allow the extension of the protocol if required by new technologies or applications.
- **Support for resource allocation.** In IPv6, the type-of-service field has been removed, but a mechanism (called *flow label*) has been added to enable the source to request special handling of the packet. This mechanism can be used to support traffic such as real-time audio and video.
- **Support for more security.** The encryption and authentication options in IPv6 provide confidentiality and integrity of the packet.

25.2   IPV6 ADDRESSES

An IPv6 address consists of 16 bytes (octets); it is 128 bits long (see Figure 25.1).

Figure 25.1   *IPv6 address*

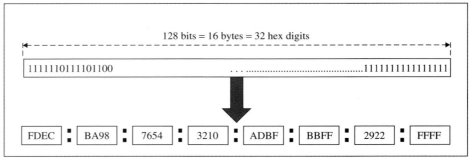

Hexadecimal Colon Notation

To make addresses more readable, IPv6 address protocol specifies hexadecimal colon notation. In this notation, 128 bits are divided into eight sections, each two bytes in length. Two bytes in hexadecimal notation require four hexadecimal digits. Therefore, the address consists of 32 hexadecimal digits, with every four digits separated by a colon.

Abbreviation

Although the IP address, even in hexadecimal format, is very long, many of the digits are zeros. In this case, we can abbreviate the address. The leading zeros of a section (four digits between two colons) can be omitted. Only the leading zeros can be dropped, not the trailing zeros. For an example, see Figure 25.2.

Figure 25.2   *Abbreviated address*

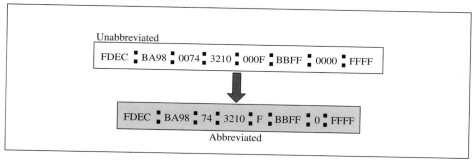

Using this form of abbreviation, 0074 can be written as 74, 000F as F, and 0000 as 0. Note that 3210 cannot be abbreviated. Further abbreviations are possible if there are consecutive sections consisting of zeros only. We can remove the zeros altogether and replace them with a double semicolon. Figure 25.3 shows the concept.

Figure 25.3   *Abbreviated address with consecutive zeros*

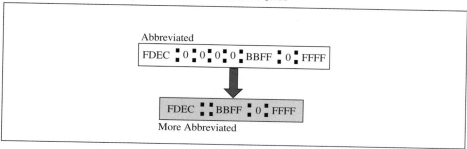

Note that this type of abbreviation is allowed only once per address. If there are two runs of zero sections, only one of them can be abbreviated. Reexpansion of the abbreviated address is very simple: Align the unabbreviated portions and insert zeros to get the original expanded address.

Sometimes we need to refer to only part of the address, not all of it. To do so, place a slash after the digits you wish to keep, and follow it with the number of digits kept. For example, Figure 25.4 shows how the first six sections can be written in a shortened form.

Figure 25.4   *Partial address*

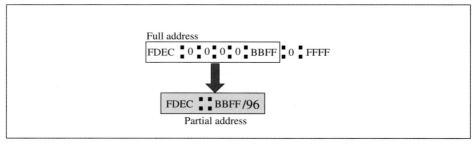

Categories of Addresses

IPv6 defines three types of addresses: unicast, anycast, and multicast.

Unicast Addresses

A unicast address defines a single computer. The packet sent to a unicast address should be delivered to that specific computer.

Anycast Addresses

An anycast address defines a group of computers whose addresses have the same prefix. For example, all computers connected to the same physical network share the same prefix address. A packet sent to an anycast address should be delivered to exactly one of the members of the group—the closest or most easily accessible.

Multicast Addresses

A multicast address defines a group of computers that may or may not share the same prefix and may or may not be connected to the same physical network. A packet sent to a multicast address should be delivered to each member of the set.

Address Space Assignment

The address space has many different purposes. The designers of the IP addresses divided the address space into two parts, with the first part called the *type prefix*. This variable-length prefix defines the purpose of the address. The codes are designed such that no code is identical to the first part of any other code. In this way, there is no ambiguity; when an address is given, the type prefix can easily be determined. Figure 25.5 shows the IPv6 address format.

Figure 25.5 *Address structure*

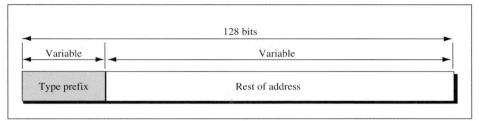

Table 25.1 shows the prefix for each type of address. The third column shows the fraction of each type of address relative to the whole address space.

Table 25.1 *Type prefixes for IPv6 addresses*

Type Prefix	Type	Fraction
0000 0000	Reserved	1/256
0000 0001	Reserved	1/256
0000 001	NSAP (Network Service Access Point)	1/128
0000 010	IPX (Novell)	1/128
0000 011	Reserved	1/128
0000 100	Reserved	1/128
0000 101	Reserved	1/128
0000 110	Reserved	1/128
0000 111	Reserved	1/128
0001	Reserved	1/16
001	Reserved	1/8
010	**Provider-based unicast addresses**	**1/8**
011	Reserved	1/8
100	Geographic unicast addresses	1/8
101	Reserved	1/8
110	Reserved	1/8
1110	Reserved	1/16
1111 0	Reserved	1/32
1111 10	Reserved	1/64
1111 110	Reserved	1/128
1111 1110 0	Reserved	1/512
1111 1110 10	Link local addresses	1/1024
1111 1110 11	Site local addresses	1/1024
1111 1111	Multicast addresses	1/256

Provider-Based Unicast Addresses

The provider-based address is generally used by a normal host as a unicast address. The address format is shown in Figure 25.6.

Figure 25.6   *Provider-based address*

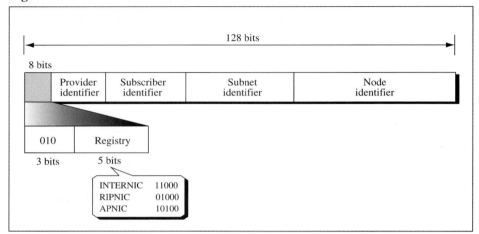

Fields for the provider-based addresses are as follows:

- **Type identifier.** This three-bit field defines the address as a provider-based address.
- **Registry identifier.** This five-bit field indicates the agency that has registered the address. Currently three registry centers have been defined. INTERNIC (code 11000) is the center for North America; RIPNIC (code 01000) is the center for European registration; and APNIC (code 10100) is for Asian and Pacific countries.
- **Provider identifier.** This variable-length field identifies the provider for Internet access. A 16-bit length is recommended for this field.
- **Subscriber identifier.** When an organization subscribes to the Internet through a provider, it is assigned a subscriber identification. A 24-bit length is recommended for this field.
- **Subnet identifier.** Each subscriber can have many different subnetworks and each network can have different identifiers. The subnet identifier defines a specific network under the territory of the subscriber. A 32-bit length is recommended for this field.
- **Node identifier.** The last field defines the identity of the node connected to a subnet. A length of 48 bits is recommended for this field to make it compatible with the 48-bit link (physical) address used by Ethernet. In the future, this link address will probably be the same as the node physical address.

We can think of a provider-based address as a hierarchical identity having several prefixes. As shown in Figure 25.7, each prefix defines a level of hierarchy. The type prefix defines the type, the registry prefix uniquely defines the registry level, the provider prefix uniquely defines a provider, the subscriber prefix uniquely defines a subscriber, and the subnet prefix uniquely defines a subnet.

Figure 25.7   *Address hierarchy*

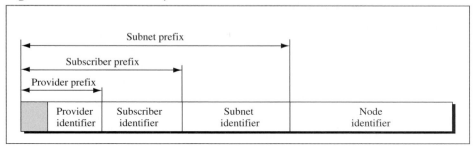

Reserved Addresses

Addresses that use the reserved prefix (00000000) will be discussed here briefly.

■ **Unspecified address.** This is an address in which the nonprefix part is also zero. In other words, the entire address consists of zeros. This address is used when a host does not know its own address and sends an inquiry to find its address. However, in the inquiry it must define a source address. The unspecified address can be used for this purpose. Note that the unspecified address cannot be used as a destination address. The unspecified address format is shown in Figure 25.8.

Figure 25.8   *Unspecified address*

■ **Loopback address.** This is an address used by a host to test itself without going into the network. In this case, a message is created in the application layer, sent to the transport layer, and passed to the network layer. However, instead of going to the physical network, it returns to the transport layer and then passes to the application layer. This is very useful for testing the functions of software packages in these layers before even connecting the computer to the network. The address as shown in Figure 25.9 consists of the prefix 00000000 followed by 119 zero bits and 1 one bit.

■ **IPv4 addresses.** As we will see later in this chapter, during transition from IPv4 to IPv6 hosts can use their IPv4 addresses embedded in IPv6 addresses. Two formats have been designed for this purpose: compatible and mapped. A *compatible address* is an address of 96 bits of zero followed by 32 bits of IPv4 address. It is used when a computer using IPv6 wants to send a message to another computer using IPv6. However, the packet should pass through a region where the networks

Figure 25.9 *Loopback address*

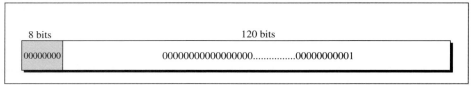

are still using IPv4. The sender uses the IPv4-compatible address to facilitate passing the packet through the IPv4 region (see Section 25.5 on Transition Strategies). For example, the IPv4 address 2.13.17.14 (in decimal dotted format) becomes 0::020D:110E (in hexadecimal colon format). The IPv4 address is prepended with 96 zeros to create a 128-bit IPv6 address (see Figure 25.10).

Figure 25.10 *Compatible address*

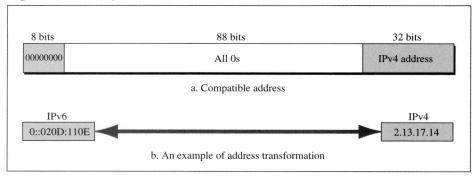

A *mapped address* comprises 80 bits of zero, followed by 16 bits of one, followed by the 32-bit IPv4 address. It is used when a computer that has migrated to IPv6 wants to send a packet to a computer still using IPv4. The packet travels mostly through IPv6 networks but is finally delivered to a host that uses IPv4. For example, the IPv4 address 2.13.17.14 (in decimal dotted format) becomes 0::FFFF:020D:110E (in hexadecimal colon format). The IPv4 address is prepended with 16 ones and 80 zeros to create a 128-bit IPv6 address (see Section 25.5 on transition strategies). Figure 25.11 shows a mapped address.

A very interesting point about mapped and compatible addresses is that they are designed in such a way that, when calculating the checksum, one can use either the embedded address or the total address because extra 0s or 1s in multiples of 16 do not have any effect in checksum calculation. This is important because if the address of the packet is changed from IPv6 to IPv4 by a router, the checksum calculation is not affected.

Local Addresses

Addresses that use the reserved prefix (11111110) are discussed here briefly.

■ **Link local address.** These addresses are used if a LAN is to use the Internet protocols but is not connected to the Internet for security reasons. This type of address-

Figure 25.11 *Mapped address*

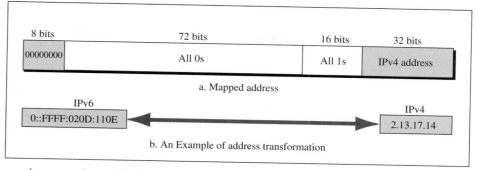

a. Mapped address

b. An Example of address transformation

ing uses the prefix 1111 1110 10. The link local address is used in an isolated network and does not have a global effect. Nobody outside an isolated network can send a message to the computers attached to a network using these addresses (see Figure 25.12).

Figure 25.12 *Link local address*

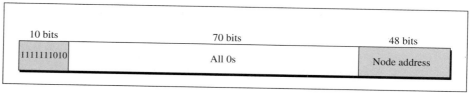

■ **Site local address.** These addresses are used if a site having several networks uses the Internet protocols but is not connected to the Internet, also for security reasons. This type of addressing uses the prefix 1111 1110 11. The site local address is used in isolated networks and does not have a global effect. Nobody outside the isolated networks can send a message to any of the computers attached to a network using these addresses (see Figure 25.13).

Figure 25.13 *Site local address*

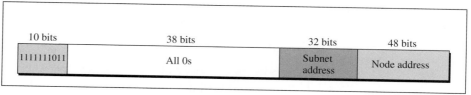

Multicast Addresses

Multicast addresses are used to define a group of hosts instead of just one. All use the prefix 11111111 in the first field. The second field is a flag that defines the group address as either permanent or transient. A permanent group address is defined by the Internet authorities and can be accessed at all times. A transient group address, on the other hand, is used only temporarily. Systems engaged in a teleconference, for example, can use a transient group address. The third field defines the scope of the group address. Many different scopes have been defined, as shown in Figure 25.14.

Figure 25.14   *Multicast address*

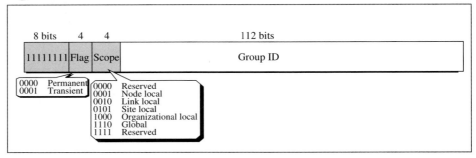

25.3   IPV6 PACKET FORMAT

The IPv6 packet is shown in Figure 25.15. Each packet is composed of a mandatory base header followed by the payload. The payload consists of two parts: optional extension headers and data from an upper layer. The base header occupies 40 bytes, whereas the extension headers and data from the upper layer usually contain up to 65,535 bytes of information.

Figure 25.15   *IPv6 datagram*

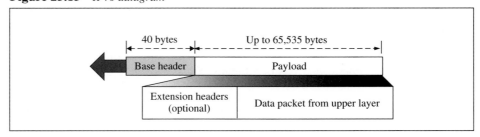

Base Header

Figure 25.16 shows the base header with its eight fields. These fields are as follows:

- **Version.** This four-bit field defines the version number of the IP. For IPv6, the value is 6.
- **Priority.** The four-bit priority field defines the priority of the packet with respect to traffic congestion. We will discuss this field later.
- **Flow label.** The flow label is a three-byte (24-bit) field that is designed to provide special handling for a particular flow of data. We will discuss this field later.
- **Payload length.** This two-byte payload length field defines the total length of the IP datagram excluding the base header.

Figure 25.16   *Format of an IPv6 datagram*

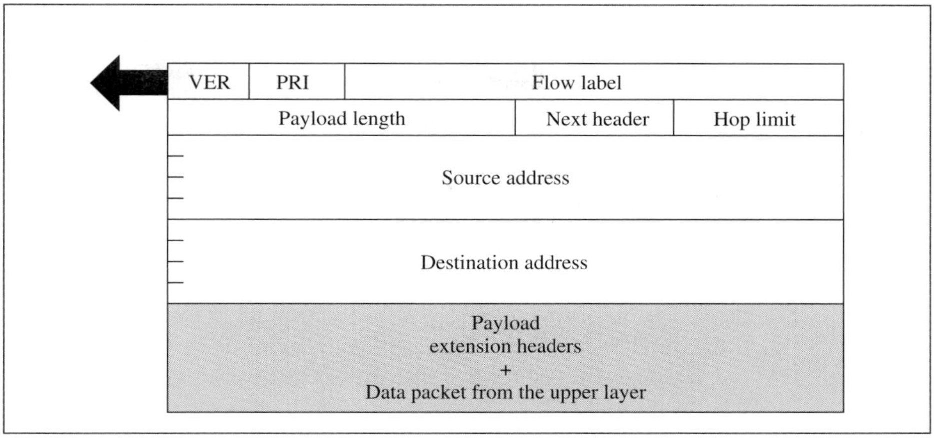

VER	PRI	Flow label	
Payload length		Next header	Hop limit
Source address			
Destination address			
Payload extension headers + Data packet from the upper layer			

■ **Next header.** The next header is an eight-bit field defining the header that follows the base header in the datagram. The next header is either one of the optional extension headers used by IP or the header for an upper layer protocol such as UDP or TCP. Each extension header also contains this field. Table 25.2 shows the values of next headers. Note that this field in version 4 is called the *protocol*.

Table 25.2   *Next header codes*

Code	Next Header
0	Hop-by-hop option
2	ICMP
6	TCP
17	UDP
43	Source routing
44	Fragmentation
50	Encrypted security payload
51	Authentication
59	Null (No next header)
60	Destination option

■ **Hop limit.** This eight-bit hop limit field serves the same purpose as the TTL field in IPv4.

■ **Source address.** The source address field is a 16-byte (128-bit) Internet address that identifies the original source of the datagram.

■ **Destination address.** The destination address field is a 16-byte (128-bit) Internet address that usually identifies the final destination of the datagram. However, if source routing is used, this field contains the address of the next router.

Priority

The priority field of the IPv6 packet defines the priority of each packet with respect to other packets from the same source. For example, if one of two consecutive datagrams must be discarded due to congestion, the datagram with the lower priority will be discarded. IPv6 divides traffic into two broad categories: congestion-controlled and non-congestion-controlled.

Congestion-Controlled Traffic

If a source adapts itself to traffic slowdown when there is congestion, the traffic is referred to as *congestion-controlled traffic*. For example, the TCP protocol, which uses the sliding window protocol, can easily respond to the traffic. In congestion-controlled traffic, it is understood that packets may arrive delayed or even lost or received out of order. Congestion-controlled data are assigned priorities from 0 to 7, as listed in Table 25.3. A priority of 0 is the lowest; a priority of 7 is the highest.

Table 25.3   *Priorities for congestion-controlled traffic*

Priority	Meaning
0	No specific traffic
1	Background data
2	Unattended data traffic
3	Reserved
4	Attended bulk data traffic
5	Reserved
6	Interactive traffic
7	Control traffic

The priority descriptions are as follows:

- **No specific traffic.** The priority 0 is assigned to a packet when the process does not define a priority.
- **Background data.** This group (priority 1) defines data that is usually delivered in the background. Delivery of the news is a good example.
- **Unattended data traffic.** If the user is not waiting (attending) for the data to be received, the packet will be given priority 2. E-mail belongs to this group. A user initiates an e-mail message to another user, but the receiver does not know that an e-mail will arrive soon. In addition, an e-mail is usually stored before it is forwarded. A little bit of delay is of little consequence.
- **Attended bulk data traffic.** The protocol that transfers the bulk of data while the user is waiting (attending) to receive the data (possibly with delay) is given priority 4. FTP and HTTP belong to this group.
- **Interactive traffic.** Protocols such as TELNET that need interaction with the user are assigned the second highest priority (6) in this group.

■ **Control traffic.** Control traffic has been given the highest priority (7) in this category. Routing protocols such as OSPF and RIP and management protocols such as SNMP use this priority.

Noncongestion-Controlled Traffic

This refers to a type of traffic that expects minimum delay. Discarding of packets is not desirable. Retransmission in most cases is impossible. In other words, the source does not adapt itself to congestion. Real-time audio and video are good examples of this type of traffic.

Priority numbers from 8 to 15 are assigned to noncongestion-controlled traffic. Although there are not yet any particular standard assignments for this type of data, the priorities are usually assigned based on how much the quality of received data can be affected by discarding some packets. Data containing less redundancy (such as low-fidelity audio or video) can be given a higher priority (15). Data containing more redundancy (such as high-fidelity audio or video) should be given lower priority (8). See Table 25.4.

Table 25.4   *Priorities for noncongestion controlled traffic*

Priority	Meaning
8	Data with most redundancy
.	.
.	.
.	.
15	Data with least redundancy

Flow Label

A sequence of packets, sent from a particular source to a particular destination, that needs special handling by routers is called a *flow* of packets. The combination of the source address and the value of the *flow label* (see above) uniquely defines a flow of packets.

To a router, a flow is a sequence of packets that share the same characteristics, such as traveling the same path, using the same resources, having the same kind of security, and so on. A router that supports the handling of flow labels has a flow label table. The table has an entry for each active flow label; each entry defines the services required by the corresponding flow label. When the router receives a packet, it consults its flow label table to find the corresponding entry for the flow label value defined in the packet. It then provides the packet with the services mentioned in the entry. However, note that the flow label itself does not provide the information for the entries of the flow label table; the information is provided by other means such as the hop-by-hop options or other protocols.

In its simplest form, a flow label can be used to speed up the processing of a packet by a router. When a router receives a packet, instead of consulting the routing table and going through a routing algorithm to define the address of the next hop, it can easily look in a flow label table for the next hop.

In its more sophisticated form, a flow label can be used to support the transmission of real-time audio and video. Real-time audio or video, particularly in digital form, requires resources such as high bandwidth, large buffers, long processing time, and so on. A process can make a reservation for these resources beforehand to guarantee that real-time data will not be delayed due to a lack of resources. The use of real-time data and the reservation of these resources requires other protocols such as Real Time Protocol (RTP) and Resource Reservation Protocol (RSVP) in addition to IPv6.

To allow the effective use of flow labels, three rules have been defined:

1. The flow label is assigned to a packet by the source host. The label is a random number between 1 and $2^{24} - 1$. A source must not reuse a flow label for a new flow while the existing flow is still alive.

2. If a host does not support the flow label, it sets this field to zero. If a router does not support the flow label, it simply ignores it.

3. All packets belonging to the same flow should have the same source, same destination, same priority, and same options.

Comparison between IPv4 and IPv6 Headers

Table 25.5 compares IPv4 and IPv6 headers.

Table 25.5 *Comparison between IPv4 and IPv6 packet header*

Comparison
1. The header length field is eliminated in IPv6 because the length of the header is fixed in this version.
2. The service type field is eliminated in IPv6. The priority and flow label fields together take over the function of the service type field.
3. The total length field is eliminated in IPv6 and replaced by the payload length field.
4. The identification, flag, and offset fields are eliminated from the base header in IPv6. They are included in the fragmentation extension header.
5. The TTL field is called hop limit in IPv6.
6. The protocol field is replaced by the next header field.
7. The header checksum is eliminated because the checksum is provided by upper layer protocols; it is thereby not needed at this level.
8. The option fields in IPv4 are implemented as extension headers in IPv6.

Extension Headers

The length of the base header is fixed at 40 bytes. However, to give more functionality to the IP datagram, the base header can be followed by up to six extension headers. Many of these headers are options in IPv4. Figure 25.17 shows the extension header format.

Figure 25.17 *Extension header format*

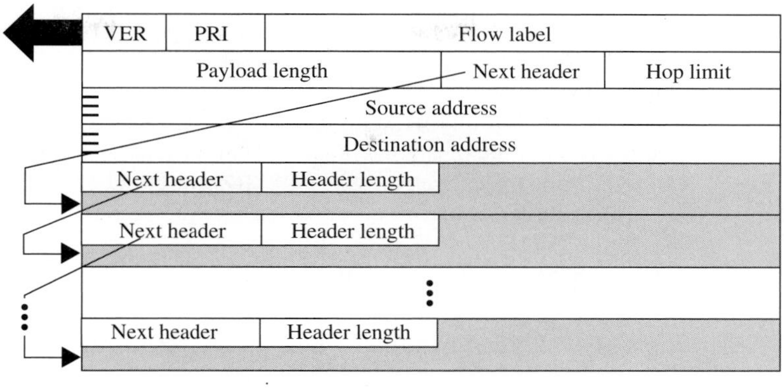

Six types of extension headers have been defined. These are hop-by-hop option, source routing, fragmentation, authentication, encrypted security payload, and destination option (see Figure 25.18).

Figure 25.18 *Extension header types*

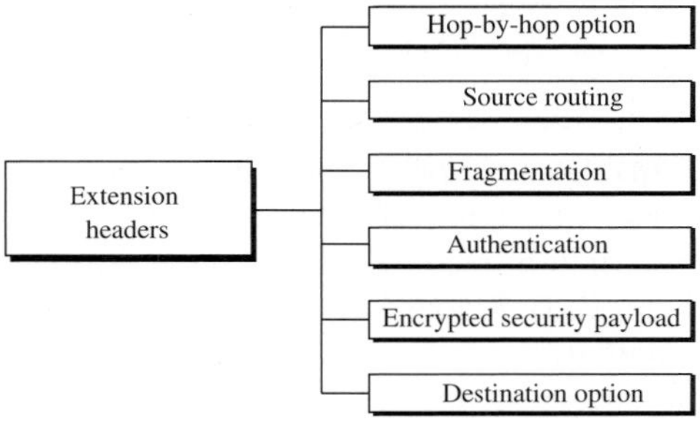

Hop-by-Hop Option

The hop-by-hop option is used when the source needs to pass information to all routers visited by the datagram. For example, perhaps routers must be informed about certain management, debugging, or control functions. Or, if the length of the datagram is more than the usual 65,535 bytes, routers must have this information. Figure 25.19 shows the format of the hop-by-hop option header. The first field defines the next header in the chain of headers. The header length defines the number of bytes in the header (including the next header field). The rest of the header contains different options.

So far, only three options have been defined: Pad1, PadN, and jumbo payload. Figure 25.20 shows the general format of the option.

Figure 25.19   *Hop-by-hop option header format*

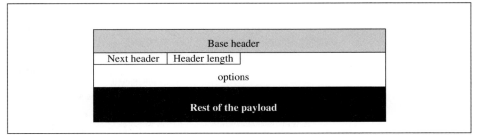

Figure 25.20   *The format of options in a hop-by-hop option header*

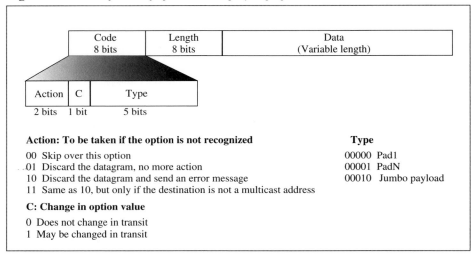

- **Pad1.** This option is one byte long and is designed for alignment purposes. Some options need to start at a specific bit of the 32-bit word (see the jumbo payload description to come). If an option falls short of this requirement by exactly one byte, Pad1 is added to make up the difference. Pad1 contains neither the option length field nor the option data field. It consists solely of the option code field with all bits set to 0 (action is 00, the change bit is 0, and type is 00000). Pad1 can be inserted anywhere in the hop-by-hop option header (see Figure 25.21).

- **PadN.** PadN is similar in concept to Pad1. The difference is that PadN is used when two or more bytes are needed for alignment. This option consists of one byte of option code, one byte of the option length, and a variable number of zero padding bytes. The value of the option code is 1 (action is 00, the change bit is 0, and type is 00001). The option length contains the number of padding bytes. See Figure 25.22.

- **Jumbo payload.** Recall that the length of the payload in the IP datagram can be a maximum of 65,535 bytes. However, if for any reason a longer payload is required, we can use the jumbo payload option to define this longer length. The one-byte option code has a value of 194 (11 for action, 0 for the change bit, and 00010 for

Figure 25.21   *Pad1*

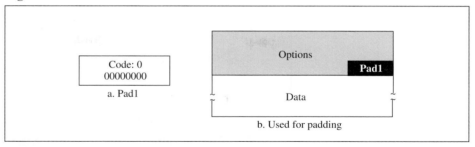

Figure 25.22   *PadN*

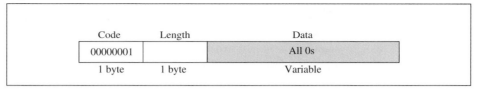

type). The one-byte option length defines the size in bytes of the next field and has a fixed value of 4. This means that the maximum length of the jumbo payload is $2^{32} - 1$ (4,294,967,295) bytes.

This option has an alignment restriction. The jumbo payload option must always start at a multiple of four bytes plus two from the beginning of the extension headers. The jumbo payload option starts at the $(4\,n + 2)$ byte, where n is a small integer. See Figure 25.23.

Figure 25.23   *Jumbo payload*

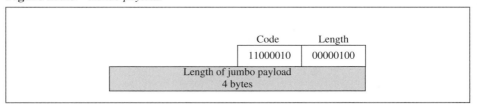

Source Routing

The source routing extension header combines the concepts of the strict source route and the loose source route options of IPv4. The source routing header contains a minimum of seven fields (see Figure 25.24). The first two fields, next header and header length, are identical to that of the hop-by-hop extension header. The type field defines loose or strict routing. The addresses left field indicates the number of hops still needed to reach the destination. The strict/loose mask field determines the rigidity of routing. If set to strict, routing must follow exactly as indicated by the source. If, instead, the mask is loose, other routers may be visited in addition to those in the header.

The destination address in source routing does not conform to our previous definition (the final destination of the datagram). Instead, it changes from router to router. For

Figure 25.24   *Source routing*

Base header			
Next header	Header length	Type	Addresses left
Reserved	Strict/loose mask		
First address			
Second address			
:			
Last address			
Rest of the payload			

example, in Figure 25.25, Host A wants to send a datagram to Host B using a specific route: A to R1 to R2 to R3 to B. Notice the destination address in the base headers. It is not constant as you might expect. Instead, it changes at each router. The addresses in the extension headers also change from router to router.

Figure 25.25   *Source routing example*

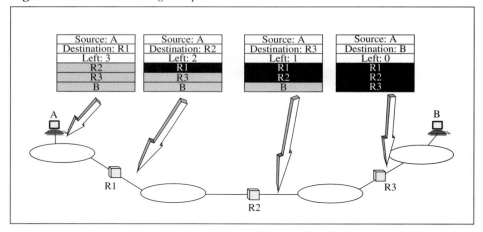

Fragmentation

The concept of fragmentation is the same as that in IPv4. However, the place where fragmentation takes place differs. In IPv4, the source or a router is required to fragment if the size of the datagram is larger than the MTU of the network over which the datagram should travel. In IPv6, only the original source can fragment. A source must use a Path MTU Discovery technique to find the smallest MTU supported by any network on the path. The source then fragments using this knowledge.

If the source does not use the Path MTU Discovery technique, it should fragment the datagram to a size of 576 bytes or smaller. This is the minimum size of MTU required for each network connected to the Internet. Figure 25.26 shows the format of the fragmentation extension header.

Figure 25.26 *Fragmentation*

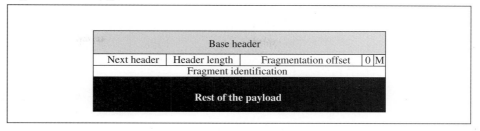

Authentication

The authentication extension header has a dual purpose: it validates the message sender and ensures the integrity of data. The former is needed so the receiver can be sure that a message is from the genuine sender and not from an imposter. The latter is needed to check that the data is not altered in transition by some hacker.

The format of the authentication extension header is shown in Figure 25.27. The security parameter index field defines the algorithm used for authentication. The authentication data field contains the actual data generated by the algorithm.

Figure 25.27 *Authentication*

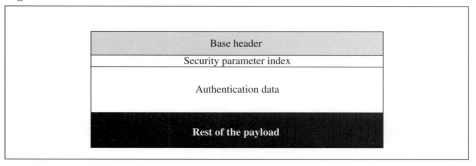

Many different algorithms can be used for authentication. Figure 25.28 outlines the method for calculating the authentication data field. The sender passes a 128-bit security key, the entire IP datagram, and the 128-bit security key again to the algorithm. Those fields in the datagram with values that change during transmission (for example, hop count) are set to zero. The datagram passed to the algorithm includes the authentication header extension, with the authentication data field set to zero. The algorithm creates authentication data which is inserted into the extension header prior to datagram transmission.

The receiver functions in a similar manner. It takes the secret key and the received datagram (again, with changeable fields set to zero) and passes them to the authentication algorithm. If the result matches that in the authentication data field, the IP datagram is authentic; otherwise, the datagram is discarded.

Figure 25.28 *Calculation of authentication data*

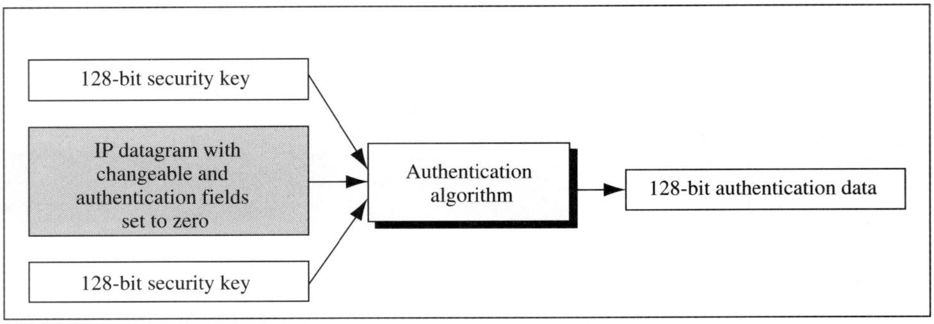

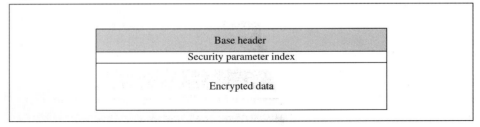

Encrypted Security Payload

The encrypted security payload (ESP) is an extension that provides confidentiality and guards against eavesdropping. Figure 25.29 shows the format. The security parameter index field is a 32-bit word that defines the type of encryption/decryption used. The other field contains the data being encrypted along with any extra parameters needed by the algorithm. Encryption can be implemented in two ways: transport mode and tunnel mode.

Figure 25.29 *Encrypted security payload*

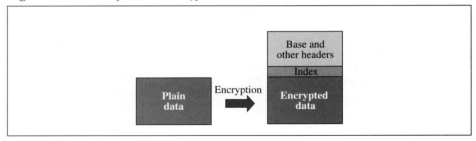

- **Transport mode.** In the transport mode, a TCP segment or a UDP user datagram is first encrypted and then encapsulated in an IPv6 packet. The transport mode of encryption is used mostly to encrypt data from host to host (see Figure 25.30).

Figure 25.30 *Transport mode encryption*

■   **Tunnel mode.** In the tunnel mode, the entire IP datagram with its base header and extension headers is encrypted and then encapsulated in a new IP packet using the ESP extension header. In other words, you have two base headers: one encrypted, one not. The tunnel mode of encryption is mostly used by security gateways to encrypt data. Figure 25.31 shows the idea.

Figure 25.31   *Tunnel-mode encryption*

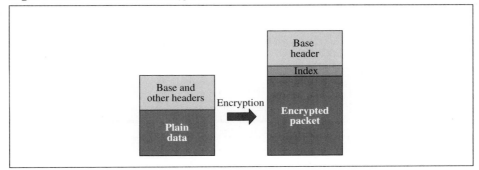

Destination Option

The destination option is used when the source needs to pass information to the destination only. Intermediate routers are not permitted access to this information. The format of the destination option is the same as the hop-by-hop option (refer back to Figure 25.19). So far, only the Pad1 and PadN options have been defined.

Comparison between IPv4 and IPv6

Table 25.6 compares the options in IPv4 with the extension headers in IPv6.

Table 25.6   *Comparison between IPv4 and IPv6 packet header*

Comparison
1. The no-operation and end-of-option options in IPv4 are replaced by Pad1 and PadN options in IPv6.
2. The record route option is not implemented in IPv6 because it was not used.
3. The timestamp option is not implemented because it was not used.
4. The source router option is called the source route extension header in IPv6.
5. The fragmentation fields in the base header section of IPv4 have moved to the fragmentation extension header in IPv6.
6. The authentication extension header is new in IPv6.
7. The encrypted security payload extension header is new in IPv6.

25.4   ICMPV6

Another protocol that has been modified in version 6 of the TCP/IP protocol suite is ICMP (ICMPv6). This new version follows the same strategy and purposes of version 4. ICMPv4 has been modified to make it more suitable for IPv6. In addition, some protocols that were independent in version 4 are now part of ICMPv6. Figure 25.32 compares the network layer of version 4 to version 6.

Figure 25.32   *Comparison of network layers in version 4 and version 6*

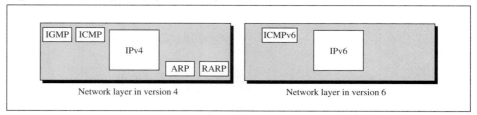

The ARP and IGMP protocols in version 4 are combined in ICMPv6. The RARP protocol is dropped from the suite because it is not used often. In addition, BOOTP does the job of RARP.

Just as in ICMPv4, we divide the ICMP messages into two categories. However, each category has more types of messages than before (see Figure 25.33). Although the

Figure 25.33   *Categories of ICMPv6 messages*

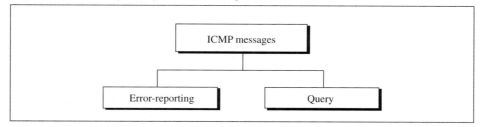

general format of an ICMP message is different for each message type, the first four bytes are common to all, as is shown in Figure 25.34. The first field, the ICMP type, defines the broad category of the message. The code field specifies the reason for the particular message type. The last common field is the checksum field, calculated in the same manner as was described for ICMP version 4.

Error Reporting

As we saw in our discussion of version 4, one of the main responsibilities of ICMP is to report errors. Five types of errors are handled: destination unreachable, packet too big, time exceeded, parameter problems, and redirection (see Figure 25.35). ICMPv6 forms an error packet, which is then encapsulated in an IP datagram. This is delivered to the original source of the failed datagram.

Figure 25.34 *General format of ICMP messages*

```
   |←—— 8 bits ——→|←—— 8 bits ——→|←—— 8 bits ——→|←—— 8 bits ——→|

   |     Type     |     Code     |        Checksum             |
   |                 Other  information                          |

                        Rest of data
```

Figure 25.35 *Error-reporting messages*

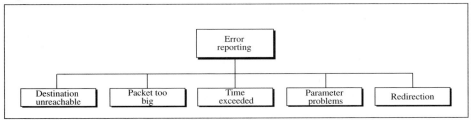

Table 25.7 compares the error-reporting messages of ICMPv4 with ICMPv6. The source-quench message is eliminated in version 6 because the priority and the flow label fields allow the router to control congestion and discard the least important messages. In this version, there is no need to inform the sender to slow down. The packet-too-big message is added because fragmentation is the responsibility of the sender in IPv6. If the sender does not make the right packet size decision, the router does not have any choice except to drop the packet and send an error message to the sender.

Table 25.7 *Comparison of error-reporting messages in ICMPv4 and ICMPv6*

Type of Message	Version 4	Version 6
Destination unreachable	Yes	Yes
Source quench	Yes	No
Packet too big	No	Yes
Time exceeded	Yes	Yes
Parameter problem	Yes	Yes
Redirection	Yes	Yes

Destination Unreachable

The concept of the destination unreachable message is exactly the same as we described for ICMP version 4. Figure 25.36 shows the format of the destination-unreachable message. It is similar to the one defined for version 4, with the type value equal to 1.

Figure 25.36 *Destination-unreachable message format*

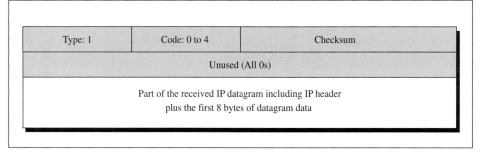

The code field for this type specifies the reason for discarding the datagram and explains exactly what has failed:

- **Code 0.** No path to destination.
- **Code 1.** Communication is prohibited.
- **Code 2.** Strict source routing is impossible.
- **Code 3.** Destination address is unreachable.
- **Code 4.** Port is not available.

Packet Too Big

This is a new type of message added to version 6. If a router receives a datagram that is larger than the maximum transmission unit (MTU) size of the network through which the datagram should pass, two things happen. First, the router discards the datagram and then an ICMP error packet is sent to the source. Figure 25.37 shows the format of the packet. Note that there is only one code (0) and that the MTU field informs the sender of the maximum size packet accepted by the network.

Figure 25.37 *Packet-too-big message format*

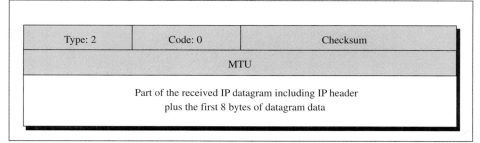

Time Exceeded

This message is similar to the one in version 4. The only difference is that the type value has changed to 3. Figure 25.38 shows the format of the time-exceeded message.

Figure 25.38 *Time-exceeded message format*

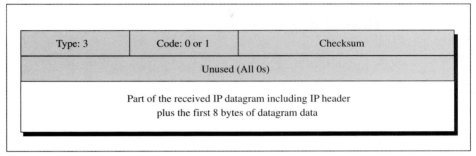

As in version 4, code 0 is used when the datagram is discarded by the router due to a hop-limit field value of zero. Code 1 is used when fragments of a datagram are discarded because other fragments have not arrived within the time limit.

Parameter Problem

This message is similar to its version 4 counterpart. However, the type value has been changed to 4 and the size of the offset pointer field has been increased to four bytes. There are also three different codes instead of two. The code field specifies the reason for discarding the datagram and the cause of failure:

- **Code 0.** There is error or ambiguity in one of the header fields. In this case the value in the pointer field points to the byte with the problem. For example, if the value is zero, then the first byte is not a valid field.
- **Code 1.** This defines an unrecognizable extension header.
- **Code 2.** This defines an unrecognizable option.

Figure 25.39 shows the format of the parameter problem message.

Figure 25.39 *Parameter-problem message format*

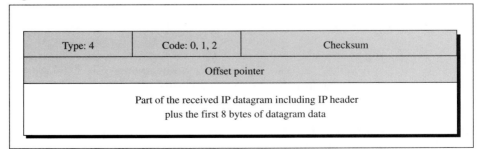

Redirection

The purpose of this message is the same as we described for version 4. However, the format of the packet is changed to accommodate the size of the IP address in version 6. Also, an option is added to let the host know the physical address of the target router (see Figure 25.40).

Figure 25.40   *Redirection message format*

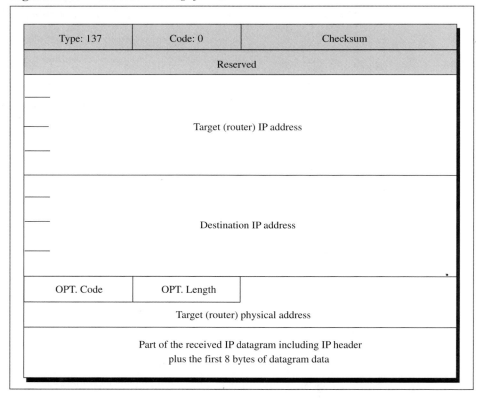

Query

In addition to error reporting, ICMP can also diagnose some network problems. This is accomplished through the query messages. Four different groups of messages have been defined: echo request and reply, router solicitation and advertisement, neighbor solicitation and advertisement, and group membership (see Figure 25.41).

Table 25.8 shows the comparison between the query messages in versions 4 and 6. Two sets of query messages are eliminated from ICMPv6: timestamp request and reply and address mask request and reply. The timestamp request and reply messages are eliminated because they are implemented in other protocols such as TCP and because they were not used in the past. The address-mask request and reply messages are eliminated in IPv6 because the subnet section of an address allows the subscriber to use up to $2^{32} - 1$ subnets. Therefore, subnet masking, as defined in IPv4, is not needed here.

Figure 25.41   *Query messages*

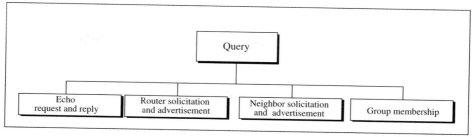

Table 25.8   *Comparison of query messages in ICMPv4 and ICMPv6*

Type of Message	Version 4	Version 6
Echo request and reply	Yes	Yes
Timestamp request and reply	Yes	No
Address mask request and reply	Yes	No
Router solicitation and advertisement	Yes	Yes
Neighbor solicitation and advertisement	ARP	Yes
Group membership	IGMP	Yes

Echo Request and Reply

The idea and format of the echo request and reply messages are the same as those in version 4. The only difference is the value for the type as shown in Figure 25.42.

Figure 25.42   *Echo request and reply messages*

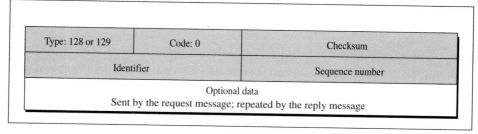

Router Solicitation and Advertisement

The idea behind the router-solicitation and advertisement messages is the same as in version 4. The router-solicitation format is the same as the one in ICMPv4. However, an option is added to allow the host to announce its physical address to make it easier for the router to respond. The router-advertisement format is different from the one in ICMPv4; here the router announces just itself and not any other router. Options can be added to the packet. One option announces the router physical address for the convenience of the host. Another option lets the router announce the MTU size. A third option allows the router to define the valid and preferred lifetime. Figure 25.43 shows the format of the router-solicitation and advertisement messages.

Figure 25.43 *Router-solicitation and advertisement message formats*

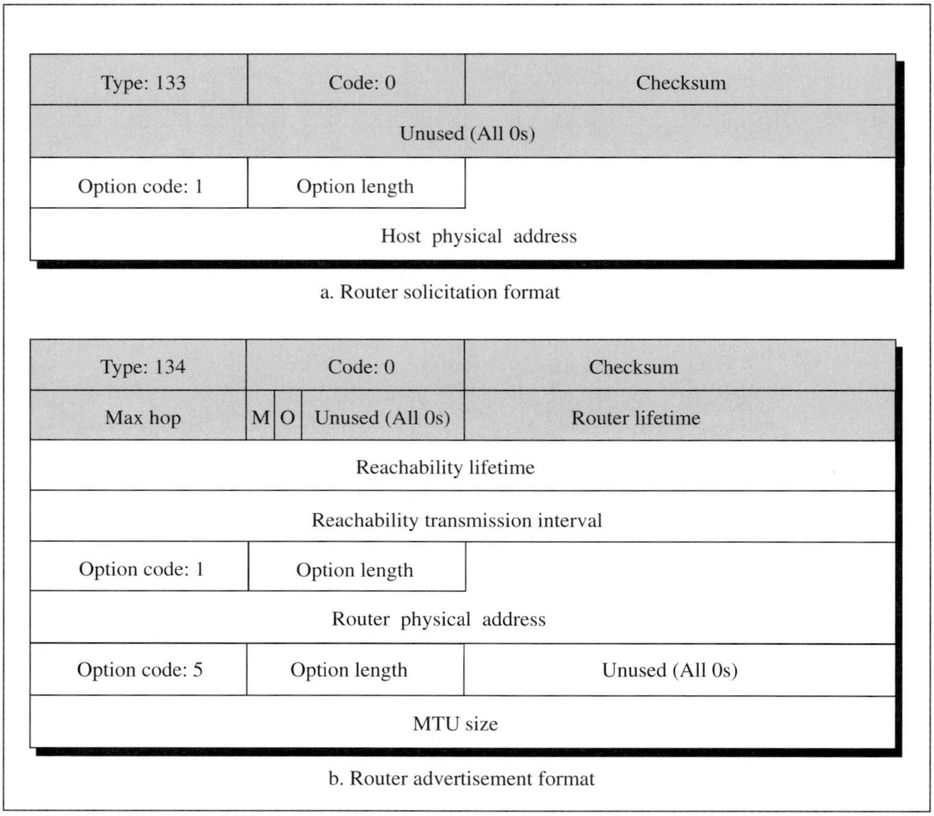

Type: 133	Code: 0	Checksum
Unused (All 0s)		
Option code: 1	Option length	
Host physical address		

a. Router solicitation format

Type: 134		Code: 0	Checksum
Max hop	M O	Unused (All 0s)	Router lifetime
Reachability lifetime			
Reachability transmission interval			
Option code: 1	Option length		
Router physical address			
Option code: 5	Option length	Unused (All 0s)	
MTU size			

b. Router advertisement format

Neighbor Solicitation and Advertisement

As previously mentioned, the network layer in version 4 contains an independent protocol called ARP. In version 6, this protocol is eliminated, and its duties are included in ICMPv6. The idea is exactly the same, but the format of the message has changed. Figure 25.44 shows the format of neighbor solicitation and advertisement. The only option announces the sender physical address for the convenience of the receiver.

Group Membership

As previously mentioned, the network layer in version 4 contains an independent protocol called IGMP. In version 6, this protocol is eliminated, and its duties are included in ICMPv6. The purpose is exactly the same, but membership termination is handled by an explicit message. In version 4, no response from the host or router indicates termination.

Figure 25.44 *Neighbor-solicitation and advertisement message formats*

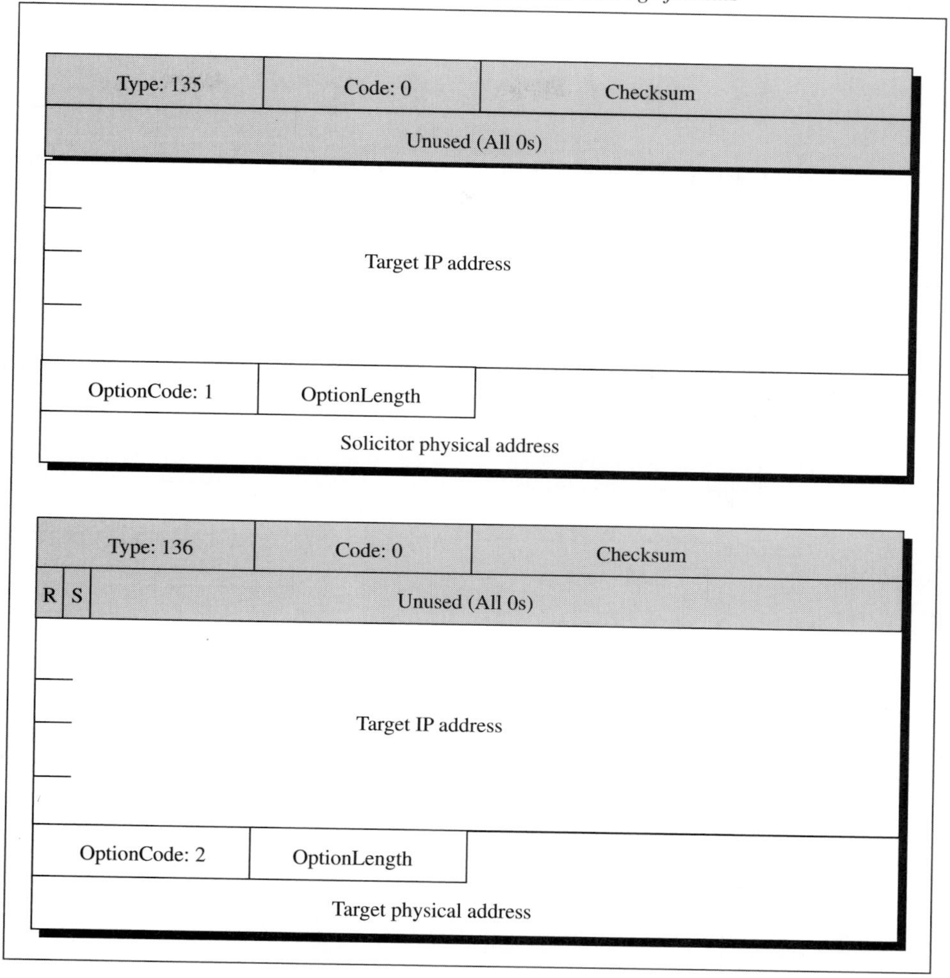

Type: 135
Code: 0
Checksum
Unused (All 0s)
Target IP address
OptionCode: 1
OptionLength
Solicitor physical address
Type: 136
Code: 0
Checksum
R
S
Unused (All 0s)
Target IP address
OptionCode: 2
OptionLength
Target physical address

Group membership has three types of messages: report, query, and termination (see Figure 25.45). The report and termination messages are sent from the host to the router. The query message is sent from the router to the host. Figure 25.46 shows the format of group membership messages.

Figure 25.45 *Group membership messages*

Host
Report
Router
R
Query
Termination

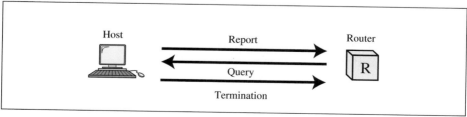

Figure 25.46 *Group-membership message formats*

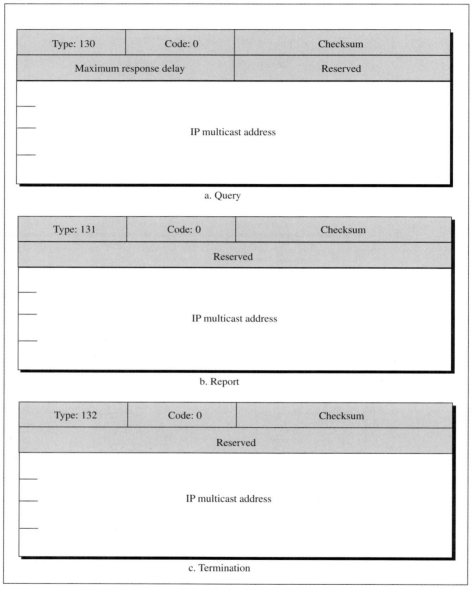

a. Query

b. Report

c. Termination

As we noted in our discussion of version 4, four different situations involve group-membership messages; these are shown in Figure 25.47. The only difference between versions 4 and 6 in this respect is that termination is explicitly declared by the host using the termination message.

Figure 25.47   *Four situations of group-membership operation*

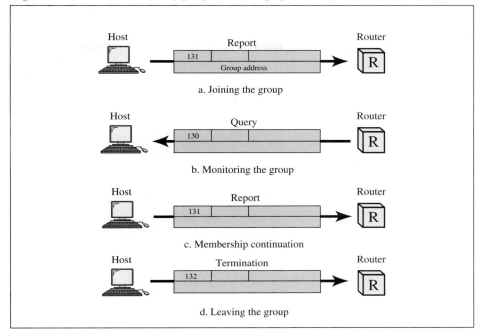

a. Joining the group

b. Monitoring the group

c. Membership continuation

d. Leaving the group

25.5   TRANSITION FROM IPV4 TO IPV6

Because of the huge number of systems on the Internet, the transition from IPv4 to IPv6 cannot happen suddenly. It takes a considerable amount of time before every system in the Internet can move from IPv4 to IPv6. The transition should be smooth to prevent any problems between IPv4 and IPv6 systems.

Three strategies have been devised by the IETF to make the transition period smoother (see Figure 25.48).

Figure 25.48   *Three transition strategies*

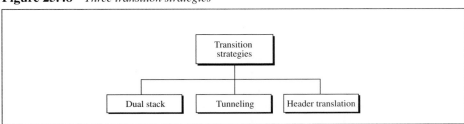

Dual Stack

It is recommended that all hosts, before migrating completely to version 6, have a dual stack of protocols. In other words, a station should run IPv4 and IPv6 simultaneously until all of the Internet uses IPv6. See Figure 25.49 for the layout of dual-stack configuration.

Figure 25.49   *Dual stack*

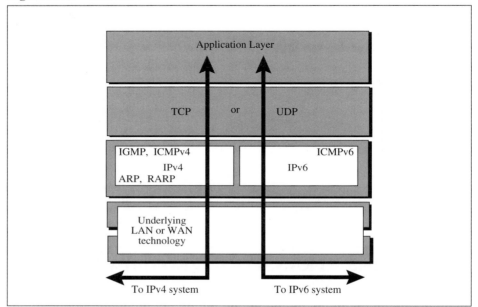

To determine which version to use when sending a packet to a destination, the source host queries the DNS. If the DNS returns an IPv4 address, the source host sends an IPv4 packet. If the DNS returns an IPv6 address, the source host sends an IPv6 packet.

Tunneling

Tunneling is a strategy used when two computers using IPv6 want to communicate with each other when the packet must pass through a region that uses IPv4. To pass through this region, the packet must have an IPv4 address. So the IPv6 packet is encapsulated in an IPv4 packet when it enters the region, and it leaves its capsule when it exits the region. It seems as if the IPv6 packet goes through a tunnel at one end and emerges at the other end. To make it clear that the IPv4 packet is carrying an IPv6 packet as data, the protocol value is set to 41. Tunneling uses the compatible addresses discussed in Section 25.2.

Automatic Tunneling

If the receiving host uses a compatible IPv6 address, tunneling occurs automatically without any reconfiguration. The sender sends the receiver an IPv6 packet using the IPv6 compatible address as the destination address. When the packet reaches the boundary of the IPv4 network, the router encapsulates it in an IPv4 packet, which should have an IPv4 address. To get this address, the router extracts the IPv4 address embedded in the IPv6 address. The packet then travels the rest of its journey as an IPv4 packet. The destination host, which is using a dual stack, now receives an IPv4 packet. Recognizing its IPv4 address, it reads the header, and finds (through the protocol field value) that the packet is carrying an IPv6 packet. It then passes the packet to the IPv6 software for processing (see Figure 25.50).

Figure 25.50 *Automatic tunneling*

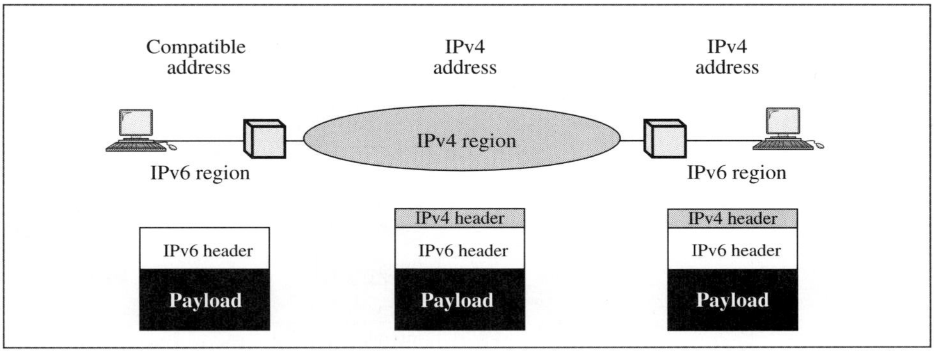

Configured Tunneling

If the receiving host does not support an IPv6-compatible address, the sender receives a noncompatible IPv6 address from the DNS. In this case, the sender sends the IPv6 packet with the receiver's noncompatible IPv6 address. However, the packet cannot pass through the IPv4 region without first being encapsulated in an IPv4 packet. The two routers at the boundary of the IPv4 region are configured to pass the packet encapsulated in an IPv4 packet. The router at one end sends the IPv4 packet with its own IPv4 address as the source and the other router's IPv4 address as the destination. The other router receives the packet, decapsulates the IPv6 packet, and sends it to the destination host. The destination host then receives the packet in IPv6 format and processes it (see Figure 25.51).

Header Translation

Header translation is necessary when the majority of the Internet has moved to IPv6 but some systems still use IPv4. The sender wants to use IPv6, but the receiver does not understand IPv6. Tunneling does not work in this situation because the packet must be in the IPv4 format to be understood by the receiver. In this case, the header format must be changed totally through header translation. The header of the IPv6 packet is converted to an IPv4 header (see Figure 25.52).

Figure 25.51   *Configured tunneling*

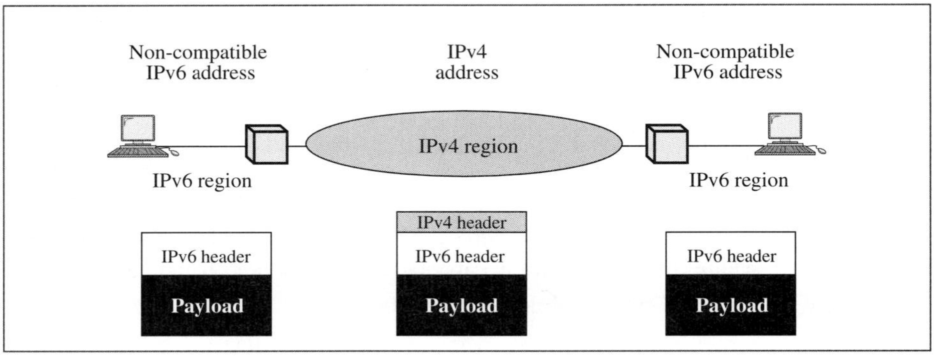

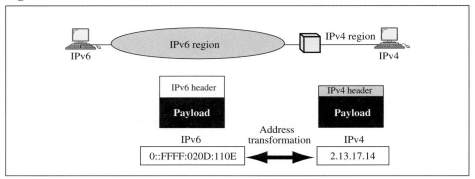

Figure 25.52   *Header translation*

Header translation uses the mapped address to translate an IPv6 address to an IPv4 address. Table 25.9 lists some rules used in transforming an IPv6 packet header to an IPv4 packet header.

Table 25.9   *Header Translation*

Header Translation Procedure
1. The IPv6 mapped address is changed to an IPv4 address by extracting the right-most 32 bits.
2. The value of the IPv6 priority field is discarded.
3. Set the type of service field in IPv4 to zero.
4. The checksum for IPv4 is calculated and inserted in the corresponding field.
5. The IPv6 flow label is ignored.
6. Compatible extension headers are converted to options and inserted in the IPv4 header.
7. The length of IPv4 header is calculated and inserted into the corresponding field.
8. The total length of the IPv4 packet is calculated and inserted in the corresponding field.

25.6 SUMMARY

- IPv6, the latest proposed version of the Internet Protocol, has a 128-bit address space, a revised header format, new options, an allowance for extension, support for resource allocation, and increased security measures.

- IPv6 uses hexadecimal colon notation with abbreviation methods available.

- There are three types of addresses: unicast, anycast, and multicast.

- The variable-type prefix field defines the address type or purpose.

- An IP datagram is composed of a base header and a payload.

- The 40-byte base header consists of the version, priority, flow label, payload length, next header, hop limit, source address, and destination address fields.

- The priority field is a measure of the importance of a datagram.

- The flow label identifies the special-handling needs of a sequence of packets.

- A payload consists of optional extension headers and data from an upper layer.

- Extension headers add functionality to the IPv6 datagram.

- The hop-by-hop option is used to pass information to all routers in the path.

- The source routing extension is used when the source wants to specify the transmission path.

- The fragmentation extension is used if the payload is a fragment of a message.

- The authentication extension validates the sender of the message and protects the data from hackers.

- The encrypted security payload extension provides confidentiality between sender and receiver.

- The destination extension passes information from the source to the destination exclusively.

- ICMPv6, like version 4, reports errors, handles group memberships, updates specific router and host tables, and checks the viability of a host.

- The five error-reporting messages deal with unreachable destinations, packets that are too big, expired timers for fragments and hop counts, header problems, and inefficient routing.

- Query messages are in the form of a response and a reply.

- The echo- request and reply query messages test the connectivity between two systems.

- The router-solicitation and advertisement messages allow routers to update their routing tables.

- The group-membership messages (IGMP in version 4) can add a host to a group, terminate a group membership, monitor a group, or maintain group membership.

- Three strategies used to make the transition from version 4 to version 6 are dual stack, tunneling, and header translation.

25.7   PRACTICE SET

Multiple Choice

1. Which of the following is a necessary part of the IPv6 datagram?
    a. base header
    b. extension header
    c. data packet from the upper layer
    d. a and c

2. The _____ field in the base header restricts the lifetime of a datagram.
    a. version
    b. priority
    c. next header
    d. hop limit

3. When a datagram needs to be discarded in a congested network, the decision is based on the _____ field in the base header.
    a. version
    b. priority
    c. next header
    d. hop limit

4. The _____ field in the base header and the sender IP address combine to indicate a unique path identifier for a specific flow of data.
    a. version
    b. flow label
    c. next header
    d. hop limit

5. The source address in the base header always contains the address of the _____.
    a. last router
    b. next router
    c. original sender
    d. any of the above

6. For a maximum number of hops, set the hop limit field to decimal _____.
    a. 16
    b. 15
    c. 42
    d. 0

7. For time-sensitive data, assign the priority field a value of decimal _____.
    a. 0
    b. 7
    c. 8 to 15

    d. 16

8. Real-time packets being sent at a constant rate are classified as _____.

    a. congestion-controlled data

    b. noncongestion-controlled data

    c. low-priority data

    d. none of the above

9. _____ data can adapt itself to the network flow.

    a. Congestion-controlled

    b. Noncongestion-controlled

    c. Compressed

    d. Modulated

10. A datagram with a priority of _____ will be discarded before a datagram with a priority of 12.

    a. 11

    b. 7

    c. 0

    d. any of the above

11. A 6,000-byte packet needs to be routed through an Ethernet LAN. What extension header must be used?

    a. source routing

    b. fragmentation

    c. authentication

    d. destination option

12. Management wants to compare the transmission time for two different routes. What extension header must be used?

    a. source routing

    b. fragmentation

    c. authentication

    d. destination option

13. An IP datagram is 80,000 bytes. What extension header must be used?

    a. hop-by-hop

    b. fragmentation

    c. authentication

    d. destination option

14. The maximum size for an IPv6 datagram is _____ bytes.

    a. 65,535

    b. 65,575

    c. 2^{32}

    d. $2^{32} + 40$

15. What is the minimum length for a hop-by-hop extension header?
    a. 1 byte
    b. 3 bytes
    c. 4 bytes
    d. 8 bytes

16. To request the physical address of a host whose IP address is known, a _____ message is sent.
    a. membership-query
    b. router-solicitation
    c. neighbor-solicitation
    d. neighbor-advertisement

17. If a host needs information about routers on the network, it sends a _____ message.
    a. membership-report
    b. router-solicitation
    c. neighbor-solicitation
    d. neighbor-advertisement

18. Which of the following types of ICMP messages need to be encapsulated into an IP datagram?
    a. neighbor solicitation
    b. echo response
    c. redirection
    d. all of the above

19. The ARP function in version 4 is part of _____ in version 6.
    a. echo request and reply
    b. router solicitation and advertisement
    c. neighbor solicitation and advertisement
    d. group membership

20. The IGMP functions in version 4 are part of _____ in version 6.
    a. echo request and reply
    b. router solicitation and advertisement
    c. neighbor solicitation and advertisement
    d. group membership

21. To join a group, a host sends a _____.
    a. group-membership report
    b. group-membership query
    c. group-membership termination
    d. any of the above

22. The purpose of echo request and echo reply is to _____.
    a. report errors

    b. check node-to-node communication

    c. check group memberships

    d. find physical addresses

23. A host must respond within the _____ time if it wishes to retain membership in a group being queried.

    a. maximum-response delay

    b. hop-count

    c. maximum-transmission unit

    d. network-response

24. In error reporting the encapsulated ICMP packet goes to _____.

    a. the source

    b. the destination

    c. a router

    d. any of the above

25. In error reporting, a destination can send a _____ message.

    a. parameter-problem

    b. packet-too-big

    c. time-exceeded

    d. a and c

26. Which field is always present in an ICMP packet?

    a. type

    b. code

    c. checksum

    d. all of the above

27. An MTU field is found on the _____ error message to inform the sender about packet size.

    a. destination-unreachable

    b. time-exceeded

    c. parameter-problem

    d. packet-too-big

28. When the hop count field reaches zero and the destination has not been reached, a _____ error message is sent.

    a. destination-unreachable

    b. time-exceeded

    c. parameter-problem

    d. packet-too-big

29. When all fragments of a message have not been received within the designated amount of time, a _____ error message is sent.

    a. destination-unreachable

    b. time-exceeded

    c. parameter-problem

    d. packet-too-big

30. Errors in the header or option fields of an IP datagram require a _____ error message.

    a. destination-unreachable

    b. time-exceeded

    c. parameter-problem

    d. packet-too-big

31. If a member of a group wishes to terminate membership, it can _____ in response to a group membership query.

    a. send a group membership report

    b. send a group membership termination

    c. do nothing

    d. b or c

32. What field on a multicasting packet uniquely identifies a group?

    a. type

    b. code

    c. maximum response delay

    d. IP multicast address

33. A _____ can learn about network _____ by sending out a router solicitation packet.

    a. router, routers

    b. router, hosts

    c. host, hosts,

    d. host, routers

34. The _____ packet contains information about a router.

    a. router solicitation

    b. router information

    c. router advertisement

    d. router option

35. When a host has the _____ address of a host but needs the _____ address, it uses a neighbor solicitation packet.

    a. physical, protocol port

    b. physical, data link layer

    c. physical, IP

    d. IP, physical

36. A router can send a _____ message to a host to inform it of a more efficient path.

    a. neighbor solicitation

    b. router solicitation

    c. redirection

d. neighbor advertisement

37. Which version 4 protocols are still viable and known by their same names in version 6?

    a. IGMP

    b. ARP

    c. RARP

    d. none of the above

38. Which error-reporting message from version 4 has been eliminated in version 6?

    a. packet too big

    b. destination unreachable

    c. parameter problem

    d. source quench

39. Which error-reporting message is found in version 6 but not in version 4?

    a. packet too big

    b. destination unreachable

    c. parameter problem

    d. time exceeded

Exercises

40. Show the shortest form of the following addresses:

    a. 2340:1ABC:119A:A000:0000:0000:0000:0000

    b. 0000:00AA:0000:0000:0000:0000:119A:A231

    c. 2340:0000:0000:0000:0000:119A:A001:0000

    d. 0000:0000:0000:2340:0000:0000:0000:0000

41. Show the original (unabbreviated) form of the following addresses:

    a. 0::0

    b. 0:AA::0

    c. 0:1234::3

    d. 123::1:2

42. What is the type of each of the following addresses:

    a. FE80::12

    b. FEC0::24A2

    c. FF02::0

    d. 0::01

43. What is the type of each of the following addresses:

    a. 0::0

    b. 0::FFFF:0:0

    c. 582F:1234::2222

    d. 4821::14:22

e. 54EF::A234:2

44. Show the provider prefix (in hexadecimal colon notation) of an address assigned to a subscriber if it is registered in the USA with the provider identification ABC1.

45. Show in hexadecimal colon notation the IPv6 address compatible to the IPv4 address 129.6.12.34.

46. Show in hexadecimal colon notation the IPv6 address mapped to the IPv4 address 129.6.12.34.

47. Show in hexadecimal colon notation the IPv6 loopback address.

48. Show in hexadecimal colon notation the link local address in which the node identifier is 0::123/48.

49. Show in hexadecimal colon notation the site local address in which the node identifier is 0::123/48.

50. Show in hexadecimal colon notation the permanent multicast address used in a link local scope.

51. What are the possible first two bytes for a multicast address?

52. A host has the address 581E:1456:2314:ABCD::1211. If the node identification is 48 bits, find the address of the subnet to which the host is attached.

53. A host has the address 581E:1456:2314:ABCD::1211. If the node identification is 48 bits, and the subnet identification is 32 bits find the provider prefix.

54. A site with 200 subnets has the class B address of 132.45.0.0. The site recently migrated to IPv6 with the subscriber prefix 581E:1456:2314::ABCD/80. Design the subnets and define the subnet address using a subnet identifier of 32 bits.

55. An IPv6 packet consists of the base header and a TCP segment. The length of data is 320 bytes. Show the packet and enter a value for each field.

56. An IPv6 packet consists of a base header and a TCP segment. The length of data is 128,000 bytes (jumbo payload). Show the packet and enter a value for each field.

57. What types of ICMP messages contain part of the IP datagram? Why is this included?

58. Compare and contrast, field by field, the destination-unreachable message format in ICMPv4 and ICMPv6.

59. Compare and contrast, field by field, the time-exceeded message format in ICMPv4 and ICMPv6.

60. Compare and contrast, field by field, the parameter-problem message format in ICMPv4 and ICMPv6.

61. Compare and contrast, field by field, the redirection-message format in ICMPv4 and ICMPv6.

62. Compare and contrast, field by field, the echo-request and reply messages format in ICMPv4 and ICMPv6.

63. Compare and contrast, field by field, the router-solicitation and advertisement messages format in ICMPv4 and ICMPv6.

64. Compare and contrast, field by field, the neighbor-solicitation and advertisement messages format in ICMPv6 with the query and reply messages in ARP.

65. Compare and contrast, field by field, the group-membership messages in IPv6 with the corresponding messages in IGMP.
66. Why are the IPv4-compatible addresses and the IPv4-mapped addresses different?
67. What is the IPv4-compatible address for 119.254.254.254?
68. What is the IPv4-mapped address for 119.254.254.254?
69. How many more addresses are available with IPv6 than IPv4?
70. In designing the IPv4-mapped address, why didn't the designers just prepend 96 1s to the IPv4 address?

Programming Exercises

71. Write a function in C to convert an address in binary format to hexadecimal colon notation.
72. Write a function in C to convert an address in hexadecimal notation to its shortest length.
73. Write a function in C to convert an IPv4 address to the corresponding IPv6 compatible address.
74. Write a function in C to convert an IPv4 address to the corresponding IPv6 mapped address.
75. Write a function in C to find the type of an IPv6 address.

APPENDIX A

ASCII Code

The American Standard Code for Information Interchange (ASCII) is the most commonly used code for encoding printable and nonprintable (control) characters.

ASCII uses seven bits to encode each character. It can therefore represent up to 128 characters. Table A.1 lists the ASCII characters and their codes in both binary and hexadecimal form.

Table A.1   *ASCII table*

Decimal	Hexadecimal	Binary	Character	Description
0	00	0000000	NUL	Null
1	01	0000001	SOH	Start of header
2	02	0000010	STX	Start of text
3	03	0000011	ETX	End of text
4	04	0000100	EOT	End of transmission
5	05	0000101	ENQ	Enquiry
6	06	0000110	ACK	Acknowledgment
7	07	0000111	BEL	Bell
8	08	0001000	BS	Backspace
9	09	0001001	HT	Horizontal tab
10	0A	0001010	LF	Line feed
11	0B	0001011	VT	Vertical tab
12	0C	0001100	FF	Form feed
13	0D	0001101	CR	Carriage return
14	0E	0001110	SO	Shift out
15	0F	0001111	SI	Shift in
16	10	0010000	DLE	Data link escape
17	11	0010001	DC1	Device control 1

Table A.1   *ASCII table (continued)*

Decimal	Hexadecimal	Binary	Character	Description
18	12	0010010	DC2	Device control 2
19	13	0010011	DC3	Device control 3
20	14	0010100	DC4	Device control 4
21	15	0010101	NAK	Negative acknowledgment
22	16	0010110	SYN	Synchronous idle
23	17	0010111	ETB	End of transmission block
24	18	0011000	CAN	Cancel
25	19	0011001	EM	End of medium
26	1A	0011010	SUB	Substitute
27	1B	0011011	ESC	Escape
28	1C	0011100	FS	File separator
29	1D	0011101	GS	Group separator
30	1E	0011110	RS	Record separator
31	1F	0011111	US	Unit separator
32	20	0100000	SP	Space
33	21	0100001	!	Exclamation mark
34	22	0100010	"	Double quote
35	23	0100011	#	Pound sign
36	24	0100100	$	Dollar sign
37	25	0100101	%	Percent sign
38	26	0100110	&	Ampersand
39	27	0100111	'	Apostrophe
40	28	0101000	(	Open parenthesis
41	29	0101001	)	Close parenthesis
42	2A	0101010	*	Asterisk
43	2B	0101011	+	Plus sign
44	2C	0101100	,	Comma
45	2D	0101101	-	Hyphen
46	2E	0101110	.	Period
47	2F	0101111	/	Slash
48	30	0110000	0	
49	31	0110001	1	
50	32	0110010	2	
51	33	0110011	3	
52	34	0110100	4	

Table A.1   *ASCII table (continued)*

Decimal	Hexadecimal	Binary	Character	Description
53	35	0110101	5	
54	36	0110110	6	
55	37	0110111	7	
56	38	0111000	8	
57	39	0111001	9	
58	3A	0111010	:	Colon
59	3B	0111011	;	Semicolon
60	3C	0111100	<	Less than sign
61	3D	0111101	=	Equal sign
62	3E	0111110	>	Greater than sign
63	3F	0111111	?	Question mark
64	40	1000000	@	At sign
65	41	1000001	A	
66	42	1000010	B	
67	43	1000011	C	
68	44	1000100	D	
69	45	1000101	E	
70	46	1000110	F	
71	47	1000111	G	
72	48	1001000	H	
73	49	1001001	I	
74	4A	1001010	J	
75	4B	1001011	K	
76	4C	1001100	L	
77	4D	1001101	M	
78	4E	1001110	N	
79	4F	1001111	O	
80	50	1010000	P	
81	51	1010001	Q	
82	52	1010010	R	
83	53	1010011	S	
84	54	1010100	T	
85	55	1010101	U	
86	56	1010110	V	
87	57	1010111	W	

Table A.1   *ASCII table (continued)*

Decimal	Hexadecimal	Binary	Character	Description
88	58	1011000	X	
89	59	1011001	Y	
90	5A	1011010	Z	
91	5B	1011011	[	Open bracket
92	5C	1011100	\	Backslash
93	5D	1011101	]	Close bracket
94	5E	1011110	^	Caret
95	5F	1011111	_	Underscore
96	60	1100000	`	Grave accent
97	61	1100001	a	
98	62	1100010	b	
99	63	1100011	c	
100	64	1100100	d	
101	65	1100101	e	
102	66	1100110	f	
103	67	1100111	g	
104	68	1101000	h	
105	69	1101001	i	
106	6A	1101010	j	
107	6B	1101011	k	
108	6C	1101100	l	
109	6D	1101101	m	
110	6E	1101110	n	
111	6F	1101111	o	
112	70	1110000	p	
113	71	1110001	q	
114	72	1110010	r	
115	73	1110011	s	
116	74	1110100	t	
117	75	1110101	u	
118	76	1110110	v	
119	77	1110111	w	
120	78	1111000	x	
121	79	1111001	y	
122	7A	1111010	z	

Table A.1 *ASCII table (concluded)*

Decimal	Hexidecimal	Binary	Character	Description
123	7B	1111011	{	Open brace
124	7C	1111100	|	Bar
125	7D	1111101	}	Close brace
126	7E	1111110	~	Tilde
127	7F	1111111	DEL	Delete

APPENDIX B

Numbering Systems and Transformation

Today's computers make use of four numbering systems: decimal, binary, octal, and hexadecimal. Each has advantages for different levels of digital processing. In the first section of this appendix, we describe each of the four systems. In the second section, we show how a number in one system can be transformed into a number in another system.

B.1   NUMBERING SYSTEMS

All of the numbering systems examined here are positional, meaning that the position of a symbol in relation to other symbols determines its value. Within a number, each symbol is called a digit (decimal digit, binary digit, octal digit, or hexadecimal digit). For example, the decimal number 798 has three decimal digits. Digits are arranged in order of ascending value, moving from the lowest value on the right to the highest on the left. For this reason, the leftmost digit is referred to as the most significant and the rightmost as the least significant digit (see Figure B.1). For example, in the decimal number 1,234, the most significant digit is the 1 and the least significant is the 4.

Figure B.1   *Digit positions and their significance*

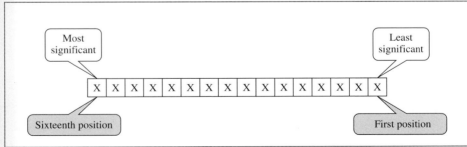

Decimal Numbers

The decimal system is the one most familiar to us in everyday life. All of our terms for indicating countable quantities are based on it, and, in fact, when we speak of other numbering systems, we tend to refer to their quantities by their decimal equivalents. Also called base 10, the name *decimal* is derived from the Latin stem *deci,* meaning ten. The decimal system uses 10 symbols to represent quantitative values: 0, 1, 2, 3, 4, 5, 6, 7, 8, and 9.

Decimal numbers use 10 symbols: 0, 1, 2, 3, 4, 5, 6, 7, 8, and 9.

Weight and Value

In the decimal system, each weight equals 10 raised to the power of its position. The weight of the first position, therefore, is 10^0, which equals 1. So the value of a digit in the first position is equal to the value of the digit times 1. The weight of the second position is 10^1, which equals 10. The value of a digit in the second position, therefore, is equal to the value of the digit times 10. The weight of the third position is 10^2. The value of a digit in the third position is equal to the value of the digit times 100 (see Table B.1).

Table B.1   *Decimal weights*

Position	Fifth	Fourth	Third	Second	First
Weight	10^4	10^3	10^2	10^1	10^0
	(10,000)	(1,000)	(100)	(10)	(1)

The value of the number as a whole is the sum of each digit times its weight. Figure B.2 shows the weightings of the decimal number 4,567.

Figure B.2   *Example of a decimal number*

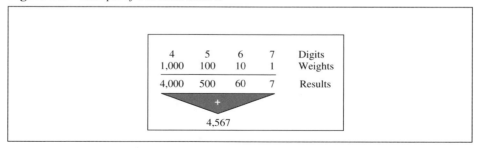

Binary Numbers

The binary number system provides the basis for all computer operations. Computers work by manipulating electrical current on and off. The binary system uses two symbols, *0* and *1,* so it corresponds naturally to a two-state device, such as a switch, with 0 to represent the off state and 1 to represent the on state. Also called base 2, the word *binary* derives from the Latin stem *bi,* meaning two.

Binary numbers use two symbols: 0 and 1.

Weight and Value

The binary system is also a weighted system. Each digit has a weight based on its position in the number. Weight in the binary system is two raised to the power represented by a position, as shown in Table B.2. Note that the value of the weightings is shown in decimal terms next to the weight itself. The value of a specific digit is equal to its face value times the weight of its position.

Table B.2 *Binary weights*

Position	Fifth	Fourth	Third	Second	First
Weight	2^4	2^3	2^2	2^1	2^0
	(16)	(8)	(4)	(2)	(1)

To calculate the value of a number, multiply each digit by the weight of its position, and then add together the results. Figure B.3 demonstrates the weighting of the binary number 1101. As you can see, 1101 is the binary equivalent of decimal 13.

Figure B.3 *Example of a binary number*

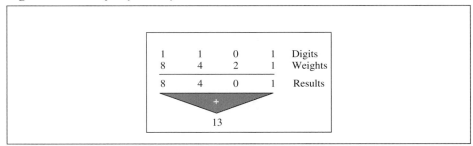

Octal Numbers

The octal number system is used by computer programmers to represent binary numbers in a compact form. Also called base 8, the term *octal* derives from the Greek stem *octa,* meaning eight. Eight is a power of two (2^3) and therefore can be used to model binary concepts. The octal system uses eight symbols to represent quantitative values: 0, 1, 2, 3, 4, 5, 6, and 7.

Octal numbers use eight symbols: 0, 1, 2, 3, 4, 5, 6, and 7.

Weight and Value

The octal system is also a weighted system. Each digit has a weight based on its position in the number. Weight in octal is eight raised to the power represented by a position, as shown in Table B.3. Once again, the value represented by each weighting is given in decimal terms next to the weight itself. The value of a specific digit is equal to its face value times the weight of its position. For example, a 4 in the third position has the equivalent decimal value 4×64, or 256.

Table B.3   *Octal weights*

Position	Fifth	Fourth	Third	Second	First
Weight	8^4	8^3	8^2	8^1	8^0
	(4,096)	(512)	(64)	(8)	(1)

To calculate the value of an octal number, multiply the value of each digit by the weight of its position, then add together the results. Figure B.4 shows the weighting for the octal number 3471. As you can see, 3471 is the octal equivalent of decimal 1,849.

Figure B.4   *Example of an octal number*

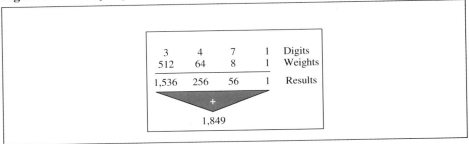

Hexadecimal Numbers

The term *hexadecimal* is derived from the Greek stem *hexadeca,* meaning 16 (*hex* means 6, and *deca* means 10). So the hexadecimal number system is base16. Sixteen is also a power of 2 (2^4). Like octal, therefore, the hexadecimal system is used by programmers to represent binary numbers in a compact form. Hexadecimal uses 16 symbols to represent data: 0, 1, 2, 3, 4, 5, 6, 7, 8, 9, A, B, C, D, E, and F.

Hexadecimal numbers use 16 symbols: 0, 1, 2, 3, 4, 5, 6, 7, 8, 9, A, B, C, D, E, and F.

Weight and Value

Like the others, the hexadecimal system is a weighted system. Each digit has a weight based on its position in the number. The weight is used to calculate the value represented by the digit. Weight in hexadecimal is 16 raised to the power represented by a position, as shown in Table B.4. Once again, the value represented by each weighting is given in decimal terms next to the weight itself. The value of a specific digit is equal to its face value times the weight of its position. For example, a 4 in the third position has the equivalent decimal value 4×256, or 1,024. To calculate the value of a hexadecimal number, multiply the value of each digit by the weight of its position, then add together the results. Figure B.5 shows the weighting for the hexadecimal number 3471. As you can see, 3471 is the hexadecimal equivalent of decimal 13,425.

Table B.4   *Hexadecimal weights*

Position	Fifth	Fourth	Third	Second	First
Weight	16^4	16^3	16^2	16^1	16^0
	(65,536)	(4,096)	(256)	(16)	(1)

Figure B.5   *Example of a hexadecimal number*

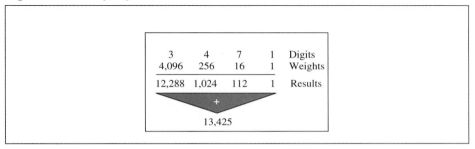

B.2   TRANSFORMATION

The different numbering systems provide different ways of thinking about a common subject: quantities of single units. A number from any given system can be transformed into its equivalent in any other system. For example, a binary number can be converted to a decimal number, and vice versa, without altering its value. Table B.5 shows how each system represents the decimal numbers 0 through 15. As you can see, decimal 13 is equivalent to binary 1101, which is equivalent to octal 15, which is equivalent to hexadecimal D.

Table B.5   *Comparison of four systems*

Decimal	Binary	Octal	Hexadecimal
0	0	0	0
1	1	1	1
2	10	2	2
3	11	3	3
4	100	4	4
5	101	5	5

Table B.5   *Comparison of four systems*

Decimal	Binary	Octal	Hexadecimal
6	110	6	6
7	111	7	7
8	1000	10	8
9	1001	11	9
10	1010	12	A
11	1011	13	B
12	1100	14	C
13	1101	15	D
14	1110	16	E
15	1111	17	F

From Other Systems to Decimal

As we saw in the discussions above, binary, octal, and hexadecimal numbers can be transformed easily to their decimal equivalents by using the weights of the digits. Figure B.6 shows the decimal value 78 represented in each of the other three systems.

From Decimal to Other Systems

A simple division trick gives us a convenient way to convert a decimal number to its binary, octal, or hexadecimal equivalent (see Figure B.7).

To convert a number from decimal to binary, divide the number by 2 and write down the resulting remainder (1 or 0). That remainder is the least significant binary digit. Now, divide the result of that division by 2 and write down the new remainder in the second position. Repeat this process until the quotient becomes zero.

In Figure B.7, we convert the decimal number 78 to its binary equivalent. To check the validity of this method, we convert 1001110 to decimal using the weights of each position. From left to right:

$$2^6 + 2^3 + 2^2 + 2^1 \quad \Rightarrow \quad 64 + 8 + 4 + 2 \quad \Rightarrow \quad 78$$

To convert a number from decimal to octal, the procedure is the same but the divisor is 8 instead of 2. To convert from decimal to hexadecimal, the divisor is 16.

From Binary to Octal or Hexadecimal

To change a number from binary to octal, we first group the binary digits from right to left by threes. Then we convert each tribit to its octal equivalent and write the result under the tribit. These equivalents, taken in order (not added), are the octal equivalent of the original number. In Figure B.8, we convert binary 1001110.

Figure B.6   *Transformation from other systems to decimal*

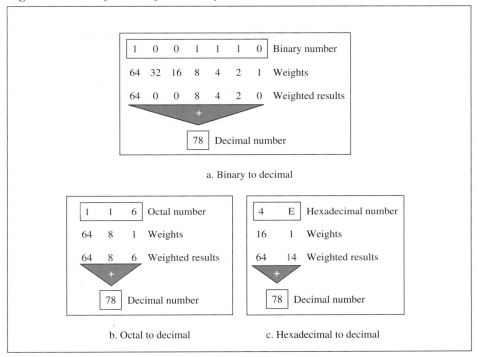

a. Binary to decimal

b. Octal to decimal   c. Hexadecimal to decimal

To change a number from binary to hexadecimal, we follow the same procedure but group the digits from right to left by fours. This time we convert each quadbit to its hexadecimal equivalent (use Table B.5). In Figure B.8, we convert binary 1001110 to hexadecimal.

From Octal or Hexadecimal to Binary

To convert from octal to binary, we reverse the procedure above. Starting with the least significant digit, we convert each octal digit into its equivalent three binary digits. In Figure B.9, we convert octal 116 to binary.

To convert a number from hexadecimal to binary, we convert each hexadecimal digit to its equivalent four binary digits, again starting with the least significant digit. In Figure B.9, we convert hexadecimal 4E to binary.

Figure B.7   *Transformation from decimal to other systems*

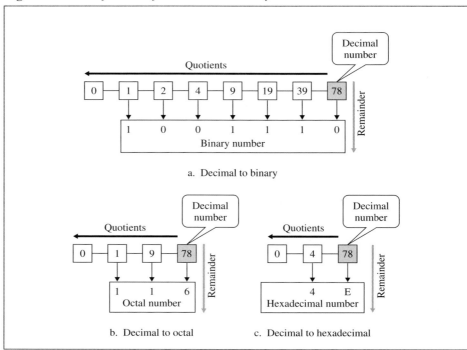

a. Decimal to binary

b. Decimal to octal   c. Decimal to hexadecimal

Figure B.8   *Transformation from binary to octal or hexadecimal*

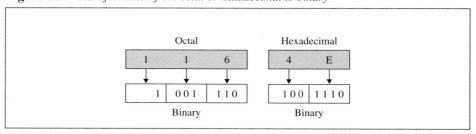

Figure B.9   *Transformation from octal or hexadecimal to binary*

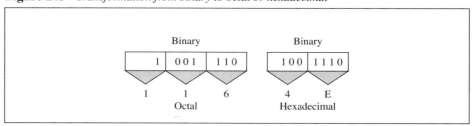

APPENDIX C

Representation of Binary Numbers

Binary numbers can be used and stored in either of two formats: unsigned or signed. *Unsigned* means without a + or − sign, and refers to positive values only. *Signed* numbers can be either positive or negative. Unsigned numbers are represented in only one format. However, computers use three different formats for representing signed numbers: sign-and-magnitude, one's complement, and two's complement (see Figure C.1).

Figure C.1 *Binary representation*

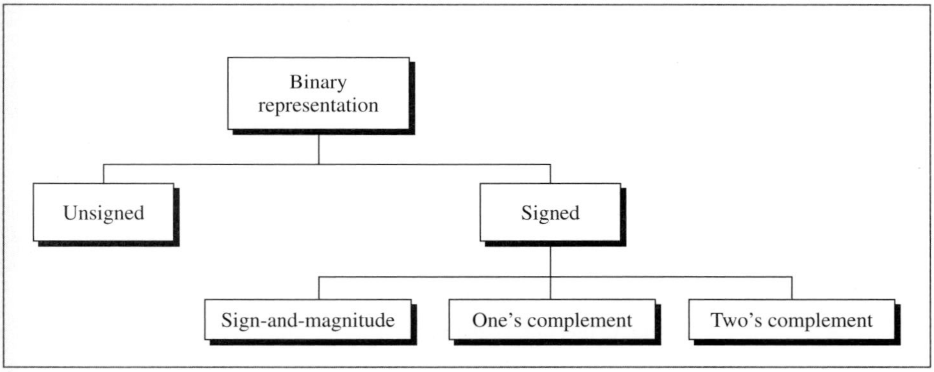

C.1 UNSIGNED NUMBERS

The buffer size limits the amount of space we have in which to store and represent information about a number. All essential information about a given value must be contained within these 16 bits, including whether a value is positive or negative. If a number is unsigned, however, it is assumed to be positive. With no need to indicate the sign, all bits become available to represent digits. In a 16-bit buffer, we can represent any whole number between 0 (0000000000000000) and 65,535 (1111111111111111); see Figure C.2.

Figure C.2   *Unsigned*

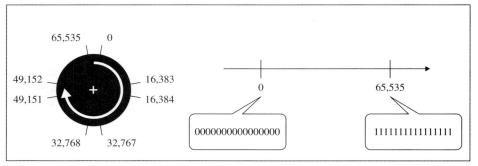

Another way to visualize the limitations of a 16-bit range is with a circle (see Figure C.2). As you can see, with 16 available bits, we can count from 0 to 65,535. When we add 1 to our maximum value of 65,535, we find ourselves back at 0. The process is called modular arithmetic. The most common example of modular arithmetic in everyday life is the 12-hour clock: when you add 1 to 12 you get 1, not 13.

From Decimal to Unsigned

To change a decimal value to its unsigned binary form, follow these steps:

    a. Change the number to its binary form.

    b. Fill in all empty cells on the left with 0s. (If you are using a 16-bit register, you need to fill all 16 cells; with an 8-bit register, you need to fill 8 cells; etc.)

Example C.1

Change 76 to its unsigned representation.

Solution:

    a. 76 in binary is 1001100.

    b. Adding 0s to make the number 16 bits long gives us 0000000001001100.

C.2   SIGNED NUMBERS

Representation of signed binary numbers presents more challenges than does representation of unsigned numbers. Given the same bit limitations, how do we include the sign (+ or −) in the number? Three methods are commonly used: sign-and-magnitude, one's complement, and two's complement.

Sign-and-Magnitude

In sign-and-magnitude representation, the most significant bit is reserved to indicate the sign. If the bit is 0, the number is positive. If it is 1, the number is negative. Notice that application of this method gives us two 0 values: +0 (0000000000000000) and −0 (1000000000000000). Reserving one bit to show sign also limits the range of values that can be represented in a given number of bits. Given a 16-bit buffer, one cell is now consumed by the sign, leaving only 15 to represent the absolute value of a number. This changes the possible range of numbers that can be represented, as shown in Figure C.3. As you can see, with only 15 possible digits, the range of representable numbers becomes −32,767 to +32,767.

Once again, the circle provides a useful way to visualize a number range. Starting from +0 (000000000000000), we add 1s, increasing the value until we reach +32,767 (011111111111111). The next added 1 changes the value to −0 (011111111111111 + 1 = 100000000000000). Continuing to advance by 1s, we move around the circle to −32,767 (111111111111111). The next added 1 changes the available bits to 000000000000000 (+0), and the cycle begins again (see Figure C.3).

Figure C.3   *Sign-and-magnitude representation*

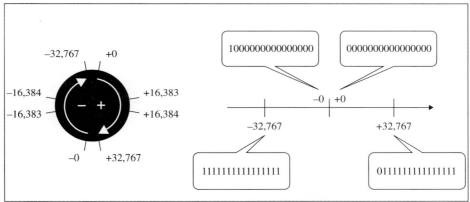

From Decimal to Sign-and-Magnitude

To change a decimal value to its sign-and-magnitude binary form, follow these steps:

  a. Ignore the sign.
  b. Change the absolute value of the number to its binary form.
  c. Fill in all empty cells, except the last one, on the left with 0s (if you are using a 16-bit register, you need to fill 15 cells; with an 8-bit register, you need to fill 7 cells; etc.).
  d. Now check the sign: if the number is positive, fill the last cell with 0. If the number is negative, fill the cell with 1.

Example C.2

 Change −77 to its sign-and-magnitude representation.

Solution:

  a. The absolute value is 77.
  b. 77 in binary is 1001101.
  c. Adding 0s to make the number 15 bits long gives us 000000001001101.
  d. The sign was negative, so we add a 1 as the last bit: **1**000000001001101.

One's Complement

In the one's complement method, all the bits, not just the most significant, take part in the representation of sign. One's complement is a symmetrical system: numbers are paired with their complements. Adding a number to its complement equals 0. To find the complement of a number, invert all of its digits. For example, inverting the digits of the number 0000000000000001 (+1), gives us 1111111111111110 (−1). This symmetry extends to zero: 0000000000000000 = +0, and 1111111111111111 = −0 (see Figure C.4).

As you can see from Figure C.4, positive numbers in this method use the same digits as those in sign-and-magnitude (and the same digits as the unsigned numbers 0 to 32,767). In this method, also, the sign of a number is immediately apparent from its most significant digit. (Positive numbers always start with 0, and negative numbers always start with 1.) However, the numerical representation of negative numbers is very different in one's complement from that in sign-and-magnitude.

One's complement is used in data communications to check the accuracy of a received transmission.

Figure C.4 *One's complement*

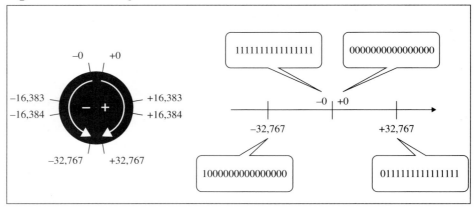

From Decimal to One's Complement

To change a decimal value to its one's complement binary form follow these steps:

    a. Ignore the sign.

    b. Change the absolute value of the number to its binary form.

    c. Fill in all empty cells on the left with 0s. (If you are using a 16-bit register, you need to fill all 16 cells; with an 8-bit register, you need to fill 8 cells; etc.)

    d. Now check the sign: if the number is positive, stop here. If the number is negative, complement the digits (invert each 0 to 1 and each 1 to 0).

Example C.5

Change −77 to its one's complement form.

Solution:

a. The absolute value is 77.

b. 77 in binary is 1001101.

c. Adding 0s to make the number 16 bits long gives us 0000000001001101.

d. The sign was negative, so we complement the number obtained in step c by inverting its digits, giving us 1111111110110010.

Two's Complement

In this method, as in one's complement, all the bits change when the sign of the number changes. The entire number, not just the most significant bit, takes part in the negation process. This time, however, we add a step, resulting in an asymmetrical system with only one representation of 0.

As Figure C.5 shows, having only a single representation of 0 results in the availability of an extra negative number: −32,768. In this way, a 16-bit integer variable can store numbers from −32,768 through +32,767.

An examination of Figure C.5 reveals another interesting fact: in two's complement 0 and −1 are bitwise inverses of each other. They are not complements of each other—adding them together does not yield 0. In fact, 0000000000000000 (0) + 1111111111111111 (−1) = 1111111111111111 (−1). In the same way, +32,767 and 32,768 are inverses of each other. These patterns allow two's complement to replicate decimal arithmetic on the machine level, as we shall see below.

Figure C.5   *Two's complement*

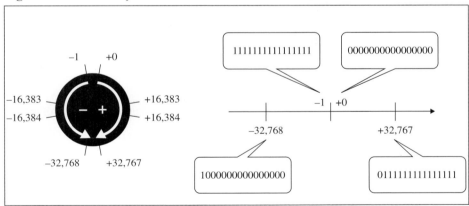

From Decimal to Two's Complement

To change a decimal number to its two's complement form, follow these steps:

a. Ignore the sign.

b. Change the absolute value of the number to its binary form.

c. Fill in all empty cells on the left with 0s. (If you are using a 16-bit register, you need to fill all 16 cells; with an 8-bit register, you need to fill 8 cells; etc.)

d. Now check the sign: if the number is positive, stop here. If the number is negative, complement the digits (invert each 0 to 1 and each 1 to 0) and then add 1 to the resulting number. If adding 1 results in a carry from the most significant digit, that carry is dropped.

Example C.7

Change −77 to its two's complement form:

Solution:

a. The absolute value is 77.

b. 77 in binary is 1001101.

c. Adding 0s to make the number 16 bits long gives us 0000000001001101.

d. The sign was negative, so we complement the number, giving us 1111111110110010. Now we add 1 to 1111111110110010, giving us the two's complement: 1111111110110011.

C.3   MORE ABOUT ONE'S COMPLEMENT

Because one's complement arithmetic is used in checksum calculation, we discuss some features of one's complement arithmetic in more detail here.

Finding the Complement

The one's complement of any number is another number, such that the sum of the two is equal to 0. For example, the one's complement of A is −A. To complement a binary number, invert every 1 to 0 and 0 to 1 (see Figure C.6).

Figure C.6   *One's complement*

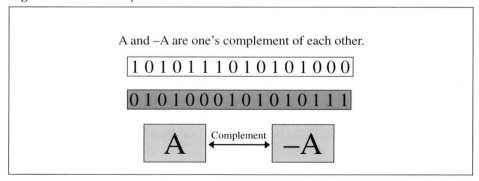

As we mentioned before, we have two 0s in this arithmetic: +0 and −0. The positive zero in a 16-bit buffer is 0000000000000000, and the negative zero in a 16-bit buffer is 1111111111111111.

We have two 0s in one's complement arithmetic:

$$+0 \;\Rightarrow\; 0000000000000000 \qquad\qquad -0 \;\Rightarrow\; 1111111111111111$$

Adding Two Numbers

To add two digits in one's complement arithmetic, we use the same steps as in base 10 addition, but in base 2. We add the two values in one column together. The box below expresses this process as a series of four simple rules.

Four simple rules of adding one column:

1. If there are no 1s, the result is 0.
2. If there is only one 1, the result is 1.
3. If there are two 1s, the result is 0 and 1 is carried to the next column.
4. If there are three 1s, the result is 1 and 1 is carried to the next column.

To add two multibit numbers, we extend this process.

Two simple rules for adding two numbers made of two or more columns:

1. Add the bits in each column.
2. If the last column generates a carry, add 1 to the result.

Figure C.7 shows an example of adding two numbers in one's complement where no carry is produced from the last column.

Figure C.7   *Adding in one's complement*

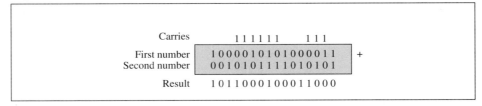

Figure C.8 shows an example of adding two numbers in one's complement where the last column generates a carry. The carry is then added to the result.

Following the above logic, if we add a number to its complement A, the result will be all 1s which, as we have seen, is equal to −0 (see Figure C.9).

Figure C.8   *Adding in one's complement with carry from the last column*

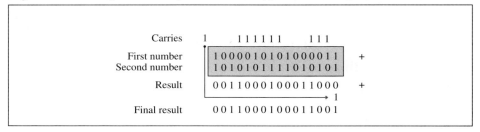

If we add a number with its complement, we get −0, which means all 1s.

Figure C.9   *Adding a number with its complement*

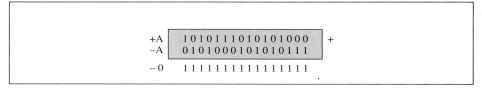

APPENDIX D

Error Detection

Networks must be able to transfer data from one device to another with complete accuracy. Anytime data are transmitted from source to destination, they can become corrupted in passage. Many factors, including line noise, can alter or wipe out one or more bits of a given data unit. Reliable systems must have a mechanism for detecting and correcting such errors.

> Data can be corrupted during transmission. For reliable communication, errors must be detected and corrected.

Error detection and correction are implemented either at the data link layer or the transport layer of the OSI model.

D.1 TYPES OF ERRORS

Whenever an electromagnetic signal flows from one point to another, it is subject to unpredictable interference from heat, magnetism, and other forms of electricity. If the signal is carrying encoded binary data, 0 can change to 1 or 1 to 0. We classify the errors as single-bit, multiple-bit, or burst errors depending on the number and position of the bit changes. Of the three, a single-bit error is the most likely to occur and a burst error the least likely (see Figure D.1).

Figure D.1 *Types of errors*

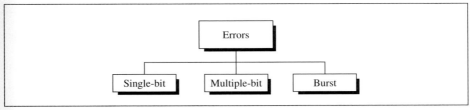

Single-Bit Error

The term *single-bit error* means that only one bit of a given data unit (such as a byte, character, data unit, or packet) is changed from 1 to 0 or from 0 to 1.

A single-bit error occurs when only one bit in the data unit has changed.

In Figure D.2, 00000010 (ASCII *STX*) was sent, meaning *start of text*, but 00001010 (ASCII *LF*) was received, meaning *line feed*. For more information about ASCII code, see Appendix A.

Figure D.2   *Single-bit error*

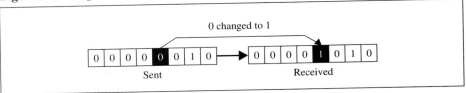

Multiple-Bit Error

The term *multiple-bit error* means that two or more nonconsecutive bits in a data unit have changed from 1 to 0 or from 0 to 1.

A multiple-bit error occurs when two or more nonconsecutive bits in the data unit have changed.

In Figure D.3, 01000010 (ASCII *B*) was sent, but 00001010 (ASCII *LF*) meaning *line feed,* was received.

Figure D.3   *Multiple-bit error*

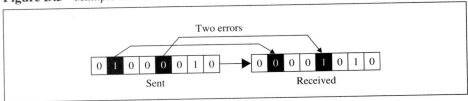

Burst Error

The term *burst error* means that two or more consecutive bits in the data unit have changed from 1 to 0 or from 0 to 1.

A burst error means that two or more consecutive bits in the data unit have changed.

In Figure D.4, 0100010001000011 was sent, but 0101101101000011 was received.

Figure D.4   *Burst error*

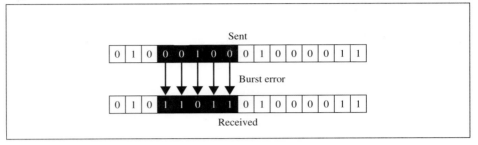

D.2   DETECTION

Now that we know the types of errors that can occur, we need a method to recognize them. We need a mechanism that is simple and completely objective.

Redundancy

One potential mechanism to recognize errors would be to send every data unit twice. The receiving device would then be able to do a bit-for-bit comparison between the two versions of the data. This system would be completely accurate (the odds of errors being introduced onto exactly the same bits in both sets of data are infinitesimally small), but it would also be insupportably slow. Not only would the transmission time double, but the time it takes to compare every unit bit by bit must be added.

The concept of including extra information in the transmission solely for the purposes of comparison is a good one. But instead of repeating the entire data stream, a shorter group of bits may be appended to the end of each unit. This technique is called redundancy because the extra bits are redundant to the information; they are discarded as soon as the accuracy of the transmission has been determined.

> Error detection uses the concept of redundancy, which means adding extra bits for detecting errors at the destination.

Figure D.5 shows a data unit and an appropriately coded redundancy check traveling over the link to the receiver. The receiver puts the entire stream through a checking function. If the received bit stream passes the checking criteria, the data portion of the data unit is accepted and the redundant bits are discarded.

Four types of redundancy checks are used in data communications: vertical redundancy check (VRC) (also called parity check), longitudinal redundancy check (LRC), cyclical redundancy check (CRC), and checksum. The first three, VRC, LRC, and CRC, are implemented in the physical layer for use in the data link layer. The fourth, checksum, is used primarily by networks, including the Internet, and is implemented in the transport layer (see Figure D.6).

Figure D.5   *Redundancy*

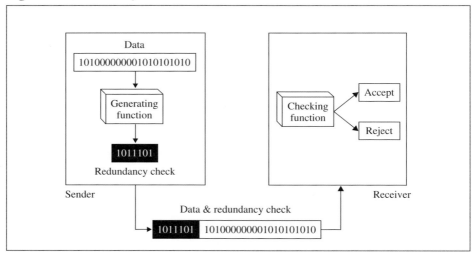

Figure D.6   *Detection methods*

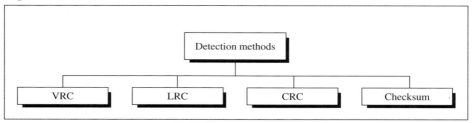

Vertical Redundancy Check (VRC)

The most common and least expensive mechanism for error detection is the vertical redundancy check (VRC), often called a parity check. In this technique, a redundant bit, called a parity bit, is appended to every data unit so that the total number of 1s in the unit (including the parity bit) becomes either even (if the system is checking for even parity) or odd (if the system is checking for odd parity).

Suppose we want to transmit the binary data unit 1100001 [ASCII *a* (97)]; see Figure D.7. We pass the data unit through a parity generator that appends the appropriate parity bit to the end. If we are using an even-parity check, the parity generator adds on a 1 parity bit (11100001): the total number of 1s is now four. At the receiver, all eight bits go through an even-parity checking function. If the receiver sees 11100001, it counts four 1s, and the data unit passes. If the receiver sees 11100101, it counts 5, an odd number. The receiver knows that an error has been introduced into the data somewhere and therefore rejects the whole unit.

In VRC a parity bit is added to every data unit so that the total number of 1s (including the parity bit) becomes even for even-parity check or odd for odd-parity check.

Figure D.7   *Even-parity VRC concept*

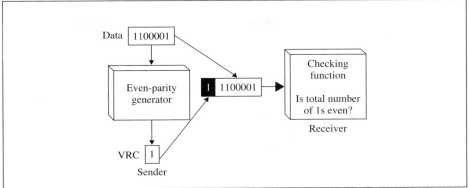

Longitudinal Redundancy Check (LRC)

Longitudinal redundancy check (LRC) is VRC in two dimensions. To increase the likelihood of detecting multiple-bit and burst errors, we look at each bit twice.

LRC error detection groups a predetermined number of data units, each already containing a VRC parity bit, together into a block. The corresponding bits of each data unit (all the first bits, all the second bits, etc.) are passed through a generator to find the parity of each position. Each position then gets its own parity bit. The parity bits of all the positions are then assembled into a new data unit, which is added to the end of the data block (see Figure D.8).

Figure D.8   *LRC*

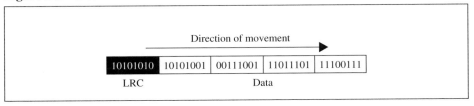

In LRC, a redundant unit is added after a number of data units. The bits in the redundant unit are calculated from the corresponding bits in the data units using VRC.

Figure D.9 shows how the LRC is calculated. The least significant bits are added together and their parity found (even or odd, depending on the LRC). Then the second bits are added and their parity found, and so on. The final bit of the LRC is both the parity bit for the LRC data unit itself and the parity bit for all the VRC parity bits in the block.

Cyclic Redundancy Check (CRC)

The third and most powerful of the redundancy checking techniques is the cyclic redundancy check (CRC). In this technique, a sequence of redundant bits, called the CRC, is

Figure D.9   *VRC AND LRC*

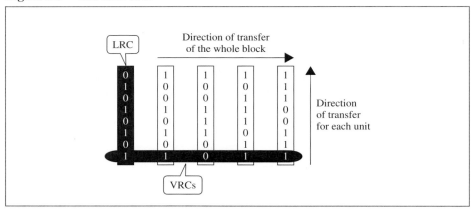

appended to the end of a data unit so that the resulting data unit becomes exactly divisible by a second, predetermined binary number. At its destination, the incoming data unit is divided by the same number. If at this step there is no remainder, the data unit is assumed to be intact and is therefore accepted. A remainder indicates that the data unit has been damaged in transit and therefore must be rejected (see Figure D.10).

Figure D.10   *CRC generator and checker*

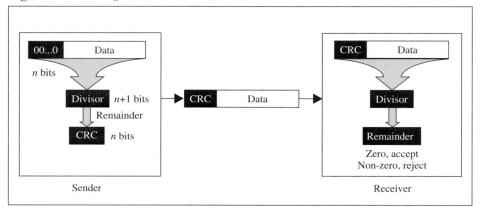

At the sender, a string of n 0s is appended to the end of the data unit. The number n is one less than the number of bits in the predetermined divisor, which is $n + 1$ bits.

The newly elongated data unit is divided by the divisor using a process called *binary division*. The remainder resulting from this division is the CRC.

The CRC of n bits replaces the appended 0s at the end of the data unit. If the derived remainder has fewer than n bits, the missing, leftmost bits are presumed to be 0s. If the division process has not yielded a remainder at all—that is, if the original data unit is already divisible by the divisor—then n 0s take the place of a remainder as the CRC. The resulting bit pattern is exactly divisible by the divisor.

The data unit arrives at the receiver data first, followed by the CRC. The receiver treats the whole string as a unit and divides it by the same divisor that was used to find the CRC remainder.

If the string arrives without error, the CRC checker yields a remainder of zero and the data unit passes. If the string has been changed in transit, the division yields a non-zero remainder and the data unit does not pass.

The CRC Generator

A CRC generator uses modulo-2 division. Figure D.11 shows this process. In the first step, the four-bit divisor is subtracted from the first four bits of the dividend. Each bit of the divisor is subtracted from the corresponding bit of the dividend without disturbing the next higher bit. In our example, the divisor, 1101, is subtracted from the first four bits of the dividend, 1001, yielding 100 (the leading 0 of the remainder is dropped off).

Figure D.11   *Binary division*

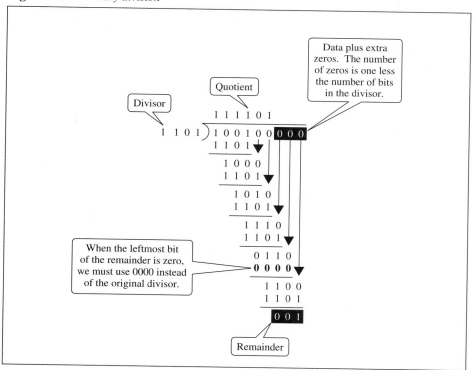

The next unused bit from the dividend is then pulled down to make the number of bits in the remainder equal to the number of bits in the divisor. The next step, therefore, is 1000 ± 1101, which yields 101, and so on.

Polynomials

The CRC generator (the divisor) is most often represented not as a string of 1s and 0s, but as an algebraic polynomial (see Figure D.12).

Figure D.12   *A polynomial*

$$x^7 + x^5 + x^2 + x + 1$$

The relationship of a polynomial to its corresponding binary representation is shown in Figure D.13. The standard polynomials used by popular protocols for CRC generation are shown in Figure D.14. The numbers 12, 16, and 32 refer to the size of the CRC remainder. The CRC divisors are 13, 17, and 33 bits, respectively.

Figure D.13   *A polynomial representing a divisor*

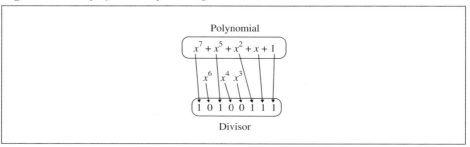

Figure D.14   *Standard polynomials*

CRC-12	CRC-16	CRC-ITU
$x^{12} + x^{11} + x^3 + x + 1$	$x^{16} + x^{15} + x^2 + 1$	$x^{16} + x^{12} + x^5 + 1$

CRC-32
$x^{32} + x^{26} + x^{23} + x^{22} + x^{16} + x^{12} + x^{11} + x^{10} + x^8 + x^7 + x^5 + x^4 + x^2 + x + 1$

Checksum

The error-detection method used by the higher layer protocols is called checksum. We discussed the concept and calculation of the checksum in Chapter 7.

APPENDIX E

Encryption/Decryption

To carry sensitive information, such as military or financial data, a system must be able to assure privacy. Microwave, satellite, and other wireless media, however, cannot be protected from the unauthorized reception (or interception) of transmissions. Even cable systems cannot always prevent unauthorized access. Cables pass through out-of-the-way areas (such as basements) that provide opportunities for malicious access to the cable and illegal reception of information.

It is unlikely that any system can completely prevent unauthorized access to transmission media. A more practical way to protect information is to alter it so that only an authorized receiver can understand it. Data tampering is not a new issue, nor is it unique to the computer era. In fact, efforts to make information unreadable by unauthorized receivers date from Julius Caesar (100–44 B.C.). The method used today is called the encryption and decryption of information. **Encryption** means that the sender transforms the original information to another form and sends the resulting unintelligible message out over the network. **Decryption** reverses the encryption process in order to transform the message back to its original form.

Figure E.1 shows the basic encryption/decryption process. The sender uses an encryption algorithm and a key to transform the plaintext (as the original message is called) into a ciphertext (as the encrypted message is called). The receiver uses a decryption algorithm and a key to transform the ciphertext back to the original plaintext.

Encryption and decryption methods fall into two categories: conventional and public key (see Figure E.2).

E.1 CONVENTIONAL METHODS

In conventional encryption methods, the encryption key (Ke) is known only to the sender and the decryption key (Kd) is known only to the receiver. Neither is public.

The conventional methods started a long time ago. In the beginning, encryption was achieved by what is called *monoalphabetic substitution*: In this type of encryption (sometimes called Caesar Cipher because it was used by Julius Caesar), each character is replaced by another character.

Figure E.1   *Concept of encryption and decryption*

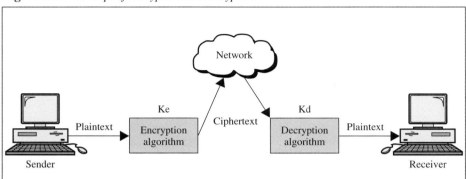

Figure E.2   *Encryption/decryption methods*

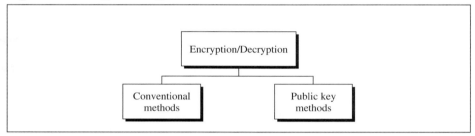

The safer form of character substitution is polyalphabetic substitution. Here again, we substitute one character for another. In this method, however, the same plaintext character is replaced by different ciphertext characters; substitution depends not only on the identity of the character but also on the position of the character in the text. For example, each of the three occurrences of the character O in the message GOOD MORNING would be replaced by a different cipher character.

An even better method is transpositional encryption. In this method, the characters retain their plaintext form but their positions are changed to create the ciphertext. This type of encryption is most efficiently accomplished by organizing the text into a two-dimensional table, then interchanging the columns according to a key. For example, we can organize the plaintext into a six-column table and then reorganize the columns according to a key that indicates which column is transposed with which other column.

Most of the above methods are obsolete. The conventional encryption methods used today are based on bits, not characters. In bit-level techniques, data are first divided into blocks of bits, then altered by substitution, transposition, swapping, exclusive-or, circular shifting, and so on.

DES

One interesting example of bit-level encryption is the data encryption standard (DES). DES was designed by IBM and adopted by the U.S. government as the standard encryption method for nonmilitary and nonclassified use. The algorithm takes a 64-bit plaintext and 56-bit key. The text is put through 19 different and very complex procedures to create a 64-bit ciphertext.

Figure E.3 shows a schematic diagram of DES. The first and last two steps are relatively simple. However, steps 2 through 17 are complex, each requiring substeps that are combinations of transposition, substitution, swapping, exclusive-or, and circular shift. Although steps 2 through 17 are the same, each uses a different key derived from the original key. Additional complexity is achieved by having each step use the output of the previous step as input.

Figure E.3 *DES*

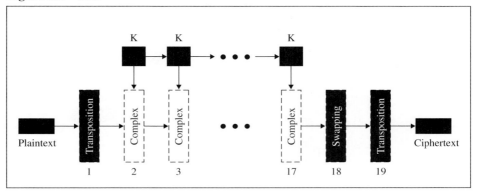

E.2 PUBLIC KEY METHODS

In conventional encryption/decryption methods, the decryption algorithm is always the inverse of the encryption algorithm and uses the same key. Anyone who knows the encryption algorithm and key can deduce the decryption algorithm and key. For this reason, security can be assured only if the entire process is kept secret. In cases where there are many senders and one receiver, however, this level of secrecy can be inconvenient. For example, imagine that a bank wants to give customers access to their accounts. To limit each customer's access to only his or her own account using conventional encryption, the bank would have to create millions of encryption algorithms and keys. This solution is impractical, particularly with old customers leaving and new customers joining the bank all the time. On the other hand, if the bank were to give the same encryption algorithm and key to every customer, it could not guarantee the privacy of any customer.

The solution is public key encryption. In this method, every user has the same encryption algorithm and key. The decryption algorithm and key, however, are kept secret. Anyone can encrypt information, but only an authorized receiver can decrypt it. The decryption algorithm is designed in such a way that it is not the inverse of the encryption algorithm. The encryption and decryption algorithms use completely different functions, and knowing one does not enable a user to know the other. In addition, the keys are different. Even with the encryption algorithm and encryption key, an intruder still will be unable to decipher the code (at least not easily).

Figure E.4 illustrates the idea of using public keys for customer access to bank services. The encryption algorithm and key are publicly announced. Every customer can use them. The decryption algorithm and key are kept secret and used only by the bank.

Figure E.4   *Public key encryption*

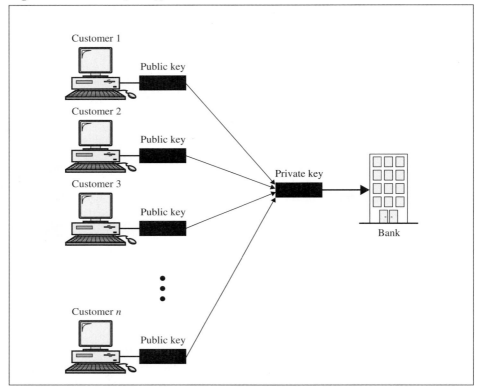

RSA Encryption

One public key encryption technique is called RSA (for Rivest, Shamir, and Adleman). Figure E.5 shows a simplified form of the RSA algorithm, which is based on number theory.

In this example, the letter F is encrypted as number 41 using the following procedure:

■   Encode character F to 6 (F is the sixth character in the alphabet).

■   Choose two prime numbers (we chose 7 and 17).

■   Subtract 1 from each prime and multiply the two results: $(7 - 1) \times (17 - 1) = 96$.

■   Choose a number that is relatively prime with 96 (we chose 5). This number is the Ke (Ke = 5).

■   Multiply the two original numbers (17×7 gives us 119).

■   Calculate $6^{Ke} \% \ 119$ (modulo division), which is 41.

Figure E.5   *RSA encryption and decryption*

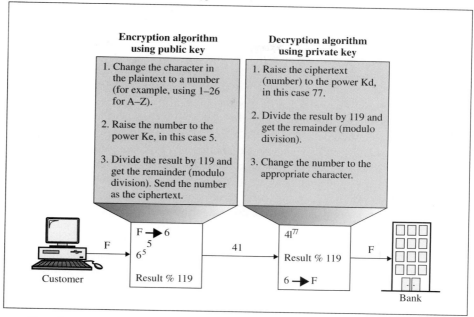

Now the encrypted text (41) is sent along the network. Note that even if an intruder knows the whole encryption procedure and the Ke (5), he or she cannot decipher the original character F easily because the procedure is not reversible.

At the receiver, the number 41 is decrypted as F using a different procedure and a different key as follows:

- Subtract 1 from each prime and multiply the two results: $(7 - 1) \times (17 - 1) = 96$.
- Multiply the two original numbers (17×7 gives us 119).
- Find a number, Kd, such that when we divide (Kd $\times$ Ke) by 96 the remainder is 1. We did and came up with 77 (Kd = 77).
- Calculate the $41^{Kd}\%$ 119 (modulo division), which is 6.
- Decode 6 as F.

It may appear that anyone with the public Ke (5) and the number 119 could find the secret Kd (77) by trial and error. However, if the private key is a large number and another very large number is chosen in place of 119, it is extremely difficult and time-consuming to do so.

E.3   AUTHENTICATION

Authentication means verifying the identity of a sender. In other words, an authentication technique tries to verify that a message is coming from an authentic sender and not from an imposter. Although many methods have been developed for authentication, we introduce only a method called *digital signature*, which is based on public key encryption/decryption.

The concept of a digital signature is similar to that of signing transaction documents when you do business with a bank. To withdraw large amounts of money from your bank, you go to the bank and fill out a withdrawal form. The bank requires that you sign the form and keeps the signed form on record. The signature is required in case there is any question later about authorization for the withdrawal. If, for example, you say later that you never withdrew money in that amount, the bank can show you your signature (or show it to a judge in court), proving that you did.

In network transactions you cannot personally sign the request for withdrawal. You can, however, create the equivalent of an electronic or digital signature by the way you send data.

Digital signatures add another level of encryption and decryption to the process discussed above. This time, however, a private (secret) encryption key is developed and kept by the customer while the corresponding private decryption key is kept and used by the bank. In this case, the customer uses one public and one private key (Ke) for encryption and the bank uses one private and one public key (Kd) for decryption.

Figure E.6 shows how a digital signature works. The customer encrypts the plaintext (P) using a secret key (Ks-1, chosen and kept by the customer) and creates the first level of ciphertext (C1). The first ciphertext is encrypted again using the public key (Kp-1) to create the second ciphertext (C2). C2 is sent through the network and received by the bank. The bank uses the secret key (Ks-2) to decipher C2 into C1. It then uses the public key (Kp-2) to decipher C1 into the original plaintext. Before it does so, however, it copies C1 and stores it in a separate file.

Figure E.6   *Signature authentication*

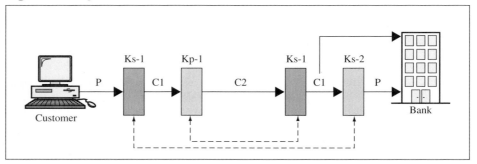

If one day the customer claims not to have made such a transaction, the bank can take C1 out of its file and apply Kp-2 to it to show that it creates P. This decryption would not be possible unless the customer had originally applied Ks-1 to P to create C1. Unless the customer had, in fact, sent the transaction, the C1 would not exist. The customer cannot claim that the bank created C1 because the bank does not have the Ks-1 required to do so. The customer may claim, of course, that an unauthorized user obtained access to the Ks-1. In that case, however, the court can point out that it was the customer's responsibility to keep the Ks-1 secret, thereby absolving the bank of liability.

APPENDIX F

MIB Objects

In Chapter 21 we discussed MIB objects. These objects are categorized in several groups: Here, we list the objects, their object identifiers, and their brief descriptions for six of the groups. The other groups are not discussed because they are currently undergoing changes. The groups are under the *mib* object in the object identifier tree (see Chapter 21).

F.1 SYSTEM GROUP

The system group gives information about the whole system. The system group simple variables are shown in Table F.1.

Table F.1 *System group variables*

Id	Name	Type	Description
1	sysDescr	String	System description
2	sysObjectId	ObjectID	Vendor identification
3	sysUpTime	TimeTicks	Time of last boot
4	sysContact	String	Person to contact
5	sysName	String	Domain name
6	sysLocation	String	Location
7	sysService	Integer	Total services rendered

F.2 INTERFACE GROUP

The interface group gives information about the interface. The only simple interface group variable is shown in Table F.2.

Table F.2 *Interface group variable*

Id	Name	Type	Description
1	ifNumber	Integer	Number of interfaces

The only table in the interface group, ifTable, is a sequence of sequences (array of records) with each sequence (record) having 22 fields (columns). The index is the value of the ifIndex field (see Table F.3).

Table F.3 *Interface group table, ifTable*

Id	Name	Type	Description
2.1.1	ifIndex	Integer	Index of the interface
2.1.2	ifDescr	String	Description of the interface
2.1.3	ifType	Integer	Type of interface
2.1.4	ifMtu	Integer	MTU of interface
2.1.5	ifSpeed	Gauge	Speed (bits/second)
2.1.6	ifPhysAddress	PhysAddress	Physical Address
2.1.7	ifAdminStatus	Integer	Desired state
2.1.8	ifOperStatus	Integer	Current state
2.1.9	ifLastChange	TimeTicks	Time since the last system came up
2.1.10	ifInOctets	Counter	Total number of bytes received
2.1.11	ifInUcastPkts	Counter	Number of unicast packets delivered
2.1.12	ifInNUcastPkts	Counter	Number of non-unicast packets delivered
2.1.13	ifInDiscards	Counter	Number of received packets discarded
2.1.14	ifInErrors	Counter	Number of received packets in error
2.1.15	ifInUnknownProtos	Counter	Number of received packets with unknown protocol
2.1.16	ifOutOctets	Counter	Total number of bytes sent
2.1.17	ifOutUcastPkts	Counter	Number of unicast packets received from higher level protocols
2.1.18	ifOutNUcastPkts	Counter	Number of nonunicast packets received from higher level protocols
2.1.19	ifOutDiscards	Counter	Number of outbound packets discarded
2.1.20	ifOutErrors	Counter	Number of outbound packets in error
2.1.21	ifOutQLen	Gauge	Number of packets in output queue
2.1.22	ifSpecific	ObjectID	Reference to the MIB definition

F.3   IP GROUP

The IP group defines the pieces of information kept by the database about the IP packets. The IP group simple variables are shown in Table F.4.

Table F.4 *IP group variables*

Id	Name	Type	Description
1	ipForwarding	Integer	Shows if the system is forwarding or not
2	ipDefaultTTL	Integer	The default value of TTL
3	ipInReceive	Counter	Number of datagrams received
4	ipInHdrErrors	Counter	Number of datagrams with header errors
5	ipInAddrErrors	Counter	Number of datagrams with address errors
6	ipForwDatagrams	Counter	Number of datagrams forwarded
7	ipInUnknownProtos	Counter	Number of datagrams with unknown protocols
8	ipInDiscards	Counter	Number of input datagrams discarded
9	ipInDelivers	Counter	Number of datagrams delivered to upper protocols
10	ipOutRequests	Counter	Number of datagrams passed to IP for transmission
11	ipOutDiscards	Counter	Number of output datagrams discarded
12	ipOutNoRoutes	Counter	Number of datagrams for which no route was found
13	ipReasmTimeout	Integer	Reassembly timeout
14	ipReasmReqds	Counter	Number of datagrams to be reassembled
15	ipReasmOKs	Counter	Number of datagrams reassembled
16	ipReasmFails	Counter	Number of reassembly failures
17	ipFragOKs	Counter	Number of datagrams fragmented
18	ipFragFails	Counter	Number of datagrams requiring fragmentation, but not fragmented
19	ipFragCreates	Counter	Number of fragments created
20	ipRoutingDiscards	Counter	Number of routing entries discarded

The first table, ipAddrTable, is a sequence of sequences (array of records) with each sequence (record) having five fields (columns). The index is the value of the ipAdEntAddr field (see Table F.5).

Table F.5   *The first IP group table, ipAddrTable*

Id	Name	Type	Description
21.1.1	ipAdEntAddr	IpAddress	IP address for an interface
21.1.2	ipAdEntIfIndex	Integer	Interface number
21.1.3	ipAdEntNetMask	IpAddress	Subnet mask
21.1.4.	ipAdEntBcastAddr	Integer	Broadcast address
21.1.5	ipAdEntReasmMaxSize	Integer	Size of largest packets to reassemble

The second table, ipRouteTable, is a sequence of sequences (array of records) with each sequence (record) having 13 fields (columns). The index is the value of the ipRouteDest field (see Table F.6).

Table F.6   *The second IP group table, ipRouteTable*

Id	Name	Type	Description
22.1.1	ipRouteDest	IpAddress	Destination IP address
22.1.2	ipRouteIfIndex	Integer	Interface number
22.1.3	ipRouteMetric1	Integer	Primary routing metric
22.1.4	ipRouteMetric2	Integer	Alternative routing metric
22.1.5	ipRouteMetric3	Integer	Alternative routing metric
22.1.6	ipRouteMetric4	Integer	Alternative routing metric
22.1.7	ipRouteNextHop	IpAddress	IP address of the next hop
22.1.8	ipRouteType	Integer	Route type
22.1.9	ipRouteProto	Integer	Routing protocol
22.1.10	ipRouteAge	Integer	Number of seconds since last update
22.1.11	ipRouteMask	IpAddress	Subnet mask
22.1.12	ipRouteMetric5	Integer	Alternative routing metric
22.1.13	ipRouteInfo	ObjectID	MIB object for this routing protocol

The third table, ipNetToMediaTable, is a sequence of sequences (array of records) with each sequence (record) having four fields (columns). The index is the combination of values of the ipNetToMediaIfIndex and the ipNetToMediaNetAddress fields (see Table F.7).

Table F.7   *The third IP group, ipNetToMediaTable*

Id	Name	Type	Description
23.1.1	ipNetToMediaIfIndex	Integer	Interface number
23.1.2	ipNetToMediaPhysIndex	PhysAddress	Physical address

Table F.7   *The third IP group, ipNetToMediaTable (concluded)*

Id	Name	Type	Description
23.1.3	ipNetToMediaNetAddress	IpAddress	IP address
23.1.4	ipNetToMediaType	Integer	Types of mapping

F.4   ICMP GROUP

The ICMP group stores information about the ICMP package. ICMP group simple variables are shown in Table F.8.

Table F.8   *ICMP group simple variables*

Id	Name	Type	Description
1	icmpInMsgs	Counter	Total number of messages received
2	icmpInErrors	Counter	Number of received messages with error
3	icmpInDesUnreachs	Counter	Number of destination-unreachable messages received
4	icmpInTimeExcds	Counter	Number of time-exceeded messages received
5	icmpInParmProbs	Counter	Numbers of parameter-problem messages received
6	icmpInSrcQuenchs	Counter	Number of source-quench messages received
7	icmpInRedirects	Counter	Number of redirect messages received
8	icmpInEchos	Counter	Number of echo-request messages received
9	icmpInEchoReps	Counter	Number of echo-reply messages received
10	icmpInTimestamps	Counter	Number of timestamp-request messages received
11	icmpInTimestampReps	Counter	Number of timestamp-reply messages received
12	icmpInAddrMasks	Counter	Number of mask-request messages received
13	icmpInAddrMaskReps	Counter	Number of mask-reply messages received
14	icmpOutMsgs	Counter	Total number of messages sent
15	icmpOutErrors	Counter	Total number of messages not sent because of error
16	icmpOutDesUnreachs	Counter	Number of destination-unreachable messages sent
17	icmpOutTimeExcds	Counter	Number of time-exceed messages sent
18	icmpOutParmProbs	Counter	Number of parameter-problem messages sent
19	icmpOutSrcQuenchs	Counter	Number of source-quench messages sent
20	icmpOutRedirects	Counter	Number of redirect messages sent
21	icmpOutEchos	Counter	Number of echo-request messages sent

Table F.8   *ICMP group simple variables (concluded)*

Id	Name	Type	Description
22	icmpOutEchoReps	Counter	Number of echo-reply messages sent
23	icmpOutTimestamps	Counter	Number of timestamp-request messages sent
24	icmpOutTimestampReps	Counter	Number of timestamp-reply messages sent
25	icmpOutAddrMasks	Counter	Number of mask-request messages sent
26	icmpOutAddrMaskReps	Counter	Number of mask-reply messages sent

F.5   TCP GROUP

The TCP group stores information about the TCP segments. The TCP group simple variables are shown in Table F.9.

Table F.9   *TCP group simple variables*

Id	Name	Type	Description
1	tcpRtoAlgorithm	Integer	Algorithm to calculate retransmission timeout
2	tcpRtoMin	Integer	Minimum retransmission timeout
3	tcpRtoMax	Integer	Maximum retransmision timeout
4	tcpMaxConn	Integer	Maximum number of connections
5	tcpActiveOpens	Counter	Number of active open messages
6	tcpPassiveOpens	Counter	Number of passive open messages
7	tcpAttempFails	Counter	Number of failed attempts to connect
8	tcpEstabResets	Counter	Number of resets
9	tcpCurrEstab	Gauge	Number of current connections
10	tcpInSegs	Counter	Total number of segments received
11	tcpOutSegs	Counter	Total number of segments sent
12	tcpRetransSegs	Counter	Total number of segments retransmitted
13	tcpInErrs	Counter	Total number of segments received with an error
14	tcpOutRsts	Counter	Total number of RST segments sent

The table in the TCP group, tcpConnTable, is a sequence of sequences (array of records) with each sequence (record) having five fields (columns). The index is the combination of values of the last four fields (see Table F.10).

Table F.10   *TCP group table, tcpConnTable*

Id	Name	Type	Description
15.1.1	tcpConnState	Integer	State of connection (1 to 12)

Table F.10   *TCP group table, tcpConnTable (concluded)*

Id	Name	Type	Description
15.1.2	tcpConnLocalAddress	IpAddress	Local IP address
15.1.3	tcpConnLocalPort	Integer	Local port number
15.1.4	tcpConnRemAddress	IpAddress	Remote IP address
15.1.5	tcpConnRemPort	Integer	Remote port number

F.6   UDP GROUP

The UDP group stores information about the UDP user datagram. The four UDP group simple variables are shown in Table F.11.

Table F.11   *UDP group simple variables*

Id	Name	Type	Description
1	udpInDatagrams	Counter	Number of user datagrams delivered
2	udpNoPorts	Counter	Number of user datagrams with no assigned ports
3	udpInErrors	Counter	Number of user datagrams with errors
4	udpOutDatagrams	Counter	Number of user datagrams sent

The table in the UDP group, udpTable, is a sequence of sequences (array of records) with each sequence (record) having two fields (columns). The index is the combination of values of both fields (see Table F.12).

Table F.12   *UDP group table, udpTable*

Id	Name	Type	Description
5.1.1	udpLocalAddress	IpAddress	IP address of this listener
5.1.2	udpLocalPort	Integer	Port address of this listener

APPENDIX G

High-Level Data Link Control (HDLC)

High-level data link control (HDLC) is a bit-oriented data link protocol designed to support both half-duplex and full-duplex communication over point-to-point and multipoint links. Systems using HDLC can be characterized by their station types, configurations, and response modes.

G.1 STATION TYPES

HDLC differentiates between three different types of stations: primary, secondary, and combined. A primary station is the device in either a point-to-point or multipoint line configuration that sends commands to the secondaries. A primary issues commands, a secondary issues responses. An example of the relation of a primary to a secondary is that of computer to terminal. A combined station can both command and respond.

> Stations in HDLC are of three types: primary, secondary, and combined. A primary station sends commands. A secondary station sends responses. A combined station sends commands and responses.

G.2 CONFIGURATIONS

Primary, secondary, and combined stations can be configured in three ways: unbalanced, symmetrical, and balanced (see Figure G.1). Any of these configurations can support both half-duplex and full-duplex transmission.

An unbalanced configuration (also called a master/slave configuration) is one in which one device is primary and the others are secondary. Unbalanced configurations can be point-to-point if only two devices are involved; more often they are multipoint, with one computer controlling several peripherals. An example of an unbalanced configuration is a computer and one or more terminals.

A symmetrical configuration is one in which each physical station on a link consists of two logical stations, one a primary and the other a secondary. Separate lines link

Figure G.1 *HDLC configurations*

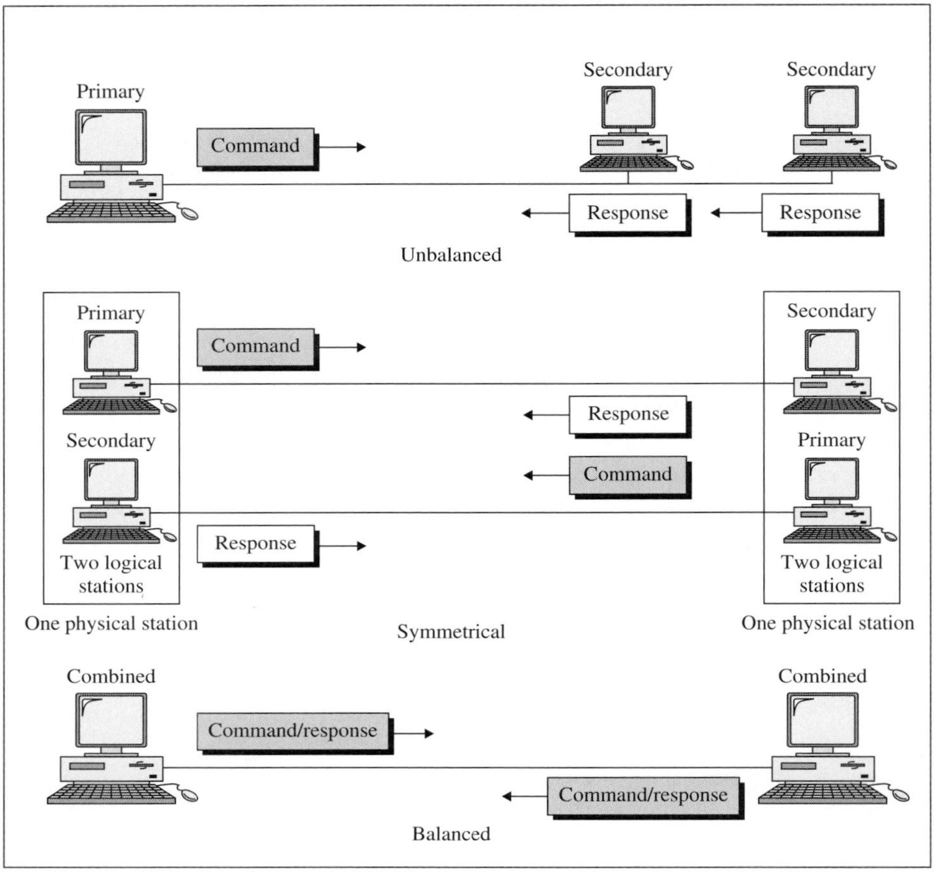

the primary aspect of one physical station to the secondary aspect of another physical station. A symmetrical configuration behaves like an unbalanced configuration except that control of the link can shift between the two stations.

A balanced configuration is one in which both stations in a point-to-point topology are of the combined type. The stations are linked by a single line that can be controlled by either station. HDLC does not support a balanced multipoint configuration. This necessitated the invention of media access protocols for LANs.

G.3 MODES OF COMMUNICATION

A mode in HDLC is the relationship between two devices involved in an exchange; the mode describes who controls the link. HDLC supports three modes of communication between stations: normal response mode (NRM), asynchronous response mode (ARM), and asynchronous balanced mode (ABM).

NRM

Normal response mode (NRM) refers to the standard primary–secondary relationship. In this mode, a secondary device must have permission from the primary device before transmitting. Once permission has been granted, the secondary may initiate a response transmission of one or more frames containing data.

ARM

In asynchronous response mode (ARM), a secondary can initiate a transmission without permission from the primary whenever the channel is idle. ARM does not alter the primary–secondary relationship in any other way. All transmissions from a secondary (even to another secondary on the same link) must still be made to the primary for relay to a final destination.

ABM

In asynchronous balanced mode (ABM), all stations are equal and therefore only combined stations connected in point-to-point are used. Either combined station may initiate transmission with the other combined station without permission.

Figure G.2 shows the relationships between these modes and station types.

Modes:

■   Normal response mode (NRM)
■   Asynchronous response mode (ARM)
■   Asynchronous balanced mode (ABM)

Figure G.2   *HDLC modes*

	NRM	ARM	ABM
Station type	Primary & secondary	Primary & secondary	Combined
Initiator	Primary	Either	Any

G.4   FRAMES

HDLC defines three types of frames: information frames (I-frames), supervisory frames (S-frames*)*, and unnumbered frames (U-frames)*;* see Figure G.3. I-frames are used to transport user data and control information relating to user data. S-frames are used only to transport control information, primarily data link layer flow and error controls. U-frames are reserved for system management. Information carried by U-frames is intended for managing the link itself.

Figure G.3 *HDLC frame types*

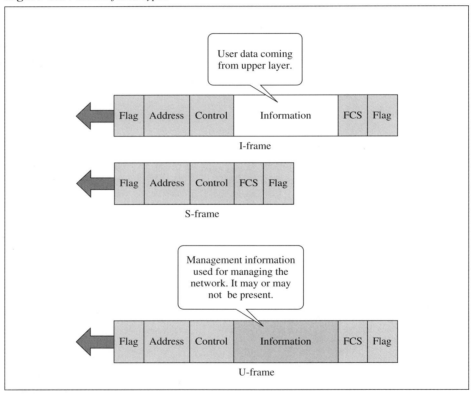

Each frame in HDLC can contain up to six fields: a beginning flag field, an address field, a control field, an information field, a frame check sequence (FCS) field, and an ending flag field. In multiple frame transmissions, the ending flag of one frame can double as the beginning flag of the next frame.

■   **Flag field.** The flag field of an HDLC frame is an eight-bit sequence with a bit pattern 01111110 that identifies both the beginning and end of a frame and serves as a synchronization pattern for the receiver. Figure G.4 shows the placement of the two flag fields in an I-frame.

Figure G.4   *HDLC flag field*

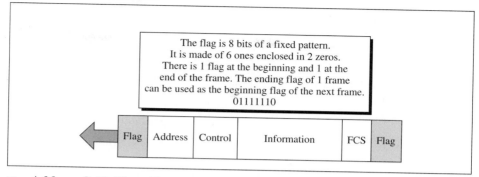

The flag is 8 bits of a fixed pattern.
It is made of 6 ones enclosed in 2 zeros.
There is 1 flag at the beginning and 1 at the
end of the frame. The ending flag of 1 frame
can be used as the beginning flag of the next frame.
01111110

| Flag | Address | Control | Information | FCS | Flag |

- **Address field.** The address field of an HDLC frame contains the address of the secondary station that is either the originator or destination of the frame (or the station acting as secondary in the case of combined stations). If a primary station creates a frame, it contains a *to* address. If a secondary creates the frame, it contains a *from* address (see Figure G.5).

Figure G.5   *HDLC address field*

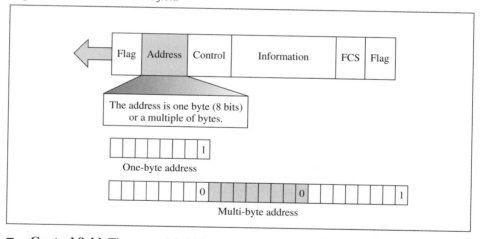

| Flag | Address | Control | Information | FCS | Flag |

The address is one byte (8 bits)
or a multiple of bytes.

One-byte address

Multi-byte address

- **Control field.** The control field is a one- or two-byte segment of the frame used for flow management. We will limit our discussion to the one-byte case. The two-byte case is similar (see Figure G.6). Control fields differ depending on frame type. If the first bit of the control field is 0, the frame is an I-frame. If the first bit is a 1 and the second bit is 0, it is an S-frame. If both the first and second bits are 1s, it is a U-frame. The control fields of all three types of frames contain a bit called the poll/final (P/F) bit (discussed below). An I-frame contains two 3-bit flow- and error-control sequences, called N(S) and N(R), flanking the P/F bit. N(S) specifies the number of the frame being sent (its own identifying number). N(R) indicates the number of the frame expected in return in a two-way exchange; thus N(R) is the acknowledgment field. If the last frame received is error-free, the N(R) number is that of the next frame in the sequence. If the last frame is not received correctly,

Figure G.6   *Control field*

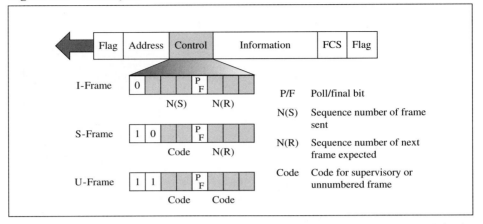

the N(R) number is the number of the damaged frame, indicating the need for its retransmission. The P/F field is a single bit with a dual purpose. It has meaning only when it is set (bit = 1) and can mean poll or final. It means *poll* (the primary selects a secondary to receive data or polls secondaries to see if they have data to send) when the frame is sent by a primary station to a secondary. It means *final* (the final packet) when the frame is sent by a secondary to a primary (see Figure G.7).

Figure G.7   *Poll/final field in HDLC*

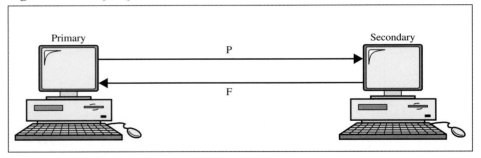

■   **Information field.** The information field contains the user's data in an I-frame, and network management information in a U-frame (see Figure G.8). Its length can vary from one network to another but is always fixed within each network. An S-frame has no information field.

■   **FCS field.** The FCS is HDLC's error-detection field. It can contain either a two- or four-byte CRC (see Figure G.9).

G.5   MORE ABOUT FRAMES

As we discussed before, three types of frames are defined in HDLC: I-frame, S-frame, and U-frame.

Figure G.8   *Information field in HDLC*

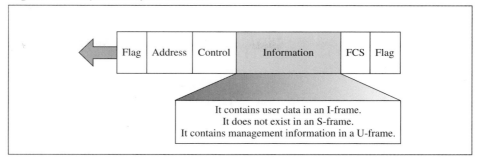

Figure G.9   *Frame check sequence (FCS) field in HDLC*

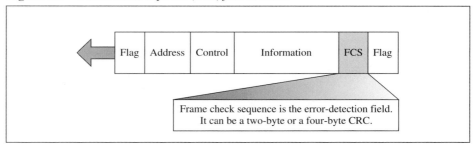

I-frames

Of the three frames used by HDLC, the I-frame is the most straightforward. I-frames are designed for user information transport and piggybacked acknowledgments—nothing else.

S-frames

Supervisory frames are used for acknowledgment, flow control, and error control whenever piggybacking that information onto an I-frame is either impossible or inappropriate (such as when the station either has no data of its own to send, or needs to send a command or response other than an acknowledgment). See Figure G.10.

U-frames

Unnumbered frames are used to exchange session management and control information between connected devices. Unlike S-frames, U-frames contain an information field; it is used for system management information rather than user data.

Figure G.10   *S-frame control field in HDLC*

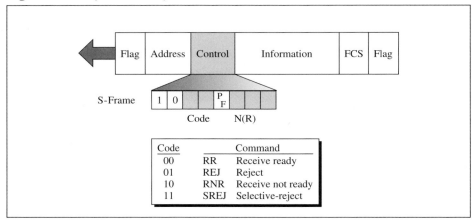

G.6   LINK ACCESS PROCEDURES (LAPS)

Several protocols under the general category **link access procedure** (LAP) have been developed. Each of these protocols is a subset of HDLC tailored for a specific purpose. Link Access Procedure, Balanced (LAPB), Link Access Procedure for D-Channel (LAPD), and Link Access Procedure for Modems (LAPM) are the most common of these.

LAPB

LAPB is a simplified subset of HDLC used only for connecting a station to a network. It therefore provides only those basic control functions required for communication between a DTE and a DCE (e.g., it does not include poll and select characters).

LAPB is used only in balanced configurations of two devices, where both devices are of the combined type. Communication is always in asynchronous balanced mode (ABM). LAPB is used today in Integrated Services Digital Network (ISDN) on B channels.

LAPD

LAPD is another simplified subset of HDLC used in ISDN. It is used for out-of-band (control) signaling. It uses ABM.

LAPM

LAPM is a simplified subset of HDLC for modems. It is designed to do asynchronous-synchronous conversion, error detection, and retransmission. It has been developed to apply HDLC features to modems.

APPENDIX H

Project 802

In 1985, the Computer Society of the IEEE started Project 802, a drive to set standards to enable intercommunication between equipment from a variety of manufacturers. Project 802 does not seek to replace any part of the OSI model. Instead, it is a way of specifying functions of the physical layer, the data link layer, and to a lesser extent the network layer to support interconnectivity of major LAN protocols.

> In 1985, the Computer Society of IEEE developed Project 802. It covers the first two layers and part of the third level of the OSI model.

The relationship of Project 802 to the OSI model is shown in Figure H.1. The IEEE has subdivided the data link layer into two sublayers: logical link control (LLC) and media access control (MAC).

Figure H.1 *LAN compared with the OSI model*

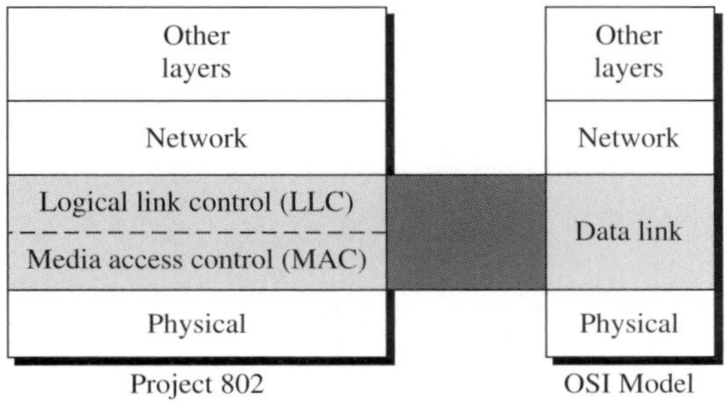

The LLC is nonarchitecture-specific; that is it is the same for all IEEE-defined LANs. The MAC sublayer, on the other hand, contains a number of distinct modules; each carries proprietary information specific to the LAN product being used.

Project 802 has split the data link layer into two different sublayers: logical link control (LLC) and media access control (MAC).

The strength of Project 802 is modularity. By subdividing the functions necessary for LAN management, the designers were able to standardize those that can be generalized and isolate those that must remain specific. Each subdivision is identified by a number: 802.1 (internetworking); 802.2 (LLC); and the MAC modules 802.3 (CSMA/CD), 802.4 (token bus), 802.5 (token ring), and others (see Figure H.2).

Figure H.2   *Project 802*

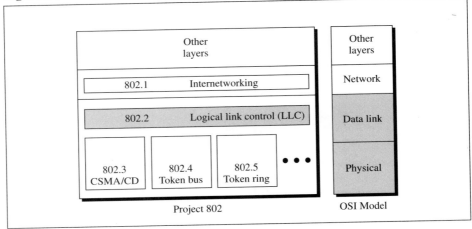

H.1   PROJECT 802.1

802.1 is the section of Project 802 devoted to internetworking issues in LANs and MANs. It seeks to resolve the incompatibilities between network architectures without requiring modifications in existing addressing, access, and error-recovery mechanisms, among others.

IEEE 802.1 is an internetworking standard for LANs.

H.2   PROJECT 802.2

802.2 is the section of Project 802 related to the physical and data link layers. It divides the data link layer into two sublayers: LLC and MAC.

LLC

In general, the IEEE Project 802 model takes the structure of an HDLC frame and divides it into two sets of functions. One set contains the end-user portions of the frame: the logical addresses, control information, and data. These functions are handled by the IEEE 802.2 LLC protocol. LLC is considered the upper layer of the IEEE 802 data link layer and is common to all LAN protocols.

> IEEE 802.2 logical link control (LLC) is the upper sublayer of the data link layer.

PDU

The data unit at the LLC level is the protocol data unit. The PDU contains four fields familiar from HDLC: a destination service access point (DSAP), a source service access point (SSAP), a control field, and an information field (see Figure H.3).

■ **DSAP and SSAP.** The DSAP and SSAP are addresses used by the LLC to identify the protocol stacks on the receiving and sending machines that are generating and using the data. The first bit of the DSAP indicates whether the frame is intended for an individual or a group. The first bit of the SSAP indicates whether the communication is a command or response PDU (see Figure H.3).

Figure H.3   *PDU format*

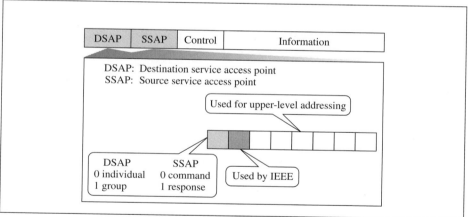

■ **Control.** The control field of the PDU is identical to the control field in HDLC. As in HDLC, PDU frames can be I-frames, S-frames, or U-frames and carry all of the codes and information that the corresponding HDLC frames carry (see Figure H.4).

MAC

The second set of functions, the media access control sublayer, resolves the contention for the shared media. It contains the synchronization, flag, flow, and error control specifications necessary to move information from one place to another, as well as the phys-

Figure H.4   *Control fields in a PDU*

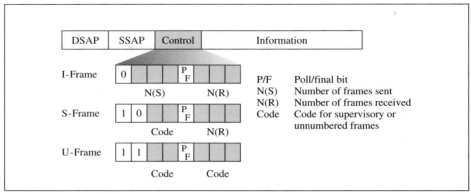

ical address of the next station to receive and route a packet. MAC protocols are specific to the LAN using them (Ethernet, token ring, and token bus, etc.).

Media access control (MAC) is the lower sublayer of the data link layer.

In the MAC layer, Project 802 is itself divided into several projects to answer the de facto standards used by the industry. Two of them are related to the LANs we discussed in Chapter 3.

■   Project 802.3 defines a LAN using a CSMA/CD access method similar to Ethernet.
■   Project 802.5 defines a LAN with token ring access method.

APPENDIX I

ASN.1

ASN.1 is a language defined by ISO to describe the structure of objects. It is similar to the data declaration in a high-level programming language such as C or C++. *Types* define the structures and *values* define the contents of those structures. The standard is so large and complex that it can easily take up a whole book. We discuss the standard here very briefly to give the reader an introduction to the concept.

I.1   DATA TYPES AND VALUES

ASN.1 defines two broad categories of data types, simple and structured, as shown in Figure I.1.

Figure I.1   *Data types*

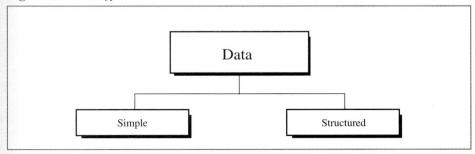

Simple Type

The simple type is the atomic data types, which ASN.1 explicitly defines. We list several simple data types below:

■   **BOOLEAN.** The type BOOLEAN represents a true or false *value*. The following shows how we can define an identifier of type BOOLEAN:

> **Status ::= BOOLEAN**

733

■ **INTEGER.** The type INTEGER represents an integral number. It can be positive, negative, or zero. The following shows how we can define an identifier of type INTEGER:

    Num ::= INTEGER

■ **ENUMERATED.** The type ENUMERATED defines an explicit set of integer values that a data type can have. The following shows how we can define an entity of type ENUMERATED. The values inside the parentheses show the integer value of each identifier.

    Month ::= ENUMERATED
        {
                jan(1) , feb(2) , mar(3) , apr(4) , may(5) , jun(6) ,
                jul(7) , aug(8) , sep(9) , oct(10) , nov(11) , dec(12)
        }

■ **REAL.** The type REAL represents a real number with arbitrary precision.

■ **BIT STRING.** The type BIT STRING represents a string of single bits (0 or 1).

■ **OCTET STRING.** The type OCTET STRING represents a string of octets (8 bits).

■ Other strings have been defined such as **NumericString** (digits 0 to 9 and space), **PrintableString, TeletexString, VideoString, VisibleString, IA5String** (International Alphabet 5), **GraphicString,** and **GeneralString.**

■ **GeneralizedTime.** This type represents date and time. The date is in the form of a four-digit year, a two-digit month, and a two-digit day. The time is in the form of hours, minutes, seconds, and an optional difference between the local time and the universal time.

■ **UTCTime.** This type represents date and time. It is the same as GeneralizedTime except that the year is in two-digit format.

■ **NULL.** This type represents a placeholder.

■ **OBJECT IDENTIFIER.** This type identifies entities and objects. They belong to the tree of objects defined by ISO and ITU (see Chapter 21). An object is defined by a series of integers separated by dots. To make the object identifiers more readable, a list of ObjectDescriptors has been defined.

■ **EXTERNAL.** This represents a type in another (external) document.

Structured Type

By combining simple and structured data types, we can make new structured data types. ASN.1 defines six structured data types.

■ **SEQUENCE.** The type SEQUENCE is a combination of simple data types, not necessarily of the same type. It is analogous to the concept of a *struct* or a *record* in programming languages such as C. The following shows how to define an identifier (Date) of type SEQUENCE. Note that month is already defined.

    Date ::= SEQUENCE
        {
                day INTEGER ,
                month Month ,
                year INTEGER
        }

- **SEQUENCE OF.** This represents a combination of data types of all the same type. It is analogous to the concept of an *array* used in programming languages such as C. The following shows how to define an identifier (Dates) of type SEQUENCE. Note that the Date is already defined.

  Dates ::= SEQUENCE OF Date

- **SET.** This is similar to a SEQUENCE except that there is no ordering.

- **SET OF.** This is similar to a SEQUENCE OF except that there is no ordering.

- **CHOICE.** This is a list of alternatives. It is similar to the concept of a *union* in C. The following shows how to define an identifier (Id) of type CHOICE.

  Id ::= CHOICE
      {
          name OCTET STRING ,
          number INTEGER
      }

- **ANY.** This is a data type that is not known at the time of specification. It can be defined later.

Tags

ASN.1 associates a tag with each data type. The tags consist of a class definition and a number that defines different types in a specific class. For example, UNIVERSAL 6 defines a tag for an OBJECT IDENTIFIER. Four classes have been defined:

- **Universal.** This class defines generally useful types that are application independent.

- **Application-wide.** This class defines types that are relevant to a specific application.

- **Context-specific.** This class is the same as the application-wide class, but the types are limited to a particular context.

- **Private.** This class relates to the types defined by users and not covered in any standard.

Subtyping

ASN.1 allows the definition of subtypes. A subtype is derived from a type by restricting the set of values. For example, we can define an integer that takes only values between 1 to 5:

Integer5 ::= INTEGER (1 | 2 | 3 | 4 | 5)

There are several ways one can define subtyes. Check the literature for details.

Values

ASN.1 allows the user to assign values to data types. Both simple and structured types can receive values. The following shows some examples:

firstmonth Month ::= jan

num INTEGER ::= 4

newyeardate Date :: { 1 , jan , 1991 }

I.2 MODULES AND MACROS

Modules and macros expand the horizon of the predefined types and values.

Modules

The notations we have used so far can be very complex and long. Modules are defined to encapsulate part of large definitions into small modules. The following shows an example of a module. It contains the definition of date and a value for date. The module can export the definition of Time to other modules, but not the value. It cannot import anything from other modules.

```
TimeModule DEFINITION ::=
BEGIN
IMPORTS
EXPORTS  Time ;
Time ::= SEQUENCE
            {
            hours            INTEGER ,
            minutes          INTEGER
            }
meeting  Time ::= {14, 20}
END
```

Macros

ASN.1 allows users to introduce their own new types and values by using a macro definition, which can be very complex. The general format is given below:

```
NEWTYPE MACRO ::=
BEGIN
        TYPE    NOTATION  ::=   define the type here
        VALUE   NOTATION  ::=   define the value here
END
```

APPENDIX J

Spanning Tree

The spanning tree algorithm is used in data structures to create a tree out of a graph. The tree should include all the vertices (nodes), with a minimum number of edges (lines) connecting the vertices. Any vertex can be selected as the root of the spanning tree. Even after selecting one specific root, we can have several spanning trees based on which subsets of branches are selected to connect each vertex to the root. However, after selecting the root, we are normally interested in one specific spanning tree, the one in which each vertex has the shortest path to the root. The shortest path is defined as the sum of the weights from a specific vertex to the root. If the graph is not weighted, each edge is assigned a weight of 1. (For more information on spanning trees, see Gilberg/Forouzan, *Data Structures: A Pseudocode Approach with C.*)

Figure J.1 shows a weighted graph and its spanning tree. Vertex A was chosen as the root.

Figure J.1   *A graph and its spanning tree*

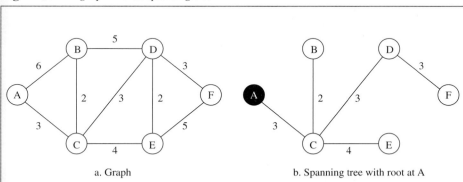

a. Graph   b. Spanning tree with root at A

J.1   SPANNING TREES AND BRIDGES

In Chapter 3, we discussed bridges and mentioned that learning bridges can determine to which LAN segment a host is connected. To create redundancy in case a bridge fails, LAN segments are normally connected by more than one bridge. However, redundancy creates loops in which a packet or several copies of a packet go from one bridge to another for ever. Let us give a very simple example. In Figure J.2, two LAN segments are connected by two bridges (Br1 and Br2).

Figure J.2   *Two LANs connected by two bridges*

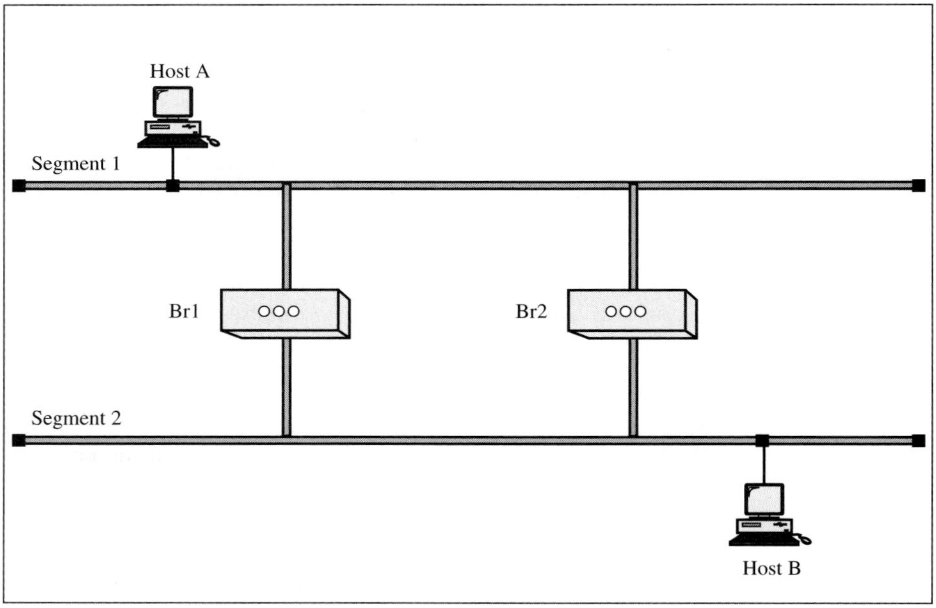

Imagine host B has not sent out any packet, so neither bridge knows to which segment host B is connected. Now consider this sequence of events:

1. Host A sends a packet to host B.
2. One of the bridges, we will say Br1, receives the packet first and, not knowing where host B is, forwards the packet to segment 2.
3. The packet goes to its destination (host B), but, at the same time, Br2 receives the packet via segment 2.
4. The packet source address is host A; its destination address is host B. Br2 erroneously assumes that host A is connected to segment 2 and updates its table accordingly. Because it does not have any information about host B, Br2 forwards the packet to segment 1.
5. The packet is then received for the second time by Br1. Br1 thinks it is a new packet from host A and, because it has no information about host B, Br1 forwards the packet to segment 2.

6. Now Br2 receives the packet once again, and the cycle will repeat endlessly.

This situation occurs due to three factors:

■   We are using learning bridges that do not have information about the location of hosts until they receive at least one packet from them.

■   The bridges are not aware of the existence of other bridges.

■   We have created a graph instead of a tree.

The situation can be corrected if we create a spanning tree out of the graph.

Algorithm

Although most data structures books give the algorithm to form a spanning tree out of a graph, they assume that the topology of the graph is already known. However, when a learning bridge is installed, it does not know the location of other bridges. The spanning tree, therefore, must be formed dynamically.

An ID number is assigned to each bridge. The ID can be any arbitrary number determined by the network manager or the address of one of the ports, normally the smallest one.

Each port is assigned a cost. Normally the cost is determined by the bit rate supported by the port. The higher the bit rate, the lower the cost. If bit rate is irrelevant, then the path cost for each port is set to 1 (hop count).

The process of finding the spanning tree can be summarized in three steps:

1. The bridges choose a bridge to be the *root* of the tree. This is done by assigning an ID to the bridge and then finding the bridge with the smallest ID.

2. Each bridge determines its *root port*, the port that has the least *root path cost* to the root. The root path cost is the accumulated cost of the path from the port to the root.

3. One *designated bridge* is chosen for each segment.

All the bridges regularly exchange a special frame called the *bridge protocol data unit* (BPDU). Each BPDU contains the bridge ID of the source, the accumulated root path cost, and some other information. When a BPDU is initiated from a bridge, the accumulated root path cost is zero.

Finding the Root Bridge

When a bridge receives a BPDU, it compares the source's bridge ID with its own ID.

■   If its own ID is larger than the source's bridge ID, it increments the root path cost by the cost of the receiving port and forwards the frame. It also stops sending its own BPDU because it knows that it will not be chosen as the root bridge (another bridge has a lower ID).

■   If its own ID is smaller than the source's bridge ID, the bridge discards the BPDU.

It is obvious that after a while, the only BPDU that is being circulated is the one with the smallest source bridge ID, the root bridge. In this way, every bridge knows which is the root bridge.

Finding the Root Port

After the root bridge has been established, the bridge records the accumulated root cost of every BPDU received for each port. The root port is the port whose BPDU has the minimum accumulated root cost. Note that the root bridge does not have a root port.

Choosing the Designated Bridge

After the root port is determined for each bridge, all bridges connected to the same segment send BPDUs to each other. The bridge that can carry a frame from the segment to the root with the cheapest root cost is selected as the designated bridge and the particular port that connects the bridge to that segment is called the *designated port*. Note that the root port cannot be chosen as a designated port. Also, note that although a bridge can have only one root port (except the root bridge, which has no root port), it can have more than one designated port.

Forming the Spanning Tree

After the root bridge, the root port for each bridge, and the designated ports for each bridge are determined, the ports of a bridge are divided into two separate groups. The *forwarding ports* are the root port and all of the designated ports. The rest of the ports are considered to be *blocking ports*. When a bridge receives a data frame, it forwards it through its *forwarding ports*. It does not forward the frame through the blocking ports.

Example

Figure J.3 shows an example of five LAN segments connected together by five bridges. Each bridge has an ID number (shown inside the box). The cost of handling a packet from a bridge to the LAN segment is shown next to the connecting line.

Figure J.4 shows the topology after using the spanning tree algorithm. The bridge with the lowest ID (Br1) is chosen as the root bridge. Each bridge has one root port (shown by an arrow). Because there are five LAN segments, we have five designated ports (marked as Des.). All the ports of bridges Br1, Br2, and Br4 are forwarding ports. Bridges Br3 and Br5 each have one blocking port.

We claim that with this configuration each LAN segment will receive one and only one copy of a frame sent by any host on any other segment; this guarantees loop-free operation.

■ A frame sent by a host on segment 1 will reach segment 2 through Br1, will reach segment 3 and segment 4 through Br1-Br2, will reach segment 5 through Br4.

■ A frame sent by a host on segment 2 will reach segment 1 through Br1, will reach segment 3 and segment 4 through Br2, will reach segment 5 through Br1-Br4.

■ A frame sent by a host on segment 3 will reach segment 4 and segment 2 through Br2, will reach segment 1 through Br2-Br1, will reach segment 5 through Br2-Br1-Br4.

■ A frame sent by a host on segment 4 will reach segment 3 and segment 2 through Br2, will reach segment 1 through Br2-Br1, will reach segment 5 through Br2-Br1-Br4.

Figure J.3   *A LAN before using spanning-tree algorithm*

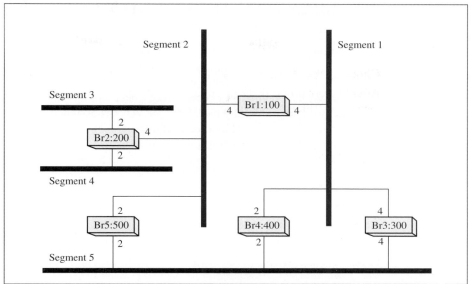

Figure J.4   *The LAN after using spanning-tree algorithm*

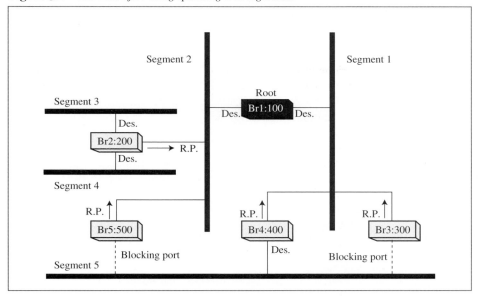

■   A frame sent by a host on segment 5 will reach segment 1 through Br4, will reach segment 2 through Br4-Br1, will reach segment 3 and segment 4 through Br4-Br1-Br2.

J.2   SPANNING TREES AND MULTICAST ROUTING

The spanning tree concept is also used in multicast routing to produce a loop-free forwarding path for datagrams in the IP layer. The idea is essentially the same as that for bridges. Here, bridges are replaced by routers, and LAN segments are replaced by LANs or WANs. The routers choose a root router among themselves. Each router then finds its root port and finally each LAN or WAN is assigned a designated router. The ports of a router are divided into forwarding and blocking ports. When a router receives a multicast datagram, it forwards only through its forwarding ports.

APPENDIX K

Contact Addresses

We have listed below contact addresses for various organizations mentioned in the text.

- **ATM Forum**
  2570 West El Camino Real, Suite 304
  Mountain View, CA 94040-1313
  Telephone: 650 949-6700
  E-mail: info@atmforum.com

- **Federal Communications Commission (FCC)**
  1919 M Street NW, Room 254
  Washington, DC 20554
  Telephone: 202 418-0200
  E-mail: psd@fcc.gov

- **Institute of Electrical and Electronics Engineers (IEEE)**
  Operations Center
  445 Hoes Lane
  Piscataway, NJ 08855-1331
  Telephone: 732 981-0060

- **International Organization for Standardization (ISO)**
  1, rue de Varembe
  Case postale 56
  CH-1211 Geneve 20
  Switzerland
  Telephone: 41 22 749 0111
  E-mail: central@iso.ch

- **International Telecommunication Union (ITU)**
  Place des Nations
  CH-1211 Geneva 20
  Switzerland

Telephone: 41 22 730 5111

E-mail: itumail@itu.int

- **Internet Architecture Board (IAB)**
  E-mail: IAB@isi.edu
- **Internet Corporation for Assigned Names and Numbers (ICANN)**
  E-mail: edyson@edventure.com
- **Internet Engineering Steering Group (IESG)**
  E-mail: iesg@ietf.org
- **Internet Engineering Task Force (IETF)**
  E-mail: ietf-infor@ietf.org
- **Internet Research Task Force (IRTF)**
  E-mail: weinrib@intel.com
- **Internet Society (ISOC)**
  12020 Sunrise Valley Drive
  Suite 210
  Reston VA 20191-3429
  Telephone: 703 648-9888
  E-mail: isoc@isoc.org

APPENDIX L

RFCs

There are approximately 2,500 RFCs. In Table L.1, we list alphabetically, by protocol, those that are directly related to the material in this text. The main RFCs for each protocol are in boldface. For a complete listing, go to http://www.ietf/cnri.reston.va.us/rfc.

Table L.1 *RFCs for each protocol*

Protocol	RFC
ARP and RARP	**826, 903**, 925, 1027, 1293, 1329, 1433
BGP	1092, 1105, 1163, 1265, 1266, 1267, 1364, 1392, 1403, 1565, 1654, 1655, 1665, 1745
BOOTP and DHCP	**951**, 1048, 1084, 1395, 1497, 1531, 1532, 1533, 1534, 1541, 1542, 2131, 2132
DHCP	See BOOTP and DHCP
DNS	799, 811, 819, 830, 881, 882, 883, 897, 920, 921, **1034, 1035**, 1386, 1480, 1535, 1536, 1537, 1591, 1637, 1664, 1706, 1712, 1713
FTP	114, 133, 141, 163, 171, 172, 238, 242, 250, 256, 264, 269, 281, 291, 354, 385, 412, 414, 418, 430, 438, 448, 463, 468, 478, 486, 505, 506, 542, 553, 624, 630, 640, 691, 765, 913, **959**, 1635
HTML	1866
HTTP	**2068**, 2109
ICMP	777, **792**, 1016, 1018, 1256, 1885
IGMP	988, 1054, 1112
IP	760, 781, **791**, 815, 950, 919, 922, 1025, 1063, 1141, 1190, 1191, 1624
IPv6	1365, 1550, 1678, 1680, 1682, 1683, 1686, 1688, 1726, 1752, 1826, 1883, 1884
MIME	See SNMP, MIME, SMI

Table L.1   *RFCs for each protocol (concluded)*

Protocol	RFC
OSPF	1131, 1245, 1246, 1247, 1370, 1583, 1584, 1585, 1586, 1587
RARP	See ARP and RARP
RIP	1131, 1245, 1246, 1247, 1370, 1583, 1584, 1585, 1586, 1587, 1722, 1723
SMI	See SNMP, MIB, SMI
SMTP, MIME, POP	196, 221, 224, 278, 524, 539, 753, 772, 780, 806, **821**, 934, 974, 1047, 1081, 1082, 1225, 1460, 1496, 1426, 1427, 1652, 1653, 1711, 1725, 1734, 1740, 1741, 1767, 1869, **1870**, 2045
SNMP, MIB, SMI	1065, 1067, 1098, 1155, **1157, 1212, 1213**, 1229, 1231, 1243, 1284, 1351, 1352, 1354, 1389, 1398, 1414, 1441, 1442, 1443, 1444, 1445, 1446, 1447, 1448, 1449, 1450, 1451, 1452, 1461, 1472, 1474, 1537, 1623, 1643, 1650, 1657, 1665, 1666, 1696, 1697, 1724, 1742, 1743, 1748, 1749
TCP	675, 721, 761, **793**, 879, 896, 1078, 1106, 1110, 1144, 1145, 1146, 1263, 1323, 1337, 1379, 1644
TELNET	137, 340, 393, 426, 435, 452, 466, 495, 513, 529, 562, 595, 596, 599, 669, 679, 701, 702, 703, 728, 764, 782, 818, **854, 855**, 1184, 1205
TFTP	**1350**, 1782, 1783, 1784
UDP	768
WWW	1614, 1630, 1737, 1738

APPENDIX M

UDP and TCP Ports

Table M.1 lists the common well-known ports ordered by port number.

Table M.1   *Ports by port number*

Port Number	UDP/TCP	Protocol
7	TCP	ECHO
13	UDP/TCP	DAYTIME
19	UDP/TCP	CHARACTER GENERATOR
20	TCP	FTP-DATA
21	TCP	FTP-CONTROL
23	TCP	TELNET
25	TCP	SMTP
37	UDP/TCP	TIME
67	UDP	BOOTP-SERVER
68	UDP	BOOTP-CLIENT
69	UDP	TFTP
70	TCP	GOPHER
79	TCP	FINGER
80	TCP	HTTP
109	TCP	POP-2
110	TCP	POP-3
111	UDP/TCP	RPC
161	UDP	SNMP
162	UDP	SNMP-TRAP
179	TCP	BGP
520	UDP	RIP

Table M.2 lists the ports ordered alphabetically by protocol.

Table M.2 *Port numbers by protocol*

Protocol	*UDP/TCP*	*Port Number*
BGP	TCP	179
BOOTP-SERVER	UDP	67
BOOTP-CLIENT	UDP	68
CHARACTER GENERATOR	UDP/TCP	19
DAYTIME	UDP/TCP	13
ECHO	TCP	7
FINGER	TCP	79
FTP-CONTROL	TCP	21
FTP-DATA	TCP	20
GOPHER	TCP	70
HTTP	TCP	80
POP-2	TCP	109
POP-3	TCP	110
RIP	UDP	520
RPC	UDP/TCP	111
SMTP	TCP	25
SNMP	UDP	161
SNMP-TRAP	UDP	162
TELNET	TCP	23
TFTP	UDP	69
TIME	UDP/TCP	37

Solutions to
Multiple-Choice Questions
and Selected Exercises

CHAPTER 1

Multiple Choice

1. d 2. c 3. a 4. a 5. a 6. b 7. d 8. a 9. c 10. b
11. a 12. c

Exercises

19. RFC 2418: The Internet Engineering Task Force (IETF) has responsibility for developing and reviewing specifications intended as Internet Standards. IETF activities are organized into working groups (WGs). This document describes the guidelines and procedures for formation and operation of IETF working groups. It also describes the formal relationship between IETF working groups and the Internet Engineering Steering Group (IESG).

    RFC 1603: This is the RFC that was obsoleted by RFC 2418.

CHAPTER 2

Multiple Choice

1. c 2. b 3. d 4. c 5. b 6. c 7. c 8. b 9. a 10. c
11. d 12. b 13. a 14. c 15. d

Exercises

17.

   a. Network layer
   b. Data link and transport layers
   c. Application layer
   d. Application layer
   e. Presentation layer
   f. Network layer

22. The equivalent of FTP in the OSI model is File Transport, Access and Management (FTAM). FTP transfers files. FTAM transfers files and can also manage files.

25. There are two protocols in the network layer of the OSI model: Connection-Oriented Network Protocol (CONP) and Connectionless Network Protocol (CLNP).

CHAPTER 3

Multiple Choice

1. b	2. b	3. a	4. b	5. d	6. c	7. c	8. a	9. a	10. c
11. b	12. a	13. a	14. c	15. c	16. c	17. c	18. b	19. d	20. b
21. a	22. b	23. c	24. d	25. b	26. d	27. d	28. b	29. c	30. b
31. d	32. c	33. d	34. d	35. c	36. b	37. b	38. a	39. b	40. c
41. b	42. c	43. d	44. c	45. a	46. d	47. b	48. a	49. b	50. d

Exercises

54. See Figure S.1.

Figure S.1   *Exercise 54*

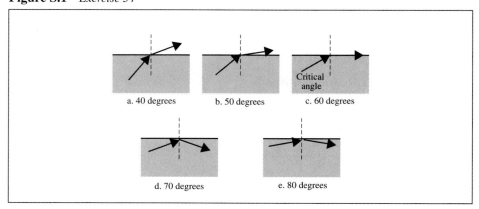

56. In 10BASE5, the transceiver is part of a separate unit called a Medium Attachment Unit (MAU) that is also used to tap into the cable. In 10BASE2, the transceiver circuitry is part of the Network Interface Card (NIC). In 10BASE-T, instead of indi-

vidual transceivers, the networking operations are placed inside of an intelligent hub with a port to each station.

74. Smallest Ethernet frame: 72 bytes (26 byte header + 46 bytes of data)

Largest Ethernet frame: 1,526 bytes (26 byte header + 1,500 bytes of data)

85. The token size is 3 bytes.

3 bytes × 8 bits / byte = 24 bits.

If the data rate is 16 Mbps, 24 bits can be generated in:

24 bits / 16,000,000 bits/second = 1.5 microseconds

CHAPTER 4

Multiple Choice

1. a   2. d   3. b   4. d   5. a   6. b   7. b   8. d   9. c   10. c

11. a   12. b   13. a   14. d   15. c   16. d   17. d   18. a   19. c   20. b

21. b

Exercises

23.
   a. 127.240.103.125
   b. 175.192.240.29
   c. 223.176.31.93
   d. 239.247.199.29
   e. 247.243.135.221

26.
   a. netid: 114   hostid: 34.2.8
   b. netid: 19   hostid: 34.21.5
   c. netid: 23   hostid: 67.12.1
   d. netid: 127   hostid: 23.4.0 (actually a loopback address)

33. This message must travel through a router because it is moving from network 128.23.0.0 to network 14.0.0.0.

36. This message must travel through a router because it is moving from network 195.23.67.0 to network 195.23.41.0.

40. Network 8.0.0.0: Class A

Network 131.45.0.0: Class B

See Figure S.2.

53. Source address: 124.67.89.34

Destination address: 127.X.Y.Z (where X, Y, and Z can be anything)

Figure S.2   *Exercise 40*

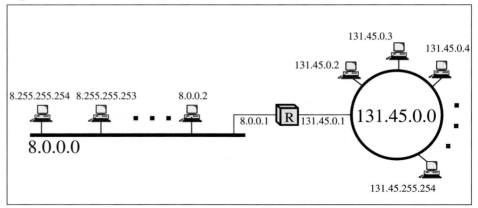

CHAPTER 5

Multiple Choice

   1. a   2. b   3. d   4. c   5. a   6. b   7. c   8. a   9. d   10. d
  11. c   12. d   13. b   14. c   15. b   16. d   17. d   18. b

Exercises

21. 150.20.193.5 to 150.20.193.6

28.

    a. 255.255.255.248

    b. 255.255.255.224

    c. 255.255.248.0

30. Subnetwork address: 120.14.0.0

    Hostid: 22.16

34.

    a. 255.128.0.0

    b. 255.224.0.0

    c. 255.248.0.0

    d. 255.252.0.0

    e. 255.254.0.0

    f. 255.255.0.0

43.

    a. $2^{10} - 2 = 1{,}022$

    b. $2^2 - 2 = 2$

c. $2^{11} - 2 = 2,046$
d. $2^{16} - 2 = 65,534$

CHAPTER 6

Multiple Choice

1. c   2. d   3. b   4. a   5. d   6. b   7. c   8. d   9. b   10. a
11. b   12. a   13. c   14. b   15. d   16. c

Exercises

22. 111.15.17.32 through interface m0
27. 111.30.31.18 through interface m0
30. See Table S.1. The interface to the rest of the Internet is m0; the interface to the network 111.0.0.0 is m1.

Table S.1 *Routing table for router R2 in Exercise 30*

Mask	Destination	Next Hop	F.	R.C.	U.	I.
255.0.0.0	111.0.0.0		U	0	0	m1
255.255.255.255	194.17.21.16	111.20.18.14	UGH	0	0	m1
....	....	....	....	.....	...	...
255.255.255.0	193.14.5.0	111.25.19.20	UG	0	0	m1
255.255.255.0	192.16.7.0	111.15.17.32	UG	0	0	m1
255.255.255.0	194.17.21.0	111.20.18.14	UG	0	0	m1
0.0.0.0	0.0.0.0		U	0	0	m0

CHAPTER 7

Multiple Choice

1. b   2. d   3. d   4. a   5. d   6. c   7. d   8. d   9. d   10. a
11. d   12. b   13. b   14. d   15. d   16. c   17. a   18. b   19. d   20. b
21. a   22. d   23. c   24. d

Exercises

25. If no fragmentation occurs at the router, then the only field to change in the base header is the time to live field. If any of the multiple-byte options are present, then

there will be changes in the option headers as well (to record the route and/or timestamp). If fragmentation does occur, the total length field will change to reflect the total length of each datagram. The more fragment bit of the flags field and the fragmentation offset fields may also change to reflect the fragmentation. If options are present and fragmentation occurs, the HLEN field of the base header may also change to reflect whether or not the option was included in the fragments.

29. In this case, we use a Loose Source Route option with only one entry. See Figure S.3.

Figure S.3   *Exercise 29*

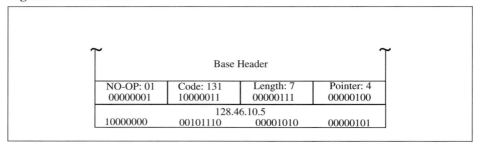

33. If the size of the option field is 20 bytes, then the total length of the header is 40 bytes (20 byte base header + 20 bytes of options = 40 bytes). The HLEN field will be the total number of bytes in the header divided by 4, in this case 10 (1010 in binary).

35. HLEN field: 5 (0101)

    Total length field: 1044 (00000100 00010100)

38. Since the fragmentation offset field shows the offset from the beginning of the original datagram in multiples of 8 bytes, an offset of 100 indicates that there were 800 bytes of data sent before the data in this fragment.

CHAPTER 8

Multiple Choice

1. d   2. a   3. b   4. a   5. a   6. a   7. d   8. a   9. c   10. b
11. c   12. d   13. b   14. c

Exercises

17. 28 bytes.
21. 0xFFFFFFFFFFFF
22. See Figure S.4.

Figure S.4 *Exercise 23*

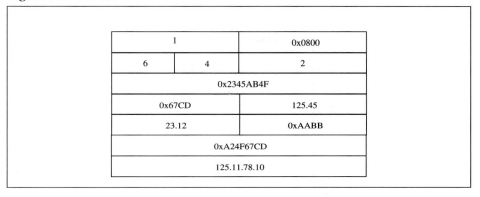

1		0x0800
6	4	2
0x2345AB4F		
0x67CD		125.45
23.12		0xAABB
0xA24F67CD		
125.11.78.10		

CHAPTER 9

Multiple Choice

1. a   2. d   3. b   4. a   5. d   6. d   7. b   8. b   9. a   10. d
11. c   12. c   13. d   14. c   15. d   16. b   17. c   18. b   19. c   20. a

Exercises

22. Hostid: 27   Class: C

24. It could happen that host B is unreachable, for some reason. The error message could then be lost on its way back to host A. It could also happen that host A is on an isolated network that does not contain host B or any router.

31. The minimum size of an ICMP packet is 8 bytes (router solicitation packet). The largest of the ICMP packets is the router advertisement packet which can list as many as 255 listings. The maximum size is then:

    255 listings $\times$ 8 bytes/listing + 8 bytes for the ICMP header = 2,048 bytes

35. See Figure S.5. The checksum is 1101001110011001.

Figure S.5 *Exercise 35*

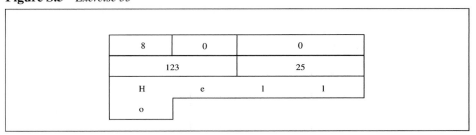

8	0	0
123		25
H	e	l	l
o			

36. See Figure S.6.

Figure S.6   *Exercise 36*

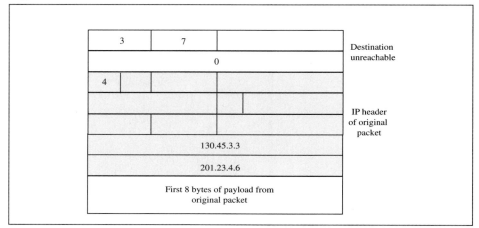

3	7		Destination unreachable
0			
4			
			IP header of original packet
130.45.3.3			
201.23.4.6			
First 8 bytes of payload from original packet			

43. Sending time = 13,562,000 – 13,560,000 = 2,000 milliseconds
     Receiving time = 13,567,000 – 13,564,300 = 2,700 milliseconds
     Round trip time = 2000 + 2700 = 4,700 milliseconds
     Difference in clocks = 13,562,000 – (13,560,000 + (4700 / 2)) = –350
     milliseconds, which means that the sending clock is 350 milliseconds ahead of the
     receiving clock. This assumes that the one-way transmission time is one-half of the
     round trip transmission time.

CHAPTER 10

Multiple Choice

1. b   2. d   3. d   4. d   5. d   6. d   7. b   8. d   9. c   10. b
11. a   12. b   13. c   14. d

Exercises

17. 00000001 00000000 01011110 00011000 00111100 00001001
20. The host must send 5 different report messages at random times in order to pre-
     serve membership in 5 different groups.
22. See Figure S.7.
37.
     a. This is a type 1 message (a query).
     b. The checksum is 0xEEFF (11101110 11111111).
     c. The groupid is all 0s (this is a query, after all).

Figure S.7 *Exercise 22*

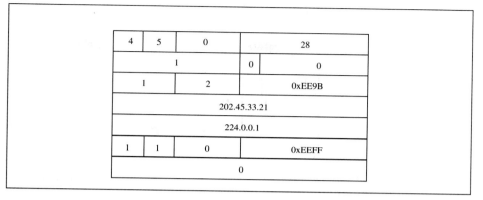

CHAPTER 11

Multiple Choice

1. c   2. a   3. c   4. d   5. a   6. b   7. a   8. d   9. d   10. c
11. d   12. b   13. c   14. a   15. a   16. c   17. d   18. a   19. a   20. c
21. c   22. d   23. c

Exercises

25. IP and UDP are both connectionless and unreliable protocols. The main difference in their reliability is that IP only calculates a checksum for the IP header and not for the data while UDP calculates a checksum for the entire datagram.

29. FTP uses the services of TCP, not UDP.

43.

   a. Port number 1586
   b. Port number 13
   c. 28 bytes
   d. 20 bytes (28 − 8 byte header = 20 bytes)
   e. From a client to a server
   f. Daytime

CHAPTER 12

Multiple Choice

1. c	2. a	3. a	4. d	5. b	6. c	7. b	8. b	9. a	10. d
11. c	12. c	13. c	14. d	15. a	16. d	17. b	18. d	19. b	20. a
21. a	22. c	23. b	24. a	25. d	26. a	27. b	28. d	29. c	30. a
31. b	32. c	33. a	34. b	35. b					

Exercises

36. RTT $= 90\% \times 4 + 10\% \times 5 = 4.1$ seconds

46. About 71.6 minutes.

50. 8000 bytes.

60.
   a. 1330
   b. 23
   c. 1
   d. 0
   e. 20 bytes.
   f. A SYN segment used for connection establishment.
   g. 2047 bytes.

CHAPTER 13

Multiple Choice

1. b	2. d	3. a	4. d	5. c	6. a	7. b	8. a	9. d	10. c
11. a	12. b	13. a	14. b	15. b	16. d	17. c	18. c	19. a	20. b
21. b	22. d	23. a	24. d	25. b	26. a	27. b	28. b	29. b	30. a
31. d	32. c	33. d	34. a	35. b	36. c	37. b	38. c	39. a	40. a
41. b	42. a	43. d							

Exercises

46. The expiration timer is 6 times that of the periodic timer because RIP relies on the services of UDP which is a connectionless and unreliable communications protocol. To do this, RIP must allow for some missed communication between routers.

59. net1   3   C
    net2   2   C

net3   1   F
net4   5   G

60. $2 + 10 \times N =$ Empty bytes in a message advertising N networks
70. See Figure S.8.

Figure S.8   *Exercise 70*

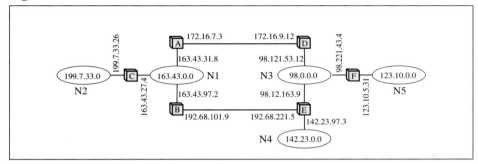

73. See Figure S.9.

Figure S.9   *Exercise 73*

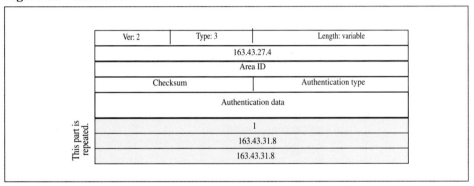

76. Transient networks: N1, N2, N5, and N6. Stub networks: N3 and N4.

CHAPTER 14

Multiple Choice

1. c   2. d   3. c   4. d   5. d   6. b   7. d   8. d   9. a   10. b
11. b   12. d   13. c   14. a   15. d   16. d   17. d   18. c   19. b   20. a
21. a

Exercises

25.
```
pid = fork ( ) ;
  if ( pid == 0 )
  {
  parent_pid = getppid ( ) ;
  printf ( " My parent is %d\n", parent_pid ) ;
  }
```
26. Four lines containing "Hello" and 4 lines containing "Bye". These lines may appear in any order depending on the order of execution of the various processes involved.
29. 1 line containing "Hello".

   2 lines containing "Bye".

   1 line containing "Hi".

   2 lines containing "Dear".

   4 lines containing "Friend".

   These lines may appear in any order depending on the order of execution of the various processes involved.

CHAPTER 15

Multiple Choice

1. d   2. c   3. b   4. a   5. c   6. b   7. d   8. a   9. c   10. d
11. d   12. d   13. c   14. a   15. d   16. d

Exercises

18. 236 bytes for the BOOTP packet

   8 bytes for the UDP header

   20 bytes for the IP header

   26 bytes for the Ethernet frame

----

290 bytes total

Efficiency $= 236 / 290 = 0.8138$

28 bytes for the RARP packet
18 bytes of padding
26 bytes for the Ethernet frame

----

72 bytes total

Efficiency $= 28 / 72 = 0.3889$

28. A newly added host needs to know its subnet mask because this allows the host to extract its subnet address from its IP address.

32. See Figure S.10.

Figure S.10   *Exercise 32*

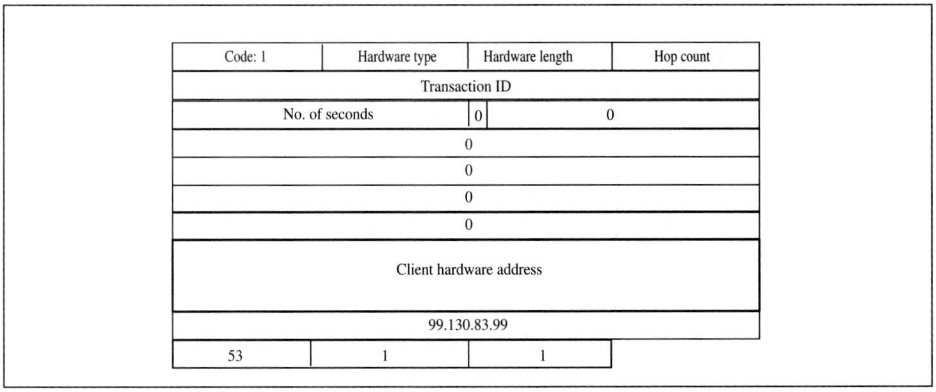

Code: 1	Hardware type	Hardware length	Hop count
Transaction ID			
No. of seconds	0	0	
0			
0			
0			
0			
Client hardware address			
99.130.83.99			
53	1	1	

42. DHCP Client:
   1. Upon booting, broadcast a DHCPDISCOVER message to the network.
   2. If no DHCPOFFER message received:
        1. Try 4 more times (every 2 seconds)
        2. If still no DHCPOFFER message received:
           1. Sleep for 5 minutes.
           2. Start over from beginning.
   3. Else
        1. Choose an offer and send DHCPREQUEST packet to offering server.
        2. If client receives DHCPACK message from server:
           1. Set a timer.
        3. While address still in use:
           1. Wait 50% of time and send another DHCPREQUEST to renew lease.
           2. If client receives DHCPACK:

    1. Reset timer.
  3. Else if client receives DHCPNACK:
    1. Stop using address
    2. Start over from the beginning.
  4. Else
    1. Wait until 87.5% of time has expired.
    2. Repeat steps for last try.
4. If lease expires:
  1. Stop using address.
  2. Start over from the beginning.
5. When finished with address:
  1. Send DHCPRELEASE message to server.

CHAPTER 16

Multiple Choice

1. d	2. a	3. c	4. b	5. a	6. b	7. d	8. a	9. d	10. d
11. c	12. d	13. b	14. a	15. c	16. a	17. a	18. d	19. d	20. a

Exercises

25.
  a. PQDN
  b. FQDN
  c. PQDN
  d. FQDN

27. 0000000100000000 = 0x0100

30. 0000010100000011 = 0x0503

This flag should never occur. The QR bit is not set, so it is a request, but the rCode field shows 3, which means "Domain reference problem". The rCode field is only used in a response message.

40. The size of the response message depends on the length of the domain name returned.

43. See Figure S.11.

Figure S.11   *Exercise 43*

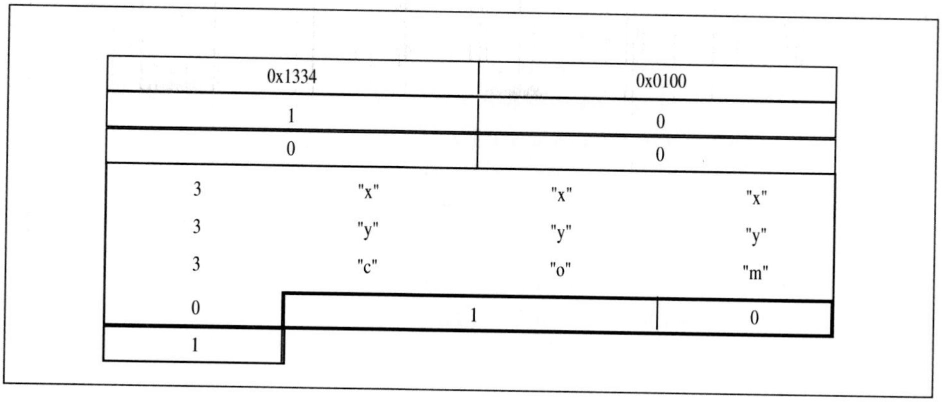

0x1334		0x0100	
1		0	
0		0	
3	"x"	"x"	"x"
3	"y"	"y"	"y"
3	"c"	"o"	"m"
0		1	0
1			

CHAPTER 17

Multiple Choice

1. b	2. c	3. d	4. c	5. b	6. c	7. d	8. c	9. a	10. d
11. b	12. d	13. b	14. d	15. c	16. b	17. b	18. d	19. a	20. d
21. c	22. b	23. a	24. b	25. b	26. a	27. d	28. a	29. b	30. a
31. d									

Exercises

32. Client to Server: IAC DO BINARY
    1111111111111110100000000
    Server to Client: IAC WILL BINARY
    1111111111111101100000000
    Client to Server: 11110011 00111100 11111111 11111111
    Note: The last byte is duplicated because it is the same as IAC, and so must be repeated in order to be interpreted as data.

35. Four transmissions, each with a minimum size of 72 bytes, means a total of 288 bytes or 2304 bits.

40. Client to Server: IAC DONT ECHO
    Server to Client: IAC WONT ECHO
    Client to Server: IAC DONT SUPPRESS GO AHEAD
    Server to Client: IAC WONT SUPPRESS GO AHEAD
    Server to Client: IAC GA
    Client to Server: IAC DO LINE MODE
    Server to Client: IAC WILL LINE MODE

43.

a. IAC WILL ECHO

b. IAC DONT ECHO

c. IAC IP (Interrupt Process)

d. IAC GA (Go Ahead)

47. Server to Client: FF F9

Client to Server: FF FD 03

Server to Client: FF FB 03

Client to Server: FF FD 01

Server to Client: FF FB 01

Server to Client: "Login:"

CHAPTER 18

Multiple Choice

1. d   2. a   3. c   4. d   5. b   6. c   7. a   8. a   9. d   10. d
11. c   12. d   13. b   14. a

Exercises

16. The client issues an active open for the control connection because the server, which is always running, is waiting for a client with a passive open on this port. The client must be the one to issue the passive open on the data port because it is the client that initiates all of the communication via the control connection. If the server were to issue a passive open on an ephemeral port number, it would have no way to send that port number to the client.

20. See Figure S.12.

24. Server to Client: 220 (Service Ready)

Client to Server: USER forouzan

Server to Client: 331 (User name OK, password is needed)

Client to Server: PASS xxxx

Server to Client: 230 (User login OK)

(Client issues a passive open on an ephemeral port number)

Client to Server: PORT 1267

(Server issues an active open on the given port number)

Server to Client: 150 (Data connection will open shortly)

Client to Server: TYPE EBCDIC

Server to Client: 200 (Command OK)

Client to Server: STRU R

Server to Client: 200 (Command OK)

Figure S.12 *Exercise 20*

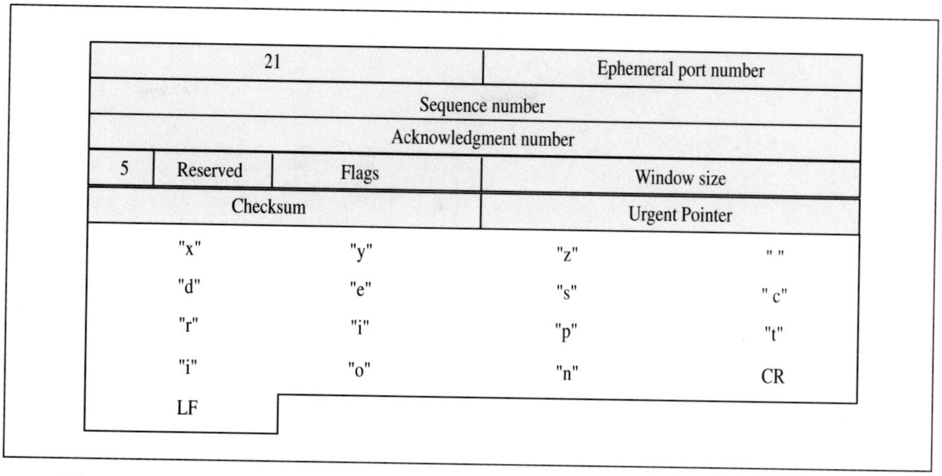

21			Ephemeral port number	
Sequence number				
Acknowledgment number				
5	Reserved	Flags	Window size	
Checksum			Urgent Pointer	
"x"	"y"	"z"	" "	
"d"	"e"	"s"	" c"	
"r"	"i"	"p"	"t"	
"i"	"o"	"n"	CR	
LF				

Client to Server: STOU /usr/user/report
Server to Client: 250 (Requested file action OK)

< Records of file are transferred from the client to the server >

Server to Client: 226 (Closing data connection)
Client to Server: QUIT
Server to Client: 221 (Service Closing)

If the file being transferred to the server already exists, the filename of the new file will be made unique.

CHAPTER 19

Multiple Choice

1. d 2. a 3. d 4. d 5. c 6. a 7. b 8. a 9. d 10. d
11. c 12. a 13. d 14. d 15. d 16. a

Exercises

21. See Figure S.13.

Figure S.13   *Exercise 21*

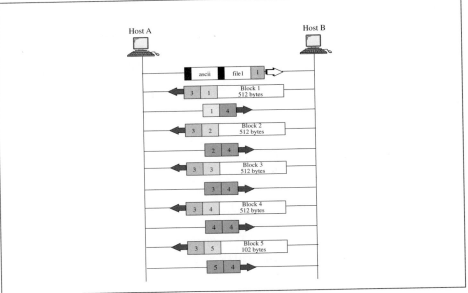

CHAPTER 20

Multiple Choice

1. d	2. c	3. b	4. d	5. a	6. c	7. d	8. b	9. b	10. d
11. c	12. a	13. c	14. b	15. a	16. b	17. c	18. d	19. a	20. d
21. d	22. a	23. d	24. b	25. a	26. c	27. a	28. b	29. c	30. c
31. c									

Exercises

37. Client to Server: MAIL FROM: aaa@xxx.com

Server to Client: 250 (Request Command Completed)

Client to Server: RCPT TO: bbb@yyy.com

Server to Client: 250 (Request Command Completed)

Client to Server: DATA

Server to Client: 354 (Start mail input)

Client to Server: From: A.A.

Client to Server: To: bbb

Client to Server: Date: 3/6/99

Client to Server: Subject: Howdy!

Client to Server: Good morning my friend.

Client to Server: .

Server to Client: 250 (Request Command Completed)

39. (Connection is established with yyy.com)

Server to Client: 220 (Service ready)

Client to Server: HELO xxx.com

Server to Client: 250 (Request Command Completed)

Client to Server: MAIL FROM: aaa@xxx.com

Server to Client: 250 (Request Command Completed)

Client to Server: RCPT TO: bbb@yyy.com

Server to Client: 250 (Request Command Completed)

Client to Server: DATA

Server to Client: 354 (Start mail input)

Client to Server: From: A.A.

Client to Server: To: bbb

Client to Server: Date: 3/6/99

Client to Server: Subject: Howdy!

Client to Server: Good morning my friend.

Client to Server: .

Server to Client: 250 (Request Command Completed)

Client to Server: QUIT

Server to Client: 221 (Service closing transmission channel)

(Connection is established with zzz.com)

Server to Client: 220 (Service ready)

Client to Server: HELO xxx.com

Server to Client: 250 (Request Command Completed)

Client to Server: MAIL FROM: aaa@xxx.com

Server to Client: 250 (Request Command Completed)

Client to Server: RCPT TO: ccc@zzz.com

Server to Client: 250 (Request Command Completed)

Client to Server: DATA

Server to Client: 354 (Start mail input)

Client to Server: From: aaa

Client to Server: To: ccc

Client to Server: Date: 3/6/99

Client to Server: Subject: Howdy!

Client to Server: Good morning my friend.

Client to Server: .

Server to Client: 250 (Request Command Completed)

Client to Server: QUIT

Server to Client: 221 (Service closing transmission channel)

CHAPTER 21

Multiple Choice

1. d   2. c   3. d   4. b   5. a   6. c   7. a   8. d   9. d   10. a
11. c   12. d   13. d   14. a   15. a   16. b   17. d   18. c   19. b   20. d
21. c   22. b   23. c   24. a   25. a   26. d

Exercises

32. 30 18
      02 04 00 00 09 29
      02 04 00 00 04 D4
      02 04 00 00 00 7A
      02 04 00 00 04 D4

38. GetRequest:
  30 29
    02 01 00
    04 06 70 75 62 6C 69 63
    A0 1C
      02 04 00 01 06 14
      02 01 00
      02 01 00
      30 0E
        30 0C
        06 08 01 03 06 01 02 01 05 05
        05 00

  GetResponse:
  30 2E
    02 01 00
    04 06 70 75 62 6C 69 63
    A2 21
      02 04 00 01 06 14
      02 01 00
      02 01 00
      30 13
        30 11
        06 09 01 03 06 01 02 01 05 05 00
        41 04 00 00 00 A7

CHAPTER 22

Multiple Choice

1. b   2. b   3. a   4. d   5. d   6. d   7. c   8. a   9. d   10. a
11. d   12. c   13. b   14. d   15. d   16. c   17. b

Exercises

19. HTTP/1.1 200 OK
    Date: Tue, 09-Mar-99 16:46:26 GMT
    Server: Challenger
    MIME-version: 1.0
    Content-length: 4623

    (Body of document)

20. HTTP/1.1 302 Moved Permanently
    Date: Tue, 09-Mar-99 16:46:26 GMT
    Server: Challenger
    Location: /usr/deads/doc.1
34. HTTP/1.1 200 OK
    Date: Tue, 09-Mar-99 17:43:02 GMT
    Server: Challenger
    MIME-version: 1.0
    Content-type: text/html
    Content-length: 6324
    Expires: 09-May-99 00:00:00 GMT

CHAPTER 23

Multiple Choice

1. c 2. d 3. a 4. b 5. c 6. b 7. a 8. b 9. d 10. a
11. c 12. b 13. d 14. d 15. b 16. c 17. d 18. c 19. c 20. d
21. d 22. a 23. d 24. c 25. d 26. b 27. d 28. d

Exercises

29. This is
    a line of
    HTML

32. This will appear as an unordered list of 3 items.
34. This will create a link to "www.mhhe". The publisher name will appear as a link in
    the page.

CHAPTER 24

Multiple Choice

1. d 2. c 3. c 4. a 5. d 6. a 7. b 8. c 9. a 10. d
11. d 12. a 13. d 14. b 15. a 16. b 17. c 18. d 19. d 20. a
21. c 22. b 23. b 24. a 25. b 26. d 27. a 28. c 29. d 30. d
31. b 32. c 33. b 34. c 35. b

Exercises

39.
```
activeSocket = socket ( AF_INET, SOCK_STREAM, 0 ) ;
memset ( &remoteAddr, 0, sizeof ( remoteAddr ) ) ;
remoteAddr.sin_family = AF_INET ;
remoteAddr.sin_port = htons ( 23 ) ;
hptr = gethostbyname ( "xxx.yyy.edu" ) ;
memcpy ( ( char * ) &remoteAddr.sinaddr.s_addr,
         hptr -> h_addr_list [ 0 ], hptr -> h_length ) ;
if ( connect ( activeSocket, &remoteAddr, sizeof ( remoteAddr ) )  ==  -1 )
{
  printf ( "\n\a ====  Bad Connection  ====\n\n" ) ;
  exit ( 101 ) ;
```

```
    }
43.  for ( ; ; )
     {
        childSocket  =  accept ( passiveSocket, &clientAddr, &clientAddrLength ) ;
        pid  =  fork ( ) ;
        if ( pid  != 0 )
         {
            close ( childSocket ) ;
            continue ;
         } /* if parent process */
        else
         {
            close ( passiveSocket ) ;

            ...
         } /* else child process */
     } /* for ( ever ) */
```

CHAPTER 25

Multiple Choice

1. d	2. d	3. b	4. b	5. c	6. b	7. c	8. b	9. a	10. d
11. b	12. a	13. a	14. b	15. a	16. c	17. b	18. d	19. c	20. d
21. a	22. b	23. a	24. a	25. d	26. d	27. d	28. b	29. b	30. c
31. b	32. d	33. d	34. c	35. d	36. c	37. d	38. d	39. a	

Exercises

41.
   a. 0000:0000:0000:0000:0000:0000:0000:0000
   b. 0000:00AA:0000:0000:0000:0000:0000:0000
   c. 0000:1234:0000:0000:0000:0000:0000:0003
   d. 0123:0000:0000:0000:0000:0000:0001:0002

42.
   a. Link local address
   b. Site local address
   c. Multicast address (permanent, link local)
   d. Loopback address

45. 0000:0000:0000:0000:0000:0000::8106:0C22 or 0::8106:C22

51. FF01: Permanent node local

FF02: Permanent link local

FF05: Permanent site local

FF08: Permanent organization local

FF0E: Permanent global

FF11: Transient node local

FF12: Transient link local

FF15: Transient site local

FF18: Transient organization local

FF1E: Transient global

55. See Figure S.14.

Figure S.14   *Exercise 55*

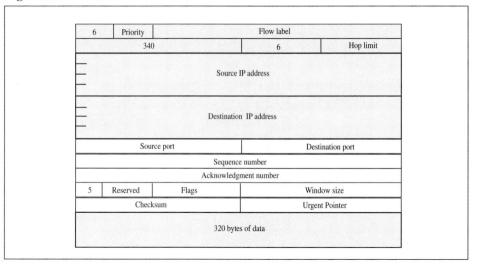

Acronyms

A

AA	Authoritative answer.
AAL	Application adaptation layer.
ABM	Asynchronous balanced mode.
AC	Access control.
ACK	Acknowledgment.
ACM	Association for Computing Machinery.
AMI	Alternate mark inversion.
ANS	Advanced Networks and Services.
ANSI	American National Standards Institute.
ANSNET	Advanced Networks and Services Network.
API	Application programming interface.
ARM	Asynchronous response mode.
ARPA	Advanced Research Project Agency.
ARPANET	Advanced Research Project Agency Network.
ARQ	Automatic repeat request.
AS	Autonomous system.
ASCII	American Standard Code for Information Interchange.
ASN.1	Abstract syntax notation 1.
ATM	Asynchronous transfer mode.

B

B-ISDN	Broadband ISDN.
BCC	Block check count.
BECN	Backward explicit congestion notification.
BER	Basic Encoding Rules.
BGP	Border Gateway Protocol.
BOOTP	Bootstrap Protocol.
BPDU	Bridge protocol data unit.

bps	Bits per second.
BRI	Basic Rate Interface.

C

C/R	Command/response.
CAD	Computer-aided design.
CCITT	Consultative Committee for International Telegraphy and Telephony.
CERN	European Laboratory for Particle Physics.
CGI	Common Gateway Interface.
CIDR	Classless Inter-Domain Routing.
CLNS	Connectionless network service.
CLP	Cell loss priority.
CLTS	Connectionless Transport Service.
CONS	Connection-oriented network service.
COTS	Connection-oriented transport service.
CR	Carriage return.
CRC	Cyclic redundancy check.
CS	Convergence sublayer.
CSMA	Carrier sense multiple access.
CSMA/CD	Carrier sense multiple access with collision detection.

D

DAC	Dual attachment concentrator.
DARPA	Defense Advanced Research Projects Agency.
DAS	Dual attachment station.
DCA	Defense Communication Agency.
DCE	Data circuit-terminating equipment.
DDN	Defense Data Network.
DDNS	Dynamic domain name system.
DEC	Digital Equipment Corporation.
DES	Data encryption standard.
DHCP	Dynamic Host Configuration Protocol.
DNS	Domain name system.
DOD	Department of Defense.
DS	Directory Service.
DSAP	Destination service access point.
DSU	Data service unit.
DTE	Data terminal equipment.
DVMRP	Distance Vector Multicast Routing Protocol.

E

EA	Extended address.
EBCDIC	Extended binary coded decimal interchange code.

ED	End delimiter.
EGP	Exterior Gateway Protocol.
EHF	Extremely high frequency.
EIA	Electronics Industries Association.
EMI	Electromagnetic interference.
EOF	End of file.
EOR	End of record.
EOT	End of transmission.
ESP	Encrypted security payload.

F

FC	Frame Control.
FCC	Federal Communications Commission.
FCS	Frame check sequence.
FDDI	Fiber distributed data interface.
FECN	Forward Explicit Congestion Notification.
FQDN	Fully qualified domain name.
FS	Frame status.
FTAM	File transfer, access, and management.
FTP	File transfer protocol.

G

GA	Go ahead.
GFC	Generic flow control.
GFI	General format identifier.
GHz	Gigahertz.
GIF	Graphics Interchange Format.
GOSIP	Government Open Systems Interconnection Profile.

H

HDLC	High-level Data Link Control.
HEC	Header error control.
HF	High frequency.
HLEN	Header length.
HTML	Hypertext markup language.
HTTP	Hypertext transfer protocol.
Hz	Hertz.

I

IAB	Internet Architecture Board.
IAC	Interpret as control.
IANA	Internet Assigned Numbers Authority.

ICANA	Internet Corporation for Assigned Names and Numbers.
ICMP	Internet control message protocol.
IDN	Integrated digital network.
IEEE	Institute of Electrical and Electronics Engineers.
IESG	Internet Engineering Steering Group.
IETF	Internet Engineering Task Force.
IGMP	Internet Group Management Protocol.
IGP	Interior Gateway Protocol.
IMP	Interface message processor.
INTERNIC	Internet Network Information Center.
IP	Internetworking Protocol.
IPng	IP next generation.
IRSG	Internet Research Steering Group.
IRTF	Internet Research Task Force.
ISDN	Integrated Services Digital Network.
ISN	Initialization sequence number.
ISO	International Standards Organization.
ISOC	Internet Society.
ITU	International Telecommunications Union.
ITU–T	International Telecommunications Union–Telecommunication Standardisation Sector.

J
JPEG	Joint Photographic Experts Group.

K
Kbps	Kilobits per second.
KHz	Kilohertz.

L
LAN	Local area network.
LAP	Link access procedure.
LAPB	Link access procedure, balanced.
LAPD	Link access procedure for D channel.
LAPM	Link access procedure for modems.
LCGN	Logical channel group number.
LCN	Logical channel number.
LF	Low frequency or line feed.
LLC	Logical link control.
LRC	Longitudinal redundancy check.
LSA	Link state advertisement.
LSP	Link state packet.

M

MA	Multiple access.
MAC	Media access control.
MAN	Metropolitan area network.
MAU	Medium attachment unit or multistation access unit.
MBONE	Multicast backbone.
Mbps	Megabits per second.
MF	Middle frequency.
MHz	Megahertz.
MIB	Management information base.
MIC	Media interface connector.
MILNET	Military Network.
MIME	Multipurpose Internet mail extension.
MOSPF	Multicast open shortest path first.
MPEG	Motion Picture Experts Group.
MSS	Maximum segment size.
MTA	Mail transfer agent.
MTS	Message transfer system.
MTU	Maximum transfer unit.

N

NAK	Negative acknowledgment.
NCP	Network Control Protocol.
NFS	Network file system.
NIC	Network interface card or Network Information Center.
NL	New line.
NLRI	Network layer reachability information.
NNI	Network-to-network interface.
NRM	Normal response mode.
NSF	National Science Foundation.
NSFNET	National Science Foundation Network.
NT1	Network termination 1.
NT2	Network termination 2.
NVT	Network virtual terminal.

O

OSI	Open system interconnection.
OSPF	Open shortest path first.

P

PDU	Protocol data unit.
P/F	Poll/final.
PING	Packet Internet Groper.

PLP	Packet layer protocol.
POP	Post Office Protocol.
PPP	Point-to-Point Protocol.
PQDN	Partially qualified domain name.
PRI	Primary rate interface.
PT	Payload type.
PTR	Pointer.
PVC	Permanent virtual circuit.

Q
QAM	Quadrature amplitude modulation.
QR	Query response.

R
RA	Recursion available.
RARP	Reverse address resolution protocol.
RD	Recursion Desired.
RFC	Request for Comment.
RIP	Routing information protocol.
ROM	Read only memory.
RPC	Remote procedure call.
RRQ	Read request.
RSA	Rivest, Shamir, and Adleman.
RSVP	Resource Reservation Protocol.
RTM	Real-time Transport Protocol.
RTT	Round-trip time.
RZ	Return to zero.

S
SA	Source address.
SAP	Service access point.
SAR	Segmentation and reassembly.
SAS	Single attachment station.
SD	Start delimiter.
SDH	Synchronous digital hierarchy.
SDLC	Synchronous data link control.
SFD	Start frame delimiter.
SHF	Superhigh frequency.
SLIP	Serial line IP.
SMI	Structure of management information.
SMTP	Simple mail transfer protocol.
SNI	Subscriber network interface.
SNMP	Simple network management protocol.

SOA	Start of authority.
SONET	Synchronous Optical Network.
SPDU	Session protocol data unit.
SSAP	Source service access point.
STP	Shielded twisted-pair.

T

TA	Terminal adapter.
TC	Truncated.
TCP	Transmission control protocol.
TCP/IP	Transmission control protocol /internetworking protocol.
TDM	Time-division multiplexing.
TE1	Terminal equipment 1.
TE2	Terminal equipment 2.
TELNET	Terminal Network.
TFTP	Trivial file transfer protocol.
THz	Terahertz.
TLI	Transport Layer Interface.
TOS	Type of service.
TPDU	Transport protocol data unit.
TTL	Time to live.

U

UA	User agent.
UDP	User datagram protocol.
UHF	Ultrahigh frequency.
UNI	User network interface.
URL	Uniform resource locator.
UTP	Unshielded twisted-pair.

V

VCI	Virtual channel identifier.
VER	Version.
VHF	Very high frequency.
VLF	Very low frequency.
VPI	Virtual path identifier.
VPI/VCI	Virtual Path Identifier/Virtual Channel Identifier.
VRC	Vertical redundancy check.
VT	Virtual tributary, virtual terminal, or vertical tab.

W

WAN	Wide area network.
Web	Synonym for World Wide Web (WWW).
WRQ	Write request.
WWW	World Wide Web.

Glossary

1Base5   The IEEE 802.3 standard for low-data-rate Ethernet. The standard specifies a star topology using twisted-pair cable with a maximum segment length of 500 meters. The data rate is defined to be 1 Mbps. It is also known as starLAN.

10Base-T   The IEEE 802.3 standard for twisted-pair Ethernet. The standard specifies a star topology using twisted-pair cable. The data rate is defined to be 10 Mbps.

10Base2   The IEEE 802.3 standard for Thin Ethernet. The standard specifies a bus topology using thin coaxial cable with a maximum segment length of 185 meters. The data rate is defined to be 10 Mbps. (Also called cheapernet or cheapnet.)

10Base5   The IEEE 802.3 standard for Thick Ethernet. The standard specifies a bus topology using thick coaxial cable with a maximum segment length of 500 meters. The data rate is defined to be 10 Mbps.

100Base-T   A version of the IEEE 802.3 standard for Fast Ethernet. The standard specifies a star topology using twisted-pair cable. The data rate is defined to be 100 Mbps.

802   See *IEEE Project 802.*

802.1   See *IEEE Project 802.1.*

802.2   See *IEEE Project 802.2.*

802.3   See *IEEE Project 802.3.*

802.4   See *IEEE Project 802.4.*

802.5   See *IEEE Project 802.5.*

AW

AAL   See *application adaptation layer.*

AAL1   An AAL layer in the ATM protocol that processes constant-bit-rate data.

AAL2   An AAL layer in the ATM protocol that processes variable-bit-rate data.

AAL3/4   An AAL layer in the ATM protocol that processes connectionless or connection-oriented packet data.

AAL5   An AAL layer in the ATM protocol that processes data with extensive header information from upper layer protocols; also called the simple and efficient adaptation layer (SEAL).

ABM   See *asynchronous balanced mode.*

abort   To terminate a process abruptly.

abstract syntax notation 1 (ASN.1)   A formal language using abstract syntax for defining the structure of a protocol data unit (PDU).

access control field   A field in a token ring frame containing priority, token, monitor, and reservation bits.

ACK   See *acknowledgment.*

acknowledgment (ACK)   A response sent by the receiver to indicate the successful receipt and acceptance of data.

active close   Closing a TCP connection by a client.

active document   In the World Wide Web, a document executed at the local site using Java.

active hub   A hub that repeats or regenerates a signal. It functions as a repeater.

active open   Establishment of a connection with a server by a client.

address field   A field containing the address of a sender or receiver.

address mask   32 bits that extract a network address or a subnetwork address.

address resolution protocol (ARP)   In TCP/IP, a protocol for obtaining the physical address of a node when the Internet address is known.

Advanced Networks and Services (ANS)   The owner and operator of the Internet since 1995.

Advanced Networks and Services Network (ANSNET)   The high-speed Internet backbone.

Advanced Research Project Agency (ARPA)   The government agency that funded ARPANET.

Advanced Research Project Agency Network (ARPANET)   The packet switching network that was funded by ARPA.

agent   A router or a host that runs the SNMP server program.

alternate mark inversion (AMI)   A digital-to-digital bipolar encoding method in which the amplitude representing 1 alternates between positive and negative voltages.

American National Standards Institute (ANSI)   A national standards organization that defines standards in the United States.

American Standard Code for Information Interchange (ASCII)   A character code developed by ANSI and used extensively for data communication.

AMI   See *alternate mark inversion.*

angle of incidence   In optics, the angle formed by a light ray approaching the interface between two media and the line perpendicular to the interface.

angle of reflection   In optics, the angle formed by a reflected light ray at the interface between two media and the line perpendicular to the interface.

angle of refraction   In optics, the angle formed by a refracted light ray at the interface between two media and the line perpendicular to the interface.

anonymous FTP   A protocol in which a remote user can access another machine without an account or password.

ANS   See *Advanced Networks and Services.*

ANSI   See *American National Standards Institute.*

ANSNET   See *Advanced Networks and Services Network.*

applet   A computer program for creating an active Web document. It is usually written in Java.

AppleTalk   A protocol suite developed by Apple Computer, Inc.

application adaptation layer (AAL)   A layer in ATM protocol that breaks user data into 48-byte payloads.

application layer   The seventh layer in the OSI model; provides access to network resources.

ARP See *address resolution protocol.*

ARPA See *Advanced Research Project Agency.*

ARPANET See *Advanced Research Project Agency Network.*

ARQ See *automatic repeat request.*

ASCII See *American Standard Code for Information Interchange.*

ASN.1 See *abstract syntax notation 1.*

asynchronous balanced mode (ABM) In HDLC, a communication mode in which all stations are equal.

asynchronous protocol A set of rules for asynchronous transmission.

asynchronous time division multiplexing Time division multiplexing in which link time is allocated dynamically according to whether a terminal is active or not.

asynchronous transfer mode (ATM) A wide area protocol featuring high data rates and equal-sized packets (cells); ATM is suitable for transferring text, audio, and video data.

asynchronous transmission Transfer of data with start and stop bit(s) and a variable time interval between data units.

ATM See *asynchronous transfer mode.*

ATM consortium A group of ATM software and hardware vendors.

ATM forum A group of parties interested in the promotion and rapid development of ATM.

ATM switch An ATM device providing both switching and multiplexing functions.

authentication Verification of the sender of a message.

authority zone The domain over which a server is responsible.

automatic repeat request (ARQ) An error-control method in which correction is made by re-transmission of data.

autonomous system A group of networks and routers under the authority of a single adminis-tration.

B

B-channel An ISDN channel type with a 64-Kbps data rate; the basic user channel; also known as the bearer channel.

B-ISDN See *broadband ISDN.*

backbone The major transmission path in a network.

bandwidth The difference between the highest and the lowest frequencies of a composite sig-nal. It also measures the information-carrying capacity of a line or a network.

base 2 A number system based on two symbols; also called the binary system.

base 8 A number system based on eight symbols; also called the octal system.

base 10 A number system based on 10 symbols; also called the decimal system.

base 16 A number system based on 16 symbols; also called the hexadecimal system.

base header In IPv6, the main header of the datagram.

baseband Referring to a technology in which a signal is transmitted directly onto a channel without modulating a carrier.

basic rate interface (BRI) In ISDN, an electrical interface providing two B channels (64 Kbps) and one D channel (16 Kbps). The total data rate is 192 Kbps, which includes some overhead.

baud rate The number of signal elements transmitted per second. A signal element consists of one or more bits.

bearer services In ISDN, a service that does not manipulate the content of the transmission.

Bellcore   Bell Communication Research; provides research and development resources for the advancement of communications technology.

Bellman-Ford algorithm   An algorithm used to calculate routing tables in the distance vector routing method.

BGP   See *Border Gateway Protocol.*

big endian   A format in which the most significant byte is stored or transmitted first.

binary number system   A method of representing information using only two symbols (0 and 1).

bit   A binary digit; the smallest unit of information; 1 or 0.

bit rate   The number of bits transmitted per second.

bit-oriented protocol   A protocol in which a frame is seen as a bit stream.

bits per second (bps)   A measurement of data speed; bits transmitted per second.

blocking   An event that occurs when a switching network is working at its full capacity and cannot accept more input.

BOOTP   See *Bootstrap Protocol.*

Bootstrap Protocol (BOOTP)   The protocol that provides configuration information from a table (file).

Border Gateway Protocol (BGP)   An interautonomous system routing protocol based on path vector routing.

bps   See *bits per second.*

BRI   See *Basic Rate Interface.*

bridge   A network device operating at the first two layers of the OSI model with filtering and forwarding capabilities.

broadband   Referring to a technology in which a signal shares the bandwidth of a medium.

broadband ISDN (B-ISDN)   ISDN with a high data rate based upon cell-relay delivery.

broadband transmission   Transmission of a signal using a modulated carrier wave.

broadcasting   Transmission of a message to all nodes in a network.

brouter (bridge/router)   A device that functions as both a bridge and a router.

browser   An application program that displays a WWW document. A browser usually uses other Internet services to access the document.

BSD UNIX   The UNIX version developed by University of California, Berkeley; includes TCP/IP protocols.

buffer   Memory set aside for temporary storage.

burst error   Error in a data unit in which two or more consecutive bits have been altered.

bus topology   A network topology in which all computers are attached to a shared medium (often a single cable).

byte   A group of eight bits.

byte rate   The number of bytes transmitted per second.

C

carrier   An analog signal whose amplitude, frequency, or phase can be altered to represent data.

carrier sense multiple access (CSMA)   A contention access method in which each station listens to the line before transmitting data.

carrier sense multiple access with collision detection (CSMA/CD)   An access method in which stations transmit whenever the transmission medium is available and retransmit when collision occurs.

CCITT   See *Consultative Committee for International Telegraphy and Telephony.*

cell   A small, fixed-size data unit; also, in cellular telephony, a geographical area served by a cell office.

cell network   A network using the cell as its basic data unit.

cell relay   A communication technology using a fixed-size data unit as the packet; used by ATM.

cellular   A wireless communication technique in which an area is divided into cells. A cell is served by a transmitter.

CGI   See *Common Gateway Interface.*

channel   A communications pathway.

channel service unit (CSU)   A device that transmits and receives digital signals, performing functions such as filtering and signal shaping.

cheapernet   See *10Base2.*

cheapnet   See *cheapernet.*

checksum   A field used for error detection. It is formed by adding bit streams using one's complement arithmetic and then complementing the result.

CIDR   See *Classless Inter-Domain Routing.*

ciphertext   The encrypted data.

circuit switching   A switching technology that establishes an electrical connection between stations using a dedicated path.

cladding   Glass or plastic surrounding the core of an optical fiber; the optical density of the cladding must be less than that of the core.

class of address   The category of an IPv4 address.

Classless Inter-Domain Routing (CIDR)   A technique to reduce the number of routing table entries when supernetting is used.

client   A program that initiates communication with another program called the server.

client-server model   The model of interaction between two application programs in which a program at one end (client) requests a service from a program at the other end (server).

CLNS   See *connectionless network service.*

CLTS   See *connectionless transport service.*

coaxial cable   A transmission medium consisting of a conducting core, insulating material, and a second conducting sheath.

code   An arrangement of symbols to stand for a word or an action.

collision   The event that occurs when two transmitters send at the same time on a channel designed for only one transmission at a time; data will be destroyed.

combined station   In HDLC protocol, a station that can function as a primary or secondary station at the same time.

common carrier   A transmission facility available to the public and subject to public utility regulation.

common gateway interface (CGI)   A standard for communication between HTTP servers and executable programs. CGI is used in creating dynamic documents.

communication network   A collection of connected devices for the exchange of information.

communication   The exchange of information between two entities.

compression   The reduction of a message without significant loss of information.

congestion   Excessive network or internetwork traffic causing a general degradation of service.

congestion control   A method to manage network and internetwork traffic to improve throughput.

connection establishment   The preliminary setup necessary for a logical connection prior to actual data transfer.

connection request   A message sent to establish a connection.

connection termination   A message sent to end a connection.

connection-oriented network service (CONS)   A network-level data protocol with formal rules for establishment and termination of a connection.

connection-oriented service   A service for data transfer involving establishment and termination of a connection.

connection-oriented transmission   Data transfer involving establishment and termination of a connection.

connection-oriented transport service (COTS)   A transport-level protocol with formal establishment and termination of a connection.

connectionless network service (CLNS)   A network-level protocol without formal rules for connection establishment or termination.

connectionless service   A service for data transfer without connection establishment or termination.

connectionless transmission   Data transfer without connection establishment or termination.

connectionless transport service (CLTS)   A transport-level data transfer protocol without formal connection establishment or termination.

CONS   See *connection-oriented network service.*

Consultative Committee for International Telegraphy and Telephony (CCITT)   An international standards group now known as the ITU-T.

contention   An access method in which two or more devices try to transmit at the same time on the same channel.

conventional encryption   A method of encryption in which the encryption and decryption algorithms use the same key, which is kept secret.

convergence sublayer (CS)   In ATM protocol, the upper AAL sublayer that adds a header or a trailer to the user data.

COTS   See *connection-oriented transport service.*

country domain   A subdomain in the Domain Name System that uses two characters as the last suffix.

CRC   See *cyclic redundancy check.*

critical angle   In refraction, the value of the angle of incidence that produces a 90-degree angle of refraction.

crossbar switch   A switch consisting of a lattice of horizontal and vertical paths. At the intersection of each horizontal and vertical path, there is a crosspoint that can connect the input to the output.

crosspoint   The junction of an input and an output on a crossbar switch.

crosstalk   The noise on a line caused by signals traveling along another line.

CS   See *convergence sublayer.*

CSMA   See *carrier sense multiple access.*

CSMA/CD   See *carrier sense multiple access with collision detection.*

CSU   See *channel service unit.*

cycle   The repetitive unit of a periodic signal.

cyclic redundancy check (CRC)   A highly accurate error-detection method based on interpreting a pattern of bits as a polynomial.

D

D channel (data channel)   An ISDN channel used primarily to carry control signals. It can also be used for low-rate data transfer.

DAC   See *dual attachment concentrator.*

DARPA   See *Defense Advanced Research Projects Agency.*

DAS   See *dual attachment station.*

data circuit-terminating equipment (DCE)   A device used as an interface between a DTE and a network.

data communication   The interchange of information between two or more entities.

data compression   The reduction of the amount of data to be transmitted without significant loss of information.

data encryption standard (DES)   The U.S. government standard encryption method for nonmilitary and nonclassified use.

data link layer   The second layer in the OSI model. It is responsible for node-to-node delivery.

data service unit (DSU)   A device used in conjunction with a CSU to ensure proper signal shaping and encoding.

data terminal equipment (DTE)   A device that is an information source or an information sink. It is connected to a network through a DCE.

data transfer   The movement of data from one location to another.

datagram   In packet-switching, an independent data unit.

DCE   See *data circuit-terminating equipment.*

DDN   See *Defense Data Network.*

de facto protocol   A protocol that has not been approved by an organized body but adopted as a standard through widespread use.

de jure protocol   A protocol that has been legislated by an officially recognized body.

decimal dotted notation   A notation devised to make the IP address easier to read; each byte is converted to its decimal equivalent and then set off from its neighbor by a period.

decimal number system   A method of representing information using 10 symbols (0, 1, ... to 9).

decoding   Process of restoring an encoded message to its pre-encoded form.

decryption   Recovery of the original message from the encrypted data.

Defense Advanced Research Projects Agency (DARPA)   A government organization, which, under the name of ARPA funded ARPANET and the Internet.

Defense Data Network (DDN)   The military portion of the Internet.

demodulation   The process of separating the carrier signal from the information-bearing signal.

demodulator   A device that performs demodulation.

demultiplexer   A device that separates a multiplexed signal into its original components.

DES   See *data encryption standard.*

destination address   The address of the receiver of the data unit.

DHCP   See *Dynamic Host Configuration Protocol.*

dialog   The exchange between two communicating devices.

differential Manchester   A digital-to-digital polar encoding method that features a transition at the middle of the bit interval as well as an inversion at the beginning of each 1 bit.

digital data   Data represented by discrete values or conditions.

digital pipe   A high-speed path composed of time-multiplexed channels.

digital signal   A discrete signal with a limited number of values.

digital signature   A method to authenticate the sender of a message.

digital transmission   Data transfer using digital signals.

Dijkstra's algorithm   In link state routing, an algorithm that finds the shortest path to other routers.

direct broadcast address   A special address used by a router to send a packet to all hosts in a specified network.

directory service (DS)   A service that can provide the e-mail address of an individual.

disconnect   To end a connection.

Distance Vector Multicast Routing Protocol (DVMRP)   A protocol based on distance vector routing that handles multicast routing in conjunction with IGMP.

distance vector routing   A routing method in which each router sends its neighbors a list of networks it can reach and the distance to that network.

distortion   Any change in a signal due to noise, attenuation, or other influences.

distributed processing   A strategy in which services provided for the network reside at multiple sites.

DNS   See *domain name system.*

domain name system (DNS)   A TCP/IP application service that converts user-friendly names to IP addresses.

DTE   See *data terminal equipment.*

dual attachment concentrator (DAC)   In FDDI, a device that connects a combination of SASs or DASs to the dual ring. It makes the combination look like a single SAS unit.

dual attachment station (DAS)   In FDDI, a station that can be connected to two rings.

duplex mode   See *full-duplex mode.*

DVMRP   See *Distance Vector Multicast Routing Protocol*

dynamic document   A Web document created by running a CGI program at the server site.

dynamic host configuration protocol (DHCP)   An extension to BOOTP that dynamically assigns configuration information.

E

E-lines   The European equivalent of T-lines.

EBCDIC   See *extended binary coded decimal interchange code.*

EGP   See *Exterior Gateway Protocol.*

EHF   See *extremely high frequency.*

EIA   See *Electronics Industries Association.*

EIA-232   A common 25-pin interface standard developed by the EIA.

EIA-449   An interface standard specifying a 37-pin connector and a nine-pin connector developed by the EIA.

EIA-530   An interface standard based on EIA-449 that uses DB-25 pins.

electromagnetic interference (EMI)   A noise on the data transmission line that can corrupt the data. It can be created by motors, generators, and so on.

electronic mail (e-mail)   A method of sending messages electronically based on mailbox addresses rather than a direct host-to-host exchange.

Electronics Industries Association (EIA)   An organization that promotes electronics manufacturing concerns. It has developed interface standards such as EIA-232, EIA-449, and EIA-530.

e-mail   See *electronic mail*.

EMI   See *electromagnetic interference*.

encapsulation   The technique in which a data unit from one protocol is placed within the data field portion of the data unit of another protocol.

encoding   Transforming information into signals.

encryption   Converting a message into an unintelligible form that is unreadable unless decrypted.

end-to-end message delivery   Delivery of all parts of a message from the sender to the receiver.

ENQ/ACK   A line discipline method used in point-to-point connections. An ENQ frame is transmitted by a station wishing to send data; an ACK is returned if the station is ready to receive the data.

ephemeral port   A port number used by the client.

error   A mistake in data transmission.

error control   The detection and handling of errors in data transmission.

error correction   The process of correcting bits that have been changed during transmission.

error detection   The process of determining whether or not some bits have been changed during transmission.

error handling   The methods used to detect or correct errors.

error recovery   The ability of a system to resume normal activity after errors are detected.

ether   An imaginary substance believed by the ancients to fill all of outer space.

Ethernet   A local area network using CSMA/CD access method. See *IEEE Project 802.3*.

even parity   An error-detection method in which an extra bit is added to the data unit so that the total number of 1s becomes even.

extended binary coded decimal interchange code (EBCDIC)   An eight-bit character code developed and used by IBM.

extension header   Extra headers in the IPv6 datagram that provide additional functionality.

Exterior Gateway Protocol (EGP)   A protocol that handles routing between autonomous systems.

extremely high frequency (EHF)   Radio waves in the 30-GHz to 300-GHz range using space propagation.

F

Fast Ethernet   See *100Base-T*.

FCC   See *Federal Communications Commission*.

FCS   See *frame check sequence*.

FDDI   See *fiber distributed data interface*.

Federal Communications Commission (FCC)   A government agency that regulates radio, television, and telecommunications.

fiber distributed data interface (FDDI)   A high-speed (100-Mbps) LAN, defined by ANSI, using fiber optics, dual ring topology, and the token passing access method. Today an FDDI network is also used as a MAN.

fiber-optic cable   A high-bandwidth transmission medium that carries data signals in the form of pulses of light. It consists of a thin cylinder of glass or plastic, called the core, surrounded by a concentric layer of glass or plastic called the cladding.

file server   A computer in a local area network that provides shared access to files.

file transfer, access, and management (FTAM)   In the OSI model, an application layer service for remote file handling.

file transfer protocol (FTP)   In TCP/IP, an application layer protocol that transfers files between two sites.

filter   A device that passes only signals containing certain frequencies.

final bit (F bit)   An HDLC control bit sent by the secondary station to indicate whether or not more frames are coming. See *P/F bit.*

flag   In HDLC, a field that alerts the receiver of the beginning or ending of a frame.

flat namespace   A method to map a name to an address in which there is no hierarchical structure.

flooding   Saturation of a network with a message.

flow control   A technique to control the rate of flow of frames (packets or messages).

forum   An organization that tests, evaluates, and standardizes a specific new technology.

fragmentation   The division of a packet into smaller units to accommodate a protocol's MTU.

frame   A group of bits representing a block of data.

frame check sequence (FCS)   The HDLC error-detection field containing either a two- or four-byte CRC.

frame relay   A packet-switching specification defined for the first two layers of the OSI model. There is no network layer. Error checking is done on end-to-end basis instead of on each link.

frequency   Number of cycles per second of a periodic signal.

FTAM   See *file transfer, access, and management.*

FTP   See *file transfer protocol.*

full-duplex mode   A transmission mode in which communication can be two way simultaneously.

G

gateway   A device used to connect two separate networks that use different communication protocols.

generic domain   A subdomain in the Domain Name System that uses generic suffixes.

go-back-*n* ARQ   An error-control method in which the frame in error and all following frames must be retransmitted.

GOSIP   See *Government Open Systems Interconnection Profile.*

Government Open Systems Interconnection Profile (GOSIP)   The protocol used in government agencies that is very similar to the OSI model.

guided media   Transmission media with a physical boundary.

H

half-duplex mode   A transmission mode in which communication can be two-way but not at the same time.

handshaking   A process to establish or terminate a connection.

hardware address   An address used by a data-link layer to identify a device.

H-channel   In ISDN, a hybrid channel available in a variety of data rates; suitable for high-data-rate applications.

HDLC   See *high-level data link control.*

header   Control information added to the beginning of a data packet.

hertz (Hz)   Unit of measurement for frequency.

hexadecimal colon notation   In IPv6, an address notation consisting of 32 hexadecimal digits, with every four digits separated by a colon.

hexadecimal number system   A method of representing information using 16 symbols (0, 1, … 9, A, B, C, D, E, and F).

HF   See *high frequency.*

high frequency (HF)   Radio waves in the 3-MHz to 30-MHz range using line-of-sight propagation.

high-level data link control (HDLC)   A bit-oriented data link protocol defined by the ISO. It is used in X.25 protocol. A subset of it, called link access procedure (LAP), is used in other protocols. It is also a base for many data link protocols used in LANs.

hop count   The number of nodes along a route. It is a measurement of distance in routing algorithms.

host   A station or node on a network.

hostid   The part of an IP address that identifies a host.

HTML   See *hypertext markup language.*

HTTP   See *hypertext transfer protocol.*

hub   A central device in a star topology that provides a common connection among the nodes.

hybrid topology   A topology composed of more than one basic topology.

hypertext markup language (HTML)   The computer language for specifying the contents and format of a Web document. It allows additional text to include codes that define fonts, layouts, embedded graphics, and hypertext links.

hypertext transfer protocol (HTTP)   An application service for retrieving a Web document.

Hz   See *hertz.*

I

I.430   An ITU-T standard for BRI physical layer specifications.

I.431   An ITU-T standard for PRI physical layer specifications.

IAB   See *Internet Architecture Board.*

ICMP   See *internet control message protocol.*

IDN   See *integrated digital network.*

IEEE   See *Institute of Electrical and Electronics Engineers.*

IEEE Project 802   A project by IEEE to define LAN standards for the physical and data link layers of OSI model. It divides the data link layer into two sublayers called logical link control and medium access control.

IEEE Project 802.1   The standard developed by IEEE Project 802 for local area networks. It covers the internetworking aspect of LANs.

IEEE Project 802.2   The standard developed by IEEE Project 802 for local area networks. It covers the LLC sublayer.

IEEE Project 802.3 The standard developed by IEEE Project 802 for local area networks. It covers the MAC sublayer for networks using the CSMA/CD access method. It provides a formal definition for Ethernet.

IEEE Project 802.4 The standard developed by IEEE Project 802 for local area networks. It covers the MAC sublayer for networks using a bus topology and token-passing access method. It provides a formal definition for token bus.

IEEE Project 802.5 The standard developed by IEEE Project 802 for local area networks. It covers the MAC sublayer for networks using a ring topology and token-passing access method. It provides a formal definition for token ring.

IESG See *Internet Engineering Steering Group.*

IETF See *Internet Engineering Task Force.*

I-frame In HDLC, an information frame that carries user data and control information.

IGMP See *Internet Group Management Protocol.*

IGP See *Interior Gateway Protocol.*

inband signaling A method of signaling in which both control and user data use the same channel.

infrared light Electromagnetic waves with frequencies just below the visible spectrum.

Institute of Electrical and Electronics Engineers (IEEE) A group consisting of professional engineers which has specialized societies whose committees prepare standards in members' areas of specialty.

integrated digital network (IDN) The integration of communication functions using digital technology in a telecommunication network.

integrated services digital network (ISDN) An ITU-T standard for an end-to-end global digital communication system providing fully integrated digital services.

intelligent modem A modem that has extra functions such as automatic answering and dialing.

interface The boundary between two pieces of equipment. It also refers to mechanical, electrical, and functional characteristics of the connection.

interior gateway protocol (IGP) A protocol such as RIP or OSPF that handles routing inside an autonomous system.

International Standards Organization (ISO) A worldwide organization that defines and develops standards on a variety of topics.

International Telecommunications Union–Telecommunication Standardization Sector (ITU–T) A standards organization formerly known as the CCITT.

internet A collection of networks connected by internetworking devices such as routers or gateways.

Internet A global internet that uses the TCP/IP protocol suite.

Internet address A 32-bit or 128-bit network-layer address used to uniquely define a host on an internet using the TCP/IP protocol.

Internet Architecture Board (IAB) The technical adviser to the ISOC; oversees the continuing development of the TCP/IP protocol suite.

Internet Control Message Protocol (ICMP) A protocol in the TCP/IP protocol suite that handles error and control messages.

Internet Engineering Steering Group (IESG) An organization that oversees the activity of IETF.

Internet Engineering Task Force (IETF) A group working on the design and development of the TCP/IP protocol suite and the Internet.

Internet Group Management Protocol (IGMP)   A protocol in the TCP/IP protocol suite that handles multicasting.

Internet Network Information Center (INTERNIC)   An agency responsible for collecting and distributing information about TCP/IP protocols.

Internet Protocol   See *Internetworking Protocol.*

Internet Research Task Force (IRTF)   A forum of working groups focusing on long-term research topics related to the Internet.

Internet Society (ISOC)   The nonprofit organization established to publicize the Internet.

internetworking   Connecting several networks together using internetworking devices such as routers and gateways.

internetworking devices   Electronic devices such as routers and gateways that connect networks together to form an internet.

Internetworking Protocol (IP)   The network-layer protocol in the TCP/IP protocol suite governing connectionless transmission across packet-switching networks.

INTERNIC   See *Internet Network Information Center.*

IP   See *Internetworking Protocol.*

IP address   See *Internet address.*

IP address class   In IPv4, one of the five groups of addresses; classes A, B, and C consist of a netid, hostid, and class ID; class D holds multicast addresses; class E is reserved for future use.

IP datagram   The Internetworking Protocol data unit.

IPng (IP next generation)   See *IPv6.*

IPv4   The Internetworking Protocol, version 4. It is the current version.

IPv6   The Internetworking Protocol, version 6. A proposed internetworking protocol that features major IP addressing changes.

IRTF   See *Internet Research Task Force.*

ISDN   See *integrated services digital network.*

ISO   See *International Standards Organization.*

ISOC   See *Internet Society.*

ITU–T   See *International Telecommunications Union–Telecommunication Standardizaton Sector.*

J
Java   A programming language used to create active Web documents.

joint photographic experts group (JPEG)   A standard for compressing continuous-tone picture.

JPEG   See *joint photographic experts group.*

K
Karn's Algorithm   An algorithm that does not include the retransmitted segments in calculation of round-trip time.

Kbps   Kilobits per second.

L
LAN   See *local area network.*

LAP   See *link access procedure.*

LAPB   See *link access procedure, balanced.*

LAPD   See *link access procedure for D channel.*

layer   One of the seven levels involved in data transmission in the OSI model; each level is a functional grouping of related activities.

LF   See *low frequency.*

line configuration   The relationship between communication devices and their pathway.

line discipline   A data link layer procedure that defines which device has the right to send data; also referred to as access control.

line layer   A SONET layer responsible for the movement of a signal across a physical line.

link access procedure (LAP)   A bit-oriented data link protocol derived from HDLC.

link access procedure, balanced (LAPB)   An LAP protocol in which stations can function only in the balanced mode.

link access procedure for D channel (LAPD)   An LAP protocol defined for the D channel in the ISDN.

link state database   In link state routing, a database common to all routers and made from LSP information.

link state packet (LSP)   In link state routing, a small packet containing routing information sent by a router to all other routers.

link state routing   A routing method in which each router shares its knowledge of changes in its neighborhood with all other routers.

little endian   A format in which the least significant byte is stored or transmitted first.

LLC   See *logical link control.*

local area network (LAN)   A network connecting devices inside a single building or inside buildings close to each other.

local loop   The link that connects a subscriber to the telephone central office.

logical address   An address defined in the network layer.

logical link control (LLC)   The upper sublayer of the data link layer as defined by IEEE Project 802.2.

longitudinal redundancy check (LRC)   An error-detection method dividing a data unit into rows and columns and performing parity checks on corresponding bits of each column.

low frequency (LF)   Radio waves in the 30-KHz to 300-KHz range.

LRC   See *longitudinal redundancy check.*

LSP   See *link state packet.*

M

MA   See *multiple access.*

MAC   See *medium access control.*

mail exchanger   Any computer capable of receiving e-mail.

mail gateway   A relay MTA that can receive both SMTP mail and non-SMTP mail.

major synchronization point   A synchronization point that must be confirmed before continuation of the session.

MAN   See *metropolitan area network.*

management information base (MIB)   The database used by SNMP that holds the information necessary for management of a network.

manager   The host that runs the SNMP client program.

Manchester encoding   A digital-to-digital polar encoding method in which a transition occurs at the middle of each bit interval for the purpose of synchronization.

MAU   See *medium attachment unit* or *multistation access unit*.

maximum segment size (MSS)   A TCP header option defining the biggest chunk of data that the destination can receive; the size is negotiated during connection establishment.

maximum transfer unit (MTU)   The largest size data unit a specific network can handle.

MBONE   See *multicast backbone*.

Mbps   Megabits per second.

media interface connector (MIC)   A type of interface card used in FDDI.

medium access control (MAC)   The lower sublayer in the data link layer defined by the IEEE 802 project. It defines the access method and access control in different local area network protocols.

medium attachment unit (MAU)   See *transceiver*.

medium bandwidth   The difference between the highest and lowest frequencies a medium can support.

message   Data sent from source to destination.

message switching   A switching method in which the whole message is stored in a switch and forwarded when a route is available.

message transfer agent (MTA)   An MHS component that accepts a message, examines it, and routes it.

message transfer system (MTS)   A group of message transfer agents (MTAs).

metropolitan area network (MAN)   A network that can span a geographical area the size of a city.

MF   See *middle frequency*.

MIB   See *management information base*.

MIC   See *media interface connector*.

microwave   Electromagnetic waves ranging from 2 GHz to 40 GHz.

microwave transmission   Communication using microwaves.

middle frequency (MF)   Radio waves in the 300-KHz to 3-MHz range.

Military Network (MILNET)   A network for military use that was originally part of ARPA-NET.

MILNET   See *Military Network*.

MIME   See *Multipurpose Internet Mail Extension*.

minor synchronization point   A synchronization point that may or may not be confirmed before continuation of the session.

modem   A device consisting of a modulator and a demodulator. It converts a digital signal into an analog signal (modulation) and vice versa (demodulation).

modulation   Modification of one or more characteristics of a carrier wave by an information-bearing signal.

monitor station   In the token ring protocol, a station that is responsible for generating and controlling the token.

motion picture experts group (MPEG)   A method to compress videos.

MPEG   See *motion picture experts group*.

MSS   See *maximum segment size*.

MTA   See *message transfer agent*.

MTS   See *message transfer system*.

MTU   See *maximum transfer unit*.

multicast address   An address used for multicasting.

multicast backbone (MBONE)   A set of internet routers supporting multicasting through the use of tunneling.

multicasting   A transmission method that allows copies of a single packet to be sent to a selected group of receivers.

multihomed host   A host connected to more than one network.

multimode graded index fiber   An optical fiber with a core having a graded index of refraction.

multimode step index fiber   An optical fiber with a core having a uniform index of refraction. The index of refraction will change suddenly at the core/cladding boundary.

multiple access (MA)   A line access method in which every station can access the line freely.

multiple bit error   Error in a data unit in which two or more nonconsecutive bits have been altered.

multiplexer   A device used for multiplexing.

multiplexing   The process of combining signals from multiple sources for transmission across a single data link.

multipoint   A line configuration in which three or more devices share a common transmission line.

Multipurpose Internet Mail Extension (MIME)   A supplement to SMTP that allows non-ASCII data to be sent through SMTP.

multistation access unit (MAU)   In token ring, a device that houses individual automatic switches.

N

Nagle's algorithm   An algorithm that attempts to prevent silly window syndrome at the sender's site; both the rate of data production and the network speed are taken into account.

NAK   See *negative acknowledgment*.

National Science Foundation (NSF)   A government agency responsible for Internet funding.

National Science Foundation Network (NSFNET)   A backbone funded by NSF.

negative acknowledgment (NAK)   A message sent to indicate the rejection of received data.

netid   The part of an IP address that identifies the network.

network   A system consisting of connected nodes made to share data, hardware, and software.

network byte order   The format used by TCP/IP protocol suite for data storage and transmission; it is the same as the big endian format.

network file system (NFS)   A TCP/IP application protocol that allows a user to access and manipulate remote file systems as if they were local. It uses the services of remote procedure call protocol.

network interface card (NIC)   An electronic device, internal or external to a station, that contains circuitry to enable the station to be connected to the network.

network layer   The third layer in the OSI model, responsible for the delivery of a packet to the final destination.

network termination 1 (NT1)   In ISDN, devices between a user site and the central office that perform functions related to the first layer of the OSI model.

network termination 2 (NT2)   In ISDN, devices that perform functions related to the first three layers of the OSI model.

network-to-network interface (NNI)   In ATM, the interface between two networks.

network virtual terminal (NVT)   A TCP/IP application protocol that allows remote login.

NFS   See *network file system.*

NIC   See *network interface card.*

NNI   See *network-to-network interface.*

node   An addressable communication device (e.g., a computer or router) on a network.

node-to-node delivery   Transfer of a data unit from one node to the next.

noise   Random electrical signals that can be picked by the transmission medium and result in degradation or distortion of the data.

normal response mode (NRM)   In HDLC, a communication mode in which the secondary station must have permission from the primary station before transmission can proceed.

NRM   See *normal response mode.*

NSF   See *National Science Foundation.*

NSFNET   See *National Science Foundation Network.*

NT1   See *network termination 1.*

NT2   See *network termination 2.*

NVT   See *network virtual terminal.*

O

octal number system   A method of representing information using eight symbols (0, 1, ..., 6, and 7).

octet   Eight bits.

odd parity   An error-detection method in which an extra bit is added to the data unit such that the sum of all 1-bits becomes odd.

one's complement   A representation of binary numbers in which the complement of a number is found by complementing all bits.

open shortest path first (OSPF)   An interior routing protocol based on link state routing.

open system   A set of protocols that allows dissimilar systems to communicate.

open system interconnection (OSI)   A seven-layer model for data communication defined by ISO.

optical carrier (OC)   The hierarchy of fiber-optic carriers defined in SONET. The hierarchy defines up to 10 different carriers (OC-1, OC-3, OC-12, ..., OC-192), each with a different data rate.

optical fiber   See *fiber-optic cable.*

OSI   See *open system interconnection.*

OSPF   See *open shortest path first.*

out-of-band signaling   A method of signaling in which control data and user data travel on different channels.

overhead   Extra bits added to the data unit for control purposes.

P

packet   Synonym for data unit; mostly used in the network layer.

packet header   Control and address information added to the data unit.

Packet Internet Groper (PING)   An application program to determine the reachability of a destination using an ICMP echo request and reply.

packet layer protocol (PLP)   The network layer in X.25 protocol.

packet lifetime   The number of stations a packet can visit before being discarded.

packet-switched network   A network in which data are transmitted in independent units called packets.

packet-switching   Data transmission using a packet-switched network.

parallel transmission   Transmission in which bits in a group are sent simultaneously, each using a separate link.

parity bit   A redundant bit added to a data unit (usually a character) for error checking.

parity check   An error-detection method using a parity bit.

passive hub   A hub used only for connection; it does not regenerate the signal.

path   The channel through which a signal travels.

path layer   A SONET layer responsible for the movement of a signal from its optical source to its optical destination.

PDU   See *protocol data unit.*

peer-to-peer protocol   A protocol defining the rule of communication between two equal layers in the OSI model.

P/F bit   See *poll/final bit.*

phase   The relative position of a signal in time.

phase shift   The phase change of a signal.

photonic layer   The SONET layer that corresponds to the OSI model's physical layer.

physical layer   The first layer of the OSI model, responsible for the mechanical and electrical specifications of the medium.

piggybacking   The inclusion of acknowledgment on a data frame.

PING   See *Packet Internet Groper.*

pixel   Picture element; the smallest unit of an image.

plaintext   In encryption/decryption, the original message.

PLP   See *packet layer protocol.*

point-to-point connection   A dedicated transmission link between two devices.

Point-to-Point Protocol (PPP)   A protocol for data transfer across a serial line.

poll   In the primary/secondary access method, a procedure in which the primary station asks a secondary station if it has any data to transmit.

poll bit   See *poll/final bit.*

poll/final (P/F) bit   A bit in the control field of HDLC; if the primary is sending, it can be a poll bit; if the secondary is sending, it can be a final bit.

port address   In TCP/IP protocol an integer identifying a process.

PPP   See *Point-to-Point Protocol.*

preamble   The seven-byte field of an IEEE 802.3 frame consisting of alternating 1s and 0s that alert and synchronize the receiver.

presentation layer   The sixth layer of the OSI model responsible for translation, encryption, authentication, and data compression.

PRI   See *primary rate interface.*

primary rate interface (PRI)   An ISDN electrical interface providing 23 B channels (64 Kbps) and one D channel (64 Kbps). The total data rate is 1.544 Mbps, which includes some overhead.

primary station   In primary/secondary access method, a station that issues commands to the secondary stations.

private key In conventional encryption, a key shared by only one pair of devices, a sender and a receiver. In public key encryption, the private key is known only to the receiver.

Project 802 The project undertaken by the IEEE in an attempt to solve LAN incompatibility.

promiscuous ARP (proxy ARP) A technique that creates a subnetting effect; one device answers ARP requests for multiple hosts.

propagation delay The difference between the time a signal is sent and the time it is received.

protocol Rules for communication.

protocol converter A device such as a gateway that changes one protocol to another.

protocol data unit (PDU) A data unit defined in each layer of the OSI model. In particular, a data unit specified by IEEE 802.2 in the LLC sublayer.

protocol port See *port address.*

protocol suite A stack or family of protocols defined for a complex communication system.

proxy ARP See *promiscuous ARP.*

pseudoheader Information from the IP header used only for checksum calculation in UDP and TCP packets.

public key In public key encryption, a key known to everyone.

public key encryption A method of encryption based on a nonreversible encryption algorithm. The method uses two types of keys: The public key is known to the public; the private key (secret key) is known only to the receiver.

push data Data that must be sent with minimum delay; marked by setting the push bit in the TCP header.

Q

Q.931 The ITU-T standard that defines network layer functions of the ISDN related to the D channel.

quadbit A unit of data consisting of four bits.

queue A waiting list.

R

R reference point In ISDN, the interface between a TE2 and a TA.

radio wave Electromagnetic energy in the 3-KHz to 300-GHz range.

RARP See *reverse address resolution protocol.*

reassembly A network layer function in which all fragments of a message are correctly ordered.

receiver The target point of a transmission.

redirection An ICMP message type that informs the sender of a preferred route.

redundancy The addition of bits to a message for error control.

reflection The phenomenon related to the bouncing back of light at the boundary of two media.

refraction The phenomenon related to the bending of light when it passes from one medium to another.

regulatory agency A government agency that protects the public interest.

reliable delivery Receipt of a message without duplication, loss, or out-of-sequence packets.

remote login The process of logging on to a remote computer from a terminal connected to a local computer.

remote procedure call (RPC)   A TCP/IP protocol used by NFS.

repeater   A device that extends the distance a signal can travel by regenerating the signal.

Request for Comment (RFC)   A formal Internet document concerning an Internet issue.

return to zero (RZ)   A digital-to-digital encoding technique in which the voltage of the signal is zero for the second half of the bit interval.

reverse address resolution protocol (RARP)   A TCP/IP protocol that allows a host to find its Internet address given its physical address.

reverse domain   A subdomain in the domain name system (DNS) that finds the domain name given the IP address.

RFC   See *Request for Comment.*

ring topology   A topology in which the devices are connected in a ring. Each device on the ring receives the data unit from the previous device, regenerates it, and forwards it to the next device.

RIP   See *routing information protocol.*

rlogin   A remote login application designed by BSD UNIX.

route   A path traveled by a packet.

route discovery   The task of finding the optimum route a data unit must take.

router   An internetworking device operating at the first three OSI layers. A router is attached to two or more networks and forwards packets from one network to another.

routing   The process performed by a router.

routing algorithm   The algorithm used by a router to determine the optimum path for a packet.

routing information protocol (RIP)   A routing protocol based on the distance vector routing algorithm.

routing table   A table containing information a router needs to route packets. The information may include the network address, the cost, the address of the next hop, and so on.

RPC   See *remote procedure call.*

RS232   See *EIA-232.*

RSA encryption   A popular public-key encryption method developed by Rivest, Shamir, and Adleman.

round-trip time (RTT)   The time for a packet to leave its source, reach its destination, and be acknowledged.

RTT   See *round-trip time.*

run-length encoding   A compression method in which a run of symbols is replaced by the symbol and the number of symbols.

RZ   See *return to zero.*

S

S reference point   In ISDN, the interface between a TE1 or a TA and an NT.

sampling   The process of obtaining amplitudes of a signal at regular intervals.

sampling rate   The number of samples obtained per second in the sampling process.

SAP   See *service access point.*

SAR   See *segmentation and reassembly.*

SAS   See *single attachment station.*

SDH   See *synchronous digital hierarchy.*

SDLC   See *synchronous data link control.*

secondary station   In poll/select access method, a station that sends a response in answer to a command from a primary station.

section layer   A SONET layer responsible for the movement of a signal across a physical section.

security   The protection of a network from unauthorized access, viruses, and catastrophe.

segment   The packet at the TCP layer.

segmentation   The splitting of a message into multiple packets; usually performed at the transport layer.

segmentation and reassembly (SAR)   The lower AAL sublayer in the ATM protocol in which a header and/or trailer may be added to produce a 48-byte element.

select   In poll/select access method, a procedure in which the primary station asks a secondary station if it is ready to receive data.

selective-reject ARQ   An error-control method in which only the frame in error is resent.

sender   The originator of a message.

sequence number   The number that denotes the location of a frame or packet in a message.

serial line IP (SLIP)   A protocol that prepares IP datagrams for serial line transmission.

serial transmission   Transmission of data one bit at a time using only one single link.

server   A program that can provide services to other programs, called clients.

service access point (SAP)   A type of address that identifies the user of a protocol.

session layer   The fifth layer of the OSI model, responsible for the establishment, management, and termination of logical connections between two end users.

session management   The control and handling of sessions between two end users.

session protocol data unit (SPDU)   The data unit defined in the session layer of the OSI model.

SFD   See *start frame delimiter.*

S-frame   An HDLC frame used for supervisory functions such as acknowledgment, flow control, and error control; it contains no user data.

SHF   See *superhigh frequency.*

shielded twisted pair (STP)   Twisted-pair cable enclosed in a foil or mesh shield that protects against electromagnetic interference.

signal   Electromagnetic waves propagated along a transmission medium.

signed number   A representation of binary numbers including the sign (plus or minus). Signed numbers can be represented using three different formats: sign-and-magnitude, one's complement, and two's complement.

silly window syndrome   A situation in which a small window size is advertised by the receiver and a small segment sent by the sender.

simple mail transfer protocol (SMTP)   The TCP/IP protocol defining electronic mail service on the Internet.

simple network management protocol (SNMP)   The TCP/IP protocol that specifies the process of management in the Internet.

simplex mode   A transmission mode in which communication is one way.

single attachment station (SAS)   In FDDI, a station that can be connected only to one ring.

single-bit error   Error in a data unit in which only one single bit has been altered.

single-mode fiber   An optical fiber with an extremely small diameter that limits beams to a few angles, resulting in an almost horizontal beam.

sliding window   A protocol that allows several data units to be in transition before receiving an acknowledgment.

sliding window ARQ   An error-control protocol using sliding window concept.

SLIP   See *serial line IP.*

slot   A space for data.

slow start   A congestion-control method in which the congestion window size increases exponentially at first.

SMTP   See *simple mail transfer protocol.*

SNMP   See *simple network management protocol.*

SOA   See *Start of Authority.*

socket   An end point for a process; two sockets are needed for communication.

socket address   A structure holding an IP address and a port number.

SONET   See *synchronous optical network.*

source address   The address of the sender of the message.

source quench   A method, used in ICMP for flow control, in which the source is advised to slow down or stop the sending of datagrams because of congestion.

source route   A path, specified by the source, that must be adhered to by the datagram.

source-to-destination delivery   The transmission of a message from the original sender to the intended recipient.

SPDU   See *session protocol data unit.*

spectrum   The range of frequencies of a signal.

standard   A basis or model to which everyone has agreed.

standard creation committee   A group that produces a basis or model to which everyone has agreed.

star topology   A topology in which all stations are attached to a central device (hub).

starLAN   A LAN using star topology with a 1-Mbps data rate in which the stations can be daisy chained.

start bit   In asynchronous transmission, a bit to indicate the beginning of transmission.

start frame delimiter (SFD)   A one-byte field in the IEEE 802.3 frame that signals the beginning of the readable (nonpreamble) bit stream.

Start of Authority (SOA)   A DNS keyword to mark the start of the authoritative record.

static document   On the World Wide Web, a fixed-content document that is created and stored in a server.

static routing   A type of routing in which the routing table remains unchanged.

stop bit   In asynchronous transmission, one or more bits to indicate the end of transmission.

stop-and-wait   A flow-control method in which each data unit must be acknowledged before the next one can be sent.

stop-and-wait ARQ   An error-control protocol using stop-and-wait flow control.

store and forward   Another name for message switching.

STP   See *shielded twisted-pair.*

subnet   See *subnetwork.*

subnet address   The network address of a subnet.

subnetwork   A part of a network.

superhigh frequency (SHF) Radio waves in the 3-GHz to 30-GHz range using line-of-sight and space propagation.

supernet A network formed from two or more smaller networks.

switch A device connecting multiple communication lines together.

synchronization points Reference points introduced into the data by the session layer for the purpose of flow and error control.

synchronous data link control (SDLC) A precursor of HDLC pioneered by IBM.

synchronous digital hierarchy (SDH) The ITU-T equivalent of SONET.

synchronous optical network (SONET) A standard developed by ANSI for fiber-optic technology that can transmit high-speed data. It can be used to deliver text, audio, and video.

synchronous transmission A transmission method that requires a constant timing relationship between the sender and the receiver.

T

T-1 line A 1.544-Mbps digital transmission line.

T-2 line A 6.312-Mbps digital transmission line.

T-3 line A 44.736-Mbps digital transmission line.

T-4 line A 274.176-Mbps digital transmission line.

T reference point In ISDN, the interface between an NT1 and an NT2.

T-lines A hierarchy of digital lines designed to carry speech and other signals in digital forms. The hierarchy defines T-1, T-2, T-3, and T-4 lines.

TA See *terminal adapter.*

TCP See *transmission control protocol.*

TCP/IP See *transmission control protocol /internetworking protocol.*

TCP/IP protocol suite A group of hierarchical protocols used in an internet.

TDM See *time-division multiplexing.*

TE1 See *terminal equipment 1.*

TE2 See *terminal equipment 2.*

telecommunication Exchange of information over distance using electronic equipment.

teleconferencing Audio and visual communication between remote users.

telephony Voice communication.

teleservice In ISDN, a service in which the network may change or process the contents of the data.

teletext A method of broadcasting text using a portion of a TV channel bandwidth.

telex A method of point-to-point communication using a variety of devices.

TELNET See *Terminal Network.*

terminal adapter (TA) A device that allows the use of non-ISDN terminals to be connected to ISDN network.

terminal equipment 1 (TE1) An ISDN standard terminal.

terminal equipment 2 (TE2) A non-ISDN terminal.

Terminal Network (TELNET) A general purpose client-server program that allows remote login.

terminator An electronic device that prevents signal reflections at the end of a cable.

TFTP See *trivial file transfer protocol.*

thick Ethernet   See *10Base5.*

Thick-net   See *thick Ethernet.*

thin Ethernet   See *10Base2*

Thin-net   See *thin Ethernet*

three-way handshake   A sequence of events for connection establishment or termination consisting of the request, then the acknowledgment of the request, and then confirmation of the acknowledgment.

time to live (TTL)   See *packet lifetime.*

time-division multiplexing (TDM)   The technique of combining signals coming from low-speed channels to share time on a high-speed path.

time-division switching   A circuit-switching technique in which time-division multiplexing is used to achieve switching.

TLI   See *transport layer interface.*

token   A small packet used in token-passing access method.

token bus   A LAN using a bus topology and token-passing access method.

token passing   An access method in which a token is circulated in the network. The station that captures the token can send data.

token ring   A LAN using a ring topology and token-passing access method.

topology   The structure of a network including physical arrangement of devices.

TOS   See *type of service.*

TPDU   See *transport protocol data unit.*

traceroute   A program that identifies the path of a datagram.

transceiver   A device that both transmits and receives.

transceiver cable   In Ethernet, the cable that connects the station to the transceiver. Also called the attachment unit interface.

translation   Changing from one code or protocol to another.

transmission control protocol (TCP)   A transport protocol in the TCP/IP protocol suite.

transmission control protocol /internetworking protocol (TCP/IP)   A five-layer protocol suite that defines the exchange of transmissions across the Internet.

transmission medium   The physical path linking two communication devices.

transparency   The ability to send any bit pattern as data without it being mistaken for control bits.

transparent bridge   Another name for a learning bridge.

transparent data   Data that can contain control bit patterns without being interpreted as control.

transport layer   The fourth layer in the OSI model; responsible for reliable end-to-end delivery and error recovery.

transport layer interface (TLI)   An application programming interface defined for System V UNIX.

transport protocol data unit (TPDU)   The data unit defined in the transport layer of the OSI model.

tree topology   A topology in which stations are attached to a hierarchy of hubs. Tree topology is an extension of star topology with more than one level.

trellis coding   A modulation technique that includes error correction.

tribit   A unit of data consisting of three bits.

trivial file transfer protocol (TFTP)   An unreliable TCP/IP protocol for file transfer that does not require complex interaction between client and server.

TTL   See *time to live.*

twisted pair   A transmission medium consisting of two insulated conductors in a twisted configuration.

twisted-pair Ethernet   An Ethernet using twisted-pair cable; 10BaseT.

two's complement   A representation of binary numbers in which the complement of a number is found by complementing all bits and adding a 1 after that.

type of service (TOS)   A criteria or value that specifies the handling of the datagram.

U

U reference point   In ISDN, the interface between an NT1 and the rest of the network.

UA   See *user agent.*

UDP   See *user datagram protocol.*

U-frame   An HDLC unnumbered frame carrying link management information.

unicast   The sending of a packet to just one destination.

universal time   A standard time reference formerly known as Greenwich Mean Time.

UHF   See *ultrahigh frequency.*

ultrahigh frequency (UHF)   Radio waves in the 300-MHz to 3-GHz range using line-of-sight propagation.

unbalanced configuration   An HDLC configuration in which one device is primary and the others secondary.

unguided medium   A transmission medium with no physical boundaries.

UNI   See *user network interface.*

uniform resource locator (URL)   A string of characters (address) that identifies a page on the World Wide Web.

UNIX   The operating system used in the Internet.

unshielded twisted pair (UTP)   A cable with wires that are twisted together to reduce noise and crosstalk. See also *twisted pair* and *shielded twisted pair.*

unsigned number   A representation of binary numbers without sign (plus or minus).

uplink   Transmission from an earth station to a satellite.

urgent data   In TCP/IP, data that must be delivered to the application program as quickly as possible.

URL   See *uniform resource locator.*

user agent (UA)   An SMTP component that prepares the message, creates the envelope, and puts the message in the envelope.

user datagram   The name of the packet in the UDP protocol.

user datagram protocol (UDP)   A connectionless TCP/IP transport layer protocol.

user network interface (UNI)   The interface between a user and the ATM network.

UTP   See *unshielded twisted pair.*

V

V series   ITU-T standards that define data transmission over telephone lines.

vampire tap An Ethernet transceiver used in thick Ethernet (10Base5). The transceiver is housed in a clamplike device with a sharp metal prong that "bites" Thicknet cable.

VCI *See virtual channel identifier.*

vertical redundancy check (VRC) An error-detection method based on per-character parity check.

very high frequency (VHF) Radio waves in the 30-MHz to 300-MHz range using line-of-sight propagation.

very low frequency (VLF) Radio waves in the 3-KHz to 30-KHz range using surface propagation.

VHF See *very high frequency.*

videoconferencing A service that allows a group of users to exchange information over a network.

videotex The process of accessing remote databases interactively.

virtual channel identifier (VCI) A field in an ATM cell header that defines a channel.

virtual circuit A logical circuit made between the sending and receiving computer. The connection is made after both computers do handshaking. After the connection, all packets follow the same route and arrive in sequence.

virtual path identifier (VPI) A field in an ATM cell header that identifies a path.

virtual path identifier/virtual channel identifier (VPI/VCI) Two fields used together to route an ATM cell.

virtual terminal (VT) The OSI remote login protocol.

virtual tributary (VT) A partial payload that can be inserted into a SONET frame and combined with other partial payloads to fill out the frame.

virus Unauthorized software introduced for destructive purposes onto a computer.

VLF See *very low frequency.*

VPI *See virtual path identifier.*

VPI/VCI *See virtual path identifier/virtual channel identifier.*

VRC See *vertical redundancy check.*

VT See *virtual tributary or virtual terminal.*

W

WAN See *wide area network.*

Web Synonym for World Wide Web (WWW).

well-known port A port number that identifies a process on the server.

wide area network (WAN) A network that uses a technology that can span a large geographical distance.

working group An IETF committee concentrating on a specific Internet topic

World Wide Web (WWW) A multimedia Internet service that allows users to traverse the Internet by moving from one document to another via links that connect them together.

WWW See *World Wide Web.*

X

X.21 An ITU-T standard defining the interface between a DTE and a DCE.

X.25 An ITU-T standard that defines the interface between a data terminal device and a packet-switching network.

X.400   An ITU-T standard for electronic mail and message handling.

X.500   An ITU-T standard for directory service.

Y

zone of authority   In DNS, the domain names for which the server is responsible.

References

Bates, Bud, and Donald Gregory. *Voice and Data Communications Handbook.* Burr Ridge, IL: McGraw-Hill, 1996.

Beyda, William J. *Data Communications*, 2nd ed. Upper Saddle River, NJ: Prentice-Hall, 1996.

Black, Uyless. *Data Link Protocols*. Upper Saddle River, NJ: Prentice-Hall, 1993.

Black, Uyless. *Emerging Communications Technologies*. Upper Saddle River, NJ: Prentice Hall, 1994.

Comer Douglas E. *Internetworking with TCP/IP,* vol. 1. Upper Saddle River, NJ: Prentice-Hall, 1995.

———. *Internetworking with TCP/IP,* vol. 2. Upper Saddle River, NJ: Prentice-Hall, 1999.

———. *Internetworking with TCP/IP,* vol. 3. Upper Saddle River, NJ: Prentice-Hall, 1996.

———. *The Internet Book.* Upper Saddle River, NJ: Prentice-Hall, 1995.

Dickie, Mark. *Routing in Today's Internetworks.* New York, NY: Van Nostrand Reinhold, 1994.

Forouzan, Behrouz. *Introduction to Data Communication and Networking.* Burr Ridge, IL: McGraw-Hill, 1998.

Halsall, Fred. *Data Communications, Computer Networks and Open Systems,* 4th ed. Reading, MA: Addison-Wesley, 1995.

Hardy, James K. *Inside Networks.* Upper Saddle River, NJ: Prentice-Hall, 1995.

Herrick, Clyde N., and C. Lee McKim. *Telecommunication Wiring.* Upper Saddle River, NJ: Prentice-Hall, 1992.

Hioki, Warren. *Telecommunications*, 2nd ed. Upper Saddle River, NJ: Prentice-Hall, 1995.

Huitema, Christian. *Routing in the Internet*. Upper Saddle River, NJ: Prentice-Hall, 1995.

Johnson, Howard W. *Fast Ethernet*. Upper Saddle River, NJ: Prentice-Hall, 1996.

McClimans, Fred J. *Communications Wiring and Interconnections*. Burr Ridge, IL: McGraw-Hill, 1992.

Miller, Philip. *TCP/IP Explained*. Newton, MA: Digital Press, 1997.

Morley, John, and Stan Gelber. *The Emerging Digital Future*. Danver, MA: Boyd & Fraser, 1996.

Moy, John. *OSPF*. Reading, MA: Addison-Wesley, 1998.

Naugle, Matthew G. *Network Protocol Handbook*. Burr Ridge, IL: McGraw-Hill, 1994.

Partridge, Craig. *Gigabit Networking*. Reading, MA: Addison-Wesley, 1994.

Pearson, John E. *Basic Communication Theory*. Upper Saddle River, NJ: Prentice-Hall, 1992.

Perlman, Radia. *Interconnections: Bridges and Routers*. Reading, MA: Addison-Wesley, 1992.

Shay, William A. *Understanding Data Communications and Networks*. Boston, MA: PWS, 1994.

Smith, Philip. *Frame Relay*. Reading, MA: Addison-Wesley, 1993.

Stallings, William. *Data and Computer Communications,* 5th ed. Upper Saddle River, NJ: Prentice-Hall, 1997.

Stevens, W. Richard. *TCP/IP Illustrated,* vol. 1. Reading, MA: Addison-Wesley, 1994.

———. *TCP/IP Illustrated,* vol. 3. Reading, MA: Addison-Wesley, 1996.

Tanenbaum, Andrew S. *Computer Networks,* 3rd ed. Upper Saddle River, NJ: Prentice-Hall, 1996.

Siyan, Karanjit S. *Inside TCP/IP,* 3rd ed. Indianapolis, IN: New Riders, 1997.

Thomas, Stephen A. *IPng and the TCP/IP Protocols*. New York, NY: Wiley, 1996.

Washburn, Kevin, and Jim Evans. *TCP/IP: Running a Successful Network,* 2nd ed. Reading, MA: Addison-Wesley, 1996.

Wright, Gary R., and W. Richard Stevens. *TCP/IP Illustrated,* vol. 2. Reading, MA: Addison-Wesley, 1995.

Index

Numerics
10BASE2 48
  advantages 48
  connectors and cables 48
  data rate 48
  disadvantages 48
  topology 48
  transceiver 48
10BASE5 48
  connectors and cables 48
  segment length 48
  signaling 48
  topology 48
10BASE-T 48
  cable 49
  data rate 48
  hub 49
  length 48
  topology 48
802.1 730
802.2 730
802.3 730
802.4 730
802.5 730

A
AAL 66
  encapsulation 67
AAL1 67
AAL2 67
AAL3/4 67
AAL5 67
ABM 723
  LAPD 728
  transmission initiation 723
Abstract Window Toolkit 586
accept call 610, 620

arguments 610
  new socket 610
access control 23
access method
  CSMA/CD 46
  Ethernet 46
  FDDI 54
  Token Ring 51
ACK 677
ACK message 481
  delayed 485
ACK segment 294, 295, 296
acknowledgment 287
  delayed 286
  TCP 275
active close 295, 372
active document 583
  binary code 583
  binary format 583
  browser 584
  client site 583, 584
  code execution 584
  compilation 584
  creation 583
  example 583
  server site 584
active open 294, 371
  FTP control connection 460
  FTP data connection 461
address
  broadcast 98
  direct broadcast 91
  FDDI 55
  internet 32
  IP 32
  limited broadcast 91
  link 31

logical 24
loopback 93
multicast 96
need for multiple 179
network 91
physical 31
port 33
private network 99
service-point 25
specific host on this network 93
this host on this network 93
types 31
unicast 96
address mask
  ICMPv6 658
address mask message 215
Address Resolution Protocol. See
    ARP
address to name resolution 411
address transformation 605
addressing 31
  Ethernet 47
  Token Ring 52
Adobe Post Script 514
Advanced Research Projects
    Agency. See ARPA
agent 525, 526
  database 526
  function 536
  MIB 532
  passive open 544
  trap 526
alias
  many-to-one expansion 502
  one-to-many expansion 501
alignment
  end of option option 158

American National Standards
      Institute. See ANSI
American Standard Code for
      Information Interchange. See
      ASCII
angle of incidence 44
anonymous FTP 473
ANSI 3
   members 3
ANSNET 11
anycast address 636
API 599
APNIC 638
applet 585, 586
   bytecode 587
   client process 587
   compilation 587
   creation 587
   HTML 587
Application Adaptation Layer. See
      AAL
application layer 27
   directory services 28
   file manipulation 28
   mail services 28
   NVT 27
   responsibilities 27
   services 27
   TCP/IP 28, 31, 369
application program 370
   activity 371
   client 370
   server 370
   universal program 371
application programming
      interface. See API
architecture
   OSI model 18
area 332
   id 333
   virtual link 333
area border router 332
   backbone router 333
ARM 723
   transmission initiation 723
ARP 28, 30, 179, 180, 181
   algorithm 186
   broadcast physical addres 180
   broadcast query 181
   concept 30
   design 186
   direct delivery 132
   dynamic mapping 181
   encapsulation 183
   four cases 184

hardware length field 182
hardware type field 182
host to host on different
      networks 184
host to host on single
      network 184
ICMPv6 633, 660
indirect delivery 133
IP to physical address
      mapping 181
operation 183
operation field 182
packet components 181
packet format 182
process 183
protocol length field 182
protocol type field 182
proxy 184
query packet 181
response packet 181
router to host on different
      networks 184
router to host on same
      network 184
sender hardware address
      field 182
sender protocol address
      field 183
steps involved 183
target hardware address
      field 183
target protocol address field 183
unicast response 181
ARP design
   cache memory 186
   cache-control module 190
   components 186
   example 191
   FREE state 190
   input module 189
   output module 188
   PENDING state 188, 189
   queues 188
   RESOLVED state 188, 189
ARP packet
   reply 189
   request 189
ARPANET 9
   original nodes 9
   TCP/IP 10
ASCII 677
   table 677
   transformation to decimal 605
ASCII code 677, 700
ASN.1 733

application-wide tag 735
BIT STRING 734
BOOLEAN data type 733
CHOICE structured data
      type 735
context-specific tag 735
data types 733
enumerated data type 734
external data type 734
integer data type 734
modules 736
object identifier data type 734
private tag 735
purpose 733
real data type 734
sequence structured type 734
simple data type 733
simple type examples 529
SMI 527
SNMP 526
structured type 734
subtyping 735
tag 735
universal tag 735
values 735
Asynchronous Balanced Mode. See
      ABM
Asynchronous Response Mode.
      See ARM
Asynchronous Transfer Mode. See
      ATM
ATM 65
   AAL layers 67
   ATM layer 66, 67
   cell 65
   cell loss priority field 68
   connection-oriented 65
   generic flow control field 67
   header error control field 68
   layers 66
   medium 68
   payload type field 67
   physical layer 66, 68
   switch 65
   virtual channel identifier
         field 67
   VPI/VCI 65
ATM Consortium 4
ATM Forum 4, 65
   address 743
ATM layer 67
   functions 67
   size 67
attachment unit interface. See AUI
attended bulk data traffic 644

attenuation 69
attribute 571
AUI 48
authentication 331, 633, 651, 711
  algorithm 651
  format 331
  receiver 651
  security key 651
  security parameter index
    field 651
  sender 651
automatic tunneling 665
autonomous boundary router 351
autonomous system 320, 332
  area 332
  backbone 333
  hop count limit 327
  path vector routing 351

B
backbone 333
  area id 333
  virtual link 333
backbone router 333
background data 644
backward explicit congestion
  notification. See BECN
balanced configuration 722
  point-to-point 722
bands
  radio 45
base 10
  one's complement 693, 694
base 8 685
base header 642
base16 686
Basic Encoding Rules. See BER
BECN 64
Bellman-Ford algorithm 321
BER 529
  class subfield 529
  format 529
  format subfield 530
  integer example 531
  IP address example 532
  length field 531
  number subfield 529, 530
  object identifier example 532
  SNMP 526, 539
  string example 531
  tag field 529
  value field 531
best-effort delivery 29, 147
  example 147
BGP 319, 320, 350

encapsulation 357
  header 353
  keepalive message 356
  length field 354
  marker field 354
  notification message 356
  open message 354
  packet format 353
  path vector routing 350
  port 747
  types of messages 353
  update message 355
bidirectional edge 335
big-endian byte order 603
binary number 684
  example 685
  formats 691
  representation 691
  signed 691
  symbols 684
  to hexadecimal 689
  to octal 688
  unsigned 691
  weight and value 685
bind call 608, 614, 618
block descriptor 464
blocking port 740
body 571
Boolean 733
boot
  initial 387
BOOTP 387
  binding 392
  boot filename field 389
  broadcast message 391
  client hardware address
    field 389
  client IP address field 388
  client port 390
  DHCP 392
  encapsulation 390
  gateway IP address field 388
  hardware length field 388
  hardware type field 388
  hop count field 388
  masking 215
  multiple users 391
  number of seconds field 388
  operation 390
  operation code field 388
  options field 389
  packet format 387
  RARP 387
  remote server 391
  server IP address field 388

server name field 389
server port 390
static configuration protocol 392
static protocol 392
TFTP 391, 489
transaction ID field 388, 391
UDP port 391
unicast reply message 391
your IP address field 388
bootstrap process 387
Bootstrap Protocol. See BOOTP
border gateway protocol. See BGP
BPDU 739
bridge 68, 70
  as filter 70
  data link layer 70
  function 70
  logic 70
  loops 738
  network division 70
  operation 70
  OSI model 69, 70
  repeater 70
  security 70
  segment 71
  spanning tree 738
bridge protocol data unit. See
  BPDU
broadcast address 96
broadcast physical address 31
broadcasting 56
  UDP 260
browser 568, 570
  architecture 568
  client program 568
  components 568
  controller 568
  dynamic document 577
  HTML 570
  interpreter 568
  markup language 570
buffer
  server 618
buffer size 691
burst error 699, 700, 701
  definition 700
  example 700
bus topology 22
  Ethernet 48
byte manipulation functions 606
byte-order transformation 604
  htonl 605
  htons 605
  ntohl 605
  ntohs 605

C

cable
  coaxial 43
  twisted-pair 42
cache memory 186
  ARP 186
  space 186
cache memory table
  attempts 188
  hardware address 188
  hardware length 187
  hardware type 187
  interface number 187
  protocol address 188
  protocol length 187
  protocol type 187
  queue number 188
  state 187
  time-out 188
caching 412
  counter 413
  problems 413
  time-to-live 413
  unauthoritative source 413
Caesar cipher 707
carrier sense multiple access with
      collision detection. See
      CSMA/CD
CDDI 54
cell 65
  size 65
cell relay 65
Cerf, Vint 9
CGI 578
  body 580
  Bourne shell example 581
  C example 582
  concept 578
  content_length header 580
  content_type header 580
  environment variable 579
  examples 581
  expires header 580
  form 580
  header 580
  HTML example 581
  input 579
  location header 580
  MIME 580
  output 580
  parameter passing 579
  Perl example 582
  pragma header 580
  program 578
  query string 580

question mark 580
  redirection 581
  status header 580
checksum 163, 216, 287, 701, 706
  at receiver 164
  at sender 163
  calculation 217, 255
  complement 163
  example 165, 217, 255
  fragmentation 154
  header coverage 165
  Internet 701
  IP packet 165
  method 163
  one's complement
      arithmetic 255
  optional 256
  protocol field 254
  receiver 255
  sender 255
  TCP 281
  testing 217
  UDP 254, 256
child process 620
child server 374, 618
child socket 610
CIDR 121
ciphertext 707
circuit switching 57
  dedicated path 57
  example 57
  in voice communication 57
  link reduction 57
cladding 44
Clark's solution 286
class A address 87, 98
  hostid 87
  netid 87
  netid and hostid 89
class B address 87, 98
  hostid 87
  netid 87
  netid and hostid 89
class C address 88
  netid 88
  hostid 89
class D address
  multicasting 88, 89
class E address 88
  reserved 90
Classless Inter Domain Routing.
      See CIDR
classless routing 113
client 248, 370, 371, 614
  active close 372

active open 371
close call 620
concurrent 372
connect call 620
connection-oriented
    concurrent 620
  definition 371
  iterative 372
  opening a socket 614, 620
  read call 620
  repeated steps 614, 620
  socket address 274
  write call 620
client program
  activity 371
  port number 249, 273
client-server
  definitions 249
  example 249
  local host 272
  remote host 272
  remote login 431
client-server model 599
  application programs 371
  client-server relationship 371
  concept 369
  concurrency 372
  process concept 374
  process-to-process
      communication 272
client-server paradigm 248
clock synchronization 214
close call 614, 620
CLOSED state 298, 299
CLOSE-WAIT state 299
coax 43
coaxial cable 41, 43
  and optical fiber 45
  frequency range 43
  noise 43
  outer conductor 43
  sheath 43
collision
  domain 49
  Ethernet 46
  Fast Ethernet 51
combined station 721
  configuration 721
Common Gateway Interface. See
    CGI
complement 163, 694
  of binary number 696
compression
  DNS 419
  FTP 464

concurrency 372
  clients 372
  servers 372
conductor
  unguided media 45
conferencing 97
configuration
  HDLC 721
configured tunneling 665
congestion 207
  buffer 207
  concept 299
  destination host 207
  ICMPv6 655
  routers 207
congestion control 299
  decreasing strategy 300
  increasing strategy 300
  network role 300
  receiver role 300
  strategies 300
  window size 300
congestion-controlled traffic 644
connect call 609
connecting device 24, 41, 68
connection 293
  establishment 293
  termination 295
  transport layer 248
connection control 25
connection establishment 293
  procedure 293
  SMTP 508
  TFTP 483
  three-way handshaking 293
connection resetting 296
  purpose 296
connection termination 295
  four-way handshaking 295
  procedure 295
  SMTP 509
  TFTP 483
connectionless
  concept 131
connectionless iterative
  communication 612
connectionless iterative server 372
connectionless service
  UDP 256
connectionless transport layer 25
connection-oriented
  concept 131
connection-oriented concurrent
  communication 618
connection-oriented concurrent

server 373, 618
connection-oriented service
  TCP 30
connection-oriented transport
  layer 25
connection-oriented vs.
  connectionless services 131
connector
  STP 43
contact address 743
contention 731
contiguous mask 113
control block table 261
control field PDU 731
control traffic 645
controller 568
conventional encryption 707
  bit-level techniques 708
  method 707
convergence sublayer. See CS
corrupted segment 287
country domain 409
  example 409
  mapping 411
CR 677
CRC 701, 703, 704
  calculation 704
  divisor representation 706
  generation 705
  generation example 705
  generator 705
  HDLC 726
  overview 703
  polynomial 706
  receiver 704, 705
  remainder 704
  sender 704
  standard polynomials 706
CRC field
  Ethernet 48
CRC generator 706
CRC-32
  Token Ring 53
critical angle 44
CS 67
CSMA/CD 46
  Project 802.3 730
CSNET 10
cyclical redundancy check.See
  CRC

D
DAC 56
DAS 55
DATA 480

data compression 27
data encryption standard. See DES
data field
  Ethernet 48
data frame
  Token Ring 52
data link layer 22
  access control 23
  addressing 22
  devices 69
  error control 23
  error handling 699
  flow control 23
  framing 22
  function 22
  LLC 731
  physical addressing 22
  Project 802 729
data link protocol
  HDLC 721
data rate
  Ethernet 47
  FDDI 55
  Token Ring 52
data transfer
  TFTP 483
data type field
  Ethernet 48
database
  DHCP 392
database description message 344
  B flag field 345
  contents 344
  I flag field 345
  link state header field 345
  M flag field 345
  M/S flag field 345
  message sequence number
    field 345
  T flag field 344
datagram 30, 147
  format 147
  in IP 147
  in switching 58
  IP 29
  version field 480
datagram approach 58
  example 58
  independence of packets 58
  links 58
  multiple channels 58
datagram socket 602
DDNS 423
  DHCP 423
de facto standard 2

de jure standard 2
decapsulation
  UDP 258
decimal
  transformation to ASCII 605
decimal number 683, 684
  example 684
  symbols 684
  to binary 688
  to octal 688
  to one's complement 694
  to sign-and-magnitude 693
  to two's complement 695
  transformation from 688
  transformation to 688
  weight and value 684
decryption 707
decryption algorithm
  public key method 709
default delivery 137
default router 210
default routing 135
DEL 681
delayed delivery 499
DELAYING state 234
delivery
  direct 132
  end-to-end 24
  indirect 132
  source-to-destination 23, 24
  station-to-station 23
delivery and routing of IP
    packets 131
demultiplexing
  UDP 259
Department of Defense. See DOD
DES 708
  method 709
designated port 740
destination address
  Ethernet 48
destination host
  reassembly 153
destination option 653
  format 653
Destination Service Access Point.
    See DSAP
destination unreachable 204
  code field 204, 210
  code meanings 205
  message creation 206
destination unreachable message
  code field 656
  ICMPv6 656
DHCP 392

address leasing 392
BOOTP 392
databases 392
DDNS 423
dynamic configuration
    protocol 392
flag field 394
message types 392
operation 392
options field 394
packet format 394
TFTP 489
dialog control 25
digit 683
  least significant 683
  most significant 683
  ordering of 683
  significance example 683
digital signature 711
  concept 712
  example 712
Dijkstra algorithm 339, 340,
    341, 351
direct broadcast address 91
direct delivery 132, 137
  address mapping 132
  determination 132
direct vs. indirect delivery 132
directory services 28
Distance Vector Multicast Routing
    Protocol. See DVMRP
distance vector routing 321
  BGP 351
  routing table 322
  sharing at intervals 321
  sharing information 321
  sharing with neighbors 321
DLE 677
DNS 401
  caching 413
  compression 419
  country domain 409
  divisions 407
  domain 405
  encapsulation 424
  example 420
  generic domain 407
  Internet 407
  inverted-tree structure 402
  labels 402
  levels 402
  message 413
  offset pointer 419
  primary server 407
  question record 416

record types 416
resolver 410
resource record 418
reverse domain 409
secondary server 407
server 405
TCP 424
UDP 424
updating 423
zone 405
DNS example 421
DNS message
  additional information
      section 416
  additional records field 416
  answer records field 416
  answer section 416
  authoritative records field 416
  authoritative section 416
  flags field 415
  header 414
  identification field 414
  question records field 415
  question section 416
DNS response
  answer records field 416
  question records field 416
DO command 438
do not fragment bit 154
DOD 9
domain
  country 409
  generic 408
  inverse 409
domain name 402, 403
  full 402
  SMTP 499
Domain Name System. See DNS
DONT command 438
draft standard 5
DSAP 731
Dual Attachment Concentrator.
    See DAC
Dual Attachment Station. See DAS
dual ring 55
dual stack 664
duplicate segment 288
DVMRP 358
  algorithm 358
  MBONE 358
dynamic database 392
dynamic document 577
  definition 577
  example 577
  URL 577

Dynamic Domain Name System.
   See DDNS
Dynamic Host Configuration
   Protocol. See DHCP
dynamic mapping 180, 181
   protocols 180
dynamic port 250
dynamic routing 135
dynamic routing table 136
dynamic table 319

E

eavesdropping 652
EBCDIC code 677, 689
echo request and reply message
   concept 212
   functioning node 212
   ICMPv6 659
   identifier field 212
   ping 212
   reachability of host 212
   sequence number field 212
EHF 45
EIA 3, 42
   interfaces 3
   manufacturing concerns 3
electromagnetic spectrum 45
Electronic Industries Association.
   See EIA
electronic mail. See e-mail
e-mail 495
   address 499
   domain name 499
   local part 499
   mail gateway 499
encapsulation 332
   ARP 183
   BOOTP 390
   DNS 424
   IGMP 233
   OSPF 350
   RARP 195
   UDP 257
encrypted security payload. See
   ESP
encryption 633, 707
   as inverse of decryption 709
   authentication 711
   bank example 709
   categories 707
   ciphertext 707
   conventional 707
   conventional methods 709
   definition 707
   DES 708

Julius Caesar 707
key 707
monoalphabetic
   substitution 707
need for 707
plaintext 707
polyalphabetic substitution
   708
presentation layer 27
public key 707, 709
RSA 710
substitution methods 707
transpositional method 708
encryption key
   digital signature 712
end-of-option option 157, 278
EOT 677
ephemeral port 249, 273
   BOOTP 391
   FTP control connection 460
   FTP data connection 461
   queue 258
   server 374, 618
   TFTP 486
error
   burst 700
   multiple-bit 700
   single-bit 700
   sources 699
   types 699
error control 25, 287
   HDLC 727
   TCP 272
   TFTP 484
   transport layer 24, 248
   UDP 257
error correction 287, 699
   counters 287
   mechanism 287
error detection 287, 699, 701
   acknowledgment 287
   checksum 163, 706
   corrupted segment 287
   duplicate segment 288
   HDLC 726
   implementation 699
   lost acknowledgment 289
   lost segment 287
   LRC 703
   out-of-order segment 288
   redundancy 701
   tools 287
   transport layer 699
   VRC 702
error message 481

ICMP design 218
error reporting 654
   ICMP 203
   ICMP v4 and v6 655
error-reporting message
   ICMP 202
ESC 678
escape character 444
ESP 652
   format 652
   transport mode 652
   tunnel mode 653
ESTABLISHED state 298, 299
ETB 678
Ethernet 46
   access method 46
   acknowledgment 47, 206
   address 31
   address conversion 232
   addressing 47
   broadcast address 180
   collision domain 49
   CRC 48
   data field 48
   data rate 47
   data type field 48
   destination address 48
   frame format 47
   implementation 48
   in sample network 95
   IPv6 address 638
   media 42
   multicasting 232
   NIC 47
   source address 48
   switched 71
   thick 48
   thin 48
   topology 48
   twisted-pair 48
ETX 677
Eudora 497, 503
experimental level 5
expiration timer 327
extension header 646
   authentication 651
   destination option 653
   ESP 652
   fragmentation 650
   hop-by-hop option 647
   source routing 649
exterior routing 320
external link ad 349
extremely high frequency.
   See EHF

F

Fast Ethernet 47, 49
  collision domain 51
  data rate 51
  need for 49
  topology 51
FCC 4
  address 743
FDDI 54
  access method 54
  addressing 55
  concept 54
  CRC 55
  DAS 56
  data field 55
  data rate 55
  frame types 55
  implementation 55
  layers 55
  MIC 55, 56
  primary ring 55
  secondary ring 55
FECN 64
Federal Communications
    Committee. See FCC
FF 677
fiber optic cable 41
file transfer 459
  problems 459
File Transfer Protocol. See FTP
FIN segment 296
final 726
finite state diagram
  client 298
  server 299
finite state machine 297
  example 297
FIN-WAIT-1 298
FIN-WAIT-2 298
flooding 333, 346
flow control 25, 281
  congestion 207
  definition 281
  HDLC 727
  in IP 206
  sliding window 282
  TCP 272
  TFTP 484
  transport layer 24, 248
  UDP 257
flow label 634, 645
  faster processing 646
  real-time transmission 646
  rules for use 646
fork call 620

fork function 377
  returned values 378
forums 2, 4
forward explicit congestion
    notification. See FECN
forwarding port 740
four-way handshaking 295
  example 296
FQDN 403
  DNS server 404
fragmentation 152, 650
  checksum 154
  definition 153
  do not fragment bit 154
  example 154
  fields copied 154
  flags field 154
  fragmentation offset 154
  header fields 154
  ICMP error message 154
  identification field 154
  IPv6 650, 655
  more fragment bit 154
  offset 155
  reassembly 153
  reassembly steps 155
frame 22
frame check sequence 727
frame format
  Ethernet 47
  FDDI 55
  Token Ring 52
frame relay 62
  addressing fields 62
  BECN 64
  command/response field 62
  discard eligibility field 64
  DLCI 62, 64
  error checking 62
  extended address field 63
  FECN field 64
  frame format 62
  issues 4
  layers 62
  operation 64
  physical layer 62
  PVC 64
Frame Relay Forum 4
frames
  HDLC 724
FREE state 234
FTP 459, 553, 569
  access commands 465
  active open 460
  anonymous FTP 473

ASCII file 463
attributes of communication 463
binary file 463, 464
binary file storage example 471
block mode 464
client components 459
client definitions 462
client in data connection 461
command 464
command form 464
command processing 464
communication 461
compressed mode 464
connections 459, 460
control connection 459, 460,
    461
damaged message 484
data connection 459, 460, 462
data connection steps 461
data formatting commands 465
data structure 463
EBCDIC file 463
ephemeral port 460, 461, 466
file management commands 465
file printability 463
file retrieval 469
file retrieval example 470
file storage 469
file structure 463, 464
file transfer 469
file transfer commands 466
file type 463
first digit of response 467
HTTP 551
image file 463
minimize delay TOS 460
miscellaneous commands 467
nonprint attribute 463
NVT 461
page structure 464
passive open 460, 461
port 459, 747
port number 466
port-defining commands 466
record structure 463, 464
response 464, 467
second digit of response 467
sending a directory or file
    name 469
server components 459
server in control connection 460
server in data connection 461
stream mode 464
TELNET 463
text file 464

third digit of response 468
transmission mode 464
UNIX interface 472
user interface 472
user interface example 472
full domain name 402
full-duplex 22
full-duplex service 275
Fully Qualified Domain Name. See
  FQDN

G
garbage collection timer 327
gateway 10, 68, 73
  compared to router 73
  function 73
  OSI layers 73
  OSI model 69
  protocol converter 73
  protocol translation 73
generator
  CRC 705
  LRC 703
generic domain 407
  first level 408
  mapping 411
gethostbyname 607
GIF 514, 574
gopher 553, 569, 747
government regulatory
  agencies 2
group membership message 661
  termination 662
  types 661
group table 234
  group address 234
  interface no 234
  reference count 234
  state field 234
groupid 228
guest password 473
guided media 41
  conductor 41
  definition 41
  optical fiber 41
  twisted-pair 42

H
half-duplex 22
HDLC 721, 722, 723, 725, 726,
  727
  ABM 723
  address field 725
  ARM 723
  balanced configuration 721

combined station 721
communication modes 722
configurations 721
control field 725
definition 721
error control 725
error detection 726
FCS field 726
flag field 724
flow control 725
flow management 725
frame format 724
frame types 726
frames 724
I-frame 724
information field 726
LAPB 728
LAPD 728
LAPM 728
line configuration 721
mode definition 722
no balanced multipoint 722
NRM 723
PDU 731
PDU control field
  similarities 731
primary station 721
Project 802 731
secondary station 721
S-frames 724
station types 721
symmetrical configuration 721
system qualities 721
transmission mode 721
U-frame 724
unbalanced configuration 721
header 20
header error 209
header translation 665
hello message 343
  backup designated router IP
    address 344
  dead interval field 344
  designated router IP address 344
  E flag 343
  hello interval field 343
  neighbor IP address field 344
  network mask field 343
  priority field 343
  T flag 343
hello packet
  network mask field 355
hexadecimal colon notation 634
hexadecimal number 686
  binary number

representation 686
  example 687
  symbols 686
  to binary 689
  weight and value 686
hierarchy
  name server 405
historic level 5
homepage 567
hop-by-hop option 647
  jumbo payload 648
  Pad1 647
  PadN 647, 648
  payload 647
hop-count 319
host
  ARP query 181
  connection to network 86
  group membership list 230
  routing table 210
host file 401
host specific delivery 137
hostent 607
hostid
  extraction 89
  of network address 91
  subnet 110
host-specific routing 134
host-to-host communication 248,
  272
host-to-host protocol 30
HTML 569
  A tag 574
  anchor 574
  applet 587
  APPLET tag 575
  ASCII document 571
  attribute 571
  BODY tag 573
  bold tag 573
  browser 571
  bulleted list tag 574
  center tag 573
  example 570, 575
  format example 576
  graphic image 574
  HEAD tag 573
  Hn tag 573
  HTML tag 573
  hyperlink example 577
  image example 576
  IMG tag 574
  italic tag 573
  line break tag 573
  list item tag 574

HTML (*cont.*)
markup language 570
numbered list tag 574
skeletal tag example 575
structure of a web page 571
subscript tag 573
superscript tag 573
tag 571
TITLE tag 573
underline tag 573
htonl 605
htons 605
HTTP 551, 569
client 552
concept 551
COPY method 555
data sending example 561
DELETE method 555
embedded commands 551
entity header 560
examples 560
FTP similarity 551
general header 559
GET method 554
HEAD method 554
header 558
header categories 558
information retrieval example 561
LINK method 555
message format 551
message types 552
methods 554
MIME-like header 551
MOVE method 555
OPTION method 555
PATCH method 555
port 747
POST method 555
PUT method 555
request header 559
response header 560
response message 555
retrieval example 561
server 552
SMTP similarity 551
status code field 556
status line 556
status phrase field 557
transaction 552
UNLINK method 555
URL 553
version field 554, 556
www 551

hub
10BASE-T 48
hyperlink 574
hypermedia 567
hypertext 567
example 567
information storage 567
pointer 567
HyperText Markup Language. See HTML
Hypertext Transfer Protocol. See HTTP

I

IAB 8
address 744
IETF 8
IRTF 8
RFC 8
IANA 8, 250
other systems 250
range 250
ICANN 8
address 744
ICMP 29, 30, 201
address mask messages 214
checksum 216
checksum field 203
code field 203
data section 203
destination unreachable message 204
diagnostics 210
echo request 213
echo request and reply messages 211
encapsulation 201
error correction 203
error handled 204
error handling 30
error message 204
error reporting 203
error-reporting message 202
fragmentation problem 205
host unreachable 205
ICMP type field 203
input module 218
IP header 204
isolated source host 206
loop 208
message format 203
message types 202
messages 30
modifications 633
network unreachable 205

nongeneration of message 204
parameter problem error 657
parameter problem message 209
port numbers 204
port unreachable 205
precedence problem 206
prohibited communication 206
protocol unreachable 205
purpose 203
query message 202, 211
redirect message 209
restricted by filter 206
router solicitation and advertisement 215
source quench message 206
source routing problem 205
time exceeded error 657
time exceeded message 208
timestamp messages 212
TOS problem 206
unknown destination host 206
unkown destination network 205
violation of host precedence 206
ICMP design 217
modules 218
output module 219
ICMPv6 633, 654
checksum field 654
code field 654
compared to ICMPv4 654, 655
destination unreachable message 656
echo request and reply 659
error packet 654
error reporting 654
format 654
group membership 660
IGMP 660
neighbor solicitation and advertisement 660
packet too big 656
parameter problem 657
query messages 658
redirection 658
router solicitation and advertisement 659
time exceeded 657
type field 654
IDLE state 234
IEEE 3, 730
address 743
Project 802 729
IESG 8
address 744

IETF
    address 744
    working group 8
I-frame
    control field 725
    flow control 725
    function 727
    information field 726
    Nr bit 725
    Ns bit 725
    retransmission indicator 726
ifTable 714
IGMP 29, 30, 227, 228
    address mapping 232
    checksum field 229
    continuing membership 230
    domain 233
    encapsulation 233
    example 231
    group address field 229
    host function 230
    ICMPv6 633, 660
    in TCP/IP 228
    IP address to physical
        address 232
    IP multicast address 229
    IP protocol 228
    joining a group 230
    leaving a group 231
    loyal member 229
    membership list 230
    message format 228
    message types 228
    monitoring group
        membership 230
    multicasting 227
    multicasting case 232
    no multicasting case 232
    operation 229
    operation in an internet 231
    physical multicast address 229
    purpose 228
    query for membership
        continuation 230
    query message 228
    report message 228
    request for group
        membership 230
    spanning tree algorithm 231
    TTL 233
    tunneling 232
    type field 229
    use of 230
    version field 229
IGMP design 234

components 234
example 238, 239, 240
group table 234
group-joining module 236
group-leaving module 236
input module 237
output module 237
timers 235
IMP 9
implementation
    FDDI 55
in_addr 600
indirect delivery 132
    address mapping 133
    concept 132
inet_aton 605
inet_ntoa 605
information field
    HDL 726
information frame. See I-frame
information technology 3
informational level 5
initialization sequence number.
    See ISN
instance suffix 533
Institute of Electrical & Electronics
    Engineers. See IEEE
interactive traffic 644
interconnectivity 2
interface
    OSI model 19
interface group 713
    ifTable 714
Interface Message Processor. See
    IMP
interior routing 320
International Standards
    Organization. See ISO
International Telecommunications
    Union. See ITU
International Telecommunications
    Union–Telecommunication
    Standards Sector. See ITU-T
Internet 1, 9, 87
    addressing 86
    administration 7
    application programs 370
    birth of 9
    communication 370
    concept 85, 179
    current 11
    DNS 407
    definition 9, 319
    e-mail 495
    example 95

history 9
info required by each
    computer 387
IP address 179
link state routing graphical
    representation 336
logical address 179
packet 179, 319
packet delivery 179
physical address 179
purpose 431
timeline 11
internet address. See IP address
Internet Architecture Board. See
    IAB
Internet Assigned Numbers
    Authority. See IANA
Internet Control Message Protocol.
    See ICMP
Internet Corporation for Assigned
    Names and Numbers. See
    ICANN
Internet Engineering Steering
    Group. See IESG
Internet Engineering Task Force.
    See IETF
Internet Group Management
    Protocol. See IGMP
Internet Protocol, Next Generation.
    See IPng
Internet Protocol, Version 6. See
    IPv6
Internet Protocol. See IP
Internet Research Steering Group.
    See IRSG
Internet Research Task Force. See
    IRTF
Internet Society. See ISOC
Internet standard 4, 5
Internet-draft 4
internetwork
    purpose 370
internetwork protocol. See IP
internetworking 730
    Project 802 730
    Project 802.1 730
internetworking devices 69
internetworking protocol. See IP
INTERNIC 638
interoperability 2
interpret as control. See IAC
interpreter 569
interrupt
    rlogin 451

inverse domain 409
  mapping 411
  server 409
inverse query 409
IP 10, 28, 29, 147
  advantages 29
  analogy 147
  best-effort delivery 147
  congestion 207
  congestion handling 148
  connectionless 131, 147
  connectionless protocol 29, 479
  datagram 29, 147
  deficiencies 201
  flow control 206
  host-to-host communication 248
  host-to-host protocol 30
  incomplete delivery 248
  lack of error handling 201
  lack of management
    communication 201
  multiplexing 151
  network layer protocol 28
  paired with TCP 147
  protocols 28
  reliability 147
  routing 30
  TCP/IP 147
  unreliable 147
IP address 31, 32, 85
  application 98
  ARP 30, 181
  authorities 99
  binary form 88
  broadcast 33
  class A 87
  class B 87
  class C 88
  class D 88
  class determination 87
  class E 88
  classes 87
  decimal notation 86, 89
  definition 85
  diskless machine 193
  example 33
  extracting netid and hostid 89
  format 32, 86
  hierarchy 109
  host 250
  hostid 86
  location 193
  multicast 33
  need for 32
  node location 90

node's connection 90
  of network 91
  RARP 30
  socket address 274
  special address 91
  structure 87
  subnet 109, 111
  subnetid 110
  supernet 109
  unicast 33
  uniqueness of 85
  universality 85
IP algorithm 165
IP datagram
  checksum field 152
  destination address field 152
  destination protocol 151
  flag field 151
  fragmentation 150, 153
  fragmentation offset field 151
  header length calculation 150
  header length field 148
  hop limit field 643
  hops allowed 151
  identification field 150
  loop problem 151
  need for total length field 150
  option error 209
  options 156
  padding 150
  precedence subfield 148
  priority 148
  protocol field 151
  reassembly 153
  service type field 148
  size 150
  source address field 152
  time-to-live field 151
  TOS bits subfield 149
  total length field 150
  version field 147
IP design 165
  components 165
  fragmentation module 169
  header-adding module 166
  MTU table 169
  processing module 167
  queues 168
  reassembly module 170
  reassembly table 170
  routing module 169
  routing table 168
IP group 715
IP packet
  delivery 131

  routing 131
ipAddrTable 715
IPng 35, 147
IPv4
  address space problems 633
  audio and video problems 633
  compared to IPv6 header 646
  comparison to IPv6 653
  deficiencies 633
  security problems 633
  transition to IPv6 663
  tunneling 664
IPv4 address
  IPv6 639
IPv6 35, 633
  address abbreviation 635
  address notation 634
  address space 634
  authentication 651
  compared to IPv4 header 646
  comparison to IPv4 653
  destination option 653
  ESP 652
  extension header 646
  extension of the protocol 634
  features 634
  flow label 645
  flow of packets 645
  fragmentation 650
  header format 634
  hop-by-hop option 647
  improvements 35
  jumbo payload 648
  local address 640
  new features 633
  new options 634
  pad1 648
  padN 648
  reserved address 639
  resource allocation 634
  routing protocols 633
  runs of zero 635
  source routing 649
  transition from IPv4 663
  tunneling 664
IPv6 address 634
  abbreviation example 635
  anycast 636
  categories 636
  consecutive zeros 635
  fields 638
  IPv4 639
  IPv4 compatible 639
  IPv4 mapped 640
  link local 641

multicast 636, 641
provider-based 638
reserved 639
shorthand notation 635
site local 641
slash 635
type prefix 636
unicast 636, 638
unspecified 639
IPv6 packet 642
base header 642
base header fields 642
extension header 642
format 642
payload 642
priority field 644
IPv6 traffic 644
congestion-controlled 644
flow label 645
noncongestion-controlled 645
priority assignments 644
redundancy 645
IRSG 8
IRTF 8
address 744
ISDN
LAPB 728
LAPD 728
ISN 294
ISO 2, 3, 17
address 743
frame relay 4
purpose 17
ISOC 7
address 744
iterative resolution 412
ITU
address 743
ITU-T 3

J
Java 569, 585
Applet 586
C++ 585
class 585
concept 585
data types 585
example 587
inheritance 585
instantiation 585
java.applet package 586
java.awt package 586
java.io package 586
java.lang package 586
java.net package 586

java.util package 586
line example 589
method types 585
object 585
packages 585
rectangle example 589
repaint example 590
string example 587
triangle example 590
typed language 585
JPEG 514, 574
jumbo payload option 647

K
Kahn, Bob 9
Karn's algorithm 292
keepalive message 354, 356
keepalive timer
purpose 292

L
label
country domain 409
generic domain 408
LAN 41, 46
TCP/IP 28
LAPB 60, 728
configuration 728
ISDN 728
X.25 61
LAPD 728
LAPM 728
LAST-ACK state 299
lexicographic ordering 535
LF 677
light 44
refraction 44
limited broadcast address 91
link 23
point-to-point 334
stub 335
transient 334
virtual 336
link access procedure, balanced.
See LAPB
link access procedure, for
modems. See LAPM
link access procedure. See LAP
link address 31
link local address 640
link state acknowledgment
message 350
link state acknowledgment
packet 350
Link State Advertisement. See LSA

link state database 339
Dijkstra algorithm 339
link state request message 345
purpose 345
link state routing 333
BGP 351
concept 334
graphical representation 336
hello message 343
routing table 341
sharing knowledge 333
sharing when there is
change 334
sharing with router 333
topology 334
link state update message 345
LSA 345
LSA field 346
number of advertisements
field 346
LIST command 469
listen call 609, 618
arguments 610
LISTEN state 299
little-endian byte order 603
LLC 729, 730, 731
addressing 731
data link layer 731
Project 802.2 730
local address 640
local area network. See LAN
local login 432
mechanism 433
procedure 433
LocalTalk address 31
locator 553
logical address 24, 179
RARP 193
Logical Link Control. See LLC
login 432
local 432
remote 433
longitudinal redundancy check. See
LRC
loop 151
time exceeded message 208
loop prevention 352
loopback 168
loopback address 93, 639
loose source route 649
loose source route option 161
lost acknowledgment 289
lost segment 287
LRC 701, 703
calculation 703

LRC (*cont.*)
final bit 703
mechanism 703
VRC 703
VRC parity bit 703
LSA 336
advertising router field 347
checksum field 347
E flag field 347
external link 338
external link ad 349
length field 347
link state age field 346
link state database 339
link state ID field 347
link state type field 347
network link 337
network link ad 348
network link advertisement 348
router link 337
router link ad 347
sequence number field 347
summary link to AS boundary
ad 349
summary link to AS boundary
router 338
summary link to network 338
summary link to network ad 348
T flag field 347

M

MAC 729, 730, 731
functions 731
modules 730
protocol specific 732
macros 736
magic cookie 389
mail exchanger 499
mail gateway 496
mail transfer agent. See MTA
mailbox 498
MAN
TCP/IP 28
Management Information Base.
See MIB
manager 525, 526
active open 544
database 526
functions 526, 536
remote reboot 526
mapped address 640
mapping
address to name 411
dynamic 180
host file 401

logical to physical address 179,
180
name to address 411
static 179
markup language
necessity of 570
masking 111
bit-wise and operation 112
concept 111
contiguous 113
hostid 112
ICMP example 215
netid and subnetid 112
noncontiguous 113
operation 112
purpose 215
supernet 120
with subnets 112
without subnets 111
master/slave configuration 721
maturity level 5
maximum segment size option 279
format 279
size determination 279
window scale factor 279
maximum transmission unit. See
MTU
MBONE 234
DVMRP 358
MOSPF 358
tunnels 358
media
guided 41
unguided 45
media access control. See MAC
Media Interface Connector. See
MIC
memcmp 606
memcpy 606
memset 606
mesh topology 22
message switching 57
metric 319, 333
OSPF 333
TOS 319
type of service 333
MIB 526, 532
accessing simple variable 533
agent 532
example 533
indexes 535
instance definition 535
interface group 713
IP group 715
lexicographic ordering 535

object categories 532
object identifier tree 532, 713
system group 713
table identification 534
MIB objects 527, 713
MIC 55
MILNET 10
MIME 511
7bit encoding 515
8bit encoding 515
alternative multipart
subtype 513
application data type 514
audio content type 514
audio data type 514
base64 encoding 515
basic audio subtype 514
binary encoding 515
CGI 580
concept 511
content subtype 512
content-description header 517
content-Id header 517
content-transfer-encoding
header 514
content-type header 512
data boundary 513
digest multipart subtype 513
extended header 511
extension to SMTP 511
external-body subtype 514
gif 514
headers 511
id parameter 513
image data type 514
jpeg 514
message data type 513
message fragments 513
message/rfc822 513
mixed multipart subtype 513
mpeg 514
multipart data type 513
number parameter 513
NVT ASCII 511
octet-stream application
subtype 514
parallel multipart subtype 513
partial message subtype 513
postscript application
subtype 514
quoted-printable encoding 516
rfc822 message subtype 513
text data type 513
total parameter 513
types of data 512

version header 512
video data type 514
minimize delay 460
modular arithmetic 692
monoalphabetic substitution 707
more fragment bit 154
MOSPF 358
    Dijkstra algorithm 358
    islands 358
    MBONE 358
    spanning tree 358
movie picture expert group. See
        MPEG
MPEG 514
MSS 294
MTA 495, 502
    client 502
    functions 496
    intermediate 501
    relay functions 496
    sendmail 502
    server 502
MTU 152, 656
    fragmentation 650
    IP design 169
    maximum length 153
    minimum size 650
    values for protocols 153
multicast address 31, 96, 227,
        636
    addresses available 228
    as destination only 228
    assigned 97
    conferencing 97
    format 227
    groupid 228
    IPv6 641
    IPv6 permanent 641
    IPv6 transient 641
    scope field 642
Multicast Backbone. See
        MBONE
Multicast Open Shortest Path First.
        See MOSPF
multicast router 229
    function 231
    IGMP report 230
    purpose 230
multicast routing 358
    spanning tree 742
multicasting 88, 227
    applications 227
    IGMP 227
    MBONE 234
    multicast address 227

UDP 260
multihomed device 90
multiple-bit error 699, 700
    definition 700
    example 700
multiplexing
    UDP 259
multipoint configuration 22
Multipurpose Internet Mail
        Extensions. See MIME

N

Nagle's algorithm 285
NAK 678
name server
    hierarchy 405
name space 401, 402
    central authority 402
    distribution 405
    flat 401
    hierarchical 401, 402
name-address resolution 410
NCP 9
neighbor solicitation and
        advertisement message 660
neighborhood concept
    path vector routing 351
netid
    extraction 89
    vs. network address 91
network
    definition 9
    private 99
    switched 57
network address 91
    ICMP 214
    masking 112
network byte order 604
Network Control Protocol. See
        NCP
Network Interface Card. See NIC
network layer 23
    devices 69
    logical addressing 24
    packet 23
    Project 729, 802
    responsibilities 24
    routing 24
    TCP/IP 28
network link ad
    attached router field 348
    network mask field 348
network link LSA 348
network link packet
    fields 348

network service
    connectionless 131
    connection-oriented 131
network specific delivery 137
network support layers 20
network to network interface. See
        NNI
network virtual terminal.
        See NVT
network-specific routing 134
next hop 131
next hop routing 133
NIC 9, 47
    10BASE2 48
    as device id 181
    station address 30
no operation option 157, 279
no specific traffic 644
node
    IP address 90
node functionality 212
noise
    repeater 69
    STP 43
noncongestion-controlled
        traffic 645
no-operation option 278
normal response mode. See NRM
notification message 356
    error code field 357
    error data field 357
    error subcode field 357
NRM 723
NSFNET 11
ntohl 605
ntohs 605
NUL 677
null suffix 404
number
    signed 692
    unsigned 691
numbering systems 683
    comparison 687
    transformation 687
NVT 27, 433
    ASCII 434
    character set 434
    control characters 435
    data characters 434
    FTP 461
    TCP/IP stack 433
    TELNET 433
    tokens 433
NVT ASCII
    MIME 511

O

OACK 487
object identifier 527
octal number 685
octal system 683, 685
  binary number
    representation 685
  example 686
  symbols 685
  to binary 689
  weight and value 686
one's complement 694
  adding two numbers 697
  carry 697
  determination of 696
  example 694, 697
  representation of zero 697
one's complement arithmetic 163,
    217, 255
one-to-all communication 98
one-to-many communication 96
one-to-one communication 96
open message 354
  BGP identifier 354
  hold time field 354
  my autonomous system
    field 354
  optional parameter length
    field 355
  optional parameters field 355
  version field 354
open shortest path first. See OSPF
open system 17
Open Systems Interconnection. See
    OSI
operating system
  local login 432
  NVT 433
optical fiber
  advantages 45
  components 44
  disadvantages 45
  reflection 44
  sizes 45
Option Acknowledgment. See OACK
options
  class subfield 157
  code field 156
  copy subfield 156
  data field 157
  end of option 157
  format 156
  function 156
  IP datagram 156
  length field 157

loose source route 161
no operation option 157
number subfield 157
record route option 158
strict source route 159
timestamp 161
types 157
OSI
  interoperability 18
  layer communication 18
  Project 802 729
OSI model 3, 17, 20, 29
  and TCP/IP 369
  application layer 27
  architecture 18
  bridge 70
  data link layer 22
  devices 68
  gateway 73
  grouping of functions 18
  header 20
  layer interface 19
  layer overview 20
  layers 17, 18, 21
  layers traversed 18
  network layer 23
  network support layers 20
  organization 20
  peer-to-peer process 18
  physical layer 18, 21
  presentation layer 26
  router 72
  session layer 25
  TCP/IP 17, 28
  trailer 20
  transport layer 24
  user support layers 20
OSPF 319, 320, 332
  database description
    message 344
  encapsulation 350
  hello message 343
  hello packet 354
  link state acknowledgment
    message 350
  link state request message 345
  link state routing 333
  link state update message 345
  link types 334
  metric 333
  network as a link 334
  packet format 342
  packet header 342
  packet types 342
  path vector routing 351

point-to-point link 334
stub link 335
transient link 334
virtual link 336
OSPF header
  area identification field 343
  authentication data field 343
  authentication type field 343
  checksum field 343
  message length field 342
  source router IP address 343
  type field 342
  version field 342
out-of-band signalling 443
out-of-order segment 288

P

P/F bit 725, 726
packet 319
  control information 57
  definition 57
  format 57
  length 57
  router 72
packet internet groper. See ping
packet layer procedure. See PLP
packet level protocol layer
    X.25 60
packet switching 57
  approaches 58
  datagram approach 58
  IP 147
  need for 57
  virtual circuit approach 58
packet too big 656
pad1 option 647
padding 278
  end of option option 157
padN option 647
page 567
parameter problem message 209
  code field 209, 657
  header ambiguity 209
  ICMPv6 657
  missing option 209
parent process 620
parent server 374, 618
parity 702
  even 702
  LRC 703
  odd 702
parity check. See VRC
parity generator 702
Partially Qualified Domain Name.
    See PQDN

PASS command 470, 471
passive close 296
passive open 294, 372
    FTP control connection 460
    FTP data connection 461
passive socket 618
PASV command 461, 466
path attributes 352
    AS_PATH 353
    NEXT-HOP 353
    non-transitive 353
    ORIGIN 353
    transitive 353
path MTU discovery
        technique 650
path vector routing 350, 351
    example 352
    loops 352
    messages 351
    path attributes 352
    policy routing 352
PDU 731
    control field 731
    format 731
    types 731
peer-to-peer process 18
periodic timer 327
    effect of others 327
    operation 327
persistence timer
    operation 292
    probe 292
physical address 31, 86, 179
    ARP 30, 181
    authority 31
    Ethernet 31
    examples 32, 179
    multicast 31
    need for 180
    RARP 30, 193
    size and format 31
    unicast 31, 32
physical layer 21
    ATM 68
    bit representation 21
    bit synchronization 21
    data rate 21
    devices 69
    OSI model 18
    purpose 21
    TCP/IP 28
    topology 22
    transmission mode 22
    X.25 60
pid_t 376

piggybacking 275, 277, 727
ping 212
plaintext 707
PLP 61
    LAPB 61
    X.25 61
pointer query 409
point-to-point 721
    sample network 95
point-to-point configuration 22
point-to-point link 334
point-to-point protocol. See PPP
poison reverse 330
    example 330
policy routing 352
poll 726
Poll/Final bit. See P/F bit
polyalphabetic substitution 708
polynomial 706
    binary representation 706
    CRC 706
POP 517
    purpose 517
port
    ephemeral 250
    registered 250
    well-known 250
port address 31, 33, 272
    example 34
    need for 33
    size 33
PORT command 461, 466, 470,
    471
port number 248, 249, 272
    ephemeral 249
    example 249, 273
    ICMP 204
    process 250
    process to process
        communication 271
    range 272
    socket address 274
    universal 249
    well-known 249, 251
Post Office Protocol. See POP
Post Script 514
PPP 59
    address field 60
    control field 60
    CRC 60
    flag field 60
    frame format 59
    protocol field 60
PQDN 404
    suffix 404

preamble
    Ethernet 47
presentation layer 26
    compression 27
    encryption 27
    responsibilities 26
    translation 26
primary server 407
primary station 721
priority field 644
private key
    digital signature 712
private networks 99
probe 292
process 374
    analogy to object-oriented
        programming 375
    child 378
    concept 375
    concurrent server 379
    creation 377
    example 377
    example of fork function 377
    fork function 377
    grandchild 378
    identification 376
    instance of program 375
    processid 376
    program 375
    structure 375
processid 376
process-to-process
        communication 248, 271, 272
    port address 272
program
    process 375
Project 802 729
    modularity 730
    OSI model 729
Project 802.1 730
Project 802.2 730
Project 802.3 732
Project 802.5 732
promiscuous ARP 184
proposed standard 5
protocol data unit. See PDU
protocols 1, 18
provider-based address 638
    subnet identifier field 638
proxy ARP 184
pseudoheader 254
    purpose 254
pseudoterminal driver 433
public key encryption
    concept 709

public key encryption (*cont.*)
  decryption algorithm 709
  digital signature 711, 712
  example 710
  RSA 710
push operation 302

Q
query
  DNS 413
query message 211
  example 420, 422
  ICMP 202
  ICMP v4 and ICMPv6 658
  ICMPv6 658
  IGMP 228
question record 416
  format 416
  query class field 418
  query name field 416
  query type field 417
queue
  client-server model 372
  overflow in UDP 258
  socket interface 612
  UDP 258
  UDP client site 258
  UDP overflow 259
  UDP port 258
  UDP server site 259
queuing 301
QUIT command 470, 472

R
RARP 29, 30, 179, 180, 193
  alternative solutions 195
  BOOTP 387
  encapsulation 195
  first boot 30
  ICMPv6 633
  IP address 387
  logical address 193
  masking 215
  packet format 193
  physical broadcast address 180
  physical machine 193
  purpose 30
  unicast address 180
RARP reply 193
RARP request 193
raw socket 602
read call 611, 620
  arguments 611
read request. See RRQ
real-time audio 633

record route option 158
  example 159
  pointer 159
  pointer field 159
  pointer-length comparison 159
recursive resolution 412
recvfrom call 611, 614
redirection message 209
  code field 210
  example 210
  host-specific route 210
  ICMP design 218
  ICMPv6 658
  purpose 210
  TOS 210
redundancy 701, 702
  bridge 738
  CRC 703
  definition 701
  transport layer 701
redundancy check 701
  physical layer 701
  types 701
reflection 44
registered port 250
regulatory agencies 4
relay agent 391
remainder 704
remote control characters 435
remote host 607
remote login 433
  problems 433
repeater 68, 69
  function 69, 70
  OSI model 68
  physical layer 69
report message
  IGMP 228
Request for Comment. See RFC
requirement level 6
reserved address
  loopback address 639
resolution
  iterative 412
  name to address 410
  recursive 412
resolver 410
resource record 418
  domain class field 419
  domain name field 418
  domain type field 419
  format 418
  resource data field 419
  resource data length field 419
  time to live field 419

response
  DNS 413
response message
  example 421, 422
RETR command 469
retransmission time 291
  round trip time 291
retransmission timer 290
  retransmission time 291
Reverse Address Resolution
    Protocol. See RARP
RFC 4, 745
  complete listing 745
  draft standard 5
  elective 6
  experimental 6
  historic 5
  informational 6
  Internet standard 5
  limited use 7
  maturity levels 5
  not recommended 7
  proposed standard 5
  recommended 6
  requirement level 6
ring topology 22
RIP 319, 320, 321
  address field 325
  broadcasting 332
  command field 325
  distance field 325
  encapsulation 332
  entry 325
  expiration timer 327
  family field 325
  garbage collection timer 327
  hop count limit 327
  instability 328
  instability example 328
  instability remedy 329
  message format 325
  path vector routing 351
  periodic timer 327
  poison reverse 330
  port 747
  port assignment 332
  requests and responses 325
  shortcomings 327, 331
  slow convergence 327
  solicited response 325
  split horizons 330
  timers 326
  triggered update 329
  unsolicited response 325
  updating algorithm 322

updating algorithm example 322
version 2 331
version field 325
RIP v2 331
  authentication field 331
  message format 331
  multicasting 332
  next hop address field 331
  route tag field 331
  subnet mask field 331
RIP version 2. See RIP v2
RIPNIC 638
rlogin 431, 448
  character mode 450
  client to server command 450
  commands 449
  connection 448
  escape character 451
  flow control 449
  interrupt 451
  interrupt key 452
  local flow control 449
  mode 450
  remote flow control 449
  security 452
  server to client command 450
  TCP connection 449
  TCP port 448
  UNIX 448
root bridge 739
root port 740
root server 406
round trip time. See RTT
router 24, 68, 72, 73, 319
  address 215
  addresses 72
  area border 332
  as multihomed device 90
  as network station 72
  autonomous system
    boundary 332
  backbone 333
  compared to gateway 73
  corruption 151
  example 72
  fragmentation 152
  function 72
  internet 72
  multicast 229
  network layer address 72
  OSI layers 72
  OSI model 69
  packets 72
  subnet 110
router advertisement message 215

address preference level 216
default router 216
format 216
router hierarchies 73
router link ad 347
  data field 347
  identification field 347
  metric field 348
  TOS field 348
  type field 347
router solicitation and
    advertisement message 215
  format 216
  function 215
  ICMPv6 659
routing 131
  default 135
  distance vector 321
  distance vector vs link state 334
  DYNAMIC 135
  example 139, 140, 141, 320
  host specific 134
  interior and exterior 320
  link state 333
  multicast 358
  network layer 24
  network specific 134
  next hop 133
  static 135
  steps 111
Routing Information Protocol. See
  RIP
routing methods 133
routing module 137, 139
  function 139
  hierarchical matching 139
routing module and routing table
  design 137
routing protocol 319, 320
routing table 133, 137, 319, 341
  added by redirection flag 138
  destination field 138
  dynamic 136
  entries 322
  example 322
  fields 137
  flags field 138
  gateway flag 138
  host-specific flag 138
  initialization 323
  interface field 138
  link state routing 333
  mask field 137
  modified by redirection flag 138
  next hop address field 138

next hop field 323
reference count field 138
shortest path tree 341
static 136, 319
up flag 138
updating 323
updating of 210
use field 138
RPC
  port 747
RSA encryption 710
  example 710
RTT 291
  as function of previous
    RTTs 291
  calculation 291
  Karn's algorithm 292
  timestamp option 291
run-length encoding 464

S
s_addr 600
SAR 67
SAS 55
secondary server 407
secondary station 721
  HDLC 721
security
  TFTP 487
segment 25, 275
  bridge 71
  definition 275
  format 275
  header fields 275
  IP datagram 30
  size 275
  TCP 30
  TCP/IP 30
segmentation and reassembly
  sublayer. See SAR
semantics 2
sendmail 502
sendto call 610, 614
  arguments 610
sequence number
  ICMP 204
server 248, 370, 372
  accept call 620
  bind call 618
  buffer 374, 618
  clients 370
  close accepting socket 620
  close the listening socket 620
  closing the communicating
    socket 620

server (*cont.*)
  concurrent 372
  connectionless iterative 372,
    613
  connection-oriented
    concurrent 373, 618
  definition 372
  ephemeral port 374, 618
  fork call 620
  iterative 372
  listen call 618
  open call 618
  opening a socket 613
  passive open 372
  primary 407
  processing data 620
  queue 372, 612
  read call 620
  receive call 614
  repeat call 620
  repeated steps 620
  root 406
  secondary 407
  socket address 274
  TCP 373, 618
  transport layer protocol 372
  UDP 372
  UDP queue 259
  well-known port 373
  write call 620
server program 249
  activity 371
  port number 249, 273
server socket interface 613
service-point address 25
service-point addressing 24
session layer 25
  dialog control 25
  responsibilities 25
  synchronization 25
SFD 48
S-frame
  control field 725
  function 727
shielded twisted-pair. See STP
shift count 280
shortest path tree 341
sign-and-magnitude 692
  example 693
  most significant bit 692
  range 693
signed number 691, 692
  one's complement 691, 692, 694
  sign-and-magnitude 691, 692
  two's complement 691, 692

silly window syndrome 284
  cause 284
  Clark's solution 286
  created by receiver 286
  created by sender 285
  delayed acknowledgment 286
  Nagle algorithm 285
simple mail transfer protocol. See
  SMTP
simple network management
  protocol. See SNMP
simplex 22
single attachment station. See SAS
single-bit error 699
  definition 700
  example 700
site local address 641
sliding window 279, 282
  acknowledgment 282
  buffer 282
  decreasing the window size 283
  example 282
  fixed-size window 282
  increasing the window size 283
  management 283
  receiving TCP 283
  sending TCP 283
  silly window syndrome 284
  TCP 272
  variable-size window 282
  window management
    example 284
  window size 284
sliding window size
  formula 280
slow convergence 327
slow start 300
SMI 526
  ASN.1 527
  BER 529
  data type 526
  encoding 529
  encoding method 526
  functions 526
  object identifier 527
  object name 527
  object representation 527
  object type 527
  objects 526
  sequence of structured type 529
  simple data type 528
  simple type 529
  simple type examples 529
  structured data type 528
  tree structure 527

SMTP 495
  address system 498
  alias 501
  alias expansion 501
  client commands 503
  command format 503
  commands 503, 505
  concept 502
  connection establishment 508
  connection termination 509
  DATA command 505, 509
  delayed delivery 499
  delivery 499
  domain name 499
  example 502
  EXPN command 506
  HELO command 505, 508
  HELP command 506
  HTTP 551
  intermediate delay 501
  limitations 511
  local part of address 498
  MAIL command 509
  mail exchangers 499
  MAIL FROM command 505
  mail transfer phases 508
  many-to-one expansion 501,
    502
  message transfer 509
  MTA 502
  NOOP command 506
  off-line PC 517
  OK command 509
  one-to-many expansion 501
  permanent negative completion
    reply 507
  port 747
  positive completion reply 507
  positive intermediate reply 507
  QUIT command 506, 509
  RCPT command 505, 509
  receiver-site delay 500
  relaying 496
  responses 507
  return mail address 509
  returned mail 499
  RSET command 506
  SAML command 507
  SEND command 506
  sender-site delay 499
  service not available 508
  service ready 508
  SOML command 506
  spooling system 499
  TCP connection

establishment 508
transient negative completion
    reply 507
TURN command 506
user mail box 498
VRFY command 506
SNI 60
SNMP 525, 536
agent 525
agent address field 538
agent database 526
BER 539
client program 526
client-server mechanism 544
community field 537
components 526
concept 525
datagram example 540
encoding 539
enterprise field 538
error index field 538
error status field 538
error types 538
examples 540
function 525
GetNextRequest 537, 543
GetRequest 537, 540
GetRequest Message 542
GetResponse 537, 541, 543
management basics 526
manager 525, 526
message components 539
message format 537
messages 536
port 747
request ID 537
retrieval example 543
server program 526
SetResponse 537
SMI and MIB 526
specific code field 539
subnet mask example 542
time stamp field 539
trap 537
trap example 543
trap type field 539
trap types 539
triplet 539
UDP ports 544
VarBindList field 538
version field 537
sockaddr_in 600
socket 600
bind call 614
byte order transformation 604

byte ordering 602
closing 614
datagram 602
definition 600
family field 600
Internet Address structure 600
local socket address field 601
protocol field 601
raw 602
receiving 614
remote socket address field 601
repeated steps 614
send call 614
sending 614
stream 602
type field 601
types 602
socket address 252, 274, 600
client 274
defined 274
definition 252
IP header 252
pair 252, 274
port number 252
server 274
socket call 608, 614, 618, 620
arguments 608
socket descriptor 608, 614
socket interface 599
client 620
client program 623
connectionless iterative
    server 612
connection-oriented concurrent
    server 618
data types 599
server program 615, 622
UNIX BSD. 599
socket interface client
    program 616
socket system call 608
SOH 677
sorcerer's apprentice bug 485
source address
Ethernet 48
source quench message 206, 655
purpose 207
recipient 207
usefulness of 208
source routing 649
destination address 649
format 649
source service access point. See
    SSAP
SP 678

spanning tree 737
algorithm 739
blocking port 740
designated bridge 739
designated port 740
example 740
finding root bridge 739
finding root port 740
formation 740
forwarding port 740
MOSPF 358
multicast routing 742
need for 738
port cost 739
root 739
root path cost 739
root port 739
structure 737
vertex 737
weighted graph 737
special address 91
specific host on this network 93
split horizons 330
example 330
selectivity 330
spooling system 499
SSAP 731
standards 2
categories 2
creation committees 2
definition 1
need for 2
ratification 4
star topology 22
start frame delimiter.
    See SFD
state transition diagram 297
static database 392
static documents 569
static mapping 179, 180
limitations 179
overhead 180
table 180
static routing 135
static routing table 136
static table 319
static vs. dynamic routing 135
station address 30
station types 721
stop bit 702
STOR command 469, 472
store and forward 59
STP 43
and UTP 43
characteristics 43

STP (*cont.*)
  conductor 43
  cost 43
  shielding 43
stream
  definition 30
stream data service 274
  delivery 275
  example 275
  receiver 275
  receivingbuffer 275
  sender 274, 275
  write operation 275
stream socket 602
strict source route 649
strict source route option 159
  concept 159
  example 161
  pointer-length comparison 160
  rules 159
STRU command 472
structure of management
    information. See SMI
structured data type 734
stub link 335
STX 677
subnet 109
  Class A example 114
  Class B example 114
  Class C example 117
  concept 109
  examples 113
  hostid 110, 111
  need for 109
  netid 111
  router function 110
  special address 113
  subnetid 111
  three levels of hierarchy 111
  variable length 117
subnet masking
  ICMPv6 658
subnetid 110
subnetting 109, 633
  need for 109
subnetwork 109
  example 110
subnetwork address
  ICMP 214
  masking 112
subscriber network interface.See
  SNI
subtyping 735
suffix 404
summary link to AS boundary

ad 349
summary link to network ad 348
  metric field 349
  network mask field 349
  TOS field 349
supernet
  concept 109
  example 120
supernet mask 120
supernetting 109, 119, 633
  example 119
  need for 119
supervisory frame. See S-frame
switch 24
  definition 57
switched Ethernet 71
switching 41, 56
  circuit 57
  methods 57
  packet 57
symmetrical configuration 721
SYN 678
SYN segment 294
synchronization points 25
SYN-RCVD state 299
SYN-SENT state 298
syntax 2
system group 713

T
tag 571, 735
  attributes 571
  common 572
  data flow 573
  executable contents 575
  format 571, 573
  hyperlink 574
  image 574
  list 574
  skeletal 573
TCB 304
  fields 305
TCP 10, 30, 147, 247, 271
  acknowledgment 275
  and IP 147
  buffer 301
  buffers 275
  checksum 281
  client-server model 372
  connection-oriented
    protocol 293
  decapsulation 301
  demultiplexing 301
  DNS 424
  encapsulation 301

  error control 287
  flow control 282
  full-duplex 275
  full-duplex mode 293
  function 30
  ICMP 204
  input processing module 309
  multiplexing 301
  operation 301
  OSI 28
  output processing module 309
  ports 747
  position in suite 271
  pseudoheader 281
  push bit 303
  push operation 302
  pushing data 301
  queueing 301
  reliable service 275
  responsibilities 272
  segment 275
  segment re-ordering 30
  segmentation 30, 464
  sequence number 30
  services 274
  sliding window 282
  split 10
  stream data service 274
  stream transport protocol 30
  stream-oriented protocol 303
  timers 290
  transport layer protocol 28
  urgent data 303
  well-known port number 251
TCP design 304
  main module 306
  TCB 304
  timers 306
TCP header
  acknowledgment number
    field 276
  checksum field 277
  control field 277
  destination port address
    field 276
  header length field 277
  options 278
  options field 278
  reserved field 277
  sequence number field 276
  source port address field 276
  urgent pointer field 277
  window size field 277
TCP option
  end-of-option 278

maximum segment size 278
multiple-byte option 278
no operation 278
one-byte option 278
timestamp 278
window scale factor 278
TCP/IP 29
addresses 31
and OSI model 369
application layer 28, 31, 369
application layer and OSI
model 31, 369
ARPANET 10, 34
data link layer 28
datagram format 147
file transfer 459
hierarchy 28
IP 147
layers 28
mail gateway 496
network layer 28
NVT 433
OSI model 17, 28
physical and data link layers 28
physical layer 28
standard file transfer 459
transport layer 28, 30
UDP 30
UNIX 10
version 4 34
version 5 35
version 6 35
TCP/IP protocol 10
TCP/IP protocol suite 28
telephone system media 42
TELNET 431, 553, 569
abort output 442
are you there 442
authentication 452
binary option 437
character mode 446
client 434
client abort 444
controlling the server 442
default mode 446
disabling an option 439
DM 443
DONT command 439
echo option 437
embedding 436
enabling an option 438
erase character 442
erase line 442
escape character 444
example 445

go ahead 445
IAC 440
infinite loop 443
interrupt 442
interrupt process 442
line mode 445
line mode option 437
mode 445
offer to disable 439
offer to enable 438
option 436
option negotiation 437
option negotiation example 440
out-of-band signaling 443
port 436, 747
program abort 442
pseudoterminal driver 433
remote login 433
request to disable 440
request to enable 439
security 452
sending control character 436
sending data 436
server 434
status option 437
suboption character 441
suboption negotiation 441
suppress go ahead option 437
symmetry in option negotiation
441
synchronization character 443
terminal speed option 437
terminal type option 437
TFTP 487
timesharing 431
Timing Mark option 437
urgent TCP segment 443
user interface 447
WILL command 439
WONT command 439, 440
terminal 432
terminal network. See TELNET
TFTP 479
ACK 483
ACK message 481
applications 489
block number field 480, 481
BOOTP 391, 489
connection 482
connection establishment 482,
483
connection establishment for
reading 483
connection establishment for
writing 483

connection termination 483
DATA 483
data field 481
DATA message 480
data transfer 483
DHCP 489
duplicate message 485
duplication of messages 485
ephemeral port 486
error 481, 483
error control 484
error message field 482
error number field 482
example 487
file retrieval 484
file storage 484
filename field 480
flow control 484
lack of checksum field 484
lost acknowledgment 485
lost message 484
messages 479
mode field 480
need for 479
opcode field 480, 481, 482
port 747
port usage 486
reading a file 479, 483
RRQ 480, 481, 483
RRQ message 480
security 487
sorcerer's apprentice bug 485
Telnet 487
termination 482
timeout 484
UDP 482
well-known port 486
writing a file 479
WRQ 481, 483
WRQ message 480
TFTP server
multiple clients 486
thick Ethernet. See 10BASE5
this host on this network 93
three-way handshaking 293
example 294
time exceeded message 208
code field 208
ICMPv6 657
late fragments 208
time-to-live field 208
time-out 287
dynamic retransmission 291
timer 290
expiration 327

timer (*cont.*)
  garbage collection 327
  keepalive 292
  periodic 327
  persistence 292
  retransmission 290
  RIP 326
  time-waited 293
timesharing 431
  login 432
  password checking 432
timestamp
  ICMPv6 658
timestamp message
  clock synchronization 212
  original timestamp field 213
  receive timestamp field 213
  reply 213
  request 213
  round trip time 214
  round-trip time 212
  transmit timestamp field
    213
  trip times 213
timestamp option 161, 280
  flags field 162
  format 280
  operation 280
  overflow field 162
  round trip time 281
time-to-live
  caching 413
time-to-live field 208
TIME-WAIT state 299
time-waited timer
  purpose 293
Token Bus
  Project 802 730
token frame
  fields 53
token passing
  FDDI 54
Token Ring 51
  abort frame 53
  access control 53
  access method 51
  addressing 52
  concept 51
  configuration 53
  CRC 53
  data field 53
  data frame 52
  data rate 52
  destination address 53, 55
  disabled station 53

end delimiter 53
frame control 53
frame format 52
frame passing 53
frame status 53
frame types 52
implementation 53
in sample network 95
MAU 54
media 42
operation 51
ordered transmission 51
Project 802.5 730
source address 53, 55
start delimiter 52
structure 53
switch 53
token frame 53
token passing 51
TOS 149
  categorizing 150
  interpretations 149
  values for application
    programs 149
trailer 20
transformation 687
transient link 334
  cost assignment 335
  graphical representation 335
transition 663
  dual stack 664
  header translation 665
  IPv4 to IPv6 663
  strategies 663
  tunneling 664
translation
  presentation layer 26
transmission control block. See
    TCB
Transmission Control Protocol. See
    TCP
transmission media 41
transport layer 24, 30, 31
  connection control 25
  connection mechanism 248, 272
  delivery to application
    program 248
  error control 25
  error handling 699
  flow and error control 248
  flow control 25
  ordering of datagrams 58
  process-to-process
    communication 272
  protocols 30, 247, 271

reassembly 25
receiving process 248
responsibilities 24, 248, 271
responsibility 25, 30
service-point addressing 24
TCP 30
TCP/IP 28, 30
transpositional encryption 708
trap 526
triggered update 327, 329
  example 329
triplet 539
Trivial File Transfer Protocol. See
    TFTP
TTL 168, 233
tunneling 232, 664
  automatic 665
twisted-pair 42
  and optical fiber 45
  Category 1 42
  Category 2 42
  Category 3 42
  Category 4 42
  Category 5 43
twisted-pair cable 41
two's complement 695
TYPE command 472
type of service. See TOS
type prefix 636

U
UA 495, 497
  envelope 497
  envelope addresses 497
  functions 496
  mail format 497
  mail summary 498
  mailbox 498
  mailbox name 502
  message 497
  message body 497
  message header 497
  programs 497
  receiving mail 498
  user-interface 497
UDP 28, 30, 247, 271
  advantages 248
  checksum 256, 257, 258
  client-server model 372
  compared to TCP 30
  components 261
  connection establishment 482
  connectionless 248
  connectionless service 256
  data link layer 257, 258

decapsulation 257, 258
demultiplexing 259
design 260
DNS 424
encapsulation 257
example 263
flow and error control 257
for simple communication 260
function 248
ICMP 204
incoming queue 259
internal control mechanism 260
IP 257
management programs 260
MBONE 234
multicasting and
  broadcasting 260
multiplexing 259
operation 256
outgoing queue 258
physical layer 257
port creation 258
port number 249
port unreachable 259
ports 747
position in TCP/IP suite 247
process-to-process protocol 30
queue overflow 258
queuing 258
route-updating protocols 260
server program 615
size restriction 256
SNMP 544
socket address 252
termination 482
TFTP 482, 483
transport layer protocol 28
unreliable 248
uses 260
well-known port number 251
UDP design
  control block module 261
  control block table 261
  example 263, 264
  input module 262
  input queue 261
  output module 262
UDP example 263
UDP port 486
UDP programs 614
U-frame
  control field 725
  HDLC 727
  information field 726
unattended data traffic 644

unbalanced configuration 721
  multipoint 721
  point-to-point 721
underlying technologies 41
unguided media 41, 45
unicast address 31
unicast address 96, 636
unicasting 227
UNIX 10
unnumbered frame. See U-Frame
unreachable network 327
unshielded twisted-pair. See UTP
unsigned number 691
  example 692
  modular arithmetic 692
unspecified address 639
update message 355
  network layer reachability
    information field 356
  path attributes field 356
  path attributes length field 355
  unfeasible routes length
    field 355
  withdrawn routes field 355
upward multiplexing 293
URG bit 303
urgent byte 303
urgent data 303
URL
  alias 554
  anchor 574
  components 553
  document retrieval 553
  dynmaic document 577
  host 554
  HTTP 553
  locators 553
  method 553
  pathname 554
  port number 554
user agent. See UA
USER command 470, 471
user datagram 253
  checksum example 255
  checksum field 254
  destination port number
    field 253
  format 253
  length calculation 253
  length field 253
  pseudoheader 254
  source port number field 253
user datagram protocol. See UDP
user network interface. See UNI
user support layers 20

UTP 42
  advantages 42
  categories 42
  connector 43

V
vertical redundancy check. See
  VRC
very low frequency. See VLF
video 633
virtual circuit approach 58
  concept 58
  difference from circuit
    switching 58
virtual link 333, 336
VLF 45
VRC 701, 702, 703
  example 702
  LRC 703
  parity check 702
  parity generator 702
  redundant bit 702
VT 677

W
WAN 41, 59
  TCP/IP 28
web page 569
  body 571
  head 571
  structure 571
  tag 571
  text 571
web site 567
weighted graph 737
well-known port 250, 373, 613
  list 747
  queue 259
  server 374, 618
  TFTP 486
wide area network. See WAN
WILL command 438
window scale factor 280
  connection setup 280
  format 280
  shift count 280
window size
  basis of 300
World Wide Web. See WWW
write call 612, 620
  arguments 612
write request. See WRQ
WRQ 480
WWW 554, 567
  active document 583

WWW (*cont.*)
  concept 567
  document types 569
  dynamic document 577
  homepage 567
  hypertext and hypermedia 567
  information distribution 567
  pointers 567
  static document 569

X
X.21 61
X.25 60

conceptual overview 60
connection definition 60
control field 62
data link layer 61, 62
definition 60
error checking 62
error checking example 62
facilities 60
general format identifier 61
interface 60
layers 60
logical channel group
    number 61

necessity for error checking 62
network layer 61
physical layer 61
SNI 60
source-to-receiver checking 62
station-to-station checking 62
traffic 62
virtual circuit approach 60

Z
zone 405